Wissenschaftliche Untersuchungen
zum Neuen Testament

Begründet von Joachim Jeremias und Otto Michel
Herausgegeben von
Martin Hengel und Otfried Hofius

44

Baptism and Resurrection

Studies in Pauline Theology against
Its Graeco-Roman Background

by

A. J. M. Wedderburn

J. C. B. Mohr (Paul Siebeck) Tübingen

CIP- Kurztitelaufnahme der Deutschen Bibliothek

Wedderburn, A. J. M.:
Baptism and resurrection: studies in Pauline theology against its Graeco-Roman
background / by A. J. M. Wedderburn. –
Tübingen: Mohr, 1987.
(Wissenschaftliche Untersuchungen zum Neuen Testament: 44)
  ISBN 3-16-145192-9
  ISSN 0512-1604

NE: GT

© 1987 by J. C. B. Mohr (Paul Siebeck), P.O. Box 2040, D-7400 Tübingen.

Typeset by Sam Boyd Enterprise in Singapore; printed by Gulde-Druck GmbH in Tübingen;
bound by Heinrich Koch KG in Tübingen.

Printed in Germany.

To

C. F. D. Moule

Preface

This study on 'Baptism and Resurrection' has occupied my attention for perhaps rather more years than I like to think; at first sight it might have seemed but a small step from the study of the background to the contrast of Adam and Christ contained in Romans 5.12–21 and 1 Corinthians 15, which was the subject of my doctoral work at Cambridge, to the background of Romans 6 and 1 Corinthians 15. In fact in the former I had to deal with the fashionable hypothesis of a background in Gnostic mythology; in the latter case it is the even more fashionable hypothesis of a background in the soteriology of the mystery-cults of the Graeco-Roman world; for some these two backgrounds may not seem that far removed from one another, but in fact the overlap is very slight, as will become clear in the course of this study. That fact alone might make one ponder whether Paul was likely thus to shift from one set of background ideas to another within the space of a few verses.

Hence this work has taken me into pastures with which I had not yet become acquainted during my doctoral studies. Moreover these pastures were somewhat extensive, with a terrain in which a sheep might all too easily get lost. Leaving the pastoral metaphor, one could also observe that it was a field of study where the literature on a whole range of relevant topics was vast. Inevitably the non-specialist in a field like Egyptian religion must depend upon the work of others and hope that he or she has picked the right mystagogues to follow. Again, when the literature is as vast as it is upon topics like the mysteries, resurrection or baptism, one has to hope that one has picked the important writings which bear significantly upon the thesis which one is putting forward; if I have overlooked some scholar's work which would indeed affect my thesis materially, I beg their pardon; there comes a point where one must blow a whistle and let one's work see the light of day. I am all too conscious that in the brief space of time that has elapsed since I completed the manuscript of this study there has appeared a work that would be highly relevant to my thesis, particularly to the first and fourth chapters, namely Gerhard Sellin's magisterial *Der Streit um die Auferstehung der Toten: eine religionsgeschichtliche und exegetische Untersuchung von 1 Korinther 15* (FRLANT 138, Göttingen, 1986); happily, as I had been conscious from my all too brief contact with the author, his work and my own, as far as they overlap

in scope, are in most respects largely in agreement, however much I may
have occasionally reached different conclusions in earlier work; as regards
the present large measure of agreement I leave it to others to judge what
sort of minds it is that think thus alike.

As I have picked my way all too slowly and painfully through these
complex fields of study there are a great many others to whose ideas and
advice and encouragement I have been greatly indebted. In particular I
should mention Michel Austin, Christoph Burchard, Walter Burkert, Hans
Cavallin, Gerhard Delling, Richard Fardon, Eric Heaton, Harry Hine, Ian
Kidd, Ronald Mellor, Stephen Neill, Ron Piper, John Richardson, David
Riches, Donald Russell, Martin West and Christian Wolff. Especial thanks
are also due here to my former colleague Robin Wilson, not least for most
generously volunteering to cast his vastly experienced scholarly and editorial eye over the proofs of this volume – a Herculean task with this
particular stable. I am also most grateful to the Study Leave Committee
of the University of St Andrews for three spells of leave which enabled
me to concentrate on the research for, and writing of, this book, to the
Research Fund of the Faculties of Arts and Divinity in this University for
help with the costs of preparing the text, and to the British Academy for a
research award to help with the cost of a brief but invaluable period of
study in Oxford which enabled me to make use of both the Ashmolean
and Bodleian Libraries there. Miss Maisie Blackwood and Miss Gail Mackie
of the St Mary's College office have greatly helped in the preparation of
the text for publication. Above all I have for many years enjoyed the
friendly encouragement and support of the editor of this series, Martin
Hengel, and my warmest thanks are due to him and his co-editor, Otfried
Hofius, for the publication of this volume in this series, and to Georg
Siebeck, Ulrich Gaebler and the rest of the staff of J.C.B. Mohr (Paul
Siebeck) in Tübingen and to their assistants in Singapore, who have done
so much to steer this work so swiftly and efficiently through to publica-
tion.

Finally, as the dedication indicates, I would like in this volume to salute
one whose wisdom and kindness guided me through my initiation into
New Testament research at Cambridge, C.F.D. Moule; one could not have
wished for a better mystagogue.

St Andrews, Scotland   A.J.M. Wedderburn

Contents

1. The Problem and the New Testament Evidence

1.1. The Problem

The problem with which this study is concerned first caught my attention at the beginning of my postgraduate studies when reading Robert C. Tannehill's book, *Dying and Rising with Christ*[1]. There it was assumed, without much argument, that when in Col 2.11–13 rising with Christ is spoken of in the past tense, as something that has already taken place in Christians' baptism, this is a 'more primitive form' of this idea than that found in Rom 6 where Paul seems to confine the resurrection of Christians to the future; there he was modifying an already existing idea of a 'past resurrection with Christ' rather than creating a new idea.

This assumption became a little less perplexing when it became plain that Tannehill was here simply adopting what had in many circles, particularly on the Continent, become an accepted axiom of New Testament studies. It has, for instance, received almost 'canonical' form in Eduard Lohse's *Umwelt des Neuen Testaments*, an introductory volume for the influential *Neues Testament Deutsch* series of commentaries. This work at the same time, as might be expected, makes plain the religio-historical perspective underlying this explanation of the New Testament evidence. The ideas of the Hellenistic mystery-religions influenced the early church, partly unconsciously, partly consciously:

> The consequence of the cultic drama in which the myste (*sic*)[2] participates – that is, his incorporation into the destiny of the cultic deity – was also the interpretation given to the Christian baptism. Anyone who is baptized into Christ is incorporated into his death and resurrection, so that the powers of immortality flow through him. (ET 242)

The conception that flows from this, of the automatic and irreversible bestowal of life and salvation and resurrection in the present, is combat-

---

Notes on 1.1

1 Here p. 10; cf. also Brandenburger, 'Auferstehung' 21f; Conzelmann, 'Schule' 95; Gäumann, *Taufe*, 64f (also 48); Jervell, *Imago* 257; Käsemann, 'Apocalyptic' 125, and *Testament* 15; Mearns, 'Development' (1984) 25; Wengst, *Formeln* 187, etc.

2 I.e. initiate.

ted by Paul in passages like Rom 6.1–5 and 1 Cor 10.1–13. The degree of
his agreement with Tannehill is even clearer and more explicit in an earlier
article on baptism and justification in Paul's thought[3]: in Col 2.12 there
emerges 'the hellenistic Christian view which was widely held before and
during Paul's time. Paul has decisively corrected this view in Rom 6.4'
(314, n. 19).

More recently this consensus was spelt out in Jürgen Becker's brief
monograph, *Auferstehung der Toten im Urchristentum*, particularly in a
chapter devoted to 'baptism and resurrection'[4]. He argues there that there
developed in early Christianity a concept of the resurrection which asserted
that dying and rising with Christ occurred in baptism; this arose independently of Paul. He grants that the reconstruction of these traditions is
hypothetical, but asserts that this belief in a present participation in
Christ's death and resurrection could not have arisen without the direct
or indirect influence of the mysteries, in which 'the participation in the
deity's fate which one experiences in the cult is the constitutive element
in the bestowal of salvation in the present' (55f)[5]. The roots of these
traditions lie in the churches of Antioch and Syria, but their full bloom
probably appeared in that of Corinth, with its consciousness of eschatological fulfilment attested most clearly in 1 Cor 4.8; it was perhaps the first
to understand baptism as a dying and rising with Christ[6]. The influence of
the mysteries with their dying and rising gods also lies behind the baptismal traditions of Gal 3.26–28 which speak of the inseparable union of
the Spirit-endowed Christian with the heavenly Spirit of the exalted Christ,
a union in which he – or she – transcends the relationships of this world.
A one-sided stress on such traditions lies behind the problems of the Corinthian church. Turning his attention to Col 2.9–13 he notes the similarity of the traditions there to those rejected in 2 Tim 2.18 and asks whether
'these post-Pauline baptismal statements which speak of Christians'
identification with and participation in the death and resurrection of the
Lord cannot be traced back into the Pauline period at least in their essen-
tials' (60)[7]. Is it not possible, he asks, that Paul, after an initial argument
with proponents of this position, found himself stating his view of baptism in terms which were dependent on the mystery-religions but at the

---

3 'Taufe'; cf. also his *Grundriß* §23a, 105f; 'Wort' 52.
4 Chap. 7, 55ff; see also the following chap. on 1 Cor 15.
5 Thus he expressly aligns himself with Gäumann, *Taufe*, and Wengst, *Formeln*, against Wagner,
   Baptism.
6 Schnelle, *Gerechtigkeit* 80, also notes the Corinthian provenance of Romans, and sees that
   city as the source of a 'nebenpaulinisch' baptismal theology which is used with slight modifica-
   tions in Rom 6 (81).
7 He cites in support Brandenburger, Gäumann, and Käsemann, *Testament*, as in n. 1 above,
   and Lohse, 'Taufe'.

same time were an appropriate correction of their views? The indirect modification of these views in Rom 6 is in other words far from typical of early Christianity; the views reflected in 1 Cor 10 and 4.8 are far more representative, views which also led some of the Corinthians to deny a future resurrection of the dead; if one wished to escape death, they argued, one must rise with Christ now in this life. Even Jesus had for them risen in his baptism and had then received the Spirit (94).

Yet it should not be assumed that this is altogether a new theory, although the regularity and the certainty with which it is now advanced may be relatively new. Already in that most influential of works, Rudolf Bultmann's *Theology of the New Testament*, the main outlines of this theory are clear; the interpretation of baptism as a participation in Christ's death and resurrection originated in the Hellenistic churches where this rite was understood on the analogy of the initiation rites of the mysteries. Paul presupposes this tradition in Rom 6, but artificially turns the present resurrection demanded by the logic of this tradition into an ethical appeal (1, 140f). The Gnostics at Corinth, too, were opposed to the realistic views of resurrection in Jewish and primitive Christian thought, and held a spiritualized view of resurrection, which could also be expressed by saying that resurrection had already occurred, as in 2 Tim 2.18 (1, 169; cf. also Jn 5.24f; Eph 5.14). One slight difference is that he does not so much emphasize that Ephesians and Colossians allowed earlier tradition to re-emerge after Paul's modification of it, but rather argues that in these letters 'the school of Paul follows his thought that the life mediated by baptism is already at work in the present' (1, 141).

In writing thus Bultmann was, however, in many respects giving expression to the findings of the *religionsgeschichtliche Schule*. In 1887 Otto Pfleiderer had anticipated some of the views of this school by likening the putting on of Christ to the putting on of animal masks in the Mithras rites; Paul 'had some slight knowledge of the heathen cults practised' in Tarsus, and it is not inconceivable that ideas drawn from the mysteries were recalled 'from the background of his consciousness' when he came to express 'his doctrines of the mystical ceremonies of Baptism and the Lord's Supper'[8]. By 1905 his views were more under the sway of the growing influence of the *religionsgeschichtliche Schule*, and he reckoned it possible, even unavoidable, that Paul had been influenced by the gods of the mysteries who died and returned to life, a rescue that guarantees a like rescue for their adherents; their rites visualized 'the fact that the wor-

---

8 *Christianity* 1, 63; 415f. This coincides therefore with the period during which the *religionsge-schichtliche Schule* is usually regarded as having had its beginnings in the works of Rohde, Usener, Dieterich, Wendland and Cumont (Kümmel, *New Testament* 245–8).

shippers partook of the god's life by the mystical participation in his death'[9]. In 1897 Heinrich Julius Holtzmann set Paul's doctrine of baptism in Rom 6.3f against the background of the ideas of the Greek mysteries; this doctrine he sees as furthest removed in spirit from the soil of the religion of the Jews and the message of Jesus[10]. Two years before Pfleiderer's later work just referred to, in 1903, Wilhelm Heitmüller had also stressed the realistic view of the sacraments held by Paul, in common with the rest of early Christianity; he too compared with the Eucharist the rites of a number of primitive cults, including that of Dionysus, and the more refined meal of the Mithras-cult. Such analogies were hardly surprising when the air was at the time of the birth of Christianity full of 'mystery-bacilli', so to speak, and the Christian faith grew up on a soil fertilized by the decaying and mingling together of various religions[11]. He pointed to 1 Cor 15.29 as evidence of the sacramental views of the Corinthians and their belief in the magical effects of baptism[12]. Later, in 1911, under the influence of the studies of Hepding, Cumont and Reitzenstein[13], he extended his mystery-religions hypothesis more explicitly to Paul's doctrine of baptism: it was only by chance that Paul never spoke expressly of 'rebirth', since Paul was responsible for introducing this idea and that of identification with the dying and rising god in an initiation rite into early Christianity[14]. In 1903 too Hermann Gunkel had advanced the thesis that Paul's interpretation of baptism in Romans 6 was influenced by the Egyptian mysteries of Osiris[15]. For Wilhelm Bousset too the dying and rising gods of the mysteries provided the background to Paul's statements in Romans 6, for there he presupposes an already existing view that baptism as an act of initiation was analogous to those of the mysteries, an act in which the initiate merges with and puts on the deity (Gal 3.26f)[16]. Richard Reitzenstein was responsible for introducing a comparison with the Mandaean texts, in which he found the idea of baptism as a voluntary death and entrance into life as in the oldest Christian interpretations of the rite, including Rom 6.2f and Col 2.12[17]. The bestowal of life in bap-

---

9 *Origins* 175f.
10 *Lehrbuch* 2, 178–81.
11 *Taufe* (1903); the last ref. is to p. 52.
12 Ibid. 15f; cf. also *'Im Namen Jesu'* 324f.
13 Hepding, *Attis*; Cumont, *Religions*; Reitzenstein, *Poimandres*.
14 *Taufe* (1911) 17, 22–5.
15 *Verständnis* 83ff; this he prefers to the earlier suggestion of Holtzmann (see n. 10 above) that Paul's view derived from the Greek mysteries.
16 *Kyrios* 107f, 140.
17 *Mysterienreligionen* 227, 230–3 (he also found a similar view in Egyptian royal baptismal rites); *Vorgeschichte* 30, 158.

tism came through the granting of the Spirit and knowledge, a sacral view of spiritual endowment which he could only derive from the mysteries[18].

Yet Bultmann went beyond any of the explicit theories of the *religionsgeschichtliche Schule* before him in his attempts to trace the development of these traditions with the help of texts like 1 Cor 15 and 2 Tim 2.18. It may be no accident that the publication of the first volume of his *Theologie* in 1948 was followed shortly afterwards by the posthumous publication of Julius Schniewind's influential article on the denial of the resurrection in Corinth[19]. A further sign of the emergence of this consensus about that time can be seen from a comparison of Martin Dibelius' commentary on the Pastoral Epistles with the third edition of the same work revised by Hans Conzelmann in 1955; Dibelius refers to the spiritualized view of the resurrection taught by the Gnostic opponents who were countered in 2 Timothy, but Conzelmann adds to this the information, apparently without the least hesitation, that this doctrine was that which Paul had already countered in 1 Cor 15[20].

In the light of this Hans von Soden and Jean Héring can be regarded as heralds of this view in that in 1931 and 1932 respectively they both anticipated Schniewind in taking the view that the Corinthians were in fact saying that the resurrection had already taken place[21]. Wilfred L. Knox, too, a few years later expressly linked the views of the Corinthians with those of Hymenaeus and Philetus[22]. Yet it is only with the work of Bultmann and after him that of Lohse and others that this view began to gain ground and to become a dominant one.

And yet, it must be noted, this theory, apart from any other weaknesses, is forced to argue that earlier views are more explicitly represented in what are generally agreed to be later documents, whether by Paul himself or, as in my view is more likely, by followers of his; that the earliest, 1 Cor 15, is to be understood in terms of the latest, 2 Tim 2.18[23], and the next earliest, Rom 6, presupposes what only appears for the first time in Ephesians and Colossians. Is this really likely[24]?

The purpose of this study, then, is to call into question this dominant theory. The rest of this first chapter will attempt to survey the exegetical

---

18 *Mysterienreligionen* 379f.
19 'Leugner'.
20 Dibelius, *Pastoralbriefe* (1931²) 69; Dibelius-Conzelmann, *Pastoralbriefe* (1955³) 83.
21 V. Soden, 'Sakrament' 361 n. 28; Héring, 'Saint Paul' 317–20; cf. also § 1.2.1.3.
22 *St Paul* (1939) 127 n. 1.
23 Cf. however J. A. T. Robinson, *Redating* 67ff, who assigns 2 Tim to 58 C.E.
24 Contrast Lähnemann, *Kolosserbrief* 157: 'it can be shown that, following the generally recognized sequence of the letters (Gal 2.19f; Rom 6.1–14; Col 2.12f; Eph 2.5f; 2 Tim 2.11f), the statements (about dying and rising with Christ) are progressively more clearly and simply formulated' (cf. also Lindemann, *Aufhebung* 143).

basis in the New Testament upon which this hypothesis has been built, and in particular the earlier texts in the agreed letters of Paul, 1 Cor. 15 and Rom 6; that done, an attempt will be made to provide an alternative religio-historical account of the development of these traditions and the influences which contributed to them, an account built around the questions which the exegetical survey of the New Testament material has thrown up, but left unanswered. This account will also give heed to the advances in our understanding of the mystery-cults of the Graeco-Roman world which have taken place, advances which have, in my judgment, fatally undermined the religio-historical foundation upon which the *religionsgeschichtliche Schule* built up its reconstruction of the development of early Christian soteriology and baptismal theology.

1.2. The Denial of the Resurrection in Corinth

Quot homines, tot sententiae; of few passages in the New Testament can this more justly be said than of 1 Corinthians 15. When one considers the complex history of the exegesis of this chapter and the varied attempts to decide what the Corinthians actually believed and why they believed it, one is confronted by a baffling array of divergent views[1]. Nor is this surprising since the apparently conflicting evidence within the chapter itself combines with the many different assessments of the Corinthian church's problems which are disclosed by the letter as a whole to produce a bewildering range of different possible solutions. Over all these looms the question how far Paul knew of, understood, or represented correctly, the views of the Corinthians; for, although it might seem at first sight a rash undertaking to try to reconstruct the Corinthians' views while taking Paul's representation of them with a very considerable pinch of salt, there have not been lacking in recent years and before that a considerable number of scholars who have ventured to do this[2]. Equally, however, there is seemingly almost total agreement that Paul knew what he was talking about when he says that they believed that 'there is no resurrection of the dead' (15.12f); in this at least he was reproducing accurately the be-

---

Notes on 1.2

1 Cf. the brief survey of the history of exegesis of this chapter in Spörlein, *Leugnung* 1–19, and of some more recent attempts in Brakemeier, *Auseinandersetzung* 1–10; a longer critical account is also to be found in Murphy, *Dead* 9–161.

2 Cf. Spörlein, ibid. 14f, 18f.

liefs of the Corinthians[3]. So P. Hoffmann argues that this formulation is Paul's only secure point of contact with the views of the Corinthians[4]. But even when one accepts this as an accurate representation of the Corinthians' views it is by no means agreed what they meant by this statement.

1.2.1.1. The first possibility is that they were *denying any future life at all.* After all Paul's argument seems to treat them as if this were what they believed, as if, that is, they held views like those of the Epicureans. In support of this is v 32 in particular: 'if the dead are not raised, "let us eat and drink, for tomorrow we die"' (quoting from Isa 22.13). V 19, too, points in the same direction: 'If it is for this life only that Christ has given us hope, we of all men are most to be pitied' (*NEB*). This interpretation is traced by B. Spörlein back to Didymus of Alexandria[1], but of particular interest is the view of G. Billroth, who held that the Corinthians took this line because they could not conceive how the decayed body could ever be revived; however, he also left room for the possibility that they held that the resurrection had already come in their spiritual rebirth which could be termed a 'resurrection' (cf. § 1.1.1.3 below)[2].

Yet this view has never found all that much favour; for one thing it is hard to see how the Corinthians could then practise a vicarious baptism for the dead such as is referred to in v 29[3]. Surely they could not be quite so inconsistent in their thinking, for this practice surely presupposes a hope of survival beyond the grave? And yet, if the groups of those denying the resurrection and those baptizing for the dead do partially overlap (even if they are not completely identical), Paul would indeed be accusing them of inconsistency at this point; would this not simply confirm that he was correct? But it will not do to accuse them of the same sort of promiscuous syncretism which seems to mark texts like that of Pseudo-Phocylides with its jumble of apparently mutually incompatible beliefs about an afterlife[4]; for one thing the Corinthians were not apparently so all-encompassing

---

3 Cf. however Roetzel, *Letters* 57, 60.

4 *Toten* 242; see also Becker, *Auferstehung* 71; Brakemeier, ibid. 11; Pearson, *Terminology* 15; Schottroff, *Glaubende* 154; this is true even of Schmithals, *Gnosis* 148, despite the extent to which he thinks that Paul was misinformed or misunderstood the Corinthians' position.

Notes on 1.2.1.1

1 *Leugnung* 2, citing K. Staab, *Pauluskommentare aus der griechischen Kirche* (NTA 15, Münster, 1933) 6–12; for Didymus the Corinthians held that the soul too was perishable.

2 Spörlein, ibid. 8f, citing Billroth's commentary of 1833.

3 That this is what is referred to is argued convincingly by Rissi, *Taufe;* there is more room for argument over how the Corinthians understood this practice.

4 At least that is the picture which Cavallin paints (*Life* 151–5); however Fischer, *Eschatologie* 125–44, gives a much more unified account of the beliefs represented in this work, although some of the tension between different traditions remains (see below § 3.1.2).

in their beliefs as to find room for 'resurrection'. However, are we certain that it was the same people who denied the resurrection and who prac-tised this vicarious baptism? Spörlein holds that the 'some' who did the former were not practising this baptism; Paul is appealing to a practice in the Corinthian church, but not one in which the deniers of the resurrec-tion participated[5]. Against this Brakemeier argues that the deniers of the resurrection were not a clearly defined group within the church; theirs was a belief that was widely influential among its members. Moreover, Paul could not hope to convince them by referring to the practice of others[6]. His second argument is more convincing than the first, but even here it could be replied that Paul also appeals to his own practice in vv 30–32. Brakemeier's argument will only carry weight when as good a case as can be has been made out for the view that Paul's appeal to his own practice would impress the deniers of the resurrection because they took as the starting-point for their own beliefs and practices the message and life of Paul. Then, and only then, does it become plausible to say that the example of those who baptized for the dead would carry weight with them for similar reasons.

1.2.1.2. Another, more popular, interpretation of the Corinthians' posi-tion is to say that they were in fact denying the resurrection of the body or the flesh because, positively, they *asserted the immortality of the soul.* Yet this implies that Paul has at least misread the situation so much that his argument misses the point. Apt here is Philipp Bachmann's question, quoted by Spörlein: 'Why has Paul not come to grips better with that possibility in which the sceptics in Corinth had taken refuge? Why is his polemic against them not more direct? Here lies the heart of the problem of this fifteenth chapter from the historical point of view'[1]. Thus Hoff-mann, for instance, although he grants that Paul reproduces the Corinth-ians' affirmation correctly, believes that Paul misunderstood what they meant by this statement; their view was in fact similar to that of those whom Justin Martyr criticizes in *Dial.* 80, who said 'that there is no resur-rection of the dead, but that at the moment of death their souls are taken up to heaven'[2]. Paul misunderstands their position because he could not

---

5 Ibid. 82f; contrast Wolff, *1 Kor* 190.

6 Ibid. 74; however Paul does argue from his own practice and experience in the following verses. Cf. also Machalet, 'Paulus' 194: baptism for the dead was 'certainly' practised by those who denied the resurrection.

Notes on 1.2.1.2

1 Spörlein, *Leugnung* 12, quoting Bachmann, *1 Kor* 457.

2 *Toten* 243; cf. also Grosheide, *1 Cor* 356 (*pneuma*); Lietzmann-Kümmel, *1–2 Kor* 79; Manson, *Studies* 206; H. A. W. Meyer, *1 Kor* 323; Morris, *1 Cor* 209; Robertson-Plummer, *1 Cor* 329.

conceive of a disembodied *Vollendungszustand*; he may have seen that they did have some expectation of survival, but this disembodied condition could not match up to his expectation of what salvation involved (245f). But in that case Hoffmann has granted too much; if Paul knew that they had some expectation of survival, why does he not only misrepresent them but also then fails to argue that disembodied survival is inadequate and that only survival in bodily form is adequate[3]? To that extent the view that he misunderstood them and supposed that they believed that with death everything is over is more satisfactory[4]. Yet it would be surprising if a Hellenistic Jew like Paul were not familiar with the idea of the survival of a disembodied, immortal soul after death. However, if Paul's representation of their views in this chapter is indeed mistaken or misdirected, then the correction of his account can only be made in the light of evidence drawn from elsewhere in 1 Corinthians, or indeed perhaps in 2 Corinthians as well. And it would be a rash man that would claim that that evidence is unambiguous.

More recently this line of interpretation has found support from R. A. Horsley's assessment of the views of the Corinthian 'strong', in which he sets them against the background of Hellenistic popular philosophy, a background which he illustrates chiefly from the writings of Philo of Alexandria. Seen against this background the Corinthian 'strong' would be led to deny the resurrection of the dead because it was an 'antithesis to their liberation from bodily and earthly realities, a threat to their heavenly immortality, and the loss of their intimate relation with Sophia and the perfection thus attained'[5]. Horsley, like those who believe that Paul misunderstood the situation, bases his analysis of it on the evidence of the rest of the letter; however, *he* does not charge Paul with any misunderstanding. Yet it is doubtful whether he has shown any better than his predecessors that Paul's argument fits the situation, and indeed, despite the title of his article which deals with this topic, he does not really come to grips with the problems of 1 Corinthians 15.

1.2.1.3. The view of the Corinthian situation which is of greatest interest to us here is that which connects the beliefs of the Corinthians with the

---

Cf. also Sandelin, *Auseinandersetzung* 149–53 (his hypothesis is that some Corinthians held that Christ's soul, like that of the righteous wise of Wis 2.10–3.9, had passed into heaven; i.e. they denied all resurrection, making no exception in the case of Jesus – pp. 13–20; contrast, e.g., Schütz, *Paul* 84). Of course that they so believed does not follow from the fact that Paul understood their denial of the resurrection to mean that (or at least represented their position as entailing that) – cf. Sandelin, ibid. 17.

3 A point forcibly made by Spörlein, ibid. e.g. 98f.

4 So Bultmann, *Theology* 1, 169; also Schmithals, *Gnosis* 147 (and 'Verhältnis' esp. 383).

5 'Elitism' 231 (cf. also his 'Pneumatikos').

position condemned in 2 Tim 2.18, the claim of Hymenaeus and Philetus that '*the resurrection has already taken place*'. What seems to mark this interpretation off from the previous ones is that, whereas the latter implied that 'resurrection' was by definition something that involved the body and was thus offensive to Hellenistic ways of thinking, this argues that the term 'resurrection' can be so spiritualized as to be able to be used of the present life of the redeemed.

The use of 2 Tim 2.18 to interpret 1 Cor 15 can be traced back as far as Thomas Aquinas[1]: some have seen the origins of this interpretation in John Chrysostom[2], but Spörlein has shown that this is a misunderstanding of what Chrysostom is actually saying[3]. The prevalence of this view in modern times, is however, due in large part to the influential essay by Julius Schniewind[4], mentioned above, who maintained that Paul's Corinthian opponents were Gnostics; they had misunderstood Paul's proclamation that Jesus had already proleptically fulfilled the eschatological resurrection and that the dead were now risen with him and in him (116f; cf. 120); the Corinthians interpreted this as meaning that they were already in Christ's kingdom and that this meant that they already shared the divine substance

---

Notes on 1.2.1.3

1 Spörlein, *Leugnung* 3.

2 E.g. Bartsch, 'Argumentation' 266; Bartsch's own suggestion, that Paul stresses the necessity of death, not the bodily nature of the resurrection, against the Corinthians' contention that they already enjoyed eschatological existence now, still fails to explain why they maintained that there is no resurrection, rather than saying that there already had been one.

3 *Leugnung* 16f.

4 'Leugner'; cf., in addition to the scholars cited in the text below (Brakemeier, Wilson), e.g. Altermath, *Corps* 4–5 (tentatively); Aune, *Setting* 18 n. 2; Barrett, *1 Cor* 347f; G. Barth, 'Erwägungen' 516, and *Taufe* 85f, 96; Bartsch, 'Eschatology' 395; Bauer, *Leiblichkeit* 90; Baumgarten, *Paulus* 99f; Becker, *Auferstehung* 69–76; Brandenburger, *Adam* 70f, and 'Auferstehung' 18; Dinkler, 'Taufaussagen' 93; Dunn, *Unity* 279; E. S. Fiorenza in *IDB* Suppl. 275a; Fuller, *Formation* 19; Godet, *1 Cor* 2, 323f; Goppelt, *Theologie* 643; Harnisch, *Existenz* 28; Haufe, 'Taufe' 565; Käsemann, 'Questions' 19f, 'Apocalyptic' 125f, and *Röm* 152; Kaiser, *Bedeutung* 243f; Klaiber, *Rechtfertigung* 113; W. L. Knox, *Paul* (1939) 127 n. 1; Kruse, *Foundations* 115; Lietzmann-Kümmel, *1–2 Kor* 192; Martin, *Spirit* 94; Meeks, 'Image' 202, and *Christians* 182 (yet he there goes on to speak in terms of 'exaltation', which need not be quite the same thing); Moffatt, *1 Cor* 241 (tentatively); J. M. Robinson, 'Kerygma' 33; Rudolph, *Gnosis* 189, 301; Schütz, 'Authority' 440, and *Paul* 85f; Schweizer, *Lordship* 112, and 'Dying' 5; v. Soden, 'Sakrament' 361 (259) n. 28; H. -F. Weiß, 'Paulus' 119f; H. D. Wendland, *1–2 Kor* 120; Ziesler, *Christianity* 133 (tentatively).

Mearns, 'Development' (1984) 24f, following Héring, 'Saint Paul' 317–20, comes to a rather similar position by a rather different route: Paul had originally preached a baptismal resurrection to the Corinthians and he 'then assumed that the Corinthians' denial of future final resurrection amounted to denying "the resurrection"'; this position seems to be reached without any specific statement as to the religio-historical background to such a belief in baptismal resurrection; in Héring's case it seems to be simply a logical inference from the idea of complete union with Christ in baptism (316); see further § 3.1.1 n. 4.

(129; cf. 135). Yet, despite this interpretation, Schniewind gives no hint that Paul's argument is misplaced, nor that Paul in the least misrepresented the Corinthians. They did indeed reject the idea of resurrection, so that even the resurrection of Jesus' flesh was offensive to them (123). But, as E. Güttgemanns points out[5], Schniewind does not clarify the relationship between their saying that the resurrection has already occurred and their denial of Jesus' bodily resurrection. For the most convincing, if not the only, reason for speaking of one's present experience as 'resurrection' is that one sees this experience as somehow the consequence of Jesus' 'resurrection'; yet it is perverse to say that 'resurrection' in one sense of the word (bodily) does not happen, even in the case of Jesus, and that in another sense (figurative, spiritualized) it not only does happen, but already has happened, if one does not at the same time make clear these different senses of 'resurrection'.

Schniewind thus paves the way for that group of scholars who hold both that Paul represents the Corinthians correctly and that they actually believed that the resurrection had already taken place. Brakemeier, too, takes a similar line: he sees no contradiction in the Corinthians' holding together a denial of the resurrection, a belief in life after death and a lack of hope[6]. Rightly their view has been connected with that mentioned in 2 Tim 2.18. The Corinthians believed that in baptism they had been raised with Christ. They already possessed the full benefits of salvation, so what more could they expect? Like Schniewind he finds Paul's argument apposite, but there are moments of real difficulty in his exegesis of the chapter as he attempts to substantiate this claim. For Paul probably deliberately ignores their belief in an immortal soul or, more likely, spirit (74). But what is his justification for overlooking this? And in v 29 Paul is not, as most suppose, pointing to a discrepancy between the Corinthians' assertions and their actions, but rather is showing them the implications of their position (75). Yet is this a very convincing distinction? Again, v 32b is an inference which Paul draws from the Corinthian position; he shows them a consequence of their position which they had not previously appreciated (77f). But were they unable to see these implications for themselves? And do they really follow from the Corinthians' premise if they in fact did believe that the spirit survived beyond the grave? The punishments and purgations of the soul in the after-life were a common enough idea in the Hellenistic world and Paul is unlikely to have been unaware of them. Thus it is doubtful whether Brakemeier's handling

---

5 *Apostel* 60.
6 *Auseinandersetzung* 13f, but on 48 he seems to want to say that the Corinthians did have a hope 'for this life only' (on 1 Cor 15.19).

of the text is ultimately any more convincing than Schniewind's which he criticizes (5).

Whereas Schniewind saw the Corinthians' views as arising from a mis-understanding of Paul's preaching of Jesus' proleptic fulfilment of the eschatological resurrection, J. H. Wilson argues that they had understood Paul's original message to be about Jesus' exaltation to heaven and not a bodily resurrection[7]. This distinction presumably implies that he was thought to have been exalted as a disembodied soul or spiritual being. Paul's original preaching had said nothing about a general resurrection of the dead or of all Christians, and, since they expected the Parousia at any moment, they had not anticipated the death of many of their number before it. This problem Paul had already faced in Thessalonica (1 Thess 4.13–17). But the Corinthians' position was rather different in that they believed themselves to be already exalted like Jesus through the Christian sacraments; they were already so decisively changed that death was now no obstacle to them. But, like the majority of proponents of such a view, Wilson has difficulty with those statements of Paul's which suggest that the Corinthians believed that there was no after-life, for he attributes to them the current Hellenistic dualistic concept of the after-life (103). Furthermore, if the Corinthians equated 'resurrection' with exaltation, then presumably they were prepared to say that they themselves had been 'resurrected' in the same sense of the word. So why should they deny the possibility of 'resurrection'? And if they held these Hellenistic views they would certainly not wish to deny that dead men could be exalted. Indeed it would be the fact that the exalted living remain in the body which would pose a problem for them.

At this point we should note the distinctive position of E. Güttgemanns on this point. He too holds that the Corinthians believed that the resurrec-tion had already occurred[8]. They also believed in the close relationship of Redeemer and redeemed of which Paul makes use in his contrast of Adam and Christ; indeed they went further than Paul was prepared to go and actually identified the Redeemer and the redeemed; thus the universal resurrection of the redeemed happened with the resurrection of the Redeemer with whom they are identical (71). But there is no resurrection for the dead, for they are no longer 'in Christ'[9]. Yet it is not satisfactorily explained why death and the destruction of the body should debar one from being in Christ; if anything one would expect the dissolution of the body to free the sparks of divine Spirit in the redeemed or those sparks

---

7 'Corinthians' 100, 102.
8 *Apostel* 70f; cf. the critique in Hyldahl, 'Auferstehung' 126.
9 Ibid. 76; on 67 he particularly stresses the qualification 'of the dead' (against Schmithals).

which are the redeemed so that they might ascend to their true home, according to Güttgemanns' account of the Corinthians' beliefs. Moreover, if the Corinthians were prepared to spiritualize the concept of 'resurrection', it is surprising that they were not prepared to extend the figure of speech a very natural step further and to speak of the resurrection of those who are spiritually 'dead' in much the same way as Eph 2.1 does later[10]. In that case they would not wish to deny that there were some 'dead' who rose.

However, a weakness in this whole approach to the problem is that these scholars are generally reluctant to say that Paul misunderstood or misrepresented the Corinthians. Now it may be true that, as W. G. Kümmel, a proponent of this solution, argues

> That Paul has here misunderstood his opponents in that he assumes their view to be that with death everything is over is hardly to be inferred from 15.19, 32[11].

There are, as we have seen and will see again, ways of so interpreting these verses that it need not be inferred that Paul actually thought that they held that death was the end of everything. Kümmel in fact seems to take the line that Paul is insisting that salvation depends upon resurrection (193f); the implication would then be that the survival in which they believed was in his view something less than salvation, and it would not instil in man a godly fear before his Creator to whom he would have to render account. Paul's point may be correct, but why does he then have to make it in this way?

Yet, even if we can avoid what seems still to be the implication of vv 19 and 32, 'there is no resurrection of the dead' (vv 12f) is an odd representation of the Corinthians' views if in fact they believed that there was a resurrection and that it had happened already and had happened to them. It would have invited misunderstanding had they put it thus, and Paul could hardly be blamed for failing to see what they meant. Had he seen what they in fact believed according to this view then his argument would have had to take a very different form, arguing about the true and proper meaning of the term 'resurrection'. Thus it is hard to avoid the conclusion that either Paul did not realize what the Corinthians believed or they did not in fact assert that the resurrection had already taken place, however much their views may otherwise have had in common with those of Hymenaeus and Philetus[12].

---

10 Cf., e.g., Rudolph, *Gnosis* 190: the 'dead' are 'those without knowledge'; cf. Luz, *Geschichtsverständnis* 338 n. 75.

11 In Lietzmann-Kümmel, *1–2 Kor* 193.

12 Cf. Schottroff, *Glaubende* 156.

1.2.1.4. Finally *Spörlein's solution* of this intractable problem deserves separate mention[1]. He rejects any influence from Hellenistic ideas of immortality of the soul. If anything the Corinthians' problem arose from their observation of the decay of the mortal body. This was aggravated by their belief that salvation would come to them at the Parousia; for they could not comprehend how the return of Christ could benefit those who had thus perished. Spörlein leaves it open what they expected to happen to the dead, whether it was the shadowy existence in Hades of popular belief or total annihilation; what mattered was that they had lost the chance to participate in the salvation which their Lord would bring with him (189–198). He likens the Corinthians' beliefs to those of the Thessalonians: they too expected all salvation to come from the return of Christ (128).

Spörlein can then maintain the aptness of Paul's answers to this position, as long as he is allowed to argue that those who had thus lost hope for the dead were not the same as those who practised vicarious baptism for the dead in v 29. Furthermore, a verse like 1 Cor 4.8 does, as we shall see (§ 1.2.3.1), give us grounds for thinking that for the Corinthians, or at least some of them, the enjoyment of salvation was not wholly a future affair. Moreover there is a subtle difference between the position that seems to be reflected in 1 Thessalonians and that of 1 Cor 15: in the former the Thessalonians' worries are most easily explicable if they had not heard anything of a future hope in the form of a resurrection of believers[2], whereas in the latter the statement 'there is no resurrection of the

---

Notes on 1.2.1.4

1 Murphy, *Dead,* provides another distinctive, but not very plausible, solution when he argues that (a) death is here understood 'comprehensively' as what Paul's opponents regard as 'gnosis-death', i.e. exclusion from salvation, and (b) the salvation of the faithful of Israel is at stake in this chapter.
   Hurd, *Origin* 286, argues that the Corinthians rejected the resurrection of the dead largely out of 'antipathy to a new idea', since Paul had formerly preached to them of Christ's Parousia which they would live to see, a belief supported for them by their conviction that they were protected against death by the Eucharist. However it is far from clear that the Corinthians were in principle averse to anything new, and so we need to ask why this idea was so repugnant to them.

2 Cf. Lüdemann, *Paulus* 1, 229f; there is no suggestion in 1 Thess that the Thessalonians were opposed to the idea of resurrection although Héring ('Saint Paul' 318) refers to 'les antiré surrectionistes de Thessalonique'; see further Lüdemann, 221–6.
   At this point too mention should be made of the thesis of Mearns, 'Development' (1980/1) 137–157, that at its earliest stage Christian eschatology was 'realized', and that the futurist teaching of the Thessalonian letters was a later correction of views which Paul had also held and proclaimed at Thessalonica; this reversal of the normal view of the development of Christian thought acknowledges the influence of Hurd's methods, but shares with him all the perils of arguing back to a period for which we have no direct evidence; moreover it would have been hard to argue, as Mearns suggests, that *all* previous Christian deaths were a punishment on sin and the like, since this period included the deaths of martyrs like Stephen and James the son

dead' presupposes that they have heard of the idea of such a resurrection and have rejected it. The position has shifted: whereas Paul could hope to reassure the Thessalonians by telling them of the resurrection, he must bring arguments against the Corinthians to convince them of the error and perversity of their rejection of this idea. It is necessary then to account for this rejection and Spörlein has not adequately done so. It is the strength of the various religio-historical solutions that they take this problem seriously. So, before turning to the wider context of 1 Corinthians in search of clues to the problems of chap. 15 and their solution, we should give some consideration to the question of the outside influences which have been held responsible for the Corinthians' denial of the resurrection.

1.2.2. Spörlein is in fact unusual in this respect, in that he does not invoke any *outside influence on the Corinthians* at this point. For the majority of scholars have postulated some sort of influence here, mostly Hellenistic or Gnostic. But we will see that there is no agreed correlation between the different theories as to the Corinthians' views and the influences which are supposed to have affected them. One particular background can be invoked to explain more than one attitude to the resurrection and there can be different religio-historical explanations of one position.

1.2.2.1. One exception to the prevalent support for the theory of Hellenistic or Gnostic influences is to be found in the views of *Albert Schweitzer and Adolf Schlatter*[1]. The former aligned the deniers of the resurrection with the *Psalms of Solomon* and the Old Testament prophets; they were 'representatives of the ultra-conservative eschatological view that there was no resurrection'; for them 'only those have anything to hope for who are alive at the Return of Jesus'[2]. Schlatter, following through his interpretation of 1 Corinthians in the supposed light of that most obscure of verses, 1 Cor 4.6, argued that the deniers of the resurrection were pursuing

---

of Zebedee; what future was expected for them? It is more likely that earlier deaths, particularly in Jewish Christian circles, presented no problem for the church since their vindication by resurrection was assumed, tacitly or explicitly; in other words it may be significant that the problem arises for the first time in a predominantly Gentile church (cf. further §1.2.3.3 and n. 4 there).

Notes on 1.2.2.1

1 Meyer, *1 Kor* 322 (ET 2, 36), also lists a number of older scholars who attributed the denial of the resurrection to former Sadducees; cf. Beet, 'Sadducees'.

2 *Mysticism* 93; Schmithals, *Gnosis* 147, considers that the vicarious baptism of v 29 refutes this suggestion.

their policy of 'going beyond what is written'. Against Lütgert he maintains that the advocates of this policy were Jews; the opposition to Paul in Corinth arose, not from a misunderstanding of his gospel, but from outside, introduced by some completely independent of Paul who were motivated by Jewish influences[3]. For them resurrection was unnecessary because they possessed perfection in the present[4]. They belittled the body[5]. For them, however, the dead were not lost, but Christ's coming would be for the living community alone. Yet what Christ's coming would bring was already fulfilled for them; already they reigned. Their position was really a return to that which Israel had formerly held: joy and peace were to be found in union with God in this life (63—65).

There is much in Schlatter's account which is worthy of note, but his thesis is weakened both by his dependence on the fickle support of 1 Cor 4.6 and by his treatment of the problems of 1 and 2 Corinthians as fundamentally the same in origin, as well as by a certain imprecision as to the origins of this Palestinian Jewish Christian group and the influences which affected them. Why, for instance, did they belittle the body? Is that the product of Hellenistic influence[6]?

1.2.2.2. Various attempts have also been made to derive the Corinthians' beliefs from *Hellenistic religious and philosophical ideas*. Vv 30—34 have led at least one scholar to specify Epicureans as the influence on the Corinthians[1]. But rightly Schmithals doubts whether Epicureans could become Christians without a radical change of view[2]. Thus those taking this line have more usually appealed to popular Hellenistic ideas rather than any particular school of philosophy[3].

---

3 *Theologie* 36; the work of W. Lütgert referred to is the influential study, *Freiheitspredigt und Schwarmgeister in Korinth: ein Beitrag zur Charakteristik der Christuspartei* (BFChTh 12.3, Gütersloh, 1908).

4 Ibid. 28; Schlatter is aware that at first sight denial of the resurrection is a contradiction of scripture, not a going beyond it. Yet he feels that his interpretation is not open to this objection.

5 Ibid. 63, citing as evidence 1 Cor 15.35ff. He cites as further evidence the Corinthians' use of prostitutes and opposition to marriage and their view of foodstuffs as morally and religiously indifferent.

6 Cf. ibid. 38: Schlatter denies that the Corinthians' asceticism arises out of any general view, e.g. of spirit and matter; rather it is the result simply of their evaluation of sexual intercourse. But that could not explain their denial of the resurrection.

Notes on 1.2.2.2

1 So W. M. L. de Wette, *Kurze Erklärung der Briefe an die Korinther* (Leipzig, 1845[2]) 129, quoted by Spörlein, *Leugnung* 8.

2 *Gnosis* 147.

3 Commentators who favour this approach are listed in Spörlein, *Leugnung* 9—12; see also Manson, *Studies* 206; Davies, *Paul* 303f; Keck-Furnish, *Letters* 67; Brandon, *Man* 219, specifies Orphic and Platonic teaching on the soul.

Yet any attempt to trace the problems of the Corinthians with the resurrection to this cause, and in particular to the belief in the immortality of the soul, is confronted with Schniewind's cogent counter-arguments[4]: why does Paul not stress the bodily nature of the resurrection in vv 12– 19? Why does he not argue that belief in immortality of the soul is inadequate? In vv 29–34 he seems to argue against crass materialists; however, instead of pointing out the inconsistency of their seeking to combine the beliefs of Platonism and those of Epicureanism, Paul shows that their theory and their practice both repudiate any life after death. In vv 35–57 he omits to define the relationship between the destiny of the soul and the resurrection of the body, and he is so far from Hellenistic usage that he speaks of man's lower, mortal existence as being that of the soul. Vv 50ff moreover suggest that the Corinthians shared Paul's eschatology and held to a belief in Jesus' resurrection. The expectation of the return of Christ was as un-Greek as the idea of resurrection. To these arguments of Schniewind could also be added the observation that the argument of vv 23–28 about the order of the eschatological events does not have much point if directed against this position.

However it is doubtful whether these arguments do more than show that the Corinthians' denial of the resurrection, *if* Paul represents them correctly, did not arise purely and simply from their adoption of the usual Hellenistic doctrine of the immortality of the soul. After all Gnostic anthropology, which Schniewind himself advances as an explanation of the Corinthians' views, had in this respect much in common with that of the Orphic and Pythagorean traditions of Greek philosophy: for it too the mortal body was a tomb incarcerating the divine and immortal element which is one's true self. Spörlein was perfectly justified in raising the question, 'what are the differences between an expectation of the after-life which is an expression of a gnostic dualism and one which is influenced by the devaluation of the corporeal that arises from a Platonic philosophical anthropology'[5]? Horsley's position too presumably involves attributing to the Corinthian 'strong' a belief in an immortal soul, but it is clear from the small proportion of his article devoted to the question of their denial of the resurrection[6] that there was far more to their position than simply the substitution of immortality of the soul for resurrection of the body. It is questionable how far Schniewind's arguments are effective against this position or any other which postulates the Hellenistic belief in immor-

---

4 'Leugner' 110–13; yet Schniewind's arguments hold good only against this view as usually found in Greek thought; he does not raise the question how this idea might be modified and altered in Hellenistic *Christian* circles (see further in this section and in chap. 3).

5 *Leugnung* 15; cf. Fascher, 'Korintherbriefe' 289.

6 'Elitism' 223–5.

tality of the soul as but one element among others in the Corinthian position.

1.2.2.3. We have already seen that the suggestion of *Gnostic influence* is not in essence greatly different from the theory of Hellenistic philosophical influence; thus, *prima facie*, it is hard to see what advantages it has over the latter, and yet it has often been preferred to the latter as an explanation of the Corinthians' position.

According to Spörlein J. L. Mosheim was the first expressly to compare the Corinthians' position with that of Gnosticism[1], but this thesis was first advocated in this century by W. Lütgert and since then has steadily gained ground[2]. Lütgert attributed the denial of the resurrection to the 'Christ party' apparently mentioned in 1.12[3]. That it is not unambiguously clear who was responsible for the denial of the resurrection is, however, shown by the fact that at various times the followers of Paul, Peter or Apollos have been held responsible[4]. However, Lütgert felt that he could maintain this position because of the points of contact between the beliefs of the deniers of the resurrection and those of Paul's opponents elsewhere in 1 Corinthians in passages where he had also detected a refutation of the Christ party's views. In particular vv 33f showed the contact between the denial of the resurrection and the libertinism attacked elsewhere in the letter (128–130). These views he attributed to 'Gnosticism'

Notes on 1.2.2.3

1 *Erklärung des Ersten Briefs des heiligen Apostels Pauli an die Gemeinde zu Corinthus* (Altona/Flensburg, 1741) 910f, cited by Spörlein, *Leugnung* 12f.

2 See §1.2.2.1 n. 3; cf., e.g., Rudolph, *Gnosis* 189.

3 Only 'apparently' since, in my view, the most convincing explanation of this puzzling reference is that it is Paul's retort to the other slogans (so first v. Dobschütz, *Life* 72). This verse and the following could then be paraphrased thus: 'I hear that you quarrel among yourselves, brethren. I have heard that one of you will say "I am Paul's" and another "I am Apollos'" and another "I am Cephas'". And I am Christ's and that allegiance is absolute and is not subdivided among his various servants. That loyalty and allegiance is *sui generis*, for none of his servants can claim to have been crucified for you, nor was it the name of any lesser person that you took upon you in baptism. Both of these constitute unique claims.' This interpretation has the advantage that it is in harmony with Paul's use of language about 'being Christ's' elsewhere in the Corinthian letters (1 Cor 3.22f; 2 Cor 10.7); otherwise it would surely be unwise of Paul to seem to endorse the slogan of one group. Moreover it is noteworthy that although Paul refers to the claims of the other three groups in 1 Cor 3.22, as does *1 Clem* 47.3, nowhere is a Christ party mentioned again. Barrett, 'Christianity' 274, objects that (1) the parallelism of the four phrases in 1.12, and (2) the lack of any indication that Paul had ceased to quote the Corinthians tell against this view (cf. his *1 Cor* 45). However the Corinthians could be expected to recognize which were their slogans and which were not, and the incongruity of putting Christ on the same level as the other three would be clear to them, even if Paul had not emphasized it in v 13. Further, it is notoriously difficult to tell at some points whether Paul is quoting the Corinthians or expressing his own view (e.g. 6.12f – see §1.2.3.2 below; 6.18; 7.1, 26; 8.1, 4, 8; 10.23, 29f).

4 Cf. Spörlein, *Leugnung* 5.

in the sense that 'a gnosis surpassing faith, which depends upon revelation and which results in Christian perfection for its possessor, is seen as the essence of Christianity' (134).

As we have seen, Schniewind's influential article also espoused this solution to the problem. Acknowledging his debt to Lütgert, he also argued that the denial of the resurrection was one aspect of the views of a single party who formed the opposition to Paul in Corinth, and 'Paul's opponents in Corinth are Gnostics. The whole of Paul's polemic in the letters to the Corinthians can be treated as parts of one single struggle against gnosis'[5]. And yet when he contrasts Paul's gospel and the message of Gnosticism on the grounds that the former said that Jesus had conquered the real opposition of the cosmic powers, while the Gnostics said that these powers did not exist[6], it is doubtful whether Schniewind has represented typical Gnostic views correctly. More typically the Gnostic believed that through his possession of gnosis he was superior to, and liberated from, these powers, without in any way denying their existence. 'Deliverance for the gnostic is . . . from the body, from this world, from the power of the archons who control it'[7].

More recently W. Schmithals in his thorough-going Gnostic interpretation of the beliefs of the Corinthians has sought to incorporate chap. 15 within his theory, but, unlike Schniewind, only at the expense of charging Paul with misunderstanding the Corinthians. Paul, writing in his letter to the Corinthians which Schmithals identifies as Letter A[8], was so incompletely informed about the Corinthians' beliefs as to treat them as denying any after-life at all (147); he does so despite the fact that the polemic in v 46 clearly reveals the Gnostic basis to their beliefs (158f). Moreover 'the denial of the resurrection of the body is a fundamental doctrine for gnosis' (148). However, v 46 also leads Schmithals into difficulties; so apposite is it, so perfectly does it hit the Gnostic nail on the head that he suggests that it may be a gloss and not part of the original letter (160f n. 2). Like Hoffmann[9], Schmithals too seems prepared to argue that Paul quotes the Corinthians correctly when he attributes to them the statement that 'there is no resurrection (of the dead)'. It is in his interpretation of this as denial of any form of life after death that Paul betrays his lack of

---

5 'Leugner' 114.

6 Ibid. 117; cf. the critique in Schottroff, *Glaubende* 162.

7 R. McL. Wilson, 'Soteriology' 850.

8 *Gnosis* 85; he notes how chap. 15 interrupts the series of answers to the Corinthians' letter, coming between the treatment of the question about 'spiritual people/gifts' in chaps 12—14 and that about the collection in 16.1—4.

9 *Toten* 242; Hoffmann largely follows Schmithals in his religio-historical analysis of the Corinthians' beliefs at this point. But, as noted above, he is not prepared to follow Bultmann and Schmithals when they charge Paul with completely misunderstanding the Corinthians.

knowledge of the true situation. He expressly rejects any identification of their position with that of Hymenaeus and Philetus with a somewhat cryptic statement: 'Precisely in his ignorance of the actual situation Paul would not have been able to cite the Gnostic doctrine with "ἀνάστασις οὐκ ἔστιν" if people in Corinth were asserting "ἀνάστασιν ἤδη γεγονέναι" '[10]. Presumably what Schmithals means is that Paul was so much in the dark that he had to use what evidence he had; it was not that he knew the situation and summed it up in his own words as a denial of the resurrection; rather he had somehow heard that they said that there was no resurrection and he had then interpreted this (incorrectly according to Schmithals). If Paul is not quoting something which he has heard we are thus at a loss to explain whence this summary of the Corinthians' views arose.

L. Schottroff also defines the Corinthians' views as Gnostic and holds that Paul differed from them principally in his view of the relation of believers to this world[11]. However, she is prepared to say that baptism for the dead is not a typically Gnostic practice, but that this practice betrayed the Corinthians' 'complex syncretistic religiosity' as they adopted the practices of the mystery-cults[12]. Moreover, their form of a religion of the Spirit is not an integral feature of Gnosticism. She explicitly criticizes Schmithals for assuming that all that happened in the Corinthian church was Gnostic[13]. Yet, once one concedes that certain features of the Corinthians' beliefs and practices were not Gnostic then the case for interpreting other features as Gnostic becomes that much weaker and more difficult to sustain; for if one feature alone were doubtful and all other evidence pointed to a Gnostic background, then there would be a strong presumption in favour of treating this ambiguous feature as also being Gnostic; the more features that are ambiguous, let alone clearly non-Gnostic, the less can one presume that all other features, however ambiguous, are in fact Gnostic.

For at this point certain fundamental problems in the handling of the evidence for Gnosticism in the New Testament present themselves: is 'Gnosticism', the phenomenon known to us from the second century C.E. onwards in certain groups and sects, to be distinguished from 'gnosis', an attitude or set of attitudes which produced this phenomenon among

---

10 *Gnosis* 148, quoted according to the ET of Schmithals' work (157f), cf. also Schottroff, *Glaubende* 156.

11 Ibid. 162.

12 Ibid. 164f; so also Schmithals, *Gnosis* 245, 348.

13 Ibid. 165; this is perhaps unfair in the light, e.g., of his treatment of 1 Cor 7, where he argues that the asceticism reflected in that chapter is a reaction by followers of Paul to Gnostic libertinism (Schmithals, ibid. 221–4).

others[14]? If it is, then 'gnosis' may be an apt description of the mentality of the Corinthians, at least at certain points, but it is not a complete explanation of the ideas and motifs which they used to give expression to that mentality, nor does it rule out the possibility that they derived both the ideas and the mentality from elements in the surrounding culture which would not normally be classed under the heading of 'Gnosticism'. Moreover, to invoke Gnosticism as an explanation may be to blind ourselves to the light which a situation like that in the Corinthian church may shed on the way in which Gnosticism could arise in certain Christian circles: the attitudes and claims of the Corinthians may show us a type of Christianity *en route* to Gnosticism, but one which has not yet advanced to any developed or systematic exposition of its beliefs.

Finally it must be noted, against those attempts to identify the cause of the Corinthians' denial of the resurrection as Gnostic views, that very often later Gnostics were prepared to use the Christian language of resurrection and to reinterpret it in their own way. Thus H.-M. Schenke can point to a positive use of the idea of resurrection widespread in Gnosticism[15]. However it is still possible that this *modus vivendi* with Christian tradition was only reached gradually and that at an earlier stage this Christian tradition met with outright rejection. (Cf. § 3.3.1 below.)

1.2.2.4. It may be questionable how far the last religio-historical explanation to be considered is separable from the previous Gnostic hypothesis. For this explanation, which invokes the influence of the *mystery-religions,* in doing so appeals to a body of material which proved a congenial and useful breeding ground for Gnostic speculations and interpretations. Nowhere is this better illustrated than in the Naassene traditions quoted by Hippolytus in his *Refutatio omnium haeresium* (5.6.3–11.1), with their plentiful appeals to, and reinterpretations of, the traditions of different mystery-religions[1].

---

14 Cf. Bianchi, *Origins* xx–xxxii; R. McL. Wilson, *Gnosis* 6ff; but cf. Rudolph, '"Gnosis"', esp. 24f, and the lit. cited there.

15 'Auferstehungsglaube'; cf. Güttgemanns, *Apostel* 68–70. Of the two examples of denial of the resurrection cited by Schottroff, *Glaubende* 155, one (Iren., *Haer.* 1.24.5=Harvey 1.19.3) does not mention resurrection, but only says that Basilides held that only the soul was saved, for the body is of transitory nature; the other (Pol., *Phil.* 7.1) is again a Christian characterization of heretical beliefs and does not quote what the opponents in question actually said about resurrection; a third passage cited by Schottroff (ibid.; cf. 77f) only rejects Christ's resurrection *in corpore mundiali* (Iren., *Haer.* 1.30.13=Harvey 1.28.7). See now further Wisse '"Opponents"' 108–14.

Notes on 1.2.2.4.
1 Cf. §2.2.1 below.

This explanation is particularly congenial to those who maintain that the Corinthians believed the resurrection already to have taken place, for it is possible for them to argue that what led the Corinthians to this position was their assimilation of the Christian gospel to the beliefs held by the adherents of the cults of the various dying and rising deities[2]. As the devotees of these cults believed that in the cultic acts they participated in the fate of their respective deities, so the Corinthians believed that in the sacrament of baptism they had already shared in Christ's death and resurrection.

Thus J. H. Wilson holds that the background to the Corinthians' beliefs lies in the popular cults of the day; from these they adopted their belief in the magical efficacy of their sacraments. Through them, they believed, they received the Spirit and shared in Jesus' exaltation[3]. Güttgemanns also seems to hint at a possible influence here from the mystery-cults when he points out that occasionally these cults spoke of the resurrection of their deities (but not apparently of their devotees)[4]. The most determined attempt to derive the belief in an already present resurrection from the mysteries is perhaps that of Brakemeier, who rejects a Gnostic explanation in favour of this one: like the adherents of the mysteries they enjoyed a present bliss in the form of an enhancement of their earthly lives (*Lebenssteigerung*); they interpreted baptism on the analogy of the initiatory rites of the mysteries: in it there took place a repetition (*Nachvollzug*) of the Christ-event in which the initiate was drawn into the fate of the deity, literally sharing its death and resurrection (*im naturhaften Sinn*). Colossians and Ephesians preserve this belief in a pure form[5].

1.2.3. A decisive question in this discussion is whether one is prepared to grant that Paul misunderstood his opponents or not. However all seem prepared to see in the statement 'there is no resurrection (of the dead)' an accurate representation of what the Corinthians were saying. Yet this assumption can seemingly be reconciled with a considerable variety of interpretations of what the Corinthians meant and why they said this, particularly if what Paul says subsequently in reply to them can be rejected as misplaced polemic based on ignorance or misunderstanding or

---

2 Not that it is only those holding this view who are prepared to invoke the influence of the mysteries; Schmithals, *Gnosis* 245, holds that the practice of baptism for the dead arose from the influence of the mysteries. Schniewind, 'Leugner' 126, also appealed to the mysteries to explain this verse, but did not do so to explain the Corinthians' beliefs about resurrection.

3 'Corinthians' 99.

4 *Apostel* 68 n. 80.

5 *Auseinandersetzung* 13–15.

both. Few attempts to reconstruct their true beliefs are, however, based on the apparently conflicting evidence of chap. 15 alone; rather scholars seek to fit the Corinthians' beliefs about resurrection into a system or set of beliefs detected in the rest of 1 Corinthians or even of 1–2 Corinthians. This, along with the internal coherence of the reconstructed beliefs, is the yardstick according to which *the plausibility of the various reconstructions* is evaluated[1].

This way of proceeding does, of course, presuppose that the denial of the resurrection is of a piece with all or some of the views found elsewhere in the letter. If, therefore, the 'some' who denied the resurrection were a group whose views were not reflected elsewhere in the problems which Paul handles in 1 Corinthians this approach would be invalidated[2]. So the most that can be said is that, if an interpretation of their denial of the resurrection can be found which is consonant with other views reflected in Paul's exchange with the Corinthian church, then this has a certain claim to probability. When Brakemeier claims that, although Paul only addresses 'some', he has the whole church in mind[3], he goes beyond the actual evidence and makes a claim which can only be justified by his reconstruction of the situation in the church as a whole. In fact, in view of

---

Notes on 1.2.3

1 Such are the imponderables in the situation that some scholars are reluctant to commit themselves to any decision as to the background to this denial of the resurrection: cf. Conzelmann, *1 Kor* 310; Bruce, *1–2 Cor* 144.

2 Senft, *1 Cor* 185, argues that the division of our 1 Cor into a series of fragments from different letters, which he like many others (cf. the list in Hurd, *Origin* 45, plus Schenk, '1 Korintherbrief'; Jewett, 'Redaction') proposes, calls into question the assumption that Paul's view of the Corinthians in 1 Cor 15 is of one piece with his view of them in other parts of the letter; for a critique of such analyses cf. Michaelis, 'Teilungshypothesen', and, more recently, Aland, 'Entstehung'; certainly considerable difficulties beset such hypotheses – the motivation of the editor(s), the rationale of their compositions, the absence of any textual evidence.

Whether one divides 1 Cor up or maintains its unity, it is hard to explain the presence of 1 Cor 15 sandwiched between answers to various points raised in the Corinthians' letter to Paul (12–14, 16.1ff), unless there is some continuity between the problems dealt with in chaps 12–14 and that of the denial of the resurrection (or at least unless Paul or an editor thought that he – or she – could see some connection). 1 Cor 11.2–16 also interrupts the sequence of answers to the Corinthian letter, but this is perhaps because the appeal to imitate Paul (11.1) leads him (or an editor) on to a point where they have deviated from the traditions which he has bequeathed – though an exceptional point perhaps (11.2, 16). What about 1 Cor 15? No such connection appears on the surface, but I should like to argue that it perhaps lies in the fact that some of those most preoccupied with the headier things of the Spirit had least time and respect for the body, including its fate in the world to come. Compare here the interesting argument of Gager, 'Body-Symbols', esp. 348–50, that the Corinthian denial of the resurrection was part and parcel of a sectarian viewpoint in which the Corinthians adopted a more pessimistic or negative view of society in general than Paul himself, and had a view of Christianity 'in which individual values take clear precedence over corporate life'. (He bases himself here on the work of Mary Douglas.)

3 *Auseinandersetzung* 18.

the all too apparent differences of opinion within the church at Corinth, it would be rash to assume that a view held by 'some' was shared by all. Better is the argument of Wolff, that elsewhere in chap. 15 (vv 14, 17, 33f, 58) Paul addresses the congregation as a whole[4]; yet that might only be because he wished to warn all of them against the view propounded by 'some'.

But are there then signs elsewhere in 1 Corinthians of views which might throw some light on the denial of the resurrection by some? Two verses in particular may be of especial relevance here, 4.8 and 6.13[5].

1.2.3.1. In *4.8* Paul comments

> All of you, no doubt, have everything you could desire[1]. You have come into your fortune already. You have come into your kingdom – and left us out. How I wish you had indeed won your kingdom; then you might share it with us! (*NEB*)

The irony of Paul's words here is plain[2]; the Corinthians, or some of them at least, are making claims and assumptions about themselves which he considers unjustified. The translation quoted here conveys well the tone of Paul's words, but paraphrases and expands the original to a certain extent. A more literal rendering would be

> Already you are satisfied; already you have become rich (aorist); you have come into your kingdom (aorist of the verb 'reign') without us; and I wish that you had indeed come into your kingdom, so that we too might reign with you.

Here the twofold 'already' ($\check{\eta}\delta\eta$)[3] points clearly to the relevance of this text to the suggestion that the Corinthians, like Hymenaeus and Philetus, also said that the resurrection had already ($\check{\eta}\delta\eta$) taken place. Is this part and parcel of the same set of beliefs? Or is the omission of 'risen' from the list of blessings already enjoyed significant?

The Corinthians' choice of language calls for some comment, and different explanations are possible of the origins of these claims made by the Corinthians which are reflected in this verse. One could point to the

---

4 *1 Kor* 173.

5 Cf. Barrett, *1 Cor* 109, 147, 347f; it has been suggested by Murphy-O'Connor, 'Slogans', that 6.18*b* is also evidence for the same view as represented in 6.13, but it would be easier to see a reference to the moral indifference of the body there if the sentence had read ὃ ἐὰν ποιήσῃ ἄνθρωπος (μόνον) τῷ σώματι οὐχ ἁμάρτημά (ἐστιν) or the like.

Notes on 1.2.3.1

1 Orr-Walther, *I Cor* 176, 178, treat these as questions, following Westcott and Hort (and Luther); whatever the punctuation the irony remains clear in the second part of the verse; cf. McHugh, 'Present' 181. Κορέννυμι is used figuratively here (BAG s.v.).

2 Cf. BDF §495(2); *pace* Jewett, 'Redaction' 407, it is hard to think that even Gnostic followers a half-century later could have missed the implications of the last part of this verse.

3 J. Weiß translates this word 'wahrlich, schon (seid Ihr gesättigt . . .)' (*1 Kor* 106).

claims made by the Cynic-Stoic tradition for the truly good and wise man[4]: he lacked nothing good[5], possessed true wealth[6], and alone was worthy to be called a king[7]. These Hellenistic philosophical views find their echo in the writings of Philo of Alexandria, especially, as might be expected, in his treatise *Quod omnis probus liber sit*, as well as in his portrayal of Moses[8]. In the former work he describes how he can call the most destitute wealthy (§ 8)[9]; he who has God for his leader is in turn set over all things on earth (§ 20)[10]; the good are more rightly called 'shepherds of the people' than kings are (§ 31); the companions of the gods are 'rulers of all and kings of kings' (§ 42). This last theme is also found in *De mutatione nominum* 151–153 and elsewhere; those born of virtue are rulers by nature, and so Abraham, though a migrant, was rightly called a king (Gen 23.6)[11]. These ideals Philo finds exemplified in the Essenes in *Omn. prob.* 75–87: though moneyless they are considered very wealthy (§ 77); their communal living ensures in a practical way that no one lacks anything necessary. Yet, more than all these parallels, the most interesting text of all in connection with 1 Cor 4.8 is Philo's description of the Therapeutae in *De vita contemplativa* 13: they, longing for the immortal and blessed life, believe that their mortal life is already (ἤδη) ended and leave their possessions to their relatives or friends, thus living

---

4 Cf. Allo, *1 Cor* 74; Dupont, *Gnosis* 302, 305; R. M. Grant, 'Wisdom' 52; Horsley, 'Elitism' 210, 228; J. Weiß, ibid. 106; Moffatt, *1 Cor* 49, compares Stoic ideas; cf. Morris, *1 Cor* 79. Conzelmann, *1 Kor* 106 n. 28, describes these ideas as 'protognosis', and Bruce, *1–2 Cor* 49, sees here an anticipation of the second-century Gnostic Prodicus; H. D. Wendland, *1–2 Kor* 35, ascribes them to 'enthusiastic gnosis'.
Significantly Conzelmann, ibid. 105, calls the style of 4.7 'diatribenartig'; cf. Stowers, *Diatribe* 84.

5 E.g. Cic., *Fin.* 4.27.74; Diog. L. 6.37, 72; Epict., *Diss.* 3.22.48; Plut., *Compendium argumenti Stoicos absurdiora poetis dicere* 4.1058C; Sen., *Ben.* 7.2.5; 7.3.2f; 7.4.1; 7.8.1; 7.10.6; *Ep.* 9 passim, 55.4; 59.14, 111.2–4; *De constantia* 5.4–6.8; *SVF* 3.589–91, 596, 599, 618; cf. also, earlier, Antisthenes frg. 80 (ed. Caizzi).

6 E.g. Cic., *Paradoxa Stoicorum* 42–52; *Fin.* 4.3.7; Dio Chrys., *Or.* 1.62; Hor., *Ep.* 1.1.106; *Sat.* 1.3.124; Luc., *Hermot.* 16; Maximus Tyr. 36.5E; Plut., *Adulat.* 16.58E; *Compendium* (as previous n.) 4.1058B–D; *Ep. Socrates* 6.8 (ed. Malherbe 236.18); *SVF* 3.593–5, 597–600, 618f, 655; Xen., *Sym.* 4.37–44; cf. Wis 7.8, 11; 8.5, 18.

7 E.g. Cic., *Fin.* 3.22.75; 4.3.7; Clem. Alex., *Strom.* 2.4 (19.3) – Speusippus; Crates frg. 5 (Diels, *Poetarum*); *Ep. Diogenes* 4 (ed. Malherbe 94.23); Diog L. 6.29f; 7.122; Epict., *Diss.* 3.22.49, 63, 79 (cf. 3.26.31); Hor., *Ep.* 1.1.107; *Sat.* 1.3.125; Luc., *Hermot.* 16, 81; Maximus Tyr. 36.5D; Plut. as in the previous n.; Sen., *Ben.* 7.10.6; *Ep.* 108.13; *SVF* 3.599, 617–22, 655; Varro, *Sat. Men.* frg. 245 (ed. Astbury); cf. additionally Socrates in Xen., *Mem.* 3.9.10; Wis 6.20, ἐπιθυμία ἄρα σοφίας ἀνάγει ἐπὶ βασιλείαν (also 8.14). See McHugh, 'Present' 187 (contrast Barrett's comments on 202).

8 For reff. cf. Holladay, *Aner* esp. 108–22.

9 Cf. *Rer. div. her.* 27 (also *Leg. all.* 1.34; 3.163; *Sacr AC.* 43; *Plant.* 65, 69; *Virt.* 8, etc.).

10 Cf. *Sobr.* 56, and Moses in *Vit. Mos.* 1.155–8.

11 Cf. *Poster. C.* 128; *Plant.* 68; *Sobr.* 57; *Migr. Abr.* 197; *Abr.* 261 (the wise as king; so also *Som.* 2.244; cf. *Abr.* 272; *Virt.* 216–18; *Quaest. in Gen.* 4.76); cf. *Ep. Arist.* 211, 290.

out what Philo holds up as the practice of the true disciple of Moses (*Deus imm.* 148ff).

That the Corinthians should adopt such popular philosophical claims is the more probable if, as G. Theißen plausibly argues[12], the 'wise' and the 'strong' in the Corinthian church were in the main drawn from the ranks of the well-to-do and educated. For, although these need not have belonged to any particular philosophical school, they would almost certainly be familiar with these ideas.

It should also be remarked that these claims could, in the eyes of converts to Christianity who had been brought up in this Hellenistic culture, find their justification in the traditions of the teachings of Jesus[13]: there one could find promises of satisfaction for the hungry (Lk 6.21 par.) and of the supplying of all one's needs (Matt 6.33 par.) in full measure (Lk 6.38); riches were promised to them (Mk 10.21 pars) and perhaps not just in the world to come (Lk 18.30); they were to rule over and judge the world (Matt 19.28 par.). The most likely reason for the Corinthians' claims is that they had fused together the Hellenistic traditions just mentioned with this sayings material, or with traditions emanating from this element in Jesus' teaching, thus reinterpreting the words of Jesus or the church teaching derived from them in the light of their own very different culture, and claiming that they already enjoyed what were largely promises for the world to come. This would be all the more probable if Paul then went on to reflect the tradition of Jesus' teaching himself in vv 11–13: the apostles manifest in the present the conditions of humiliation to which Jesus promised a share in God's reign in the future (but only in the future)[14].

---

12 'Starken'.

13 Cf. Robertson-Plummer, *1 Cor* 84; J. Weiß, *1 Kor* 106; Klauck, *1 Kor* 38, sees the influence of both the tradition of the sayings of Jesus and of popular philosophy here.

This would be further evidence for the argument advanced by J. M. Robinson and others (lit. in Tuckett, '1 Corinthians' 607–12) that the Corinthians were making use of sayings of Jesus; Tuckett, however, has shown that there is little evidence that their source was 'Q'; 1 Cor 4.8 (and 13.2) he counts as the strongest evidence of their use of sayings material, but it is doubtful whether the background of 1 Cor 4.8 can be pinpointed as, e.g., Luke's 'Sermon on the Plain' (J. M. Robinson, 'Kerygma' 43).

Wettstein, *Novum Testamentum* 2, 114, also compared OT passages like Hos 12.8 and Isa 47.7, but these are not so much examples to be copied as ones to be avoided; they would hardly have lured the Corinthians to such claims.

This may be connected with the unusually frequent references to the kingdom or reign of God or Christ in 1 Cor in comparison with the rest of Paul's letters (4.20, 6.9f; 15.24, 50). This usage may point to the Corinthians' interest in, and use of, this language, and 4.8 would then suggest that they regarded themselves as sharing now the reign of God and/or Christ; Paul's warnings about the conditions for 'inheriting' that kingdom (in the future) would then have an added point (6.9f; 15.50).

14 Cf. J. M. Robinson, 'Kerygma' 44; Walter, 'Paulus' 509.

Yet it might be rash to claim that the Corinthians held an 'over-realized eschatology' on the basis of this verse in chap. 4 alone, unless there is other evidence in the letter to support this analysis, but it does make a good starting-point for the argument, and a far better one than such controversial keys for the rediscovery of the Corinthians' theology as 4.6 or 12.3[15]. It does, moreover, fit in well with other evidence in the letter, notably the argument on the order of the eschatological events in 15.23ff[16]. At least it is clear that the Corinthians were conscious, too conscious in Paul's eyes, of being already in possession of extensive spiritual blessings; in so far as these were usually regarded as being 'eschatological' we are justified in calling their position one of an '(over-) realized eschatology'.

However, if the Hellenistic parallels to these claims surveyed above are indeed the origin, or a part of the origin, of the Corinthians' beliefs, then we should not expect to find resurrection mentioned among them; Philo never mentions the hope of resurrection, and it is even less likely that non-Jews in the Graeco-Roman world would gladly or readily have adopted it for themselves, as we shall see in § 3.2 below. Here it needs to be emphasized that this list of what the Corinthians claimed already to enjoy does *not* include resurrection either[17].

1.2.3.2. The other verse which we must consider, *6.13*, is less straightforward in many respects:

> (12: All things are lawful for me, but not all are beneficial. All things are lawful for me, but I will not have the law laid down for me by anything)[1].
> 13: (*a*) Food is for the stomach and the stomach is for food. (*b*) And (or 'but') God will destroy both the stomach and food. (*c*) But the body is not for fornication but for the Lord, and the Lord for the body.
> (14: And God both raised the Lord and will raise us up by his power).

The following problems are of immediate concern here:

(1) To what extent (if any) is Paul quoting the views of the Corinthians here?

---

15 Cf. the argument of Thiselton, 'Eschatology', against Ellis, 'Christ' 73f; cf. also Lincoln, *Paradise* 33.
4.6, as mentioned above, was Schlatter's point of departure, 12.3 that of Schmithals (*Gnosis*).
16 Cf. Schottroff, *Glaubende* 161; 15.46 would also fit in with this if it were translated 'but the spiritual nature does not come at first, but rather the psychic, and only then subsequently the spiritual' (cf. my ' "Man" ' 301f).
17 Cf. Doughty, 'Presence' 75.

Notes on 1.2.3.2

1 An attempt to capture something of the word-play contained in the cognate words ἔξεστιν and ἐξουσιασθήσομαι. Fuchs, 'Herrschaft' 186, gives examples of Epictetus' use of ἔξεστι (and σύμφερον).

(2) What is the connection between the statements about food and those about sexual relations?

(3) What is the connection between 13*a* and 13*b*?

(1) Many have seen in parts of 6.12f quotations from the Corinthians' letter to Paul mentioned in 7.1 or quotations of their views which he has heard from other sources. So J. C. Hurd lists 22 scholars who think that 'all things are lawful' (v 12) is such a quotation and 15 who think that 'food is for the stomach and the stomach for food' (v 13*a*) is another[2]. With 6.12 quite a strong case can be made out, since the same phrase recurs in 10.23, although without the personal pronoun μοί. The addition of that pronoun in 6.12, however, shows that Paul has probably adopted their words and, as it were, taken them on his own lips. This draws our attention to a difficulty which besets any attempt to identify these' quotations: there are good reasons for thinking that in many respects the views of the Corinthians were very similar to those of Paul himself, nor is this surprising in a church that he founded; so the fact that the Corinthians said something does not rule out the fact that Paul himself could equally well have said precisely the same thing, with or without qualification. The problem becomes acute when the attempt is made to explain notoriously difficult statements in 1 Corinthians as quotations of the Corinthians' views just because of their difficulty and, implicitly, the scholar's reluctance to accept that Paul could have said such a thing. One instance of this is in 6.18[3], another in 10.29*b*–30[4].

Now in the present instance Hurd only lists 13*a* as a possible quotation of the Corinthians[5], but 13*b* might also come into the reckoning too[6], depending upon one's assessment of the relationship of that statement to 13*a*; is the connecting δέ any more adversative than that at the beginning of v 14?

(2) At first sight 6.13*a* would be far more appropriate in the context of the discussion of chaps 8–10; there such a principle could easily have been used in justification of eating anything, regardless of any previous contact with idolatrous worship. But here it seems to be used in the context of a discussion of sexual relationships. It is hard to see why it should

---

2 *Origin* 68; to the latter list should now be added Barrett, *1 Cor* 146; Bruce, *1-2 Cor* 62; Conzelmann, *1 Kor* 133; Thrall, *1–2 Cor* 45f.

3 Cf. Hurd, ibid. 67 n. 1; see now Murphy-O'Connor, 'Slogans'.

4 Cf. Hurd, ibid. 130 n. 2, for a survey of the different solutions, including treating this as an objection voiced by a 'strong' Christian.

5 So also in his own reconstruction of the letter (ibid. 146).

6 So Barrett, *1 Cor* 146, prints it as part of a quotation of the Corinthians' views; cf. Thiselton, 'Eschatology' 517; implied by Klauck, *1 Kor* 47; see also Héring, *1 Cor* 46; Bruce, *1–2 Cor* 63, considers this possible.

be unless the same principle, the moral and religious indifference of the stomach, was also applied to other bodily functions, including that of sexual activity. But that it is introduced here, without any apparent connection with the subject under discussion, may be a sufficient argument for seeing it as a principle invoked by the Corinthians as a justification of their behaviour in sexual matters[7].

(3) There are various possible relationships between 13a and 13b. 13b might (i) contradict 13a[8], (ii) agree with 13a but qualify it[9], or (iii) support 13a[10]. Now in other instances where Paul may be quoting the Corinthians and then goes on to contradict them or, more often if not always, to qualify their view, the conjunction which he usually employs to introduce his qualification seems to be the strong adversative ἀλλά ('but'). It is this which he uses in 6.12 (twice) and in 8.1 with 8.7[11]. Here, however, 13a and 13b are connected by δέ which need not be adversative at all; it is certainly not so in v 14, although it is in 13c. More telling is the difficulty that it is hard to see how 13b qualifies 13a, let alone contradicts it, unless it is that it simply sets a time limit upon this mutual relationship of food and stomach: they may be meant for one another now, but that will come to an end. But that is an odd qualification to introduce here, since the qualification which Paul wishes to make is to distinguish the stomach and the body (σῶμα). The one is transitory (13b), the other will be raised up by God's power as is implicitly stated in v 14; the one may just be for food, but the body is for the Lord. In that case, however, 13b is better regarded as a reason for, a confirmation of, 13a: what one does with food and what goes into the stomach *are* of no significance ethically or religiously, since they are ephemeral. At the same time this prepares the way for the distinction between the transitory stomach and the body which belongs to the Lord and will be raised by God (vv 13c–14). This is rather different to the reason given by Paul in 10.26 for saying that in itself no food is capable of contaminating the one who eats it: 'the earth is the Lord's and all its fulness'. The latter argument asserts the essential goodness of all created things, while 6.13b argues that their transitory nature is a reason for considering all permissible. The one is a very positive reason, the other a rather negative one.

---

7 So, e.g,, Barrett, ibid. 147; cf. Senft, *1 Cor* 83.

8 Morris, *1 Cor* 99, seems to hold that 13b contradicts 13a or at least the argument which the Corinthians wished to base on the slogan of 13a; also Fascher, *1 Kor* 175f.

9 Cf. Moffatt, *1 Cor* 68; Robertson-Plummer, *1 Cor* 120, 123.

10 So most commentators; cf. also Thiselton, 'Eschatology' 517.

11 Of Hurd's other quotations (*Origin* 67) it is disputed whether some are in fact quotations (e.g. 7.1: cf. Baltensweiler, *Ehe* 156f; Niederwimmer, *Askese* 80f n. 3), and others are not statements with which Paul would wish to disagree (e.g. 8.4).

Yet that is not to say that Paul is not capable of using both arguments; indeed that of 10.26 would be of no use to him in 6.12ff, since he wishes there to distinguish between the transitory stomach and the body which will be raised: for it would imply that the stomach and food were the Lord's too, as well as the body. But, equally, it is not impossible that the Corinthians might have justified the statement about food and the stomach by such an argument. If it is true that Paul's position was in many respects near to that of the Corinthians, then we may not be compelled to choose between Paul and the Corinthians as the source of this statement. However, the role that 13*b* plays in his argument, in that it aids the distinction which he wishes to draw between the transitory belly and the body which is to be raised to new life, may be sufficient reason for our seeing this statement as Paul's own comment[12].

Yet that need not mean that the Corinthians would disagree with this statement; it may in fact echo their arguments. If, of course, they held that the body was something evil, then that would be a different reason for their behaviour and would show a clear Gnosticizing, if not Gnostic, tendency in their thinking[13]. Logically that would cast doubt upon the goodness of the Creator or his power and there is no hint of that in their thinking; 8.4 seems to indicate that they adopted the monotheism of Hellenistic Jewish and Jewish-Christian propaganda[14]. On the other hand Paul seems to assume that they held to most of the elements of early Christian eschatology: he speaks to them of the coming judgment (3.1ff; 4.5; 6.2f; 11.32; cf. 9.27), of the coming end of the present age (7.29, 31; 10.11; 13.8, 10, 12; 15.24ff, 50ff) and of the return of Christ (11.26; 15.23; 16.22; cf. 1.7f). He speaks to them as if he could assume their consent to the basic elements of the Christian gospel (11.2; 15.1f, 11). All this is compatible with the Corinthians regarding this coming consummation and end of the present age as a valid reason for their treating what they saw as very much part of this age as something transitory and therefore unimportant. (Equally, if they in fact held a view which represented parts of

---

12 Paul also devalues the things of this world on the grounds that 'the form of this world is passing away' in 1 Cor 7.29–31 (on this passage cf. Schrage, 'Stellung'; I doubt, however, whether he has really made out a case for Paul's quoting apocalyptic traditions here; cf. also Baumgarten, *Paulus* 221–4. The extent of Paul's modification of apocalyptic traditions detected by these scholars means, at any rate, that the quotation would be limited – perhaps just 'the time is short/has been shortened' – v 29; cf. Barrett, *1 Cor* 176 – and the majority of the contents of these verses is the work of Paul).

13 Schottroff, *Glaubende* 166f, holds that Paul's argument is directed against a dualism which holds the body and matter to be not only inferior, but also 'feindlich und mächtig'; however it is doubtful whether she has shown that the dualism which Paul combats is definitely of this character nor whether, even if it were, it would be exclusively and peculiarly Gnostic.

14 Cf. too 10.26, which would certainly not fit in with Gnostic dualism; Paul's appeal to this text contains no suggestion that he was aware of any such basis to their views.

this creation as inherently evil then Paul was arguing at cross purposes with them throughout large portions of this letter.) Doubtless, however, it may be suggested, they would have been the readier to adopt this attitude towards their bodily functions because their Hellenistic upbringing also suggested to them that the body was of inferior nature and that bodily existence was a transitory experience of their true selves. Thus their eschatology contains elements both of early Christian preaching and of Hellenistic ideas, the latter interpreting and reinforcing the former.

However this suggestion should be distinguished from the common assertion that the Corinthians were denying the resurrection because they held the Greek view of the immortality of the soul (cf. §§ 1.2.1.2; 1.2.2.2). It is only the negative corollary of this Greek view, namely the mortality and consequent inferiority of the body, which the Corinthians would have adopted.[15]. Otherwise their views are distinguished from the usual Greek view by two factors in particular, their eschatology and their enthusiasm[16]. There is an eschatological dimension to their thinking which is not found in typical Greek representations of this view, but has its origins in Jewish apocalyptic writings; that is attested both by 6.13 and by Paul's arguments about the order of the eschatological events in 15.23–28 if they are at all apposite to the Corinthians. The Corinthian church is also a, if not the, prime example of the other factor, the Spirit-filled enthusiasm of early Christianity; in this what gave them confidence of survival after death and of salvation was the presence in them of God's Spirit, present, however, in them but not in all people. The basis of their confidence was the divine πνεῦμα, but not the ψυχή which was in all people[17]; for the Spirit which was God's eschatological gift to humanity had been poured out on them and this distinguished them from the rest of the human race[18]. And, we may surmise, it is unlikely that

---

15 Cf. Allo, *1 Cor* 399; Beker, *Paul* 164–6.

16 Cf. Knox, *Paul* (1939) 126f.

17 Cf. Klauck, *1 Kor* 112: they derived their own immortality from the conferring of the indestructible πνεῦμα in baptism.

However it should be noted that on occasions Greek writers used a dualism of πνεῦμα (instead of ψυχή) and σῶμα: Eur., *Suppl.* 532–4; frg. 971 (Nauck); Diog L. 9.19 (Xenophanes); Epicharmus in Diels-Kranz, *Fragmente* 23 (13) B 9; Kaibel, *Epigrammata* 250.6; 613.6; cf. Ps 104 (LXX 103).29f; Eccl 12.7 (cf. H. Kleinknecht in *TDNT* 6, 336 §4; Fischer, *Eschatologie* 137). Here, however, πνεῦμα is something possessed by all and not the prerogative of a few (likewise when πνεῦμα is the substance of the soul: cf., e.g., *SVF* 1.136, 140; 2.715, 774; Epict., *Diss.* 2.1.17; 3.3.22).

18 It can be seen how far Paul shared their beliefs from his arguments in 1 Cor 2.6ff. The origins of this distinction are obscure: cf. Pearson, *Terminology*; Schade, *Christologie* 69ff; Wilckens, '1 Kor 2, 1–16' 528–37 (in contrast to his earlier *Weisheit*); Winter, *Pneumatiker*; see further §4.3.1 n. 7, and Horsley, 'Pneumatikos' referred to there.

An interesting comparison here is with Jas 2.15f which has in common with 1 Cor 1–2 a contrast of two wisdoms, a negative use of ψυχικός, and a context of strife (cf. also the ref. to

those who had received this gift would in fact believe that all was ended for the individual with the moment of physical death, despite the impression that some of Paul's arguments in 1 Corinthians 15 give (see the next section)[19].

1.2.3.3. The consideration of these two passages may have seemed to lead us in *two opposite directions*: 4.8 seemed to suggest a sort of 'realized eschatology' and 6.13 and other passages a futuristic one, both held by the Corinthians. We should be the more reluctant to give up the former interpretation of the Corinthians' beliefs in that it is against such a view that an argument about the eschatological order of events like that found in 15.23–28 makes best sense: Paul reminds the Corinthians that the full consummation of God's purposes for them has not yet taken place, but is still a thing of the future. Yet the Corinthians also seem to have accepted that there were future eschatological events to come. How are these beliefs to be held together?

Now it has been argued, very plausibly, that we should see most, if not all, of the problems of the Corinthian church as arising out of a misunderstanding or perversion of Paul's original gospel, which he then has to cor-

---

the 'Lord of glory' in 2.1), although Pearson, ibid. 14, argues that the language is dependent on Paul. It may be suggested that this distinction arose, not out of a (Gnostic) desire to devalue the natural endowment of the human race, but out of a desire in Christian circles interested in 'wisdom' and critical of the 'wisdom' claimed by others to find language that could express their sense of a supernatural and eschatological endowment and which would distinguish it from the (merely) natural endowment of others who advanced competing claims to wisdom (cf. Luck, 'Weisheit'). In turn it is probably correct to see these Christian wisdom circles arising out of Hellenistic Jewish wisdom circles (cf. Schade, ibid. 80f). Schade may be correct, too, to see a contrast in Jewish exegesis between the $\psi v \chi \acute{\eta}$ of Gen 2.7 and the $\pi v \epsilon \tilde{v} \mu a$ of Ezek 37.14 (79, see further in §4.3.1 n. 7 again).

In one sense the contrast which they thus introduced was not new; some Greek thinkers had long distinguished the natural, material powers of the human soul from a divine something that came to humans from beyond this world, whether that something was mind or $v o \tilde{v} \varsigma$ (cf. Rohde, *Psyche* 493–7, on Aristotle, and Plut., *Fac. lun.* 28.943A–C; cf. Dillon, *Platonists* 211f), or a daemon (Empedocles in Diels-Kranz, *Fragmente* 31 B 115.5, 13; Plato, *Tim.* 90A; cf. Rohde, ibid. 380–4; Kirk-Raven, *Philosophers* 355–60). Both are mentioned in Plut., *Gen. Socr.* 22.591DE – Timarchus' vision; cf. Dillon, *Platonists* 212f; but 'daemon' seems preferred. In Stoic thought this daemon could sometimes be spoken of as an external spirit guiding and leading a person (cf. Rohde, ibid. 524f n. 44).

Here in Christian thought the divine Spirit that makes the spiritual person spiritual is not common to all; it comes to some and not to others. (This too has Hellenistic parallels: Dillon, ibid. 213f) Nor does it belong to anyone by nature; when it comes it comes by grace and God's decision. The Corinthians may also have been aware of something of this too, as well as Paul; it is, after all, possible so to misunderstand grace as to become conceited at being a recipient of it.

19 Cf. Klauck, *1 Kor* 112.

rect[1]. So, for instance, in sexual matters some could appeal to Paul's message of freedom from the law as grounds for licence, while others could appeal to Paul's own personal example to justify celibacy (7.7). If that is the case then we can look, not, as M. E. Thrall suggests[2], to the later 2 Corinthians, but to the earlier 1 Thessalonians for an indication of the sort of message which the Corinthians may have heard and misunderstood. And in fact 1 Thessalonians both gives a summary of the message which that church heard and indicates that some of the problems of the Corinthians may have confronted Paul in Thessalonica as well. On the one hand (1) they turned from idols to serve God and to await the appearance of Jesus from heaven, Jesus whom God had raised from the dead to be our deliverer from judgment to come (1 Thess 1.9f)[3]. Here the elements of Christ's resurrection and parousia and the coming judgment are plainly parts of the message which they had received. However there is no stress upon the cross of Christ, which may be significant in the light of the way in which Paul has to emphasize its importance to the Corinthians. Although Paul asserts the centrality of the cross to the Corinthians, and maintains its centrality in his original preaching in Corinth (1 Cor 2.2), it seems that this was lost on the Corinthians; we have to ask whether it was in fact so prominent and so evident to his Greek hearers during Paul's original ministry in Corinth. But (2) Paul also has to deal in 1 Thessalonians with a series of matters similar to those dealt with in 1 Corinthians: he has to emphasize the need for sexual purity (1 Thess 4.2–8); he calls them to even greater brotherly love (4.9–12; they were apparently more successful in this than the Corinthians); he has to reassure them about the fate of those who have died before Christ's return (4.13–18); he instructs them about spiritual manifestations and in particular prophecy (5.19), having earlier commented on their rich spiritual endowment (1.5).

If the message of Paul to the Corinthians was similar to that which he delivered to the Thessalonians then it would be surprising if the former had felt that they could have abandoned such elements in it as the return of Christ and the coming judgment. Nor is it likely that Paul could have overlooked a rejection of these parts of his message by some at Corinth. On the other hand the resurrection of dead Christians does not seem to have been something about which the Thessalonians knew, although they

---

Notes on 1.2.3.3

1 Cf., e.g., Dahl, 'Paul' 333; Hurd, *Origin* esp. 274–8; Knox, *Paul* (1925) 309f; Machalet, 'Paulus' 195, seems to imply that this was also the case with the denial of the resurrection – see n. 11 below.

2 *Pace* Thrall, 'Christ'.

3 Verses widely regarded as a traditional credal formula (cf., e.g., Best, *1–2 Thess* 81–7).

did know of Christ's resurrection (1 Thess 1.10)[4]. This comparison makes it less surprising that the Corinthians too apparently expected a future consummation and a return of Christ and accepted the message of Christ's resurrection, and yet did not include as a necessary part of their beliefs a resurrection of the dead[5]. What does distinguish them from the Thessalonians is that they *have* heard of the resurrection of the dead, and some of them have rejected the idea[6]. It would, however, be more surprising in the light of the extent of the Thessalonians' apparent knowledge if they already held Paul's view of the representative role of Christ's work which entailed believers' sharing in his experiences; moreover the idea of their sharing his resurrection should then have been a logical inference from this belief[7].

But 1 Thessalonians does not provide parallels or analogies to all the problems presented in 1 Corinthians; in particular there is no sign of the interest in wisdom and knowledge so characteristic of the Corinthians, no parallel to the claim to be 'spiritual' reflected in 1 Cor 3.1 nor of the preoccupation with tongues-speaking dealt with in chaps 12–14. In short, little sign of the distinctive features of those whom Horsley describes as a 'spiritual élite' group in the Corinthian church, and to whom he attributes the confident claims of 4.8[8]. One possible reason for the absence of parallels to these in Thessalonica is that in that city Paul did not succeed in converting so many members of the upper, better educated

---

4 Cf. Becker, *Auferstehung* 39: 'resurrection of the dead' is not in the 'Predigtschema' of 1 Thess 1.9f, although Christ's resurrection is (unless one considers 10*b* a later insertion); a future resurrection is not part of the message because of the expectation of an imminent end, but is introduced in chap. 4 as something new. (He sees the traditional message still influencing 5.23f – pp. 40f.) His explanation of how early Christianity had reacted to the deaths that had taken place earlier is less convincing (§5.6), but it is still quite possible that a Christian response to the presence of death amongst members of the church did not figure prominently in Paul's original preaching in Thessalonica. Cf. Brandenburger, 'Auferstehung' 20: 'the idea of the resurrection of believers was at least not part of the fundamental beliefs of this church' (also Marxsen, *Introduction* 35; 'Auslegung' 27f). But Beresford, *Concept* 215f, considers it most unlikely that Paul had not preached the resurrection to them (so too Perkins, *Resurrection* 297).
 The attempt of Harnisch, *Existenz*, to explain the problem as arising out of Gnostic beliefs confronts the difficulty that the belief that only the living share in salvation and the dead are excluded from it is hardly a Gnostic one, if 'living' and 'dead' are taken in their normal physical senses; for 'the redemption guaranteed by means of "knowledge" . . . is first realized by the gnostic at the time of his death' (Rudolph, *Gnosis* 171); this is similar to Greek dualistic views at this point.
5 Cf. Hurd, *Origin* 285f. Schottroff, *Glaubende* 157, argues that their dualistic views must have led them to a docetic view of Christ's death but this is unnecessary; death could still be a reality, but also a gateway to an incorporeal life, for Christ and for believers; their view of death may not have been as radical as Paul's, but that does not make it unreal.
6 But cf. Marxsen, 'Auslegung' 28: they had not necessarily heard of it from Paul.
7 *Pace* Güttgemanns, *Apostel*; cf. above §1.2.1.3.
8 'Elitism'; cf. above §1.2.1.2.

classes; we hear in Acts 17.5f, 9 only of a certain Jason, whereas there seems to have been a small but disproportionately influential group of such converts in Corinth[9]. This latter group, according to G. Theißen, are not to be described as Gnostics so much as regarded as a parallel phenomenon to the later Gnostics, in that both groups represent 'a transformation that was typical of Christian belief as it made its way up into the higher levels of society'; both were on a similar 'intellectual plane' and held to a soteriology based on one's knowledge and combined a consciousness of being an élite group within the Christian movement with a desire to keep in touch with the surrounding pagan world[10]. Such a group already had the knowledge and the spiritual power which meant so much to them, so that it is reasonable to see in them those who claimed already to be satisfied and rich and to have come into their kingdom[11].

We have also seen that 6.13 makes it likely that some Corinthians held a negative view of the body and its functions and the Christian message of a coming consummation seemed to confirm their belief that bodily existence was not something of permanent value but was something that would pass away[12]. Indeed, in so far as this age had already been penetrated by the divine powers of the age to come, and they had been possessed by those powers in their rich spiritual endowment, it behoved them to live as citizens of the new age and to place little importance on bodily existence. (After all living now as if the coming world were already here . seems implicit in Paul's teaching in passages like 1 Cor 6.3; 7.29–31.) For they were 'spiritual people', or so they claimed (3.1). It would only be consistent to live now the life of the world to come, and in that world, they seem to have felt, the body and its functions played no part.

This line of argument suggests that that reasoning is correct which argues that 15.29 shows that they cannot have denied any form of life after death at all[13]. Nor is it really conceivable that those who believed

---

9 Cf. Theißen, 'Schichtung'(also Malherbe, *Aspects* 71–84).

10 'Starken' 166f.

11 Schottroff's contention that their present eschatology did not entail 'eine Verfügbarkeit des Heils in der Gegenwart' (*Glaubende* 161f) arises from her conviction that the Corinthians were Gnostics and that for Gnosticism salvation was not a 'verfügbarer Besitz'; however it is easiest to treat the polemic of 10.1–13 as countering some such view. Schottroff in fact has to concede that Paul's eschatology is 'not so different' from that of Gnosticism, which makes it harder to see the point of 15.23ff.

11 Machalet, 'Paulus' 195, makes the interesting suggestion that Paul's words in 1 Cor 15.50 represent the starting-point for the speculations of those who denied the resurrection. Confirmation of a Corinthian belief in a disembodied after-life may also be seen in 2 Cor 5.3 if that view is correct which sees Paul as arguing against some who held that we exist 'naked'= 'disembodied' after death (cf. Lincoln, *Paradise* 66f; Lang, *2 Korinther 5,1–10* chap. 7).

12 Cf. Wisse, ' "Opponents" ' 104f.

13 So Schweizer in *TDNT* 6, 420; G. Barth, *Taufe* 89, argues that this ref. shows that Paul was

themselves to be 'spiritual' in this life could believe that their existence
would be snuffed out with the death of their physical bodies[14]: rather the
evidence seems to suggest that they felt that they should live now in as
great a detachment and independence of their bodies as possible, not
worrying overmuch about what happened to those bodies.

But still we are left with those verses which seem to suggest that Paul
regarded them as pure materialists, as denying any form of existence
beyond the grave (15.19, 32). One answer to this, as we have seen, is to
say that Paul misunderstood their position or was ignorant of it. To make
that excuse for him may be to assume that he always argued with complete fairness and objectivity. That a disembodied after-life was in his eyes
no adequate form of life at all may have seemed in his eyes sufficient
justification for representing the deniers of the resurrection in this light[15].
In our eyes it may seem to be hardly a fair caricature of their beliefs, and
we may be right; after reading 1 Cor 11.2—16 it would be hard to be confident that all Paul's arguments were always thoroughly good and valid.
He was not playing a game of cricket. This is not, however, to say that his
position here is therefore not a valid one. Perhaps a disembodied soul is a
poor continuation of our present bodily existence and a body is necessary
for a sense of identity and for meaningful being. But the methods by
which he sustained that position are perhaps not above approach, although
he would not be the only one in the ancient world to have wielded
weapons suitable for the criticism of Epicureanism against opponents who
are by no means to be classed as Epicureans; indeed it could be claimed

---

'very well informed' about the various views represented in the Corinthian church (contrast
Schmithals' views referred to in §1.2.2.3).
Cf. Klauck in §1.2.3.2 n. 17, but contrast Doughty, 'Presence' 75f; Wolff, *1 Kor* 190f, points
out that this argument would hardly have convinced the Corinthians if they believed that the
rite affected the soul by bestowing the divine Spirit.

14 Cf. P. Hoffmann in *TRE* 4, 454, who sees in 1 Cor evidence of a form of religion which through
the power of the Spirit knows itself to have transcended the limitations of this age, especially
the power of death, and in the context of dualistic anthropology can dispense with any part for
the body in salvation. Keck-Furnish, *Letters* 68, go further: in baptism they participated in
Christ's resurrection, anticipating their release from the body in their experiences. This line of
interpretation, i.e. spiritual existence now as release from any sort of body, is more convincing than Schweizer's suggestion (*TDNT* 6, 420) that they believed that all had a spiritual body
already; cf. Pearson, *Terminology* 16. But such a release, either theirs or Christ's, would not
strictly be 'resurrection (of the body)', but 'exaltation' or 'glorification' or the like which
removed one away from the sphere of the body.

15 I.e. he did not show 'understanding' for their views only in the sense of 'sympathy'; Wolff,
1 Kor 175, aptly compares his description of non-Christians in 1 Thess 4.13. Cf. also Schottroff's interpretation of Paul's arguments in vv 13—19 (*Glaubende* 160) and v 29 (163). Hurd,
Origin 197, speaks of him exaggerating, although 1 Cor 8.13 which he cites is not quite the
same as a misrepresentation of his opponents.

that this polemical approach had the legitimacy accorded it as a recognized convention[16].

No solution of the problems of 1 Corinthians 15 seems entirely satisfactory: the alternatives range between a complete agnosticism (we just do not know enough to say anything at all about the reasons for the denial of the resurrection), a characterization of the Corinthians as completely muddled (although some were apparently clear enough that there was no resurrection of the dead), and a reconstruction of their beliefs which calls into question the validity of at least some of Paul's counter-arguments. But for our present purpose it may be enough to have shown that the view that the Corinthians held the belief rejected in 2 Tim 2.18, that their resurrection had already taken place (in baptism), is not the only possibility, and indeed is not even the best possibility, for solving the problems of this chapter. What may serve to confirm this and to show what is the most likely solution is to follow up the suggestions made above as to (a) the most likely understanding of the idea of resurrection of the dead among Gentile Christians, and (b) the way in which they would have regarded their spiritual endowment. These will be the subject matter of chapters 3 and 4 respectively.

1.3. Paul's Use of Traditional Material in Romans 6

The sixth chapter of the letter to the Romans occupies a fundamental position in the hypothesis which we are questioning; whereas the most that could be argued from 1 Corinthians 15 was that a tradition of an already present resurrection existence was circulating in early Christianity, that some Corinthians held this belief and that Paul expressly rejects it, Romans 6 can be used to show that Paul was prepared to adopt and adapt these traditions; moreover, it is argued, that he introduces these traditions in the context of a reference to baptism clearly shows the baptismal connections of these traditions: the rite of baptism was the occasion when, according to these views of Hellenistic Christianity, believers entered upon this present resurrected existence. Furthermore, it is significant that baptism should be the place where this happened, since it suggests that what has happened is that the Christian rite was interpreted on the analogy of

---

16 Cf. Malherbe, 'Beasts' esp. 79 (also F. C. Grant, *Hellenism* 72f; Jungkuntz, 'Fathers').

the rites of the Hellenistic mystery-cults[1]. If that is the case, then it can be argued that Paul is indebted to these cults to a greater or lesser extent for one of the most fundamental aspects of his theology, his statements of the Christian's union with Christ.

It was this contention that led the Baptist scholar, Günter Wagner, to write his immensely learned and thorough monograph on *Pauline Baptism and the Pagan Mysteries* to refute the suggestion that the mystery-cults are of any help to us in interpreting Romans 6. But already the previous paragraph enables us to detect a weakness in Wagner's approach: for most proponents of this thesis today there is no question of a direct dependence of Paul upon the mystery-cults; their influence upon him has been mediated *via* Hellenistic Christian baptismal traditions which he does not take over wholesale[2]; rather he decisively modifies them in the light of his own theology. Wagner, however, has tended to pose the question in terms of an 'all or nothing', seeking in the mystery-cults a fairly complete parallel to all the aspects of Paul's discussion of baptism in Romans 6:

> can we find a myth of a dying and rising or resuscitated god whose fortune is regarded as fundamental for the cult, and in whose worship rites actualising, repeating, or representing that fortune are celebrated – rites that give the person by whom or to whom they are done such a fellowship with the god that allows his initiates to share in his fortune? (61)

Noteworthy here is that he does not specify that the rites need be baptismal ones[3], but he seeks in the mysteries rites of any sort which effect a sacramental union of the god and his devotees analogous to that which Paul sees effected in baptism between Christ and Christians. But the relevant point here is that if Paul has modified traditions formed on the anal-

---

Notes on 1.3

1 Cf. Becker, *Auferstehung* 55f (cf. 57); Bornkamm, 'Taufe' 37 n. 5 (ET 85 n. 5); Bousset, *Kyrios* esp. 140; Bultmann, *Theology* 1 §13.1, 140–4; §34.3, 311f; *Christianity* 233; Conzelmann, 'Schule' 95; Gäumann, *Taufe* 46; Käsemann, 'Apocalyptic' 125; *Röm* 153; Leipoldt, 'Taufe' 70f; Lietzmann, *Röm* 30f; Lohse, 'Taufe' 313–16; Merk, *Handeln* 23 n. 110; Michel, *Röm* 139; Wengst, *Formeln* 187.

I leave aside here the suggestion of O'Neill, *Rom* 109f, that 'Paul's original argument has been overlaid with commentary that boldly adopted the language of the Mysteries' (i.e. vv 4a, 5–7), let alone chap. 6's lucky escape from being deleted *in toto* as a gloss (115); cf. my review in *SJTh* 29 (1976), 291–3.

Worthy of mention here is the suggestion that Corinth was the place where this baptismal theology of dying and rising with Christ on the analogy of the mysteries was formulated: so Becker, ibid. 61–4; Schnelle, *Gerechtigkeit* 80.

2 Pokorný, 'Epheserbrief' 166, 177, also argues that baptism was the entry-point by which Gnostic speculations on the Primal Man entered Christianity.

An alternative possibility is that the influence of the mystery-cults was mediated to Paul via the Hellenistic Jewish Diaspora synagogue (cf. Gäumann, *Taufe* 39).

3 Schweitzer, *Paul* 210, had earlier argued that the mysteries contained 'no analogue to this dying and rising again effected solely by the use of water'; cf. also H. W. Schmidt, *Röm* 107.

ogy of the mysteries the parallels between his ideas and those of the mysteries need only be partial, fragmented ones. Peter Siber puts it thus in his study *Mit Christus leben*, which contains one of the most thorough recent discussions of the question of the traditions used by Paul in Romans 6:

> we would have to ask whether the ideas of the mysteries could have influenced the various earlier stages in the development of these traditions. In doing so we would not only have to ask whether the mystery-religions knew of the whole concept of cultic participation in the death and resurrection of the cult god, but we would also have to reckon with the influence of various aspects of the mysteries[4].

Here Siber states admirably and concisely the way the question has to be posed if we take seriously the possibility of Paul's using tradition here. This does not detract from the value of the religio-historical material which Wagner has so painstakingly gathered and evaluated[5], but it does set a question-mark against the conclusions which he draws from his survey[6], the resounding 'No' to the suggestion of any influence of the mysteries upon Paul's thought (e.g. 268).

1.3.1. But *does Paul use Christian traditional material in Romans 6*? While Wagner does not rule out this suggestion *per se*, but only the suggestion that the tradition in question was modelled on the rites of the mysteries, he makes no real attempt to gauge what other traditions might be being used here[1]. Many scholars would criticize him for this; for a common view is that Paul here corrects a tradition which held that Christians had already both died and risen with Christ in baptism, and that he corrects it by reserving the resurrection of Christians for the future[2], or by emphasizing that life in the present takes the form of obedient service to God[3].

---

4 *Mit Christus* 213 n. 62; cf. my 'Paul'.

5 Cf. the review by C. Colpe in *Gn.* 38 (1966), 47–51.

6 This is probably the commonest, and most important, reason for the rejection of his findings by scholars; cf., e.g., Käsemann, *Röm* 151; Lohse, *Grundriß* §14c, 67; Lona, *Eschatologie* 166; Tannehill, *Dying* 2.

Notes on 1.3.1

1 *Baptism* 279.

2 Cf., e.g., G. Barth, *Taufe* 95f; Conzelmann, *Schule* ' 91; Dunn, *Jesus* 268 (tentatively); Gäumann, *Taufe* 48; Güttgemanns, *Apostel* 218 n. 45; Jervell, *Imago* 257; Käsemann, 'Apocalyptic' 125; *Testament* 15; *Röm* 153, 157; Lohse, 'Taufe' 314 n. 19; 'Wort' 50; Tannehill, *Dying* 10; Walter, ' "Eschatologie" ' 345; Wengst, *Formeln* 47.

Other see here no correction: e.g. Carlson, *Baptism* 176; Kuss, *Röm* 299, 304; Schlier, *Röm* 194; Schnackenburg, *Baptism* e.g. 71. Lona, *Eschatologie* 160, holds that we can see in Rom 6.1–11 Paul carefully avoiding any talk of a resurrection accomplished in baptism, but he does not say that this is because he is correcting another view. What Paul is here correcting is not a different baptismal theology, but a false inference from his theology of grace (170).

3 Braun, ' "Stirb" ' 155; Merk, *Handeln* 24.

This is, however, not so much an outright rejection of other Christians' beliefs as in the case of the denial of the resurrection in 1 Cor 15; here the beliefs of other Christians would be being adapted as a means of rebutting the charge that Paul's gospel encouraged immorality (6.1, 15; cf. 3.8).

Two features of Romans 6 point to the use of traditional material:

1.3.1.1. There is the use of the introductory phrase ἤ ἀγνοεῖτε ὅτι . . . in 6.3 which suggests that Paul is reminding the Roman Christians, members of a church which he has neither founded nor visited, of things which they already knew. Wagner, however, is inclined here to follow H. Lietzmann and O. Kuss in interpreting these words as 'imparting some pieces of new information to those to whom he is writing . . . in the tones of "courteous instruction"'[1]. Yet Lietzmann himself, commenting on Rom 6.3, insisted that ἤ ἀγνοεῖτε (and ἤ οὐκ οἴδατε) always refers to something that is already known[2], and this would be the most natural sense here; so Lietzmann favours such an interpretation of this verse[3].

Moreover, unfortunately for those who wish to suggest that Paul is imparting new information in 6.3, the one other occasion on which he

---

Notes on 1.3.1.1.

1 Kuss, *Röm* 297 (cf. also his 'Frage' 15 n. 94), quoted by Wagner, *Baptism* 278, who also appeals to Lietzmann, *Röm* 34 (on 7.1); cf. also. Frankemölle, *Taufverständnis* 40. Nock, too, comments ('Christianity' 115) that 'the phrase need be no more than a trick of style', and compares *Corp. Herm.* 10.20 (ἤ οὐχ ὁρᾷς); 13.14 (ἀγνοεῖς), and Lucretius' frequent *nonne vides*. Cf. Lona, *Eschatologie* 166; certainly it is true that the singular ἀγνοεῖς and similar phrases in the second person singular are frequently used in Graeco-Roman philosophical material – see Stowers, *Diatribe* 89 (also 137) –, but it is equally true that this introduces something which the feigned interlocutor ought to have known, at least in the opinion of the speaker. Note particularly Stowers' observation on Rom 11.2: 'ἤ οὐκ οἴδατε . . . in Paul introduces basic traditional Christian or scriptural material which should be a matter of common in-group knowledge'(152); he holds the same to be true in 6.3, 16.
Yet Brandon, *History* 26 n. 4, maintains that in this chap. Paul 'enunciates a completely new interpretation' of baptism – only to qualify this by saying that he 'must have been reminding his readers of what they already knew', perceiving 'suddenly a deeper significance in the existent custom'.
Mußner, 'Tauflehre' 189, paraphrases 'has no one told you of this?' in the sense that 'it seems that no one has told you this'.
2 *Röm* 30; cf. Braumann, *Taufverkündigung* 54f; Tannehill, *Dying* 12.
3 *Röm* 30; so also Barrett, *Rom* 121 ('is, or ought to be, common knowledge'); G. Barth, *Taufe* 95; Best, *Rom* 66; Bornkamm, 'Taufe' 37 n. 5; Braumann, ibid. 54f; Bultmann, *Theology* 1 §13.1, 141; Cranfield, *Rom* 1, 300; E. Dinkler in *RGG*³ 6, 631, and 'Taufaussagen' 72 (which goes too far in saying that the phrase is frequently used in citations of credal statements; this particular phrase is only used twice in the NT, here and in Rom 7.1, hardly a credal statement), and 'Römer 6,1–14' 86 ('an introductory formula for an already familiar credal or doctrinal statement'; cf. Jeremias, ibid. 111); Gäumann, *Taufe* 72f; Halter, *Taufe* 41; Käsemann, *Röm* 155; Kaye, *Structure* 60; Kirby, *Ephesians* 155; Leenhardt, *Rom* 152; Meyer-Weiß, *Röm* 295; Michel, *Röm* 130; Murray, *Rom* 1, 214; Ridderbos, *Paul* 397 n. 4; H. W. Schmidt, *Röm* 108; Schnackenburg, *Baptism* 32; Wilckens, *Röm* 2, 11, 50.

uses the phrase ἤ ἀγνοεῖτε ... ὅτι, Romans 7.1, does clearly presuppose some knowledge on the part of his readers: Paul interjects γινώσκουσιν γὰρ νόμον λαλῶ. Now it may be uncertain to which law he refers and of which he assumes a prior knowledge, the Mosaic law, Roman law or law in general[4], but it is still true that he seems to imply that his readers will know what he is talking about.

Yet that is not to say that he expects his readers already to be familiar with the argument which he wishes to develop from this principle. It is only that he expects them to be familiar with this starting-point of his argument. Wagner indeed seems to acknowledge the force of this in the case of 6.3 also when, after arguing that ἤ ἀγνοεῖτε could be translated 'do you not grasp?' or 'do you perhaps not understand?', i.e. as referring not to the possession of factual knowledge but to their understanding of the knowledge which they did possess, he suggests that Paul here 'points out to the Christians in Rome˙something that (in theory at any rate) they were in a position to know, and whose implications they ought to have understood' (279)[5]. This surely implies that the Roman Christians *were* in possession of certain information, yet perhaps without fully realizing its significance.

In support of his contention Wagner can also point to the existence of a range of similar introductory phrases of which the closest is (ἤ) οὐκ οἴδατε[6]. Sometimes this introduces an idea which might be thought to be self-evident, for instance that one is the slave of that which one obeys

---

4 Mosaic: e.g. Althaus, *Röm* 62; Diezinger, 'Toten' 271; Leenhardt, ibid. 177; Lietzmann, *Röm* 34; Murray, ibid. 240; Räisänen, *Paul* 58 and n. 78; Schlatter, *Gerechtigkeit* 224 ('understand the law'); Wilckens, ibid. 64.
  Roman: suggested by several as possible, but generally not favoured (but cf. Meyer-Weiß, ibid. 328f).
  Law in general: Best, *Rom* 76; Denney, *Rom* 637; Käsemann, ibid. 177; Knox, *Rom* 488; Lagrange, *Rom* 160; Michel, ibid. 141; Sanday-Headlam, *Rom* 172.
  'Religion': K. Barth, *Rom* 230.
5 Cf. too Siber, *Mit Christus* 195: in 7.1 Paul starts from his readers' knowledge, but places his question and the knowledge that he presupposes entirely at the service of the ideas which he himself develops. One could also appeal to the use of ἀγνοῶν ὅτι in Rom 2.4, where surely 'that God's goodness calls you to repentance' is something that Paul's reader should have known? So too Lagrange, ibid. 144, comments on Rom 6.3 that 'Paul assumes that Christians know what he is going to say, but his language does not rule out that he would have been aware of imparting a truth that had not been appropriated in sufficient depth'. Cf. also Bruce, *Rom* 136; Sanday-Headlam, *Rom* 156.
6 Others are. οὐ θέλω/θέλομεν . . . ὑμᾶς ἀγνοεῖν (Rom 1.13; 11.25; 1 Cor 10.1; 12.1; 2 Cor 1.8; 1 Thess 4.13; cf. Jeske, 'Rock' 246; yet this formula could far more easily be interpreted as conveying new information than the interrogative form could – so Lüdemann, *Paulus und das Judentum* 34); γνωρίζω/γνωρίζομεν . . . ὑμῖν (1 Cor 15.1; 2 Cor 8.1; Gal 1.11); γινώσκειν . . . ὑμᾶς βούλομαι (Phil 1.12). It seems that all these are better suited to conveying fresh information than the two interrogative formulae mentioned above. See further Jewett, *Terms* 283.

(Rom 6.16); again they can be assumed to know the words of the Old Testament in Rom 11.2; that a little leaven pervades the whole lump of dough should be a matter of everyday experience (1 Cor 5.6) and they should have observed that the temple servants are fed by the temple and the altar (1 Cor 9.13)[7], and that there is only one winner in a race (1 Cor 9.24). At times the information introduced by this phrase *may* be new: that they or their bodies are God's temple (1 Cor 3.16; 6.19)[8], that God's holy ones will judge the world and even angels (1 Cor 6.2f), that the unrighteous will not inherit God's kingdom (1 Cor 6.9)[9], that their bodies are Christ's limbs (1 Cor 6.15), or that if one joins oneself to a prostitute the two become one body (1 Cor 6.16). In some of these cases Paul's way of putting things may be his own and original but the basic idea should have been familiar to his readers: thus, for instance, it can be argued that 1 Cor 6.2 refers to a piece of early Christian cate- chetical material[10] and that 6.9 uses traditional material[11]. 1 Cor 6.16*b* may imply that they should have known what is asserted in 6.16*a* from their knowledge of Gen 2.24. It could even be argued that 1 Cor 6.15 merely presupposes that they should have known that they belonged to Christ, body and all, and that therefore their bodies (and limbs) were his[12]. Thus in the majority of these instances of ($\dot{\eta}$) $o\dot{v}\kappa$ $o\ddot{i}\delta\alpha\tau\epsilon$ it seems likely that Paul presupposed some knowledge of what he was saying; possibly this was true in all these instances, or at least Paul thought it was[13].

Yet, at the same time, this has not settled the question *how much* the Roman Christians were supposed to know[14]. Kuss is therefore perfectly

---

7 Siber, *Mit Christus* 195 n. 14, describes this as an OT statement, but this is no quotation like Rom 11.2 nor is it necessarily only applicable to the Jewish cult (cf., e.g., Conzelmann, *1 Kor* 185).

8 On 6.19 cf. Keck-Furnish, *Letters* 83: 'We may assume that he is reminding them of something that, in person, he had explained previously'.

9 That should only be a novelty if Paul's doctrine of the ungodly had been pushed to extremes by his followers; Braumann, *Taufverkündigung* 73, argues that Paul's unusual use of the word 'kingdom' points to this being a traditional statement known to the congregation (but see above §1.2.3.1 n. 13).

10 So Conzelmann, *1 Kor* 126f, though it is hard to see where this is expressly stated in 1 Thess 4.13ff or 5.1ff which he cites.

11 Conzelmann, ibid. 128.

12 Treating 'limbs' and 'body' (singular) as equivalent to one another; I am doubtful whether the the idea of the collective 'body of Christ' lies in the background here, since v 15*b* seems to imply that the individual Christian has 'limbs' (plural) to offer to Christ or to a prostitute, rather than that he himself is a 'limb' (singular) of Christ's body (cf. Rom 6.13; also my 'Body' 74f).
Of 6.15 Barrett, *1 Cor* 148, comments 'Paul implies that his readers ought to know'.

13 The same may be true of Jn 19.10; Jas 4.4.

14 Cf., e.g., Schnackenburg, 'Todes- und Lebensgemeinschaft' 42: 'Paul only assumes that all Christians knew of baptism's effect of bringing them into fellowship with the Lord, and insin- uates to his readers his own understanding of what that entailed'.

justified in commenting that 'at any rate the introductory formula "or do you not know?" does not give us a decisive argument for deriving the baptismal theology of dying and rising with Christ, hitherto regarded as specifically Pauline, from a "pre-Pauline" Hellenistic Christianity'[15]. How much prior knowledge Paul could or should have reckoned with is a question to which we shall have to turn in the following sections (§§1.3.2–3).

1.3.1.2. A second feature of this chapter is a possible tension between the present life and the future resurrection of Christians, which is suggested above all when Paul calls upon the Roman Christians to offer themselves to God as if they were living persons who had once been dead (ὡσεὶ ἐκ νεκρῶν ζῶντας, 6.13). Paul does elsewhere in this passage refer to the present life of Christians: 6.4, '. . . so that . . . we also might walk in newness of life'; 6.11, 'so you also must consider yourselves to be dead as far as sin is concerned but living in the sight of God in Christ Jesus'[1]. However it is v 13 which would be most markedly different from the stress which

---

15 Kuss, *Röm* 297; cf. Beasley-Murray, *Baptism* 127f: 'The "Do you not know" of Rom 6.3 could presume the currency of teaching analogous to that of Paul, without its possessing the precise features of Rom 6. . . . An interpretation of baptism that regarded it as involving appropriation by the crucified and Risen Lord, forgiveness through His death and the gift of the Spirit could justly be regarded by Paul as one with his, even though none other than he stated its implications in the manner of Rom 6.1ff.' See also Carlson, *Baptism* 215f.

Notes on 1.3.1.2
1 The datives have here been interpreted as datives of relation or respect (cf. BDF §197; Althaus, *Röm* 52, 'in Beziehung auf'; Moule, 'Death'; Frankemölle, *Taufverständnis* 39, translates τῇ ἁμαρτίᾳ as 'betreffs der Sündenmacht' despite his earlier description of this as a dative of disadvantage (34), and Schnackenburg, *Baptism*, similarly opts for a dative of disadvantage (33) and then uses phrases like 'over against the power of sin' to express its meaning – 37; cf. 62). Comparable here are the datives in 4 Macc 7.19; 16.25 (where the difference from the sense of advantage may be indicated by the fact that 'dying for God' is expressed by διά with the accusative); Lk 20.38. Although no parallel construction is used in Wis 3.1ff, it may be an apt parallel in sense, contrasting the fate of the righteous in the eyes of the foolish (seemingly dead), with their actual fate in the sight of God and in his presence (at peace, with the hope of immortality), although of course this speaks of existence after death and has no counterpart to Paul's personified powers like sin here. However this 'relation' is not that of a neutral observer, contemplating things from a certain perspective, but is that of the potential masters of human life, God and sin/death/the law; thus BDR §188 (3), though putting this usage under the heading of the dative of (dis)advantage, comments that it expresses more the relationship of the possessor (cf. §189); however this usage lacks the verbs characteristic of that dative (εἶναι, γίνεσθαι), so that it seems apter to compare it with the dative of relation or respect (§197). See too the suggestive parallels in Burkert, 'Craft' 18, although this grammatical construction is not paralleled in the examples which he cites.
'Living to/for God' is harder to gauge (cf. the reff. cited by Nickelsburg, *Resurrection* 160; it could so easily be a dative of advantage. But it is worth noting the instances from 4 Macc and Lk cited above and recalling how these grammatical categories are not watertight compartments, and that the native Greek speaker could easily pass from one nuance of usage to another, perhaps even unconsciously; cf. my 'Observations').

some scholars detect elsewhere in the chapter, the stress on resurrection — and life in its fullest sense — as being something for the future (6.5, 8 — συζήσομεν)[2]. If, however, Paul is *not* deliberately correcting a view that resurrection has already taken place then it is possible that these futures are as much logical as temporal[3], or, putting it another (perhaps better) way, they refer to a state of affairs that already obtains in some measure, however much it still looks to the future for its full consummation (as in 5.19?). Yet in v 13 the phrase ἐκ νεκρῶν seems at first sight to echo the language of resurrection (cf. v 9: Christ is ἐγερθεὶς ἐκ νεκρῶν), so that we have to ask whether Paul thought that Christians were already risen as opposed to a present 'life' or gradual transformation, however hidden (2 Cor 3.18)[4].

The phrase ἐκ νεκρῶν in v 13 is, however, not quite parallel to the same phrase used with a verb like 'raise', since there it must be translated as 'from (amongst) the dead'[5]; here it must mean something like '(passed) from (the state of) the dead'[6]. The 'dead' are here not the company that

---

2 So, e.g., Käsemann, *Röm* 159, on v 5: 'the future is clearly eschatological' (cf. 157; but also n. 9 below on the ambiguity of the word 'eschatological' here); or Barrett, *Rom* 124, who describes the future of v 8 as 'undoubtedly temporal'; cf. also Conzelmann, 'Paulus' 232; Dinkler, 'Römer 6,1–14' 90f (yet see 92 – Paul also refers to eternal life being effective in the present); Kuss, *Röm* 303, 306 (but cf. 321); Mußner, 'Tauflehre' 192; Schlier, *Röm* 196; Schnelle, *Gerechtigkeit* 77; Thüsing, *Per Christum* 70f, 139–41. Wilckens describes these features as eschatological (*Röm* 2, 15), yet refuses to see a tension between this and the present tense in vv 4b and 11. Bouttier, *En Christ* 46f, treats these futures as *both* eschatological *and* ethical (logical). It is too drastic a short-cut to assert that Paul says that Christians die and rise with Christ (Percy, *Probleme* 107; cf. however 109f; in his *Leib* 31f Percy treats these futures as logical).

3 Cf. e.g., Caird, *Letters* 194; Frankemölle, *Taufverständnis* 61, 81f; Lagrange, *Rom* 145; Larsson, *Christus* 71; Leenhardt, *Rom* 161; G. Otto, *Formulierungen* 54 (but cf. 81: συζήσομεν in 6.8 is primarily eschatological in meaning 'even if the fact of living with (Christ) is *wurzelhart, keimhaft* present in Christians'); Schnackenburg, *Baptism* 38, on v 5 (contrast 41 on v 8). Cranfield considers that there are three alternative possibilities for the futures: purely logical, referring to the moral life (his choice), or referring to the eschatological fulfilment (*Rom* 1, 308); but it is only by treating the futures as at least in part logical that one can make them refer to the present life of Christians (as well as to the future), and the moral demand for the present is based on the fact that the life of the new age (i.e. eschatological life) is to be lived now. Thus the alternatives should probably be posed as either (1) referring exclusively to the still future eschatological consummation or (2) applying to present existence as well. The reference to 5.19 above illustrates well how Paul uses the aorist to refer to a past event that still unfolds and the future to refer to a future event that is already unfolding (contrast the aorist participle of 5.1; cf. my 'Structure' 352f).

4 Hickling, 'Centre' 204, argues, with particular reference to 2 Cor 2.17, that 'it seems extremely hard to think that . . . Paul could have included resurrection within that part of the Last Things that is already accessible to Christians', against Héring, 'Saint Paul'.

5 BAG s.v. ἐκ §1b: 'with a group or company from which the separation takes place'; Grimm-Thayer[2] s.v. I.2.

6 BAG ibid. §1c: 'of situations and circumstances out of which someone is brought', comparing *inter alia* Rom 11.15, 'life from the dead' (cf. J. A. Fitzmyer in *JBC* 2, 323; Perkins, *Resurrection* 295f); see also Demosth., *Or.* 18.131; Lys. 28.1; Soph., *Oed. tyr.* 454; *Ant.* 1093; Xen-

they have left, but themselves in their former state which they have now left behind. Thus it is not quite accurate to speak in Rom 6.13 of a ' "spiritual" resurrection'[7] nor to translate the phrase 'since you have risen from the realm of the dead to life'[8].

Related to this are the very different views of death in this verse and elsewhere in the passage. In this verse death is the state from which we must be saved, a state of lostness[9]. Earlier in this chapter death is a saving event, for it is a death with Christ to sin (as far as sin is concerned); it is the necessary presupposition for life, an integral part of the Christian's path to God. At this point 6.13 is closer to the thought of Ephesians (and Colossians in part) where, as Kuss notes[10], ' "being dead" is not associated with Christ . . . and thus does not belong to the side of salvation . . ., but designates nothing less than the state of being unsaved'. Thus, although the ideas of death and resurrection or life in Rom 6 may not be incompatible with one another (at least if we do not stress the futurity of the resurrection, let alone regard it as a deliberate correction of a belief in a present resurrection), yet we can detect two rather different strands of thought in Paul's statements: (1) the Christian's former sinful existence as death which is replaced by life, and (2) the Christian's gaining life through death (with Christ). Although not necessarily contradictory they are undeniably different.

Undoubtedly it is the latter sense of death as saving that is more characteristic of Paul with his distinctive paradoxical affirmations about Christian, and particularly apostolic, existence; this is most clearly seen in passages like 2 Cor 4.10–12 or, above all, 6.9, where Paul speaks of the apostles' existence 'as dying, and behold we live' (*RSV*); death is a characteristic mark of his existence as an apostle and yet it is precisely there that the presence of true life is most apparent (2 Cor 4.10; cf. further § 6.4.1 below).

Not that Paul is inconsistent with himself in his use of the former sense of death and life; not at least if one does not treat the futures of vv 5 and 8 as referring exclusively to that which is still in the future and if one emphasizes the word ὡσεί. So, for instance, Käsemann sees this word as

---

oph., *An.* 7.7.28; *Cyrop.* 3.1.17; also LSJ s.v. I.3; Grimm-Thayer[2] s.v. I.5. In such cases ἐκ could well be rendered 'in place of', if one does not wish to supply a verb of motion.

7 *Pace* Beker, *Paul* 225; cf. 229. At least such language is misleading in that it obscures this different nuance in the meaning of the preposition.

8 As Michel, *Röm* 133.

9 Cf. C. C. Black, 'Perspectives' 424, who describes death here as the 'antecedent, existential experience from which we have been liberated'.

10 *Röm* 327: so in Eph (cf. Lona, *Eschatologie* 362) and in Col 2.13 (contrast Col 1.12, 20; 3.3; cf. Dinkler, 'Taufaussagen' 102).

preserving Paul's 'eschatological proviso'; Christians participate proleptically in their Lord's resurrection only in the form of their new obedience, while, conversely, their service for him proclaims that the power of
resurrection has already grasped them and transported them to the new
life and the new age[11]. This reserve is even clearer if we translate ὡσεί as
'as if' as Wilckens does, rejecting the causal interpretation of this word[12].
The combination of this idea with his postponement of the resurrection
to the still future end only really becomes difficult if that postponement
is seen as a deliberate correction of a view which held that that resurrection had already taken place; in that case Paul's use of language here is,
to say the least, unguarded. But it is precisely this sort of correction
which, as we have seen, some scholars find in Rom 6, and which this
study seeks to challenge.

1.3.2. But if tradition is being used here *how widely is it used and how is
it used*? Is it quoted *verbatim* or paraphrased loosely or even rephrased by
Paul?

1.3.2.1. Tannehill argued that Paul was drawing upon tradition quite
extensively in this chapter. He criticized Kuss and Schnackenburg for
failing, first, 'to see the subordinate place of the reference to baptism in
Rom 6'[1]. And, secondly, they had failed to see that ἢ ἀγνοεῖτε in v 3 was
picked up by a series of phrases with a similar function later in the chapter: εἰ in v 5 has a meaning close to 'since'[2], giving the conditional protasis
'the same function as ἢ ἀγνοεῖτε in v 3, for it also refers to what Paul
believes can be taken as an accepted fact and so as a basis for argument'.
In v 6, too, τοῦτο γινώσκοντες, ὅτι should be translated 'since we know

---

11 Käsemann, *Röm* 168; for Barrett, *Rom* 128, this word combines the sense of 'as if you were'
and 'as in fact you are', for in one sense Christians have been raised, in another sense not; cf.
Schmidt, *Röm* 113. Many commentators stress the 'as in fact you are' (='because you are')
aspect: cf. Schlier, *Röm* 204, etc.
    It is important to emphasize that this life, and so the future tenses in this passage, may still
be 'eschatological' even if they are not referring to something solely in the future, but to something already anticipated to some extent in the present.
12 *Röm* 2, 21 and n.76: ὡσεί corresponds to the comparative sense of ὡς, not the causal – BDF
§453(3); BDR §425 n. 5 ('gleichsam'='as it were'); BAG s.v.; LSJ s.v. (For an example of the
causal sense see Barrett's rendering in the previous note.)

Notes on 1.3.2.1
    1 *Dying* 13, quoting Kuss, *Röm*, and Schnackenburg, *Baptism* 33f; cf. K. Barth, *Dogmatik* 4.4,
    128f.
    2 He compares BDF §372.

this, that . . .'[3]. Similarly in vv 8–9 we find a conditional sentence with
εἰ followed by the indicative and then a participle (εἰδότες). He concludes that 'Paul is using in this chapter an interpretation of Christian
baptism which is known beyond his own churches', an interpretation
which asserts that in baptism 'the Christian has already died with Christ'[4].

Taken at its face value this argument would suggest that already Paul's
readers in Rome were aware of the ideas that (a) they were baptized into
Christ (v 3), (b) this baptism was a baptism into his death (v 3), (c) they
had been 'united with the likeness of his death' (v 5), (d) their old nature
had been crucified with Christ (v 6), (e) they had died with Christ (v 8),
and (f) Christ's resurrection meant that he had for ever escaped death's
clutches (v 9). In other words they were fairly fully acquainted with the
essential features of Paul's view of baptism, including his distinctive σὺν
Χριστῷ concept[5].

Yet how much do these further pieces of presupposed information add
to that initially assumed in v 3? How much further do they go than
repeating the implications (or what Paul felt to be the implications) of
the belief that Christians have been baptized into Christ's death[6]? Certainly
the view that they had been 'united with the likeness of his death' (v 5)[7]
could be regarded as re-expressing the same idea as v 3: the death of their
old nature could be regarded as a corollary of that baptism (v 6)[8], as could

---

3 Yet Frankemölle, *Taufverständnis* 73, suggests that this participle might be equivalent to an
imperative (cf. BDF §468(2)).

4 *Dying* 14. Beasley-Murray, *Baptism* 127, interprets Michel, *Röm* 148ff, as if he thought that
Paul was quoting a baptismal liturgy or hymn; it is true that Michel does say that Paul uses the
first person plural of a confession (148) in contrast to 5.12–21 and that 'through the glory
of the Father' has a credal ring (153). But on 149 he says that in vv 1f and 15 the first person
plural is to be seen as rhetorical and *dialogisch*, but in vv 4–6 and 8 it is *bekenntnisartig;* that
is not to say that he is actually quoting extensively nor would the style of the passage suggest
that; yet it is possible that there may be isolated allusions to such material in individual words
and phrases.

5 Cf. also Gäumann, *Taufe* 46f.

6 Cf. Best, *Rom* 68: vv 5–7 'carry on the thought of verses 3–4'.

7 This phrase has received a considerable amount of attention: see, e.g., Schrage, 'Kirche', who
departs from the view of Bornkamm, 'Taufe' 41–3, that 'the likeness of his death' refers to
Christ's death, i.e. the reference is to the person of Christ; rightly Schrage asks (210) why Paul
did not say so, but his suggestion that the 'likeness' is the body of Christ, the church, is surely
rather unexpected. The collective sense is clear in the first person plurals, but is it not easier
to treat ὁμοίωμα as equivalent in sense to εἰκών in 1 Cor 15.49? Christian existence bears
the mark now of its Lord's death; that is the sort of existence into which baptism has ushered
us. Cranfield, *Rom* 1, 308, aptly compared the phrase συμμορφιζόμενος τῷ θανάτῳ αὐτοῦ in
Phil 3.10 and holds it to be similar in sense to σύμφυτοι . . . τῷ ὁμοιώματι τοῦ θανάτου αὐτοῦ;
cf. Tannehill, *Dying* 38f. This perhaps comes near to Fazekaš, 'Taufe' 311, when he proposes
'the concrete form of his death and resurrection, his earthly and glorified body' (and also notes
tellingly that the future ἐσόμεθα is hard to understand if the ὁμοίωμα refers to their – past –
baptism).

8 Cf. Käsemann, *Röm* 159; also R. Bultmann in *TDNT* 1, 708.

their dying with Christ (v 8)[9]. It is only with v 9 that really new information is presupposed, but that Christ has once and for all escaped death's
clutches is not a particularly esoteric piece of information and could he
assumed to be widely known among Christians (cf., e.g., Acts 2.24; 1 Pet
3.18, 22; Rev 1.18)[10].

It is not clear, moreover, that Tannehill's data rule out Schnackenburg's
evaluation of this evidence, namely that the baptismal traditions of the
early church linked this sacrament to Jesus' death in a general way only,
and that Paul may be deliberately (or even unintentionally?) over-estimat-
ing his readers' knowledge, and giving his own deeper interpretation of
'the symbolism and significance of the bath of baptism'. And so, he
argues, 'there is no evidence to show that the interpretation of baptism in
terms of a dying (and rising) with Christ, as expounded by Paul, was
already current in the Church'[11]. Is then the evidence so ambiguous that
both interpretations are equally possible, or can we gauge with more
precision the extent of the Roman Christians' familiarity with Paul's
ideas?

1.3.2.2. F. Hahn, on the other hand, argues that vv 3*b*–4 contain too
much that is characteristically Pauline to be a quotation of tradition[1]. Yet
Paul assumes more than just the existence of a formula like being 'baptized into Christ', and 'if he appeals to a tradition in writing to the Roman
church, he must cite it in its entirety and he cannot give it in an altered
form of words'[2]. Such a quotation he sees in v 8 with its uncharacteristic
use of πιστεύειν. But is the tradition then in exactly this form, complete
with conditional clause? Or does the traditional material follow πιστεύομεν
ὅτι? But v 8*b* alone would hardly support Paul's claim to base himself on
tradition in vv 3f. So was the form of the tradition something like '(we
believe that) we died with Christ and will live with him'? Yet, as we shall
see, there is good reason to doubt whether the 'with Christ' language is
any more traditional, any less characteristically Pauline than the rest of
the language of vv 3f. So, if Paul could not presuppose knowledge of that
in a church which he has not visited, what Christian traditions could he
assume?

---

9 Cf. Käsemann, ibid. 161.
10 It could be argued that the confession of 1 Cor 15.3f is also in the background here, with its
   reference to Christ's death and burial and resurrection (Frankemölle, *Taufverständnis* 26–30,
   etc.).
11 *Baptism* 33f; Rese, 'Formeln' 94, argues that we should be cautious in assuming a *verbatim*
   quoting of traditional material.

Notes on 1.3.2.2
 1 'Taufe' 19; 'Verständnis' 140.
 2 'Verständnis' 140.

1.3.2.3. It is with this question that *P. Siber* is largely concerned in the third chapter of his book, *Mit Christus leben*. He agrees with Tannehill about 'the subordinate place of the reference to baptism'[1]; put more precisely, Paul could equally well have made much the same point about dying with Christ as far as sin is concerned without mentioning baptism, as he in fact does in a number of other passages: 'you were put to death as regards the law through Christ's body' (Rom 7.4); 'we have been separated from the law by dying as far as that under which we were confined is concerned' (7.6); 'one man died for all; so all died; and he died for all in order that those who live should no longer live for themselves but for him who died and was raised from the dead for their sake' (2 Cor 5.14f); 'for through the law I died with regard to the law in order that I might live before God. I have been crucified with Christ' (Gal 2.19); 'those who are Christ's have crucified the flesh' (5.24); '. . . the cross of our Lord Jesus Christ, through whom the world has been crucified as far as I am concerned and I as far as it is concerned' (6.14). Now it is true that in many of these texts scholars have seen quotations of, or allusions to, baptismal traditions, but that is an assumption which needs to be questioned. Here, as elsewhere, there is the tendency to assume the presence of baptismal traditions where there is little real evidence for it[2]. It may be granted that motifs which can also be applied to Christian existence as a

---

Notes on 1.3.2.3

1 Quoting Tannehill, *Dying* 13, as in §1.3.2.1 n. 1; cf. Dunn, *Jesus* 335: 'the major development of the theme of suffering and dying with Christ . . . is not dependent on the metaphor or event of baptism. It would therefore be a mistake to seek elucidation of Paul's experience by constantly harking back to his baptism; it was much too contemporary, too day-to-day an experience for that.' See also Althaus, *Röm* 56; Best, *Body* 46; Bonnard, 'Mourir' 103f; Hoffmann, *Toten* 305f n. 87; but contrast Schnelle, *Gerechtigkeit* 75.

2 Cf. Betz, *Gal* 187: 'we ought not . . . to interpret baptism into these passages'; M. Barth, *Eph* 2, 544: 'Eph 4:22−24 is a piece of instruction well suited to the preparation for, or the liturgy of, baptism. But its usefulness for a given service does not necessarily demonstrate the original *Sitz im Leben*' (similarly elsewhere in this work; cf. §1.4.2); Bouttier, *En Christ* 48; Dibelius, 'Isis Initiation' 96; Kennedy, *St Paul* 226: 'The great bulk of Paul's utterances concerning death with Christ have no reference whatever to baptism'; G. Otto, *Formulierungen* 43 (Otto also emphasizes − 85 − that another similar text, Phil 3.10, 'that I . . . may share his sufferings, becoming like him in his death' − *RSV*, is in no way related to baptism). Braumann, *Taufverkündigung*, seems at least partially aware of the difficulties involved in deciding what elements in Paul's thought were derived from an earlier baptismal context (cf. 8−13), and he does recognize that certain motifs would fit other contexts equally well (e.g. redemption and forgiveness, 38), but his study seems to be undermined by his failure to ask whether a given motif belongs peculiarly or even primarily to a baptismal context. A similar criticism could be levelled at Schnelle, *Gerechtigkeit*. In other words is it always the case that Paul takes motifs from baptismal traditions and sets them in the context of the apostolic preaching in general or in other contexts (Braumann, ibid. 42), or that from time to time he and others used to interpret baptism motifs which are part of the apostolic preaching which baptism presupposes? See further G. Barth, *Taufe*, 130ff; Dunn, *Unity* 145−7.

whole can also appropriately be applied to that rite which marks the beginning of that existence, and *vice versa*, but too often it is assumed that the movement, the influence, is from the rite to the understanding of Christian existence, and not the other way round. Certainly in the present case the latter seems more probable: language used of Christian existence in general is in Rom 6 applied to baptism[3].

And, it may be suggested, it is applied to baptism since that rite is the common starting point for all Christians' existence[4]; thus no Christian is exempted from that radical break with sin which Paul refers to as 'dying to sin'. It is a fundamental and integral part of his existence if he belongs to Christ. Thus Paul can counter the charge that his understanding of Christian existence encourages a Christian to continue sinning (6.1; cf. 6.15).

This would be in line with W. Marxsen's observation that Paul in passages like Rom 6 reflects, not upon the meaning of baptism, but upon the meaning of having been baptized, i.e. upon the nature of Christian existence[5]. A corollary of this would seem to be that this present existence prescribes to a large extent the terms in which Christian beginnings in baptism or elsewhere are depicted – and, according to Marxsen, it can be 'elsewhere' since 'Paul can describe this beginning in quite different ways. The reference to the past event of baptism is only one among many possibilities' (e.g. faith, receiving the Spirit – 173). That surely implies that Paul thus describes baptism because he does so in the light of his experience of Christian existence as a warfare against sin, as a sharing in Christ's sufferings, as a freedom from the domination of sin and the law[6].

But Siber does part company with Tannehill and does so above all where the latter argues that the tradition to which Paul alluded involved the idea of a union with Christ in his death and resurrection. The 'with Christ' language which Siber had investigated earlier in his study, that is, the ideas of being with Christ in the resurrection (especially in 1 Thess 4.13–18)[7] and living or being glorified with him after suffering with him (especially in Phil 3.10f, 20f and Rom 8.17–20) was Paul's own language and so too this striking usage might be his coinage; certainly it is not

---

3 So, e.g. Best, *Rom* 67; cf. Carlson, *Baptism* 217; Dodd, *Rom* 87, but contrast, e.g., Käsemann, *Röm* 153; v. d. Osten-Sacken, 'Christologie' 256–62; Wilckens, *Röm* 2, 54.

4 Just as 'Jesus is Lord' may be a baptismal confession (but cf. G. Barth, *Taufe* 133), cited in 1 Cor 12.3 to bear witness to the fact that all Christians have the Spirit.

5 'Erwägungen'; cf. Bornkamm, 'Lehre' 50 n. 22.

6 Cf. Tannehill, *Dying* 41: 'the presence of the death of Christ in baptism is merely one aspect of the presence of the death of Christ in the new dominion as a whole.'

7 Kuss, *Röm* 321, compares Rom 6.8*b* with the 1 Thess passage, but Siber, *Mit Christus* 10, rightly notes that the latter lacks the idea of the future life being a sharing in Christ's resurrection.

found elsewhere than in Paul's writings and those influenced by him (and that includes Ephesians and Colossians). Although Siber grants that Christians before Paul believed that they were already resurrected, they did not believe that they had risen *with Christ*; that was part of Paul's contribution to the development of these ideas. He took these traditions of the Hellenistic church which spoke of the resurrection of Christians as something that had taken place in their baptism and (1) linked all life, both present and future, to Jesus' resurrection, and understood it as a sharing in that resurrection; (2) he viewed that life as being in the present simply a new way of behaviour and service to God, and distinguished it from the future resurrection of the dead; (3) he held fast to this still future resurrection and designated it alone as life 'with Christ'.

Paul's statements about dying with Christ were even more distinctively his own. He could, it is true, draw upon Christian traditions which associated the forgiveness of sins with baptism, a forgiveness which was then in its turn seen as mediated to us by Christ's death. 'Paul's question in Rom 6.3 shows that he presupposed that the understanding of baptism as baptism into Christ's death was either known or at least lay close to hand' (208). Suggestive, too, is the juxtaposition of the allusions to Christ's death for us and baptism in his name in 1 Cor 1.13. Yet such ideas 'only bring baptism and the forgiveness of sins granted in it into a very loose connection with Jesus' death as Paul does in Rom 6' (ibid.). In contrast to Paul 1 Pet 2.24 associates Jesus' death with a dying to sin and a new life that comes to the Christian, but this dying is not called a sharing in Jesus' death and this life is not called a sharing in his resurrection. 'So Paul was the first to describe the purification from sins in baptism', an idea current in Christian tradition, 'as a dying to the power of sin, and so to regard liberation from sin as a participation in Christ, or, more precisely, in his death. So his σύν-statements can be seen to be Paul's own theological achievement' (213).

In my view Siber has made out a convincing case for the originality of Paul's 'with Christ' language, at least as far as he speaks of a Christian's having died with Christ in the past[8]. It is striking how no real parallels

---

8 While many of his terms may be paralleled, his way of using them is distinctive (Schnackenburg, *Baptism* 139, 174f; also 'Adam-Christus-Typologie' 52: the 'with Christ' language 'may in this context be Paul's own creation'); cf. also W. Grundmann in *TDNT* 7, 782 ('Paul did not take over the formula σὺν Χριστῷ from anyone else. He coined it, attracted by its simplicity.'); Cranfield, *Rom* 1, 312; Frankemölle, *Taufverständnis* 102 ('specifically Pauline, almost without analogy'); Froitzheim, *Christologie* 191; Hoffmann, *Toten* 302; Kuss, *Röm* 328 (more cautiously on 336 — the formula could be an early Christian one, though its content here is Pauline); Schulz, *Nachfolge* 184; Wagner, *Baptism* 284. Contrast Gäumann, *Taufe* 55f; Käsemann, *Röm* 152. Lohmeyer, 'Σὺν Χριστῷ' 229–31, 248, 256f, while rejecting most of the possible religio-historical derivations of Paul's 'with Christ' language, yet argues that, since

have been found, even in the literature relating to the mystery-religions which are so frequently asserted to be the source of these ideas, and one question which will need further consideration is the relationship between the initiate and the deity in these cults: is it the case that their ideas were similar to Paul's, and he then adopted their ideas and formulated his own terminology to express them, or are their ideas as well as their language fundamentally different to his? (See chap 5 below.)

If there is one point at which Siber is less convincing it is in his acceptance that Paul here used a tradition which spoke of Christians having risen already in baptism. He argues for this on the basis of a comparison with the later text, Eph 5.14, which he regarded as being an early Christian baptismal hymn:

> Arise, sleeper,
> and rise from the dead,
> and Christ will shed his light upon you.

In this many would agree with him, but there is no clear evidence in the context that this quotation has a setting in a baptismal liturgy[9]. Moreover, his case is rather spoilt by the passages which he compares: from the literature relating to the mystery cults he cites Firmicus Maternus, *Err. prof. rel.* 22.1 which can hardly be described as a call to awake since the initiates there have not been asleep but have been lamenting the dead deity:

> Be of good cheer, initiates, now that the god has been saved;
> for we shall have salvation from our troubles.

The other text which he quotes, Aristophanes, *Ran.* 340, seems to be either an invocation to the god Iacchus (not the initiate) to arise (intransitive) like the morning star, or to raise (transitive) the flaming torches in his hands[10]. In his citation of these passages he is following the commentary of M. Dibelius and H. Greeven[11], which also compares the Manichaean Turfan fragment M7:

Paul presupposes a knowledge of this usage, he must be deriving it from early Christian usage. This seems questionable, at least as regards dying with Christ. See further §5.3.

9 The weakness of the evidence is plain in Schille, *Hymnen* 95, who says of such calls to awake that 'unfortunately their setting in the liturgy of an initiation rite can only be shown in a few cases, presumably because their form is derived from evangelistic language'; in fact the evidence turns out to be only two passages, Eph 5.14 and Aristoph., *Ran.* 340ff.

10 The *LCL*'s 'from sleep arising' is perhaps misleading and is based on the reading ἐγείρου; the MSS and most edd. seem to have the active ἔγειρε, though the Budé translation takes this intransitively too.

Leipoldt even suggested that this hymn was based on an Eleusinian chant ('Taufe' 72; cf. 'Christentum' 58; see Wagner, *Baptism* 71, 74f).

11 *Eph* 91; cf. also Schlier, *Eph* 241.

> Shake off the drunkenness in which thou hast slumbered,
> awake and behold me!
> Good tidings to thee from the world of joy
> from which I am sent for thy sake[12]

However Jonas sets this in the context of the myth of the Primal Man[13]; moreover in its context it is in fact a dialogue between Zarathustra and his soul or self[14]. An apter comparison would be the text which Jonas cites immediately afterwards, from 'the so-called "Abridged Mass of the Dead"':

> My soul, O most splendid one, . . . whither hast thou gone? Return again. Awake, soul of splendour, from the slumber of drunkenness into which thou hast fallen . . . .

This call, though it echoes that addressed to the Primal Man, is, Jonas thinks, directed to 'the soul in general'[15]. But its setting, like that of many similar calls which he cites, is not in any rites of initiation, but is part of the evangelistic call to the slumbering dead[16]. It would only be appropriate in a rite of initiation in so far as that rite recapitulated the prior moment of spiritual awakening. Thus we find here a similar problem to that noted already apropos of the baptismal setting claimed for the idea of dying with Christ: the rite encapsulates a certain understanding of one's previous existence and of the new existence which it inaugurates; language appropriate to describing the old and the new may therefore be applied to baptism, but it does not necessarily follow that whenever that language is used it derives from this ritual usage, nor that the writer who uses it has that rite in mind.

Another difficulty for Siber's position is the relative lateness of the quotation in Ephesians: this letter is, by general consent, later than Romans, although not necessarily much later[17], and is one which, like Colossians, views Christians as having not only died with Christ but also as having already risen with him too. In other words, if this call is meant

---

12 Quoted according to Jonas, *Religion* 83; cf. Reitzenstein, *Mysterienreligionen* 58. Lindemann, *Aufhebung* 235 n. 167, argues against K. -M. Fischer that a Gnostic understanding of existence provides a better analogy than the mystery-cults; Rudolph, *Gnosis* 120, also refers to Eph 5.14 as a 'gnostic call'.

13 Ibid.; cf. Lidzbarski, *Ginza* 430 (=L. 1.2.10; ET in Foerster-Wilson, *Gnosis* 2, 274); *Act. Thom.* 110.43 (Hennecke-Schneemelcher-Wilson 2, 500).

14 The wider context is translated in Asmussen, *Literature* 48.

15 *Religion* 83; but cf. M. Boyce in *HO* 1.4.2.1, 74.

16 Cf. Schnackenburg, 'Tauflehre' 164; K. G. Kuhn, 'Epheserbrief' 342, rejects these Gnostic parallels on the grounds that the basic idea here of a call out of ignorance of one's true self to knowledge that one's soul is in fact a spark of light from the world of light is lacking; such *Substanzdenken* is alien to Eph. Here it is a question of a decision to change one's conduct, from sinning to a way pleasing to God.

17 J. A. T. Robinson, *Redating* 61ff, argues that it was only a year and a bit later, but most would argue for a later date.

to be realized in this life then it may well reflect the same development of Paul's thought that is found elsewhere in this letter and in Colossians (see § 1.4); this application of this call would then be a secondary development of Paul's thought as well.

1.3.2.4. In other words, Siber too fails to present a convincing case for the hypothesis that Paul could presuppose in Romans 6 a tradition which viewed baptism as a resurrection of the baptized. The entry to life, yes, but the case for resurrected life is, in my judgment, not proved. But we saw in § 1.3.1. that there were indeed signs that Paul was drawing upon traditional ideas of different sorts in this chapter, and so we must now turn to the question of the nature of these ideas. Our account of them, to be satisfactory, must show them to be sufficiently extensive to account both for Paul's implying that the Roman Christians should have known something of what he was telling them and for the diversity of views of life and death in the chapter.

1.3.3. So, then, what sort of traditions are reflected in Romans 6, and what ideas did they contain?

1.3.3.1. In the first place Paul could assume that the rite of baptism *somehow united one with Christ*[1]. Just quite how it was thought to do this in early Christian tradition would be clearer if we were more certain of the background and meaning of the expression 'to be baptized into the name of Christ', a usage of which Paul knew and which was evidently known in his churches (1 Cor 1.13, 15). It was evidently known there since Paul elsewhere more characteristically speaks of being 'baptized into Christ'[2]; that he uses this longer phrase, which is uncharacteristic of his usage, suggests that this was nevertheless a way of speaking with which he expected his readers to be familiar. Moreover other New Testament writers occasionally use εἰς rather than ἐν or ἐπί with references to the name of Christ in baptismal contexts (Matt 28.19; Acts 8.16; 19.5)[3].

Various backgrounds have been suggested for the phrase 'in(to) the name of Christ'. For Heitmüller it was the world of Hellenistic commerce;

Notes on 1.3.3.1

1 Cf. G. Barth, *Taufe* chap. 2; Wilckens, *Röm* 2, 8.

2 The nearest he approaches this usage elsewhere is 1 Cor 6.11, 'you were washed . . . in the name of the Lord Jesus Christ and in the Spirit of our God' (*RSV*) (assuming that the prepositional phrases qualify 'you were washed' as well as 'you were justified').

3 Baptizing ἐν τῷ ὀνόματι: Acts 2.38 v.1; 10.48 (cf. 1 Cor 6.11); ἐπὶ τῷ ὀνόματι: Acts 2.38 v.1; n.b. also Acts 19.3, εἰς τί . . . ἐβαπτίσθητε; *Did.* 7.1; Just., *Apol.* 61.3 has ἐπ᾽ ὀνόματος.

to be baptized into the name of Christ meant that one had become his property, one was, so to speak, credited to his account[4]. However there is a certain incongruity in the idea of baptizing someone into an account[5], yet in favour of this explanation it is clear that belonging to Christ is for Paul a consequence of being baptized into him (not into his name): in Gal 3.27—29 he speaks of those who have been baptized into Christ having put him on, being in him, and belonging to him. However we must reckon too with the possibility that if $\beta \alpha \pi \tau i \xi \epsilon \iota \nu$ $\epsilon \iota \varsigma$ $(\tau \dot{o}$ $\ddot{o} \nu o \mu \alpha)$ was a Semitic concept (see below) which was then used in a Hellenistic context it might then take on new nuances of meaning[6]: the $\epsilon \iota \varsigma$, for a start, could be taken as a spatial metaphor, just as one can be baptized 'into' the Jordan (Mk 1.9), although this construction is rare[7]. Or the similarity to commercial language might have led to the interpretation of an originally Semitic phrase in the light of this commercial usage.

The suggestion that this phrase is a literal translation of a Semitic idiom might well imply that its use goes back to the earliest days of the Christian mission. However this idiom has been variously interpreted. Strack-Billerbeck interprets the phrase $\epsilon \iota \varsigma$ $\ddot{o} \nu o \mu \alpha$ $= l e \check{s} \bar{e} m$ in Matt 10.41 as either final (with regard to something which should be the case) or causal (with regard to something because of which or for whose sake). The latter is preferable in Matt 10.41 and 18.5: 'because he is a prophet', 'for my sake'[8]. With regard to Matt 28.19 they do not clearly state whether a cause or purpose is implied, although the parallel examples cited from rabbinic rites clearly suggest that in these cases the purpose of the rites is expressed. Interestingly they comment that in baptism 'into' the name of the Father, Son and Holy Spirit 'the element of obligation is not to be overlooked: baptism is the basis of a relationship between the triune God

---

4 *'Im Namen Jesu'* e.g. 109, 127 (distinguishing $\epsilon \nu / \epsilon \pi i$ $\tau \tilde{\omega}$ $\dot{o} \nu \dot{o} \mu \alpha \tau \iota$ from $\epsilon \iota \varsigma$ $\tau \dot{o}$ $\ddot{o} \nu o \mu \alpha$). Cf. Dinkler, 'Taufaussagen' 117; Leenhardt, *Rom* 152; A. Oepke in *TDNT* 1, 539, and in 2, 433; Schlier, *Röm* 192.
Bultmann, *Theology* 1, §13.1, 137, suggests that Paul's use of the term 'seal' of baptism presupposes a similar background (2 Cor 1.22; cf. Eph 1.13; but it is only in later literature that the connection of this image with baptism becomes explicit, e.g. in *Herm. Sim.* 9.16.4; cf. also G. Barth, *Taufe* 75ff; G. Fitzer in *TDNT* 7, 949, 952f).

5 Cf. H. Bietenhard in *TDNT* 5, 275f; Wilckens, *Röm* 2, 49. And yet Dinkler, 'Taufaussagen' 93—6, points out how Paul applies various terms used in secular Greek commercial language to describe baptism (or entering into Christian existence, for baptism is not explicitly mentioned) in 2 Cor 1.21f. But against this G. Barth, ibid. 51, points out that the idea of *Ubereignung* is not inherent in the $\epsilon \iota \varsigma$ τo $\ddot{o} \nu o \mu \alpha$ formula, but only takes on that sense through preceding verbs like $\pi \rho o \sigma \tau i \theta \eta \mu \iota$, and it is very doubtful whether $\beta \alpha \pi \tau i \xi \epsilon \iota \nu$ could count as one of these verbs. The idea of becoming Christ's possession was one added to the phrase later, and not inherent in it (58f, 75).

6 Cf. Hartman, 'Name' 435.

7 Cf. Fazekaš, 'Taufe' 306f and n. 7; Frankemölle, *Taufverständnis* 49f; Tannehill, *Dying* 23.

8 Str. -B. 1, 591.

and the baptized to which the latter must assent and which he must realize through his confession of the God in whose name he has been baptized'[9]. As L. Hartman observes, this comes very close to Heitmüller's interpretation of the meaning of the phrase; he notes the telling comment of Kuss that 'it is not of fundamental importance whether one derives the formula *eis to onoma* from the Greek . . . or from the Semitic . . . usage'[10].

Hartman himself prefers a Semitic backgound for the phrase, but points out how widely the Hebrew or Aramaic phrases *lešēm, lešûm*, could be used. In particular, in connection with various rites, they 'introduce the type, reason or purpose of the rite as well as its intention'. So in *m. Nid.* 5.6, ' "We know in whose name we have vowed it" or "in whose name we have dedicated it" ', the phrase denotes not 'by what or whom one has promised, but a kind of fundamental reference for the vow. In a similar way "Jesus" could be the fundamental reference for baptism. The phrase then characterized the rite in a fundamental way: it was a "Jesus baptism" '[11]. 'Into the name of Jesus' 'especially delimited Christian baptism from that of John'[12].

And yet is this not altogether too vague? Does it not leave out of consideration the meaning which the rite was held to have? Acts 19.1–7 shows how John's rite was considered to be a baptism of repentance; baptism 'into the name of the Lord Jesus' (it is not called 'Jesus' baptism' or 'the Lord's baptism') is associated with the gift of the Spirit, and, in 2.38, with the forgiveness of sins. Moreover, Hartman's appeal for support to *m. Nid.* 5.6 is surely suspect: the vow or dedication was made invoking the name of the thing or person in whose presence the vow or dedication was made. So Jesus quotes as Old Testament teaching the principle that 'you shall repay your vows to the Lord' (Matt 5.33)[13]; God was something more than the rather vague phrase, 'the fundamental reference' for the vow: he was the one to whom the person who had sworn was accountable[14].

---

9 Ibid. 1055; cf. Bietenhard in *TDNT* 5, 268, 274–6.

10 Hartman, 'Name' 433 and n. 1, quoting O. Kuss, 'Zur vorpaulinischen Tauflehre im Neuen Testament', *ThGl* 41 (1951), 289–309, repr. *Auslegung und Verkündigung* 1 (Regensburg, 1963), 93–120, here 98; cf. also J. Jeremias in de Lorenzi, *Battesimo* 106.

11 Ibid. 439.

12 Ibid. 440.

13 Not in fact an express OT quotation, although it could claim to paraphrase a text like Deut 23.21 (22).

14 Cf. Bietenhard in *TDNT* 5, 255: 'the name thus pronounced (in oaths, etc.) guarantees Yahweh's presence, attention, and active intervention.' G. Barth, *Taufe* 57, argues that the reference to the 'name' in the phrase *lešēm* was not nearly so full of meaning in Jewish usage, but that it is 'conceivable' that, used in the context of Christian worship, it came to take on a fuller meaning for an early Christianity which summed up the saving activity of God in Jesus by reference to the 'name' of Jesus.

But an apter comparison than oaths here might be those references to rabbinic ritual washings using the phrase *lešēm* which Strack-Billerbeck cites (and which Hartman strangely seems to ignore)[15]. Especially note-worthing is *b. Yebam.* 45*b*:

> If a man bought a slave from an idolater and [that slave] forestalled him and performed ritual ablution with the object of acquiring the status of a freed man (*lešēm ben ḥôrîn*, literally: 'for the name of a son of freedom') he acquires thereby his emancipation[16].

Seemingly the *lešēm* phrase designates the purpose of the bath and ex-presses the status (or name) that the one washed takes on himself, 'a son of freedom'. But clearly those baptized 'into the name of Christ' do not style themselves Christs[17], and to that extent the Christ rite has no anal-ogy in the Jewish rites, nor would we expect it to have any; yet neverthe-less they still in a sense bear the name of Christ as his followers.

Thus Strack-Billerbeck's argument that the phrase indicated how the baptized was bound to the one into whose name he was baptized and that this bond carried with it an obligation may be held to have survived the objections raised against it by Hartman[18]. Moreover, when Paul speaks of belonging to Christ as a corollary of being baptized into him in Gal 3.27–29, it may well be that the amount of reinterpretation of the Semitic idiom which this involves may be slight. In baptism the first Christians were conscious of becoming members of the community of the Messiah, enjoying fellowship with him, and being marked out from the rest of Juda-ism by their allegiance to him[19]. The omission of the reference to 'the name' in Gal 3.27 and Rom 6.3 may be daring[20], but nonetheless it makes plain the sense of joining Christ already implicit in the longer phrase 'into the

---

15 Str. -B. 1, 1054; Bietenhard in *TDNT* 5, 268; Jeremias, *Baptism* 29.

16 Soncino ed./trans.

17 Not yet at least, but cf. the ref. to Cyril of Jerusalem in Leipoldt, 'Taufe' 71.

18 Cf. Halter, *Taufe* 138: 'Regardless of the derivation of the terminology almost all have come to the same conclusion with regard to the meaning of this phrase used in the context of baptism: it is a matter of the transference of ownership, be it the ownership of the baptized transferred to the Lord (the usual explanation) or, *vice versa*, the saving event or the cross event being transferred to the possession of the baptized (Delling).'

19 Cf. Schweizer, *Gemeinde* §3g, 34f.

20 Käsemann, *Röm* 56, argues that 'into' and 'into the name' are independent of each other (so Tannehill, *Dying* 22; also Dunn, *Baptism* 141, and *Unity* 158; cf. Best, *Body* 65–73). Con-trast, e.g., Barrett, *Rom* 122; G. Barth, *Taufe* 44, 46, 99; Gäumann, *Taufe* 73f; Leenhardt, *Rom* 152; Oepke in *TDNT* 1, 539; Schlier, *Röm* 192; Schnackenburg, *Baptism* 25; Wilckens, *Röm* 2, 11 (on 48 he describes it as a 'general view' that 'into' is a Pauline interpretation of 'into the name of'). Certainly this derivation from 'into the name of' seems to lie closest to hand; what is going too far, however, is to suggest that not only are 'into the name of the Lord Jesus' and 'in the name of . . .' identical, but that these are also synonymous with 'into (Christ Jesus)', 'being Christ's', 'putting on Christ' and 'in Christ' (Beker, *Paul* 272 n.).

name of Christ'[21]. At the same time baptism was seen not just as imposing obligations upon the baptized; it was an act by which the baptized appealed to Jesus and to God for deliverance; that much is implied by the reference to washing away sins and calling on Jesus' name in Acts 22.16, and possibly also by the enigmatic reference of 1 Pet 3.21 to baptism as 'the appeal to God of a good conscience' (or perhaps 'for a good conscience'). One declared one's allegiance to this new master, but at the same time sought from him protection and deliverance[22]. Thus Kuss may be correct in assuming that Paul could presuppose the belief that by this rite the individual obtained a share in the salvation won once and for all through Christ's saving act[23].

This does not mean, however, that we need to go as far as Tannehill seems to do when he argues that being baptized 'into Christ' can only be understood in terms of entering Christ as the corporate person of the new aeon[24]. That *may* be how Paul understood it, but if it is implied by Rom 6.3 that the Roman Christians too were familiar with this language (as Tannehill thinks they were) there are still other ways in which one might feel onself to be under someone's lordship and protection. Need one, for instance, suppose that Paul in 1 Cor 10.2 speaks of baptism into Moses because he thinks of entry into another corporate person[25]? On the contrary Christian Wolff considers this usage an argument against a local sense of εἰς in this phrase[26]. The Israelites were placed under Moses' leadership, yes, but it would be unwise to insist that whenever βαπτίζεσθαι εἰς is used it must have the full sense that Paul elsewhere gave it. Thus other early Christians may have used the same language without this deep and complex sense which Paul gives it. For them it may simply have

---

21 Cf. Cranfield, *Rom* 1, 301. It may, however, be correct to see this change of language as 'strengthening and intensifying' this relationship of the baptized to Christ (Kuss, *Röm* 308; cf. Hermann, *Kyrios* 79–81; Schnackenburg, *Baptism* 111).

22 So Kuss, *Röm* 307: 'the baptized became Jesus' possession and one committed to his care'; cf. Bultmann, *Theology* 1, §13.1, 138; Schlier, *Röm* 192. So Pokorný, 'Christologie', stresses the link baptism signified between the baptized and the risen Jesus who by his resurrection was shown to be able to offer these things to his people. Dinkler, 'Taufaussagen' 96, finds the same two ideas of possession and protection inherent in the Jewish background to the idea of 'sealing' applied by Paul to baptism (or just to becoming a Christian – see nn. 4f above) in 2 Cor 1.22; cf. Leipoldt, 'Taufe' 70. This seems to be a more precise way of stating the relation presupposed than that of, e.g., Lagrange, *Rom* 151, who suggests that baptism, like all rites of initiation, unites the initiated with the deity (is that true?).

23 *Röm* 309.

24 *Dying* 22 and esp. 42: 'The motif of dying and rising with Christ, and the corporate patterns of thought associated with it, were connected with baptism in the early church.'

25 It is true that Moses may, like Adam or Christ, represent a(n) (*Un*)*heilsordnung* (Tannehill, ibid. 24), but is that quite the same as being 'an inclusive or corporate person'?

26 *1 Kor* 41 n. 231.

meant that they were united with and joined to Christ in the sense of entering the people placed under his lordship and protection.

Quite how far this union with Christ in baptism was viewed particularly as a union with Christ in his death is another matter, for, as Wilckens comments, 'there is no other evidence for the parallel formulation εἰς τὸν θάνατον αὐτοῦ in early Christianity'[27]. The stress upon Christ as the one who died is characteristic of Paul, but it is an emphasis with which his readers would be bound to agree; after all, there was no other Christ with whom one could be united in baptism than the one who had died for those baptized[28]. And yet, as Wilckens also notes, the meaning of εἰς with an event (like Jesus' death) cannot be exactly the same as that of εἰς (τὸ ὄνομα) with a person; Paul does not say that we are baptized into the crucified one; Wilckens' answer to this problem is to give the verb 'baptize' its full, concrete sense of 'immerse'[29]. Presumably the force of εἰς here is then similar to that of Mk 1.9, although one would immediately have to say that although the latter spoke of a literal immersion in water Rom 6.3 uses this idea figuratively, just as the idea of baptism is used figuratively in Mk 10.38 and Lk 12.50. However it is by no means clear that 'into his death' is a figurative extension of being dipped into water rather than an extension of the idea of being united with a person, an extension of it to a being caught up in the events of that person's life (just as the Israelites were 'baptized into Moses' through certain shared experiences, referred to as 'the cloud' and 'the sea', in 1 Cor 10.2)[30]. At the same time the abbreviation of 'into the name of' to 'into' makes it possible that Paul was also conscious of the analogy with the water in which one was immersed. If we try to pin him down to either a mere abbreviation of εἰς τὸ ὄνομα[31] or an adaptation of the idea of being immersed in water we run the risk of overlooking the fluidity and complexity of his language (and indeed of most language).

This sharing in Christ's death in baptism should, however, be distinguished from the views that baptism as an initiation rite or 'rite of passage' inevitably involved in it the idea of the death of the baptized[32], or

---

27 Wilckens, *Röm* 2, 11; cf. also 50; G. Barth, *Taufe* 99; for another view cf. J. Jeremias and M. Barth in de Lorenzi, *Battesimo* 112, 115 (the former arguing from 1 Cor 1.13). Kuss, 'Frage' 15f, regards it as possible that Hellenistic Christians preceded Paul in understanding baptism as a death.

28 Cf. Schnackenburg, *Baptism* 25; also Halter, *Taufe* 139 and esp. 41 where he argues that Paul is here presupposing 'belief in the Lord who was killed and raised at work in the church in the present.'

29 *Röm* 2, 11.

30 Cf. Schnackenburg, *Baptism* 111.

31 Counselled against by Bouttier, *En Christ* 37f, who stresses the element of the 'movement' of incorporation contained in the phrase.

32 Cf. King, *Death*; see further below §6.3.

that the rite of baptism was viewed as a form of death in earlier Christian tradition[33]. For the reference here is not just to death, but to the past death of one particular man. Put most starkly, but probably correctly, by Ridderbos, 'baptism is not a grave and resurrection . . . but baptism incorporates us into, makes us participate in, Christ's death on Golgotha and resurrection in the garden'[34]. Here lies the main difficulty, and at the same time perhaps the most distinctive feature, of Paul's thought here[35].

To sum up, it seems most likely that 'baptism into Christ' was originally an abbreviation of 'baptism into the name of Christ', and that the latter meant that the one baptized came under Christ's lordship and protection. The shorter phrase did, however, lend itself to a figurative local sense, thus giving a more intimate, and less purely formal, sense of union between the baptized and Christ. Paul, characteristically, stresses that the Christ with whom one was united in baptism is none other than the Christ who died.

1.3.3.2. Secondly, we saw in Acts 2.38 how baptism is connected with the *forgiveness of sins*, and this forgiveness in turn is connected with Christ's death. The latter connection is clearly implied by the traditional material quoted in 1 Cor 15.3, that 'Christ died for our sins according to the scriptures'[1], as well as by at least part of the tradition of the words of Jesus at his last supper with his disciples: 'This is my blood of the covenant which is poured out for many for the forgiveness of sins' (Matt 26.28). This too

---

33 Cf. Bartsch, 'Taufe' 84–96 (also Reitzenstein, 'Religionsgeschichte' 11; Thyen, 'Βάπτισμα' 133 n. 6); for Bartsch even Jesus' baptism was viewed as a death and rebirth; it is not quite clear whether this was Jesus' own view of baptism (both at his baptism and in his utterance of the words of Mk 10.38 and Lk 12.50) or merely an interpretation of baptism by the early church (how early?); the former is surely historically doubtful. Kuss, however, in 'Frage' 11f, argues that 'the image of baptism in Mk 10.38 and 39 (and Lk 12.50) has as little to do with Christian baptism as it has to do with Jesus' baptism in the Jordan'; it was precisely because it did not speak of Christian baptism, but could be misunderstood as doing so, that Matt omitted this part of the logion. Jesus' reference was primarily to suffering (which could indeed include death).

34 *Paul* 404 (rightly, above all, in the light of 2 Cor 5.14, see further below in §5.3.1–2).

35 The difficulty of this idea can be seen from the brief surveys of the different interpretations of it by Kuss, *Röm* 328–44; Schnackenburg, *Baptism* 139–54; Tannehill, *Dying* 3–6, and elsewhere.

Notes on 1.3.3.2

1 Material thought by many to lie behind the assertions about Christ's death, burial and resurrection in Rom 6: so, e.g., G. Barth, *Taufe* 100; Carlson, *Baptism* 216f; Frankemölle, *Taufverständnis* 28; Gäumann, *Taufe* 62–4; Hahn, 'Verständnis' 142; Michel, *Röm* 130; Schnackenburg, *Baptism* 34; Wilckens, *Röm* 2, 12. However Dinkler, 'Römer 6,1–14' 89, warns against assuming that the credal material itself, rather than the events to which it refers, lies behind Rom. 6.3f.

was clearly something which Paul could assume to be known to his readers in Rome, as part of the Christian proclamation shared by all (1 Cor 15.11)[2].

The connection between baptism and the forgiveness of sins which Paul here could assume goes back to the probable roots of the Christian rite in the baptizing movement of John who preached 'a baptism of repentance leading to the forgiveness of sins' (Mk 1.4; Lk 3.3 ; contrast Jos., *Ant*. 18.5.2 §117)[3]. This same effect of Christian baptism is found, as we have seen, in Luke-Acts (Lk 24.47; Acts 2.38; 22.16)[4] and it is an interpretation which arises naturally out of the symbolism of washing[5]. Yet Black notes that Christian baptism differed from John's in that the former was integrally related to Christ's death for sins[6], and it is indeed likely that from very early on this connection was made in some way by the early Christians. However, as Kuss notes[7], Paul has a far more radical view of the plight from which we are saved (and of the salvation into which we enter), although his use of the word ἀπελούσασθε in 1 Cor 6.11 is most easily understood simply of cleansing from sin in baptism (cf. Acts 22.16; also Eph 5.26; Tit 3.5)[8].

Nevertheless Siber is correct to regard the connection between baptism, the forgiveness of sins and the death of Christ in the earliest period of the church as 'loose' in the sense of ill-defined[9]. The connections are there, but how they are made is not spelt out; the beginnings of such a spelling out we can see in Paul's exposition in Romans 6.

1.3.3.3. Thirdly, baptism was seen as a *break with one's sinful past life*[1] *and the start of a new life*. The break with sin was clearly implied by the

---

2 So Wilckens, ibid. 8, 50.

3 See also *Sib*. 4.162–70. Most recognize in John's baptizing a precursor, if not the sole one, of the Christian practice, whether or not they accept the Fourth Gospel's account of Jesus' followers also baptizing during his ministry (Jn 3.22; 4.1f); so, e.g., Wilckens, ibid. 54, describes this connection as 'clear and generally recognized'; cf. G. Barth, *Taufe* 37; Dinkler, 'Taufaussagen' 63; Kraft, *Entstehung* 216; Rowland, *Origins* 153, 238.

Braumann, *Taufverkündigung*, emphasizes this role of John's rite and in particular sees Paul's view of baptism in Rom 6 as sharing with John the view that baptism marked a break in the baptized's life (cf. §1.3.3.3), that it was eschatologically orientated (6.22f), and that it led to an appropriate way of life (p. 16). For Pokorný, 'Christologie' 374, the two baptisms are linked by the question how a sinner can survive God's judgment.

4 Cf. also 1 Cor 6.11; Eph 5.26; Heb 10.22; ?1 Pet 3.21; *Herm. man.* 4.3.1.

5 So Bultmann, *Theology* 1, §13.1, 133, 136; cf. Thyen, 'Βάπτισμα' 166f: 'Almost everywhere in the NT the forgiveness of sins appears in a close and primary connection with baptism!'

6 Black, *Rom* 93.

7 *Röm* 308.

8 Schnackenburg, *Baptism* 3, suggests a causative sense for the middle: 'you had yourselves washed'; cf. Ridderbos, *Paul* 398. Carlson, *Baptism* 350, questions the ref. to baptism.

9 *Mit Christus* 208; cf. Schnackenburg, ibid. 33. Kuss, *Röm* 309, tentatively raises the possibility that Hellenistic Christians may have preceded Paul in forging closer ties between baptism and Christ's death (cf. also 'Frage' 15).

idea of repentance which was linked with the rite by John the Baptist
(Matt 3.2, 8, 11; Mk 1.4; Lk 3.3, 8; Acts 13.24; 19.4) and was seemingly
taken up by the early church (Acts 2.38); for John, moreover, baptism
was linked with a life of rigorous obedience to the law (Jos., *Ant.* 18.5.2
§117)[2]. The same idea of a radical break with the past eventually came
to be expressed with the vivid image of rebirth (Jn 3.5; Tit 3.5)[3], but,
however much this imagery may be in continuity with earlier ideas, it
should not be assumed that it was *immediately* adopted (from the mysteries?)[4] to express those ideas; it only appears in relatively late strata of the
New Testament and, although Paul uses the comparable idea of 'new
creation' (2 Cor 5.17; Gal 6.15)[5] he does not expressly link it with the
rite of baptism, nor does he, as opposed to the follower of his who probably wrote the Letter to Titus, ever use the imagery of rebirth[6].

In keeping with this baptism was associated with the gift of the Spirit,
the power of this new life (Acts 2.38; cf. Jn 3.5; Acts 10.47; 19.2–6;
Barn. 11.11)[7]. This may well be reflected in 1 Cor 6.11, where washing,
sanctification and justification are associated with the name of Christ
and God's Spirit[8], and in 1 Cor 12.13, where all Christians are baptized

---

Notes on 1.3.3.3

1 And so, put vividly by Paul as the death of the 'old self' (Wilckens, *Röm* 2, 8). Dahl, 'Observations' 33, notes how the 'soteriological contrast pattern' (cf. Bultmann, *Theology* 1, 105f)
   is frequently associated with the mention of baptism which marks 'the change from the "once"
   prior to faith to the "now" of faith'.

2 Cf. Pokorný, 'Christologie' 374.

3 Cf. Justin, *Apol.* 1.61.3; 66.1; *Dial.* 138.2.

4 Bultmann, *Theology* 1, 142; Bartsch, 'Taufe' 86ff, 97f (yet he distinguishes the Christian
   view from that of the mysteries; for the former the dying in baptism is 'an actual death, and not
   just a death without any sting, in the form of mystical experience'); Schnackenburg, *Baptism*
   10–17 (more guarded – n.b. 17). Schweizer, 'Dying' 6, suggests that in Tit 3.5 the term παλιγγενεσία (not the usual one for the mysteries) derives from Jewish apocalyptic usage (cf. Matt.
   19.28) which in turn drew upon Hellenistic usage, primarily the Stoic cosmic sense, rather than
   the individual one of the mysteries. Besides the possible derivation from the mysteries it should
   be noted that the baptized proselyte was regarded as a newborn child; perhaps this is too
   natural an imagery for 'parallels' necessarily to imply influence or borrowing. Cf. Sahlin,
   '"Beschneidung"' 22, who argues that because Christian baptism was a 'circumcision' which
   was for Jews a new birth, baptism came to be regarded as a new birth too. See further chap. 6
   below.

5 Cf. Davies, *Paul* 119–21. On the symbolism of garments, old and new, in baptism cf. J. Z.
   Smith, 'Garments'.

6 Davies, ibid. 120 n. 4 and lit. cited there; cf. Simon, *'Schule'* 140 (but see F. C. Grant, *Hellenism* 159).

7 Cf. the reff. to baptizing in the Spirit (Mk 1.8 pars; Jn 1.33; Acts 1.5; 11.16); cf. also G. Barth,
   Taufe chap. 3; Bultmann, *Theology* 1, 138–40. This link between Spirit and baptism is unparalleled in any of the rites of washing in the mystery-cults: so Kennedy, *St Paul* 230.

8 Lohse, 'Taufe' 321f, considers this verse to be a quotation of early Christian baptismal teaching; cf. now Schnelle, *Gerechtigkeit* 37ff. Since this is written to a Pauline church it is possible
   that the Corinthians were taught these ideas by Paul; yet on balance they are probably not to
   be regarded as peculiar to his churches (cf. also 1 Cor 12.13; Tit 3.5).

'into one body'[9] in the one Spirit and have been given one Spirit to drink[10]. It is quite possible that this association goes back to the earliest days of the church[11]. For it was this gift of the Spirit which the early Christians felt distinguished their baptism from John's[12], as well as its association with the name of Jesus; this distinction probably led them to set a similar contrast on John's lips in Mk 1.8 pars (cf. Acts 1.5; 11.16).

1.3.3.4. Fourthly, that old, sinful life could be regarded as a *state of death from which one must be rescued.* That is a view characteristic of Ephesians (2.1, 5) and Colossians (2.13), but such a figurative use of νεκρός 'dead' is found more widely: Lk 15.24, 32 (cf. Jn 5.25; 1 Tim 5.6; 1 Jn 3.14; Rev 3.1; *Herm. sim.* 9.16.3−6)[1]. Nor is this surprising, since such a figurative use of 'death' and 'dead' was found also in Greek (especially Stoic) philosophy[2] and in Hellenistic Judaism, where Philo speaks of the life of the wicked in estrangement from God as true death, a death of the soul (as opposed to that of the body which is liberation)[3]. Such a figurative usage is also found in rabbinic literature as well . Thus, in all likelihood, Paul could expect such a figure of speech to be readily intelligible to his readers.

What, however, has not been shown is that Paul could draw upon a tradition in which the passing from death to life was already described in the language of resurrection, however near at hand such an extension of this imagery may have lain, at least among those familiar with this form of expectation of a life after death. And what we shall have to ask

---

9 The parallel use of βαπτίζεσθαι εἰς would suggest that the primary reference here is to the crucified body of Christ; contrast *NEB* 'we were all brought into one body by baptism'. In favour of the first interpretation cf. J. Cambier in de Lorenzi, *Battesimo* 113, following L. Cerfaux.

10 Or 'have been watered' with it (cf. Cuming, 'ἐποτίσθημεν'; cf. Schnackenburg, *Baptism* 85f).

11 So Schnackenburg, ibid. 109, against G. Kittel, 'Die Wirkungen der christlichen Wassertaufe nach dem Neuen Testament', *ThStKr* 87 (1914), 33−42. Haufe, 'Taufe' 565f, argues that baptism and the Spirit were not originally linked; this connection only arose in a Hellenistic, pagan area (Syria). After all John' baptism had not been associated with the Spirit. But the association may still have originated very early.

12 Kraft, *Entstehung* 20, argues that in reality 'the Baptist regarded his baptism as an announcement of the Spirit-baptism, that is, as a prophetic sign for the outpouring of the Holy Spirit.' Originally the early church may also have regarded baptism as announcing a coming outpouring of the Spirit, but immediately they experienced that baptism brought the Spirit, i.e. experienced the rite as an effective sign (215).

Notes on 1.3.3.4

1 Cf. R. Bultmann in *TDNT* 4, 893, in 2, 863 n. 267, and in 3, 17f (n.b. also Rom 7.10).

2 Cf. Bultmann in *TDNT* 3, 12: especially Stoicism (cf. L. Coenen in *DNTT* 1, 443−6); cf. Epict., *Diss.* 1.3.3; 5.7; 9.19; 3.23.28; Philostr., *Vit. Ap.* 1.9; Sen., *Ep.* 1.2.

3 Cf., e.g., Philo, *Leg. all.* 1.76; 3.52; *Det. pot. ins.* 70; *Deus imm.* 89; *Congr.* 57; *Fug.* 55, 78, 113; *Som.* 1.151; 2.66, 234; *Praem. poen.* 70, 72; *Quaest. in Gen.* 1.16, 45, 51, 76; 4.152, 173.

is the question how widespread such an expectation was, particularly in the Hellenistic environment in which Paul founded his churches, and thus how readily this figurative use of the idea of resurrection could have arisen. A figurative idea of the state of death and of what it meant to be dead was commonplace enough. A figurative resurrection as a remedy to that was anything but common. (See chap. 3.)

1.3.3.5. Fifthly, there is a contrasted view of *death as liberating and freeing one from sin*; this idea is far more widespread in the Pauline homologoumena than the previous one (the state of sin as death) and may be regarded as a characteristic Pauline emphasis even if it is not peculiar to him. For within Greek dualistic thought death was often regarded as the soul's liberation from its bondage in the body, and this too is reflected in Philo's writings: when we die the soul lives its own proper life, liberated from the 'dead' body in which it had previously been incarcerated[1]. But Paul speaks more of liberation from sin and from death as a state of God-forsakenness, death under God's curse (but cf. Rom 7.24). We have to be snatched from the clutches of this power which holds us captive[2].

At first sight Rom 6.7 might be thought to be clear evidence of Paul's use of a rather different tradition to the Hellenistic one at this point, for it is widely thought that he is here quoting a maxim, perhaps one familiar in Jewish thought[3]. And yet if there were such an adage to the effect that death clears all debts or that death removes the possibility of sin this is hardly what Paul means here, for in his eyes death is the moment when sin catches up with the sinner (6.23); it is the continuing dominion of sin which makes death a bitter thing and no joyous liberation, in contrast particularly with the Greek dualistic view outlined above (1 Cor 15.56). Thus there is much to be said for Cranfield's view that Paul is here saying that 'the man who has died with Christ in baptism . . . has been justified from his sin'[4]. That in turn comes near to the suggestion

---

4 One might see evidence for such a usage among the rabbis in a saying like *m. Pesaḥ*. 8.8: 'He that separates himself from his uncircumsicion is as one that separates himself from a grave' (Danby 148; cf. *m. ʿEd.* 5.2). But see the end of §6.3 for a different interpretation of this text. For further rabbinic reff. cf. Str. -B. 1, 489; 3, 652.

Notes on 1.3.3.5

1 E.g., *Leg. all.* 1.108; *Quaest. in Gen.* 4.152; so Philo comes to speak of two deaths, that of the human person (i.e. the separation of the soul from the body) which is welcome, and that of the soul which is the true evil: *Leg. all.* 1.105; 2.77 (cf. *Conf. ling.* 36).

2 Cf. Schnackenburg, 'Adam-Christus-Typologie' 53.

3 Cf. Str. -B. 3, 232; K. G. Kuhn, 'Rm 6,7'; Dinkler, 'Römer 6,1–14' 91; G. Schrenk in *TDNT* 2, 218. Yet, if it is a rabbinic tradition that 'in general death atones, even when one has not repented' (Kuhn, ibid. 307), it is unlikely that Paul would have endorsed it. *Pace* Schrenk, ibid., the rabbinic and the Pauline statements are not 'fully identical in substance'.

4 *Rom* 1, 311; cf. also Feuillet, 'Mort' 490; Kuhn, ibid.

that this is a Christological statement: in the first place the one who has died is Christ, although with him all died as well (2 Cor 5.14)[5]. It is his death which set him free (cf. v 9) and with him all those whom he represents. Christ has passed from the lordship of sin and death into God's domain, leading us with him. It is this Christological evaluation of death which takes as its starting point Christ's death under a curse (Gal 3.13) and then views that death for us from the perspective of God's raising of him from the dead which distinguishes Paul's treatment of death from the Hellenistic and rabbinic views that we have just considered.

Thus his positive view of death as liberating and saving is undergirded for Paul by his characteristic language of the Christian both having died with Christ and dying with him in the present (cf. §1.3.1.). In the past he died with Christ (Rom 6.8), was crucified with him (Gal 2.19; cf. Rom 6.6), and was put to death as far as the law was concerned through Christ's death (Rom 7.4). Now Paul dies daily (1 Cor 15.31), bearing about in his body 'the death that Jesus died' (2 Cor 4.10, *NEB*), suffering with him (Rom 8.17).

It should be noted that not only the 'with Christ' language but also the past tenses which are so clear in Rom 6 are hard to parallel: 'we were buried with him' (6.4), 'our old nature was crucified with him' (6.6), 'we died with Christ' (6.8)[6]. That the moment of this death is not just that of baptism, but is also, perhaps even primarily, that of Jesus' death on Golgotha is indicated above all by the statement of 2 Cor 5.14 that 'one died for all; therefore all died'; it seems desperately difficult to understand 'all died' as a reference to anything but the moment of the death of the one[7]. So to interpret the believer's death helps to explain how it could be argued above that Paul's 'with Christ' language was independent of the rite of baptism and baptismal traditions (cf. §1.3.2.2.).

However Halter justly warns us against too extreme an espousal of this line of argument[8]; although this position is favoured particularly in Barthian circles[9] this leads to the view that baptism is no sacrament, indeed is simply superfluous as such; it is no more than an act of acknowledgment of what happened then on the cross for and to all. One must then violently

---

5 Cf. Frankemölle, *Taufverständnis* 76–7; Kearns, 'Interpretation'; Scroggs, 'Romans vi.7'.

6 Cf. also Gal 2.19.

7 Cf. Hughes, *2 Cor* 195: 'The two aorist verbs . . . point back to the one event, namely, the crucifixion of Christ.' Cf. Feuillet, 'Mort' 483–7. So, on Rom 6, G. Barth, *Taufe* 270f; Güttgemanns, *Apostel* 212 ('The real liberating event has taken place in (the experiences of) Christ'), 217, 219 and n. 50, 221–223; G. Otto, *Formulierungen* 37, 42; Percy, *Leib* 26.

8 *Taufe* 43–6: he wishes to distinguish Christ's death in the past for all and our dying with him in baptism – the 'with' is not temporal, but speaks of sharing in the eschatological Christ-event, sharing in the soteriological 'effect' of the Christ-event.

9 See the lit. in ibid. 535 n. 39.

'de-sacramentalize' all passages speaking of baptism as saving or interpret them of a pure spiritual baptism not connected directly with water-baptism, or one lets them stand but criticizes them as inconsistent with the 'centre' of Paul's theology. But why does Paul then again and again speak of baptism, and why does he not just say in Rom 6.2 'Or do you not know that one died for all and so all died with him?'? This is unfortunately not the place to go too deeply into Pauline hermeneutics (but see further in §5.3), but something nevertheless needs to be said here: the tension between a death with Christ at Golgotha and a death with him in baptism perhaps becomes more comprehensible if one regards both deaths as primarily 'word events' or, better, 'communicative events' (however much or little Paul was conscious that this was how he was treating them). They are, in other words, events which are significant for us not because they automatically do something to us, but because they communicate something to us, they let us know of something, in this case of God's judgment on sin and his promise of life; that was the message of Golgotha and of Easter; it is also the message of baptism. It needs to be proclaimed once and for all, in the past, but it needs also to be repeated again and again so that individuals may hear it and respond to it. But because it is a repetition of something already said in the past Paul speaks of us already dying with Christ in the past, when we shared in the verdict delivered upon him.

It is this language of suffering and dying with Christ and, in particular, having died with him in the past that is really unparalleled. Some of the ideas which he otherwise uses may be expressed in different words: so the future existence of Christians with Christ may be paralleled by statements about the future fellowship of the Son of man with the elect (e:g. in Mk 13.26f; Rev 14.1 – $\mu\epsilon\tau\,'a\dot{v}\tau o\tilde{v}$)[10] or of the Messiah with his people; so too ideas like suffering in the present in order to obtain glory to come are found elsewhere and in other language. But when Wilckens cites one such passage, 1 Pet 1.3–10, to show that 'all aspects of Paul's $\sigma\acute{v}v$-statements, sacramental, eschatological and also those concerning Christian or apostolic suffering, have their origins . . . in the context of baptism' and to show that Paul developed his 'with Christ' language out of an earlier form of baptismal theology[11] he goes too far. As he grants (51) the 'with Christ' language is missing there, and if that is missing then a whole dimension, and a fundamental one at that, of Paul's thought is also missing. For, as P. Althaus comments, the presupposition of Paul's teaching on baptism

---

10 Cf. *1 Enoch* 62.14, 'with that Son of Man shall they eat and lie down and rise up for ever and ever'.
11 *Röm* 2, 47.

is his 'conviction that Christ's death and resurrection are facts which contain a comprehensive reality that affects the whole of humanity'[12], and it is this conviction to which he gives expression in his 'with Christ' language. All died with Christ, when he died. It is this idea which is lacking from passages like 1 Pet 1.3—10 and other non-Pauline works, a fundamental and distinctive element in Paul's thought. It is, however, this element which some have suggested was borrowed from the Hellenistic mystery-cults via Hellenistic Christianity, although Althaus again would say that this idea was wholly different to theirs[13]. This argument over the relation of the cult-god and his initiates and over the relation of Christ to the believer is one which we will have to consider further: are these two sets of relationships, cult-god and initiates, Christ and believers, sufficiently similar to allow us to postulate that the latter was influenced by the former, or are they so different that we must postulate a different background to Paul's ideas? (see chap. 5.)

1.3.3.6. For the present, however, we may say that many of Paul's statements in Romans 6 would have echoed, at least in part, teaching which the Roman Christians would have received: it would come as no surprise to them that they had been united with Christ in baptism and that this meant a break with sin; the fact that they knew that would mean that Paul's gospel would have been viewed with suspicion if it was thought to imply that Christians could persist in sin; that would conflict with what they had been taught. The same knowledge made their experience of baptism a logical starting point for Paul's argument that they had broken with sin. They knew all too well that baptism meant a break with their sinful past and a new beginning, a life lived in the service of the Son of the righteous God of the Jews; they perhaps even viewed the new obedience which they had undertaken as involving obedience to the Jewish law[1]. That amount of common ground (which of course did not include the obedience to the Jewish law, at least in the way the synagogue demanded it) between Paul and his readers in Rome is perhaps sufficient to justify the implications of his introductory ἢ ἀγνοεῖτε (6.3).

And yet, it must be noted, that common ground needs no hypothesis of the influence of the mystery-cults to explain it. Rather its origins lie

---

12 *Röm* 55; this significance arises, he argues, from Christ's God-given position as head and representative of humanity.
13 Ibid. 56.

Notes on 1.3.3.6
1 Cf. 'Ambrosiaster', Prologue to comm. on Rom (in Migne *PL* 17, 46); Schmithals, *Römerbrief* 56ff.

in Jewish Christianity and in the adoption and adaptation by the early church in Palestine of the rite which marked the ministry of John the Baptist. There is no need to postulate that these traditions bore the impress of ideas characteristic of the mysteries.

But what of Paul himself? If the 'with Christ' language is peculiar to him, does it reflect the influence of the mystery-cults and their theology, although Paul has chosen his own way of expressing that theology? Was Paul modelling his portrayal of Christ on the dying and rising gods of the cults? These are questions that still need answering, although this way of posing them comes closer to the way in which Wagner posed them and answered them to his own satisfaction at least (cf. § 1.3); yet they can also be posed, not in terms of an entire structure of thought, a whole package of ideas, but in terms of a series of individual motifs and ideas which may have gone to make up that view of baptism which Paul presents in Romans 6[2].

1.3.4.1. We noted at the beginning of this section (§1.3) that the rite of baptism was widely regarded as the matrix in which the ideas of union with Christ and participation in his life and death were nurtured, and that this Christian rite was the point of contact with the Hellenistic cults which enabled their ideas to infiltrate early Christianity, the bridge over which these new and alien ways of thought crossed over into the Palestinian Jewish faith of the first followers of Jesus. But if the association of these concepts of union with Christ on the one hand and the rite of baptism on the other is a secondary one, if these ideas originally had an existence in Christianity independent of any association with baptism, then this point of contact is lost and an alternative route for their arrival in early Christianity must be sought. And if an alternative route then quite possibly an alternative place of origin as well. So this very naturally raises the question where this alternative place of origin might be.

1.3.4.2. In looking at 1 Cor 15 we noted two lines of enquiry to be pursued further: how Gentile Christians would understand the idea of the resurrection of the dead and its terminology, and how they would have regarded their spiritual endowment. The importance of the first has now been underlined by our questioning whether Siber was correct to suppose that Paul used a tradition which asserted that Christians were already resurrected in their baptism; we noted that Paul merely speaks of Christians as living, without saying that they gained this life through their resurrection. Need the one imply the other? The second line of enquiry is also

---

2 As in Siber, *Mit Christus* 213 n. 62 quoted above in §1.3.

suggested by the references to this present life, although the theme of the Spirit is not treated fully until Romans chap. 8: it is not far away in chap. 6, however, in such phrases as 'walk in newness of life' (v 4), especially when we find the rather similar phrase 'serve in newness of the Spirit' in 7.6[1]. Moreover the interconnection between these two questions can readily be seen from the fact that new life (in the Spirit) appears in Paul's text where the flow of logic would rather suggest a reference to our resurrection: we died with Christ when he died; do we not rise when he rose?

But, in noting the novelty of Paul's language of dying and rising with Christ, we have raised a further question: if Paul did not derive his ideas of union with Christ in his death and life from the Graeco-Roman mystery-cults, whence did he derive them? Does the fact that the cults do not echo his language mean that he does not echo their ideas; if it is hard to find *any* close parallel to Paul's language, does that not mean that these cults are still as likely as any to provide the background to Paul's thought at this point? Or is there another background which, while not using the same language, provides a closer analogy to his thought? So that we shall have to investigate, first, whether this novel language of Paul's does indeed reflect a basic dissimilarity of thought to that of the mysteries, and then, secondly, what alternative backgrounds there are to Paul's ideas. (See chap. 5.)

There is one final point to be considered which also arises out of our treatment of Romans 6, the evaluation of the rite of baptism as a dying. For it has often been argued that this is a point which baptism has in common with the initiation rites of the Graeco-Roman mystery-cults. Does this Christian rite in fact fit into a pattern common to all initiatory rites, including those of the mysteries? But, in looking for such patterns we shall at the same time also have to bear in mind that this dying is not just the individual's death, but that he shares in *Christ's* death, and we shall have to ask whether this aspect of Paul's thought does not distinguish his view from all other common patterns of initiation rites and rites of passage. (See chap. 6.)

Notes on 1.3.4.2
1 Cf. Hahn, 'Verständnis' 146.

1.4. Colossians and Ephesians

In investigating the evidence of Colossians and Ephesians we do not need to be drawn too deeply into the questions of the authors of both letters and of the relationship between the two writings. One thing, however, perhaps needs to be said here in the case of Colossians: on the one hand there are those features of the letter which have led scholars to deny that it is the work of Paul's hand — differences of style and particularly of theology[1]. On the other hand there are the clos relationship of this letter to the brief letter to Philemon, whose authenticity few have doubted[2], and the possibility that the city of Colossae was laid low by the same earthquake as devastated the nearby Laodicea in 60–61 C.E.[3] Orosius reports that Laodicea, Hierapolis and Colossae had fallen in an earthquake (singular — *Historia adversus paganos* 7.7.12)[4], and, while it may be true that this might refer to separate events[5], there is the strong possibility that Colossae shared Laodicea's fate on that occasion, but lacked her wealthier neighbour's resources and thus remained unrestored, at least for a while[6]. The idea of a later pseudonymous letter written to a city that was in ruins and to a church there that perhaps no longer existed and which Paul had never visited (Col 2.1) seems too macabre to be likely, especially since the letter makes no mention of this disaster that had overtaken the city[7]. This silence is even stranger if the letter is written

---

Notes on 1.4

1 Cf. Lohse, *Col* 84–91; also Bujard, *Untersuchungen* esp. 220; Conzelmann, *Kol* 177f; Gnilka, *Kol* 19–23; Marxsen, *Introduction* 184f; Schenke-Fischer, *Einleitung* 1, 165–7; Vielhauer, *Geschichte* 196–200.

2 Cf. Kümmel, *Introduction*[2] 349f: 'only tendenz-criticism could doubt the authenticity of this letter' (cf. Gnilka, *Philemonbrief* 3f); also Houlden, *Letters* 138. See also the use made of Col's connection with Philemon by Abbott, *Eph-Col* lvii–lix; Johnston, *Eph* 53; Moule, *Col* 13f; Ollrog, *Paulus* 238; Robinson, *Redating* 61f.

3 Tac., *Ann.* 14.27. Mr E. J. D. Smith informs me in a letter that seismologists date this to 60 C.E.

4 Cf. also Eus., *Hieronymi Chronicon* 183.21f (64 C.E.).

5 So Lohse, *Col* 9.

6 Reicke, 'Setting' 430–2, argues that it 'never regained any real importance'; Colossae does, however, appear on an inscription and coins in the 2nd and 3rd centuries (Magie, *Rule* 986 n. 22; cf. *MAMA* 6, nos 38 and 40 and p. 142, Magie appeals to *IGRR* 4, no. 870, and F. Imhoof-Blumer, *Kleinasiatische Münzen* (Wien, 1901–2), 260f, 525f) and Houlden argues from this that it maintained 'respectable city-status in Imperial times, with the usual complement of officers and institutions' (*Letters* 119); cf. also Bruce, *Col* 5, who disputes the evidence (Strabo) for the decline of Colossae. But we can argue that its recovery was probably slower than that of Laodicea (cf. Gnilka, *Kol* 2); why, after all, does Rev 2–3 contain no letter to the church at Colossae (nor is Hierapolis mentioned)? But certainty here is hindered by the absence of evidence (*MAMA* 6, xi).

7 And yet Lohse seems to countenance this possibility: *Col* 181; cf. Lindemann, *Kol* 12f.

soon after the earthquake[8], and, even if Colossae was relatively untouched by the earthquake, the church there was in touch with that in Laodicea (Col 4.16); it is unlikely that it remained oblivious to the latter's fortunes or that the writer of Colossians would wish it to be so.

The best way to reconcile these data seems to be the hypothesis that Colossians was written by a close follower of Paul during the apostle's lifetime, perhaps in a situation where Paul's imprisonment (Col 4.3, 10, 18) meant that he had to leave the composition of the letters to Colossae and to Philemon rather more in the hands of his associates than he had previously been accustomed to do[9]. In the case of Colossians Timothy is the most obvious candidate for such an associate (1.1)[10]. The other alternative to such an early date is to say that Colossians was written much later, perhaps some way into the second century, to a church in the rebuilt Colossae, or perhaps to no particular church if the address to the Colossian church is also a fiction[11].

If this argument is correct then it has certain implications for the relationship between Paul's views in Romans 6 and the passages in Colossians which deal with dying and rising with Christ. If Colossians is written during Paul's lifetime then it is extremely unlikely that the letter is reviving a view which Paul deliberately corrected (and by implication rejected) in his letter to the Romans, namely that in baptism believers had already risen. This would, of course, be even more unlikely if Colossians were written by Paul himself, although such a change of heart and thought, even in the course of so few years, is possible[12]. Such a correction only becomes more plausible if Colossians is written later — and we have argued above that this was likely to be quite a lot later — by someone with

---

8 But Gnilka makes this a pseudonymous letter of ca. 70 C.E. (*Kol* 22; cf. Schenke, 'Weiterwirken' 513; Schenke-Fischer, *Einleitung* 1, 168; contrast Schweizer, 'Letter' 12, and Scott, *Col* 6).

9 It is arguable that developments, in church order particularly, which scholars have tended to see as the product of a later period after Paul's death, may in fact have begun earlier: with his Caesarean imprisonment Paul began a period of extended confinement, unable to visit his churches, perhaps at times finding it difficult even to write freely to them; while the conditions of his imprisonment in Rome are reported to have been relatively easy (Acts 28.30) we certainly cannot assume that this was always the case; such a situation of prolonged captivity would introduce many of the factors, such as the lack of his presence and control, which made these developments of church discipline necessary (cf. Gnilka, *Kol* 25); one need not wait till the period after Paul's death (contrast Schenke, ibid. 512). Benoit too ('Rapports' 331–4) argues for a date during Paul's life for both Eph and Col.

10 So Schweizer, *Kol* 26f, and 'Letter' 13f; cf. Gnilka, *Kol* 22 (Timothy, but writing after Paul's death); O'Brien, *Col* xlix (very tentatively); Ollrog, *Paulus* esp. 241; this is perhaps preferable to the suggestion of Epaphras (cf. Lähnemann, *Kolosserbrief* 181f. n. 82).

11 Schenke-Fischer, *Einleitung* 1, 167f; but this is also questionable if placed as early as they wish to place Col, namely ca. 70 C.E.

12 For the defenders of Pauline authorship cf. the list in Kümmel, *Introduction*[2] 340 n. 12. The same would be true of Eph: cf. Schlier, *Eph* 111.

no direct contact with Paul and with the situations in which he wrote his letters, at a time when it was no longer appreciated that Paul had had in Romans 6 to set his face against an already realized resurrection. At a very much later date there is, moreover, less likelihood of the spontaneous re-emergence of primitive pre-Pauline traditions; their appearance is more probably the result of deliberate revision.

Nor have there been lacking those who have defended the Pauline authorship of Ephesians[13]. However, more significantly, amongst the proponents of non-Pauline authorship there have been occasional voices raised in support of an author who derived his knowledge of Paul's thought from a personal acquaintance with the apostle, rather than from reading his letters or being the recipient of oral tradition[14]. If that were so, then the same arguments would apply to this epistle as applied to Colossians.

On the whole, the suggestion that the authors of Ephesians and Colossians have expressed ideas which Paul himself corrected (see §1.3.1) is less likely than the hypothesis that rather they develop views already hinted at in Paul's own writings[15]. This, however, still leaves room for the possibility that these views were current already before Paul wrote Romans 6; he would then have taken over these traditions, but either modified them or did not allow them to emerge in his writings in their full form[16]. Yet, although this is possible, I do not see any firm evidence for the existence of these earlier traditions[17]. The evidence of Colossians and Ephesians, I shall argue, points to their use of Romans 6, but it is merely speculative to try to penetrate back behind Romans 6 for the origin of their ideas. Moreover, I suggest, such a hypothesis is not necessary to account for the data which we have.

1.4.1. The statements in *Colossians* which concern us here, especially 2.12f and 3.1, are regarded by perhaps the majority of scholars as later elaborations upon Romans 6[1]; this is true whether they are the work of a follower of Paul or of Paul himself[2].

---

13 See the list in Kümmel, ibid. 357 n. 26; also van Roon, *Authenticity*.

14 E.g. Beare in *IntB* 10, 600; Knox, *Paul* (1939) 184, 203. This view is sympathetically received by Kirby, *Ephesians* 54, 165.

15 So Schlier, *Eph* 111 — 'an exposition of the apostle's earlier understanding of baptism'; also E. Dinkler in *RGG*[3] 6, 633f (cf. 972); Gnilka, *Kol* 11 (but contrast 14 — Col goes back to traditions older than Rom 6); Lähnemann, *Kolosserbrief* 163.

16 Cf. Gnilka, *Kol* 135 (opting for one of the two alternatives named on 119).

17 Cf. Halter, *Taufe* 194.

Notes on 1.4.1

1 Cf., e.g., Bouttier, *En Christ* 52; Conzelmann, *Kol* 190; Kuss, *Röm* 315; Lindemann, *Aufhebung* 140; Lona, *Eschatologie* 155, 168, 171; Wilckens, *Röm* 2, 43.

2 Cf. Lincoln, *Paradise* 122f, 131f: the differences are not such as to preclude the Pauline authorship of Col; cf. also Martin, *Col* 34, 101, and Percy, *Probleme*.

Not all would agree with E. P. Sanders in regarding the first of these passages, Col 2.12f, as evidence of a later *literary* dependence upon Paul's letters, as opposed to reminiscences of phrases characteristic of Paul by a follower of his[3]. The difference, however, is not great, except perhaps in the implications for the dating of the letter. So Sanders' arguments have still a considerable relevance here, even if I am inclined to date Colossians at an earlier date when its author was more likely to be recalling from memory the teaching of Paul than to be fabricating a patchwork of citations and allusions on the basis of his collected letters. Sanders argues (1) that the end of Col 2.12, 'God who raised him from the dead', conflates Rom 6.4, 4.24, and Gal 1.1 (Eph 1.19 is closer to the second of these); these relationships might, however, be better explained as independent echoes of a credal formula[4]. (2) ʽσυνεγείρω is peculiar to Colossians and Ephesians in the NT, and is one of those verbs which our author has developed by adding a prefix to a Pauline word', and (3) this is also true of συζωοποιέω. (4) Colossians avoids the μέν . . . δέ of Rom 6.11 ; this construction is frequent in Paul's letters, but is not found in Colossians[5]. (5) The switch from 'you' to 'us' at the end of Col 2.13 is due to the influence of Rom 8.32. (6) The same allusion to Rom 8.32 involves the use of χαρίζομαι in two different senses, 'bestow' in Rom 8.32 and 'forgive' in Col 2.13 (this is hardly an argument for the use of the one by the other). The idea conveyed by the latter sense in Col 2.13, namely the forgiveness of sins, is infrequent in Paul's writings, but 'a central motif' of Colossians[6]. However, both of these last two points would be equally well, if not better, explained by the use of traditional material at the end of v 13 and in the following two verses; in favour of this is (1) the change from second person to first, (2) the series of participles, and (3) the profusion of uncommon expressions[7]. The last of these three reasons is not altogether convincing in a letter characterized as a whole by so many *hapax legomena*[8]. An alternative would be to explain the change of person in v 13 by saying that the forgiveness of sins and what is described in vv 14f is 'common Christian experience', common to both Jewish and Gentile

---

3 'Dependence' 40−2, followed by Carlson, *Baptism* 176−80.

4 Cf. Burger, *Schöpfung* 96f; Gnilka, *Kol* 135f; Kramer, *Christ* §3f, 23.

5 Cf. Bujard, *Untersuchungen* 26f.

6 Cf. Lohse, *Col* 106; Percy, *Probleme* 85.

7 So Lohse, ibid.; Deichgräber, *Gotteshymnos* 167−9; Schille, *Hymnen* 32−4; cf. Wengst, *Formeln* 186−94 (the citation starts at the beginning of v 13 − originally καὶ ὄντας ἡμᾶς . . .; this is a 'piece of baptismal liturgy' − 186); Burger, *Schöpfung* 85, 102, seems mistaken in suggesting that Lohse only sees the citation beginning at v 14 (cf. also Lohse, 'Bekenntnis' 430−2: he does suggest that the author of Col has set 13c at the start of the quotation of the hymn, but 13c is still a 'Satz gemeinchristlichen Bekenntnisses', as the title of his article makes clear).

8 Cf. Lohse, *Col* 84−8.

Christians[9]; a further possibility would be the observation that the writer had switched from confronting opponents to describing God's activity[10].

Sanders' case here is thus hardly established beyond question. Stronger evidence for the dependence of this passage on Paul's teaching, if not directly upon his letters, may well be the echoes of Romans 6 found here: συνθάπτομαι is found in the New Testament only here and in Rom 6.4, in both cases in the context of an explicit allusion to baptism[11]. The echo of 6.11 which Sanders detects is less certain; it amounts to the presence of the second person plural personal pronoun, in one case in the nominative, in the other in the accusative, νεκρούς, followed by the dative, and, naturally enough, a reference to a subsequent, contrasted life (ζῶντας ... τῷ θεῷ, Rom 6.11; συνεζωοποίησεν ... σὺν αὐτῷ, Col 2.13). We must note, however, that the construction of the dative following the νεκρούς in each instance is rather different: in the case of Rom 6.11 it is the distinctive 'dead to' construction which I argued involved a dative of relation or respect[12]; in the case of Col 2.13 it is a dative of accompanying circumstances, 'dead *in* transgressions and the uncircumcision of your flesh'[13]. However Conzelmann is in my view correct when he argues that Col 2.12 gives expression to the meaning of baptism in terms borrowed from Romans 6[14]; that holds good whether or not we detect in this passage an echo of Romans 6.11.

As we saw earlier (§1.1), there are those who argue that Col 2.12f goes back to traditions which are already presupposed in Romans 6. There is nothing in Colossians itself to support such a conclusion; we have seen evidence of its dependence upon a knowledge of Paul's words, whether

---

9 Dibelius-Greeven, *Kol* 31.

10 Gnilka, *Kol* 121, appealing to Bujard, *Untersuchungen* 83f.

11 Cf. Sellin, ' "Auferstehung" ' 231.

12 See above §1.3.1.2 and n. 1. For this sense, or something quite close to it, Col seems to use ἀπό and the genitive (2.20); cf. Schweizer, *Kol* 126 (the different construction indicates that it is not a question of escaping from the domain of sin's power, but of liberation from the various tabus listed in the following verses; this is closer to Paul's idea of freedom from the law).

13 Cf. Moule, *Col* 97, who notes that some MSS read ἐν here (cf. also Best, 'Dead' 12; O'Brien, *Col* 122). The difference is noted by Lohse, *Col* 107 (who translates the datives with an 'in' – 92 – and yet describes this as a causal dative – 107 n. 90, comparing BDF §196, which rather strangely includes Acts 15.1 as an example: 'according to the custom of Moses' – cf. Moule, *Idiom Book* 45); also Conzelmann, *Kol* 191; Dibelius-Greeven, *Kol* 31; Larsson, *Christus* 83, Best, ibid. 10, notes the switch from death in baptism in vv 11f to this sense of 'death' as the non-Christian's state in 'his pre-baptismal non-believing period' in 13a and back again to the sense of vv 11f in 2.20. Burger, however, wants to interpret the phrase in 2.13 as 'dead to' and as parallel to our burial with Christ (*Schöpfung* 98f); for this sense I would have expected an aorist ptc.

14 *Kol* 190; cf. too his 'Schule' 90, and Schweizer, *Kol* 112; also Gäumann, *Taufe* 63–5; Kuss, *Röm* 315f; Lindemann, *Kol* 42f; Perrin, *New Testament* 123; Lähnemann, *Kolosserbrief* 176, holds that the idea of dying and rising with Christ in Col has been taken over from Rom 6.

the writer of Colossians had a written text of Romans before him (Sanders) or whether, as seems to me more likely, he recalled from memory characteristic ideas and phrases which the apostle used: the idea of a 'burial with Christ' in baptism, the formation of words with the prefix συν- to express the 'with Christ' ideas so characteristic of Paul (Sanders' points 2 and 3 above), and the idea of passing to a new life through union with Christ's death. As I remarked (§1.4), it is strange if we have here an instance of a writer so indebted to Paul correcting his (or her) leader. It is, however, wrong to see the alternatives here as either a contrast or an 'authentic commentary on Rom 6'[15]. There is in fact a whole range of possibilities from a deliberate correction of Paul at one extreme to a simple explication of what he implied at the other; in between lie various other alternatives, including a divergence through ignorance of what Paul meant (a possibility that becomes stronger the later Colossians is dated), and a possible development of Paul's ideas which is, however, not the only one possible (compare 2 Tim 2.18!)[16]. Neither of the extremes seems to me to be very likely; the other two alternatives that I have mentioned seem to me to be far likelier candidates.

Col 3.1 repeats the motif of a past resurrection of Christians with Christ. It provides no further evidence for or against the derivation of this idea from Paul's thought rather than from pre-Pauline tradition. It does show, however, both the similarity and the difference of Colossians' thought to that of Ephesians. 'Things above', itself a phrase not found in the Pauline *homologoumena*[17], corresponds to 'heavenly things/places' (τὰ ἐπουράνια) in Ephesians, and yet the two letters express this in different ways. More noteworthy still is the way in which this state of having been raised is qualified in Col 3.1–4: (1) the tension of indicative and imperative is retained ('you have been raised . . . seek . . . set your minds (φρονεῖτε) . . . you died and your life is hidden')[18], and (2) the tension between a present and future realization is retained in this passage[19]. The

---

15 Cf. Lohse, *Col* 104 and n. 72. An example of the 'authentic commentary' view would be Percy, *Probleme* 107–13, in that he holds that the author of Col was Paul himself: 'the assumption that someone other than the apostle wrote this would mean that he knew how to express the apostle's view better than he did himself' (113) – which is not impossible.

16 There we find a view which might well be very similar, or at least seem similar, to that of Col (cf. Conzelmann, *Eph* 97, and 'Schule' 90, 93; Gräßer, 'Kol 3,1–4' 150; H. -F. Weiß, 'Motive' 315; also Lähnemann, *Kolosserbrief* 162, on its similarity to the thought of Eph); it is denounced in the name of Paul; it is perhaps presuming too much to distance Col from the views of Hymenaeus and Philetus by describing the latter as 'a fanatic enthusiasm' (Lohse, *Col* 105).

17 Lohse, ibid. 132; cf. Lincoln, *Paradise* 123, and Gräßer, ibid. 156f.

18 Cf. Gnilka, *Kol* 171f; Lindemann, *Kol* 52f; Percy, *Probleme* 116–22; Schweizer, *Kol* 132.

19 Cf. also P. Hoffmann in *TRE* 4, 457; Lona, *Eschatologie* 189; Percy, ibid. 115f; but, according to Lindemann, *Kol* 54, not a future resurrection – there is no room left for that –, but only glorification (cf. Bornkamm, 'Hoffnung' 211 (62), but contrast Lona, ibid. 186f).

tension is, however, expressed in a rather different way to Paul's: it is a tension between that which is 'hidden with Christ in God' and that which is to be 'revealed with him in glory'[20]. Thus the language of this passage is perceptibly closer to that characteristic of Ephesians than to that of Paul.

1.4.2. It is unquestionably true that *Ephesians* has a special relationship to Colossians[1], although the nature of that relationship and the way in which it has come about are much disputed. Many reject the idea that this relationship stems from common authorship; against this are signs of Ephesians' literary dependence upon Colossians and those points at which the thought of the two is markedly different, even though the vocabulary is similar[2]. Some would argue that the author of Ephesians had a hand in

---

20 Even the word κρύπτω does not appear in Paul's generally acknowledged writings although the compound ἀποκρύπτω does (1 Cor 2.7); cf. Gnilka, *Kol* 174. Gräßer argues that Paul would seek to convey something of the same idea by means of the distinction between faith on the one hand and sight or hope on the other ('Kol 3,1–4' 160); cf. further Steinmetz, *Heils-Zuversicht* 29–31, 43f; H. -F. Weiß, 'Motive' 320; also Lindemann, *Aufhebung* 40–4. Lona, ibid. 165, 171, sees here particularly the replacement of Paul's temporal categories by spatial ones, although the former are not completely superseded. However he draws attention to Phil 3.19f as a Pauline precursor to this language (177).
Bornkamm, ibid. 208 (59), argues that the difference in content is masked by the retention of language at home in the temporal categories of Jewish apocalyptic writings (cf. 212 (64)).

Notes on 1.4.2
1 So Kümmel, *Introduction*[2] 358: 'The kinship of Eph with Col is undoubtedly far greater than the kinship of any other letter of Paul with the rest of the Pauline corpus'; cf. Polhill, 'Relationship' 439f; Goodspeed, *Meaning* 82ff, and Mitton, *Epistle* 279ff, 319ff, set out the correspondence in parallel columns.
If, however, the writer knew the other Pauline letters as well his relatively greater use of Col is surprising. It is odder still if the author of Eph had 'the wording of Col before him only for 6:21f.' (Kümmel, *Introduction*[2] 365) – odd that he should have just this bit, odd that his letter should then have this special relationship to the rest of Col (cf. Kirby, *Ephesians* 51). This problem might be solved by saying that the same man was the author of Col and Eph, but was not the author of the other letters, although he was familiar with them or at least with the ways in which their author, Paul, expressed himself. But then the divergences between Eph and Col are a problem, and so a better solution would be to suggest that both were written by members of a Pauline 'school', or a group of Paul's followers, who shared a veneration for the apostle and a certain similarity of style (cf. Conzelmann, 'Paulus' esp. 234, and 'Schule' 88–95; Lindemann, *Paulus* 36ff; Schenke-Fischer, *Einleitung*, esp. 186). This would account for the other factors which Gnilka postulates as accounting for the relationship between Col and Eph over and above any literary dependence: traditions of a liturgical, paraenetic and catechetical kind; the relationship is such as to demand a common authorship or the living traditions of a school (*Eph* 10f; cf. 15 n. 3, and 21).
2 The strongest arguments for literary dependence are (a) the close agreement of Eph 6.21f and Col 4.7f, and (b) instances where Eph echoes the language of Col, but in doing so expresses itself awkwardly (cf., e.g., Col 3.7 and Eph 2.2f: οἷς in the former is neuter, but masculine in the latter, presumably referring in the context to the 'sons of disobedience').

writing at least parts of Colossians; most recently this has been propounded by Schmithals[3], but the parts of Colossians supposedly written by the author of Ephesians include some passages where Colossians' thought differs from that of Ephesians, and the original Pauline parts of Colossians (in his reconstruction) contain some of the linguistic data which have led scholars to argue that Paul did not write Colossians[4].

1.4.2.1. Thus the weight of evidence seems to suggest that *Ephesians follows Colossians* rather than *vice versa*[1]. This would be true of the pas-

---

Differences can be seen, e.g., in comparing Col 1.26f (God's 'mystery' now revealed is Christ 'in' or 'among' the Colossians) with Eph 3.3ff (although it echoes the language of Col the 'mystery' is now the fact that Gentiles share in the inheritance promised to the Jews); cf., though, Percy, *Probleme* 379–81.

I wonder whether the writer of Eph wanted to draw upon Col because of the authority invested in the latter epistle, for instance because Paul had had some hand in its composition, even if indirectly.

That he draws so much upon Col rather than upon other Pauline letters becomes an acuter problem the later Eph is dated, since, with the passage of time, the likelihood of familiarity with more letters of Paul increases.

3 Sanders, 'Dependence' 28, holds that this view 'seems to be gaining ground', but Schnackenburg, *Eph* 29 n. 36, considers such theories 'almost universally rejected'.

4 Schmithals, *'Corpus'* 119–21; on 124 n. 19 he quotes earlier proponents of similar theories (to which should be added Harrison, *Paulines* 43f and 65–79); see also Sanders, ibid. 28 n. 3, as well as Benoit, 'Rapports' 332f; Mitton, *Epistle* 72–4; Percy, *Probleme* 3f and n. 21; Polhill, 'Relationship' 444–6.

Schmithals' original Pauline letter (Col 1.1–8, 24–9; 2.1a, 4f, 16f, 20–3; 3.1–15a; 4.1–18) contains exactly half of the 34 *hapax legomena* which are found nowhere else in the NT, and 16 of the 28 words not found elsewhere in the Pauline *homologoumena*. Of the 11 words found only in Col and the other Pauline letters, but not in the rest of the NT, 8 are found in the suggested deutero-Pauline interpolations (using the tables in Lohse, *Col* 85f). Very many of the stylistic peculiarities listed by Lohse 88f occur also in the original letter. Only with the 10 words peculiar to Col and Eph and the 15 shared by these two letters and the rest of the NT, excluding the Pauline epistles, can any correlation be detected between Schmithals' interpolations and these stylistic data: all of the first group are found in these passages and only 2 of the second are found in the original letter. Some of the ideas which make scholars suspect that Col is not by Paul occur also in Schmithals' original letter: Paul's completion of Christ's sufferings for the church (1.24) and his role in revealing God's mystery to the Gentiles (1.25–7); the way Col speaks of legal observances in 2.17 (cf. Schweizer, *Kol* 21f). Many of the shifts in thought between Col and Eph which scholars have detected are also to be found in passages of Col which Schmithals assigns to the author of Eph: Eph 2.20 echoes Col 1.20, but inserts the non-Pauline ἔργα ἀγαθά; Eph 2.16 speaks of Christ as the agent of reconciliation, but in Col 1.20 it is God; in Eph God's mystery is not Christ as in Col 1.26f; 2.2; 4.3, but 'the unity of the Gentiles and the Jews in the body in Christ' (Eph 3.4f; the quotation is from Kümmel, *Introduction*[2] 360); whereas Christians' foundation is Christ in Col 2.7 as in 1 Cor 3.11, it is the apostles and prophets in Eph 2.20f.

Notes on 1.4.2.1

1 So Schweizer, *Kol* 20: Eph is dependent on Col (cf. Benoit, 'Rapports'; Best, 'Dead' 10; Conzelmann, *Eph* 87; Johnston, *Eph* 7, 54; Kirby, *Ephesians* 135f; Kümmel, *Introduction*[2] 346; Lähnemann, *Kolosserbrief* 158, 166, 169; Lindemann, *Aufhebung* 47, and *Paulus* 41; Lona,

sage which most concerns us here, Eph 2. (1), 5f[2]; in it there are strong
signs that it is Ephesians which takes up and modifies Colossians: (1) Best
notes that the introductory καί of Eph 2.1 'can be accounted for most
easily by its use in Col 2.13', as can that in 2.5[3]. (2) If we set the very
similar wording of Col 2.13 and Eph 2.5f side by side we see that the
former has the second person plural personal pronoun, the latter the first
person plural, at least to start with; it follows from this change that the
phrase in Col 2.13, 'and in the uncircumcision of your flesh', would have
to be omitted from a letter purporting to be from Paul[4]. (3) Eph 2.6 adds
to the idea of making us alive with Christ those of raising us with him and
making us sit with him 'in the heavenly places', a phrase characteristic
of Ephesians[5]. To this might be added the point that (4), while Col 2.13
has σὺν αὐτῷ after συνεζωοποίησεν in contrast to Paul's normal practice
of following συν- compounds with a simple dative[6], its 'parallel' in Eph 2.5
omits the σύν; this stylistic difference tells against the suggestion that the
non-Pauline features of Colossians can be explained by seeing the hand of
the author of Ephesians at work in it; here Ephesians is more 'Pauline'
than Colossians[7]. (5) Unlike Colossians (and Romans 6) Ephesians makes
no mention of union with Christ's death or burial[8]. Further, (6) Gnilka
argues that the absence in Ephesians of any counterpart to Col 3.1—4 is
due to the further development of its theology beyond that represented
in Colossians[9]. Finally, (7) it is interesting that Ephesians has no parallel

---

Eschatologie 35—40; Mitton, *Eph* 5, 27; Ollrog, *Paulus* 238; Schenke, 'Weiterwirken' 513;
Schenke-Fischer, *Einleitung* 1, 183—6). Percy, who holds that both letters were by the same
author, Paul, also holds that Eph is later than Col (*Probleme* 397—9, 418f). It is less certain
how much later Eph is than Col; Gnilka, e.g., makes much of the development presupposed
by the differences between Col and Eph, but if the authors were different people then they
might have written almost simultaneously, the one being more 'developed' in his, or her, thinking than the other (cf. Gnilka, *Eph* 12f). Occasionally it has been suggested that Col is an
imitation of Eph or is dependent on it: e.g. Coutts, 'Relationship'.

2 Lona, ibid. 360.

3 'Dead' 11 (cf. 14f).

4 However the same is not true of the other 'parallel' in Eph 2.1 (cf. Best, ibid. 15). For another
evaluation of the relationship of these passages cf. Coutts, 'Relationship' 202—4; cf. also Lindemann, *Aufhebung* 135: Col and Eph here use traditional material independently of each other
(yet cf. 140: Col 2.10ff is the immediate *Vorlage* of Eph 2.1—10).

5 Cf. Conzelmann, 'Schule' 94; also Schnackenburg, *Eph* 22. Lona, *Eschatologie* 361, sees this as
increasing the use of spatial categories.

6 Lohse, *Col* 108 n. 95; Benoit, 'Rapports' 319f, notes that Eph and Col share the rare word
συνεζωοποίησεν.

7 Unless we read ἐν τῷ Χριστῷ in Eph 2.5 and interpret συνεζωοποίησεν there as a reference to
the fellowship of Jews and Gentiles (an idea entertained but rejected by Schlier, *Eph* 109: this
section is primarily concerned, not with the unity of Jews and Gentiles, but with the relationship of what God has done in Christ to what he does for believers).

8 Cf. Houlden, *Letters* 284; also Abbott, *Eph-Col* xix—xx; M. Barth, *Eph* 1, 43f; Lona, *Eschatologie* 361f; contrast Schnackenburg, 'Tauflehre' 161.

9 Gnilka, *Kol* 16; cf. Schnackenburg, *Eph* 95.

to the explicit reference to baptism in Col 2.12[10]. This should perhaps be noted; M. Barth comments that 'the reasons for imposing a sacramental interpretation upon Eph 2:5–6, or upon the whole context 2:4–10, are insufficient'[11]. Otherwise the wording of the two passages in Colossians and in Ephesians is sufficiently close to make a literary relationship of some sort possible, a relationship which makes far better sense of the evidence if Ephesians is taken as dependent upon Colossians and not the other way round[12].

Baptism, we should note, is mentioned only twice (possibly) in Ephesians (4.5; 5.26)[13], but that has not deterred many from seeing references to baptism in the passages which concern us[14], and indeed in the letter as a whole[15]. There is not really much to be said for this. As we have seen just above the express reference to baptism in Col 2.12 has no place in its Ephesians counterpart, and, as Best notes, 'baptismal ideas, wherever they enter (e.g. 1.13, 18; 4.5, 30; 5.25–7), are presented under other images and baptism is never treated with the same direct attention which it receives in Col 2.11f.'[16]. What M. Barth asserts of Eph 4.22–24 may well be true of much of the other material in Ephesians which scholars have wished to give a baptismal setting: 'Eph 4:22–24 is a piece of instruction well suited to the preparation for, or the liturgy of, baptism. But

---

10 Cf. Best, 'Dead' 11; Lona, *Eschatologie* 361f; Benoit, 'Rapports' 320, suggests that this was because the author of Eph did not have to combat a return to circumcision.

11 *Eph* 1, 234; cf. Lindemann, *Aufhebung* 140: 'it is extremely unlikely that Eph 2.1–10 contains a baptismal liturgy'; however baptism and its effects on Christians' lives may be in the background here.

12 The same is true of the echo of the previous verse, Col 2.12, in Eph 1.19f; the latter is marked by a piling up of genitives at the end of v 19, a stylistic feature of Eph, although one shared also by Col to some extent (Gnilka, *Kol* 17). There too there is a reference in v 20 to Christ's being seated at God's right hand 'in the heavenly places'.
Gnilka warns us, however, against thinking that the relationship can be explained solely in terms of the literary dependence of Eph on Col: *Eph* 10f; *Kol* 15f. For a denial of any such dependence cf. Percy, *Probleme* 275f and n. 20.

13 Most see in the latter passage a reference to baptism (cf. M. Barth, *Eph* 2, 692ff and n. 33; he reviews the evidence thoroughly but doubts whether the case has been proved; he suggests a reference to baptism in the Spirit). Kirby, *Ephesians* 153, takes two references to sealing with the Spirit (1.13; 4.30) as 'direct references to baptism'; 'both these passages must refer to baptism'. Contrast G. Fitzer in *TDNT* 7, 949: 'There is no direct reference to baptism or circumcision' in 2 Cor 1.22; Eph 1.13; 4.30; that is more accurate, however close at hand the idea of baptism may be. It is in *Hermas* that 'baptism is for the first time clearly and unambiguously called a σφραγίς' (952). See also M. Barth, *Eph* 1, 135–43.

14 E.g. Schnackenburg, *Baptism* 73-8, and 'Tauflehre' 161, 169.

15 E.g. Coutts, 'Ephesians i.3–14'; Dahl, cited with approval by Sahlin, 'Beschneidung' 5 n. 1; Dibelius-Greeven, *Eph* 92 (tentatively); Kirby, *Ephesians* 150–61 (Gnilka, *Eph* 25, describes Kirby's thesis as 'quite fantastic'; cf. also Mitton, *Eph* 23f); Moule, *Birth* 25 (tentatively); Pokorný, 'Epheserbrief' 178, 180–91; Schille, *Hymnen* 102; Williams, 'Catechesis'; also Dahl, 'Adresse' (1.3–14).

16 'Dead' 12.

its usefulness for a given service does not necessarily demonstrate the original *Sitz im Leben*'[17].

1.4.2.2. A special case is *Eph 5.14* which is widely regarded, as we have seen (§1.3.2.3), as a fragment from a baptismal liturgy[1], a belief that has important consequences for the investigation of early Christian beliefs about baptism and resurrection. But we have already noted that the parallels often appealed to are either references to initiates or mysteries but not parallels (Firm. Mat., *Err. prof. rel.* 22.1; Aristophanes, *Ran.* 340), or are parallels but not ones belonging to a context of initiation (the Manichaean texts cited above). The words introducing this quotation, διὸ λέγει, elsewhere (4.8) introduce a quotation from the Old Testament, and there have been attempts to see in 5.14 at least a vague recollection of several Old Testament texts[2]. Unconvinced by that, others have suggested a text from some apocryphal writing[3], others a Christian text[4]. The reference to Christ certainly suggests the last proposal. The further contention that this text had its place in the baptismal liturgy is supported by an appeal to Clement of Alexandria who cites this verse with three further lines added:

---

17 *Eph* 2, 544.

Notes on 1.4.2.2

1 Cf. the list in Schlier, *Eph* 240 n. 4; further Beare in *IntB* 10, 711; Best, 'Dead' 17 ('probably'); Bruce, *Eph* 376; Caird, *Letters* 86; Conzelmann, *Eph* 117; Coutts, 'Ephesians i.3−14' 127; Dinkler, 'Taufaussagen' 108; Ernst, *Eph* 371; Gnilka, *Eph* 260−3; Goodspeed, *Meaning* 59; Houlden, *Letters* 327; Johnston, *Eph* 22 (tentatively); Kirby, *Ephesians* 160; K. G. Kuhn, 'Epheserbrief' 342; Lona, *Eschatologie* 356−60 (though he grants that there is no emphasis on its cultic background in this context − 357); Moule, *Birth* 25, and *Worship* 56 (tentatively); Pokorný, 'Epheserbrief' 187; Schenke-Fischer, *Einleitung* 1, 176; Schille, *Hymnen* 95f; Schnackenburg, 'Tauflehre' 160f, and *Eph* 234; Simpson-Bruce, *Eph* 122 n. 20; Williams, 'Catechesis' 93. However Mitton thinks it more suitable in the setting of preparation for baptism, looking back to the catechumen's conversion-experience (*Eph* 186f). M. Barth, *Eph* 2, although cited by Best as if he upheld a baptismal setting for the verse (ibid. 24 n. 58), in fact questions it: 'we may ask whether all references to light in Eph 5, especially the hymn quoted in vs 14, contain an allusion to baptism; it certainly cannot be demonstrated that in the NT the verb "to enlighten" and the cognate nouns "light" and "enlightenment" always refer to baptism. Many, perhaps all, ways of communication and receiving the word of salvation can be meant' (601).

2 Gnilka, *Eph* 259 n. 2, refers to the comm. of W. M. L. de Wette (Leipzig, 1847[2]) *ad loc.*; cf. however Noack, 'Zitat' 52−5. It was the late Stephen Neill who drew my attention to the rare form ἀνάστα and suggested a reference to the book of Jonah (cf. Jonah 1.6 LXX, but ἀνάστηθι in 1.2; 3.2; cf. BDF §95 (3)).

3 Cf. Epiph., *Haer.* 42.12.3 (ed. Holl-Dummer 2, 179.25−180.2); Resch, *Agrapha*[2] 33 (contrast lst ed. 222ff: dominical saying); see the rather varied ascriptions by various patristic writers gathered by Stone-Strugnell, *Books* 75−81.

Arise, sleeper,
and rise from the dead,
and Christ the Lord will shed his light upon you,
the sun of the resurrection,
the one begotten before the morning star,
he who bestows life through his own rays[5].

Gnilka maintains that this clearly refers to baptism[6], but what evidence is there for that? He finds confirmation of this in the Syriac *Didascalia* 21, and, above all, in Rom 6.13. The former says that its Gentile readers have been baptized into Christ and a great light has arisen over them[7]; however it says equally that this light has come upon them with Christ's appearance to them and with their conversion[8]. Romans 6, as we have seen (§1.3.2.3), applies a variety of ideas to baptism in order to explain to the Romans the significance of the rite; that is not to say that these ideas are inseparably connected with baptism.

B. Noack took an independent line in questioning whether this verse was a piece of a baptismal liturgy, referring to a metaphorical rising from the sleep and death of one's previous sinful life[9]. Certainly the first line is metaphorical, but a metaphor for what? Nowhere else is rising from the dead (ἀναστῆναι ἐκ τῶν νεκρῶν) used in a metaphorical sense in the New Testament. The metaphor of the first line could refer to the same thing, a literal resurrection of the dead, since this figurative use of 'sleep' for death is found elsewhere[10]. Only once does the New Testament use ἐγείρω figuratively (Rom 13.11). In his judgment 'the citation as such contains nothing which prevents a literal interpretation (of resurrection from the dead here); all of it gives a good, clear sense, even without a reference to baptism' (61). He grants that in its context, where 'dead' is sometimes used figuratively (Eph 2.1, 5; contrast 1.20), a figurative sense may be possible; immediately it is lifted out of that context it becomes far less likely[11]. Then the most likely setting for it is an 'eschatological hymn, whose words, strictly speaking, have never yet rung out, but will first do so on the last day' (62). They are the sort of words which the archangel will utter on that day (1 Thess 4.16; cf. Jn 5.25). For such an interpreta-

---

4 So first Theodoret of Cyrrhus in Migne *PG* 82, 544f.

5 *Prot.* 9.84.2. Probably these extra lines are not to be considered as an original part of the hymn but a development of it (Schnackenburg, 'Tauflehre' 166).

6 *Eph* 260.

7 Ed. Achelis-Flemming 110.6f.

8 Ibid. 109.36ff.; cf. also Philo, *Abr.* 70, which refers to Abraham's conversion (Gnilka, *Eph* 262); Philo also uses φωτίζω of the coming of God's command or word to the soul (*Fug.* 139).

9 'Zitat'; cf. the tentative support of Beresford, *Concept* 278f.

10 He cites for καθεύδειν 1 Thess 5.10 (?); Ps 87.6 LXX; Dan 12.2; κοιμᾶσθαι is also used in this sense; cf. Oepke in *TDNT* 3, 436; Bultmann, ibid. 14 n. 60.

11 Contrast K. G. Kuhn, 'Epheserbrief' 343.

tion he appeals to Jerome and Epiphanius for support[12], although it is doubtful whether these really help his case.

There is a great deal to be said for this interpretation. Noack's case is probably the stronger the further that this quotation is pushed back into the history of early Christianity; the earlier it is the less likely it is, I suggest, that such a passage would speak figuratively of resurrection. There is a certain weakness in Noack's arguments when it comes to defining the setting for which such a passage would first have been composed. I would suggest that it would make best sense in an apocalypse like, for instance, the proclamations in Rev 12.12; 14.7; 18.4; 19.5. However it is also true that the 'realized eschatology' of the writer to the Ephesians would cause him to view such an eschatological context rather differently. Yet it is important to note that such a reinterpretation would first arise at the time when the 'realized eschatology' of the writer and his fellows came into being. This is not to be confused with the earlier setting and meaning of the fragment, although it is possible that baptism might at an earlier stage have been viewed as proleptic, as anticipating the eschatological events; the baptized would then hear already, in a vivid and daring use of language, the command that was to resound at the end. Yet its sole connection with baptism need still only be the connection that arose later from the association of baptism with the bestowal of resurrection life in this realized eschatology. All the same, a proleptic anticipation of the end in baptism would increase the tendency towards a realized eschatology. To understand the rising of Eph 5.14 figuratively might only have become possible once rising from the dead had come to be thought of as something possible for Christians here and now, and that stage may not have been reached much before the time of composition of Ephesians and Colossians. In short, a realization of the leap in understanding involved in giving a figurative sense to 'resurrection' (see further in chap. 3) should render us cautious about seeing in this text all that early a witness to the idea of a realized resurrection.

1.4.3. But how did the authors of these two letters, Colossians and Ephesians, come to speak of an already accomplished resurrection with Christ? I have argued that there are problems confronting the suggestion that they were reverting to an earlier tradition, earlier than the statements which Paul makes in Romans 6; the problems are all the greater if Romans 6 is

---

12 Jerome's comm. *ad loc.* in Migne *PL* 26, 559; Epiph., *Haer.* 64.71.15, 19 (ed. Holl-Dummer 2, 520.20–2, 521.10–14).

held to be an implicit correction of these earlier traditions. But how else could such an idea arise[1]?

One very obvious answer is the pressure of the broken parallelism in Romans 6. Just as one argument in favour of Paul's correction of earlier traditions was the awkwardness of the symmetry of Rom 6.4 in particular, so this same awkwardness could lead followers of Paul to say that, if Christians shared in the past death of Jesus, so they also shared in his past resurrection[2].

It may, however, also be the case that the circumstances in which these two letters were written had something to do with this development of Paul's thought, particularly in the case of Colossians. Whereas Paul, especially in 1 Corinthians, had been confronted earlier with the problem of enthusiastic followers of his who claimed too much for their present status as 'spiritual men', the writer to the Colossians, whoever he was, seems to have had a very different situation to contend with: he had to emphasize the sufficiency and adequacy of the salvation brought by Christ over against the attempt to supplement that salvation by various means, worship of angels (Col 2.18) and regard for spiritual powers (cf. 1.16f; 2.10, 15), ritual and ascetic observances (2.16, 18, 20–23), and possibly visionary experiences (2.18)[3]. In the light of such tendencies to belittle the significance of Christ it would be very natural to stress the completeness of what Christians had received from him: instead of the physical circumcision which was perhaps demanded of the Colossian Christians they are reminded of the circumcision that they have already received in their union with Christ, namely the far more drastic 'putting away of the fleshly body' which comes from union with him in his death and burial; they have been raised with him in his resurrection and they are called upon to trust in the power of the same God who raised Jesus; he has given them life, he has wiped away their sins, he has blotted out the legal indictment that stood against them and has triumphed over those powers which they regard with such awe (2.11–15). Thus drawing what so obviously seemed to be the corollary of Paul's statement that we died with Christ, namely that we also shared his resurrection, served a valuable purpose. In a somewhat similar way the writer of the Letter to the Hebrews countered the danger of a reversion to Judaism by stressing the sufficiency of Christ's saving work in terms of the Jewish priestly cult. The

---

Notes on 1.4.3

1 Lona, *Eschatologie* 170, 172, sees the influence of the mysteries as responsible for the baptismal theology of Col, an influence that is clearer here than in Rom 6.

2 Cf. Bouttier, *En Christ* 52.

3 Cf. Ernst, *Kol* 203; Lindemann, *Kol* 45f; Lona, *Eschatologie* 170f, 235–40; O'Brien, *Col* 121.

writer to the Colossians has a different response, one closer to the thought of Paul himself, but his objective is similar.

This lead, we may suggest, was followed by the author of Ephesians, who wrote without the same polemical intent, but still breathed much of the same intellectual and spiritual atmosphere as the author of Colossians and spoke much the same language, though with certain turns of phrase that are peculiar to him.

These two letters in their turn, it may be argued, paved the way for the later development of the idea of a resurrection already realized in baptism[4]; that development is not to be understood without reference to the part played by these deutero-Pauline writings; they are far more than simply witnesses to its pre-Pauline stages; they actually help to bring it into being.

1.5. Philippians 3 and Conclusions

We have now covered the main New Testament texts upon which has been based the argument for an early influence of the Hellenistic mystery-religions upon the sacramental theology of the first Christians. Other texts could be cited in support, but these are the principal ones. In particular appeal could be made to *Philippians chap. 3*, were it not for the uncertainties which beset this letter, and in particular this chapter; there too it could be argued, as in the case of 1 Corinthians, that Paul rebukes the excesses of his followers. There, as in Romans 6, Paul stresses conformity with Christ's death as a present reality and speaks of the present experience both of the power of Christ's resurrection and of sharing his sufferings (v 10). He speaks in v 11, again as in Romans 6, of his desire to attain to resurrection himself (cf. Rom 6.5*b*, 8 — it might be more accurate to describe this as a hope or confidence rather than a desire) and stresses that he has not 'already' ($\check{\eta}\delta\eta$; cf. 1 Cor 4.8)[1] got that or something else unexpressed[2], nor is he already 'perfected ($\tau\epsilon\tau\epsilon\lambda\epsilon\acute{\iota}\omega\mu\alpha\iota$, v 12)', although he seems to align himself to some extent with those who are

---

4 Cf. §3.3.1 (the Gnostic debt to Eph and Col); Lona, *Eschatologie* 371f.

Notes on 1.5

1 Cf. Baumbach, 'Irrlehrer' 302.

2 The object of $\check{\epsilon}\lambda\alpha\beta o\nu$ is not expressed; for the various possibilities cf. Collange, *Phil* 133; Hawthorne, *Phil* 151.

'perfect' or 'mature' (τέλειοι, v 15; cf. 1 Cor 2.6; 14.20)[3]. It would be most natural to see here a criticism of those who did maintain that they already shared Christ's resurrection[4]; there is a shift of emphasis here, an explicit denial, which is altogether lacking in Romans 6[5]. If Philippians is a later letter, and if Colossians (and possibly also Ephesians) was written within Paul's lifetime (cf. §1.4), that would not be surprising, although it would mean that the followers of his who wrote Colossians and Ephesians were less guarded in the way in which they wrote of the relation between Christ's resurrection and that of Christians. These may seem big assumptions; the second, however, that Colossians and possibly Ephesians were written before Paul's death, I have already sought to provide with a certain plausibility. My readiness to accept the first, the late date for Philippians, stems from the feeling that, despite the attractions of an Ephesian setting for the writing of this letter, the reference of Phil 1.13 could very well be to the praetorian guard and not to a provincial governor's residence[6]; it would then be personal, like the following καὶ τοῖς λοιποῖς πᾶσιν which is joined to it[7]. The reference to 'those of Caesar's household' in 4.22 also perhaps points to a Roman setting[8]. That would indicate a date either as late as, or even later than, the composition of Colossians at least, according to the dating which I have suggested, and perhaps also Ephesians[9]. If the authors of these last two letters, or only that of Colossians, had by then developed Paul's ideas as expressed in Romans 6 so as to speak of Christians having risen with Christ, there is no reason why other supporters of Paul could not have made the same step by the time of the writing of Philippians; however they may well have failed to preserve both the tension between the 'already' and the 'not yet' apparent still in Col 3.1–4 and the stress on Christians' ethical obligations which is

---

3 Hence the first person plural φρονῶμεν: cf. Baumbach, 'Irrlehrer' 303. There is a comparable first person plural in Rom 15.1; 1 Cor 8.1, 4.

4 Cf. Köster, 'Purpose' 323; Martin, *Phil* (NCeB) 135, and (TNTC) 150; Siber, *Mit Christus* 118; Vielhauer, *Geschichte* 165.

5 Cf. Collange, *Phil* 134f; Gnilka, *Phil* 198.

6 It is true that elsewhere in the NT πραιτώριον refers to a governor's residence (cf. Collange, ibid. 54), but then not much of the NT has a Roman setting. It would, however, be rather unlikely that praetorian guards would be found in any number outside Rome at this stage, unless the emperor were travelling or there was a military campaign. And Paul is unlikely to have been caught up in either of these.

7 Elsewere Paul uses φανερός with ἐν and a personal dative: Rom 1.19 (some do not distinguish this from a plain dative of the indirect object; e.g. *RSV*); 1 Cor 11.19 (if the ἐν ὑμῖν is not to be taken more closely with the οἱ δόκιμοι – so most translate it; but the position of the ἐν ὑμῖν is then rather strange); cf. Martin, *Phil* (NCeB) 71, and Beare, *Phil* 56–8.

8 Cf. however Collange, *Phil* 155; Houlden, *Letters* 116, and most commentators. The matter becomes even more complex if Phil is divided up into different letters from different places of origin, written at different times (Gnilka, *Phil* 18).

9 Note the interesting comparisons with Col introduced by Köster, 'Purpose' 328f.

so clear in Col 3.5ff and elsewhere in the letter. There would then be no reason to suppose that Philippians provides us with any better evidence than the texts considered in §§1.2–4 for a belief in a past or present resurrection being held by Christians prior to, and independently of, Paul's utterance in Romans 6.

However, as long as a Roman (or Caesarean) setting for Philippians remains so controversial and so strong a case continues to be made for Ephesus as its place of origin, so late a dating of the letter is precarious[10]. If an Ephesian setting were to be correct, then the date of the letter would be earlier, close to 1 Corinthians in time. If we could then be sure that Paul was refuting a belief that Christians had already risen in 3.12, then we would have to agree that somewhere at least in Paul's churches such a belief had arisen before the writing of Romans. However we cannot even be sure of this while there is no agreement as to the unexpressed object of ἔλαβον in that verse. Perhaps only two scholars, W. Lütgert and R. A. Lipsius[11], understand it to be the same as the object of the verb in v 11, namely 'resurrection from the dead'. It must be granted that this seems the easiest solution to this problem, although it is hard to parallel the idea of 'receiving' resurrection[12]. The compound καταλαμβάνω, on the other hand, is used of the Christian's goal or prize in vv 12f, and λαμβάνω is also used in this sense in 1 Cor 9.24, as well as καταλαμβάνω. If another object is preferred, be it the 'prize' of v 14[13] or a deliberately vague one[14], then the position which Paul is criticizing comes nearer to that which we have suggested for the Corinthians. Paul maintains his reserve towards a too precipitate assumption of completeness and fulfilment, a reserve which becomes all the more significant if Philippians is to be dated later, at a time when Ephesians and Colossians might already have been written. This would then be a further argument against seeing in these latter epistles an undiluted expression of Paul's own theology. But certainty is impossible here[15].

---

10 One factor that might prove troublesome for an Ephesian setting is the absence of reference to the collection for the Jerusalem church.
  The same arguments as for a Roman setting would hold good for a Caesarean setting for Phil; for the arguments for that cf. Hawthorne, *Phil* xxxvi–xliv.
11 W. Lütgert, *Die Vollkommenen im Philipperbrief und die Enthusiasten in Thessalonich* (BFChTh 13.6 Gütersloh, 1901) 10–14, cited by Gnilka, *Phil* 198; Lipsius, *Phil* 238.
12 The construction with τυγχάνω in Lk 20.35; Heb 11.35 is nearer the sense of Phil 3.11 (καταντάω).
13 E.g. Beare, *Phil* 103, 129; Bonnard, *Phil* 67; cf. also Delling in *TDNT* 4, 7 (tentative).
14 E.g. Collange, *Phil* 133; Gnilka, *Phil* 198; Schmithals, *Paulus* 71; Hawthorne, *Phil* 148, translates 'grasped the meaning of Christ'; the difficulty here is that the object must be supplied from the following relative clause.
15 The verdict of Kümmel, *Introduction*[2] 332.

Fortunately the other evidence which we have considered seems to me less ambiguous. We have seen that the hypothesis that the Corinthians denied the resurrection of the dead because they believed that they had already risen was by no means the most likely solution of the problems of 1 Corinthians 15. We have seen that Romans 6 is unlikely to be a correction of such a belief in an already realized resurrection; Paul's appeal to the Roman Christians' knowledge of baptismal traditions is quite intelligible without that hypothesis. Nor is it likely, if he had corrected such a belief, that his followers who were the probable authors of Ephesians and Colossians would forthwith reinstate it; not, at least, unless they were writing their pseudonymous letters so much later that they were oblivious to what Paul had been doing. Rather their theology is best seen as a development from the sort of ideas expressed by Paul in Romans 6, not an appeal back to even earlier traditions. If Philippians had already been written, and I am by no means sure of that, they were either unaware that Paul was so against a realized resurrection or failed to see that that was what he was contradicting; we have just seen that they could be excused for that in view of the vagueness of Paul's launguage.

Yet if we have argued against one way, one channel, by which the Graeco-Roman cults and Graeco-Roman culture in general influenced early Christian thinking about the sacraments and particularly the rite of baptism, this does not exclude all influence from these sources upon this area of early Christian theology. Rather, the texts which we have considered have thrown up a number of questions which call for some sort of answer:

(1) when and how easily was the language of *'resurrection'* spiritualized in such a way that it could be used to refer to an existence which was, at least outwardly, still being lived out in this world and on this side of death? Did it not originally have such physical and material connotations that it was only with difficulty that Christians came to reinterpret it figuratively, so that 'resurrection' could apply to an existence still in this world subject to decay and death[16]? In that case it would be unlikely that Hellenistic Christians early or easily came to think of themselves as already risen from the dead; rather this idea should be seen as a development which took place under the influence of Paul's idea of Christians' sharing in Christ's death and resurrection; they came to use 'resurrection'

---

16 Cf. Lona, *Eschatologie* 163: 'resurrection' is for Paul 'eindeutig', but for Col and Eph 'zweideutig'. The reason, he suggests, lies in the significance of our bodily nature (*Leiblichkeit*) for Paul (187); if that is to explain his reservation of resurrection for the future we must also add the assumption that I am arguing for here, namely that 'resurrection' is for him bodily. In that he was at one with his fellow Jews – cf. chap. 3. If Paul found it difficult to speak figuratively of resurrection so did others.

in this daring way under the compulsion of the logic of Paul's 'with Christ' language. Later, too, the normative place assumed in early Christian theology by the hope of resurrection forced Hellenistic Christians to whom this doctrine was repugnant so to reinterpret it as to avoid the implication of the eternal survival of the despised human body.

(2) The possession of the *Spirit* or the experience of its presence and influence was a common factor uniting all members of the earliest church, however much it may have been manifested in different ways and with differing outward manifestations, some more spectacular than others; early on, perhaps from the very first, they connected this possession, this endowment, with the rite of baptism. But how did they understand this gift? Did it bring the life of the new age, and, if so, what of the trappings of the old age? What of the body and bodily existence? Was it taken up into the new age, or was it left behind? In the former case this new life could reasonably be called resurrection life, but not in the latter. And did they misunderstand this gift and misuse it? Did it lead them into a misplaced confidence in themselves and their new nature? These questions particularly need to be asked of Hellenistic Christians, such as the members of the Corinthian church. We need to know in what ways their culture would have prepared them for the interpretation of the spiritual endowment which they received in Christian baptism.

(3) Paul's discussion of Christian existence is characterized by, among other things, his talk of Christians *dying with Christ*. How did this language arise? Can it only be explained as analogous to the views which initiates into the mystery-cults held of their relationship with their respective cult deities? Or did they view this relationship so differently that any suggestion that Paul derived this concept from them, directly or indirectly, must be reckoned highly improbable? But then how else could this idea and language have suggested themselves to him?

(4) Finally there is the suggestion that *'life through dying'* was a common theme, found not only in Paul, but also in the mystery-cults. How common was it in fact, and how likely is it that Paul derived it from these cults, e.g. through the assimilation (by Paul or his predecessors) of Christian beliefs and practices to those of the initiatory rites of the mysteries?

However, before we tackle any of these questions it would be as well to reflect on some of the basic problems involved in any discussion of the *mystery-cults*. We should be mindful how some scholars have categorically and scornfully dismissed any suggestion that early Christianity was indebted to these cults[17]. To others the position as regards the study of these seems so uncertain, with so many issues unresolved, that there is

---

17 Cf. Schweitzer as cited in §2 below.

little or no point in opening up the question of Paul's dependence upon them at this point of time[18]. A decision about the rightness or wrongness of such a verdict may have to rest upon the evidence of the ensuing chapters, but it is at least incumbent upon such a study as this to face these problems.

---

18 This was the substance of observations made to me in a letter by the late Professor W. C. van Unnik; but cf. the point made by Morenz, *Begegnung* 99, that it is doubtful whether the increasing amount of archaeological material is going to advance our knowledge of the beliefs found in the Egyptian cults beyond what we already know from Apuleius (*Met.* 11), except perhaps for their beliefs about the dead; the same is likely to be true of other cults in large measure; the new materials and others yet to be discovered may do little to answer the questions concerning the soteriology of the mysteries which chiefly concern us here. In other words waiting is not going to help to clear up the problem!

2. The Mystery-Religions
and the World of Early Christianity

That so many can raise the question of the influence of the mystery-cults on early Christianity and come to such very different answers[1] is in itself eloquent testimony to the problems that beset any who would venture into this field. These problems were already raised acutely by Albert Schweitzer when he argued that it was only from the early second century C.E. onwards that the mysteries enjoyed wide currency in the Roman Empire; it was only then that they fell under the influence of late Greek religious thought and aspirations, and were transformed from imported cults into universal mystery-religions. Hence 'Paul cannot have known the mystery-religions in the form in which they are known to us, because in this fully-developed form they did not yet exist'[2]. Thus Schweitzer draws attention to two problems confronting the investigation of a possible background to early Christianity in the mysteries, that Christianity was born when the mysteries' hey-day still lay in the future[3], and that the mysteries were then yet to undergo a considerable transformation and reinterpretation.

Implicit in Schweitzer's argument is the fact that most of our main sources for the theological thinking of the mysteries come from this later period when the mysteries were at the height of their influence and when they were being thus transformed and reinterpreted; as we shall see, it is true that much of the material used to construct a 'theology of the mystery-religions' is drawn from such sources. In other words our sources

---

Notes on 2

Bibliographies on the mystery-religions can be found especially in *OrRR*; Metzger, 'Considerations', and in *ANRW* 2.17.3, 1259–1423; Wagner, *Baptism*; Wiens in *ANRW* 2.23.2, 1279–84. A bibliography, chiefly of works in English, also appears in Dungan-Cartledge, *Sourcebook* 355–74.

1 Cf. the survey in Wagner, *Baptism* 7–57.

2 *Paul* 191f; cf. Rahner, *Myths* esp. 11, 18.

3 Cf. F. C. Grant, *Hellenism* 77f: '. . . the main period of *floruit* of the mystery religions was not the first century but the second and third – much too late to have provided Christianity with sacraments, ministry, or the fundamental doctrines of salvation, regeneration, or the death and resurrection of a divine Saviour . . .'. On this *non sequitur* cf. §2.1.

for the nature and beliefs of these cults during the first century C.E. are limited to say the least, and Schweitzer implied that the case for the influence of the Hellenistic mysteries on Paul, and presumably this applies to the rest of first century Christianity too, is based on these later, misleading sources.

However, that is not the only problem that the sources present; in addition, many of them stem from Christian writers, and this is particularly true of very many which have tended to interest those investigating the relationship of early Christianity and the mysteries; that is understandable, since it was where early Christian writers felt that the mysteries were a dangerous imitation of Christian rites and beliefs that they were most likely to refer to them and criticize them, and it is these similarities which are the basis for arguments about Christianity's borrowing from, and dependence upon, the mysteries (though the influence might be, and sometimes was, in the opposite direction, from Christianity upon the mysteries)[4]. Whatever these early Christian writers were discussing about the mysteries, they were their rivals, and so they were hardly unbiased witnesses[5]. Nilsson describes their accounts of the secret initiatory rites of the mysteries as 'thoroughly unreliable'[6].

An even more serious problem perhaps is that presented by the vow of secrecy by which initiates were forbidden to disclose the contents of the rites which they had undergone. It is clear that in many cases this obligation was taken very seriously, and that initiates felt themselves constrained to guard the secrets entrusted to them very carefully indeed. In earlier times certainly they had to, under fear of death, at least in some cults; the secrecy of the Eleusinian cult, for instance, is attested by the *Homeric Hymn to Demeter* which tells how Demeter taught her rites and mysteries, 'awful mysteries which no one may in any way transgress or pry into or utter, for deep awe of the gods checks the voice'[7]. Mylonas records the evidence for the seriousness with which that command was taken[8]: breaches of it were viewed as seriously as threats to the very constitution of the state[9]; Alcibiades and others were condemned for performing the

---

4 Cf., e.g., Duthoy, *Taurobolium* 119–21; Simon, *'Schule'* 141; more tentative in Hepding, *Attis* 200 n. 7.

5 Nilsson, *Geschichte* 2, 682–5.

6 Ibid. 351f; for a detailed substantiation of this with regard to the Eleusinian rites cf. Mylonas, *Eleusis* 287–316.

7 Lines 478f (tr. Evelyn-White); cf. Eur., *Ba.* 472.

8 *Eleusis* 224–6; in addition to the texts cited below cf. also Soph., *Oed. Col.* 1050–4; Hdt. 2.171; Mylonas also surmises that additions to the cult when celebrated in other centres were not guarded with as great strictness (302). For later evidence that it was still observed cf. also Luc., *Menippus* 2; Achill. Tat. 5.26.3.

9 Isoc. 16.6.

mysteries in a private house[10], and Diagoras the Melian was condemned to death for divulging these secrets[11]; Aeschylus and Andocides only just escaped a like fate[12]. In the second century C.E. Pausanias still felt the sacred precincts of Demeter in Athens and Eleusis to be too holy to describe, and spoke of a dream forbidding him to do so[13]. Sometimes the goddess herself was believed to punish those responsible for breaking those vows[14].

In the same century as Pausanias, Apuleius, one of our chief sources for what knowledge we have of the ancient mysteries, though threatened with a charge of sorcery, insists that he will not betray what is secret: accused of having 'kept something mysterious wrapped up in a handkerchief among the household gods in the house of Pontianus', a something which gave a hold to his accusers in their charge of magic (*Apol.* 53), he tells how he has 'taken part in initiatory rites (*sacrorum pleraque initia*) in Greece'[15] and keeps carefully certain 'emblems (*signa*) and mementoes' given to him by the priests. This is quite common practice, as those who have only been initiated into the rites of Liber will vouch: they keep certain things at home which they worship silently, 'away from all profane persons (*absque omnibus profanis*)'. How much more is this true of him, with his multiple initiations (§55). These secret objects he keeps wrapped in a linen handkerchief, linen being the cloth used by Egyptian priests to cover holy things. If any present at his trial took part in the same rites as himself he should give a sign (*signum*), and he can then hear what Apuleius has been keeping. But, regardless of the risk to himself, he will not be forced to declare to profane persons what he has been given to keep secret[16].

---

10 Andocides 1.11–13; cf. 16; Plut., *Alcibiades* 19–22; Xenophon, *Hellenica* 1.4.14f.

11 Schol. on Aristoph., *Av.* 1072 (cf. on *Ran.* 320); cf. also Pseudo-Lys. 6.17; Melanthius in *FGH* §326 frg. 3; Livy 31.14.17f; Sopater in Walz, *Rhetores* 8.110.20–2.

12 Aristotle, *Eth. Nic.* 3.1.17 (1111*a*); Heraclides Ponticus frg. 170 (Wehrli); Clem. Alex., *Strom.* 2.14.60.3; this also seems to have been one of the charges levelled against Andocides (Pseudo-Lys. 6.51).

13 1.14.3; 38.7; cf. also the reports of violations of temples of Isis near Tithorea and in Coptos: 10.32.17f; further Livy 39.13.5.
    Burkert, *Homo* 279, argues that the secrecy increased with the passage of time (in the period of the Roman Empire even the hierophant's name could not be mentioned) and that 'the heightened secrecy veiled the sinking power of the mysteries' (ET 253).

14 Cf. Horace, *Odes* 3.2.25–9, also Callimachus 6.116f. On the secrecy of the rites of the Samothracian mysteries cf. Diod. S. 5.49.5 and the texts in Lehmann-Lewis, *Samothrace* 1, 100–2 (nos 221–225*a*).

15 §55: I depart here from Butler's translation, 'Greek mysteries', since the phrase which Apuleius uses means that it is possible that he, like Lucius in *Met.* 11, was initiated into the rites of Isis in Greece; cf. Solmsen, *Isis* 106; Griffiths, *Isis-Book* 1–7.

16 Cf. the reff. to Pausanias and Horace above in nn. 13f; for the risk involved cf. Festugière, *Religion* 77; Solmsen, *Isis* 100.

Yet in his *Metamorphoses* Apuleius seems to make his hero Lucius describe the actual process of his initiation into the rites of Isis: 'I ap-proached the boundary of death and, treading on Proserpine's threshold, I was carried through all the elements, after which I returned. At dead of night I saw the sun flashing with bright effulgence. I approached close to the gods above and the gods below and worshipped them face to face'[17]. For some these are Apuleius' own words[18], for others they are a quota-tion of a sacred formula[19], similar to other formulae preserved for us by Christian writers, formulae characterized, like Apuleius' words, by a series of aorists or perfects in the first person singular, following upon one another, often in asyndeton, occasionally with past participles added. So, for instance, Clement of Alexandria quotes what he calls an Eleusinian σύνθημα: 'I fasted; I drank the draught (cyceon); I took from the chest; having done my task[20], I placed in the basket and from the basket into the chest'[21]. Arnobius quotes the same formula in Latin, calling these words *symbola* and saying that they are the reply given when asked 'in receiving the sacred things (*in acceptionibus*)'[22]. Firmicus Maternus quotes a similar formulation from the cult of Cybele and Attis: 'I have eaten from the *tympanon*: I have drunk from the *cymbalon*; I have become an initiate of Attis'[23]. Clement quotes another version of this too, calling the

---

17 §23, tr. Griffiths, *Isis-Book* 99.
18 So Griffiths, ibid. 295: 'whereas the *symbola* describe ritual actions, Lucius describes his move-ments and what he has seen, and all this in a heightened symbolical sense'; cf. Krämer, 'Isis-formel' 101–3; Sänger, *Judentum* 135; Wagner, *Baptism* 106 n. 94.
19 Dibelius, 'Isis Initiation' 64f; Nilsson, *Geschichte* 2, 634.
20 I find it hard to justify translating ἐργασάμενος as 'having handled'; but cf. Deubner, *Feste* 79. Nor are there sufficient grounds for accepting Lobeck's emendation ἐγγευσάμενος (*Aglao-phamus* 25). Burkert, *Homo* 300–2 (ET 272–4), argues that this is a reference to grinding corn with a mortar and pestle, all these being contained in the chest; he compares the Roman *confarreatio*. Whittaker, *Jews* 224, seems to omit the word.
21 *Prot.* 2.21.2 (tr. Butterworth 43); according to Nilsson, *Geschichte* 1, 659; 2, 95, this formula belongs to the Alexandrian cult of Demeter; cf. also Mylonas, *Eleusis* 300–3; they quote also H. G. Pringsheim, *Archäologische Beiträge zur Geschichte des eleusinischen Kults* (Diss. Bonn, 1905) 49, 58 n. 1 (the κάλαθος may have a mystic role in the Alexandrian cult of Demeter; cf. Callimachus 6.1, 3, 120; also Diels-Kranz, *Fragmente* §1 B 23, p. 20.6). Nilsson, *Religion* 45, is prepared to grant that the reff. to fasting and drinking the cyceon come from Eleusis; it is the second half which he suspects comes from Alexandria. But cf. Burkert, *Homo* 298 (ET 270) and n. 20, pointing to a use of *kalathoi* elsewhere in Demeter rites. For a full discussion cf. Fraser, *Alexandria* I, 200f (also 2, 338 n. 80; 340–2 n. 95); see also below §2.3.
Eliade, *History* 1, 297, also attributes to the Alexandrian rites the ritual described by Asterius, *Homily* 10 in Migne, *PG* 40, 323f.
22 *Adversus nationes* 5.26 in Migne, *PL* 5, 1137 (tr. Bryce and Campbell: 'I have fasted and drunk the draught; I have taken out of the [mystic] cist (*cista*), and put into the wicker-basket; I have received (*accepi*) again, and transferred to the little chest (*cistula*)').
23 *Err. prof. rel.* 18.1; he precedes this with a Latin rendering of the formula, substituting for the last clause 'I have learnt thoroughly the secrets of the religion'.

words σύμβολα: 'I ate from the drum; I drank from the cymbal; I carried the sacred dish; I stole into the bridal chamber'[24].

But do any of these formulations lay bare to us the innermost secrets of these cults? Obviously, if any of them are authentic, they are important evidence in an area where evidence of any sort is hard to come by. But what place had they in the cults? Mylonas argues that the σύμβολον was a credal confession, the σύνθημα a password 'used for recognition and identification'[25], but it is hard to find justification for this distinction in the sources. Firmicus seems to give the Latin word *symbolum* (or *signum*) the function which Mylonas ascribes to σύνθημα: he begins the section to which I referred above with the statement that he wishes to show 'with which signs (*signa*) or symbols (*symbola*) the wretched crowd of men recognize themselves in their rites (*superstitiones*). For they have their own signs and their own answers (*responsa*)' which they have been taught. Moreover we have seen that what Clement calls a σύνθημα Arnobius quotes as an example of *symbola*. Thus it seems that a distinction between σύνθημα and σύμβολον is not to be pressed[26].

But when were such συνθήματα or σύμβολα used? Firmicus states that the Attis formula which he quotes was uttered 'in a certain temple, in order that the one who is about to die may be admitted into the inner parts (of the temple)'. Dibelius compared Firmicus' reference to 'the one who is about to die' (*moriturus*) with the description of initiation into the cult of Isis as a 'voluntary death' in Apul., *Met*. 11.21. And so he went on to argue that Firmicus meant that this was a formula which the candidate for the highest initiation, the 'half-initiated', who had undergone certain preparatory rites, uttered before being admitted to these higher rites[27], but if Firmicus meant that, he was confused, for the introduction to 18.1 surely means that 'the following sayings would be signs for mutual recognition of the initiates, but according to Firmicus the Attis smybol was a response during the initiation'[28].

Yet *is* Firmicus confused? Has Dibelius not failed rather to recognize the polemic thrust and irony of his words? For Firmicus believed that the rites into which pagans were initiated were spiritually fatal; their sacred meals were spiritual poison. And so he continues in 18.2: 'you have con-

---

24 *Prot.* 2.15.3 (tr. Butterworth 35); Eliade, *History* 2, 287, attributes to Vermaseren the strange translation 'I have become the *kernos*', but certainly in his *Cybele* 116, 118, the latter has 'I have borne the *cernus*'; the scholiast on Plato, *Gorg.* 497C (ed. Hermann 6, 319), gives the impression that this belongs to the Eleusinian rites.
25 *Eleusis* 295.
26 Cf. Burkert, *Homo* 298 (ET 269f) n. 19.
27 'Isis Initiation' 67; cf. Griffiths, *Isis-Book* 296; Gäumann, *Taufe* 42f.
28 Ibid. 69.

sumed a pestilent and poisonous venom, and you lick a lethal cup . . . .
Death and punishment always follow that food. . . . Another food it is
which bestows salvation and life . . ., which bestows on the dying the
marks of eternal immortality. Seek Christ's bread, Christ's cup . . .'[29].
Thus Firmicus in no way suggests that the formula which he quotes was
used in the midst of the process of initiation; rather it was used to admit
to the further rites of the cult, in which only those already initiated could
participate.

What then of Dibelius' own view of the setting of these formulae, after
he had set Firmicus' view aside as confused? They are, he argues, 'most
likely sayings with which the initiate of the Eleusinian, the Attis, or the
Isis mysteries confesses himself outside in the world as a member of his
cultic community'[30]. A change of use could have taken place: what had
been 'a liturgical response at the reception of a higher initiation could
have become a recognition sign or, vice versa, a *signum* could have become
a *responsum*'[31]; by frequent use what had been secret could have become
public. The chief evidence for this use of the formulae are Apuleius'
invitation in *Apol.* 56 to fellow initiates to give a sign[32], and Firmicus'
description of these signs as the means by which the adherents of the cults
recognize one another[33].

Sänger, however, argues that the Eleusinian σύνθημα was used to gain
access to the second or third stage of the Eleusinian rites, the τελετή or
the ἐποπτεία of the Greater Mysteries at Eleusis[34]; it was a password which
signified that one had passed through the earlier μύησις or initiation in
the Lesser Mysteries at Agrae[35]. And certainly the Attis formula in Firmicus' version expressly declares that the speaker has been initiated. The
first part of the Eleusinian formula seems to refer to ritual acts which
echo the fasting of Demeter in her search for her lost daughter, a fast
which ended, according to the *Homeric Hymn*, when she accepted a drink
of cyceon[36]. Whether these ritual acts could have formed part of the

---

29 Cf. Pastorino's comm. 187, and Turcan's 288f; Dey, Παλιγγενεσία 83 (he compares also 8.3;
27.1); Gasparro, *Soteriology* 82; Nilsson, *Geschichte* 2, 649 n. 1, and 686; Wagner, *Baptism*
241.
30 'Isis Initiation' 70.
31 Ibid. 69.
32 Ibid. 74.
33 Both cited above; cf. Plautus, *Miles gloriosus* 1016.
34 *Judentum* 111; Kerenyi, *Eleusis*, does not seem to recognize any separate stage of the τελετή,
between the μύησις and the ἐποπτεία; cf. however Plut., *Demetrius* 26.2.
35 Deubner, *Feste* 80, argues that it refers rather to some rite at Eleusis prior to the τελετή; Mylonas, *Eleusis* 295, that it refers to completion both of the Lesser Mysteries and of the preliminaries to the Greater Mysteries in Athens and Eleusis; Kerenyi, *Eleusis* 65, argues that 'in all probability' (!) it was uttered at the river Rheitoi at the site of the palace of Crocon.
36 Lines 47, 208–10; cf. Berner, *Initiationsriten* 14, 17; Bianchi, *History* 114.

preliminary Lesser Mysteries or only of the Greater Mysteries is hard to determine, if not impossible; possibly both contained allusions to, and re-enactments of, the myth[37].

I would suggest that there may be four possible candidates for the context in which these formulae were used. In the first place they could be a ritual declaration before being admitted to rites to which only those who had passed through certain preliminary rites could be admitted, e.g. the sacred meals of the initiates of a cult, or further, higher rites of that cult; the former at least is a setting suggested by both Firmicus and Arnobius. And it is conceivable that this declaration could be uttered in the hearing of non-initiates debarred from these rites[38]. Again, Apuleius' trial suggests another possible use, a means of mutual identification outside a cultic setting, perhaps rather like the handshake by which Freemasons today recognize one another, and like that perhaps a rather open secret; perhaps even more open, since the manner of a handshake is less immediately apparent than the utterance of some formula[39]. Thirdly, I would tentatively suggest that another use might be on the occasion of a completed initiation, such as when the initiated Lucius is presented, in symbolic robes, to a crowd of worshippers and non-initiates (Apul., *Met.* 11.24). On such an occasion some declaration was surely necessary of the experience that the initiate had undergone, some explanation of the change effected in the one now presented to the crowds[40]. And some suitably allusive

---

37 So Mylonas, *Eleusis* 243, 259f, is uncertain whether the drinking of cyceon ended the fasting of the Lesser Mysteries or that of the 20th Boedromion, the day before initiation into the Great Mysteries. Note, however, the observation of Burkert, *Homo* 294 (ET 266) n. 7, that 'the Lesser Mysteries are no longer attested in Roman times'; we need to reckon with the possible modification of the rites, and consequently of the setting of such formulae, with the passage of time. Deubner, *Feste* 84, seems to press too much out of Proclus' comm. on Plato, *Resp.* (ed. Kroll 1, 125.20–2: 'the rites (τελεταί) of Kore and Demeter and the greatest goddess herself have handed down to us certain holy laments (θρῆνοι) in secret') when he insists that this refers to the τελετή as opposed to the μύησις or ἐποπτεία (Boyancé, 'Mystères' 481f, argues that the 'greatest goddess' is Themis who figured prominently in the Eleusinian rites).

38 Cf. Mylonas, ibid. 248: on 15th Boedromion, he suggests, an inspection of the would-be initiates in the Greater Mysteries may have taken place to see who was 'properly prepared, through their participation in the Lesser Mysteries . . . . Of course a strict examination aiming at the exclusion of undesirables was impossible, especially in the days of the Roman Empire when large crowds attended the celebration, . . .'. However a public setting would be less appropriate if the Eleusinian formula was uttered only to admit to the ἐποπτεία, but Arnobius' reference to *acceptiones* would hardly be appropriate to the ἐποπτεία alone.

39 While σύνθημα can mean a secret pass-word, it need not have any connotation of secrecy; cf. LSJ s.v.

40 This seems more satisfactory than the suggestion of Bergman, '*Per omnia*' 675, that the purpose of the formula was to prepare initiands for the rite ahead of them (who would then pronounce the formula – one already initiated?)

Need we assume that these possible uses are mutually exclusive? Dibelius, we have seen, posits a changing function ('Isis Initiation' 69); cf. also Pastorino's comm. on Firm. Mat., *Err. prof. rel.*, 184f; also n. 37 above.

reference to the preceding ritual acts might serve this purpose well. In that case it would mean that the statement was deliberately intended for the ears of non-initiates.

In this last case none of these formulae need have been secret statements. In the first two cases they were by their nature uttered in public settings where they could not be expected to remain secret for long. Certainly it is doubtful whether any of the phrases which have come down to us[41] belong to the esoteric and secret parts of the rites of these cults; they were hardly part of the secret λεγόμενα which Andocides was nearly condemned to death for revealing and without knowledge of which one could not apparently be considered properly initiated[42]. Rather, they should be seen as having their place in those parts of the rites which were open to the public, either by design or by force of circumstances and the passage of time[43]. And so there is no need to argue that Firmicus Maternus, for instance, was a former initiate, in order to explain his knowledge of the mysteries[44]. Nor is there any need to assert that Apuleius, despite all his protestations of fidelity to his vows, did in fact reveal more than he should have through the lips of his hero, Lucius, whether it be a sacred cultic formula[45], or, more likely, a summary in his own words of what the initiation involved.

Finally, however, there is the suggestion of Boyancé that some at least of these phrases may have their origin as passwords, not for human ears, but for divine, ensuring those that uttered them a favourable reception from the queen of the underworld[46]. This is not incompatible with a cultic setting like some at any rate of those suggested above if the rites involved what Nock calls 'a symbolic anticipation of what was to take place hereafter, . . . a piece of sympathetic magic which ensured safety by a simulation here and now'[47].

---

41 Listed in Dieterich, *Mithrasliturgie* 213−18.

42 Pseudo-Lys. 6.51.

43 So, for instance, with the words from the Eleusinian cult recorded in Hipp., *Ref.* 5.8.40 and 7.34 (cf. Proclus' comm. on Plato, *Tim.* ed. Diehl, 293C): the cry of the hierophant, ἱερὸν ἔτεκε πότνια κοῦρον Βριμὼ Βριμόν and the cry ὕε, κύε. (The latter is echoed on the inscription of a foreigner at Athens: cf. Perdrizet, 'Mên' 78−80; Mylonas, *Eleusis* 270f). The scholiast on Juv. 8.29 (ed. Wessner 137) attributes the words εὑρήκαμεν, συγχαίρομεν to the *populus Aegypti* (Juv. himself attests that the people acclaim the finding of Osiris), and they are quoted, slightly altered, in Sen., *Apocolocyntosis* 13.

44 F. Boll in *PRE* 6, 2365, argues that, contrary to the assumption of T. Friedrich's Gießen diss. of 1905, Firmicus' warning to the astrologers in *Mathesis* 2.30.10 (ed. Kroll-Skutsch-Ziegler= 2.28.13 ed. Sittl) implies that he had not participated in any mysteries himself, but agrees with K. Ziegler (in *RAC* 7, 956f) in the value of his knowledge of the mysteries.

45 Cf. Dibelius, 'Isis Initiation' 71: 'Is it credible that Apuleius, himself an initiate in the mysteries, would have exposed a sacred cultic formula to the public?'

46 *Culte* esp. 51−3, following a suggestion in Proclus' comm. on Plato, *Resp.* 1, 83.18−20 (Kroll).

47 *Conversion* 12.

Mostly the innermost experiences of the mysteries remain, in all probability, closed to us[48]. And yet some explanation of their goals and aspirations, their beliefs and their claims, did filter through to the general public, was even deliberately proclaimed to that public, and impressed itself upon the consciousness of that age to such an extent that, from Plato onwards, other religious and philosophical movements copied their language and their claims, however much they filled their words with another content (cf. §2.3). That is indication enough of a fair level of knowledge of, and esteem for, the mysteries, whether they were admired or feared as rivals. Their myths, in all their various forms, were public knowledge, from the time of the *Homeric Hymn to Demeter* onwards[49]. Their public rites and processions proclaimed the relevance of these myths and their claims upon the veneration of all[50]. Numerous works of art portray the deities and their rites with varying amounts of detail. Thus, despite the apparent preservation of their secrets, there is reason to think and hope that a considerable amount of their beliefs is still accessible to our view.

2.1. The Spread of the Mysteries

Schweitzer, we saw, maintained that the mystery-religions were only widely influential from the beginning of the second century C.E. and certainly it is correct that they enjoyed a possibly unparalleled degree of influence and prestige in this century, perhaps reaching a peak at its close

---

48 Cf. Mylonas, *Eleusis* 281, 316.

49 Perhaps to be dated as early as the 7th century B.C.E. (ed. Evelyn-White xxxvi; Mylonas, *Eleusis* 3); Kerenyi, *Eleusis* 27, speaks of the myth as 'a public introduction to the Mysteries'.

50 On the distinction between the secret and public parts of the Eleusinian rites cf. Mylonas, *Eleusis* 226–9. In the Isis cult Apul. records for us the public procession during which Lucius' transformation took place (*Met.* 11.8–13, 16) and the following worship (17), subsequent rites in which the uninitiated could participate (19, 22), and finally the public gathering to which the initiated Lucius is displayed (24). Sen., *Ep.* 95.64, distinguishes the *sanctiora sanctorum* known only to initiates and the *praecepta* known to others too (the latter part of the distinction is probably couched in terms rather of philosophy with which he compares the mysteries).
Nilsson, *Mysteries* 4, comments that 'whereas the old mysteries were hidden in secrecy, the Bacchic mysteries were not'; hence the many representations of their ceremonies (but cf. Rostovtzeff, *Italy* 93, 97). MacMullen, *Paganism* 23, argues that 'mystery' suggests, misleadingly, revelations in secret to a tiny number of devotees; rather 'a *mysterion* normally meant something more open and unexciting, essentially a lesson in a cult to be learned, perhaps by very large numbers at a time, as in the Eleusinian rites or in the mystery cult . . . of Cybele' (cf. 24); cf. Poland, *Geschichte* 36. Perhaps an important factor was the price charged for more

in the Severan period[1]. Many emperors were themselves initiated into various mysteries[2], and the senatorial class followed, and even anticipated, their example[3]. There was a marked tendency for new mysteries to spring up where there had been none before, a sure sign that such rites were fashionable: even the imperial cult took on the form of mysteries in Asia Minor[4], and Lucian depicts Alexander of Abonuteichos establishing his own mysteries in his home town in Paphlagonia[5].

Yet, although it may be freely granted that the mysteries reached a peak of popularity in the second century, it by no means follows from this that they were unpopular and without influence earlier. In fact the evidence suggests what is in fact *a priori* likely, that they already enjoyed a considerable degree of popularity during the two preceding centuries[6]; their rise to prominence in the second century was the outcome of a period of mounting influence and in part a response of the leadership to feelings and loyalties manifested earlier by private citizens, as well as by the subject peoples of the Empire[7]. Our evidence for the earlier period is scantier; we have no Apuleius and no Lucian for it. Yet what sparse and scattered evidence we have suggests that the influence of the mysteries in the second century was by no means a new phenomenon. So A. D. Nock,

---

secret rites (cf. §2.1 n. 31); yet it should not be forgotten that, in the Eleusinian rites at least, secrecy was insisted on for some rites and revelations, however great the numbers involved (see above).

Notes on 2.1

1 Liebeschuetz, *Continuity* 233; cf. Vidman, *Isis* 139 (followed by Hengel, *Sohn* 45=ET 27); Malaise, *Conditions* 437–43. Or is this peak simply because the output of inscriptions in general was highest then? – cf. MacMullen, *Paganism* 115f (see further at the end of this section).

2 So for Eleusis: Script. Hist. Aug., *Hadrian* 13.1; *IG* 2/3[2], 3575=Smallwood, *Documents* (1966), 71(a) – Hadrian; Script. Hist. Aug., *M. Antoninus* 27.1; Dio C. 71.31; *EphArch* 3.3 (1885) 150. 13f; *SIG*[3] 2, 872.15f – M. Aurelius, Commodus; Commodus' initiation in the rites of Isis and Mithras may be implicit in Script. Hist. Aug., *Commodus* 9.4–6 (cf. *Pescennius Niger* 6.8f).

3 Beaujeu, 'Religion' 64–74.

4 Pleket, 'Aspect'; even if Nilsson is correct in calling these 'pseudo-mysteries' (cf. *Geschichte* 2, 370f and further reff. in Pleket 335 n. 17) the existence of such imitations underlines how mysteries were in fashion.

5 Luc., *Alex.* 38–40.

6 Cf. Beaujeu, 'Religion' 74f; Kennedy, *St Paul* 70; so Walbank, *World* 221, argues that Apuleius' account in *Met.* 11, though written in the 2nd century C.E., was still 'relevant to the religious experience of the Hellenistic age'.
Nash, *Christianity* 127, describes the mysteries as 'still largely localized' in the first century; the evidence for the spread of the various cults given below hardly bears this out; some, like the Eleusinian rites, were localized, and remained so, because tied to a particular location.

7 Cf. Angus, *Mystery-Religions* 161: in their recognition or introduction of cults 'Roman rulers pretended to lead where they were in truth being led'; also Graillot, *Culte* 116, 144.
However we should avoid talking here of *religiones licitae*, an idea which Köster criticizes as 'a modern construction' apropos of the status of Judaism (*Einführung* 233, 376=ET 1, 226, 365); cf. F. C. Grant, *Hellenism* 172–8.

writing apropos of the period up to the death of Nero, speaks of it as characterized 'by a rise in the importance of the initiatory sacraments, which gave a revelation and a new status to the initiate by some rebirth or reconstitution, also by the growth of small private mysteries, such as those of Hecate associated with the so-called Chaldaic oracles . . .'[8].

One can indeed point to signs of official favour towards various oriental cults in Rome in the first century C.E. Isis had apparently been worshipped in Rome for over a century[9] when Caligula seems to have granted her cult his favour: Josephus mentions his donning female attire 'in the rites of certain mysteries' and instituting mysteries[10], and it may well be that the rites of Isis are referred to; to him may possibly be attributed the building of a temple of Isis in the Campus Martius, and the official recognition of the Isiac feast of the Finding of Osiris[11]. Lucan 8.831–4 perhaps provides a *terminus ad quem* for the official establishment of the cult:

> 'Though we have admitted to Roman temples your Isis and your dogs half divine, the rattle which bids the worshipper wail, and the Osiris whom you prove to be mortal by mourning for him, yet you, Egypt, keep our dead a prisoner in your dust.' (Tr. Duff)

Lucan died in 65 C.E.[12]

Caligula's successor, Claudius, is credited with having attempted to introduce the Eleusinian rites in Rome[13]. Less certain is whether he showed any particular favour to the rites of Cybele and Attis. The former already enjoyed considerable prestige at this time — her temple had been restored by Augustus[14]. Johannes Lydus (sixth century C.E.) also credits Claudius with the formation of a new festival including Attis in March, but this has been viewed with some scepticism[15]. Pliny the Elder also tells us

---

8 In *CAH* 10, 508; cf. Turcan, *Sénèque* 7, on the second third of the first century; also Bruhl, *Liber* 163; Grant, ibid. 37–9, 45.

9 Apul., *Met.* 11.30, dating the *collegium* of the *Pastophori* to the time of Sulla; cf. Latte, *Religionsgeschichte* 282; Versnel, 'Religion' 58; Malaise, *Inventaire* 112 no. 2, points to an inscription of the 1st century B.C.E. in which T. Sulpicius describes himself as a priest of Capitoline Isis; 124 no. 35 may also come from this century.

10 Jos., *Ant.* 19.1.5 §30; 19.1.11 §71; cf. Suidas Γ. 12 (Adler 1, 503); Jos. also mentions boys from Asia singing in mysteries celebrated by Caligula (*Ant.* 19.1.14 §104); cf. Suet., *Caligula* 57, as well as Köberlein, *Caligula*, who sets these scattered reff. in the wider perspective of Caligula's reign in general; on these Jos. reff. cf. ibid. 35.

11 Cf. the arguments of Mommsen in *CIL* 1², 333f, followed by Balsdon, *Gaius* 174; Latte, *Religionsgeschichte* 283 n. 5; Malaise, *Inventaire* 213, and *Conditions* 221–7, 400; A. D. Nock in *CAH* 10, 496; Platner-Ashby, *Dictionary* 284; Wissowa, *Religion* 353f.

12 Tac., *Ann.* 15.70.

13 Suet., *Claudius* 25.5: 'he even attempted to transfer the Eleusinian rites from Attica to Rome' (tr. Rolfe).

14 *Res Gestae* 19.2 (Ehrenberg-Jones, *Documents* 16f); cf. Platner-Ashby, *Dictionary* 324; Versnel, 'Religion' 59, says that he incorporated it into his palace: 'thus the goddess had a part to play in deification of the emperors'; cf. also Graillot, *Culte* 108ff.

15 *De mensibus* 4.59 (Wuensch 113), followed tentatively by Latte, *Religionsgeschichte* 261; Nock, *Conversion* 69; Vermaseren, *Cybele* 98, 113; less tentatively by Carcopino, *Aspects* 49

that Nero was initiated into the meals of the *magi* during Tiridates' visit
to Rome in 66 C.E.[16]

Otho was said to have been a devotee of Isis[17], and Vespasian, perhaps
because of the evidence of the favour of Sarapis which he had experienced,
or was believed to have experienced, at Alexandria[18], favoured the cults of
Isis and Sarapis[19]. His favour towards Cybele is shown by his restoration
of a temple in Herculaneum[20]. His son Titus seemingly continued his
father's patronage of these Egyptian deities[21], which now seem to have
recovered completely from the disfavour with which they were viewed
under Augustus and Tiberius. Domitian, who had reputedly escaped
Vitellius' forces by disguising himself as a devotee of Isis[22], rebuilt the
temple of Isis on the Campus Martius after it had been destroyed by fire
in 80 C.E.[23] and erected an obelisk in it representing himself being crowned
by Isis[24]. Yet, however great the Flavian emperors' support of these gods

---

−75; Cumont, *Religions* 51f; v. Doren, 'Évolution' 79; S. Giversen in *HRG* 3, 284; Graillot,
Culte 115f, 142; House, 'Tongues' 137; Momigliano, *Claudius* 28, 93 n. 20; A. D. Nock in
CAH 10, 499; Vermaseren, 'Religions' 516; Whittaker, *Jews* 231f ('presumably referring to
this'); but cf. Wissowa, *Religion* 322; also Scramuzza, *Claudius* 152−5, 287−90: at most
Lydus' words mean 'only that the emperor issued a police permit for the procession'. Lambrechts, 'Fêtes', argues, against Carcopino, that Johannes Lydus' ref. should not be regarded as
evidence for the introduction of the whole cycle of the March festival; rather this was introduced in at least two stages: (1) Claudius introduced only the festival of the *Dendrophoria* (a
funeral rite in which the tree did not necessarily represent Attis himself) after which Cybele's
statue and the sacred implements were washed in the Almo (*Lavatio*); (2) Antoninus Pius introduced the official *taurobolium* for the emperor, entrusted to the *archigallus*. Only in the
second half of the 2nd century or later did the idea of Attis rising annually appear and the
Hilaria were inserted awkwardly between the 'day of blood' (24th March) and the *Requietio*
of 26th March.
Yet Suet., *Otho* 8.3, does mention Otho setting out 'on the very day . . . when worshippers of
the Mother of the Gods begin their wailing and lamentation', which suggests the existence of
this part of the cult by the end of Nero's reign; G. Sanders, 'Kybele' 278f, points out too how
Attis certainly had a firm place in private devotion in Rome from ca. 100 B.C.E., as finds of
terracotta figures of him on the Palatine attest (cf. Vermaseren, *Cybele* 43; *CCCA* 3.14−199=
pls 28−97); see also Cosi, 'Salvatore' 52f (evidence for the cult of Attis at Ostia and in Sicily).
16 Pliny, *Hist. nat.* 30.6.17 (*initiaverat*).
17 Suet., *Otho* 12.1; Le Corsu, *Isis* 182, infers that he was a priest of Isis.
18 Tac., *Hist.* 4.81f; Suet., *Vespasian* 7.
19 Jos., *Bell.* 7.5.4 §123; cf. Malaise, *Conditions* 407−13; while the route of the Flavian rise to
   power favoured the Egyptian gods, the experiences of Julius Caesar and Octavian very naturally
   led to an aversion to Egypt and things Egyptian, including their gods, under the early Principate
   (cf. Malaise, ibid. 245f, 378−95; 395−401 outline the reasons for Caligula's changing that
   policy).
20 *CIL* 10, 1406 and *CCCA* 4.20; v. Doren, 'Évolution' 81f, is inclined also to assign *CIL* 6,
   10098 (cf. 33961) to his reign.
21 Suet., *Titus* 5.3.
22 Suet., *Domitian* 1.2; cf. Tac., *Hist.* 3.74; Le Corsu, *Isis* 184, argues that he was an initiate.
23 Cf. Eus. in Hopfner, *Fontes* 486 col. 3; Eutropius, *Breviarium* 7.23.5 in Hopfner, ibid. 555; cf.
   also Griffiths, *Isis-Book* 327f; Malaise, *Inventaire* 213.
24 Malaise, ibid. 203−7 no. 387 (cf. 296−9, Beneventum nos. 10−11).

may have been, it does not follow that they were representative of the highest strata of Roman society at this early period[25]; for evidence of widespread support at this social level we must wait another century[26], although there are signs of *some* penetration of these cults into the highest levels of Roman society early on in the first century; this is indicated by the story which Josephus tells of the seduction of Paulina through her devotion to the cult of Isis[27].

Moreover, what was true to some extent of Roman society seems to have been even more true of provincial Italian society: Malaise comments, after surveying the evidence of devotion to Egyptian deities at Pompeii, that 'the members of the municipal aristocracy embraced the Egyptian cults with more enthusiasm than the Roman patricians; they did not even hesitate to enter the class of priests, a step which, according to the evidence of our inscriptions, the high and mighty of Rome only took considerably later'[28].

And yet such public recognition of these oriental deities does not by any means attest a corresponding influence of any mysteries attached to their cults; this is a distinction which has to be very clearly made, between oriental cults which may only have public rites, and the 'mysteries' which some of them contained or developed[29]. So, for instance, the two thousand devotees of Isis estimated by Tran Tam Tinh at Pompeii prior to its destruction in 79 C.E. were not necessarily all initiates in her mysteries[30]. Far from it; they were most unlikely to be unless the esoteric rites were decidedly cheaper in the first century than in the second[31], for Lucius

---

25 Liebeschuetz, *Continuity* 182.

26 Cf. Vidman, *Isis* 107f.

27 *Ant.* 18.3.4 § §66—80; cf. Tac., *Ann.* 2.85; Suet., *Tiberius* 36; Sen., *Ep.* 108.22.
   As a result the temple of Isis was destroyed (Jos., ibid. §80; for its replacement cf. Dio C. 47. 15.4).
   For earlier penetration of such cults into the nobility cf. Versnel, 'Religion' 55.

28 *Conditions* 85; cf., however, n. 9 above. See also Tran Tam Tinh, *Essai* 26, 39ff. Whittaker, *Jews* 241, surmises that Caligula's favouring of the Egyptian cult was in response to 'popular demand' implying that the spread of the cult at lower levels of society was even greater by this stage.

29 Cf. Nock, *Conversion* 57.

30 *Essai* 60 (cf. 112); i.e. 10% of the population (cf. Griffiths, *Isis-Book* 191), an estimate of M. Della Corte, *Juventus* (Arpino, 1924) 76, combined with A. Maiuri's estimate of the population in *Pompei, i nuovi scavi, la villa dei Misteri, antiquarium* (Roma, 1958) 18; a maximum of 25,000 in *Pompei* (1935²) 14.

31 According to *IG* 2², 1672=*SIG*² 2, 587.207 (329/8 B.C.E.) the total cost of initiation at Eleusis was 15 drachmae per person; cf. Kerenyi, *Eleusis* 59f. This was little more than a week's wages for a skilled workman at this time: Mitchell, *Economics* 131. The rate for the biennial Dionysiac rites in Miletus in the 3rd century B.C.E. was a stater (Quandt, *De Baccho* 171); for the Iobacchi in Athens in the 2nd century C.E. the entrance fee was 50 denarii (half price if one's father was a member) and a libation: *SIG*³ 3, 1109.39—41 (cf. Leipoldt-Grundman, *Umwelt* 2, no. 113.4—7). Cf. Vidman, *Isis* 127: 'the mysteries of all oriental cults in the im-

tells us in Apul., *Met*. 11 that, having had certain expenses in connection with his first initiation into the rites of Isis, although apparently assisted by others (§23), he was in considerable difficulties in attempting to raise the money necessary for his subsequent initiations in Rome (§§28, 30). This was despite the fact that he was apparently possessed of some means[32]: he was travelling to Thessaly 'on business' (*Met*. 1.2), and possessed slaves (11.20); after his misadventures, he tells how his relatives[33] had provided amply for his needs; he also refers to the 'modest sum' of his fortune (§28)[34]. Nor does Apuleius' story suggest that anyone who wished to, and had the necessary means, could be initiated into the rites of Isis; rather he must await the guidance and permission of the goddess (§§21f)[35]. In this, it seems, the rites of Isis were more selective than those of Eleusis[36].

And yet the same evidence, the experiences of Lucius, may perhaps deter us from remaining too agnostic or sceptical about the influence of mysteries at an earlier period. For what reason have we to suppose that the same phenomenon did not exist, to a greater or lesser extent, in the previous century or centuries[37], the phenomenon, that is, of esoteric rites performed for a few devotees of a deity − perhaps very few −[38], but rites whose consequences and significance were at least in some measure laid bare to a far wider circle of devotees and even interested or curious spectators? Even truer perhaps in his day and in a slightly earlier one than it was in Plato's time was the saying quoted in the latter's *Phaedo* (69C) that 'there are many *thyrsus*-bearers but few *bacchi*'[39]. For, in Apul.,

perial period were very costly'; also Nock, *Conversion* 57; D. H. Wiens in *ANRW* 2.23.2, 1265. In contrast the Eleusinian initiation formerly at least counted as fairly cheap: Plato, *Resp.* 2.378A.

32 As was Apuleius himself: *Apol*. 23 − he and his brother inherited nearly two million sesterces, but he spent much of it on travels, study and gifts. There is an element of autobiography in the *Metamorphoses*, especially in Bk 11: cf. §27 − Lucius too is from Madaura. However cf. Malaise, *Conditions* 238 (Lucius' resources were scanty at the time).

33 Following Griffiths' rendering of *familiares* rather than the LCL's 'servants'.

34 Tr. Griffiths, *Isis-Book* 105 (*viriculas patrimonii*).

35 Cf. Paus. 10.32.13.

36 Gordon, 'Mithraism' 96f, speaks of two different patterns of initiation in the mysteries: less sophisticated ones offering one or two further initiations after the primary one of purging from sin, and ones like Apuleius' description, where initiation was 'unusual and expensive, a concern only of the deeply committed'. Mithraism was different to these two types. However, apart from the clear distinction of the relative cost and of the number of initiates in relation to the total number of devotees (surely not unrelated?), I do not see that this is all that clear or accurate a distinction, at least as regards the nature and meaning of the ceremonies themselves.

37 But not too much earlier; cf. Versnel, 'Religion' 61: 'it is very uncertain how far the oriental cults, like those of Cybele and Isis, had already also developed mysteries in addition to their more official manifestations in the Republican period. The problem cannot be solved, for we have no evidence.'

38 Cf. Dunand, *Culte* 3, 255; Nilsson, *Geschichte* 2, 699f.

39 =*Orph. Fr.* 5.

Met. 11, after the secret nocturnal rites, Lucius was presented in an 'Olympian stole', 'adorned like unto the sun' before a crowd of 'very many who were present', subsequently referred to as 'the people' (§ 24). Such a pattern in these cults is unlikely to have risen suddenly and without preparation in the second century. And yet the controls imposed on all sorts of *collegia* by Julius Caesar, Augustus and Claudius lest they became clandestine centres of disaffection[40] suggest that one would have had to be careful about too intimate a contact with a deity that did not enjoy imperial favour, particularly if one met with others in conditions of secrecy. That means that one would not expect very much evidence for the existence of mysteries of any deity before that deity had received official approval; if they had existed previously then they would have had to do so secretly, and certainly would not have advertised the fact on stone. Thus the data that we have considered for the official recognition of various mystery-cults or cults that could contain mysteries provide the likely *termini post quos* for the appearance of epigraphic evidence of the existence of any such mysteries.

So, although the presence of oriental cults does not imply the presence of mysteries, the existence of the cults did mean that the consciousness of the public was awakened as to these deities, their nature and their claims. It is recorded, for instance, that just before Caligula's murder rehearsals were under way for a nocturnal performance showing scenes from the underworld depicted by Egyptians and Ethiopians; it is to be expected that that would have familiarized many with the role of Osiris as king of the dead[41]. Many, that is, over and above any that may have been initiated into mysteries of Osiris.

Certainly we know of the presence in Italy of a cult generally regarded as mysteries, and calling itself such, from at least the second century B.C.E. onwards, the rites of *Dionysus*. True, they had been banned after a scandal in 186 B.C.E.[42], and there is some doubt when that ban had been lifted or had lapsed[43]. Certainly it does not seem to have been operative

---

40 Suet., *Julius* 42.3; *Augustus* 32.1 (*antiqua et legitima* excepted); Dio C. 60.6.6f. Religious associations would have been included among such *collegia*.

41 Suet., *Caligula* 57; cf. Malaise, *Conditions* 228, 399.

42 Livy 39.8—19; prior to that Dionysus, under the name of Liber, had been given a shrine on the Aventine in 496 B.C.E. or later, along with Demeter and Kore (=Ceres and Libera); cf. Dion. Hal., *Ant. Roma.* 6.17.2, 94.3; this temple was restored in 17 C.E. (Tac., *Ann.* 2.49); cf. Bruhl, *Liber* 30ff. The ban applied primarily to mysteries and not to the official and public cult of the wine-god.

Wilamowitz-Moellendorff, *Glaube* 2, 386f, remarks that the mysteries of Dionysus are 'the only mysteries which spread throughout the Hellenistic world and also over Hellenized Italy' and survived throughout the whole period. He implies that only these deserve the title of 'Hellenistic mystery-religion'.

43 Kerenyi cites as evidence that it had Servius' comm. on Vergil, *Ecl.* 5.29—31 (Thilo 57f):

by the time in the mid second century C.E. when a troop of Dionysiac initiates, listing nearly four hundred names, dedicated a statue at Torre Nova to Pompeia Agrippinilla[44]. Yet earlier their rites, along with those of Eleusis, had inspired many works of art, like the stuccos from the Villa Farnesina in Rome[45]; particularly noteworthy here are the Dionysiac scenes from the Villa of the Mysteries (Villa Item) at Pompeii[46], which perhaps reveal some admixture of Egyptian motifs[47]. In the second century B.C.E., Livy alleges, the number of initiates into the Dionysiac rites 'was very great, almost constituting a second state; among them were certain men and women of high rank (*nobiles*)'[48]. By the time of Caesar there was 'undoubtedly a Dionysiac current' flowing in Rome[49]; however Antony's identification of himself with Dionysus[50] might have put a check on the god's popularity after Octavian's victory (compare the fate of the Egyptian gods)[51], but other factors seem to have disposed Augustus to view Liber more kindly[52]. Certainly poets continued to celebrate him[53] and he remained popular in the decoration of homes and gardens[54]; most significant here are those works of art depicting scenes from the Dionysiac mysteries[55] since, for Bruhl, the fact that artists portrayed these scenes

---

'this plainly refers to Caesar who, it is agreed, was the first to bring the rites of father Liber to Rome' (*Dionysos* 363); cf. House, 'Tongues' 138; Bruhl, *Liber* 124–7, takes Servius' statement with a pinch of salt; certainly, taken at its face value it is plainly wrong: rites of Liber had long been known in Italy (cf. Coleman, comm. on Vergil, *Ecl.* 174). But the ref. to *thiasi* suggests the ecstatic cult rather than traditional viticultural rites (cf. Coleman, ibid. 161); thus, if 'Daphnis' is an allusion to Julius Caesar (cf. Coleiro, *Introduction* 147–9), Servius' information must be taken more seriously, as referring to that form only of the Dionysiac worship that was banned in 186 B.C.E. But even so it must be wrong, for what had been banned had already been introduced (though not officially, if this is what Servius means). Bruhl may be on safer ground in holding the ban to be still in force at this time, and Livy reminds his readers of that fact (*Liber* 182f).

44 Vogliano, Cumont, Alexander, 'Inscription' 215–70; the gaps on the inscription mean that the original number of dedicants was probably well over this figure.

45 Cf. Bianchi, *Mysteries* pl. 86; Bruhl, *Liber* pls 5–8; Leipoldt-Grundmann, *Umwelt* 3, pl. 51; Nilsson, *Mysteries* figs 11–13; Rostovtzeff, *Italy* pls 21–7 (chaps 2f are relevant here); cf. also Nock in *CAH* 10, 504.

46 Cf. Bianchi, ibid. pls 91f; Leipoldt-Grundmann, ibid. pls 52–4; Nilsson, ibid. fig. 10; Rostovtzeff, ibid. pls 2–7. (A good over-all impression is given by the two photographs in Macchioro, *Orpheus*.) Zuntz, 'Fresco', argues that, although these scenes do not actually depict the mysteries or initiation, they reflect the piety, and portray some of the persons, of a local Dionysiac *thiasus*.

47 Cf. Le Corsu, *Isis* 163–71; cf. also 'Oratoire'.

48 Livy 39.13.14 (tr. Sage); cf. 15.8, 'many thousands'; 17.6, '7,000'.

49 Bruhl, *Liber* 126.

50 Plut., *Antony* 24.4; 60.5; *IG* 2/1, 482.23.

51 Cf. Bruhl, *Liber* 183; Matz in *Gn. 32*, 549f.

52 Cf. the sign of favour noted in n. 46 above; cf. Bruhl, ibid. 183f.

53 Bruhl, ibid. 133–44; cf. Horace, *Odes* 1.18.11: one note of distaste among general approbation.

54 Bruhl, ibid. 145–59.

55 Cf. nn. 45f above; also Bianchi, *Mysteries* pls 85, 87f, 94; Leipoldt-Grundmann, *Umwelt* 3, pls

perhaps shows that they had clients who would understand and appreciate the meaning of these subjects[56]. Yet, probably rightly, he doubts whether the numbers of actual participants in the mysteries, or the manner in which they participated, were now comparable with those which had rocked the state in 186 B.C.E., but 'that does not prevent the knowledge of the rites of the mysteries and their meaning being quite widespread in cultured circles'[57]. Partly, perhaps, because of their familiarity, the rites of Dionysus did not enjoy the upsurge of popularity of other cults from the East at this time; the epigraphic evidence becomes more plentiful from the second century onwards, but, according to Bruhl, this was the fruit of an earlier 'inner movement'[58]. For that assertion the main support is the artistic evidence referred to above.

Nor were mysteries of *Isis* completely absent from first century Italy: an inscription at Forum Popilii mentions *telestini*, initiates[59]. On the other hand mysteries of *Cybele and Attis* are hard to find at this period (they seem best attested in Rome in the fourth century C.E.), but Attis does appear in the first century in a most suggestive setting, in the underground hall near the Porta Maggiore in Rome[60]. There, amidst four scenes of Attis in more pensive mood if not mourning, the central scene on the vault is a winged Attis carrying Ganymede up to heaven[61]. Other scenes reflect other mythological traditions, including those of Egypt and the cult of Dionysus but Attis is central. According to Vermaseren, 'one begins to wonder whether this expensive monument was erected in order to commemorate the early death of a young married couple . . .'[62]. The main

---

55f (p. 22: from the beginning of the Empire); Rostovtzeff, *Italy* pls 5, 20 (?29.2); cf. also 55–94 on the 'Homeric' house at Pompeii. For a complete list of the evidence, of varying date, cf. Matz, Τελετή 8f, and also pls 2, 8, 10, 12–25. For secondary literature cf. the discussion by Foucher in *ANRW* 2.17.2, 690–4.

56 Bruhl, *Liber* 148, 154.

57 Bruhl, ibid. 159; cf. Rostovtzeff, *Italy* 40.

58 Bruhl, ibid. 164f. For the significance of the absence of epigraphic evidence for the earlier period see below.

Petronius, *Satyricon* 17, also refers to nocturnal religious rites of Priapus performed in a shrine, *secreta* which are known to scarcely a thousand persons; this may well date to the 1st century C.E. (R. Hanslik in *KP* 4, 673); Foucher in *ANRW* 2.17.2, 696, regards this deity, an 'anthropomorphized phallus', as a symbol of new life to be reborn after death.

59 Malaise, *Inventaire* 27; cf. Budischovsky, *Diffusion* 75; also Tran Tam Tinh, *Essai* 94, 98, 111.

60 Cf. Vermaseren, *Cybele* 55–7, 78, 113 (pls 39f); *CCCA* 3, 344 (pls 202–5). This hall is dated to the reign of Tiberius or that of Claudius. For Carcopino (*Études*) this was the place of worship of a Pythagorean group, but this view does not find much favour today; the dominance of Dionysiac elements in the decoration would be one argument against such a characterization (cf. §2.2).

61 That is Vermaseren's identification; for Carcopino, *Études* 111, Ganymede is carried aloft by a winged god; though the head may be lacking, the trousers, also worn by the adjoining figures of Attis, are visible.

62 *Cybele* 56; against this v. Doren, 'Évolution', argues from the absence of any hope of bliss in

theme of the display was the conferring of immortality, an immortality at least possessed by Attis and conceivably also mediated or conferred by him. Here one needs to note that the find of terracotta figures of Attis from the previous century[63] is followed by a steady flow of representations of Attis in the first century C.E.[64] If not a god of any mysteries Attis at least seems to have possessed for some the sort of qualifications needed for a mystery-god.

Moreover, the bulk of the first century evidence which we have so far considered relates to Rome, and the rest almost entirely concerned Italy; in general our evidence for this region of the ancient world is anyhow far more extensive than it is for the provinces[65]. In Italy there remained a deep-seated suspicion of novel cults, especially ones with ecstatic and secret rites. Yet cults from the East arrived there with trade and the spoils of war, and had their first adherents among foreigners settled on Italian soil[66]; only later did they become established amongst the officially recognized cults of Rome. That implies two things: first that the signs of official recognition which we traced above were preceded by a period in which these deities were influential at lower levels of Roman society, particularly among the immigrant population[67]. Secondly, in so far as these were oriental or Hellenistic cults this implies that they already enjoyed widespread support and influence in their respective homelands even before they were introduced into Italy. And it is, of course, chiefly in the eastern provinces that Christianity arose and made its earliest advances, so that

---

CIL 6, 10098 (the Hector of which, he argues, was a *gallus*) that this cult was not yet a mystery-cult in the true sense in the time of Vespasian. That may simply mean, however, that not all worshippers of Cybele and Attis held the same hopes and beliefs simultaneously.

63 See n. 15 above.

64 Cf. *CCCA* 3.220, 310; 4.3, 21, 29, 35, ?40, 42, 69, 85, 147, ?169, 194, 203, 210, 229, 248, 259; 7.59, ?81, 85, 131, 182 (but not seemingly winged before the 2nd century C.E. as far as the *CCCA* series goes; a mourning Attis is widely found). Cf. Vermaseren, 'Religions' 502.

65 Cf. Colpe, 'Einführung' 7.

66 But cf. Malaise, *Conditions* 66–100, who rightly cautions against a too easy acceptance of this; however (a) epigraphic evidence favours the well-to-do and established who could afford inscriptions (cf. MacMullen, *Paganism* 7, 24f, 118); the impoverished new arrivals were unlikely to leave so much of a mark, except perhaps for graffiti; (b) he concedes that dating is often difficult, but for this question it is crucial; for early inscriptions the stock is small: from his prosopographical lists Malaise cites only one from the 3rd–2nd century B.C.E. (*Inventaire* p. 323), one from the (?) 2nd (320), both from Sicily; possibly three from the 1st (112 no. 2; 124 no. 35; 266 no. 27). Literary evidence may thus be more significant: e.g. Tiberius banished to Sardinia 4,000 *libertini* who were involved in Jewish and Egyptian rites (Tac., *Ann* 2.85); it is probable that this class and slaves were active in spreading the Egyptian cults earlier (cf. MacMullen, *Paganism* 114f; Malaise, *Conditions* 90f). Another factor in the cult of Isis is that 'Isis appealed especially to women, but . . . women rarely put their names and vows on stone. It is likely that the main part of her worshippers are hidden in silence' (MacMullen, ibid. 116).

67 *ILS* 3090; Nock in *CAH* 10, 491f n. 5. They were evidently also popular with the mistresses of Roman poets (Malaise, ibid. 86).

what was influential there is of prime importance for the question of the background to early Christianity.

Certainly, although it is true that *Eleusis*, that great centre of mysteries, enjoyed a great popularity in the second century, it did not lack prestige earlier in the Roman period. It was adorned with the Lesser Propylaea vowed to Demeter by the consul Appius Claudius Pulcher in 54 B.C.E. and constructed later by his two nephews[68]; in the same century Crinagoras of Mytilene echoed earlier poets in pronouncing benedictions on initiates in this life and hereafter[69], and Cicero bore eloquent testimony to the esteem in which he held these mysteries[70]. Augustus apparently set the precedent for later emperors by being initiated at Eleusis[71]. We have seen above how Claudius contemplated introducing the mysteries to Rome; why he did not or could not do so we are not told[72]. His successor, Nero, avoided Eleusis for fear of being refused initiation, and Mylonas argues that this too points to the high regard in which the sanctuary and its rites were held[73]. Finally, a first century inscription from the base of the statue of Tiberius Claudius Demostratus at Eleusis records that he was initiated ἀφ'ἑστίας[74].

Although we noted above the restraint exercised *vis-à-vis* the secret rites of *Dionysus* in Italy, a restraint that was all too natural in view of the historical precedents for that cult there[75], such inhibitions were not felt in the provinces. Nevertheless, in the first century B.C.E. and the first century C.E. the Dionysiac cults in the East do not seem to have shown the same vitality as those from Asia Minor and Egypt, or at least they have

---

68 Mylonas, *Eleusis* 156; cf. also *SEG* 21, 494; 22, 110.55; 111.1; 26, 121.21f; Prümm, *Handbuch* 222.

69 *Anth. Pal.* 11.42.3–6.

70 *De legibus* 2.14.36 – himself an initiate.

71 Dio C. 51.4.1; 54.9.10; Suet., *Augustus* 93; however this example was not followed by his immediate successors (much as Nero may have wanted to – see n. 73) until Hadrian (see above n. 2).

72 See above p. 100; also Picard, 'Patère'; there were evidently mysteries of Demeter on Italian soil in the 1st century (Statius, *Silvae* 4.8.50f).

73 Mylonas, *Eleusis* 155, citing Suet., *Nero* 34.4.

74 *SEG* 24, 220 (dating it to around 70 C.E.).
The Samothracian mysteries too seem to have kept up a steady flow of initiations throughout this period (cf. *SIG*³ 762; *IG* 12/8, 173, 188f, 195, 206–8, 210, 214f; *CIL* 3 Suppl., p. 2083 no. 12321; Lehmann-Fraser, *Samothrace* 2/1, 28–44, the last-named volume comments on the early appearance of Romans among the initiates and *epoptae* – pp. 28–44; cf. Börner, 'Untersuchungen' 3, 387ff (145ff); Cole, *Theoi* 5, 38, 90–100, also 145f (=Vidman, *Sylloge* 703).
The Andanian cult was also active in tthe 1st century B.C.E. (Burkert, *Religion* 417=ET 279, citing *IG* 5/1, 1390=*SIG*³ 736=Turchi, *Fontes* §182).

75 In addition to the scandal of 186 B.C.E. there is the hardly favourable fact that Spartacus' wife was a priestess and prophetess of the Dionysiac cult (Plut., *Crassus* 8.3); the dubious associations of the rites continue with scenes like those described in Tac., *Ann.* 11.31.

not left us much evidence of it[76]. Yet there is still sufficient evidence of the outward signs of the mysteries of Dionysus in these two centuries to make us reasonably confident of their continuing influence. Diodorus writes of the continued existence of Dionysiac rites in many Greek cities, and it is at least arguable that he refers to his own period, the first century B.C.E.[77] Nilsson refers to two inscriptions at Callatis in Thrace set up by a θίασος of Dionysus in the first century C.E.[78] and we may add another at Thessalonica in the same period or slightly earlier[79]. Towards the end of that century an inscription from Smyrna refers to two πατρομύσται[80], and Quandt cites a first century dedication from Seleucia ad Calycadnum in Cilicia to Dionysus and his initiates[81]. Finally, writing early in the second century, Plutarch reminds his wife that the 'mystic symbols' of the Dionysiac rites which they both know keep them from falling into Epicurean views of the fate of the dead[82].

Vidman maintains that we can only detect the first steps towards true mysteries of *Isis*, formed under Greek influence, in the late Hellenistic period[83]. Yet initiates and initiations are mentioned in some of the Isis aretalogies[84], and, while Nilsson may be correct in saying that these do not

---

76 Bruhl, *Liber* 268; this would apply too, perhaps to a lesser extent, to the public cult of Dionysus; there too inscriptions are not so numerous for this period.

77 Diod. S. 4.3.3; cf. Eliade, *History* 1, 372; Nilsson, *Mysteries* 7; also Dodds, *Greeks* 270f; terms like συνενθουσιάζειν and βακχεύειν make it clear that he means the traditional, orgiastic rites of Dionysus. For a slightly earlier period Henrichs, 'Glimpses' 9, points to the evidence of maenads in the 3rd and 2nd centuries B.C.E., and writes in 'Identities' 144 that the 'epigraphical evidence confirms that ritual maenadism existed in the Hellenistic period; that the maenads conducted initiations (*teletai*), went "to the mountain" (*eis oros*), handled sacred implements and were organized in *thiasoi* under the leadership of a chief maenad; and that the decline of ritual maenadism began in the second century C.E.'; yet he grants that it is hard to rule out the possibility that they were just imitating the language of maenadism in the classical period (156; cf. further his 'Maenadism' which lists – cf. 121 n. 2 – 'five Greek inscriptions of major importance' published between 1890 and 1968 'which illustrate the practice of maenadism in Greece, Asia Minor, and Italy from the third century B.C. to the second century A.D.', including *Inscr. Magn.* 215, which may include a genuine Delphic oracle of the 3rd century B.C.E. to the Magnesians copied by an initiate in the 2nd century C.E., about the importation of three maenads from Thebes, and two inscriptions from Miletus of 3rd–2nd centuries B.C.E. – 148–52).

78 *Mysteries* 50f; cf. *SEG* 24, 1026, 1034; 27, 384.

79 *SEG* 30, 622=*IG* 10, 259; cf. Daux, 'Inscriptions' 478ff.

80 *CIG* 2, 3173 (cf. Quandt, *De Baccho* 147); they seem to have belonged to an association of actors styling themselves 'initiates' of Dionysus. Cf. *SIG*³ 1115 – Pergamum, 1st century C.E.

81 Quandt, ibid. 234.

82 *Consol. ad uxorem* 10.611D; de Lacy and Einarson (LCL 7, 578) argue that this is written in his old age since he already has a granddaughter (1.608B).

83 *Isis* 126 and n. 7.

84 Those from Cyme (*IG* 12 Suppl. 98.22) and Ios (ibid. line 19) and Andros (*IG* 12/5, 739.11f) and, oldest of all, Maroneia (ca 100 B.C.E.: *SEG* 26, 821.23); cf. also *P. Oxy* 1380.111 (μύστις).

refer exclusively to Isis-mysteries, but refer to mysteries in general as part of the civilization and piety that Isis taught[85], it would be perverse if the goddess believed to have brought the mysteries of other gods had none of her own. Had she none hitherto, it is hard to believe that she would not soon have done so. It is, however, true that Vidman can only assign three Italian inscriptions relating to Isis mysteries or initiates to the first century[86]. Against that is to be set his admission that the total crop of inscriptions which certainly relate to mysteries is not all that great[87]; he only cites four more inscriptions for the mysteries of Isis and Sarapis during the following two centuries[88]. Outside Italy there is the important remark of Plutarch that the priestess Clea to whom he writes his *De Iside et Osiride* was consecrated in the rites of Osiris by her father and mother[89]. It is not clear whether this necessarily implies initiation, then or at a later stage: probably not, for dedication to Isis as an infant 'was only valid until the time of marriage and does not seem to have implied any consequent obligation or particular service for the goddess'[90]. However it is clear that Clea was still a devotee of Isis and perhaps even a priestess[91]. It is true that Plutarch's reference may take us over the threshold of the second century if this work is to be placed late in his life[92], but certainly at the time of writing there are mysteries and initiates of Isis[93]. It is also true that to describe the earlier cult of Isis as 'mysteries' as Greeks did from Herodotus onwards[94] is misleading: the secret ἱεροὶ λόγοι may not

---

85 The suggestion of D. Müller, *Ägypten* 49, that the reference is to something rather like medieval mystery-plays might apply to any Egyptian original of these aretalogies, but in them themselves we are dealing not with Egyptian religion *simpliciter* (which may have had no mysteries in the Greek sense), but with Hellenized Egyptian religion (and the aretalogies are in Greek), moreover where would 'initiates' and 'initiations' fit into such mystery-plays? But cf. Vidman, 'Isis' 141. More realistically Grandjean, *Aretalogie* 78f, argues that the links forged in the Maroneia aretalogy between Isis and Demeter would have been unlikely if Isis 'had not then had her own mysteries, ones which were sufficiently close to those of Eleusis to justify the presence of lines 35–41'; contrast, however, Bianchi, 'Iside' 18–23.

86 Vidman, *Sylloge* 390, 462, 587 (discussed in *Isis* 107, 126, 128).

87 *Isis* 131.

88 Ibid. chap. 7: *Sylloge* 295 (Roman period), 326 (2nd century), 586, 758.

89 §35.364E; it may be that this was not in Delphi itself where there is no evidence of Egyptian cults, but perhaps in nearby Tithorea (Dunand, *Culte* 2, 40). Cf. too *Inscr. Delos* 2149 in Vidman, *Sylloge* p. 70.

90 Dunand, ibid. 3, 170.

91 §2.351E; much of what is said in §§ 2f makes better sense if Clea is among οἱ τελούμενοι (351F), the ἱεραφόροι and ἱερόστολοι (352B), and claims to be an Ἰσιακή (352C); cf. Griffiths' ed. 253f; Le Corsu, *Isis* 11.

92 Cf. Jannoray, 'Inscriptions' 256ff; Griffiths, ibid. 16f.

93 §2.351F.

94 Hdt. 2.171; cf. Diod. S. 1.29.2–4, 96.4f; Erman, *Literature* 141, quotes a text referring to 'mysterious ceremonies in the temples' of Osiris.

have been secret so much as 'difficult to communicate' because of their complexity, and so closed to the simple faithful, either Greek or Egyptian[95]. And yet Apuleius' description of the priest of Isis producing strange books from the secret parts of the temple and explaining from them the necessary preliminaries to initiation shows how easily this Egyptian religion, with its antiquity and strange scripts, could lend itself to interpretation as a mystery, given the desire among Greeks to have it as such. In that case the priests of the Egyptian cults may be regarded as its earlier 'initiates', initiated into a 'book-mystery' by a process of instruction[96]. Furthermore the similarity of its myths to those of Eleusis (the search and mourning of the goddess, the restoration of the one sought) cannot but have aided this process. If the evidence is scanty then it may be that the numbers were indeed few; this perhaps reflects the admission to a status subordinate to the priests of only a small number of chosen individuals (and wealth may often have been an important criterion in the choice) to whom would be imparted some knowledge of the secret lore handed down by the priests and some share in the administration of the cult. It may be regarded as a further development from the formation of associations of worshippers in many parts of the Greek world from the third century B.C.E. onwards[97].

Mysteries of *Sabazius* are mentioned in an inscription from Pergamum in the second century B.C.E.[98]: votive hands, distinctive of this cult, have

---

95 Dunand, *Culte* 3, 246–8; cf. Erman, *Religion* 382f; Wagner, *Baptism* 94f; Moret, *Mystères* 3ff, distinguishes among the Egyptians between public mysteries, dramas like the medieval mystery-plays (6), which is presumably what Hdt. saw (2.171; see n. 94), and special rites whose meaning was only disclosed to priests and a few spectators, celebrated behind closed doors (18ff); Nagel, ' "Mysteries" ', argues that the rites which the likes of Hdt. saw were ones whose symbolism was not immediately evident to him, but they were not reserved for a circle of initiates; cf. further Bleeker, 'Initiation'; Ringgren, *Religionen* 28, 30; G. Widengren in *HO* 1.8.2, 66; also Junge, 'Isis'. Wessetzsky, 'Osirisglauben' 141, argues that the secret of Osiris' nature and fate runs as a unifying theme through the various stages of Egyptian religion.

96 So in a text of 162 C.E., *P. Tebt.* 2, 291.2.41ff, a priest shows his qualifications by reading from a hieratic text; cf. too *SEG* 26, 821.23 (Isis discovered holy γράμματα for initiates). Cf. Le Corsu, *Isis* 38f; Nock, 'Mysteries' 184 (797); Sauneron, *Priests* 41f, 47–50. Naturally this would not apply to the priesthood held only as an annual office, but only to the priesthood as a permanent, often hereditary, office. Similarly, perhaps, the Egyptian king might be regarded as a possessor of secret and mysterious knowledge: see the repeated 'he [the king] knows' of the text published by Assmann, *König* 21.11–30; the objects of knowledge include the secret utterances of the eastern souls at the appearance of the sun and of the crews of the latter's ship, the secret doors whence the sun emerges (see also Assmann's comments on this 'mystery' and knowledge on 53–7); compare here the language of the *Litany of Re*, ed. Piankoff 36= Hornung, *Buch* § §183–5; also Bleeker, 'Initiation' 57. Wessetzsky, 'Osirisglauben' 142, sees in Apuleius' account in *Met.* 11 a reference to the *Book of the Dead*, but it is hard to be so sure of this.

97 Listed in Dunand, *Culte* 3, 176ff.

98 Cf. Eisele in *ALGM* 4, 238, citing Fränkel, *Inschriften* 1, 248.54.

been found at Dangstetten on the Upper Rhine in a legionary camp occupied only in 15–9 B.C.E., in rubbish deposited at the camp at Vindonissa between 25 and 101 C.E., and at Pompeii[99].

G. Sanders, arguing from the occurrence of the term Ἀτταβοκαοί in
inscriptions from Pessinus, dates the existence of mysteries of *Attis* there
back to the first century C.E.[100] Gasparro, too, finds an 'obviously
mystery terminology' used of the cult of Cybele in the Hellenistic period,
in scholia on Pindar and Sophocles[101]; yet there is no sign that the rites
have changed their character since the fifth century; terms like τελεταί
and μυστήρια are used 'without implying a reference to a ritual complex
of the Eleusinian type, in other words to a religious institution tied to a
sanctuary and organised according to the initiatory-esoteric scheme'. More
significant are an inscription from Troezen of the second half of the third
century B.C.E. referring to τελεστῆρες[102] and a decree from Minoa of
Amorgus of the first century[103]. The latter shows an institutionalized form
of the rites emerging. Finally a Hellenistic bas-relief from Lebadeia shows
an initiate being presented to the Magna Mater[104].

When mysteries of *Mithras* first began anywhere is uncertain; Vermaseren, for example, dates this change from earlier forms of worship to the
last two centuries B.C.E.[105] In the period with which we are concerned
Mithras does not seem to have had much impact yet on Roman or Italian
society, apart perhaps from incidents like the visit of Tiridates mentioned
above; no Mithraic remains have been found at Pompeii, for instance[106].

---

99 Fellmann, 'Sabazios-Kult' 318, 323 (citing Blinkenberg, *Studien* 66ff), and 'Belege' (286: probably before 75 C.E.).

100 'Kybele' 287 (cf. Gasparro, *Soteriology* 70; see 71–4 for other evidence of the Imperial period); however if he is referring to the two listed in Hepding, *Attis* 79 nos 7f (=*OGIS* 2, 540f), it should be noted that these are dated by Hepding to the end of the 1st century (so Cosi, 'Salvatore' 47) or the beginning of the 2nd (204); these Ἀτταβοκαοί are 'fellow initiates in the mysteries of the goddess' and presumably these mysteries did not spring up the night before the dedication. Cf. Klauck, *Herrenmahl* 120 and n. 201.
Nock, *Conversion* 284, finds evidence of the mysteries of Cybele at Cyme in the 1st century C.E., but Vermaseren, *Cybele* 28, points out that Cybele is not named in the inscription in question, only Mandros, a male deity: cf. Gasparro, ibid. 73.

101 Ibid. 20–3, citing schol. on Pind., *Pyth.* 3.137*b* and 140 (Drachmann 2, 81) and on Soph., *Phil.* 391 (Papageorgius 362); cf. also *Anth. Pal.* 6.51; cf. also ibid. chap. 4.

102 *CCCA* 2, 479; cf. 469.

103 Ibid. 650.

104 Ibid. 432 (pl. 127); v. Graeve, 'Tempel' 342, also mentions evidence of mysteries of Atargatis at Thuria in Messenia at the end of the 1st century B.C.E. or the beginning of the 1st century C.E.

105 Vermaseren, *Mithras* 22; cf. Berner, *Initiationsriten* 32f; Colpe, 'Mithra-Verehrung' esp. 390–4. For Merkelbach, *Mithras* 75–7, the Mithras mysteries of the Empire were 'a new religion' and arose later than Christianity, only being widely attested from 140 C.E. onwards (146).

106 Vermaseren, *CIMRM* 1, no. 594 is the earliest Mithraic inscription from Rome (?reign of Trajan; 2, 31: ?102 C.E.).

The earliest certain reference to initiates or grades of initiates seems to be from the mid second century C.E. Vermaseren speculates that Mithraism may have been brought to Rome by the Cilician pirates captured by Pompey, basing this on Plutarch's statement that

> they . . . offered .strange sacrifices of their own at Olympus, and celebrated there certain secret rites (τελετάς τινας ἀπορρήτους), among which those of Mithras continue to the present time, having been first instituted by them[107].

Others would be disposed to regard this as an anachronism[108], but at least Plutarch knew of such mysteries by his time.

It may seem from all this that the evidence for the presence of mysteries in the first century C.E. is, after all, slender; was Schweitzer then right to play down their possible influence on early Christianity? There is one important factor to be borne in mind here: to the absence in the first century of literary sources like the writings of Apuleius and Lucian must be added the uneven distribution of epigraphic evidence during the period of the Roman Empire[109]. The rate at which Latin inscriptions were produced, at least those that have survived, during the reign of Vespasian is 5–6 times greater per year than that of the reign of Augustus and the inscriptions of the reign of Septimius Severus are 3.5 times more plentiful per year than those of the reign of Vespasian[110]. Using this evidence MacMullen shows, for instance, that, although the numbers of free-born devotees of Isis seem to have peaked at the end of the second century in the reign of Caracalla, the evidence, when represented as a proportion of the extant Latin inscriptions of the various periods, is uniformly distributed over the centuries[111]. In the light of this it could perhaps be argued that our evidence, as far as it can be dated, is surprisingly good, and that the mysteries do seem already to have established themselves in the first century; small though the quantity of evidence is, it is still as large a share of the extant inscriptions of that period as is necessary to show that they were influential then.

2.2. The Interpretation of the Mysteries

At the start of this chapter I mentioned that it was implicit in Schweitzer's dismissal of the possibility of influence on Paul from the side of the

---

107 *Pomp.* 24.5 (tr. Perrin); cf. Vermaseren, *Mithras* 28f; also Cumont, *Textes* 1, 244; Turcan, *Mithras* 1ff.
108 Cf. the scepticism of Gordon, 'Mithraism' 93 and 113 n. 10; also R. Beck in *ANRW* 2.17.4, 2073; Mellor, 'Archaeology' 131; Widengren, 'Reflections' (1980) 651f.

mystery-religions that the latter had not yet in the first century C.E. undergone a transformation and reinterpretation which would make them more suitable for a comparison with Paul's beliefs. Gasparro, however, reminds us how 'the Eleusinian ideology' endured more or less unchanged over many centuries, from the *Homeric Hymn to Demeter* to Cicero, *De legibus* 2.14.36. Here she is thinking more of the public claims of the cult, rather than the reinterpretations of it by individual adherents[1]. One could ask whether something so enduring and stable was likely to be swept aside easily in subsequent centuries; was it not likelier that the cult continued to make these same claims? Yet in part Schweitzer is correct: the mystery-religions were for instance used by the later Neoplatonist school to provide a witness to their own beliefs, and presumably it is some such reinterpretation that he had in mind. But in part this is also invalid as an argument, in that this process of reinterpretation was but a continuation of something that had already been going on for centuries. Indeed it may well be that the very nature of the mysteries and the way in which they presented their message laid them open to varying interpretations and reinterpretations, and not only laid them open to this, but demanded such a treatment. If Aristotle is correct in saying that 'those who are being initiated into the mysteries are to be expected not to learn anything but to suffer some change, to be put into a certain condition, i.e. to be fitted for some purpose'[2] then we should not expect any great degree of theological systematization common to all the initiates[3]; rather it was left to them to make what they would or could of the experience granted to them[4]. The mysteries of Isis, on the other hand, do seem to

---

109 Cf. MacMullen, *Paganism* 114–18.

110 See the graph in MacMullen, *Paganism* 115, quoting Mrozek, 'Répartition' 114; the same article shows that the number of inscriptions trebles from the 1st century C.E. to the 2nd (not quadruples: 481:1,552).

111 MacMullen, ibid. 116.

Notes on 2.2

1 *Soteriology* xxi.

2 Tr. Ross 87, quoting from Synesius, *Dio* 10.48a; text in Ross's ed. of selected frgs 84 (=Turchi, *Fontes* §87; frg. 15, Rose); there is something to be said for the Migne translation of the last clause, *posteaquam nempe idoneum se praebuerit*, though the text there prefers a pres. ptc. to an aor. (which may be better taken of an action preceding those expressed by the infinitives), and even more for that of Croissant, *Aristote* 142, 'evidently after having become fit to receive them'; cf. Boyancé, 'Mystères' 462.

3 Cf. Bianchi, 'Initiation' 162 (157); F. C. Grant, *Hellenism* 18; contrast Willoughby, *Regeneration* 28f.

4 Cf. Guthrie, *Greeks* 290; Nock, *Conversion* 268: 'Theology might be and was applied to them (the oriental mystery-religions): beliefs and hopes and interpretations clustered around them, but they were fluid and the interpretations came from outside, from Greek speculations and from the earlier habits of the Greek mind in religious things'; cf. 113, 135; also Cumont, *Lux*

have had some preliminary instruction for initiates, and this is in keeping with the character of Egyptian religion with its sacred texts. However the instruction seems largely to have been concerned with various practical matters connected with the initiation and not with its theological interpretation[5]. One possible exception may be Orphic circles in which theological teaching does seem to have played a prominent part and which were characterized by a considerable body of sacred literature[6].

For some the reinterpretation referred to above was not only desirable but also necessary; the primitive nature of many of the rites and their often horrendous myths called out for an interpretation which could find in these practices and stories a higher meaning, a more edifying doctrine of sublimer truths more congenial to the intellectual palates of the more sophisticated. Thus, for much the same reasons as those responsible for encouraging the allegorical interpretation of Homer, a higher meaning was also found in the mystery-religions[7]. Of course their interpreters could at the same time claim that their own teaching thus corresponded to revealed divine truths of considerable antiquity and prestige[8].

One type of interpretation of the mysteries which was possible was what Bianchi calls 'mysteriosophy', that is 'a special manner of seeing the cosmos, man and the history of the gods: a manner which implies a *sophia* or general mystic conception of life and of the cosmos, of its divine origins, of the perpetual and recurring cycle of changes which govern it, and also, and in particular, a doctrine of the soul as subject to an alternation of decay in this world subject to destiny (or to matter) and of final reintegration, or at least of final integration in the divine world — under the image of the concept of *soma-sema*, the body-tomb'[9].

242; Hepding, *Attis* 98; Schnackenburg, *Baptism* 143. This was also true of Egyptian religion according to Cumont, *Religions* 82f=*Religionen* 80f.

5 Cf. Apul., *Met.* 11.22: the priest indicates to Lucius from the hieratic texts (cf. Griffiths, *Isis-Book* 285) the preparations necessary for the rite, and he immediately arranges for 'those things' to be bought (§23). Boyancé, *Culte* 49, suggests that Eleusis may have had a similarly practical *logos*. The comparison might be drawn with the practical discussion that a clergyman today might enter into with an engaged couple before their marriage ceremony; rather than a discussion of the theology of marriage this is perhaps more often concerned with matters of who does what and who says what.

6 The first Greek religion to be so (Nilsson, 'Orphism' 628 (181); cf. Eur., *Hipp.* 954; Plato, *Resp.* 2.364E; also Crahay, 'Éléments' 337; Graf, *Eleusis* 8—22; Macchioro, *Orpheus* 125—9, and now, above all, West, *Poems*.

7 On Homer cf., e.g., Heraclitus, *Hom. All.* 1.1—3; cf. also Buffière, *Mythes* 49. Tate is concerned to emphasize that the apologetic concern to defend Homer and Hesiod was not the original cause of the rise of allegorical interpretation of their works (cf. 'Plato' 142—4, and 'History' 108f). Cf. also Pseudo-Demetrius, *De elocutione* 101: 'the mysteries are revealed in an allegorical form (ἐν ἀλληγορίαις) in order to inspire such shuddering and awe as are associated with darkness and night. Allegory also is not unlike darkness and night.'

8 Cf. Dörrie, 'Mysterien' 356f; Tate, 'Plato' 142, 144, and 'Beginnings' 215.

9 *Mysteries* 6; Bianchi asks just before this when the Eleusinian mysteries contemplated such a

As Bianchi's reference to the 'body-tomb' image indicates, one possible example of this sort of reinterpretation is what may in fact be a very early one, the reinterpretation in some Orphic circles of the Dionysus myths[10]. The originator or, more likely, originators of the 'Orphic movement' have, in the view of many at least, taken as the basis of their characteristic anthropology the myth of the rending of Dionysus Zagreus by the Titans, their subsequent destruction by the thunderbolt of Zeus, and the origin of the present human race from the resultant soot, although it may be more accurate to say that this account was only current in some Orphic circles[11]. Plato's reference to our 'ancient Titanic nature' is also thought

---

mysteriosophy, but in the light of my preceding argument I should prefer to ask when individual initiates saw their experiences in this way. It is unlikely that there would ever have been an 'official' mysteriosophic interpretation put out to all initiates. Cf. also his 'Initiation' 159f (154f); *History* 54f.

10 That he has this in mind is explicit in 'Initiation' 160 (155); how early this is is controversial – see below. Certainly it is a reinterpretation which is earlier than the Christian era, since Diodorus knows of the tradition of the rending of Dionysus (3.62.6–8) and comments 'with these stories the teachings agree which are set forth in the Orphic poems and are introduced into their rites, but it is not lawful to recount them in detail to the uninitiated' (tr. Oldfather). The 3rd century B.C.E. Gurob 'mystery-papyrus' (cf. Diels-Kranz, *Fragmente* §1 B 23, p. 20.7f) seems to refer to the playthings used by the Titans in their destruction of Dionysus (cf. Clem. Alex., *Prot.* 2.17.2–18.1, Stählin, quoting an Orphic hymn). It is, too, arguable that it was the myth of the rending of Dionysus that led to the identification of him with Osiris which is attested as early as Herodotus (2.42.2; 144.2); cf. Stambaugh, *Sarapis* 53f; West, *Poems* 141 (he holds that the Eudemian Theogony containing the myth was current in 4th century Athens – 174f). See also the brief survey in Burkert, *Religion* 443 =ET 298: 'One should therefore concede that the myth of the dismemberment of Dionysus is relatively old and well known among the Greeks but was consciously kept secret as a doctrine of mysteries'. On the phenomenon of 'Orphism' as an interpretation, perhaps a reform, of the mysteries, esp. the Eleusinian, cf. Burkert, ibid. 441=ET 296, and also 'Orphism' 7; Graf, *Eleusis*. (In my terms used here I have tried to accommodate the strictures of West, *Poems* 2f.)

11 Cf. *Orph. Fr.* 220 (p. 238); Brandon, *Man* 186f; Cumont, *Lux* 244f; Guthrie, *Orpheus* 82f, 120; Rohde, *Psyche* 340f, 353 n. 33; cf. also *Orph. Fr.* test. 210, and Festugière, 'Mystères' 366 n. 1 (2nd–3rd centuries C.E.?). Burkert, 'Orphism' 5, points to the primitive nature of this tradition as evidence for its antiquity. West, *Poems* 6, 140ff, argues that this was appropriately attributed to Orpheus in that this myth reflected a special type of initiation undergone by shamans; a tradition describing that myth was fittingly ascribed to Orpheus, the story of whom came from 'shamanistic' traditions in Thrace or further north. He locates this tradition within the Eudemian Theogony. Striking, however, is the positive evaluation of the Titans in *Orphic Hymn* 37 (in line 8 they sound more sinned against than sinning). On the ambivalence of the Titans' role in Greek religion in general cf. Alderink, *Creation* 67. Furthermore 'the Titans represent good as well as evil in the Orphic accounts'; *pace* Guthrie 'they were gods . . . and they remained divine' – p. 70. Different versions of the descent of the human race from the Titans existed and it would be rash to assume a unified myth in Orphic circles (any more than in Gnostic ones); cf. Rohde, ibid. 359f n. 77. Linforth argues strongly against assigning this *theologoumenon* a central place in Orphic beliefs, but without this undergirding there is the danger that 'the Orphics' and 'Orphic rites' lose any coherence over and above the fact that they appealed (for some reason) to the name of Orpheus; some may think that this is nearer the truth (cf. West, *Poems* 2f). Paus. 8.37.5 attributes the myth of the Titans as the cause of Dionysus' sufferings to Onomacritus (6th century B.C.E.) – cf. *Orph. Fr.* p. 56, test.

by many to reflect this anthropogonic myth[12]. The aversion in Orphic circles to the killing of animals and the eating of flesh can be seen as diametrically opposed to the tearing apart of live animals and the eating of raw flesh so characteristic of Dionysiac rites in their classical form[13], and

---

194; Dodds, *Greeks* 155f; Guthrie, *Orpheus* 107. (Contrast, Linforth, *Arts* 350–3, and the caution of Boulanger, 'Salut' 74 – but see Boyancé, 'Remarques' 166ff.)

12 *Leg.* 3.701BC (tr. Rice-Stambaugh, *Sources* 41); cf. Nilsson 'Orphism' 652f (202f), and *Geschichte* 1, 686; Plutarch, *De esu carnium* 1.996BC, having referred to Empedocles' view of reincarnation as a punishment 'for murder, the eating of animal flesh, and cannibalism', traces the doctrine further back to stories of the dismembering of Dionysus by the Titans and their punishment by the thunderbolt after tasting his blood; 'all this is a myth which in its inner meaning (ἠνιγμένος) has to do with rebirth' (=reincarnation; cf. *Is. et. Os.* 72.379F, tr. Cherniss-Helmbold, LCL); it is these 'Titans' in us, our irrational, disorderly, violent nature, which is δαιμονικόν, which are punished (in our reincarnations; cf. Dio Chrys., *Or.* 30.10 – though there is no mention of the sin of the Titans there being specifically their assault on Dionysus). It is important to distinguish here between an 'original sin' imitated by later generations and a 'hereditary sin' transmitted from one generation to another; cf. also *Is. et Os.* 35.364F–365A.

One cannot prove anything from so vague and deficient a text as *Orph. Fr.* 32c–e.5, but Zuntz's suggestion that this line was 'in all three cases inserted for the cases of victims of lightning stretches credulity and statistical probability rather far (*Persephone* 316, 322; tentatively supported by Garland, *Way* 99f; cf. Burkert, *Religion* 439; Rohde, *Psyche* 418 n. 54, 581 – the coincidence is even greater if the body of the one struck 'must be buried in the place where the lightning struck it'). However West, *Poems* 23, does suggest that there is here an allusion to the bolt of Zeus which despatched the Titans to their fate and which has despatched this soul to its life in a mortal body.

Also relevant here may be Olympiodorus' ascription to Plato's pupil Xenocrates of the view that our 'prison' was Titanic and εἰς Διόνυσον ἀποκορυφοῦται (*In Platonis Phaedonem* 84.22–85.3, Norvin=Xenocrates frg. 20, Heinze); Linforth, *Arts* 337: 'the exact sense . . . is obscure'; cf. Heinze, *Xenokrates* 152; Dillon, *Platonists* 27, gives its sense as 'under the command of Dionysos'; also Boyancé, 'Remarques' 167f. West, ibid. 21 n. 53, questions whether this phrase is part of the original quotation; he also helps our understanding of this reference greatly if his suggestion is correct, that 'Titanic'='analogous to the imprisonment of the Titans', and that Xenocrates regarded the myth of the Titans' imprisonment in Tartarus as an allegory of the imprisonment of bad *daimones* as souls in mortal bodies (21f). Note too the following reff. to the Titans and Dionysus in Olympiodorus, ibid. 85.4ff, Norvin; cf. also Alderink, *Creation* 69ff; Dodds, *Greeks* 156, 177 n. 134; Eliade, *History* 2, 189.

Boyancé, ibid. 168f, argues for Aristotle's knowledge of this story on the basis of a fragment published by Reinach, *Cultes* 5, 62ff=ed. Bussemaker 4, sect. 111.43 of *Problemata inedita* – p. 331; however there are grounds for doubting the authenticity of this material (*PRE* 2, 1046f; *OCD²* 115).

However on all this cf. Linforth, ibid. chap. 5, esp. 343f; on the other hand he considers the Pindar frg. in Plato, *Meno* 81B (frg. 127 Bowra=133 Snell) 'plausible evidence' for the story of the dismemberment (350; cf. 354f; Alderink, *Creation* 72f).

13 For the Orphic beliefs cf. Aristoph., *Ran.* 1032; Eur., *Hipp.* 952; Plato, *Leg.* 6.782CD (*Orph. Fr.* test. 90, 212f); usually these are said to result from their belief in metempsychosis (but then what is its mythical explanation?), but cf. Alderink, ibid. chap. 3.
For the Bacchic rites cf. Eur., *Ba.* 139–140; *TGF* 472.12 (Nauck²).
The opposition may have found its legendary deposit in the story, attributed to Aeschylus, of Orpheus' death at Dionysus' instigation (*Orph. Fr.* test. 113); cf. Detienne, *Dionysos* 91f; Guthrie, *Greeks* 315–18; Wili, 'Mysteries' 69. For a full discussion of this puzzling ref. cf. West, 'Tragica VI' 66–9: he sees the opposition as being rather between an Orpheus at home in certain Bacchic cults, and another Orpheus who appeared in Pythagorean poetry where Apollo was prominent. Aeschylus has fused these two elements together in his plot.

this lends support to that view which sees at least one strand of Orphic tradition as essentially a critique of the Dionysiac rites, perhaps arising within the context and setting of the Dionysiac tradition[14]. What is interesting is that both traditions, the rending and eating of animal flesh, and the vegetarianism of some Orphics, honour the same deity; the one, if anything, rivals the savage primal events, the other seems in horror to shy away from anything resembling them[15]. Even more curiously, but perhaps deliberately, the two seem to be combined in a fragment of Euripides'

---

14 Cf. Diod. S. 3.65.6 (Orpheus made changes in the orgiastic rites of Dionysus and so the rites established by Dionysus are also called Orphic); also, e.g., Angus, *Mystery-Religions* 47; Bianchi, 'Initiation' 172–4 (167–9); Guthrie, *Orpheus* 107–20, 199f., 218, and *Greeks* 317f (the Orphic reinterpretation in fact brings the Dionysiac religion in some respects nearer to its earlier Thracian form, a form suppressed by contemporary Greeks with their insistence on the gulf between mortal and immortal; cf. also House, 'Tongues' 137; Rohde, *Psyche* 336; yet note that in Guthrie's *Orpheus* 110f it is the Cretan Dionysus whom they reinterpret); Jeanmaire, *Dionysos* 404f; Macchioro, *Orpheus* 136; Nilsson, 'Orphism' 653 (203), and *Geschichte* 1, 686f; P. Wendland, *Kultur* 99; Willoughby, *Regeneration* 90f.

The Orphic and the Dionysiac are brought into close contact with one another in traditions like those of Diod. S. 3.62; Plut., *Alex.* 2.5f (about Olympias) and in the Derveni finds from the 4th century B.C.E. (cf. Burkert, 'Orpheus' 94, and 'Funde' 33), and in those from Olbia dating from the 5th century B.C.E. (cf. Burkert, 'Funde' 36f). The oldest ref. would be Hdt. 2.81 if we could be sure of the original text (cf. Linforth's argument for the shorter text in *Arts* 38–50, and Burkert's for the longer in *Lore* 127f). See further Alderink, *Creation* 79; West, *Poems* 24–6.

Yet cf. Linforth, ibid. 171, 188, 206–32; it must be granted that the Orphic critique would apply also to other Greek rites than those of Dionysus, although perhaps not so acutely. As Linforth observes (ibid. 189–97) Orpheus' name is also linked with the Eleusinian rites, but without any trace of criticism or opposition; cf. Eur., *Rhes.* 943; Graf, *Eleusis*, and also Alderink, *Creation* 95 and 115f n. 7. Eliade, *History* 2, 184, suggests that 'the sixth and fifth centuries saw in the mythical figure of Orpheus a founder of Mysteries who, though inspired by traditional initiations, proposed a more appropriate initiatory discipline, since it took into account the transmigration and immortality of the soul'.

The Orphic tradition was not alone in its criticism of the mysteries, especially the Dionysiac. cf. Heraclitus in Diels-Kranz, *Fragmente* §22 B 14; also B 15 on public rites.

15 Cf. Nilsson, 'Orphism' 654 (203f): 'The central rite of the Bacchic orgia . . . transmuted into a crime in the Orphic myth . . . . The Bacchants were thus put on a level with the Titans, the principle of evil'. Perhaps, even more than the relation of Jews and Christians to which Nilsson refers as an analogy, we may compare the way in which the Gnostics revalued the Old Testament and its God. Cf. also Guthrie, *Orpheus* 119, 133. According to Willoughby, *Regeneration* 101–4, the Orphics were initiated by partaking of raw flesh and then abstaining subsequently; there is little evidence for this, apart perhaps from the fragment quoted in the next note; moreover the eating of raw flesh was not a once and for all initiatory rite in the Dionysiac cult as far as we know. Detienne, *Dionysos* 72f, rightly argues against Dodds, *Greeks*, that in the myth Dionysus is not captured by pursuit and, above all, is not eaten raw; rather he is cooked, treated as a ritual sacrifice, though with the boiling and the roasting in the wrong order (cf. too Jeanmaire, *Dionysos* 387): 'the overall staging of the Orphic tale tends to show that alimentary blood sacrifice is, in the exemplary time of myth, a crime, an act of cannibalism, an allelophagic feast' (83); cf. Otto, *Dionysus* 131; West, *Poems* 160f (n. 70 lists ancient authors who thought the eating of raw flesh imitated the fate of Dionysus).

Cretans where the chorus has both celebrated the 'banquets of raw flesh' and shuns 'living food-stuffs'[16].

Implicit too in Bianchi's argument is that an Orphic reinterpretation of the Dionysiac myths lies behind the 'body-tomb' tradition and behind that Greek dualism so influential from Plato onwards[17]. It may be, however, that we should here heed some more cautious scholars who have urged that Plato seems implicitly to assign the 'body-tomb' image to another group than 'Orphics'[18]: what is more generally agreed is that the latter did liken the body to a prison[19], a view that is slightly different, but nevertheless hardly any more positive in its evaluation of the body than the 'body-tomb' image[20]. However it is doubtful how far Greek thinkers both before and after Plato were always conscious of any mythological basis for these images[21]. The Pythagoreans, for instance, who shared so many beliefs with 'Orphics', including abstention from meat and a dualism of body and soul[22], concentrated their attention on Apollo rather than

---

16 Eur., frg. 472.12, 18f (Nauck[2]); at least that is Nauck's rendering (followed by *Orph. Fr.* 210, p. 230); Porphyry (perhaps appropriately in a work *On Abstinence* – 4.19) inserts a μή in line 11, even at the cost of a syllable too many in the line. Cf. Guthrie, *Orpheus* 199; also Burkert, 'Orpheus' 104 n. 25; Festugière, 'Mystères' 373f. Alderink, *Creation* 112 n. 41, questions whether this ref. is to Orphic ritual. Suggestively Burkert sets this succession of omophagy and vegetarianism within a pattern whereby the initiates gain purity through an initiation that is often of a character that is in complete contrast to the character that is gained by it (*Religion* 447=ET 301; cf. Klauck, *Herrenmahl* 118; Professor West in a personal communication points out too that one 'can have ritual abstention at ordinary times combined with sacramental indulgence on the special prescribed occasion').

17 E.g. Plato, *Crat.* 400C; *Gorg.* 493A; *Phaedo* 62B, 65CD, 66B; *Phaedrus* 250C; Epict., *Diss.* 3.10.15; cf. Sen., *Ep.* 65.16f, 22; *Ep. Heraclitus* 5.3 (ed. Malherbe 194.28); Philo, *Leg. all.* 1.108; 3.42, 69f, 72; *Deus imm.* 111, 150; *Agric.* 25; *Ebr.* 101; *Migr. Abr.* 9, 16, 21; *Rer. div. her.* 68, 85, 273f; *Mut. nom.* 36, 173; *Som.* 1.139, 181; 2.237; *Quaest. in Gen.* 1.70, 93; 2.12, 69; 4.75, 78; cf. also Crahay, 'Éléments' 324–7; also n. 22 below (Philolaus).

Bianchi, 'L'orphisme' 190 (132), following Boulanger, 'Salut' 73, notes that in the Orphic conception the body is not so much evil in itself as the place where the soul is punished (cf. Alderink, ibid. 64f), and that the Titanic element is not limited to the human body; rather it is present in the soul itself (cf. Plato, *Resp.* 4.439ff). For Olympidorus too our bodies are Dionysiac (*In Platonis Phaedonem* 3.3, Norvin); cf. also de Vogel, '*Sōma-Sēma* Formula'; Alderink, ibid. 62, 108 n. 8 (but for an anthropology to be dualistic it is not necessary for it to regard the body as 'totally evil'; cf. 71 – there is an anthropoligical dualism in Orphism, though 'not a dualism which divides human beings into composite and contradictory elements').

18 Cf. Dodds, *Greeks* 148, 169f n. 87; also Alderink, ibid. 59–62; contrast Bianchi, ibid., 190 (132); Eliade, *History* 2, 186.

19 Plato, *Crat.* 400C; Dodds, ibid. 149; cf. Plato, *Phaedo* 62B, 82E; *Leg.* 9.854B; Pseudo-Plato, *Axiochus* 365E; Philolaus in Diels-Kranz, *Fragmente* §44 B 15.

20 Guthrie, *Greeks* 311 n. 3.

21 Cf. Nock, *Conversion* 248, of a later period: 'The mythology on which this was based had long ceased to matter.'

22 Philolaus in Diels-Kranz, *Fragmente* §44 B 14; Antiphanes frg. 135 (*FAC* 2, 226f); Aristophon frg. 9 (*FAC* 2, 524f); Clearchus frg. 38 (Wehrli); cf. West, *Poems* 7–15, on the possible contacts between the two traditions, and 18: 'by the middle of the fifth century [Orpheus] was established in Bacchic cults over a wide area'; also Burkert, *Religion* 445=ET 300, and 'Craft'.

Dionysus; they could be interpreted as often propounding, as it were, a demythologized version of Orphic beliefs[23], demythologized and perhaps then remythologized[24]. Pindar too seems to echo some aspects of Orphic teaching, but without reference to Dionysus[25], as does Empedocles slightly later[26].

This early reinterpretation of the myths in Orphic traditions is the more interesting in that it has a number of points of contact with the considerably later interpretations of the mysteries and their myths by the Gnostics and the Neoplatonists, points of contact that are by no means fortuitous; for Guthrie observes, over against Cumont and Nock, that in fact in the period of the later Republic and early Empire Orphic rites and initiations emerge, more or less for the first time, into the light, being now attested explicitly in contrast to the veil of silence drawn over them earlier[27]. Even if Nilsson's scepticism concerning his evidence is justified, on the grounds that it could simply stem from the literary tradition relative to the Orphic mysteries[28], this evidence does attest a knowledge of these rites, and consequently a possibility of interest in them and influence by them, at this period.

2.2.1. Some Orphic texts had much in common with later *Gnostic sects* — their complex theogonies, their dualism with an assertion of the divine element in human nature and a disparagement of the created world, the product of a primal fall or sin[1]. It is all the more surprising, then, to note

---

23 Cf. Guthrie, *Orpheus* 218f; *History* 1, 199; Dodds, *Greeks* 171 n. 95. It might not be too far-fetched to see the Derveni papyrus as a specimen of a similar reinterpretation of Orpheus (Burkert, 'Orpheus' 99, 104f, 109; 'Funde' 34; cf. West, *Poems* chap. 3). But n.b. Burkert, *Lore* 131f: there is no basis in the oldest sources for modern attempts to distinguish the doctrines of Orphism and Pythagoreanism.

24 Cf. Burkert, 'Orpheus' 113f.

25 E.g. *Olymp.* 2.56–83. Cf. Zuntz, *Persephone* 83–9, esp. 86 n. 3. However Guthrie, *History* 2, 253 n. 1, sees a ref. to the myth of Dionysus probably lying behind frg. 127, Bowra=frg. 133, Snell (from Plato, *Meno* 81B).

26 Cf., e.g., in Diels-Kranz, *Fragmente* §31 B 126; 128.8–10; 129 (quoted by Porphyry as a tribute to Pythagoras); 136f; 139; 148; cf. Zuntz, ibid. 183, 254, 256, 263–74; he also attributes the gold plates (cf. *Orph. Fr.* 32=Diels-Kranz, *Fragmente* §1 B 17–21) to Pythagorean rather than Orphic tradition, and one principal argument for this is the absence of any ref. to Dionysus.

27 Citing, e.g., Cic., *Nat. deorum* 3.23.58=*Orph. Fr.*, test. 94; Plut., *Caesar* 9.3.

28 *Geschichte* 2, 429.

Notes on 2.2.1

1 Cf. Bianchi, 'Initiation' 173f (168f); yet Orphism is for him a 'mysteriosophy' and not 'gnose', cf. also 'Problème' (1965) and 'Problème' (1967) 10f, 20–3; Rudolph, *Gnosis* 303=ET 286. But see also Drijvers, 'Ursprünge'. Bianchi here follows Wobbermin, *Religionsgeschichtliche Studien zur Frage der Beeinflussung des Urchristentums durch das antike Mysterienwesen*

the almost total absence of explicit references to Graeco-Roman deities, to the mystery-cults, and to Orphic traditions in the extant Gnostic literature[2]. Despite this, however, many have been quick to note and assert the affinities between Gnosticism and the mysteries. For Bousset Gnosticism came under the category of the syncretistic mystery-religions of late antiquity[3]. In this he was followed by Reitzenstein[4]; Jonas reversed the order, subsuming the mysteries under the heading of 'Gnosis'[5]. Pokorný, while recognizing the differences between the mysteries and Gnosis, yet emphasized the close connection between them; the one is a development from the other[6]. Others have been less certain and have stressed the difference between the mysteries and Gnosticism. Hegermann's criterion for distinguishing the two found favour with some: 'in the mysteries there are none who are saved by nature ($\phi \acute{v} \sigma \epsilon \iota \ \sigma \omega \zeta \acute{o} \mu \epsilon \nu o \iota$) and in Gnosticism there is no transformation (of persons)'[7]. So too Berner emphasized the consubstantiality of the Gnostic and his or her deity as an element in Gnosticism, but lacking in the mysteries[8]. In the mysteries one became what one was not before, in Gnosticism one became anew or realized afresh what one was originally and had in essence remained. But then we have to ask whether that makes the Orphic theologians, and any Orphic interpreters of the mysteries, Gnostics[9]. Or again, it could be argued that the pessimistic view of the material world in Gnosticism was very different in spirit, even completely opposed, to the vegetation-cults

---

(Berlin, 1896) 70ff, and Leisegang, *Gnosis* 185 (cf. 269, 292, 364f), but he fails to note the very different ways in which terms like 'life' and 'soul' are used in these different contexts (Drijvers 826–9). Yet the affinities between a man like Empedocles and his beliefs and later Gnostics and their views remain. Cf. Crahay, 'Éléments' 332. Burkert, 'Craft' 9, speaks of Gnosticism being the first to exploit the 'potentialities' for a religion of salvation inherent in the myth of the *Orpheotelestai*, 'especially when combined with the doctrine of transmigration and the ensuing ascetic life-style'. Suggestive too is Alderink's argument that for the Orphics 'it was the knowledge itself (of the distinction between body and soul) which brought about a change in the person' (89).

2 Cf. R. McL. Wilson, 'Gnosis' 454; also Bianchi, 'Initiation' 160 (155): he distinguishes mysteriosophy and 'gnose' in that the latter eliminates reff. to the mysteries.

3 *Hauptprobleme* 276f.

4 *Erlösungsmysterium* 93ff.

5 *Gnosis* 1, 80, qualified in *Religion* 38 ('some of the *mystery-religions* of late antiquity also belong to the gnostic circle, insofar as they allegorized their ritual and their original cult-myths in a spirit similar to the gnostic one').

6 *Epheserbrief* 82f, esp. 87.

7 *Vorstellung* 4; cf. Schenke, 'Hauptprobleme' 590–2.

8 *Initiationsriten* 126; he also compares H. -G. Gaffron, *Studien zum koptischen Philippusevangelium unter besonderer Berücksichtigung der Sakramente* (Diss. Bonn, 1969), esp. 91.

9 For Crahay, 'Éléments', esp. 329f, the Greeks, including the Orphics, lacked the characteristic theological dimension of the Gnostics' thinking which set the responsibility for evil at the door of a divine being.

underlying so many of the mysteries[10], and yet by the Imperial age the mystery-cults had developed in many ways from those origins. Problems of definition, above all, both of the terms 'Gnosticism' and 'Gnosis' and of the phenomena which they describe[11], bedevil any attempt to draw a hard and fast line between the mysteries and Gnosticism and Gnosis. In the end the small amount of evidence of any connection with the mysteries which the Gnostic sources evince may be the surest indication that they were different phenomena, or at least that they were either unconscious of their relationship or deliberately concealed it. Was it that the majority of Gnostic sects, at least to start with, came from circles, Jewish and Christian, which were implacably opposed to the mysteries? Particularly if those Gnostic groups claimed to be still part of either Judaism or Christianity, it would be felt that dependence on the mysteries or too great an affinity with them would discredit them.

The one major exception to this silence of the Gnostics about the mystery-religions is the teaching of the Naassenes described by Hippolytus in his *Refutation of All Heresies*[12]. These he accuses of borrowing their myth from the 'Mysteries ($\tau\epsilon\lambda\epsilon\tau\alpha\iota$) . . ., both the Barbarian and the Greek'; 'collecting together the hidden and ineffable mysteries ($\mu\nu\sigma\tau\dot\eta\rho\iota\alpha$) of the nations and speaking falsely of Christ' they 'lead astray those who have not seen the Gentiles' secret rites'[13]. They seek their answer to the question of the origin and nature of the soul in humankind from the

---

10 Cf. Gasparro, 'Interpretazioni' 393 ('a reversal of values and perspective'; despite that there is a certain continuity between the mysteries and Gnosticism); Bianchi, 'Initiation' 159 (154), distinguishes the true mysteries (concerned with the individual, initiatory, esoteric) from the fertility cults on which they were based (social, collective: 164 (159)).

11 Cf. Drijvers, 'Ursprünge'; also Yamauchi, *Gnosticism* 13–19, and §1.2.2.3 and n. 14 above.

12 *Ref.* 5.6.3–11.1; Drijvers, 'Quq', points to another possible example in the Edessan Quqites (cf. 121f, 126).
In the following reff. to the Naassene document I have tried to take into account Frickel's very thorough analysis of it in which he detects a number of layers superimposed one upon the other: (1) an allegorical comm. on a hymn to Attis, itself the product of the syncretistic theology of the world of the mysteries, in which all cults and myths were seen as expressions of the same wisdom and the work of the same divine power; in the comm. the phallus makes possible the identification of all the deities mentioned in the hymn and also represents the soul that gives life to all, the principle and goal of the strivings of all nature (esp. *Erlösung* 42, 46); this mystery-theology cannot really be called Gnosis (49). (2) This comm. was edited by the '*Anthropos*-Gnostic', a self-styled Christian who adopted a positive attitude towards the pagan cults and thus found the Attis-comm. a congenial basis for his work on the divine *Anthropos*. (3) Finally this is revised by the '*Pneuma*-Gnostic: whereas the '*Anthropos*-Gnostic' took a positive view of pagan cults, this editor is critical of all external cultic activities; true worship is only 'in spirit' and true knowledge belongs only to the Gnostics, born again of water and spirit. Frickel's account is convincing as long as the authors of this text were coherent and systematic in their thought; at least he shows the different strands of thought present in the document.

13 7.1 (tr. Legge); the implication of the last clause may be that Christians who knew the pagan origin of this myth would automatically shy away from it.

'mystic rites' (μυστικά)[14]: the rites (τελεταί) of the Assyrians (5.7.9) which
name the soul Adonis or Endymion (7.11) and the doctrine found also
in the story of the castration of Attis are examples of this; the last is seen
as the new *anthropos*, androgynous (7.13–15). Not only the Assyrian and
Phrygian mysteries but the Egyptian too teach of the blessed nature, for
this race are, after the Phrygians, the oldest race and 'were the first to
teach all other men after them the rites and orgies (τελεταί καὶ ὄργια) of
all the gods and their forms and activities'; they 'possess the holy and ven-
erable mysteries of Isis that must not be disclosed to the uninitiate'[15].
Osiris in their cults means water and the seven robes of Isis refer allegorically (ἀλληγοροῦντες) to the seven planets (7.23). Their mystery is the
phallus of Osiris which stands in all their temples (7.27), a phallus which
has also been adopted by the Greeks (7.28f), the unchanging source of
all being. The Greeks worship Hermes in this form, the guide of souls,
whom the Naassenes identify with Christ. Here allusion is made to the
great and unspeakable mystery of the Eleusinians, 'Rain, conceive' (ὕε,
κύε, 7.34). The Samothracian mysteries too, with their pair of ithy-
phallic statues, bear witness to the primal *anthropos* and the reborn
spiritual *anthropos* who is 'essentially the same in all respects with (that)
primal man'[16]. The Thracians and Phrygians call him Corybas (8.13) and
the latter call him Papas, 'the dead' (νέκυς) and 'god' (8.22–4), the
unfruitful (ἄκαρπος) and ·Aipolos and the fruitful one (πολύκαρπος) and
the green ear of wheat (8.31–9); the application of each of these names is
supported by often complex allegorical exegesis: 'Aipolos' may mean
'goatherd' to the ψυχικοί, but it means in fact that he is ἀείπολος because
he 'always everywhere turns all things round and changes them to his
own' (8.34–6, tr. Stead). The reference to the green ear of corn enables
the Naassenes to turn for further evidence of their views to the Eleusinian
mysteries where a harvested ear of corn is the great visionary (ἐποπτικός)
mystery shown in silence to the initiates (ἐποπτεύοντες). The Phrygians,
again, call the father of all Amygdalus (almond tree) and this is interpreted
allegorically of his begetting of his son (via the etymology of ἀμύσσω,
tear), whom they call a fluteplayer (9.1–4). They can support their views
too with their exegesis of Homer, which enables them to mock those not
initiated into the holy scriptures (8.1). Their exegesis is sprinkled with
allusions to other Greek writers and poets as well, Hippocrates (7.21)[17],

---

14 7.8 (tr. Legge; this is preferable to Stead's 'secret writings' in Foerster-Wilson, *Gnosis*).
15 7.20, 22 (tr. Stead); Frickel, *Erlösung* 75, finds here the hand of the Egyptian '*Anthropos-
   Gnostic*' at work, to whom the Egyptian mysteries were particularly suited for his brand of
   universalism rather than the Phrygian ones elsewhere so dominant in the document.
16 8.10 (tr. Stead).
17 Or is this a comparison drawn by Hippolytus, like the allusion to Thales in 9.13?

Empedocles (7.30), Anacreon (8.6), Heraclitus (8.42), and Parmenides (8.43), as well as numerous quotations of the Old and New Testaments[18]. In 9.8f we have the quotation of two short hymns to Attis: in the first he is identified with Adonis and Osiris, the 'heavenly crescent moon' to Greek wisdom; for the Samothracians he is Adamas, for the Haemonians Corybas, for the Phrygians Papas or the dead or god or the unfruitful, Aipolos or the green ear of corn or the flute-playing man ($\dot{\alpha}\nu\dot{\eta}\rho$ $\sigma\upsilon\rho\iota\kappa\tau\dot{\alpha}\varsigma$). Here the manifold identifications of the god, in a manner familiar to us from the Isis-aretalogies, are plain; here too is clearly the source of many of the non-biblical identifications of the primal *anthropos* found earlier in Hippolytus' account[19]. This 'Attis-aretalogy' was, it is claimed (9.7), one which one could hear declaimed in the theatre. The second, shorter hymn to many-formed ($\pi o\lambda\dot{\upsilon}\mu o\rho\phi o\varsigma$) Attis greets him with the cry of $\epsilon\dot{\upsilon}o\hat{\iota}$, $\epsilon\dot{\upsilon}\dot{\alpha}\nu$, as Pan and Bacchus and shepherd of the stars[20]. Those who are thus led to attend the mysteries of the Great Mother think that through the sacred actions ($\delta\rho\dot{\omega}\mu\epsilon\nu\alpha$) they will understand the whole mystery (9.10)[21]. Plain in all this account is the dominance of the Phrygian cult of Cybele and Attis in the thinking of Hippolytus' source[22]; despite their claims to be enlightened Christians its writer or writers evidently found meaning in the worship of that cult and arguably found as much inspiration in its tradition as they did in the holy writings of the Christians; their appeal to Christian traditions may even have been a later development in the history of this group, but the Jewish ingredient in this document is probably as early as its Gnostic content[23].

---

18 Cf. Bergman, 'Beiträge' 96: this section of the *Refutatio* is unusual in the number of quotations.

19 So Pokorný, *Epheserbrief* 52, 90, describes this hymn as the 'text' of the 'Naassene sermon'; cf. Bergman, ibid. 95: 'about half the document is constructed as a running commentary on the familiar Attis-Hymn'; also Berner, *Initiationsriten* 131; Schenke, *Gott* 59, and above all Frickel, *Erlösung*.

20 Cf. Vermaseren, *CCCA* 3, nos 362, 365=pls 218–20, 228: the Ostia *Attideum* is flanked by two figures of Pan; cf. also no. 366=pl. 228, a statue of Dionysus dedicated by a *tauroboliatus*, also *CCCA* 2, nos 180(?), 182, 309(?), 432. This at least shows a partial merging of the cults of the two deities, even if not an identification of the two deities themselves.

21 Schenke, *Gott* 59, maintains that the Naassenes were not 'Attisgläubiger'; Frickel, 'Naassener' 96f, suggests that they used a non-Gnostic comm. on the Attis-hymn which had originally been used by devotees of Attis (cf. further n. 12 above).

22 Cf. Jonas, *Gnosis* 1, 350; Bergman, 'Beiträge' 84–6, compares the worshippers of the snake in *Act. Phil.* 94ff, who are probably thought of as being in Ophiorhyme (which is Hierapolis – §108) and its surroundings; snakes figure more prominently in another Phrygian cult, that of Sabazius, but there are traces of them in the iconography of the Attis cult (cf. Vermaseren, *CCCA* 3, no. 446=pl. 282; 4, no. 45=pl. 19; 268=pl. 107; 7, no. 46, 90=pl. 60). It is commonly asserted that the Naassenes were so called from their partiality for the snake (from the Heb. *naḥaš*: cf., e.g., Rudolph, *Gnosis* 93; so Hipp. *Ref.* 5.6.3), but that leaves unexplained why they thus honoured the snake or which snake.

23 Cf. Reitzenstein-Schaeder, *Studien* 105f (cf. Reitzenstein, *Poimandres* 82); Schenke, *Gott*

But this document is an exception, and should not be taken as normative for all Gnosticism[24]. As I suggested above, it may be that the majority of Gnostic groups were too conscious of their roots in the Judaeo-Christian tradition, too keen to preserve those roots, however tangled they may have become, ever overtly to have acknowledged inspiration from the mysteries, which were regarded as the rivals of that tradition. Nor should this material which Hippolytus preserves be regarded as a typical interpretation of the cult of one of the mystery-deities by one of its devotees. After all it is expressly acknowledged that the person celebrating Attis in the hymn quoted in Hipp., *Ref.* 5.9.8 'declares the great mysteries without knowing what he says'[25]. From the Gnostic point of view he would be one of the $\psi\upsilon\chi\iota\kappa o\acute{\iota}$ mentioned in 8.34. It is rather that a different viewpoint is introduced to the cultic traditions from the outside, and the latter are then reinterpreted in the light of that alien perspective[26].

2.2.2. The direct line of continuity between the Orphic tradition and the other type of later reinterpretation of the mysteries which we are considering, that of *Neoplatonism*, is made plain by Nilsson's description of the Orphic literature as the Bible of the Neoplatonists[1]. Whereas one would be hard-pressed to make out a case for direct and conscious influence either of Orphism or of the mysteries upon Gnosticism in general, the debt, or at least the alleged debt, to both is openly, even aggressively at times,

---

57, 59; it does not follow, however, from their use of OT citations that they were Jews, any more than their use of Eleusinian traditions means that they were Greeks or initiates of Eleusis; can we say more than that Jews *may* have contributed to this document? Their contribution is anyway likelier to be at a later stage than the comm. on the Attis-hymn which Frickel, *Erlösung* (see n. 12 above), sees as the first stage of this Naassene text.

24 Although Hipp. states that the Naassenes were numerous and split into many groups (*Ref.* 5.6.4).

25 Tr. Stead in Foerster-Wilson, *Gnosis* 1, 279; cf. Schenke, *Gott* 59; also Berner, *Initiationsriten* 140–4; Pokorný, *Epheserbrief* 90; Reitzenstein-Schaeder, *Studien* 106. However Frickel, *Erlösung* 229, assigns the last words, 'without knowing what he says', to the latest stage of redaction of the document, that of the '*Pneuma*-Gnostic' (see n. 12 above).

This is an argument against the view of Jonas, *Gnosis* 1, 350, that this Naassene teaching is 'a valuable example of how the mysteries, originally based on ancient nature-myths, . . . in late antiquity . . . came under Gnostic influence, and perhaps even took on a completely Gnostic character and correspondingly reinterpreted their respective older cult-myths'.

26 Cf. Schenke, *Gott* 59; also Burkert, *Homo* 278.

Notes on 2.2.2

(The numbering of Julian's speeches used here is that of LCL.)

1 *Mysteries* 133; cf. Lloyd, 'Neoplatonists' 280; Wallis, *Neoplatonism* 3; P. Wendland, *Kultur* 162. This was more obviously true of later Neoplatonists like Iamblichus than it was of Plotinus; cf. Armstrong, 'Plotinus' 206.

asserted in Neoplatonist writings[2]. In particular one can point to works like the treatise *On the Gods and the Universe*, Julian's 'hymns' to Helios and even more to the Great Mother, and to writings of Porphyry which Julian knows of, but has not read, on the same subject as the latter hymn (rather it is Iamblichus whose ideas he follows); it seems likely that the reference is to works like that *On Images*[3]. Of Porphyry Cumont comments that even in his later years he 'continued to interpret the representations of the gods, the mythological legends, the rites of the sacred ceremonies, seeking a deeper meaning in their symbolism'[4]. As evidence of this he cites Augustine's reference to Porphyry's *On the Return of the Soul* in *Civ. D.* 10.32: there he finds Porphyry bearing witness that 'no one system of thought has yet embraced a doctrine that embodies a universal path to the liberation of the soul, no, neither the truest of philosophies, nor the moral ideas and practices of the Indians, nor the initiation of the Chaldaeans (*inductio Chaldaeorum*) . . . ', despite what Augustine deems his devoted study of the subject: he found this path 'neither in what he had learned from the Indians nor in what he had learned from the Chaldaeans' and, Augustine adds, 'he took over from the Chaldaeans the divine oracles to which he constantly refers'[5]. Here the Neoplatonists followed the example of the Neopythagorean Numenius of Apamea whom they claimed as a Platonist[6].

Particularly important for us here is the treatise which has already been mentioned, by Sallust *On the Gods and the Universe*, important, that is,

---

2 Cf. Boyancé, *Culte* 164: 'for the Neoplatonists the mysteries represent in truth the crown of the spiritual life'. It is hard to avoid the conclusion that the Neoplatonists felt themselves to be part of the pagan tradition in a way in which most Gnostics did not; both may have used similar philosophical traditions, but these were not felt to be inimical by the Jewish and Christian traditions (cf. Philo of Alexandria), whereas the mysteries were.

3 *Or.* 5.161C (admiration for Iamblichus: 4.146A, 150D, 157D; admiration for Iamblichus' pupil Maximus: *Ep.* 12); Eus., *Praep. Ev.* 3.11.12; cf. Hepding, *Attis* 47; also Bidez, *Vie* 27; Turcan, *Mithras* 106.

4 *Lux* 366; he sees in Plotinus, however, a certain coolness towards the cults and a desire for independence of them (359f); cf. Porph., *Vit. Plot.* 10.34–8; as for allegorical interpretation Wallis, *Neoplatonism* 93, refers to 'his casual use of Greek mythology to illustrate his metaphysics as required' (examples on 135).

5 Tr. Wiesen in LCL; cf. Des Places, *Oracles* 18–24; these oracles 'became a holy book to later Neoplatonism' (Nock, *Conversion* 111; cf. 158), cf. Marinus, *Vita Procli* 28; Cumont, *Lux* 361–3; Wallis, ibid. 3, 105–7; P. Wendland, *Kultur* 162.

6 Cf. frgs 1*a*, Des Places=9*a*, Leemans; 55, Des Places=39, Leemans. Proclus describes him as 'stitching together the words of Plato with those of the astrologers (γενεθλιαλογικά), and these with those concerned with secret rites (τελεστικά)' (*In Platonis Rem Rublicam* 2, 129.12f, Kroll=100.18–20, Leemans (cf. 35)=frg. 35, Des Places); Turcan, *Mithras* 63, argues that it is the Mithraic traditions that Proclus has particularly in mind here. Porphyry in particular was influenced, at least in some respects, by Numenius: Proclus, *In Platonis Tim.* 1, 77.2f, Diehl=87.17–19, Leemans=frg. 37, Des Places (cf. pp. 26–8 of his ed.); cf. further Festugière, *Révélation* 1, 19–21.

in view of the use made of it by Lohse (see §2.3 below)[7]. It is clear from the start that the author makes certain assumptions about the nature of the gods which are going to colour strongly his handling of the myths of the mystery-religions: the gods are unchangeable (§1; cf. §14) and they do not come into being (§2); the implications for gods who die (and rise) and for stories of their births are plain[8]. Why then the myths told about them? They are to be respected as having divine authority; they 'represent (μιμοῦνται) the gods in respect of that which is speakable and that which is unspeakable, of that which is obscure and that which is manifest, of that which is clear and that which is hidden, and represent the goodness of the gods'; the universe itself can be called a myth, revealing material things and keeping concealed souls and intellects. The apparently unedifying content of many myths by its very nature provokes us to look beyond for the real meaning of the myths (§3)[9]. He then divides the myths into various classes, theological, physical, 'psychical', material, and blended myths. He takes the myth of Kronos swallowing his children and interprets it (a) theologically of the god's nature as mind 'directed towards itself'[10], (b) physically of time (χρόνος) swallowing its parts, and (c) 'psychically' of the thoughts of the soul remaining in it. The reference to 'some' holding the physical interpretation (b) underlines that he was here drawing on a line of earlier exegetes. The fourth type, the material, is typical of the Egyptians and it is a type which he himself disparages: here material things are deified, earth as Isis, moisture as Osiris[11], heat as Typhon, water as Kronos, the fruits of the soil as Adonis, wine as Dionysus. An example of the fifth type, the blended myth, is the judgement of Paris: it is blended in that it combines different elements, theological (the banquet signifying the togetherness of the gods), physical (the golden apple signifying the cosmos), and 'psychical' (the soul living by sense-perception only sees beauty, i.e. Aphrodite, and none of the other powers in the universe). Such blended myths can also be illustrated from that of Attis[12]. Despite the apparent vicissitudes of the mother of the gods and

---

7 Probably the 'Saloustios' of this treatise is the Sallust to whom Jul., *Or.* 4 is dedicated and whose death is the subject of *Or.* 8: Nock, *Sallustius* ci; Bowersock, *Julian* 125, argues that this was most likely Secundus Salutius, praetorian prefect of the East; so too Rochefort's ed. of Sallust xiv ff; Des Places' introduction to Iamb., *Myst.* 22; Athanassiadi-Fowden, *Julian* 154.

8 Cf. Nock, ibid. xliii.

9 Cf. Jul., *Or.* 5.170AB; 7.216CD, 222CD; Pausanias speaks of the myths being in the form of riddles (8.8.3), as does Plotinus (*Enn.* 3.6. 19; 5.1.7, cf. Armstrong, 'Plotinus' 204).

10 Julian (*Or.* 5.165C) also calls Attis νοερός.

11 Cf. Hipp., *Ref.* 5.7.23.

12 A fuller and more elaborate version of this account, different in some respects, is to be found in Jul., *Or.* 5 (*Hymn to the Mother of the Gods*), which Sallust perhaps used; cf. Nock, *Sallustius* lii; Rochefort, *Saloustios* xvii; Athanassiadi-Fowden, *Julian* 142 n. 79, 155.

Attis[13] this myth in fact tells of eternal and unchanging realities, realities which are imitated in the festival of Attis: Attis is creator of transitory things or, more precisely, in Julian's words he is the substance (οὐσία) of generative and creative Mind'[14], and is to be found by the Milky Way (ὁ Γαλαξίας κύκλος = the river Gallus), the uppermost boundary of matter that is liable to change[15]. We are, like him, 'fallen from heaven'[16]. He loves a nymph, and nymphs, because of their association with that which flows, are set over coming into being (γενέσεως ἔφοροι). He leaves his genitals with her and rejoins the gods (his divine status is symbolized by his cap) so that 'the process of coming into being should stop and that what was worse should not sink to the worst' (symbolized in the rites by the cutting of the pine-tree and fasting)[17]. His worshippers celebrate his restoration to divine status, being fed on milk as though being reborn (ὥσπερ ἀναγεννωμένων) and the following rejoicings and garlandings are 'as it were a new ascent to the gods'. He finds a confirmation of this symbolism in the setting of this festival near the time of the spring equinox[18], while the rape of Kore is set near the autumn equinox 'and this signifies the descent of souls' (§4, tr. Nock). Again the text reveals that the interpretations offered are by no means universally accepted: the Egyptians, we saw, were taken to task for their 'material' interpretations, and §3 makes it clear that the right understanding of myths is for philosophers[19]. Indeed the treatise starts by saying that those wishing to learn about the gods must have been well educated from childhood, and must not have been reared among foolish opinions, and must be 'good and intelligent by nature' (§1, tr. Nock).

So it would, I suggest, be as foolish to regard the Neoplatonists as disclosing the true doctrine which had been inculcated in the mysteries by their hierophants down the centuries as it would be to regard the Naassenes as propounding an interpretation widely recognized outside their own

---

13 Julian says that her love for Attis was 'passionless' (ἀπαθής), 166B, and that Attis' madness is 'so-called', 167D; cf. esp. 171D: 'the myth says that he is led upwards as though from our earth, and again resumes his ancient sceptre and dominion: not that he ever lost it, or ever loses it now, but the myth says that he lost it on account of his union with that which is subject to passion and change' (tr. Wright).

14 *Or.* 5.161C, tr. Wright; cf. 165B, 175A.

15 A view found in Jul., *Or.* 5.165C, 171A (contrast 167D), but not elsewhere: Nock, *Sallustius* liii and n. 63.

16 Nock traces the pedigree of this view of human nature back to Empedocles and the gold plates (see §2.2 n. 25 above): ibid. liii–liv; cf. also Jul., *Or.* 5.169BC.

17 For Plotinus the eunuchs of the Great Mother symbolized the barrenness of matter (*Enn.* 3.6. 19).

18 Cf. Jul., *Or.* 5.168C ff.

19 Cf. Jul., *Or.* 5.172D.

ranks[20]. The Neoplatonists read Neoplatonist doctrines into the mysteries and we should not expect any but Neoplatonists or their adherents to find them there. At the conclusion of his study of *Mithras Platonicus* R. Turcan observes that 'the dynamic and militant optimism animating the followers of Mithras, their conception of the primordial sacrifice as an incarnation of the soldiers of Good begotten for salvation would be fairly far removed from the theories of a Porphyry concerning the fall of souls into the world of bodies'. What optimism there was in Neoplatonism stemmed from Plato's *Timaeus*, not the religion of Mithras[21]. Cumont, too, comments how different the Neoplatonist interpretation of Isis was from the popular conception of her as queen of the underworld, a view repugnant to the Platonist tradition which sought to separate divinity from the earth and matter[22]. This illustrates well the point which he had made earlier, that the 'good hope' offered by the mysteries varied in content according to the personal convictions of their participants and each philosopher interpreted it according to his own system[23]. An Isis who was queen of the underworld would not have fitted into the Neoplatonist scheme.

Thus in these two cases, the Gnostic and the Neoplatonist reinterpretations of the mystery-religions, we are dealing with interpretations carried out with the help of certain prevailing systems of belief and thought which were in fashion at particular periods in the ancient world. It should be clear that they would not necessarily have suggested themselves at all times to the devotees of the mysteries, particularly when such ways of thought were not fashionable or had not even emerged. Even when they were in fashion it is certainly not the case that all would have interpreted the mysteries in such ways; such sophistications were for the educated *élite* of society. This may seem all too obvious, but it is perhaps necessary to stress it in the light of a work like J. Godwin's recent study, *Mystery Religions in the Ancient World*[24], an attractively presented work appealing to the interested non-specialist. He sees everywhere the myths of the soul; the mysteries would not have been taken so seriously, he argues, had

---

20 Cf. Gasparro, *Soteriology* 61: 'We cannot . . . apply to the religious reality of the cult of Cybele the Neoplatonic interpretation of Julian' – nor *a fortiori* that of Sallust who depends on him 61f).

21 *Mithras* 130; cf. 68–89, and 'Salut' 183f (also Merkelbach in n. 25 below).

22 *Lux* 267; cf. Plut., *Is. et Os.* 78.382EF on Osiris (§2.2.3 below) and *Fac. lun.* 27.942E, where Kore is Hades' boundary (=the moon).

23 *Lux* 242; cf. *Religions* 12.

24 This work is marred by some odd features: it begs far too many questions, for instance, to say that Gnosticism arose in·Palestine in the 1st century B.C.E. (84), and confidence is further shaken when Basilides is put in the early 1st century C.E. (86); in so brief an account one could surely have omitted to mention the surmise that Paul was an Orphic initiate (144).

they been but referring to fertility rites (as if that were the only alternative to a myth of the soul; cf. §5.1); rather in the Eleusinian rites Persephone represents the soul alternately descending at birth for 'half a year'
in the 'underworld' of bodily existence and returning at death to its true
home (52). That this is a self-evident interpretation becomes rather less
plausible when he then also invites us to 'consider the tale of the Sleeping
Beauty . . . as a myth of the soul's descent and rebirth' (64); to whom is
it 'self-evident'? In this approach I fear that Godwin has not adequately
respected the distance between himself and the ancient sources, a respect
which is a prime requisite for historical study; he has not allowed the pre-
Neoplatonists to remain in their world, but has made them Neoplatonists
before their time, since it is only the Neoplatonist interpretation of the
mysteries which is congenial to his 'Perennial Philosophy'[25].

2.2.3. A more satisfactory way of proceeding would be to turn to interpreters of the mysteries from as near in time to the period of the New
Testament as we can get, to see what possibilities of interpretation presented themselves to them. The best example that we have, from a slightly
later period, is the work of *Plutarch of Chaeronea* (ca. 45–120+ C.E.).
The work of his which is of greatest concern to us here, his treatise *On
Isis and Osiris*, is probably among his latest writings (cf. §2.1), but even
so very likely reflects traditions of Platonist exegesis going well back into
the first century. By the time of writing it he was a priest at Delphi near
his native Chaeronea (§68.378D) and he wrote it to the priestess Clea,
also at Delphi, who was herself consecrated in the rites of Osiris (§35.
364E) and so was presumably a possible source of Plutarch's information
about them. His teacher Ammonius was an Egyptian[1] and it is to be
expected that Plutarch would have learnt much of his Platonizing exegesis
of the Egyptian rites from him, as well as perhaps his knowledge of Per-

---

25 Cf. *Mystery Religions* 8, 165: 'The Neoplatonists used the names of Greek and Roman gods to
    expound the complexities of their hierarchical scheme of "Orphic" theology, but the scheme
    must have existed long before, expressed in symbols of another sort. The beings to which they
    refer as "Jupiter", "Attis", etc., are not necessarily the same as the ones commonly worshipped
    under those names: yet these philosophers alone give us insight into an esoteric theology, with-
    out which we would be little better off than the simple syncretists.' (Compare his difficulties
    with Mithraism on 99. But contrast Merkelbach, *Weihegrade*, where Mithraism is treated
    throughout as a far more unified cult throughout its existence, having been created under the
    influence of Platonic ideas.)

Notes on 2.2.3
1 Eunapius, *Lives* 454.

sian religion[2]. Thus there is a strong possibility that some of the ways of interpreting the myths of Isis and Osiris were learnt by him in his earlier days under Ammonius in Athens, perhaps in the reign of Nero[3].

Plutarch's account in his *On Isis and Osiris* anticipates much of what we have already seen in the Neoplatonic treatise *On the Gods and the Universe* (cf. §2.2.2). The 'philosophy' of the Egyptians is veiled in myths and in words that do not hint at the truth (§9.354C), as for instance the story of the sun rising from the lotus refers in riddling form (αἰνιττόμενοι) to the kindling of the sun from the waters (§11.355C)[4]. Thus it would be a great mistake to understand the myths as factual descriptions of events; Clea must 'not think that any of these things is said to have actually happened so or to have been enacted so' (§11.355B)[5]. Elsewhere he describes the stories of transformations of Apollo and Dionysus as 'riddles and mythical tales'; these speak in a riddling way (αἰνίττονται) of the latter's sufferings and transformations as a rending and a dismemberment; this is all to be combined in some way with the assertion that the god is indes-

---

2 Cf. Dillon, *Platonists* 191, 203; however he also had brief first-hand experience of Egypt: *Quaest. conv.* 5.5.1.678C; cf. Ziegler in *PRE* 21, 654.
   We have already noted (§2.1) that Plutarch had experience of the Dionysiac mysteries (*Consol. ad uxorem* 10.611D); Griffiths leaves it open whether he was also an initiate of the Egyptian cult (Comm. 96–8).

3 *Ei Delph.* 1.385A; 7.387F; cf. Dillon, *Platonists* 185.

4 Even the garments of the Isiacs hint at truths about the gods (§3.352B); cf. also *Ei Delph.* 1.384F–385A; 2.385CD. Elsewhere Plutarch speaks disparagingly of at least some allegorical interpretations (*Aud. poet.* 4.19EF); R. P. C. Hanson's statement that Plutarch accepts ὑπόνοιαι but rejects allegory does not square with this passage where the two are identified (*Allegory* 61).
   For the use of αἰνίττεσθαι cf. Plato, *Resp.* 1.332B; *Lys.* 214D; *Charm.* 162A; *Theaet.* 152C, 194C (cf. Hersman, *Studies* 8); used of the mysteries in *Apol.* 21B; *Phaedo* 69C (cf. Tate, 'Plato' 149f).

5 Tr. Griffiths; cf. §20.358E (the tales are *prima facie* morally objectionable); §58.374E ('We must not treat the myths as wholly factual accounts (οὐχ ὡς λόγοις πάμπαν οὔσω), but take what is fitting in each episode according to the principle of likeness (to truth)', tr. Griffiths). In particular he rejects as ridiculous that interpretation whch speaks of seasonal changes as births and deaths of gods (§70.379B).
   In the light of such statements what does Griffiths mean when he says (Comm. 101) that 'it seems that Plutarch believed in the historicity of most of the Osiris-myth . . .'? (the stress on οὔτω in §11.355B on p. 289 does not really help him out of this difficulty; cf. also Betz, *Writings* 47; contrast R. P. C. Hanson, *Allegory* 61.) Mr. D. A. Russell mentioned to me privately his suspicion that οὔτω is in fact to be taken with λέγεσθαι and is displaced to avoid hiatus, as often; this would give a sense of 'don't think that any of these stories is so told because it happened . . .'; even if that is not the case and the sense is that 'none of these stories is told (so) because it happened so or was done so' it is hard to make the text fit Griffiths' interpretation.) Hersman, *Studies* 30, whom Griffiths quotes, merely says that an allegorical meaning does not necessarily rule out a non-fictitious reference to living persons (n. b. 33f, 39). What is morally objectionable applied to gods (§20.358E) is surely equally objectionable in good *daimones* destined to be promoted to gods (but cf. Hersman, ibid. 31, 39: 'a true history of the lives of demons').

tructible (ἄφθαρτος) and eternal in nature[6]. He does not here resolve the difficulty by saying that Apollo and Dionysus are, or were, *daimones* as opposed to gods, and so liable to change[7], but they are compared in this respect with the Egyptian gods or *daimones* in *Is et Os.* 25.360F[8]. Nor does he anywhere tell us expressly what it was that happened if it did not happen as narrated, nor why anything at all had to have happened if the stories were merely meant to point to certain philosophical, psychological, physical or theological truths. But it seems as if not only the stories but those primal events of which they tell, however inadequately, have this quality of pointing in riddling form to truths beyond themselves[9]. The stories are set down in this form as images of reality which turn our thought to other things as the rainbow is a reflection of the sun in a cloud (*Is. et Os.* 20.358F−359A)[10]. Thus the exercise of reason and discernment is called for in the investigation of 'what is displayed and done (τὰ δεικνύμενα καὶ δρώμενα)' in the rites of Isis and Osiris (§3.352C)[11], just as the issuing of ambiguous oracles is meant to spur us on to reasoned argument[12].

This treatise is filled with a whole plethora of different interpretations of the various myths of Isis and Osiris, so that it is often difficult to be sure what Plutarch himself accepts or rejects. The first thing to note is that all the various categories of myths listed in *On the Gods and the Universe* seem to have been known to him. The number of different allegorical interpretations is in itself a witness to the extent of the earlier

---

6 *Ei Delph.* 9.388E−389A; this does not seem to assert the unchangeability of the gods as clearly as Sallust's *De diis et mundo* 1f (see §2.2.2 above), but rather leaves room for certain mutations, as indeed would be necessary if *daimones* can become gods (see below n. 18; also Dillon, *Platonists* 223f); however cf. also Ammonius' remarks, e.g. in *Ei Delph.* 20.393AB; 21.393E−394A; *Def. orac.* 20.420E.

7 Cf. *Def. orac.* 12−13.416C−E.

8 As would be only natural if Dionysus and Osiris are identical (*Is. et Os.* 35.364E); moreover it is the role of *daimones* to be responsible for the secret rites of the mysteries (*Def. orac.* 13.417A; cf. *Fac. lun.* 30.944D). That Dionysus was a *daimōn* is implied in *Def. orac.* 21.421C; *Is. et Os.* 27.361E.

9 To this extent his position is different to (and less consistent than?) that of Sallust, *De diis et mundo* 4; passages like *Is. et Os.* 2.351E−352A may point to a more thorough-going allegorizing of the legends (Typhon scattering the sacred *logos*); cf. §49.371AB.

10 The mysteries, as opposed to other religious rites, give the best impression of, and insight into, the truth concerning the *daimones* (*Def. orac.* 14.417BC).

11 Cf. §68.378AB; also *Amat.* 17.762A. Plutarch has a great abhorrence of superstition (δεισιδαιμονία) which he considers worse than atheism: *Is. et Os.* 11.355D; cf. also *Superst.*; the Egyptian rites are free of this as well as of irrationality and the 'fabulous' (μυθῶδες, §8.354E, tr. Griffiths). Yet he recognizes that this riddling form of communication adopted in religious myths of all sorts does run the risk of leading people astray, either into superstition or into atheism (§67.378A; cf. §71.379E).

12 *Ei Delph.* 6.386EF.

exegesis of the Egyptian and other mysteries in this manner[13]. He knows of the 'theological' interpretation of myths: the relationship of Isis and Osiris expresses the truth that the female goddess has always a part in the highest god and is united with him 'through love of his good and fine qualities' (§58.374F)[14]. The 'physical' interpretation is widely attested; he too knows of the interpretation of Kronos as time (§32.363D)[15], but presumably under this head would also come the likes of the Egyptian interpretation of Typhon as the solar world and Osiris as the lunar (§41. 367CD). 'Psychical' interpretation is found when Osiris is interpreted as the intelligence and *logos* in the soul and Typhon as 'the element of the soul which is passionate, akin to the Titans, without reason, and brutish' (§49.371AB). The 'material' interpretation, which Sallust attributed particularly to the Egyptians, indeed figures prominently in this account; the Egyptians say that Osiris is the Nile, Isis is earth, Typhon the sea[16]. And, of course, the practice of allegorical interpretation does admit of finding many different levels of meaning in a given text, so that Plutarch is not compelled to opt for one correct interpretation to the exclusion of all others[17].

Yet he does have his own preferences amongst this welter of interpretations and does not simply list all the possibilities of which he knows without discriminating between them. He emphatically rejects the followers of Euhemerus in §§22—24, preferring the view that these gods are *daimones* (§25.370D—F)[18]. After mentioning the identification of Osiris with the Nile and Typhon with the sea (§32.363D) he says that 'the wiser of the priests' go further than this and identify Osiris with 'the whole principle and power (ἀρχὴ καὶ δύναμις) which creates moisture', which is the cause of generation and the essence of seed, and Typhon with all

---

13 It is clear that Plutarch knows of other similar accounts of other deities: e.g. §32.363D, 34. 364D, 40.367C (Stoics), 66.377E.
14 Tr. Griffiths; cf. §78.383A; the same level of interpretation seems to be Plutarch's own preference in §64.376F—377A; cf. also §62.376C (Griffiths, Comm. 83, seems to regard the allegory as the work of Eudoxus of Cnidos, but the interpretation might be Plutarch's and Eudoxus might only be the source for the myth).
15 Cf. *Quaest. Rom.* 12.266EF.
16 §32.363D; he compares this with Greeks identifying Kronos with time (a 'physical' interpretation for Sallust), Hera with air, Hephaestus with fire; cf. §§65—6.377B—E.
17 Cf. Hersman, *Studies* 33.
18 Cf. §30.363A: the Pythagoreans regard Typhon as a δαιμονικὴ δύναμις (cf. *Fac. lun.* 30.945B; also *Def. orac.* 15.417E, 21.421D).
For Plutarch Isis and Osiris were *daimones* later promoted to gods (§27.361E, 30.362E; cf. *Def. orac.* 10.415BC; on *daimones* in Plutarch cf. D. A. Russell, *Plutarch*, 74—78; Dillon, *Platonists* 216—221; Soury, *Démonologie*). A different theory seems to be implied by *Def. orac.* 21.421E: *daimones* are named after gods to whom they are allied.

that is dry and fiery and opposed to moisture (§33.364A)[19]. In §64 he draws his conclusions from the preceding account, rejecting the view that Osiris or Isis are water or sun or earth or sky or that Typhon is fire or drought or sea[20]. Rather to the latter is assigned 'whatever in these things is without measure and order through excess or deficiency' (376F) and we are to regard what is orderly and good and useful as belonging to Isis and as the image and copy and reason (λόγος) of Osiris (377A). In the following section he goes on to criticize those who associate the gods with seasonal and agricultural changes (§65.377BC)[21]. Those who make this mistake are no better than those who would regard sails, ropes and an anchor as a steersman, warp and woof as a weaver, a cup, a honey-drink or barley gruel as a doctor (§66.377E)[22]. Rather, of course, the gods are those who use these various natural objects and supply them to us, or are, more accurately, the one reason (λόγος) and providence (πρόνοια) and the ancillary powers (δυνάμεις ὑπουργοί) set over them (§67.377F–378A)[23].

Again, however, like Hippolytus and the Neoplatonists, Plutarch makes it quite clear that these interpretations, both his and those of others, are not shared by all, and indeed are the preserve of but a few. At the very start he recognizes that most are ignorant why Egyptian priests shave off their hair and wear linen clothes; some are not interested in knowing the reason, others give other, wrong reasons (§4.352CD). The masses are satisfied with those explanations of Isis and Osiris based on the cycle of the seasons and agriculture which Plutarch rejects in §65 (377BC). The masses in fact 'both speak and think the most abominable things about the gods themselves' (§68.378D). The majority of the Egyptians treat various animals as gods, with dire results (§71.379E). The point which Cumont made about the Neoplatonic view of Isis[24] applies equally to Plutarch's treatment of Osiris: the majority are confused by the thought that Osiris is hidden away beneath the earth in the world of the dead, but 'he is actually very far removed from the earth, being undefiled, unspotted, and uncorrupted by any being which is subject to decay and death'; he becomes lord of souls when they are freed from the body and its emotions[25].

---

19 In §39.366F the view is mentioned that Isis and Osiris are the 'essence' (οὐσία) of earth and water respectively.

20 Contrast frg. 157, Sandbach (in LCL; D. A. Russell, *Plutarch* 82, suggests that the physical interpretation given here comes from a dialogue and 'need not therefore represent Plutarch's own opinion' (so does P. Decharme quoted by Sandbach 282f)).

21 Cf. §66.377E, 70.378F–379C.

22 Cf. §71.379C; *Def. orac.* 29.426BC.

23 Cf. §76.382AB; also *Ei Delph* 21.393D; *Aud. poet.* 6.23A ff; *Def. orac.* 42.433DE.

24 Cf. §2.2.2 above.

25 §78.382EF, tr. Griffiths.

Time and time again in his work *On Isis and Osiris* Plutarch makes it plain that he is drawing on already established traditions of exegesis, either to criticize them, particularly in §§22–24 and 65–67, or with varying degrees of assent. He approves of those who reckon Typhon, Osiris and Isis to be *daimones*, not gods (§25.360DE); that is not his own original theory. He knows of the views of those having a reputation for handling such matters more philosophically and of their Egyptian representatives who identify Osiris with the Nile, Isis with the earth, and Typhon with the sea (§32.363D), but, as we have seen, he prefers the views of the wiser among the priests (§33.364A). He knows of the Stoic treatment of the Greek gods as different spirits ($\pi\nu\epsilon\acute{u}\mu\alpha\tau\alpha$) in the natural order (§40.367C) and its Egyptian counterpart (367BC). Some Egyptians combined such physical interpretations with astronomy (§41.367CD; cf. §44.368D), while others engaged in numerical symbolism (§42.367F–368A).

Now a scholion on Hom., *Il.* 20.67[26] traces back the identification of gods in Homer with physical elements or aspects of human character ($\delta\iota\alpha\theta\acute{\epsilon}\sigma\epsilon\iota\varsigma$, e.g. prudence, folly, desire, reason) to Theagenes of Rhegium in the sixth century B.C.E., the author of a work on Homer. Whatever the truth of this, both ways of handling Homer's text had a long pedigree. The identification of the gods with physical elements was particularly favoured by the Stoics[27]; Xenocrates too is said to have called his first god, the monad, Zeus and mind ($\nu o\tilde{u}\varsigma$), the second, the dyad, justice ($\delta\acute{\iota}\kappa\eta$)[28], as well as identifying powers in the various elements with gods[29].

These traditions are well established by the time of the rise of Christianity. Heraclitus, the author of the *Homeric Allegories*, is generally considered to be earlier than Plutarch; Buffière gives as his reason for this the absence from his work of the 'mystical exegesis' of the Pythagoreans which we find attested from Plutarch's writings onwards[30]. Reinhardt assigns his work to the period of the Julio-Claudians[31]. Although, as his title suggests, he is mainly concerned with the writings of Homer, he also finds support for his views in the mysteries when he finds there the view

---

26 Ed. Dindorf 4, 231.27f; but cf. Tate, 'Beginnings' 214f, who raises the claims of Pherecydes of Syros (Diels-Kranz, *Fragmente* §7 B 5; cf. B 1); cf. also 'History' 108.

27 Cf., e.g., Minucius Felix, *Octavius* 19.10; Cic., *Nat. deorum* 1.15.36, 39f; 3.24.63; *SVF* 1.539; 2.1077f.

28 But cf. Dillon, *Platonists* 25 and n. 1.

29 Frg. 15, Heinze; Zeller, *History* 2, 372 n. 5, quotes a late source (Syncellus, *Chron.* 149C) to the effect that the followers of Anaxagoras interpreted the gods of the myths in what he calls 'a moral sense': Zeus is $\nu o\tilde{u}\varsigma$, Athena $\tau\acute{\epsilon}\chi\nu\eta$; cf. Diog. L. 2.11.

30 His ed. of Heraclitus x; cf. xxi, xxvi; also *Mythes* 69, 394.

31 In *PRE* 8, 508.

that Apollo is the sun (§6.6)[32]. Indeed, he reveals that he considers the study of Homer, the great hierophant, to be like initiation in a mystery (§76.1)[33]. From the example of his treatment of Apollo amongst many others it is clear that he is a proponent of those methods of physical allegory which we have already seen ('material' exegesis in Sallust's analysis), but he also knows of 'psychical' and 'moral' allegorizing, as when he finds Plato's tripartite division of the soul in Athena's encounter with Achilles in Hom., *Il.* 1.194–200 (§§17–20) or interprets Athena and Iris as wisdom (φρόνησις) and the *logos* which speaks (εἴρων λόγος) as opposed to Hermes, the *logos* that interprets (§28.1–3, etc.). Heracles, on the other hand, is interpreted as a wise man, an initiate into heavenly wisdom, a view for which he claims the support of the 'most distinguished of the Stoics' (§33.1). The account of the pursuit of Dionysus by Lycurgus is treated as an allegory of the vine harvest by a Lycurgus who is the owner of a vineyard on the slopes of Nysa (§35).

Two figures, both Stoics, can be dated with greater certainty to the first century C.E., Cornutus and Chaeremon, of whom Eusebius records that it was from them that Origen 'learnt the figurative interpretation (τὸν μεταληπτικὸν . . . τρόπον), as employed in the Greek mysteries'[34]. Cornutus, though not uncritical of some Stoic allegorizing[35], follows many of its traditions: Zeus is the cosmic soul (*Theol. Graec.* 2) and Hera is air and Kronos is time (§3) and Poseidon the power of moisture (§4); Hermes is the *logos* (§16), Dionysus wine (§30), and Heracles is also the *logos*, that which is in the universe and which makes nature strong and powerful (§31). Chaeremon was at one point a tutor of Nero; an Egyptian priest himself, he wrote amongst other works at least one on Egypt and evidently interpreted their myths of forces and elements of nature and of heavenly bodies[36].

Buffière, we saw, gave as a reason (not a very good one) for an early date for Heraclitus' *Homeric Allegories* the absence in them of any 'mystical exegesis'; this rather vague term he exemplifies by referring to the Pythagoreans who sought in the Homeric myths 'the reflection of the

---

32 Cf., e.g., Plut., *Ei Delph.* 4.386B, 21.393Dff; *Pyth. or.* 12.400D; *Def. orac.* 42.433DE, 46. 434F–435A; Cornutus, *Theol. Graec.* 32; Buffière, *Mythes* 187ff (he suggests that the source of this tradition is in Orphic and Neopythagorean circles: 186f).

33 Cf. Buffière, *Mythes* 37; *pace* Buffière (68) his view of himself seems nearer that of an initiate than that of a hierophant (§3.3); cf. also on Philo in §2.4.2 below.

34 Eus., *Hist. eccl.* 6.19.8 (tr. Oulton). Cornutus was exiled by Nero (Dio C. 62.29.2–4).

35 Cf. Tate, 'Cornutus' 41–45; he cites, for instance, the implied criticism of Cleanthes at the end of *Theol. Graec.* 31; Tate's main thesis is that Cornutus departs from Stoic tradition especially in his view that Homer and Hesiod had distorted the myths of pre-Homeric philosophers (cf. §17).

36 Frg. 5, Schwyzer. For the tradition that he taught Nero cf. test. 3.

mysteries of the other world'[37]; it is an exegesis which 'transfers to souls the adventures of heroes in the flesh'[38]. That it was not the exclusive preserve of Pythagoreans is clear from the fact that he finds it first attested in Plutarch (and then later in the Neoplatonists)[39]. But Turcan argues that a certain Eubulus cited by Porphyry found in the rites of Mithras an illustration of the Platonic doctrine of the soul descending into the lower world and returning whence it came[40]; this Eubulus he tentatively dates to the first century C.E. or slightly earlier[41]. Certainly this sort of exegesis is not altogether absent from the writings of Philo of Alexandria: commenting on the text of Gen 15.15, 'But you shall go to your fathers in peace, nourished (so LXX) in a good old age', he interprets this of 'the incorruptibility of the soul, which removes its habitation from the mortal body and returns to the mother-city, from which it originally moved its habitation to this place'[42]. The 'fathers' are the 'incorporeal Logoi of the divine world', normally called 'angels'[43]. Immediately before he described Gen 15.13f as 'allegories of the soul'; 'for the soul of the wise man, when it comes from above from the ether and enters into a mortal and is sown in the field of the body, is truly a sojourner in a land not its own, . . .'[44]; when the mind is 'released from its evil bond, the body', then 'it goes forth and exchanges its state not only for salvation and freedom but also for possessions . . .'[45]. It is interesting that Buffière does not find evidence of his 'mystical exegesis' before Plutarch despite the fact that he quotes Bréhier's view that Philo's purpose (amongst others surely?) was 'to show in the succession of events and regulations of Jewish history the inner movement of the sinful soul, plunging itself in its failings or else hoping for salvation and entry to the invisible and better world', and comments

---

37 Ed. of Heraclitus xxvi; cf. Delatte, *Études* 109–36.
38 Buffière, *Mythes* 410; cf. in general 393ff; he distinguishes this from 'psychical' or 'moral' exegesis in that the latter is concerned with the nature and behaviour of the soul and people in this world, not in the other.
39 See above n. 30.
40 *Mithras* 24–6, citing Porphyry, *Antr. nymph.* 6 (60.1–14, Nauck), who knew of his multivolume ἱστορία περὶ τοῦ Μίθρα (*Abst.* 4.16=253.19f, Nauck); Turcan 39 points out that in the latter passage Eubulus is mentioned before Pallas, and so is probably earlier (Pallas is mentioned on 254.11ff., Nauck); cf. Seel in *PRE* 18.2, 242: he makes the more important point that Pallas is represented as developing the exegesis of Eubulus.
41 *Mithras* 43; he is earlier at least, he argues, than Pallas who, according to the more plausible interpretation of Porphyry, *Abst.* 2.56.3 (181.1–4, Nauck), wrote on the mysteries of Mithras in the reign of Hadrian (Turcan 39f; cf. Seel, ibid. 240); however contrast, most recently, the translation of Bouffartigue and Patillon (also their ed. 2, 227f n. 11).
42 Cf. also *Quaest. in Gen.* 4.178; cf. *Abr.* 258.
43 *Quaest. in Gen.* 3.11 (tr. Marcus).
44 Cf. *Quaest. in Gen.* 4.74; also *Gig.* 12–15; *Conf. ling.* 77f; *Rer. div. her.* 240; *Som.* 1.181.
45 *Quaest. in Gen.* 3.10 (tr. Marcus); cf. also *Rer. div. her.* 82; *Som.* 1.138f, 181; *Spec. leg.* 1.207.

that this corresponds to the tendencies of the Neoplatonists who sought in the adventures of Ulysses the mystical story of the soul *en route* to its true home[46]. If there is anything in this correspondence, and I think that there is, then the difference between a first century Platonist like Philo and the Neoplatonists with regard to this sort of allegorizing is but one of degree of emphasis.

2.2.4. I would not claim that the preceding sections were anything more than soundings at various points during the first four centuries of the Christian era, gauging the ways in which the mysteries (or the myths of Homer which were treated in a similar fashion) were interpreted in intellectual and philosophical circles, but I think that they have been sufficient at least to hint strongly at certain conclusions:

(1) whereas Schweitzer argued that the second century marked a significant change in the understanding of the mysteries, it is doubtful whether this is so. We have seen that there was a considerable degree of continuity in Middle Platonist exegesis of the mysteries and that this is seemingly well established by the beginning of the second century.

(2) What is perhaps a new departure in the interpretation of the mysteries is heralded by the rise of Neoplatonism under Plotinus (or, according to some, his teacher, Ammonius Saccas)[1] in the third century. This was a new interpretation in so far as Neoplatonism was new and the mysteries were invoked as witnesses to it, but even then we have to recognize the extent to which it was indebted to Middle Platonism and to figures like the Neopythagorean Numenius. The mysteries, along with other traditions (Orphic, Homeric), continued in their role as witnesses to this developing philosophical movement.

(3) In none of the cases which we have examined can it really be claimed that the interpretation offered was an official or general one; rather it was limited to the adherents either of a particular religious sect or group of sects (the Naassenes) or of a particular philosophical school, although I suppose that we come near to an official interpretation in one sense at least when the emperor (Julian) happens to belong to that

---

46 *Mythes* 38f n. 27, quoting Bréhier, *Philon* 61; Bréhier's statement concentrates on the soul in this world, which would fit in with Buffière's statement about exegesis before Plutarch, but not with his subsequent remark in this note about the Neoplatonists. While it is true that Philo says far more about the soul in this world, it is clear that he does have views about its existence before and after incarnation and does use these in his exegesis.

Notes on 2.2.4

1 Cf. Dörrie in *KP* 4, 85; Früchtel, *Vorstellungen* 2; but see Proclus, *Theologia Platonica* 1.1 (16.16–17.8, Saffrey-Westerink); Dillon, *Platonists* 383; Wallis, *Neoplatonism* 1.

school. The texts make it clear that they are offering interpretations which would not have occurred to the majority of devotees of the mystery gods, interpretations which the masses might not even have understood.

Now, unless it can be shown that, e.g., the Neoplatonist interpretation of the mysteries is alone suitable for a comparison with Paul (which I would think very doubtful), then the argument from chronology at this point has no bearing upon the relevance or otherwise of the mysteries for our understanding of Paul; the Platonist interpretation is in all probability there in the first century if it is of any help. With the Gnostic interpretation of the mysteries the position is more difficult in that it is entangled with the question of a pre-Christian Gnosticism[2]. For my part I think it wiser in the New Testament period to speak of tendencies towards Gnosticism rather than already existing Gnostic groups. Certainly it would be rash to use the mysteries themselves as evidence of a pre-Christian Gnosticism; against that is the general absence of explicit references to the mysteries in Gnostic circles; the evidence of the Naassene traditions seems to indicate that Gnosticism came to the Attis cult from outside and latched on to it as a fertile ground for the elaboration of its ideas, rather than being spawned by the cult itself. The Gnostics apart, there is little firm evidence of any marked change in the interpretation of the mysteries in the second century which would justify us in fencing off the first century from the second; if there are different interpretations the main distinction is that between philosophers on the one hand and non-philosophers on the other, who were content to take the myths of the mysteries more at their face value, although something of the philosophers' sophistications may have filtered down to them; this distinction holds good throughout the centuries that we have been considering.

2.3. A Common Theology of the Mysteries?

From these two problems posed by Schweitzer we turn to yet another of which he was conscious[1] and which speedily confronts any student of

---

2 Cf. Yamauchi, *Gnosticism,* esp. the survey of opinions on 20–8; also Rudolph, *Gnosis* esp. 315f =ET 297f (Simon Magus as founder of a Gnostic sect contemporary with early Christianity); A. F. Segal in *ANRW* 2.23.2, 1334–6; R. McL. Wilson, 'Nag Hammadi' 292f.

Notes on 2.3
1 *Paul* 192f.

the mysteries who tries to compare them with the New Testament. Among some scholars we meet the claim that amidst all the variety of the pagan cults there is a certain continuity, a common basic set of beliefs and convictions, which finds expression in these varying ways. One such scholar is Lohse in his *Umwelt des Neuen Testaments*[2]: 'Although the cultic myths of the individual mystery religions were of diverse origin, and the forms of worship variously constructed, it is still possible to discern certain basic features common to all the mystery communities notwithstanding their peculiarities' (172=ET 234). One thing which they shared was the belief that in initiation the initiate was reborn and granted immortality. This took place through cultic participation in the fate of the dying and rising deity: 'By the initiates' participation in the drama, in the fate of the deity, they are involved in its fate and are filled with divine power' (173=ET 234)[3]. They are thus granted a deliverance which is irrevocably and for ever theirs.

Such a 'becoming and passing away' was not related to a definite historical event, but is an eternal truth. In proof of this he cites a sentence from Sallust's *On the Gods and the Universe*, to the effect that all that is narrated in the Attis myth 'did not happen at any one time but always is so' (§4, tr. Nock)[4]. This text Nock also quotes in his book *Conversion*,

---

2 For other similar views cf. Albert, *Religion* 96ff; Colpe, 'Mithra-Verehrung' 381; Eliade, *History* 2, chap. 26; Le Corsu, *Isis* 41; Schneider, *Mysterien* 9, 11, 86f (e.g.); Willoughby, *Regeneration* 30f; cf. also Haufe, 'Mysterien' 102 (who yet, after giving a similar summary to that of Lohse, goes on to say that 'it is true that the differences in individual cults are so great that one can nevertheless hardly speak of a unified theology of the mysteries'; for variations within individual cults cf. Vermaseren, 'Mithras' 101). Angus, too, despite his emphasis on the lack of a systematic theology in the mysteries (e.g. *Mystery-Religions* 61) and on the varying levels of understanding of the mysteries among their devotees (e.g. 39–43), nevertheless gives the impression that the range of interpretation was constant from cult to cult and from period to period, and makes some incredible generalizations (e.g. 46: ' "all things are opposite the one to the other" was a principle universally observed by the ancient worshipper of the Mysteries'). King, too (*Death* 81), believes that Wagner's study shows, perhaps unconsciously, that 'in spite of specific differences in ritual detail and theological content, all the major mystery religions shared a common symbolico-ritual pattern and an understanding of the results effected in the existence of the initiate because of his passage through the initiatory ritual experience.' On Godwin, *Mystery Religions* cf. §2.2.2 above.

3 Here Lohse is an heir of the *religionsgeschichtliche Schule*: cf. Simon's summary in 'Schule' 135; also the critique by Gasparro, *Soteriology* xiii–xvi. But, for a start, Mithras is not a dying or suffering god: cf. Turcan, 'Salut' 178f, in criticism of A. Loisy's identification of Mithras and the bull (the same view found expression in Turcan's summary quoted in n. 11 below); also Gordon, 'Mithraism' 96; Vermaseren, 'Mithras' 111.

Even Bianchi's phrase 'gods subject to vicissitude' (*Mysteries* 5; cf. Gasparro, ibid. xvi–xvii) is not particularly appropriate for Mithras. The caution of MacMullen, *Paganism* 172 n. 22, is timely: 'of course Jupiter Dolichenus, Sabazius and Mithra are Oriental but never suffered; and resurrection in divine stories more often calls to mind fertility (planting and growing) than immortality, e.g. in the story of Attis, . . . or of Kore or Osiris!'

4 Julian's version is that 'never did this happen save in the manner that it happens now': Attis

which remains one of the best introductions to the mystery-religions available, with the comment that this interpretation is 'philosophic and yet true to the spirit of ancient belief' (234). 'Philosophic' it certainly is, but, whatever the latter part of the quotation means, it seems hard to believe that this particular reinterpretation of the Attis myth could have arisen except in the context of certain clearly formulated views of what myths were and what was the proper way to speak of the gods (cf. §2.2.2 above). To suggest that this is what in fact the ancients always believed about the myths that they heard, if that is what Nock is suggesting, is to suggest in them an anachronistic degree of sophistication. After all, we saw (in §2.2.3 above) that even one so sophisticated and ready to reinterpret the myths philosophically as Plutarch was seems to have been ready to posit a prehistory when the present gods of the myths were still only *daimones* and did undergo changes and vicissitudes[5].

Again it is Schweitzer who warned 'that those who are engaged in making these comparisons (between Christianity and the mysteries) are rather apt to give the Mystery-religions a greater definiteness and articulation of thought than they really possess, and do not always give sufficient prominence to the distinction between their own hypothetical reconstruction and the medley of statements on which it is based'. Such accounts 'manufacture out of the various fragments of information a kind of universal Mystery-religion which never actually existed, least of all in Paul's day'[6]. Arguably, too, the differences in time are as important as those either of place or between different cults[7]. That would mean, for

---

is always the Great Mother's servant and charioteer, always he yearns towards generation, always he cuts off his unlimited course (*Or.* 5.171CD).

5 Cf. Craik, *Aegean* 149: 'The Greeks viewed their myths . . . simply as early history, a record of events in the remote past, at a time when gods and men rubbed shoulders'; cf. also Widengren in *HO* 1.8.2, 75. Prümm, *Handbuch* 299, argues that it was only the minority of devotees of the mysteries who sought a deeper wisdom in the cults.

6 *Paul* 192f; cf. also Wagner's criticism in *Baptism* 268; also Brandon, 'Kings' (on the 'myth and ritual' school); Dey, Παλιγγενεσία 38f, 85; Dörrie, 'Mysterien' 342f; Gordon, 'Mithraism' 113 n. 9; F. C. Grant, *Hellenism* 39 (cf. 50, 77); Griffiths, 'Concept' 215f; Mellor, 'Archaeology' 138; Nilsson, *Geschichte* 2, 685, 693; Simon, '*Schule*' 142, and 'École' 269; Turcan, 'Salut' 175; and Wilamowitz-Moellendorff cited in §2.1 n. 42.

Henrichs, 'Identities' 151, makes the point that even within the cult of one deity there could be great variations: 'the so-called "religion of Dionysus" is a convenient modern abstraction, the sum total of the god's numerous facets, symbols and cults'; Delphic maenads and adherents of South Italian Orphic-Dionysiac sects had little in common.

Nash, *Christianity* 122, adds his voice to those denying that 'there was one common, or general, mystery religion', but then goes on to describe the annual vegetation cycle as 'central to the mysteries'; yet for a start he recognizes that Mithraism was different (147), and such generalizations run into trouble with aspects of the Dionysiac cult like the trieteric rites (cf. §3.2.3.2).

7 Cumont, *Lux* 236; cf. MacMullen, *Paganism* 106; D. H. Wiens in *ANRW* 2.23.2, 1250. This applies, however, to Cumont's own view of Roman Mithraism as a direct successor of Iranian

example, that a Neoplatonist interpreter of Attis would have more beliefs in common with a follower of one of the other mystery-deities, at least with a philosophically-inclined follower, at the same period − and indeed when multiple initiation was so prevalent he or she might well be a devotee of any of those other deities too −[8] than he would have with a devotee of Attis from the period of the establishment of the cult of the Great Mother in Rome in 204 B.C.E. or even perhaps from the Julio-Claudian period.

A subtler and more authoritative critique of the position represented by Lohse can be found by implication in Helmut Köster's *Introduction to the New Testament* (1, 196−203)[9]. In the first place he points out how mystery-religions may be defined by certain external characteristics: organization of the members into communities, initiation ceremonies, regular gatherings with a fixed ritual, certain ethical or ascetic obligations, mutual support, obedience to the leader of the cult, preservation of certain traditions, guarded in secrecy[10]. In contrast the *beliefs* of these religious groups varied: different cults changed their beliefs in the course of a considerable span of time and varied from region to region, just as early Christianity exhibited a considerable variety of beliefs[11]. Certain beliefs they did, however, share in common, but these were not peculiar to them; rather 'they are intimately linked to the typical Hellenistic view

---

religious beliefs: Mellor, 'Archaeology' 130f; but cf. Gasparro, *Soteriology* xxi, quoted above in §2.2 n. 1.

8 Cf. *CIL* 6, 504, 510, 1675, 1779 (=*ILS* 1, 1259, 1264; 2.1, 4152; cf. also 4154); Apul., *Apol.* 55; *Met.* 3.15; cf. Cumont, *Religions* 189, 204=*Religionen* 186, 203; Nock, *Conversion* 114f.

9 =*Einführung* 202−11.

10 N.b.: Köster does not argue that all these were always present in every mystery-religion (ibid. 204=ET 1, 198); cf. also Prümm, *Handbuch* 295; and §2.4.2 below.

Sänger, *Judentum* 98, defines a mystery-religion as 'a religious community into which one is initiated by a ritual action, in which the ritual action of initiation is effected under a strict regime of secrecy'; Burkert, *Homo* 274=ET 248: the basic phenomenon of the mysteries is that a person becomes a member of a group for the first time through particular ritual actions; this group focuses on a cult whose chief component is this same initiation ceremony; cf. also Widengren in *HO* 1.8.2, 43.

But Berner proposes a more theological definition: one can properly speak of a mystery-religion when a cult has as its central point a union of human and the divine destinies, even a merging of human and divine persons (*Initiationsriten* 4; cf. Colpe, 'Mithra-Verehrung' esp. 381). He also, however, agrees in seeing the secrecy of the mysteries as a decisive criterion for what was or was not a true mystery (120f) and concludes that the graded structure of their ritual was the chief criterion of their initiation rites, with further decisive marks being their once-and-for-all character and their irreversibility.

11 Cf. B. Lincoln, 'Mithra(s)' esp. 516; MacMullen, *Paganism* 99−107; Vermaseren, 'Mithras' 101; Turcan's summary of the discussions at the colloquium on the soteriology of the oriental cults in the Roman Empire in 1979: 'traditional schemata are no longer suited to the diversity of the oriental cults and of the evidence concerning them; too often they have led to inadequate generalizations' (Bianchi-Vermaseren, *Soteriologia* xvii).

of human beings and their world' (ET 1, 202=209)[12]: the cosmos has its divine order, but we are not allowed a full share in that order, since we live in the world of the senses and of matter, in the grip of disorder and finitude, under the dominion and rules of fate[13]. Yet in our soul we share in the divine world; powers and spirits are at hand to aid us and rescue us, for ultimately we are akin to them. Such ideas were far more widespread than just among the adherents of particular mystery-religions. 'Seen theologically, such language and ideas are not a specific phenomenon of the mystery religions, but of the Hellenistic history of religions in general which came to its flowering in the Roman imperial period' (ET 1, 200= 207). The symbolism and the theological interpretation of the various rites were very diverse, but they all operated within the compass of these same Hellenistic concepts. They spoke a common language, not a special preserve of the mysteries, but 'the general religio-philosophical language of Hellenism' (ibid.), a language shared by Christianity and Judaism as well[14]. In other words, the mystery-cults shared a common outward form and structure amongst themselves; in so far as they shared common beliefs these were not peculiar to them, but were shared also by many contemporary religious movements.

Notable, however, is the absence from Köster's account of any specific common theology of the mysteries involving a particular expectation attached to initiation into the cults or a particular view of the relation of the initiate to the cult-deity, a theology so important for the question of the mysteries' influence on the early Christians and on Paul as well as being so prominent in very many accounts of the common beliefs of the mystery-religions. According to some scholars one should not even expect to find such a common theology. For Hepding the rites are the constant element within each cult; how each devotee explained those rites and the view that he had of the ἱεροὶ λόγοι was of secondary importance. Hence even the myths attached to each cult varied[15]. We could add that a unified interpretation of the myths would thus be further hindered unless there was a common theology applied to all myths just as philosophers of a

---

12 Cf. F. C. Grant, *Hellenism* 115 (the mysteries used certain ideas 'in the air' at that time); Nilsson, *Geschichte* 2, 700.

13 Yet contrast the positive view of Mithraism: Turcan, 'Salut' 183.

14 Cf. S. Giversen in *HRG* 3, 282: 'in general one can . . . say that the mystery-religions are best understood as a branch of the general Hellenistic religious spirit'.

15 *Attis* 98f; cf. Nock, *Conversion* 13; Vermaseren, 'Religions' 512; Cumont, *Religions* 81f, 182f =*Religionen* 80f, 179f, stresses the variation in doctrine within the Egyptian cults. Cf. also Burkert, *Homo* 324=ET 294: 'The explanation given to the mystai through oral instruction probably underwent greater changes in the course of time than did Christian theology or religious instruction in the church. There was no dogma at Eleusis.' (See further below.)

particular persuasion found their philosophy in all sorts of different myths by means of allegory; the myths themselves could not foment this unified theology. Moreoever, Hepding was speaking of variations within a single cult; *a fortiori* the chances of finding an explanation common to all the cults are slender indeed. Again, Nock argues that, while some such unified theology may have emerged under Julian, who reigned from 360 to 363, it did not exist earlier, nor was there then 'even convergent belief in "saviour gods" '[16]. And when that unity finally emerged under Julian, what we have seen above in §2.2.2 would suggest that this consensus emerged under the impulse of a dominant philosophical school and not from any forces immanent within the mysteries themselves. Moreover Cumont remarks on how different the situation was two centuries earlier in Lucian's time; then philosophies were 'up for auction' as opposed to the dominance of Neoplatonism under Julian[17]. We shall see below (in §5.1) how diverse the views of the relationship of the initiate to the deities of the various cults were.

One city, Alexandria, may perhaps provide us with illustrative examples of two sides of this question of unity and diversity in the mystery-cults. On the one hand Cumont sees in Ptolemy IV Philopator's attempt to regulate the cult of Dionysus there evidence of the variation that had sprung up within that one cult in one country, in that Ptolemy sought to unify it[18]: persons performing the cult in the interior were to report at Alexandria 'from what persons they have received the transmission of the sacred rites for three generations back and shall hand in the sacred book (τὸν ἱερὸν λόγον) sealed up . . .'[19]. The motivation for this organization may be in doubt[20], but a desire to achieve some uniformity, for whatever reason, seems very likely; certainly, without some central control, the possibility of local variations arising would have been considerable.

On the other hand Alexandria witnessed another measure which might certainly have tended to promote some degree of homogeneity between the Alexandrian cults and those of Greece; Plutarch and Tacitus both refer to the part played in the organization of the cult of Sarapis under Ptolemy I Soter by Timotheus the Eumolpid, skilled in the Eleusinian

---

16 'Christianity' 81.

17 *Religions* 185f=*Religionen* 183 – an allusion to the title of one of Lucian's works (*Philosophies for Sale* in LCL 2); cf. also *Hermot.* 14, 25ff.

18 *Lux* 252; cf. *Religions* 196=*Religionen* 193f.

19 Tr. Hunt-Edgar, *Papyri* 2, no. 208=*BGU* 6, 1211; cf. Lenger, *Corpus* no. 29.

20 Cf. Fraser, *Alexandria* 1, 204; 2, 347 n. 116; Lenger, ibid. 68ff; Tondriau, 'Décret'; Walbank, *World* 212.

mysteries[21]. There seems little reason to doubt this tradition thus far[22], but how far does it in fact take us? Are we to infer that Timotheus gave the new cult a theology along Eleusinian lines, or did his role lie rather in organizing the outward framework of the cult? On the one hand it would be unrealistic to expect his Eleusinian expertise to be of no use to him here, but on the other there is a limit, it seems, to what could be simply transported from Eleusis to another place; it was felt, by some at least[23], that the Eleusinian cult of Demeter and Kore could only be performed at Eleusis (perhaps it was for that reason that Claudius' attempt to introduce it at Rome failed)[24]. That seems to rule out a re-enactment of the Eleusinian cult at Alexandria, but it still does not exclude the possible influence of Eleusis on the cult of Sarapis (nor possibly elements from the Eleusinian cult in the religious festival celebrated in the Alexandrian deme of Eleusis)[25]. However it is hard to detect the influence of Eleusis *via* Timotheus on the cult of Sarapis; it is Dionysiac elements that play a considerable part in the cult of this deity (scarcely surprisingly in view of the prominence of this Greek deity under the Lagides); however there is no need to derive these from any Eleusinian influence, since it is equally possible to regard them as having been taken over with the identification of this god with Osiris or Osor-Hapi, the deified Apis bull of Memphis who became one with Osiris in the underworld[26]. Finally, it is perhaps this same Timotheus who, if we may believe a late tradition[27], appears to have turned his attention also to the cult of Cybele and to have written on it; how much impact, if any, this had on the cult is hard to say, but if this is true it may suggest that Timotheus' activities in the cult of Sarapis also extended to a description of the cult and its mythology, providing it with a ἱερὸς λόγος.

Furthermore, the assimilation of Egyptian cults to Greek ones would be an inevitable consequence, at least for Greeks, of the identification of

---

21 Plut., *Is. et Os.* 28.362A; Tac., *Hist.* 4.83; Stambaugh, *Sarapis* 8–13, warns against identifying the occasion of this organisation with the creation of the god or the cult; rather it was involved with the introduction of a new cult statue from Sinope.

22 In support of the tradition cf., e.g., Cumont, *Lux* 260; Fraser, *Alexandria* 1, 251; Le Corsu, *Isis* 58; Nilsson, *Geschichte* 2, 95f; Nock, *Conversion* 38–41.

23 *P. Oxy.* 1612 (=vol. 13, 148–54); Epict., *Diss.* 3.21.13–16; cf. Kerenyi, *Eleusis* 115; O. Kern in *PRE* 16, 1250; Nilsson, ibid. 94; contrast Paus. 2.14.1; 8.15.1; 8.31.7 referred to below; cf. Alföldi, 'Regna' 553–64; Kern, ibid. 1269f; Köster, *Einführung* 185=ET 1, 180; Vermaseren, 'Religions' 508.

24 On Claudius see above §2.1.

25 Cf. Fraser, *Alexandria* 1, 210; 2, 340 n. 91; also Bell, *Cults* 18 n. 50. But Sarapis does not seem to have been a mystery-god initially – cf. §5.1.1.4 and n. 1.

26 Cf. Fraser, ibid. 1, 255; also Bell, ibid. 19; Stambaugh, *Sarapis* 59.

27 Arnobius, *Adversus nationes* 5.5; his account is paralleled, in a shorter form, in Paus. 1.17.10–12, where it is described as 'the local legend'.

Egyptian deities with Greek ones, and this is attested as early as the work of Herodotus[28]. The resultant cross-fertilization can most clearly be seen in a passage like Plutarch, *On Isis and Osiris* 16.357BC where Isis' nursing of the royal child of Byblos and her attempt to immortalize it by fire echoes the *Homeric Hymn to Demeter* (lines 233ff.)[29]. And yet, despite this influence, Griffiths warns us against following Nilsson in supposing the Egyptian cult to have been more or less completely Hellenized; as he shows again and again in his commentary on Apuleius, *Met.* 11, 'its appeal, especially that concerned with immortality, remains Egyptian'[30]. Indeed its exotic Egyptian colouring was probably a very considerable factor in its popularity in view of the fascination which things ancient and oriental exercised on the age.

Nor was the influence of Eleusis only felt by the Egyptian cults; its influence elsewhere too is perhaps more tangible at a later period. When Alexander of Abonuteichos founded his new mysteries, Lucian makes plain the analogies with Eleusis; they began with a proclamation 'as at Athens', and Lucian refers ironically to Alexander's attendants as Eumolpidae and Kerykes[31]. In this imitation he would, it seems, be following the example of other cults during the first two centuries of our era[32], but Lucian's account seems the clearest evidence of this process, unless he has scornfully exaggerated the resemblances to the Eleusinian rites to make clearer Alexander's fraud. Far earlier the introduction of initiatory rites into the cult of Cybele is ascribed to the influence of Eleusis by G. Sanders, although he warns us that the expectations and hopes of the initiates should not be too quickly presumed to be the same as those of Eleusinian initiates[33]. Naturally, too, the influence of Eleusis was most strongly felt in rites of Demeter elsewhere, even in southern Italy[34]; at Celeae near Corinth, Pausanias tells us (2.14.1), mysteries in honour of Demeter are celebrated every fourth year with different hierophants appointed for

---

28 E.g. 2.42.2; 59.2; 123.1; 144.2; cf. also Diod. S. 1.25.1f; 4.1.6; Plut., *Is. et Os.* 27.361E (attributing this to Archemachus of Euboea – 3rd century B.C.E. – and Heraclides of Pontus); cf. too the Isis-aretalogy from Maroneia (*SEG* 26, 821.35ff).

29 Griffiths, Comm. 328; Le Corsu, *Isis* 61 (immortalizing by fire is not an Egyptian idea).

30 *Isis-Book* 30, against Nilsson, *Geschichte* 2, 634, 638 (cf. also Köster, *Einführung* 190–2=ET 1, 183–7); Merkelbach, *Roman* 22 n. 2, considers the influence of Eleusis on the mysteries of Isis beyond doubt; but how great an influence? In support of Griffiths cf. Junge, 'Isis'.

31 Luc., *Alex.* 38f; it would, however, be wrong to interpret Philostr., *Vit. Ap.* 4.18 as a reference to mysteries of Asclepius (*pace* MacMullen, *Paganism* 196 n. 54) since a part of the regular Eleusinian rites is clearly meant as the hierophant's words show (cf. Deubner, *Feste* 72f.).

32 Cf. Festugière, 'Mystères' 202; F. C. Grant, *Hellenism* 78; Le Corsu, *Isis* 58; Prümm, *Handbuch* 297.

33 'Kybele' 273.

34 Cf. Statius, *Silvae* 4.8.50f; Kern in *PRE* 16, 1263; Nilsson, *Feste* 334–52. Their influence can perhaps also be detected in the Samothracian mysteries (Nock, 'Mysteries' 181=794).

each celebration; despite these differences to Eleusis the actual initiatory rites are a copy of the Eleusinian (ἐς μίμησιν); the Phliasians admit, he continues, that they copy the ritual actions (δρώμενα) at Eleusis. The same writer says also of the shrine of Demeter at Pheneus that it is said that the ceremonies there are the same as those at Eleusis (8.15.1), but it is clear that there are elements peculiar to their cult too: for a start they celebrated the greater rites every other year, reading sacred writings preserved in a container formed of two large stones. At Megalopolis too the two goddesses of Eleusis are worshipped in mysteries which are copies (μιμήματα) of the Eleusinian ones (8.13.7). Doubt has been cast on Pausanias' accuracy here by Kern[35], but in the first place he quotes these claims as made by others, so that it is not really relevant whether or not he knew the Eleusinian rites himself[36]; secondly, it is doubtful whether 1.38.7 in fact means that he did not witness the Eleusinian rites; rather it could imply that he knew them but could not write them down for the uninitiated to read. Despite local variations there are good reasons to think that cults like these were similar in many respects to the Eleusinian rites, but the local variations prevent them being an exact replica of what took place at Eleusis; moreover they would lack the sacred sites so integral to the re-enactment of Demeter's search at Eleusis.

A passage, too, like one found in Theon of Smyrna's treatise on mathematics might suggest that initiation into the mysteries took a fixed form by his day (second century C.E.) with five stages, preliminary purification, instruction in the sacred rites, vision (ἐποπτεία), binding of the head and garlanding, the bliss of acceptance by the gods and fellowship with them[37]. MacMullen refers here to 'a generalized initiatory experience, suggesting that the same procedures were found in a number of rites'[38]. This may be so, but equally other rites do not fit this scheme: those of Mithras with their seven grades do not[39]. However, if the second stage (ἡ τῆς τελετῆς παράδοσις) corresponds to initiation at Eleusis in the narrower sense of the word (as opposed to the mystic vision of the ἐποπτεία) then it may be correct to see here confirmation of the prevalence of the pattern of the Eleusinian mysteries[40].

This unifying force of Eleusis should not, however, be too quickly assumed to have brought with it a unifying of theology among the mysteries, as opposed to a similar structure and outward form to the rites.

---

35 In *PRE* 16, 1270; cf. the less sceptical use of these accounts in Nilsson, ibid. 342–4.
36 Local adherents may have exaggerated the likeness to Eleusis in order to enhance the prestige of their cults by the reflected glory of the fame of the Eleusinian rites.
37 Ed. Dupuis 20–3.
38 *Paganism* 172 n. 20.
39 Cf., e.g., Berner, *Initiationsriten* esp. 54ff.
40 On the stages of the Eleusinian rites cf. above §2 and n. 34.

Burkert, for instance, points out how the ancient interpretations of Eleusis took many forms, arising out of the many possible interpretations of what took place in them[41]. These ranged from Varro's interpretation of the rites as concerned merely with the finding of grain or with the coming of civilization, through the Stoic interpretation in terms of the spirit or vital power in the grain, to a Platonic interpretation in terms of a drama of spirit and matter. Again we come back to the point made by Hepding, that the rites may be constant, but the myths commenting on these rites vary, and, even more it seems, so too do the theological explanations of those myths.

The outcome of the preceding discussion is that, although there were forces working towards a unified theology of the mysteries, this synthesis did not emerge until the period of Neoplatonism, and then presumably only among those sufficiently educated to be influenced by this school[42]. The emergence of a dominant philosophical movement was a most powerful factor in the emergence of this synthesis, and indeed it could probably not have arisen without it. Another factor, perhaps more on the level of the cultic organization and structure of the mystery rites, was the prestigious influence of Eleusis, that cult centre of which most Hellenized citizens of the early Roman Empire would think first whenever one spoke of 'mysteries'[43]. Although this centre perhaps at times played a role with regard to mysteries in the Hellenistic world comparable to that played by Delphi in religious questions in general, it would be a mistake to assume too readily that this influence led to a suppression of the very real differences between the various mystery-gods and their cults in different places; as we have seen, even where those gods were the same as those of Eleusis their cult was never simply a repetition of that at Eleusis itself, nor was such an imitation felt, by some at least, to be desirable, nor was it perhaps even possible.

2.4. The Use of the Language of the Mysteries

We have seen how the mystery-cults had their public side, or it might be better to say that the cults of some deities had, in addition to their public rites, additional, esoteric mysteries restricted to an inner group of

---

41 *Homo* 324=ET 294 in n. 15 above, and cf. Hepding on the cult of Attis above.
42 Cf. Cumont, *Religions* 185=*Religionen* 182.
43 F. C. Grant, *Hellenism* 78, perhaps exaggerates this factor when he describes the oriental mysteries as merely ancient vegetation rites repatterned on the Eleusinian model.

initiates; better, since all the evidence is that, with the majority at least, the public worship existed prior to the esoteric. I argued from this that something at least of the message of these cults was, and was meant to be, known to the general public; it had value as propaganda. We also saw in §2.2 how the myths and rites of the mystery-cults were taken up and reinterpreted to support the beliefs of philosophers and of Gnostics. That again helped to spread knowledge of the cults, however misleading a picture of the cults it may have given. The extent of that spreading of knowledge should, of course, not be overestimated, since the appeal of these reinterpretations would have been largely confined to the educated and well-to-do sections of the population; the masses would have had little inclination or aptitude for such sophistications, although some may have fancied that they had.

This widespread awareness of the cults and of something of what went on in them and what they claimed to offer led to a frequent borrowing of their language and concepts, either in rivalry, to present a counter-claim to theirs, or, as it were, parasitically, in order to express one's own beliefs and ideas in their language; implicit in the latter was often the belief that one's own revelations were superior to theirs. We shall look especially at Plato and Plutarch as examples of the latter[1], and at Philo as an example of the former[2].

2.4.1. *Plato* adopted the language of the mysteries[1]; he esteemed them highly enough to do so, but constantly he was conscious that the philosopher trod a higher, though perhaps still a parallel, path towards a higher, truer goal[2]. It is significant that while the souls that have seen the most of the truths in their preincarnate state become the souls of phil-

---

Notes on 2.4

1 For further examples cf. Dio Chrys., *Or.* 12.33f; *SVF* 2.42 and 1008, and also Festugière, *Ideal* 120—7; Lobeck, *Aglaophamus* 129f; Nock, *Conversion* 182, and 'Mysteries' 188f =799— 801.

  Another sort of borrowing can be seen in Betz, 'Formation' 164 and 237 nn. 10—18, who lists examples of the Greek magical papyri's adaptation of mystery terminology for their purposes.

2 Cf. Wolfson, *Philo* 1, 45—55.

Notes on 2.4.1

1 Cf. Albert, *Religion* 98ff; Croissant, *Aristote* 159—64; Des Places, 'Platon'; Dillon, 'Self-Definition' 74; Dörrie, 'Mysterien' 343—6; Goodenough, 'Mystery'; also Boyancé, 'Mystères'. In this Plato perhaps followed the Pythagoreans who influenced him so greatly; cf. §2.2 and Goodenough, 'Mystery' 227.

2 It is doubtful how true it would be to speak of Plato (or Socrates) at least as 'scornful of mystic rites' (Goodenough, ibid. 228); their attitude seems often to have been a more positive one — cf. de Vogel, '*Sōma-Sēma* Formula'; that is not to say that they were not critical of some aspects of them (cf. however Boyancé, *Culte* 9—31, etc.). Goodenough himself quotes *Phaedo*

osophers, lovers of beauty, musicians and filled with love (ἐρωτικοί), and those that have seen least become tyrants, prophets and those who perform mystery rites (τελεστικοί) come halfway down his scale of values (*Phaedrus* 248DE). This is a timely reminder, for shortly after this he introduces a passage which is the most extended comparison of the philosopher and the initiate anywhere in his works. The philosophical soul, he tells us, uses the memories which it gains before incarnation and in doing so is constantly being initiated into perfect mysteries (τελέους ἀεὶ τελετὰς τελούμενος, 249C); quitting (ἐξιστάμενος) human concerns and consorting with the divine, such a man is deemed crazy by the masses who do not perceive that he is divinely inspired (ἐνθουσιάζων, 249D). The vision, too, which the preincarnate soul had of beauty is described as initiation into the most blessed of mysteries, celebrated (ὠργιάζομεν) in a state of perfection (ὁλόκληροι) and untroubled by the evils later to afflict it; it is initiated into and beholds (μυούμενοί τε καὶ ἐποπτεύοντες) these clear visions with a clear eye, purified[3] and unencumbered by the body (250BC).

In the *Symposium* too Diotima makes use of the analogy of the mysteries to contrast the mysteries of love which are within Socrates' powers with the perfect, visionary (ἐποπτικά) mysteries for whose sake the former exist and which may be beyond him (209E–210A)[4]; if the imagery is sustained until 210E we may see in the goal (τέλος) of the preceding educative process a comparison with the vision of the Eleusinian ἐποπτεία: reaching the goal of the mysteries of love, he will suddenly perceive something wondrous and beautiful in nature, that which exists eternally. Here the different stages of the Eleusinian mysteries are clearly in view[5]; in the *Phaedrus* terms like ἐνθουσιάζων (249D) and ὠργιάζομεν (250C)[6] suggest that the Dionysiac rites may also be in Plato's mind[7], though not exclusively, as he also uses ἐποπτεύοντες (250C) there. It is the culminating vision of the Eleusinian mysteries, alluded to in this last word, which seems particularly appropriate to Plato as an analogy to the philosopher's goal[8].

69C to the effect that 'those who founded the mysteries seem not to be bad fellows at all (οὐ φαῦλοι)' (230); cf. also Jaeger, 'Ideas' 110.

Ep. Crates 2 (ed. Malherbe 54.10f) also speaks of those 'initiated into philosophy'.

3 Cf. the language of purification applied to philosophers in *Phaedo* 67A–D.

4 So too in the *Meno* (76E) Socrates' instruction is likened to being initiated into mysteries; cf. *Theaet.* 155E–156A (contrast the rival rites of *Resp.* 8.560E).

5 Cf. *Gorg.* 497C.

6 Though ὄργια can be used of the Eleusinian rites (*Hom. Hymn to Demeter* 273, 476; also Aristoph., *Ran.* 386, ed. Hall-Geldart; *Thes.* 948) and others it is most frequently used of the rites of Dionysus (LSJ s.v.).

7 Cf. *Symp.* 218B; *Phaedo* 69CD.

8 Cf. also *Epinomis* 986D.

It is this vision and light, too, to which *Plutarch* appeals as an analogy. Beginning to study philosophy is likened to the awed silence that falls over the previously noisy crowd of initiands, particularly when they see the great light[9] 'as though a shrine were opened' (*De profectibus in virtute* 10.81DE). Perceiving that which must be grasped by the intellect (τὸ νοητόν) and is pure and simple is like a lightning flash passing through the soul and thus only able to be apprehended but once[10]. Thus Plato and Aristotle call this part of philosophy visionary (ἐποπτικόν, *Is. et Os.* 77.382D)[11]. The contemplation of the intelligible and eternal nature is the goal of philosophy as the vision (ἐποπτεία) is of initiation (τελετή, *Quaest. conv.* 82.718D). Yet even the best of initiations in the mysteries are, it must be remembered, but a dream (ὄνειρον) of the vision and initiatory rite (ἐποπτεία καὶ τελετή) granted to virtuous souls after ten thousand years when they are privileged to gaze on the reality, particularly in the 'Plain of Truth, in which the accounts (λόγοι), the forms and the patterns of all things that have come to pass and of all that shall come to pass rest undisturbed.' This information Cleombrotus learnt from a stranger near the Persian Gulf (*Def. orac.* 21.421A) 'as though it were in some rite of mystic initiation'[12]. The 'Plain of Truth' appears also in *Amat.* 19.764F−765A where Eros guides the soul thither during its earthly life, stirring its memories of what it saw in its preincarnate days (765B) and escorting it upward 'like a mystic guide (μυσταγωγός) beside us at our initiation'[13]. On reaching the other world and dwelling there till it is time for another incarnation, the true lover 'joins in the continual celebration of his god's mysteries' (κατωργίασται καὶ διατελεῖ περὶ τὸν αὑτοῦ θεόν, 766B).

Is it not striking that these philosophers look to the vision of some mystic truth afforded by the mysteries, like the 'harvested ear' of corn which Hippolytus claims as the great secret revealed at Eleusis (*Ref.* 5.8.39)[14]? There is no reference to the dying and rising deity or to sharing in his or her fate. Was it that such a doctrine, though central to the mysteries, was not congenial to the philosophers and could not be adapted to their frame of reference? Or was it that such a doctrine was not in fact so central, even to the mysteries, as some would have us believe? (See further in chap. 5.)

---

9 Cf. Hipp., *Ref.* 5.8.40, and §5.1.2 and n. 21.
10 Cf. Plato, *Ep.* 7.344B.
11 Cf. *Alex.* 7.3(5).668B.
12 *Def. orac.* 22.422BC, tr. Babbitt (LCL): καθάπερ ἐν τελετῇ καὶ μυήσει.
13 Tr. Helmbold (LCL); the language of initiation is also used of instruction in geometry in 765A.
14 Some, however, are unwilling to believe that so mundane an object, so frequently exposed to view in the decorations of the Eleusinian sanctuary, could really have been the great mystery of these rites: cf., e.g., Mylonas, *Eleusis* 275f.

There is, however, one passage which might support the suggestion that death and restoration to life were central in the mysteries. This is a fragment quoted by Stobaeus and attributed by him to Themistius' work on the soul but which is now more usually thought to go back to a work of Plutarch on the same subject[15]. In this the soul is said to undergo at death an experience like initiation into great mysteries (τελεταῖς μεγάλαις κατοργιαζόμενοι)[16]; hence the similarity of the verbs τελευτᾶν, to die, and τελεῖσθαι, to be initiated[17]. At first there is

> straying and wandering, the weariness of running this way and that, and nervous journeys through darkness that reach no goal, and then immediately before the consummation every possible terror, shivering and trembling and sweating and amazement[18]. But after this a marvellous light meets the wanderer, and open country and meadow lands welcome him; and in that place there are voices and dancing and the solemn majesty of sacred music and holy visions[19]. And amidst these he walks at large in new freedom, now perfect and fully initiated, celebrating the sacred rites, a garland upon his head, and converses with pure and holy men; he surveys the uninitiated, unpurified mob here on earth, the mob of living men who, herded together in mirk and deep mire, trample one another down and in their fear of death cling to their ills, since they disbelieve in the blessings of the other world[20].

But it must be granted that it is most likely that Plutarch's views of what death involves and what lies beyond it have coloured his account rather than any details of what happened in particular mystery rites; a general pattern of wandering and purposelessness, fear, illumination, freedom and bliss is enough to make valid his comparison. Undoubtedly, too, the comparison would be helped by the conviction, which we have already noted in both Plato and Plutarch, that the insight gained by the soul either before incarnation or after death or a cycle of incarnations, but at any rate liberated from the body, was like an initiation. Furthermore, and this is most important to note here, death is compared to an initiation and not

---

15 Stob., *Ecl.* 4.52.49 (ed. Wachsmuth-Hense 5, 1089–92); M. R. James, 'Clement', argued that the attribution to Themistius was impossible because of the echoes of this passage and others in Clement of Alexandria; Plutarch is the likeliest author because of the interlocutors named, the same as those of Plut., *De sera numinis vindicta*, Timon and Patrocleas. This attribution is also followed by Des Places, 'Platon' 10, as well as by the LCL Plutarch and others.

16 It is tempting to see here an allusion specifically to the Greater Mysteries of Eleusis, but cf. Mylonas, *Eleusis* 264–6. It might be thought that the Dionysiac rites with their ecstatic bands of devotees roaming the mountain sides might be as much in Plutarch's mind as Eleusis with its purposeful and dignified procession to Eleusis (cf. 'journeys . . . that reach no goal'); as a priest at Delphi Plutarch would have been only too familiar with the biennial winter rites on the slopes of nearby Parnassus (Paus. 10.4.3).

17 For another etymological play cf. *Stoic. rep.* 9.1035B: Chrysippus connected τελεταί with τέλος, arguing that theology came last among philosophical disciplines.

18 Cf. Ael. Arist., *Or.* 48=*Or. sacr.* 2.28: carrying out certain rites prescribed by Asclepius 'almost as if in an initiation, since there was great hope together with fear' (tr. Behr); cf. also §33.

19 Cf. *Fac. lun.* 28.943C.

20 Tr. Sandbach in *Moralia* 15 (LCL), 317–19 (=frg. 178).

vice versa; one cannot appeal to *this* text to support the view that initiation was viewed as a death, however likely that may be on other grounds[21]. Nor is there a restoration to life; rather one enters into a new, true life. For the initiate this may only have been possible through the gracious protection of the mystery god or goddess, but for Plutarch this is the natural destiny of the human soul. The difference between the two viewpoints is clear from the way in which he transposes the fate of the uninitiated in the underworld, plunged in mire, to speak of the fate of those not yet dead, still living on earth, whom the departed soul contemplates from its other-worldly vantage point. While initiation in the mysteries was for the initiate a promise of continued life after death, death for Plutarch is, his words at least imply, liberation from the real death of Hades-like existence here on earth; life only really begins at death.

2.4.2. An example of the former sort of adaption of the language of the mysteries, that which seeks to present a counter-claim to those of the mysteries, can best be seen in *Philo of Alexandria*. The difference in his attitude to the mysteries compared with that of Plato and Plutarch can be seen in his vigorous repudiation of, and outspoken contempt for, the pagan mysteries and pagan religion in general, as befitted a pious Jew[1]. Greeks and barbarians had their religious assemblies, the product of 'mythical fictions', full of follies (*Cher.* 91); in these were 'profane initiations' (ἀμύητοι μυήσεις) and rites that are untrue (ἀνοργίαστοι τελεταί, §94)[2]. Their robes may be pure but their hearts are not, yet it is impure animals that they disqualify for their worship (§95)[3]. These rites are forbidden by the Law of Moses and Moses' followers may neither confer nor receive initiation (*Spec. leg.* 1.319)[4]. Mythmaking too is something alien to Moses[5], and Philo is equally scathing about pagan mythology in general[6], with its crude anthropomorphisms[7].

---

21 *Pace* King, *Death* 146, following E. O. James, *Religion* 136; cf. further § §6.1, 6.3.

Notes on 2.4.2

1 Cf. Goodenough, *Light* 44; Pascher, Ὁδός 7f (who gives ample evidence of Philo's use of the language of the mysteries; doubts arise, however, the more he speaks of Philo's acquaintance with the inner 'dogmatic basis' — p. 100 — of the Isis-mysteries).

2 Cf. *Quaest. in Exod.* (ed. Harris) 262 no. 20 (cf. Harris, *Fragments* 75).

3 Cf. also *Deus imm.* 102f; *Spec. leg.* 1.56, 315, 320, 323; 3.40; cf. Hegermann, *Vorstellung* 9ff.

4 *Pace* Goodenough, *Light* 123, this is most naturally taken as a warning to his fellow-Jews not to suppose that their faith allowed them to partake in pagan rites; cf. 1 Cor 10.14—22.

5 Cf., e.g., *Op. mund.* 1f, 157; *Gig.* 58 (cf. 60); *Conf. ling.* 2—13; *Fug.* 121 (it is also alien to God: *Det. pot. ins.* 125).

6 Cf., e.g., *Op. mund.* 157; *Cher.* 91; *Sacr. AC.* 76; *Migr. Abr.* 138; *Congr.* 15; *Spec. leg.* 3.45;

Yet, despite this estimate of the pagan mysteries, Philo was quite prepared to present Judaism in terms appropriate to a mystery-religion[8]. And indeed it was such, according to some definitions at least. It is arguably one of the problems of the definition which Köster offers (see §2.3 above) that it could in many respects also fit the Judaism, if not of Philo's day, at least of the period after the fall of Jerusalem, as Köster grants[9]: it was characterized by the preservation of a tradition handed down by word of mouth alone, by the requirement of strict moral and ritual observances for all its members, by the obligation on all members to meet regularly and to help each other, and by the fact that they were sharply differentiated from outsiders. On the other hand the Jewish initiation ceremonies did not feature quite so prominently in Jewish ritual as in most pagan mysteries, and it is questionable how far one can talk of secrecy in the case of Judaism[10]; we saw (in §2.1) in the case of earlier Egyptian religion how what seemed due to secrecy to the Greeks may have been rather the result of the abstruse nature of their documents and doctrines which put them beyond the reach of simple worshippers; so too much in the Jewish religion must have seemed strange and incomprehensible to the outsider[11].

Yet Philo heightens the similarities between Judaism and the mysteries by repeatedly presenting the religion of Moses as if it were a mystery-religion, sometimes directly contrasting it with the pagan myths:

> 'when Moses convokes such people (wise men) and would initiate them into his mysteries (μυσταγωγῶν), he invites them . . ., exhorting them . . . to rise in rebellion against the mythical fables impressed on their yet tender souls from their earliest years by parents and nurses and tutors and the multitude of other familiars, . . .' (*Virt.* 178, tr. Colson).

4.178; *Virt.* 102, 178; *Praem. poen.* 8, 162; *Aet. mund.* 56f, 131; also *Rer. div. her.* 228 (against the myth of an ἐκπύρωσις); *Vit. cont.* 63 (against Aristophanes' myth in Plato, *Symp.* 189D ff); *De providentia* 2.66 (against the myth of the land of the Cyclops).

7 Cf., e.g., *Leg. all.* 1.43; *Poster. C.* 2; contrast *Deus imm.* 61f.

8 On Philo's predecessors here cf. Cerfaux, 'Influence'. Perhaps the most significant text is one attributed to Orpheus which Eus. says he found in a work by Aristobulus; the profane (βέβηλοι) are ordered to depart and Musaeus is bidden to keep the revelation secret (cf. tr. Lafargue in Charlesworth, *Pseudepigrapha* 2, 799). None of this evidence quite compares with the scale of Philo's assimilation of the language of the mysteries. Yet the possibilities of the identification by Artapanus of Moses with Musaeus and as Orpheus' teacher are considerable (in Eus., *Praep. ev.* 9.27.3f). Cf. also, rather later, Jos., *Ap.* 2.188f; also Dean-Otting's judgment that *3 Apoc. Bar.* is rooted in the language and thought of both the OT and the mystery-cults (*Journeys* 108f). Wolfson, *Philo* 1, 46, argues that Philo employs the language of the mysteries as of popular religion and of mythology because it was 'part of common speech'.

9 *Einführung* 206=ET 1, 199; cf. Früchtel, *Vorstellungen* 114.

10 Contrast the definitions of Sänger and Burkert quoted above in §2.3 n. 10.

11 Cf., e.g., Tac., *Hist.* 5.4f; Jos., *Ap.* 1.239f, 249f.

In keeping with this Moses is very frequently referred to simply as 'the hierophant'[12]; he has himself been initiated into most holy mysteries (*Gig.* 54)[13], but is no ordinary initiate but one who reveals holy things from the shrine (*Poster. C.* 173). Jeremiah too is once described as a hierophant[14] and Aaron's cultic duties in the sanctuary can be described in terms suggestive of a mystery-cult[15]. But the primarily bookish nature of this mystery can be clearly seen in the reference to the 'oracles' of the Old Testament as exercising the functions of a hierophant in *Som.* 1.207[16] and Philo's allegorical exegesis of these forms mystic rites[17].

As well as referring to his fellow followers of Moses as initiates, especially those sharing his insights into Moses' true meaning[18], Philo can at times describe the divine insight that he has been granted in terms recalling the possession of the Bacchants[19]: what he has experienced countless times (μυριάκις) is that at some times he has settled down to write something which he had in mind but has found his mind bereft of ideas, and yet at others he has sat down without any conception of what to write and has been showered with ideas from above 'so that under the influence of the Divine possession I have been filled with corybantic frenzy (ὡς ὑπὸ κατοχῆς ἐνθέου κορυβαντιᾶν) and been unconscious of anything, place, persons present, myself, words spoken, lines written' (*Migr. Abr.* 34f, tr. Colson-Whitaker). The Therapeutae, too, 'snatched up by heavenly love, like those in Bacchic or corybantic frenzy, are possessed (ἐνθουσιά-ζουσιν) until they see the object for which they yearn' (*Vit. cont.* 12). In this is it clear that Philo's ecstasy leads to literary output and it is doubtful whether the Therapeutae's is any more than a figurative usage for their wholehearted search after divine truth[20]. Rightly Pohlenz, alluding to *Cher.* 27f, observes that, although Philo's insights may be inspired and not just the product of human reasoning, yet they should not be put on the same level as prophetic visions, the sacramental experience of the mysteries or such phenomena of tongues-speaking. The artfulness of his writings is not the work of frenzied possession[21].

---

12 *Leg. all.* 3.151; *Sacr. AC.* 94; *Poster. C.* 16, 164; *Migr. Abr.* 14; *Som.* 2.3, 29; *Virt.* 75; cf. also *Deus imm.* 156; *Som.* 1.164; *Vit. Mos.* 2.153; *Spec. leg.* 1.41. Hierophant and prophet: *Leg. all.* 3.173. Hierophant and teacher of divine rites: *Gig.* 54. 'Keeper and guardian of the mysteries of the Existent One': *Plant.* 26.
13 Cf. *Vit. Mos.* 2.71.
14 *Cher.* 49; cf. *Conf. ling.* 44: a member of the θίασος of the prophetic chorus.
15 *Ebr.* 129; cf. *Vit. Mos.* 2.153.
16 *Leg. all.* 3.219; cf. *Conf. ling.* 149.
17 Cf., e.g., *Som.* 1.164f.
18 *Cher.* 42; *Fug.* 85; *Decal.* 41.
19 Cf. also §4.2 and texts cited there, also §4.2.2.
20 Cf. Nock, 'Question' 162f=465.
21 'Philon' 474; also Früchtel, *Vorstellungen* 112–15; cf. §4.2.2 and n. 35.

Two motifs drawn from the world of the mysteries are particularly striking in Philo's thought, their secrecy and their graded rites. Despite his scorn at their secrecy in *Spec. leg.* 1.320, God's unspeakable mysteries (ἀπόρρητα) are, he argues, not for all to see but only for those who can keep them safe (*Leg. all.* 2.57)[22]. They are only for the purified[23]; these beauties are not for the uninitiated (*Som.* 1.164). The various stages in the mysteries, especially in the Eleusinian rites, are also copied by Philo in his description of the soul's way to God; there too there are lesser mysteries before the greater, either, for instance, when it knows God in his actions alone as opposed to his essential nature (*Abr.* 122) or when it tames the passions through reason as a preparation for higher knowledge (*Sacr. AC.* 62). The very variety in the use of this imagery should, however, warn us against taking it too literally[24]; it is imagery used to describe the quest for philosophical[25] and religious knowledge through God's revelation in the scriptures of the Old Testament, be it the quest of an individual or the collective search of a group like the Therapeutae[26].

It is noticeable how much more frequent and pervasive the language of the mysteries is in Philo's writings than in those of Plato and Plutarch, yet it does not follow that his use of this language is any different in kind from theirs. This is argued persuasively by E. R. Goodenough in his *Introduction to Philo Judaeus*[27], where he qualifies the position set out in his earlier *By Light, Light* to guard against certain misunderstandings that the latter had occasioned[28]. He does not want to suggest that there were mystic Jews with 'distinct rites of their own' and 'distinct initiations, to which even Jews must be specially admitted'. The rites that played a part in their mysticism were the usual Jewish ones, into which a deeper meaning was read, just as they found a deeper meaning in the Jewish scriptures[29]. This meaning was a real mystery as Greek philosophers from

---

22 Cf. also *Cher.* 48; *Sacr. AC.* 60, 62, 131; *Som.* 1.191; *Quaest. in Exod.* 4.8; in this he was following Plato's example (*Theaet.* 155E); cf. also *SVF* 2.1008.

23 Cf. *Leg. all.* 3.100; *Gig.* 54; *Vit. Mos.* 2.114; *Praem. poen.* 120f; cf. *Quaest. in Exod.* (ed. Harris) 262 no. 20=Harris, *Fragments* 75.

24 Cf. also *Leg. all.* 3.100; *Cher.* 49; *Vit. Mos.* 1.62.

25 Philo refers to οἱ φιλοσοφίας θιασῶται in *Cher.* 85.

26 Cf. *Leg. all.* 3.71, 100; *Poster. C.* 101; *Plant.* 58; *Omn. prob. lib.* 14; *Vit. cont.* 25.

27 *Introduction* 154; for a brief survey of the various views on this question cf. Hegermann, *Vorstellung* 6–9; P. Borgen in *ANRW* 2.21.1, 139–42.

28 This clarification was necessary: cf. *Light* 8, 'The evidence seems on the whole to suggest that [the cult groups of mystic Jews] may have had their mystic initiation, baptism, like the Christians later', with *Introduction* 156f, 'there is no trace of an initiatory rite for Jews into the Mystery. . . . Philo has nothing to say about baptism. Whether Jews were using it in Alexandria we do not know, but it was a rite which did not come from the Pentateuch, and Philo has no occasion to mention it.' (It is presumably the earlier view which Dillon censures in 'Self-Definition' 74.)

29 *Introduction* 155.

Plato onwards had understood it in the sense of 'the miraculous elevation of the soul through its assimilation of and by the immaterial', an eleva- tion for which most men need the help of myths and rites[30]. Of course it was not then a 'mystery-religion' in the sense in which we normally use the phrase, any more than Plato's philosophy or Plutarch's, although it was more overtly a religion rather than a philosophy in so far as one can make the distinction at this stage[31]. Yet confusion could arise because Philo does use language appropriate to, and indeed often derived from, the mystery-religions, although, as we have seen, he was by no means the first to transpose this language into the service of a creed of a different sort. To the extent that this language was thus transposed it might be legitimate to call it 'figurative'; more precisely, one should perhaps say that a real 'mystery', *qua* mystic philosophy, is expressed at times in figures of speech derived from the mystery-religions[32]. And, because he is a zealous devotee of a religion, and an exclusive one at that, Philo is perhaps all the keener to use this language in order to show how his faith surpasses the religion of the pagan cults[33].

One Hellenistic Jewish work often thought to reflect an assimilation of the Jewish faith to the mysteries is *Joseph and Aseneth*[34]. Yet Berner argues that this work does not show the Jewish adoption of pagan sacra- mental ideas any more than does the thought of Philo[35]. Decisive here is the fact that the moment of Aseneth's reception into the Jewish faith and the Jewish community is not linked with any of the various symbolic rites described in the work, fasting, eating a honeycomb or a cultic meal, or the putting on of festal garments[36], but takes place between them, in

---

30 Ibid. 138; cf. 'Mystery'.

31 Yet the difference is certainly one of degree only as far as Plutarch was concerned since he too saw a deeper meaning in various religious rites and traditions; cf. Goodenough, 'Mystery' 235f. What is doubtful is whether mystic Jews ever 'formed special groups for celebrating the Jewish "sacraments" in their own way with their own explanations and comments' ('Mystery' 241; this does not seem to be reasserted in his *Introduction*; cf. 158: 'the traditional forms were quite adequate when properly understood'); cf. also E. P. Sanders, 'Covenant' 25: Philo represents 'essentially a Hellenistic mystical philosophy'.

32 Cf. Nock, 'Question'.

33 Cf. Hegermann, *Vorstellung* 13–15.

34 Cf. Sänger, *Judentum* 48ff.

35 *Initiationsriten* 156ff; cf. Sänger, ibid. 148ff.

36 Fast: *Joseph and Aseneth* 10 (Batiffol 50.18–53.4=Philonenko 10.2, 20). Putting on garments. 14 (60.2–16=14.12–17). Meal of honeycomb: 16 (62.23–65.17=16.1–17). This is described as 'the bread of life' and 'cup of immortality' and 'anointing of incorruption' (64.14f – not in Philonenko, but cf. tr. Burchard 16.16 in Charlesworth, *Pseudepigrapha* 2, 229; see also 15, 61.4–7=15.4).

In response to her fasting and prayer of repentance and after she has replaced her garments of mourning with festal ones Aseneth is told that her name was written (ἐγράφη) in the book of life (15, 61.3f =15.3) and that from that day she will be renewed and given new life; moreover she was chosen before birth (8.11; Batiffol's version differs).

response to Joseph's petition and Aseneth's confession; it is something that takes place between the proselyte Aseneth and the God of the Hebrews and not in any cultic ceremonies; the latter serve merely as what Berner calls 'accompanying ritual actions'. Here again, as in Philo's writings, it may be suggested, we have the normal Jewish rites and meals described in terms reflecting the usage of the pagan cults as a deliberate contrast to them[37].

2.4.3. When we turn to *Paul and early Christianity* we can, I think, say with as near certainty as is possible that Paul himself was never an initiate or a devotee of the mysteries or any pagan cults, despite occasional suggestions to the contrary[1]. With early Christianity as a whole one must be far more circumspect, but it seems unlikely, particularly in view of the tendency of many mysteries to extract a high price for initiation (cf. §2.1), that the number of converts to Christianity from the ranks of initiates was very high, especially in the earliest, formative years of the church and its theology. It seems to me to be assigning a disproportionate influence to this small and still completely hypothetical group of converts to suggest that they exerted a strong formative influence on the development of early Christian sacramental thinking by interpreting the Christian rites along the lines of the secret doctrines of the mystery-cults.

That being so, it is surely far more plausible to suggest that any influence which these cults exerted on early Christianity came, not from their secret rites and beliefs, but from their public ceremonies and affirmations and from those aspects of their beliefs which had become part of

---

37 §8 (49.3–8, 22f =8.5, 11; cf. Sänger, *Judentum* 172, 184; also Burchard, *Untersuchungen* 121–33, and Charlesworth, *Pseudepigrapha and the NT* 133). This is not incompatible with the basic assessment of Kee, 'Setting', that *Joseph and Aseneth* reflects a form of Judaism in the tradition of Merkabah mysticism, for, even if a deeper symbolism was read into the Jewish rites and customs, this is not to make them sacramental channels of salvation in the manner of the mysteries. Rather the type of Judaism represented by this document is presented in a way which rivals the claims of the Isis-cult, and does so by echoing some of the imagery and literary forms used by that cult (cf. Kee 410).

Notes on 2.4.3

1 Cf., e.g., §2.2.2 n. 22; contrast Nock, 'Vocabulary' 139=347: 'Many curious imaginings have flitted across the minds of men as they have sought to reconstruct the past; but there can have been few more curious than the picture of Paul listening attentively to Stoic lectures at Tarsus or making enquiries about Mithraism and later enriching Christianity from these sources'; cf. Simon, '*Schule*' 139: no one today should maintain that Paul read or studied pagan religious literature, but he could know those secrets that leaked out from the cults – or, we should add, what the cults openly proclaimed.

the common heritage of the Hellenistic world². Even Paul would have been familiar with the public face of the pagan cults and rites³, and so would any early Christians at all familiar with Graeco-Roman culture. Paul shows this when he does not hesitate to draw parallels between pagan cultic practice and belief and Christian ones in 1 Cor 10.19—21 ; the cults referred to here are of course by no means to be limited to the mysteries, but it would be arbitrary to exclude them⁴; as in the Christian cult meal so in pagan ones the table-fellowship and the attendant rites effect a real fellowship with the one in whose name the meal is held, and in the case of pagan rites that means a fellowship with demons. (This is an interpretation with which some pagans might agree, in view of the role which Plutarch assigns to his *daimones* in officiating over oracles and mystery rites⁵; the difference is that for Paul *daimones* or *daimonia* are without exception to be avoided as evil, for Plutarch they can be good or bad⁶.)

Paul's language elsewhere shows familiarity with language that could be used of the myetery-religions and perhaps either originated with them or was given certain important nuances by them, but arguably it is all language which had by his day a far wider currency. It was A.D. Nock who commented on the absence from the New Testament as a whole, including Paul, of terminology that was really distinctively that of the mysteries and Hellenistic religious vocabulary in general⁷: missing are μύστης, μυστικός, μυσταγωγός, τελέω in the sense of 'initiate' and its compounds, τέλος in the sense of 'rite', τελετή, ἀτέλεστος (like ἀμύητος), ἱεροφάντης, ὄργια, as well as a number of terms appropriate to spiritual possession, κατέχεσθαι, κάτοχος, ἔνθεος, ἐνθουσιάζω and cognates; although καθαρισμός is used (7 times) we do not find καθαρμός, καθαρσία or κάθαρσις, and so on. When μυστήριον is used it simply means 'secret'⁸ and μεμύημαι is found only in Phil 4.12 in a figurative sense. It almost seems, he con-

---

2 For an example of the figurative use of mystery language in general usage cf. Plut., *Consol. ad Apoll.* 12.107E.

3. Cf. D. H. Wiens in *ANRW* 2.23.2, 1263f.

4 Cf. Lietzmann-Kümmel, *1—2 Kor* 49—51.

5 Cf. §2.2.3 n. 8.

6 Cf. Héring, *1 Cor* 96.

7 'Vocabulary' esp. 132—4=342f; contrast the usage of Clem. Alex., *Prot.* 12.118.4; 119.1; 120.1f, 5; Orig., *Cels.* 3.59—62; cf. Dodds, *Pagan* 96; Eliade, *Birth* 118; Nock, 'Mysteries' 206f=815f; G. H. R. Horsley, *Documents* 1, 14; Wagner, *Baptism* 274f; Leipoldt, 'Taufe' 68, comments that early Christians avoided ritual actions too which were too closely associated with the mysteries.

8 Cf. G. Bornkamm in *TDNT* 4, esp. 824: 'μυστήριον is a rare expression in the NT which betrays no relation to the mystery cults.' Cf. Wischmeyer, *Weg* 56f: it is 'a frequently used concept in the general religious language of the New Testament period'. Yet contrast H. D. Betz, 'Problem', on 1 Cor 2.6ff: 'It should be obvious to anyone who has read ancient literature connected with the mystery cults that Paul has taken over and applied terminology from the mystery cults' (37).

cludes, that 'there was a deliberate avoidance' of such terms 'as having associations which were deprecated'[9]. Later he applied this insight very forcefully to the question of baptism and the Lord's supper: 'any idea that what we call the Christian sacraments were in their origin indebted to pagan mysteries or even to the metaphorical concepts based upon them shatters on the rock of linguistic evidence'[10].

If Paul and other New Testament writers thus fought shy of using so much of the Graeco-Roman religious vocabulary and displayed so many more inhibitions about using it than Philo did, is it likely that they would have felt free to use ideas which had their origin in the mystery-religions? That seems to me unlikely, to say the least. Where some have argued that Paul does use the language of the mysteries, e.g. in 1 Cor 2.6f [11], it is surely preferable, in the light of the above arguments, to say that the terminology which has been used has been, in Paul's eyes, thoroughly decontaminated; it must have been part of general Graeco-Roman usage (i.e. not specifically connected with pagan religion) and, more important, an accepted part of the vocabulary of Hellenistic Judaism, whatever connotations it may have had for his Corinthian readers.

If any direct adaption of the language or ideas of pagan religion is unlikely on the part of Paul or indeed on the part of those who have written the majority of our New Testament, what of their predecessors? Is it possible that there was a stratum before them of Hellenistic Christians who did not share their qualms and prejudices and who so firmly established an assimilation of Christian tradition to Hellenistic beliefs that their successors accepted this version of the Christian faith without detecting, or shrinking from, its pagan traits? It is always possible, I suppose, but highly unlikely. It is the service of M. Hengel that he has asked us to look realistically at the likely facts[12]: the earliest Christian congregations in Hellenistic centres like Antioch were 'mixed' in the sense that they were composed of both Jews and non-Jews — the latter, we may add, including

---

9 Contrast Reitzenstein, *Mysterienreligionen* 420; Köster, *Einführung* 196=ET 1, 191; G. Widengren in *HO* 1.8.2, 79; the claim of Noack, '*Teste*' 25, that 'Paul did in fact lavishly use the language of the mysteries' is misleading and has to be read in the light of his subsequent observation that 'he simply speaks and writes the language of his time and his milieu . . . in so far as it had adopted, in colloquial usage, disparate bits of religious and philosophical ideas'. It might rather be thought that, in the light of Nock's evidence, the dictum of Heinrici quoted with approval by Clemen, *Einfluß* 25, to the effect that Christianity was an 'anti-mystery' rather than a mystery-religion had much to be said for it.

10 'Mysteries' 200=809.

11 Cf. Reitzenstein, *Mysterienreligionen* 333ff; Wilckens, *Weisheit* 53ff; contrast G. Bornkamm, who in *TDNT* 4, 819, allows that the Corinthian Gnostics' usage can be detected behind Paul's words, but argues that Paul's understanding of it is very different; cf. Lührmann, *Offenbarungsverständnis* 113ff.

12 'Christologie' esp. 47–51=ET 32–5.

a considerable number, probably a majority, at least at first, who had been previously attached to the synagogue – and so were ineptly described as 'Gentile Christian' by the likes of Bousset[13]; moreover the timescale for any such assimilation of the Christian faith to these pagan beliefs would probably have had to be very short, particularly if it was supposed to have taken place before Paul's conversion and subsequent further instruction in the Christian faith. On any reading of the evidence the time between Jesus' death and resurrection and Paul's conversion must have been very short, perhaps as little as two years or less[14]. This hardly allows much time for a fusion of the ideas of the mysteries and Christian thinking about the sacraments to have become so established and accepted that Jewish Christians like Paul could adopt them unaware of the pagan associations which they were elsewhere so careful to avoid. Thus, if the mysteries were going to have any effect upon early Christianity it is more likely to have done so *via* Hellenistic Judaism and its beliefs; Hellenistic Judaism, as we have seen in one of its representatives, Philo, abhorred the mystery-cults of paganism and yet to varying degrees was prepared to adopt their language, using it figuratively, to present its rival claims; in this adoption and adaptation it in turn was following, to a large extent, the conventions of Greek philosophy which had also used this language, without quite the same polemical thrust, to present its claims to open the way to a higher, truer mystery. Both these traditions, Hellenistic Judaism and Greek philosophy, can thus be described as having been influenced by the mysteries, however much they opposed them on the one hand, or scorned them or considered them inadequate on the other. If, then, in the following chapters we can show any positive influence of the mysteries on early Christianity and in particular on Paul and his churches, it is likely to have been exerted to start with in this very indirect way, *via* Greek culture in general and the thought of Hellenistic Judaism in particular. Only later, as Christians without this Jewish antipathy to paganism appeared in the early church and made their influence felt, should we expect to find traces of direct influence of pagan ideas on their thinking and thus, most likely in the form of a repudiation, on the thought of their Jewish Christian leaders, including Paul. It is the gauging of these two sorts of influence that will concern us in what follows, as a positive sequel to the perhaps rather negative, but still very necessary, conclusions which we have reached up to this point.

---

13 *Kyrios* e.g. 75–7.
14 Cf. my 'Chronologies'.

2.5. Conclusions

The preceding sections have sought to show that we must be more cautious than Schweitzer was when he so curtly dismissed the possibility of Paul's being influenced by the Graeco-Roman mysteries. The mysteries were certainly very much alive in the first century of our era and, even if they were not yet enjoying the boom which they experienced in the following two centuries, they were a spiritual power to be reckoned with in Paul's day. Nor is there any adequate reason for saying that the beliefs of their devotees then were greatly different from those a century later, so that it is not illegitimate to read back whatever we may infer from, for instance, Apuleius' account of Lucius' initiation into the mysteries of Isis.

What will not do, however, is to infer that everyone initiated into the rites of Isis understood them in quite the same way, even in Apuleius' day, let alone a century earlier; still less is it true that Lucius' experiences can be read into the experiences of initiates of all the other mystery-religions as if they all shared a common theology. It is impossible to generalize from such individual pieces of evidence; the best that we can do is to say that this was true in one particular instance and may have been true in some others also. However we have no reason either for setting any such piece of evidence aside as only an isolated case; it might also be typical of many others.

A perhaps even more cogent reason for caution in postulating any influence of the mysteries on early Christianity is the difficulty of reconstructing a plausible historical setting where such an influence, if known to be such, would have been tolerated. Unlike Philo, the early Christians seem to have fought shy of using even the language of the mysteries, and any group of them who were both ready to use not only their language but their ideas as well and were on the scene early enough to have the necessary formative influence on pre-Pauline theology is an unproved, hypothetical entity, and not a very plausible one.

Later Paul did establish churches where there was a larger proportion of Greeks and non-Jews, probably including some at least with little or no personal experience of Judaism as a way of life; at that stage we may expect to encounter Christians without Jewish scruples and aversion towards the mysteries and pagan religion in general; they would, moreover, tend to interpret the faith which they had been taught in the light of their pagan religious experience, especially if through the pressures of time or persecution Paul and other Christian evangelists had not been able to instruct them as thoroughly as was necessary and desirable (cf., e.g., 1 Thess 3.10) in the principles of what was in the eyes of the ancient world a most unusually exclusive religion.

There would also have been indirect influence earlier, of course, both positively in the mark left on Graeco-Roman culture by the mysteries, and negatively in the ways in which early Christianity set itself up as a rival to these pagan cults. The spores of the mystery-cults were, on the one hand, embedded too deeply in the soil of Hellenistic culture for early Christianity to escape them entirely without losing all touch with its world (cf. 1 Cor 5.10); and, on the other, it had to present the claims of its Lord in antithesis to the 'many "gods" and many "lords"' of its world (1 Cor 8.5).

Thus, in looking for signs of Graeco-Roman influence, and in particular of influence of the mysteries, on early Christianity in the following chapters we shall have to bear in mind that Paul's letters may witness to positive influence on two possible levels:

(1) Jewish Christians, including Paul, may have unwittingly taken over from their Graeco-Roman environment ideas and language that were shared by the mysteries and pagan religion, but were not peculiar to them, even if they may have originated in them.

(2) Gentile Christians, perhaps encouraged by these similarities, may have then interpreted the Christian faith in terms of their own religious traditions, reading into it interpretations that had not previously occurred to their Jewish Christian teachers, who, once they realized them, repudiated them.

3. The Spiritualizing of 'Resurrection'

This chapter is limited in scope; the wider questions of resurrection, be it that of Jesus or of the general resurrection, have been much discussed elsewhere[1]. Rather, we are primarily concerned with two historical questions: the first is how the language of resurrection, and in particular the term ἀνάστασις and its cognates and, to a lesser extent, ἐγείρω and its cognates[2], would have been understood in the Graeco-Roman culture of the first century C.E., and the second is the question how far the concept was open to, and ripe for, reinterpretation and how and when it was reinterpreted.

In investigating the reinterpretation of the idea of resurrection we need carefully to distinguish between reinterpretation of it and substitution of another idea for it. In other words we are not concerned so much with views of an after-life simply in terms of a spiritual or non-corporeal existence[3]; rather what concerns us here is those texts which use the language of resurrection in a spiritual or non-corporeal sense. This is the distinction between saying that we shall survive but without specifying that the form of survival is that of resurrection, and saying that there is resurrection, now or in the future, but that it does not involve the raising of physical bodies from the dead. Yet a further distinction must also be made here between language which unambiguously belongs to the idea of bodily resurrection, and language which may at times be used of resurrection, but is not exclusively or properly limited to that idea. It may be granted that

---

Notes on 3

1 Recent bibliographies will be found in *ALW* 23, 112–16; *ANRW* 2.25.1, 844–90; *DNTT* 3, 305–9; Hoffmann, *Toten*[3] 365–76; Schillebeeckx, *Jesus* 329–31, 516f; Schürer-Black-Millar-Vermes, *History* 2, 539 n. 90; Stemberger, *Leib* 1–4 and nn.; *TRE* 4, 443, 449f, 463–7, 509–13.

2 Fascher, 'Anastasis' 168–70, shows that the verb ἐγείρω and the noun ἀνάστασις are the commonest terms in the NT to express the idea of resurrection. Ἔγερσις is found only once (Matt 27.53) and ἐγείρω is found approximately twice as often as ἀνίστημι in this sense (perhaps because of the stress on God as the one who raised Jesus; cf. Kramer, *Christ* §6ab, 32f); cf. also Evans, *Resurrection* 20–7.

3 Failure to make this distinction (and also the following one) mars the work of Cavallin, *Life*, as well as that of others like Nickelsburg, *Resurrection*.

ἀνάστασις in 2 Tim 2.18 is an example of the first, but what are we to make, for instance, of cases of a ζῳοποιεῖν in the present[4]?

A further important distinction to be made is that between resurrection as the means by which all people or a certain class of people enter their final, ultimate state of existence, and a raising which simply restores a particular individual to his or her previous mode of existence on earth, a mode of existence that still awaits death in the end. The one introduces a state beyond death, triumphant over death; the other is simply a prolongation of life for a time, until finally death comes again to claim its own; it is but a temporary reprieve[5]. Thus when Hengel observes that 'the notion of resurrection was not completely alien even to the Greeks'[6] the examples which he cites are of temporary restorations to life like the miracle-stories of the Gospels in which Jesus restored certain individuals to life[7]. Strictly, however, these raisings are not 'from the dead' since usually those who are thus raised have not yet entered the realm of the dead, nor have the burial rites for them been duly completed. The likes of Lazarus would be an exception (cf. John 11.17, 39)[8]; so too, even more clearly, would be the experiences of Alcestis and Eurydice, but their raising was still not a permanent rescue from the kingdom of the dead, only a temporary release[9]. It is very natural that the raising of people to renewed this-worldly life is bodily; if it liberated one from this-worldly bodily existence it is likely that it would represent a final triumph over death. Yet it must be granted that this distinction, this difference in kind, was not always observed, as, for instance, when the rabbis argued for the resurrection of the dead in the future by citing the miracles of resuscitation worked by Old Testament prophets[10].

Finally we must note that the 'spiritualizing' referred to in the title of this chapter could and did mean different things. To refer to a 'spiritual

---

4 Cf. on *Joseph and Aseneth* below in §3.3.2; here questions of the context of the work as a whole come into consideration, and also that of the context in which the work was written. 'Make alive' may more easily imply resurrection in a rabbinic text than it does in a Hellenistic one.

5 Cf. Hoffmann, *Toten* 73.

6 *Judaism* 2, 131 n. 575.

7 Mk 5.42 pars; Lk 7.15; John 11.44.

8 On the onset of putrefaction after three days: *Qoh. Rab.* 12.6; *Lev. Rab.* 18.1; Str. -B. 2, 544f.

9 See the catalogue of gods, heroes and others in Hyginus, *Fabulae* 251; cf. Pötscher, ' "Auferstehung" '. One common feature of the shaman's role is to visit the underworld in his spirit and, if need be, to heal by summoning up the soul of the sick from there; cf. West, *Poems* 5. The legend of Zalmoxis in Hdt. 4.95 is harder to gauge; presumably the sceptical, rationalist account of this Thracian god would have to say that after his staged resurrection this slave of Pythagoras lived for a while, only to die eventually (contrast 4.94).

10 Cf. Volz, *Eschatologie* 235, citing *Pesiq. Rab Kah.* 9.4 (tr. Braude-Kapstein 176) and *Pirqe R. El.* 33 (tr. Friedlander 239ff).

resurrection' could mean a great many different things (we shall see in the following chapter, apropos of 1 Corinthians 10 — see §4.1.1.3 below —, that 'spiritual' is in general a most elusive word). 'Spiritual' in the present context could mean, e.g.,

(1) 'of spirit(s)', so that a 'spiritual resurrection' means a raising of spirit(s) rather than bodies (cf. §3.1.2 below);

(2) 'of a spiritual nature or substance' as opposed to 'of a bodily or corporeal nature or substance';

(3) 'of a spiritual nature' as opposed to 'of a carnal, this-worldly nature' — such a 'spiritual resurrection' might then be bodily, but other-worldly in the sense that it is part of the inauguration of a new world-order, still physical and material, but cleansed and purged of sin and decay;

(4) 'empowered, activated, controlled by the Spirit (of God)' — here it is clear that the spirit to which the adjective 'spiritual' relates is not the human spirit but the divine, and what is 'spiritual' is in contrast with all that is opposed to, or independent of, God;

(5) 'relating to, taking place in the human spirit' — here it is more or less equivalent to 'inward and unseen'; a 'spiritual resurrection' is then a hidden and unseen one in the depths of the human spirit as opposed to the public one expected at the end of this world;

(6) much the same as 'metaphorical'[11].

Thus, when we find scholars asserting that they have found the idea of a 'spiritual resurrection' in some source or other, we need to ask very carefully what is meant by the phrase. Paul, for instance, can speak of a 'spiritual resurrection' in the sense of the resurrection of a 'spiritual body' in 1 Corinthians 15, and we should probably take this in the sense of (3) or (4) above or both; yet this is for him something that still lies in the future for all except Christ and cannot be realized in this world or on this side of the barrier of physical death, at least not in its full sense. Hence we must carefully distinguish between the use of the language of 'resurrection' to describe the survival of the human soul or spirit beyond death (senses 1 or 2 above), and its use to describe present existence in this world. The former, if evidence of it can be found, at least at an early enough date to be significant (and we shall see that some do indeed claim to have found it), is less striking as a reinterpretation than the latter. Possible examples of the former we shall consider in §3.1.2, whereas the latter will be considered under §3.3.

---

11 It is clear, e.g. from M. Delcor's remarks in *JSSt* 13, 280, that for him a 'spiritual resurrection' in the sense of the Qumran community's present exaltation is a 'metaphorical' one. The community are also metaphorically 'dead', but only metaphorically, not physically (cf. on Rom 6.13 in §1.3.1.2 above).

3.1. The Jewish Doctrine of Resurrection

3.1.1. 'Resurrection' is, of course, an idea widely attested in Jewish writings. Its emergence in its various forms has been frequently investigated, being traced back to its first clear appearance in Jewish texts in the period of the Maccabees and back beyond that[1]. What needs to be stressed is that, at least in the period up to the fall of Jerusalem and the rise to dominance of Pharisaic Judaism, there existed side by side in Judaism a variety of different hopes and beliefs about life after death[2]. However, even before the triumph of the Pharisaic movement had given resurrection a dominant position in Jewish reflections on the manner of life after death, the idea of resurrection had been established in the centre of early Christian thinking on this subject. For the reason for this we do not have to look very far: it was believed that God had raised Jesus from the dead. It was not inevitable − far from it[3] − that Jesus was held to have been vindicated by God in this way, but once it was generally accepted by the earliest Christians that he had been it was inevitable that 'resurrection' should be a central and indeed normative item in the beliefs of early Christians.

It will be the argument of this section that originally, when the Greek-speaking Jew spoke of ἀνάστασις and its cognates, or ἐγείρειν and its cognates, in the context of the after-life, then, like the non-Jewish Greek, he did so knowing 'that the severed connection between the soul and the body must be restored again'[4]. In other words, it was not expected that

---

Notes on 3.1.1

1 See Cavallin, *Life* 1, 25f nn. 22−5, on the different sources suggested for the Jewish belief in resurrection; hints or foreshadowings (to put it no stronger) of resurrection can perhaps be detected elsewhere in the OT: cf. Russell, *Method* 356, 367f; also Hoffmann, *Toten* 75f.

2 Cf. Evans, *Resurrection* 27: 'resurrection was not a universally held belief and badge of orthodoxy, but a subject of considerable speculation and debate' during the period with which we are concerned; cf. also Beresford, *Concept* Pt 1; Harvey, *Jesus* 150; Hoffmann, *Toten* 79f; Russell, *Method* 372−4; Volz, *Eschatologie* 253.

3 Harvey, ibid. 151, urges us to take seriously the puzzlement of the disciples in Mk 9.10 at the idea of rising from the dead; but contrast with this the views of Pesch, 'Entstehung' esp. 222−5, who, following Berger, *Auferstehung* esp. 146, argues that the categories for interpreting Jesus' fate as the death and resurrection of the righteous eschatological prophet lay ready to hand. Lapide, too, argues, following Schweitzer, that Jesus had expected the rising and parousia of the Son of Man to follow his death; accordingly his disciples were horrified, not at what happened, but at what failed to happen thereafter (*Resurrection* 68); it was a theological necessity that Jesus should rise (88f); yet he grants that most of Jesus' friends believed his death was the end (85) and that the wish to anoint his body 'proves that basically none of the disciples nor the women themselves . . . expected his resurrection' (96).

4 Fascher, 'Anastasis' 187; cf. Kretschmar, 'Auferstehung' 111; already this way of speaking bears the mark of later, Greek ways of thinking according to the judgment of Stemberger, who sees

there could be an ἀνάστασις that only involved the soul. I say 'originally' because we shall see that the physical connotations of the term came to be weakened and it was reinterpreted to make it more congenial to different ways of thought.

For it is perhaps misleading when Fascher speaks of Hippolytus and Clement of Alexandria as evidence of different understandings of ἀνάστα-σις among Jews and sectarian groups[5]. Already by their time a modification of the term had taken place as different groups sought to accommodate themselves to the dominance of the term in both Jewish and Christian traditions. Ἀνάστασις was now an accepted idea; if you did not like its physical connotations you had to reinterpret it; to declare your opposition to it would be to put yourself beyond the pale. The Naassenes' use of the term in Hipp., *Ref.* 5.8.24 is quite clearly a reinterpretation of the Christian tradition[6]. In another example cited by Fascher Clement of Alexandria hesitantly (τάχα μέν . . . τάχα δέ . . .)[7] relates Plato's account of the revival (ἀνεβίω, *Resp.* 10.614B) of Er to a resurrection (ἀνάστασις) or the ascent of souls through the twelve signs of the Zodiac (*Strom.* 5.14.103.4)[8]; a reinterpretation of resurrection as purely spiritual would be no surprise at this late date, but Clement elsewhere retains the resurrection of the flesh, although transformed flesh (e.g. *Paed.* 1.6.46.3)[9]. Quite clearly in the context of the *Republic*, however, Plato spoke of a resurrection to this-worldly life in which Er was able to speak of his

---

in passages like *1 Enoch* 51.1, not the reunion of separated soul and body, but the resurrection of the dead who have descended as wholes to Sheol and return as wholes (*Leib* 47; cf. 24 on 2 Macc).

Perhaps the same point can be put in the words of Brown, *Conception* 70 n. 121: with regard to the claim of Jesus' resurrection 'there was no other kind of resurrection' than a bodily one, only a question of what kind of body. But cf. Berger, ibid. 113, appealing to Mark 12.26f.

It is surely significant that Marxsen, *Resurrection* 132, asserts that in the context of a dualistic anthropology 'resurrection' 'means the "resurrection" of the soul from the body, the ascent of the soul, so to speak – its journey to heaven', and yet only a few lines later comments that in such a context 'the term is hardly ever used'.

It is one of the weaknesses of the thesis of Mearns, 'Development' (1984) 20, that he assumes that 'earliest Christian belief about the general resurrection would probably have been that it was largely accomplished already through adult believers' conversion'; this seems to leave out of account the question what 'resurrection' could with any ease have meant to the early Christians.

5 Ibid. 201f.

6 Cf. his usage at *Ref.* 9.29.1: resurrection (ἀνάστασις) is of the flesh, as distinct from the survival of the soul (both were denied by the Sadducees).

7 Though less common with the indic. this sense of τάχα is found, whereas parallels to Schmöle's 'bald . . . bald . . .' are hard to trace (*Läuterung* 97); it does not follow from the fact that τάχα can mean 'bald' that the repeated τάχα is equivalent to this German idiom. So I prefer to follow Voulet's translation in *SC* 278, 197: 'peut-être . . . peut-être . . .'.

8 Cf. 5.1.9.4.

9 Cf. Schmöle, *Läuterung* 96.

experiences during his seeming death. Such a restoration was a 'resurrection', but was not a final event such as the ascent of the soul usually was, except in cases of ecstasy; in Er's case it proved to be a very exceptional case, and was not final. In that case, Clement's use of this instance is very much his own reinterpretation of Plato's text, treating the latter's 'on the pyre' as an allusion to the purgative function of fire in the transformation of the flesh.

If, on the other hand, we go back to the earliest Jewish texts which are generally agreed to refer to resurrection, it is clear that something physical, affecting human bodies, is meant. When Dan 12.2 LXX speaks of many of those sleeping in the breadth (literally)[10] of the earth rising (ἀναστήσονται, LXX; ἐξεγερθήσονται, Theodotion) this is plainly something physical, as most admit[11]. Yet there is the reference to 'those who are wise' who 'shall shine like the brightness of the firmament' and 'those who turn many to righteousness' who shall shine 'like the stars for ever and ever' (12.3, *RSV*); this was taken to refer to a glorified, transformed corporeal existence by many later writers[12]. In describing such views as referring to a 'physical' resurrection, a 'corporeal' existence, we must bear in mind Schubert's contention that in the earlier texts the resurrection is thought of corporeally, but not as the resurrection specifically of the same body that had died[13]. It is difficult to be certain here; the vagueness of the references may, however, suggest that the ideas which they express are similarly vague.

More explicit perhaps is Isᵣ 26.19 LXX: 'the dead shall rise (ἀναστήσονται), and those in the tombs shall rise (ἐγερθήσονται), and those in the earth[14] shall rejoice'. This surely refers to a bodily resurrection, whatever doubts there may be about the Hebrew text[15]. Schubert's caution is, however, still applicable here.

Throughout the earlier period which concerns us here 'resurrection' had not, for non-Christians at least, assumed a dominant, 'canonical' position; thus there was not the motivation to mould the idea to fit one's own tastes; one could simply choose another idea more congenial to one's

---

10 BAG s.v. πλάτος: 'the broad plain'; Theodotion has ἐν . . . χώματι (?='dust' – LSJ s.v. §V, citing τὸ χῶμα τῆς γῆς in Exod 8.12f, LXX – not 8.16).

11 Cf. Stemberger, *Leib* 89; for possible exceptions cf. Cavallin, *Life* 1, 28 n. 1.

12 E.g. *1 Enoch* 104.2; *4 Ezra* 7.97, 125; *2 Apoc. Bar.* 51.10; *4 Macc* 17.5; *Bib. Ant.* 33.5. For ideas of astral immortality in Greek thought cf. Burkert, *Lore* 360ff (where one becomes a star rather than just like one).

13 'Entwicklung' 195, 198, 214; he only finds this quite clearly stated first in the relatively late *4 Ezra* and *2 Apoc. Bar.* (206–8).

14 The order of the words surely rules out Cavallin's 'rejoice in the land' (*Life* 1, 106).

15 Cf. Bousset-Greßmann, *Religion* 270; Cavallin, ibid. 109 n. 22; Moore, *Judaism* 2, 295f, Gamaliel quotes Isa 26.19 as a prophetic witness to resurrection in *b. Sanh.* 90b.

outlook, or just simply leave the nature of the after-life blurred and ambiguous. The term 'resurrection' continues to be reserved for something physical, often seemingly crudely and naively conceived[16]: so, above all, in 2 Macc 14.46 the godly Razis, sorely wounded, 'tore out his entrails, took them with both hands and hurled them at the crowd, calling upon the Lord of life and spirit to give them back to him again' (*RSV*); the third of the seven brothers martyred in chap. 7 stretched out his hands and said, 'I got these from Heaven, and because of his laws I disdain them, and from him I hope to get them back again' (2 Macc 7.11, *RSV*). In *Sib. Or.* 4.181f, too, God fashions again human bones and ashes (after the fiery final conflagration) and raises up mortals as they were before[17]. Pseudo-Phocylides also includes amongst his varied statements a reference to the remains (λείψανα) of the dead coming from the earth (103f)[18]. The *Apocryphon of Ezekiel* found in Epiphanius, *Haer.* 64.70.5ff [19] insists on the presence of both body and soul at the judgment. We find the rabbis agreeing that the end-product of the resurrection was like that of our creation in this world, but disagreeing on the order of the process: the school of Shammai argued, appealing to Ezek 37.8, that the order of the new creation was the opposite of that in this world; here skin and flesh are created first, then sinews and bones, whereas in the world to come this order will be reversed. The Hillelites, on the other hand, argued that the order was the same in both cases[20]. Another controversy, over whether the dead would rise naked or clothed, also presupposes a physical resurrection[21]. Other texts speak of the revivification of dead bodies[22].

---

16 Cf. also Job 19.26, LXX; 'seemingly' because of the argument of Stemberger, *Leib* 17, 19, 23, 25, 115f, that, although the usual interpretation of such words is that it is the same bodily parts that the martyrs expect to receive back, yet perhaps this is not the primary intention of these texts; rather they stress God's righteous requital of the martyrs' sacrifices: as they gave up their lives, so they will get life back, and as they give up their hands or entrails, so they will get hands or entrails back. 'The resurrection is bodily, but not necessarily in the sense of a resurrection of a body that is materially the same (as the old one)' (17; contrast Evans, *Resurrection* 15; Hoffmann, *Toten* 92). The work does not speak of a reunion of soul and body. The resurrection body is a new creation according to 2 Macc 7.28 (20).
The resurrection of the *flesh* was to become a commonly held doctrine in early (and later) Christianity: cf. Barrett, 'Immortality' 79–81; *Apoc. Pet.* 4; *Apoc. of Paul* 42.

17 So too in the accounts of the risen Jesus, esp. Lk 24.39; John 20.20, 27; compare too the *Book of Elijah* 8.3 (in Rießler, *Schrifttum* 238 – a late work, probably 3rd century C.E.: Schrage, *Elia-Apokalypse* 197; Rießler argues that different parts are of different dates – 1279).

18 Ed. van der Horst 185: 'a very literalistic doctrine of the resurrection'.

19 Ed. Holl-Dummer, 515.24ff (ET in Charlesworth, *Pseudepigrapha* 1, 492); cf. the similar image in *b. Sanh.* 91*ab* (also Moore, *Judaism* 2, 384 and n. 1).

20 *Gen. Rab.* 14.5 on 2.7; *Lev. Rab.* 14.9 on 12.2.

21 *B. Ketub.* 111*b*; *Pirqe R. El.* 33; *b. Sanh.* 90*b*, etc.; cf. Moore, *Judaism* 2, 380f.

22 Cf. Volz, *Eschatologie* 251f (this view lies behind passages in *2 Apoc. Bar.*, 4 Ezra, etc., as well).

In the *Apocalypse of Moses* great care is taken by God and his angels in anointing and burying the bodies of Adam and Abel in paradise in the third heaven (chap. 40)[23]; then God calls to Adam and 'the body' answers from the earth (it is not quite clear whether this earth is still that in the heavenly paradise or not; the reference is difficult if it is not); God then tells him that he is earth and so had to return to earth, but he promises him resurrection, for him and all his seed (chap. 41)[24]. In the resurrection he will be bodily enough to enjoy once more the tree of life (28.4).

It is a further sophistication when the *Syriac Apocalypse of Baruch* introduces two stages in the process of resurrection: the question is posed, 'In what shape will those live who live in Thy day?' (49.2); this is further specified as 'Will they . . . resume this form of the present . . ., or wilt Thou perchance change these things which have been in the world as also the world?' (49.3)[25]. The answer is that the earth will restore its dead[26], making 'no change in their form', in order that the dead may be recognized (50.2−4)[27]. Then a change will take place in the appearance both of the guilty and of the righteous: the former will deteriorate as they are tormented, the latter will be glorified (51.1ff); they will take on a form in keeping with the eternal world which they will inherit (51.3), an angelic form (51.5); they will be equal to the stars (51.10)[28]. This clear and specific statement of what resurrection involves makes it more plausible to see in chap. 30 an imprecise reference to an implied resurrection of the body rather than the idea of the resurrection of souls[29], although it is possible that different traditions are here juxtaposed in an uneasy combination[30].

---

23 Cf. Rowley, *Relevance*[3] 114.

24 The same work also speaks of the spirit returning to God at death (chaps 31f, 42).

25 Cavallin, *Life* 1, 87, notes that 'this is one of the very few passages, if not the only one, which explicitly treats the question of what the resurrected bodies will look like'; cf. ed. Bogaert 92.

26 Cf. *2 Apoc. Bar.* 42.7f (cf. 21.23); a similar idea is found in *1 Enoch* 51.1 (there not only the earth but also Sheol and hell give back those committed to them; cf. *4 Ezra* 4.42; *Bib. Ant.* 3.10; 33.3); *4 Ezra* 7.32 (but Stemberger points to the tensions within this verse between different traditions: *Leib* 74ff; a similar tension appears in *2 Apoc. Bar.* 21.22−4: ibid. 91f). In *Apoc. Pet.* 4 even the beasts and the birds give back what they have devoured.
   So Fuller, *Formation* 73: '"resurrection" to the Jewish mind naturally suggested resurrection *from the grave.*'

27 Cf. *Qoh. Rab.* 1.4 §2; for Volz, *Eschatologie* 253f, the preservation of identity is the prime reason for the restoration of bodies. Contrast *Bib. Ant.* 62.9.

28 Cf. n. 12 above.

29 So, e.g., Wilckens, *Resurrection* 94: 'a completely naive unreflecting use of a general imprecise anthropological concept'; but cf. Christ, 'Leben' 142.

30 Cf. Cavallin, *Life* 1, 87; also Wilckens, ibid. 94f; Stemberger, *Leib* 92−6, 116f, points to the presence of the idea of souls stored in chambers awaiting (new) bodies alongside the older one of 'the dead' being raised from Sheol or the earth (cf. also 4 Ezra). The former idea may be due to Greek influence (cf. Schubert, 'Problem' 162, 166).

Whereas for *Syriac Baruch* the resurrected live 'in the heights of that world' (51.10) other texts plainly seem to envisage a more earthly glory: in *1 Enoch* 51.5 the earth rejoices at the time of resurrection, when the 'Elect One' arises, and the righteous and elect dwell on the earth, albeit a new one (45.5); in 62.15f they are 'clothed with garments of glory', garments which do not grow old[31]. In *T. Benjamin* 10.6−8 the patriarchs rise, each set over his own tribe, and all are changed, some into glory and some into shame. Zebulun tells his tribe that he will rise again in their midst and Stemberger interprets this as referring to a resurrection on earth[32]. *T. Levi* 18.4f clearly speaks of a transformed earth, full of peace and joy[33], when God raises up a new priest, and *T. Dan* 5.12 refers to a new Jerusalem. For *Apoc. Mos.* 13.3−5 too 'all flesh' is raised, or at least all the holy people, to enjoy the delights of paradise, with God in their midst. Paradise also awaits the righteous who have been raised in 4 Ezra 7.36, although this paradise may be a heavenly one[34]. Yet this last qualification need not be a very serious one, since the present boundaries between heaven and earth tend to fade away when this earth, polluted with sin, is renewed and purged in the apocalyptic writers' expectations of the new age. Moreover, the boundary between a figurative use of corporeal images to describe spiritual existence and a literal description of spiritual corporeality is hard to define; Stemberger at times runs the risk of ignoring this difficulty[35].

In all these texts which we have considered so far, 'resurrection' seems to involve something physical, a restitution of the body which was given to the earth in burial or something which can and must also be described in terms suggesting a bodily existence; it is surely significant that, despite all the varieties of Jewish expectations for eschatological revivifying which he had just surveyed, P. Volz concluded that 'the common element in all the forms of revivification, or, more precisely, in all the ways in which one participates in the life of the time of salvation, is the assumption that the departed who have returned are of a corporeal nature'[36]. There are, it

---

31 How far is Russell, *Method* 377, correct in interpreting 'garments' of this sort as a 'figure' for 'spiritual' bodies? (He compares 4 Ezra 2.39, 45.) Contrast Stemberger, ibid. 49 (also 86 − a relatively late concept); also Haulotte, *Symbolique* 226f.

32 *T. Zebulun* 10.2; cf. also *T. Simeon* 10.2, 7; *T. Judah* 25.1, 4! See Stemberger, ibid. 66, also 71: 'the *T. 12 Patr.* teach of resurrection in the form of the return of the (naturally bodily) person to earth'.

33 Cf. *1 Enoch* 51.4f (also 45.4f).

34 Russell, *Method* 283. Stemberger, *Leib* 83f, doubts this.

35 So (ibid. 44) *1 Enoch* 108 describes the future bliss of righteous spirits in terms that are 'in some way corporeal'; on 35, however, he grants that the corporeal descriptions of the future life of the dead in *1 Enoch* 91−104 *may* all be purely figurative.

36 *Eschatologie* 249; even where the soul is regarded as immortal, it is reunited with a new body

is true, attempts to make this corporeal nature something better than the body which died, to give it a form more befitting the glorious new age which the resurrection ushers in; this is done either by a two-stage resurrection (*Syriac Apocalypse of Baruch*), with restitution followed by transformation, or by speaking of garments of glory (*Similitudes of Enoch*). But are there exceptions to this physical concept of resurrection, exceptions in which something like the human soul or spirit alone is said to be raised?

3.1.2. Up to this point we have considered texts which seem plainly to assume that resurrection is both future and physical. Some, however, have seen one exception to this rule in texts which seem to speak of an *incorporeal future resurrection*, and another in those which speak of a present figurative resurrection. It is to the former set of possible exceptions that we now turn, leaving the latter to §3.3.

Some see a resurrection of spirits implied in a passage of *Ethiopic Enoch*[1]: chap. 22 describes a vision of the three or four hollow places in which the spirits (πνεύματα) of the dead are to be stored until the day of judgment. The passage is obscured by doubt as to the number of places and the number and nature of those who occupy them. In v 2 there are four places, which the Greek text specifies as one bright and three dark[2]; in v 9 there seem to be only three places[3], and the impression is given that there are three groups of departed, one righteous and two sinful, those not judged during their lives (v 10) and another group[4]. But, it is suggested,

---

(250). Cf. also Davies, *Paul* 299–301; Hengel, 'Osterglaube' 262, 268; Moore, *Judaism* 2, 295, 313f.

Notes on 3.1.2

1 So Cavallin, *Life* 1, 41f; Nickelsburg, *Resurrection* 134ff; also (tentatively) Christ, 'Leben' 142.

2 The Eth. text rather suggests that all were dark (despite the fact that it calls them 'beautiful', vv 1, 3 – Knibb explains this as a misreading of κοῖλοι as καλοί: ed. 2, 108; cf. Sparks, *Apocryphal OT* 210 n.; Black, ed. 166; Uhlig, ed. 555 n.; Wacker, *Weltordnung* 43, agrees except that she thinks that the Greek *Vorlage* may have been corrupt); the Greek may have arisen because it was felt that the righteous should have better accommodation; on the other hand the Eth. may have omitted this passage because of the following remark suggesting that all were dark (so Wacker, ibid. 44).

3 Cf. E. Isaac in Charlesworth, *Pseudepigrapha* 1, 25 (despite the 'four' in 22.2); however cf. the translation of Black and ed. 167: 'These three . . . . And yonder one . . .'.

4 So Charles, *Apocrypha* 2, 202, wishes to emend v 2 to read 'three' and to bring it into line with this verse (contrast his ed. of 1893 *ad loc.*). It is perhaps more likely that an original 'four' was emended before the list of places in vv 9ff due to the inability to see what the four corresponding categories of the departed were, or, as Wacker suggests (*Weltordnung* 108–10), to bring the text into line with a common pattern of a threefold division of humankind according to their fate, vv 12f being taken as a reference to the generation of the flood; she further suggests that originally 22.1–4 contained no reference to divisions; these were later inserted when

this other group contains two groups, 'those who make their suit' and who were 'slain in the days of the sinners' (v 11) and another imprecisely defined group who are somehow unlike those in v 10. Of those in v 10 it is said that they shall be bound for ever and of those in v 13 that 'their spirits shall not be punished on the day of judgment nor shall they be raised ($\mu\epsilon\tau\epsilon\gamma\epsilon\rho\theta\tilde{\omega}\sigma\iota\nu$) from thence' (tr. Charles). In contrast with v 10 one might expect that these were judged during their lives on earth, but this is not stated.

The strange reference to those making suit in v 12 seems best explained by comparing vv 5−7[5]; there either the spirits of men (Eth.) or of a single man (Aram.)[6] makes suit; it is the spirit of Abel making suit against Cain. In that case it might be thought hard to regard those mentioned in v 12 as a class of sinners. If their mention there is part of the original text it would be hard to see the reason for the division of the four places into one bright (for the righteous) and three dark (for sinners?)[7]; the third is for those slain like Abel, whose blood cries out to God from the ground (Gen 4.10). Thus it might seem more likely that we are dealing with two groups of righteous and two groups of sinners, and that the second group of righteous is those who have died a violent death[9]. However, Wacker points out that there is no stress on Abel's righteousness, either here or in Jewish tradition prior to Josephus' *Antiquities*[10]. The group designated here is not to be set alongside the righteous on ethical grounds, but alongside the wicked (in the dark places) because of the manner of their death: they have died violently (cf. Ezek 32.19ff)[11]. It remains true that they are not to be classed as sinners either.

---

the rest of the chap. was added (122ff). Knibb suggests that the meaning is 'these three other places', the place for the martyred righteous having already been dealt with, by implication, in vv 5−7, although they are mentioned again in v 12 (ed. 2, 111).

5 So Moore, *Judaism* 2, 302; some see the mention of those like Abel already in vv 5−7, but cf. the criticism in Hoffmann, *Toten* 107; moreover it would leave v 12 to be assigned to one of the other classes of dead.

6 Aram., ed. Milik 229; the Gk perhaps originally read a singular, but the surviving text is confused; the singular $\dot{\epsilon}\nu\tau\upsilon\gamma\chi\acute{a}\nu\upsilon\tau\varsigma$ and $\alpha\dot{\upsilon}\tau\upsilon\tilde{\upsilon}$ suggest that it too originally had a singular (so Black, ed. 166; Knibb in Sparks, *Apocryphal OT* 211 n.; Uhlig, ed. 556 n.; Wacker, *Weltordnung* 55). Even in the Eth. vv 6 and 7 speak of a singular 'spirit'.

7 *Pace* Moore, *Judaism* 2, 302. Nickelsburg, *Resurrection* 135 n. 17, excises this reference as secondary. The division into light and dark places could result from a failure to see that those of v 12 were righteous; alternatively, if the reading is original the idea might be that the woe of these did not end with their violent death; they remain in darkness calling out for vengeance (cf. Hoffmann, *Toten* 108; Nickelsburg, ibid. 137); curiously, then, nothing is said about restitution. This explanation, which is perhaps more likely, brings us nearer Wacker's interpretation.

8 So Beresford, *Concept* 144; Knibb, ed. 2, 110f; Russell, *Method* 365.

9 So Knibb, ed. 2, 111; Nickelsburg, *Resurrection* 137.

10 *Weltordnung* 182−4; cf. Jos., *Ant.* 1.2.1 §53. Yet Black, ed. 168, says that this class 'are clearly not sinners'; this presents problems.

11 It is not clear whether they were all unavenged like Abel (cf. v 7).

Nickelsburg argues that the second class of sinners (in v 13) differ from the first (in v 10) in that they are not 'raised'; from that he infers that the first *are* raised in that they are transferred from their previous 'hollow place' to 'there' (v 11), which presumably means Gehenna[12]. But are the sinners of v 13 contrasted with the first group of sinners or with the righteous, including those so allusively mentioned in v 12? The difference in the fate of the two groups of sinners would then be that at the day of judgment the spirits of the second group are not slain (Eth.) or punished (Gk) whereas the spirits of the first are tormented on that day and are bound for ever (v 11); the second group had been punished in their lives, the first had not, but shall not therefore escape a worse fate in the afterlife to compensate for this.

But, the writer adds, the spirits of the second group are not raised. By this he does not mean to imply, I suggest, that some spirits *are* raised, as spirits only and without bodies[13]. A crucial argument against the idea of such a resurrection of spirits at this point is Stemberger's observation that this section of *Ethiopic Enoch* presupposes a return to earthly life on a purified earth[14]. This bodily form of bliss presupposes a bodily resurrection

---

12 *Resurrection* 134f.
13 Milik, *Books* 219, argues that the Ethpaʿal of קום which he restores here means 'remain permanent, retain (life, etc.) lastingly', and that the phrase in the Gk of v 13 'does not refer in any way to the doctrine of bodily resurrection' (contrast, e.g., Black, ed. 168; Rowley, *Relevance*[3] 94). The argument is confused at this point by the impression given that *1 Enoch* is distinguishing between some sinners that are raised (for judgment because they have not been punished on earth) and some that are not (because they have been punished on earth). Nickelsburg, *Resurrection* 136f, takes that line but concedes that such a distinction would be unusual (so also Beresford, *Concept* 145, rejecting the view of Snaith that *T. Benjamin* 10.6–10 is a parallel); that alone should make us question this interpretation (but cf. Hoffmann, *Toten* 109f; Str. -B. 4, 1168–73; Volz, *Eschatologie* 241, 245f). *M. Sanh.* 10.3 is not quite a parallel: at first there is a dispute whether those 'who have no share in the world to come' need to 'stand in the judgment', i.e. to be raised for judgment (Volz, *Eschatologie* 246). This seems to be the point at issue between R. Nehemiah (mid 2nd century – Strack, *Introduction* 115) and his opponents; he seems to represent the older view that only the righteous are raised, and his opponents hold that the wicked too are raised to be judged. The issue between R. Akiba and R. Eliezer is rather different: do the generation of the wilderness and the 'company of Korah' perish for ever (Akiba) or are they raised eventually (after suitable chastisement: *t. Sanh.* 13.9f; cf. 13.3; *b. Roš. Haš.* 17a)? Moore seems to want to introduce this latter idea at this point in *1 Enoch* (*Judaism* 2, 302), but his suggestion is impossible once it is granted that the group of 22.12, whom he wants to see as an intermediate group of less wicked sinners, are in fact righteous who have died violently, or at least are characterized by their having died violently rather than by any particular moral status. Another view that one might be tempted to introduce at this point, that some wicked were so punished in Gehinnom as to be annihilated and incapable of being raised, is dated by Str. -B. 4, 1173, from the early 2nd century on. All in all it seems simpler to see the distinction in v 13 to be between these wicked who are not further punished, but simply left where they are, and the righteous who are raised to life.
14 *Leib* 38, comparing *1 Enoch* 10.16–22; 25.4–6; cf. also Schubert, 'Entwicklung' 192f (this earthly existence far surpasses the present one); Moore, *Judaism* 2, 303. Wacker, *Weltordnung*

for the righteous; they shall eat of a wondrous tree, whose 'fragrance shall be in their bones' (25.6). The language of v 13 may be loose, but what seems to be meant is that these spirits are denied any resurrection, which would involve their union with bodies upon this transformed and 'healed' (10.7) and cleansed (10.20–22) earth[15]. In the light of this one can also see how it would make better sense to suppose that all the wicked were denied any resurrection, for resurrection is the way to bliss[16]. The only consideration that weighs at all against this is Beresford's argument that 27.2f implies that the sufferings of those 'accursed for ever' are visible to the righteous[17]; however, not only does this assume a doubtful degree of consistency on the part of the author or authors of this section, but it also assumes that he or they realized that corporeality was necessary for visibility and applied the logic of this strictly[18]; nor, strictly speaking, is it their sufferings that are a 'spectacle' (Ethiopic only), but their judgment. In short, whatever the correct interpretation of this confusing text there seems little need to postulate a 'resurrection' without a body for any of the groups.

Again, Nickelsburg speaks in his summary of a 'resurrection' of spirits in *1 Enoch* 102–104[19]. Yet either he is guilty of a rash use of language here or he is reading more into the text than is warranted. Contemplating the way in which the same fate has seemingly overtaken righteous and unrighteous alike — they have died and their souls have descended to

---

281–288, argues for ' "resurrection of the soul equipped with bodily functions" in the sense of a re-envigorating of the powerless shadowy being to a full human life in the time of salvation' (she adapts Schubert's language in 'Problem' 158f here); but if there is any point to the 'thence' in 22.13 it surely implies that those who are 'raised thence' leave the world of a shadowy existence for a fuller life; their 'bright place' with its 'spring of water' (v 2) was evidently not good enough for their final dwelling-place. It may not be spelled out that they are reunited with bodies; it is true that the chapter is more concerned with the fate of sinners, and it may therefore be unwise to assume that this section of *1 Enoch* had all that precise a conception of the form in which the righteous would live on, but at any rate it was incapable of describing it in other than bodily terms (Wacker points out, justifiably, how bodily are the torments of sinful 'souls' in the 'myth of Er' in Plato's *Republic* – ibid. 287).

15 Cf. also 10.16; 11.1f.

16 This is also the interpretation of Wacker, *Weltordnung* 274ff. The view that resurrection is for the righteous only is widely attested: Jos., *Bell.* 2.8.14 §163; *Pss. Sol.* 3.13–16 (10–12; cf. 13.9f = 10f; chap. 14, but see also the doubts expressed on the interpretation of *Pss. Sol.* by Stemberger, *Leib* 56–61); *1 Enoch* 46.6; *T. Zebulun* 10.1ff; *Apoc. Mos.* 13.3; *2 Apoc. Bar.* 30.2–5 (that is the impression given by these texts in themselves; what is questionable in some cases is how far this impression is given by the incorporation of unassimilated material or how far it is to be corrected in line with the views of these works as a whole). In rabbinic writings the exclusion of some wicked at least is common enough: e.g. *m. Sanh.* 10.1–4. See also Volz, *Eschatologie* 238–40; Str.-B. 4, 1183–92.

17 *Concept* 145.

18 After all 22.5 has Enoch seeing the spirit(s).

19 *Resurrection* 174; cf. Beresford, *Concept* 105; Christ, 'Leben' 142; Russell, *Method* 372.

Sheol (102.5) — the author encourages the righteous to look to the day of judgment: then the spirits of the righteous will be rewarded with life and rejoicing (103.4), with radiance like the lights of heaven (104.2), with joy like that of the angels (104.4), and with fellowship with the heavenly hosts (104.6). The term 'resurrection' is not used here, nor 'rise' or other such language[20]. Nickelsburg's assertion can only be justified by taking this passage in conjunction with 91.10, 'the righteous shall arise from their sleep'[21], or 92.3, 'the righteous one shall arise from sleep'[22]; 'rising' is of course a natural counterpart to the metaphor of 'sleep'. If it is legitimate to take these two passages together and to combine them to produce a coherent system of belief[23], one would have to agree that the spirits of the righteous do indeed 'rise' from their 'sleep'; but it is far from clear that this section contains such a coherent belief. Stemberger in fact argues that 'sleep' in 100.5 is not a reference to death but to the security of the righteous on earth once sin is destroyed[24]. Is this idea also behind 91.10 and 92.3[25]? At all events, Stemberger questions Charles' assumption that the life of the righteous was in heaven; the walking of the righteous 'in the paths of righteousness' (92.3) is a this-worldly one[26]. It is only with chaps. 102–104 that this section of *Ethiopic Enoch* speaks unambiguously of post-mortal existence[27]. Moreover this whole section (chaps. 91–104) thinks of the dead in corporeal terms; this could be a mere figure of speech, a device to avoid the difficulty of speaking of incorporeal existence, but a decisive factor is that *Ethiopic Enoch* as a whole holds a view of human nature and the dead which is not purely spiritual or incorporeal[28]. One may, however, question how decisive this in fact is, in view of the variety of different traditions and collections of material that make up this book. It is far better to reach as certain a conclusion as possible in

---

20 Cf. Cavallin, *Life* 1, 43f.

21 So Russell, *Method* 372; Schubert, 'Problem' 160, interprets this of 'the resurrection of a soul with a bodily nature'; yet Stemberger, *Leib* 40, points out that in the same verse wisdom is said to arise; rather than a reference to resurrection of the dead the verse announces the strengthening, the victorious superiority of the righteous and this on earth.

22 Uhlig, ed. 710 n.: 'a clear statement about resurrection'. Bousset-Greßmann, *Religion* 271, treats chap. 92 as 'probably a superscription to 94ff which has been added later'.

23 As Stemberger, *Leib* 44, accuses Charles of doing, 'seduced by an urge to systematize'; cf. also Hoffmann, *Toten* 126f.

24 Ibid. 41; cf. 50. Contrast Black, ed. 307.

25 He quotes with approval H. W. Kuhn, *Enderwartung* 55, to the effect that, if Hebrew thought extended the realm of death into this earthly life, then heaven too can be present now, thus 'clearly one should not separate this-worldly and other-worldly life so sharply from one another as we are wont to do in our ways of thinking'.

26 Ibid. 42.

27 Ibid. 44.

28 Ibid. 35; but Schürer-Black-Millar-Vermes, *History* 2, 540 n. 93, seems to treat chap. 103 as evidence for the belief in the immortality of the soul.

the light only of the immediate context of such passages. The certainty
that can be obtained here, it must be granted, leaves something to be
desired.

Jub. 23.30f could also be construed as speaking of a resurrection of
'spirits'; in the time of God's salvation his 'servants' will be healed and
'rise up and see great peace'; the 'righteous' will see this and rejoice;
'their bones shall rest in the earth, and their spirits shall have much
joy'[29]. What is not clear is whether the 'servants' who rise are the same as
the 'righteous' whose bones remain in the earth and whose spirits have
joy. Nickelsburg judiciously weighs up the alternatives: if the 'servants are
the same as the 'righteous' then 'we have reference to the resurrection of
the spirits of the righteous'. But the 'servants' may be those still living as
opposed to the 'righteous' who have died; the 'rising' of the former may
be from humility and subjugation (he compares 1 Sam 2.8; Isa 52.2) or a
being taken up to join the spirits of the 'righteous' who are in heaven (we
might compare 1 Thess 4.17)[30].

Not even the spiritual existence of the righteous in *Slavonic Enoch* is
really an exception: there the angels are portrayed as having a bodily
form, with faces, eyes, lips, wings (1.5), although 20.1 (AB) describes
them as 'incorporeal'[31]; Enoch is made to be like them, after he has been
anointed and dressed by Michael (22.9f). He needs no food (56.2). He
needs to have his face cooled, even frozen, in order that he may return to
earth and people may look at him (37.2, A). The idea is presumably that
in his glorified state he glows with a blazing fire and light (cf. 39.3, A). In
his cooled state he can be approached by mortals and can be kissed by
them (64.1–3). It is to be assumed that the fate of the righteous will be

---

29 Tr. Charles, *Apocrypha* 2, 49.

30 *Resurrection* 32f; cf. Charles' ed. of 1902, 150: 'the words "will rise up" have apparently no
reference to the resurrection, and mean merely that when God heals His servants . . . they
become strong'; he compares the views of *1 Enoch* 91–104. The idea of the messianic kingdom
in this chap., being introduced gradually as a 'spiritual transformation of man', does not fit in
with those of a final judgment and resurrection. When Davenport, *Eschatology* 40 n. 2, reads
into his 'The bodies rest, but the spirits rise' the idea of 'a resurrection of the spirit' this would
entail a considerable shift of thought, a shift which Davenport rejects. Hoffmann, *Toten* 100f,
also considers the 'servants' and the 'righteous' two different groups; the former share in the
eschatological time of salvation, the latter, being already dead, only witness to it; there is no
mention of a resurrection here or elsewhere in *Jub.* (cf. Str.-B. 4, 1169: *Jub.* only knows of
the survival of souls with no resurrection to follow). Berger, ed. 466, gives as an alternative to
the 'sich erheben' of the text 'auferstehen', yet in n. (e) he denies any reference to resurrection;
it is more likely the bones of the wicked who remain in the earth and the spirits of the righteous that rejoice; that seems a very difficult reading of the text. O. S. Wintermute in Charlesworth, *Pseudepigrapha* 2, 102, sees 'two quite different interpretations' of v 31 as possible:
spirits remain conscious while the bones rest in the earth, or as a 'poetic hyperbole' for the dead
who lie in the earth content that God will certainly vindicate the righteous.

31 Chap. 9 in Vaillant (ed. 22f); the reff. in the text above are to Charles, *Apocrypha* 2, 431ff.

similar, as they dwell in light and in an incorruptible paradise. If it is argued that the language of a corporeal existence is but a necessary vehicle for expressing the ultimately inexpressible nature of an incorporeal existence, then this may be true, but equally the language of resurrection is not used either, and that is critical for our purpose[32].

U. Fischer is inclined to see an 'extremely spiritualized hope of resurrection' in the *Sentences* of Pseudo-Phocylides[33]. He explains the at first sight very diverse statements of lines 103ff by supposing that in them we find a union of the Greek belief in the eternal survival of the soul and the Jewish hope of resurrection; the work contains a tripartite anthropology with a different destiny for each part when the three parts are separated at death : the body returns to the dust, the immortal soul departs to Hades and thence returns to the light and is deified as a consequence of our being in God's image. The spirit is loaned to us by God for our lives and departs at death into the air. He disagrees with F. Christ in that he sees no mention of a reunion of these parts[34]; on the face of it that is certainly correct. His interpretation rests upon taking λείψανα (line 104) of the souls referred to in line 105; that would, however, be a somewhat novel usage, as the word was elsewhere frequently used of the all too material bodily remains of the departed[35]. Moreover it is a fundamental weakness of this line of interpretation that, while it may seem to impose a sort of coherence upon lines 103—108, it destroys the connection between 103f and what precedes it. Lines 100ff have been warning against digging up graves, concluding that 'it is not good to dissolve the human frame (ἁρμο-νίην . . . ἀνθρώποιο)' (line 102) which van der Horst very reasonably takes as a reference to the dissection of corpses[36]. That makes admirable sense in the context. This is then followed by lines 103—104a[37]. In this context

---

32 U. Fischer, *Eschatologie* 62–70, argues that the original form (B) of *2 Enoch* was closer to the unified anthropology of the OT and Judaism; life after death involved body and soul. Resurrection, perhaps unexpectedly, is not mentioned; this is intelligible if eschatological judgment means annihilation for the godless and a continuation of paradisal existence for the righteous.

33 *Eschatologie* 141; contrast the view of v.d. Horst quoted in §3.1.1 n. 18 above.

34 Christ, 'Leben'; Walter, ed. 207, identifies the spirit of 106 with the soul of 105.

35 Cf., e.g., Soph., *El.* 1113. Particularly interesting here is Plato, *Phaedo* 86BC, where Simmias suggests that the soul is a mixture and harmony (κρᾶσιν . . . καὶ ἁρμονίαν) of heat, cold, moisture and dryness. The soul then perishes when the body is too relaxed or strained (the harmony of the lyre does not survive its destruction either), but the remains (λείψανα) endure for a long time until they are burnt or rot away. The occurrence of the two terms ἁρμονία (cf. line 102) and λείψανα together is suggestive here; whether or not Pseudo-Phocylides had Plato's text in mind, line 102 does seem to refer to a psychosomatic unity; if Plato's text is in the background a different translation to v. d. Horst's 'frame' would have to be found. ·

36 Ed. 183; cf. also Walter's ed. 207; Perkins, *Resurrection* 51.

37 V. d. Horst makes the connection seem clearer than it is by translating καὶ . . . δ' by 'for' (ed. 95); cf. in Charlesworth, *Pseudepigrapha* 2, 577.

it seems most plausible to regard the λείψανα as referring to the same remains as were in danger of dissection. Fischer's suggestion only becomes plausible if we make a sharp division between lines 102 and 103[38], but a good case can indeed be made out for seeing 103f as reinforcing the warning against tampering with buried corpses: they will return and they will even be immortalized as gods. This is in keeping with Cavallin's approach to this material, which is to see the paraenetic concerns of the writer as dominant and to regard these as the reason for his allowing this 'unharmonized juxtaposition of contradictory ideas about after-life'[39]. In short, what is certain is that the writer tries to combine Greek views of the eternal soul (especially clear in line 115) and the Jewish belief in the resurrection; what is very doubtful is how far this latter belief is spiritualized; it would have to be if it were to be reconciled with other views expressed here, but it is doubtful whether this reconciliation has in fact taken place.

In this survey of Jewish documents our enquiry has been made more difficult by two factors: (a) we have seen how hard it is to distinguish sharply between earthly and heavenly existence when earthly existence means existence on a new, transformed earth in the world to come; (b) corresponding to this it is difficult to be sure whether in a given case this existence on a new earth was really conceived of in bodily terms or whether this language is simply being used for want of anything better, because of the inexpressible, even inconceivable, nature of the new order of things (we shall meet in §3.2.2 a similar phenomenon in a Greek writer like Plato). But in any case it must be firmly emphasized that, even if this eschatological existence were really 'spiritual' and were really devoid of any material nature, yet this would still be very different from the idea of a spiritualized resurrection existence that one could experience in this present world: the former belongs to a world that is still to come and is part and parcel of it, the latter would be an experience of that future world enjoyed here and now. It is very far from being an easy step from the one to the other. Indeed it does not seem that the one in fact led to the other; we shall see (in §3.3.3) that the closest approximation to language of an already realized resurrection in Judaism is found in the Dead Sea Scrolls which are marked by a lack of any clear indications as to their expectations in the afterlife.

---

38 Cf. Fischer, *Eschatologie* 129.
39 Cavallin, *Life* 1, 153; cf. in *ANRW* 2.19.1, 295f.

3.2. 'Resurrection' in the Graeco-Roman World

When we turn to the Graeco-Roman world and ask how it would have understood these terms, ἀνάστασις, ἐγείρειν (ἐκ νεκρῶν)[1], and the like, a number of questions are involved:

1. within the normal views of the afterlife among the Greeks was any room found for this terminology to express ideas either of a bodily resurrection or of a 'spiritual' resurrection (in some sense of the world 'spiritual')? Did the survival of the soul, for instance, ever come to be spoken of in such language? (§3.2.1)

2. Did the Graeco-Roman world know of any bodily survival after death and, if so, how did it express such ideas? (§3.2.2)

3. We often hear of the 'dying and rising' gods of the mysteries. How far is it in fact true that they experienced 'resurrection' and in what sense, and how far did this entail a similar expectation for their devotees? (§3.2.3)

3.2.1. If the idea of *resurrection* of the dead is found *in non-biblical Greek literature* it is perhaps most frequently found as a statement of the impossible: the dead are not raised[1]. As Apollo assures the chorus in Aeschylus' *Eumenides*, 'when the dust hath drained the blood of man, once he is slain, there is no return to life (οὔτις ἔστ᾽ ἀνάστασις)' (lines 647f)[2]. In contrast Aristotle reckons with at least the theoretical possibility of resurrection (τὸ ἀνίστασθαι) if the soul, having left the body, returns to it again (*De anima* 1.3.406*b*3—5), but Hicks comments that 'This is intended by A[ristotle] as a *reductio ad absurdum* of the supposition that the soul moves in space'[3]; in other words, this is not a theoretical possibility that Aristotle seriously entertains.

Notes on 3.2
  1 Evans, *Resurrection* 20, comments that ἐγείρειν was hardly, if ever, used in ordinary Greek in connection with death and resurrection.

Notes on 3.2.1
  1 So Marxsen, *Resurrection* 131, speaks of 'an attitude . . . widespread in the Hellenistic world: the resurrection is nonsense'. Cf. Wolfson, 'Immortality' 61, citing Aug., *Enarratio in Ps 88* 5 in Migne *PL* 37, 1134; Cyr., *Catecheses* 18.1 in Migne *PG* 33, 1017; Pseudo-Justin, *Cohortatio ad gentiles* 27 (ed. Otto 2, 27.26B); also Prümm, *Handbuch* 256.
  2 Tr. Smyth; cf. *Ag.* 1361; Hdt. 3.62.3f; Hom., *Il.* 24.551, 756 (cf. 21.56); Soph. *El.* 138f; also Nilsson, *Geschichte* 2, 692. Barrett, 'Immortality' 71, reminds us that this idea is also found in the OT (he quotes 2 Sam 12.22f; Ps 88.10—12).
  3 Ed. 249.

Occasionally the possibility is left open that there may be exceptions. In Euripides' *Hercules furens* Amphitryon holds out against the mocking Lycus that a god might raise (ἀναστήσειε) his son Heracles from the dead (line 719); clearly he means that Heracles may be restored — as the audience knows that he already has been (523ff) — to continue his existence on earth and in particular to avenge Creon's death. The *Cynegeticus* attributed to Xenophon tells us that Asclepius was given the power to raise (ἀνιστάναι) the dead and heal the sick (1.6)[4]; the pairing of these two gifts suggests that what was primarily in mind was the restoration of the dead to life in this world. This is clearly the case in his restoration of Hippolytus to life in Paus. 2.27.4 for the latter goes on to be king of the Aricians[5]. This is to be distinguished from the suggestion that he eventually evaded death, being granted glory in the heavens by the gods (2.32.1). Similarly when Sextus Empiricus mentions that Stesichorus records that Asclepius raised up (ἀνιστᾷ) some of those who had fallen at Thebes the likelihood is that a restoration to present life is intended (*Math.* 1.261)[6]. With other cases there is less certainty[7]: we know, for instance, of the tradition of the raising of Tyndareus[8], but the incident is obscure; Pliny's remark that Asclepius brought him back to life (*revocavisset ad vitam*) may suggest that he too was restored to this-worldly existence (*Hist. nat.* 29.1.3)[9]. Again he is credited with attempting the restoration of Orion[10], but apparently was struck down before he could accomplish this; instead Orion was set among the stars. Another such restoration to this-worldly, bodily life would be the trick attributed (with some scepticism) by Herodotus to Salmoxis (4.95f).

Fascher's conclusion is thus that 'where the Greek speaks of ἀνιστάναι, ἀνίστασθαι and ἀνάστασις (and he does so), he knows that the severed connection between the soul and the body must be restored again'[11]. In

---

4 Cf. Paus. 2.26.5; for a similar power in Apollonius of Tyana cf. Philostr., *Vit. Ap.* 4.45 (though ἀνάστασις and its cognates are not used here) — this is clearly a case of the restoration of the dead — or seemingly dead — to this-worldly life.

5 Cf. Ovid, *Fasti* 6.746–56; Staphylus quoted by Sext. Emp., *Math.* 1.261, speaks of him healing Hippolytus (ἐθεράπευεν); cf. the restoration of Glaucus in Apollodorus, *Bibliotheca* 3.3.1 with 10.3.

6 On the identity of some of these cf. Frazer's ed. of Apollodorus' *Bibliotheca* 2, 17 n. 3.

7 For lists of such raisings cf. Apollodorus, *Bibliotheca* 3.10.3; Hyginus, *Fabulae* 49; Schol. on Pind., *Pyth.* 3.96 and on Eur., *Alc.* 1 (ed. Dindorf 4, 88f); Sext. Emp., *Math.* 1.261.

8 Apollodorus, ibid.; Lucian, *Salt.* 45; Sext. Emp., ibid.; Zenobius, *Centuria* 1.47 (ed. Leutsch-Schneidewin).

9 Cf. the same phrase used by Hyginus quoted in Robert's ed. of Eratosthenes' *Catasterismi* p. 69.

10 Telesarchus in Sext. Emp., *Math.* 1.262 (ἀναστῆσαι) — an unparalleled tradition according to *ALGM* 3, 1033.

11 'Anastasis' 187: Philo can, however, use μετανάστασις of the 'migration' of the soul from pas-

other words here too a resurrection is something involving the body, and for the majority of Greeks this was something incredible, impossible; exceptional miracles were, however, a possibility, but these involved the restoration of the dead to life on this earth, followed by eventual death[12], or else, in the case of the privileged few, by escape from death (cf. §3.2.2.1). In the light of this general rejection of the possibility of resurrection in the Greek world it is not surprising that many Diaspora Jews rejected this form of post-mortal hope and espoused a Hellenistic hope in the immortality of the soul. Philo, for instance, makes no mention of resurrection and speaks only of the latter form of expectation[13].

One further observation is worth making here: whereas the Jews and Christians largely spoke of resurrection in the context of a final consummation, in which some or all dead would be raised to a new, future existence in some form or other, the Graeco-Roman materials seem largely or solely to speak of resurrection either as what is impossible as a final destiny, or as a temporary reprieve, or as what is possible for an exceptional few as just such a temporary reprieve from their final lot; this latter idea is, of course, also known in Christian traditions, as we have seen (§3.1), as well as before them in Jewish traditions about Elijah and Elisha (1 Kgs 17.17–24; 2 Kgs 4.18–37), but it is far less prominent than the idea of resurrection as a final act[14].

3.2.2. At first sight it might seem unlikely that we should find any notion of *bodily survival after death in the Graeco-Roman world*. J. Whittaker

---

sions to virtue (*Leg. all.* 3.19) or in death to God (*Sacr. AC.* 10); it is also used of the departure of the spirit after ecstasy (*Rer. div. her.* 265).

Not really relevant here either are cases of souls 'ascending' to earth again as in the case of Alcestis in Plato, *Symp.* 179C (ἀνεῖναι); presumably she would have to be reunited with a body on earth, but Plato is not precise here. Similarly reff. to the ascent of the soul after death provide no exception to Fascher's conclusion (e.g. Kaibel, *Epigrammata* 653: ἀνιή).

12 It is, as Pötscher observes of Heracles' raising of Alcestis ('"Auferstehung"' 211), an 'Auferweckung eines Toten für eine bestimmte Zeit', not an 'Auferstehung als solche'. Just how temporary this reprieve might be is illustrated by the case of Protesilaus, allowed to return to this world perhaps for as little as three hours (Hyginus, *Fabulae* 104; cf. Apollodorus, *Epitome* 3.30).

13 Cf. *Cher.* 114; *Quaest. in Exod.* 2.46; Beresford, *Concept* 71, 75; Brandon, *Man* 143; Wolfson, *Philo* 1, 404–6. Fischer, *Eschatologie* 236, comments that 'the doctrine of the resurrection made little impact on the Jews of the Western Diaspora'. This avoidance of the doctrine is scarcely surprising when we read the comment of Dodds, *Pagan* 130 n. 1, that 'No Christian doctrine was more shocking to educated men than the resurrection of the body'; it is hardly surprising that cultured Jews of the Diaspora sought alternatives to the Jewish doctrine – cf. §3.2.2 on Josephus.

14 Cf. Selby, *Look* 105: for Jews 'either the resurrection was entirely in the future, something to be waited for as the final fulfilment of God's plan for the world, or, when it happened it would be that after which there would be no future at all . . .'.

remarks that 'the almost universal Hellenistic rejection of the body and
the identification of mind and man served to render the idea of the resurrection of the body thoroughly objectionable to the average Hellenistic
mind'[1]. Nilsson, too, states that ancient pagan beliefs decisively rejected
the idea of the resurrection of the flesh; it was incomprehensible to the
ancient Greek since he knew that the body dissolved and decayed after
death[2].

Yet there are three considerable exceptions to this rule: first there is
the occasional restoration of dead people to a resumed life on earth in
healing miracles similar to those attributed to Jesus, which have been
mentioned already in §§3 and 3.2.1. Then there is the idea that certain
privileged individuals escape entirely; their survival is then in some sense
bodily, but not strictly *after death*, except in a few cases; instances of this
sort will be considered later in this section. However, before that, mention
should also be made of the third possible exception, the idea of metempsychosis or the transmigration of souls, in which a soul passes into
another body and is reincarnated[3]. For it is interesting that when Josephus
comes to explain the Pharisaic doctrine of the resurrection of the body he
does so in terms which rather suggest metempsychosis: 'every soul . . . is
imperishable, but the soul of the good alone passes into another body
(μεταβαίνειν . . . εἰς ἕτερον σῶμα), while the souls of the wicked suffer
eternal punishment'[4]. If resurrection were thought of as being with
another body rather than with the same body as had died and been
buried, it might well be intelligible to the Hellenistic mind on the analogy
of this belief. Yet the Greek view of the migration of souls, whatever form
it took[5], never spoke of the return of the soul to the *same* body, whereas
sometimes at least Jewish thought did assert just that[6]. But not the Phari-

---

Notes on 3.2.2

1 'Plutarch' 56; cf. also §3.2.1 above.
2 *Geschichte* 2, 692; cf. also MacMullen, *Paganism* 130; Perkins, *Resurrection* 61f, citing Minucius Felix, *Octavius* 11.2–5; Schubert, 'Entwicklung' 187.
3 For this as comparable or analogous to resurrection, but in Christian eyes inferior to it, cf.
   Wolfson, 'Immortality' 62f, citing Aug., *Civ. D.* 22.27; Gregory of Nyssa, *De anima et resurrectione* 46ff in Migne *PG* 46, 108f; Iren., *Haer.* 2.33.1–34.1=Harvey 2.50–55; Lact., *Div.
   inst.* 7.23; Orig., *Cels.* 7.32; Tert., *De resurrectione mortuorum* 1.5.
4 *Bell.* 2.8.14 §163; cf. 3.8.5 §374 – put on Josephus' own lips; also *Ap.* 2.30 §218; see Fischer,
   Eschatologie 154–6; Perkins, *Resurrection* 38, 52. Compare, too, the language used to describe
   μετενσωμάτωσις by Hipp., *Ref.* 1.19.12. Harvey, *Jesus* 150, compares Diog. L. 8.5 where
   μεταβαίνειν is used of Pythagorean belief in transmigration.
5 E.g. whether the new incarnation can be into animal or vegetable forms (e.g. Empedocles in
   Diels-Kranz, *Fragmente* §31, B 117, and Xenophanes, ibid. §21 B 7; Plato, *Phaedrus* 249B;
   Resp. 10.618A, 620A–D) or only into different human individuals (a later view arising as the
   earlier was 'rejected by Platonists from Porphyry on' – Dillon, *Platonists* 377; cf. *Corp. Herm.*
   10.19; *Chaldaean Oracles* no. 160); cf. Burkert, *Lore* 133–5; Dörrie, 'Kontroversen'.
6 On this distinction cf. Tert:, *Apologia* 48.1–4 and reff. above in n. 3.

sees according to Josephus[7], nor Paul with his insistence on the difference between our mortal body and the resurrection body[8].

Apart from this influential tradition in Greek thought, the Greeks' varied beliefs concerning individual survival had, as far back as we can penetrate, included tales of the exceptional conquest of death, or rather the avoidance of it. In these exceptional cases, usually because the mortals in question had divine parentage or ancestry, heroes were snatched away from the jaws of death and transferred to another place, far away or in the bowels of the earth, to live the blessed life of those immortal by nature[9]. This continued existence was bodily, for of course the breath of life had never left their bodies at a moment of death. Thus certain privileged individuals passed from this life to continue their existence in bliss, in Elysium or the Isles of the Blessed[10]. In later sources these might be regarded as the destination of righteous *souls* and might be set in Hades or amongst the stars[11], but when that stage was reached entry into those blissful realms was not an exemption from death; it was one of the possible modes of existence of the dead, in contrast to the terrors of Tartarus awaiting the wicked. Such a blissful existence was not then one which bypassed death.

At an earlier time, however, it is plain that in the likes of the Homeric poems going to the Elysian fields at the end of the world is an escape from death: Proteus tells Menelaus that he will not die in his native Argos, but the gods will send him to Elysium as befits Zeus' son-in-law (Hom., *Od.* 4.561–569)[12]. As he avoids death he presumably goes there in bodily form and, after all, these fields are situated on this earth; there life is easiest for man. Others, however, came to such abodes of bliss *after death*. The *Aethiopis*, for instance, tells of Thetis carrying off the body of

---

7 Possibly he is correct concerning some of them at least; cf. W. D. Davies, *Paul* 308: 'there would be many Pharisees prepared to argue, as Paul does, for a transformed resurrection body.'

8 1 Cor 15.35–49; this stress on difference and discontinuity (esp. in vv 39–43) makes it very hard to regard v 44*b* as the conclusion of Paul's argument. The difficulty is increased by the appeal to scripture in v 45 which, if the existence of a 'spiritual body' were the point to be proved, would be most unfortunate: that part of the verse relevant to this (45*b*) is not a quotation of scripture. It is better to treat 44*b* as a parenthesis as Paul recalls the questions posed in v 35 before returning to the main thrust of his argument, to show the Corinthians that their present existence is still qualitatively different from the new, eschatological existence ushered in by Christ; their present confidence (4.8) is thus misplaced (cf. my 'Body' 92–4, and ' "Man"' 301f).

9 Cf. Rohde, *Psyche* 1, chaps 2f; G. Strecker in *RAC* 5, 465–70.

10 Cf. D. Roloff, *Gottähnlichkeit* 93ff.

11 Cf. Kroll, 'Elysium' 25ff.

12 Cf. Eur., *Hel.* 1676f; this passage of the *Odyssey* may be an interpolation (Rohde, *Psyche* 1, 58, 80 n. 2) and a relatively late one (Kroll, 'Elysium' 13). On the importance of divine descent here cf. Roloff, *Gottähnlichkeit* 68ff.

Achilles to Leuce[13]; there, Rohde argues, to make him immortal[14]. Certainly Pausanias (3.9.12f) tells the story of Leonymus of Crotona sailing to Leuce and finding there Achilles wedded to Helen, Ajax son of Oileus, Ajax son of Telamon, Patroclus and Antilochus[15]; this suggests a continuation of this-worldly life analogous to that presumably to be found on the Isles of the Blessed[16]. Eugammon's *Telegonia*, too, tells of Circe making Penelope, Telemachus and Telegonus immortal after Odysseus' death and after Odysseus' body had been brought to the island of Aeaea[17]; why it is specified that the body was brought is not clear, nor is it clear, either, from the text whether the immortalizing included the dead Odysseus or not. But a scholion on Lycophron's *Alexandra* says that Circe raised Odysseus up (ἀνέστησε)[18]. This would certainly explain why the body was brought thither, but not how Penelope was then apparently free to remarry according to the scholion!

Hesiod, too, speaks of some of the heroes of the fourth race of men[19] in his *Works and Days* 161–173 dying before Thebes and Troy and others being sent by Zeus to dwell in the Isles of the Blessed; these latter, as Rohde rightly remarks[20], must be thought of as not suffering death, i.e. the separation of their souls from their selves, but as being 'carried away alive in the flesh'. It is perhaps somewhat surprising to enter historical times and find that Harmodius the tyrannicide has also escaped death and is believed to be on the Isles of the Blessed with Achilles and Diomedes[21].

From early times, however, there had been the belief that the place of the dead lay underground and gradually it came to be assumed that this was where all mortals went, however privileged, even if they were simply

---

13 Proclus in T.W. Allen's ed. of Homer 5, 106; the term ἀναρπάσασα (106.14) suggests the removal of the body of Achilles; cf. Pind., *Ol.* 2.79 – ἔνεικε. It is hard to be sure, *pace* Rohde (*Psyche* 1, 64), just what is implied by Proclus' statement that the *Aethiopis* tells how Eos bestowed immortality on Memnon (in Allen, ibid. – Rohde, *Psyche* 1, 84 n. 27, grants that Proclus' statement is written with 'regrettable brevity'); Poll., *Onom.* 4.180 refers to Eos ἁρπάξουσα Memnon's body (cf. also *ALGM* 2.2, 2672f).

14 *Psyche* 1, 65.

15 Cf. Philostr., *Heroic.* 54 (ed. Lannoy 70–2); Achilles is on the Elysian plain married to Medea according to Ibycus and Simonides (Page, *Poetae*, nos 291, 558); cf. also Apollodorus, *Epitome* 5.5.

16 Contrast Homer, *Od.* 24.13ff, where the ψυχαί of Achilles and other heroes dwell as εἴδωλα on the asphodel meadow (underground? – cf. the κατά in lines 10, 13); cf. Bremmer, *Concept* chap. 3.

17 Proclus in Allen, ibid. (n. 13 above) 109.

18 Ed. Scheer 2, 253.30; 254.21; here we come closest to Judaeo-Christian ideas of resurrection.

19 Who thereby break the sequence of ages named after different metals (Rohde *Psyche* 1, 69f; ed. West 174; ed. Sinclair 17).

20 Ibid. 75; it is an 'alternative to death' (ed. West. 192, comparing also the ref. mentioned in the following note).

21 Page, *Poetae* 475 no. 894 – *Carmina convivialia*.

swallowed up by the earth and then made immortal, presumably in a bodily form of some sort[22]. Thus by the time of Plato's *Gorgias* (523Aff) both Rhadamanthys (523E8, etc.) and the Isles of the Blessed (523B1, 8; 524A3) have been assigned a different place from that which they occupied in earlier literature[23]: for the fact that Tartarus is the alternative to the Isles of the Blessed within this myth suggests that both are thought of as parts of the underworld, and this is confirmed by references to Hades in 525B8, C7, E1. But what takes place there is a judgment of *souls*, unadorned (523E2–4), who must leave behind all their finery on the earth (523E5), and are stripped of their bodies (524D5). However much the scenes in the world below may suggest that the souls were embodied, it is clear that these descriptions are in these terms just for the sake of convenience; it is difficult otherwise to describe the soul's fate in such vivid terms[24].

For, although all the stress came to be put on the survival of the soul alone, particularly when ascent to the stars became the commonest form of a hope for immortality[25], this continued existence was often described in bodily terms; nor was this altogether surprising when the Stoic tradition in particular emphasized the corporeal nature of soul and spirit[26]. We can perhaps disregard accounts like Lucian's description of the ascent of a vulture from Peregrinus' pyre, claiming that it was on its way to Olym-

---

22 So, e.g., Amphiaraus: clearest in Apollodorus, *Bibliotheca* 3.6.8; Eur., *Suppl.* 925–7; Agatharchides in Phot., *Bibl.* 443B; Philostr., *Vit. Ap.* 2.37; Xen., *Cyn.* 1.8; Soph., *El.* 837ff.
   Kroll, 'Elysium' 18, traces the transposition of Elysium to the underworld to the Eleusinian mysteries (and possibly beyond them to Minoan influence?)

23 The alternative would be to set them in the heavens: the righteous go heavenwards for a thousand years in *Resp.* 10.614C4–D1. The Pythagoreans seem to have identified the Isles of the Blessed with the sun and the moon (Iambl., *Vit. Pyth.* 82), but they distinguished the Isles from the abode of the dead (Burkert, *Lore* 364); cf. also Plut., *Fac. lun.* 28.943C; 29.944C.
   For the natural transition from an earthly place in the furthest west to the underworld as the place of the departed cf. Zemmrich, 'Toteninseln' 227, etc.: this is the place where the sun descends (218).
   On the possible Egyptian origin of the idea cf. J. G. Griffiths, 'Search'.

24 Compare the analogy developed in Plato, *Gorg.* 524B2ff, between the character and scars that would be carried by the body in its afterlife, and those that, Socrates infers, would be carried by the soul. Pind., *Ol.* 2.74, although reflecting a doctrine of the transmigration of souls (lines 68–70), yet speaks of those acquiring final bliss having hands.
   Bremmer, *Concept*, points out how for the ancient Greeks the dead soul was regarded as looking like the living person and yet behaved in many ways differently (73); this tension is perhaps the product of the fusion of the memory of the dead when alive with the memory of their corpses at the point of death (83–5).

25 Cumont, *After Life* 77, suggests that the Stoic belief in the fiery nature of the soul made it impossible to take literally accounts of its descent into the underworld, and that Pythagoreans and Platonists came to share this conviction.

26 Cf. Hengel, *Judaism* 1, 199f; 2, 133 n. 595; E. Schweizer in *TDNT* 9, 613f. Note that the use of ἀνάστασις of 'rising' to astral immortality which Hengel finds (1, 197) in *Anth. Pal.* 7.748 is a conjecture of Beckby's ed. not followed in other edd.

pus[27]; that, if taken at its face value, suggests that this was a convenient form adopted by the deified Peregrinus, similar to the animal disguises assumed at times by the Olympian gods in Greek legend[28]. It would not be thought that this was his permanent new form. It is different when Ovid describes Romulus'' translation; 'his mortal part (*corpus mortale*) dissolves into thin air, . . . and now a fair form clothes him, worthier of the high couches of the gods . . . '[29]. But this is again in a very real sense an escape from death and was seen as such[30]. Moreover it was a fate which was regarded as the prototype for the apotheoses of the Roman emperors[31]. Similarly, too, when Heracles disappeared and no bones were found it was assumed that he had been transported from the world of mortals to that of the gods[32]. Empedocles of Acragas during his lifetime told his fellow-citizens 'I go about among you all an immortal god, mortal no more'[33]; it is thus perhaps no surprise that Diogenes Laertius records concerning his 'death' that Empedocles disappeared after a feast; someone recalled hearing a voice calling Empedocles and seeing a heavenly light. Searching for him brought no success[34] and 'later he bade them take no

---

27 *Peregr. mort.* 39f.
28 We may compare the practice of releasing a caged eagle from the top of the funeral pyre of a dead Roman emperor (Dio C. 56.42.3: 'appearing to bear his spirit to heaven' – tr. Cary; i.e. an escort for the soul rather than its form in its ascent); cf. A. F. Segal in *ANRW* 2.23.2, 1348f; A. D. Nock in *CAH* 10, 488. But for the soul ascending as a bird cf. Cumont, *After Life* 157–9 (this was later modified to the idea of the bird carrying the soul).
29 *Met.* 14.824–8 (tr. Miller); cf. Livy 1.16; Plut., *Romulus* 27.5, 7; *Numa* 2.2f.
30 So Euthymus' disappearance is described by Pausanias as $\dot{\alpha}\pi o\theta\alpha\nu\epsilon\hat{\iota}\nu\ \dot{\epsilon}\kappa\phi\nu\gamma\dot{\omega}\nu$ (6.6.10); cf. Plut., *Numa* 2.3; also Heb 11.5.
31 Bickerman, *'Consecratio'* 15f; Friedrich, 'Lk 9,51' 52; G. Strecker in *RAC* 5, 469; Talbert, 'Concept' 426f; some supposed this to have happened to Aeneas too (Dion. Hal., *Ant. Rom.* 1.64.4). Sometimes, however, the emphasis is on the emperor's soul being taken up – detachment from the body is implied in Cic., *Rep.* 6.29; cf. Cumont, *After Life* 102. Perkins, *Resurrection* 56, remarks that Christian art later 'represented tthe ascent of Christ along the same lines as those employed for the *apotheosis* of the emperor' (the examples given are from the 4th century).
32 Diod. S. 4.38.4f; Soph., *Philoct.* 726–9; cf. Apollodorus, *Bibliotheca* 2.7.7. Cf. Vermaseren-Simoni, *Liber* 53, on this as a prototype of the apotheosis of Roman emperors. But this is reckoned by Friedrich, ibid., as an example of an ascent *after death*. Similarly it is not quite clear how Jos., *Ant.* 4.8.48 §326, views the end of Moses – his disappearance in a ravine amidst a cloud is described, but attention is drawn to his record of his death in Deut 34, which Moses wrote 'lest they should venture to say that by reason of his surpassing virtue he had gone back to the Deity'(tr. Thackeray, who notes the echo of the fate of Enoch, 1.3.4 §85; such a translation is also one of the possibilities entertained when Moses is on Mount Sinai – 3.5.7 §96; Jos. denying this interpretation of Moses' end?). Yet the word 'disappear' ($\dot{\alpha}\phi\alpha\nu\dot{\iota}\zeta o\mu\alpha\iota$) is frequently used of such translations (Friedrich, ibid. 54 and n. 60).
33 Diels-Kranz, *Fragmente* §31 B 112.4f (tr. Kirk-Raven, *Philosophers* 354).
34 Diog. L. 8.68; so too a three-day search by 50 men could not find Elijah in 2 Kgs 2.17; cf. too *T. Job* 39.12 and the examples in Berger, *Auferstehung* 117–22; G. Strecker in *RAC* 5, 468f; Talbert, 'Concept' 421–7. The Cynic Diogenes seems to have enjoyed a similar end according to Cercidas (Diog. L. 6.76f).

further trouble, for things beyond expectation had happened to him, and it was their duty to sacrifice to him since he was now a god' (8.67f, tr. Hicks). Cleomedes of Astypalaea seems to have had little to commend him apart from great strength and a foul temper: this combination led him to demolish a schoolhouse and, on the run, he took refuge in a chest (a large one); when it was broken open he was gone and eventually the Delphic oracle solved the mystery: Cleomedes was the last of the heroes[35]. The disappearance of the body in such instances means that the privileged individual was transferred bodily to dwell with the immortal gods[36]. For the most part these stories are told without any reflection on the question of the substance of the body in this new, immortal existence. Occasion ally, however, as in the Ovid passage quoted above, we do find some express mention of the transformation that is necessary for this new life to be entered upon. Paul, confronted by the scepticism of some of his Corinthian converts, seems to have introduced some similar qualification of the nature of resurrection existence.

Thus it is quite plausible when G. Friedrich suggests that Luke 'makes use of the language of translation since he considered it suitable for bringing home to Greeks the special nature of Jesus' resurrection'[37]. However if that is true then the solidly physical nature of the risen Jesus in Luke's account of the resurrection appearances needs to be borne in mind[38]. There is no reflection here upon the need for the old nature to be transformed; Luke's main concern seems to be to allay the suspicion that the risen Jesus was a mere spectre or phantom (Lk 24.37, 39).

Yet in none of the cases that we have considered, either of this-worldly raising of the dead to continued earthly life (§§3, 3.2.1) or of the bypassing of death by the privileged (§3.2.2), do we find a true parallel either to the Christian expectations for the future existence of believers or to what they believed had happened to Jesus. Their beliefs differed from the former in that they believed that resurrection introduced one to a final, glorious state in which death was conquered for ever[39], and they differed from the latter in that they believed that this state was entered only through death, not by escaping it or avoiding it[40]. It is only with the

---

35 Plut., *Romulus* 28.4f; Paus. 6.9.6–8; Orig., *Cels.* 3.33; Suidas s.v. Κλεομήδης (K. 1724).

36 Cf. Bickerman, *'Consecratio'* 14f: 'contemporary opinion, both pagan and Christian, agreed that the deification of a mortal, be it Romulus, a Caesar, or Jesus presupposed that the body some-how was taken up into heaven and changed into a divine being', quoting such texts as Just., *Apol.* 1.21; Minucius Felix, *Octavius* 21; Orig., *Cels.* 2.68.

37 'Lk 9,51' 56; cf. Talbert, 'Concept' 435.

38 Friedrich, ibid. 59, points to the parallel in Philostr., *Vit. Ap.* 8.12.

39 Friedrich, ibid. 56: such a view of an 'eschatological event of the breaking in of God's new world into this world of death and destruction' was 'completely alien' to the Greeks.

40 Cf. Bickerman, *'Consecratio'* 16: 'a deified emperor did not die'.

relatively few cases of exceptional individuals who do not escape death but are revivified after death that we find a near parallel: they die, they are restored to bodily life and they enjoy for ever a godlike existence. However this was largely an experience enjoyed only by heroes of the legendary past, not a figure of the recent past. Later thought tended more to think of even these individuals sloughing off their bodies and continuing existence as souls alone, whether the dwelling-place of the soul was seen as being above or below this earth: so for Plato Ajax, son of Telamon, is not on the island of Leuce (see above), but after a span of a thousand years since his death his soul is about to be reincarnated in the body of a lion (*Resp.* 10.620B1–3). This was even more true of those for whom no legend specified any fate different to the normal. There still remained the exceptional few, emperors and others, who disappeared from this world, translated bodily to another one, in such a way that it is hard to be certain whether they can really be said to have died at all. There was no question of this being a general hope for people living at that time or for the ordinary dead of the recent past.

3.2.3. Commonly it is believed that the Graeco-Roman world was familiar with the idea of resurrection from the *'dying and rising gods'* of the mystery-cults[1]. This has, however, been challenged from a number of different viewpoints. We have seen already (§2.3 n. 3) MacMullen's scepticism about these gods, as he points out that several mystery-gods never suffered and that 'resurrection in divine stories more often calls to mind fertility (planting and growing) than immortality, e.g. in the story of Attis . . . or of Kore or Osiris'[2]! Yet it is doubtful whether this scepticism is altogether well-founded. It is true that the seasonal cycles of the growth and withering of vegetation may lie behind many of these stories and that the stories may be a mythological expression of those cycles[3]; yet the

---

Notes on 3.2.3

1 E.g. Barrett, 'Immortality' 75, 77; Braun, *Jesus* 14f; Lapide, *Resurrection* 120–2.

2 *Paganism* 172 n. 22. Perkins, *Resurrection* 56, baldly states that 'resurrection was not the creation' of the varied cults of the Graeco-Roman world; but we are not so much interested in the 'creation' of the idea as its propagation. Contrast Dieterich, *Mithrasliturgie* 173, who finds a 'dying and rising god' at the heart of almost all the mystic cults of late antiquity.

3 Colpe, 'Struktur' (cf. *Gn.* 38, 50 – he differentiates less between these figures there), argues that originally Adonis, Attis and Osiris were very different figures, Adonis a Baal producing fertility by union with a female consort, Attis an androgynous figure, and Osiris a shepherd slain by hostile powers threatening his flock. But for our purposes the question is not what they originally were, but how they were understood and interpreted in the 1st century C.E. Moreover each single deity may in different times and places have represented different aspects of the natural world and different natural cycles (cf., e.g., Jacobsen, *Treasures*, on the varying backgrounds to the myths of Dumuzi). Moreover one must note the radical challenge to the

stories themselves are told of persons, human and divine, however much they are embodiments of natural processes. It is by no means evident that their hearers would always have immediately been reminded of those cycles of nature, especially once their focus of interest had shifted from that of an agricultural community to that of individuals seeking salvation for themselves. Conversely, stories about individuals, once likened to courses of nature, might, by virtue of that analogy, be transformed into a pattern of death leading to further life.

Another approach which offers perhaps more hope of success is to question how far the individual stories of the gods in question in fact speak of their resurrection. So Wagner argues that the legend of Heracles burning himself to death on Mount Oeta and ascending thence to heaven suggests 'an ascension, an apotheosis, rather than a resurrection'[4]. Dionysus represents the identity of death and life rather than their succession; in his case 'one can only speak of a "resurrection" in the most symbolic sense of the term'[5]. 'The "vivification" of Osiris is not a resurrection'; although Osiris is brought back to life, and indeed to bodily life (the reassembling of the scattered limbs of Osiris is an essential part of the process), he is merely 'awakened to a sort of existence as king of the shades . . . only a dead king, though one who in death continues to exist: he does not rise again to a new life in his former majesty, . . .'[6]. The confused and fragmentary sources for the myth of Tammuz do not support the contention that he was a dying and rising god; rather they 'give reason to believe that Tammuz's death and descent to the Nether World was regarded as an event that happened once and for all and that he remained in the Nether World'[7]. The original understanding of Attis as symbolic of the spring vegetation burnt up by the heat of summer, in which attention was focused not on his revivifying but on his death, gave way to the

---

common interpretation of Adonis (stemming from Frazer) posed by Detienne, *Gardens*: 'the whole body of Greek mythology into which the story of Myrrha's son fits revolves around a fundamental opposition between the sphere of Adonis and that of Demeter: spices are diametrically opposed to cereals and seduction to marriage' (2). Thus it may be advisable to lay aside the quest for original meanings and even intervening layers of meaning and to *try* to concentrate on the meaning(s) attached to these figures in the Graeco-Roman period. A common source for the first is at least questionable (*pace* Frazer); a unitary picture of the last may be equally elusive.

4 *Baptism* 64; Athen. 8.392DE also tells of Heracles being brought back to life (ἀναβιῶναι) by the smell of a quail after being slain by Typhon.
5 Ibid. 67, quoting A. Oepke in *TDNT* 2, 336.
6 Ibid. 119.
7 Ibid. 145. Wagner also criticizes the idea of a resurrection of Marduk (159–70); this criticism seems to be in line with the consensus of scholarly opinion, although Ringgren, *Religionen* 149=ET 87, is more cautious.

view of him as a hunter and as 'a sort of underworld god'[8]; there is no mention of his resurrection. At least down to the mid second century C.E. the rites of Attis were ones of mourning, unmixed with any joy at a resurrection of the cult hero. Wagner follows Nilsson in seeing the first mention of a resurrection of Attis in the fourth century C.E., in Firm. Mat., *Err. prof. rel.* 3.1, as due to the influence of the Eleusinian mysteries[9]. In the first century C.E. the festival of Cybele and Attis seems to have lacked the *Hilaria*, the day of joy, on 25th March; it is first attested only in the third century, in the reign of Alexander Severus (Script. Hist. Aug., *Alexander Severus* 37.6) and, anyway, no connection of this day with Attis' resurrection is to be found before the sixth century[10].

So we must first ask whether any of these deities would have been regarded in the Graeco-Roman world as rising from the dead or as offering to their followers resurrection from the dead. (Often the answer to the first question will also provide an answer to the second, since it is unlikely that a deity who provided no answer to death for himself or herself would offer anything better to his or her followers; conversely, once the deity has been exposed to the fate of death and mortality there is the possibility that the manner of his or her overcoming that fate will set the pattern for his or her followers' hopes for their own existence beyond death.) Only once these questions have been answered will we be able to consider whether these deities are likely to have exercised any formative influence upon early Christian thinking about the resurrection of Jesus or that of his followers.

3.2.3.1. But it is questionable how far one can or should be too strict in one's definition of 'resurrection' in handling these traditions. Heracles' fate may suggest ascension or apotheosis rather than resurrection to us, but how did it appear to the ancient world[1]? And, perhaps more important, how did Jesus' fate appear to that world? Were early Christians' views of Jesus' resurrection all that homogeneous, let alone the impressions gained by their unbelieving contemporaries? Those of Christians seem to range through a whole spectrum from the accounts of the crucified body being restored to life, wounds and all (cf. Lk 24.37—43; Jn

---

8 Ibid. 180.
9 Cf. Nilsson, *Geschichte* 2, 650.
10 Damascius in Phot., *Bibliotheca* 242.345A.

Notes on 3.2.3.1

1 On the ambivalence of traditions about Heracles' fate cf. Pötscher, "'Auferstehung'" 208—10, who traces this to the fusion of divinity and humanity in this particular hero. He is still prepared to speak of his resurrection. For parallel cases of confusion cf. G. Strecker in *RAC* 5, 469f.

20.25, 27), through Paul's account in 1 Cor 15 which seems to suggest that the resurrection appearances were of the same kind as his own conversion experience (a 'spiritual body' different in kind from the earthly?), to a narrative like that of the hymnic Phil 2.6–11 which speaks simply of death and exaltation[2]. In the light of that sort of range of interpretation how would the fate of Jesus compare with those of the deities mentioned? Would not that spectrum of concepts have overlapped, at least at one end, with, for instance, the description of Heracles' end? Is it not solving the problem just too easily by classifying the latter as an 'ascension' or 'apotheosis'? After all Jesus was regarded as having ascended (and it is only really Luke-Acts which attempts to distinguish that from his resurrection); would that not have seemed comparable to Heracles' end?

3.2.3.2. With regard to *Dionysus* Wagner would seem to be on firmer ground: for a start the influential shrine of Delphi maintained that his remains. ($\lambda\epsilon i\psi\alpha\nu\alpha$) were buried close by the oracle (Plut., *Is. et Os.*, 35. 365A). But we would do well to remember that by the period which concerns us the origins and the nature of Dionysus were seemingly about as puzzling and confusing to most then as they are to us today: 'we have many Dionysi', Cicero bluntly states, first the son of Jupiter and Proserpina, then the son of the Nile-god who is said to have destroyed Nysa, thirdly the son of Cabirus (so most editors emend the text) and former king of Asia in whose honour the Sabazia were founded, fourthly the son of Jupiter and Luna, in whose honour the Orphic rites are said to be performed and finally the son of Nisus and Thyone who is reputed to have established the biennial festival at Thebes (*Nat. deor.* 3.23.58). Other witnesses may list fewer candidates but still agree on the plurality of bearers of the name[1]. It would be rash to be too dogmatic about the ultimate origins of this enigmatic, and seemingly composite, deity. The best that we can do is to try to gauge the impression he may have made on men and women of the first century C.E.

---

2 And yet the context is very much in the categories of Jewish apocalyptic thought, so that there should be no question of its representing a Hellenized version of the resurrection tradition, if by that is meant a version that takes us outside the varied thought-world of the Greek-speaking Jewish Diaspora; cf. Georgi, 'Hymnus' esp. 265f.

For other similar texts cf. Evans, *Resurrection* 135–7; Anderson, *Jesus* 192f. See also Perkins, *Resurrection* 20.

Notes on 3.2.3.2

1 See the n. in Pease's ed. 2, 1121; some of the other witnesses also list five candidates, often defined rather differently to Cicero's account.

Nilsson argues that Orphic theology taught that Dionysus was slain and rose again and that he brought his mother back from the underworld and that this aroused hopes of immortality in his initiates[2]. Those hopes of immortality are referred to by Plutarch in his *Consolatio ad uxorem* 10.611D[3]. *Ei Delph*. 9.388F records the tradition that Dionysus is 'deathless and eternal in his nature' (tr. Babbitt). The wiser (οἱ σοφώτεροι) speak allusively of what he suffers and his transformation (Plutarch seems to regard Apollo and Dionysus as manifestations of the same deity) as some sort of tearing apart and dismemberment; they speak of destructions and disappearances followed by returns to life (ἀναβιώσεις) and regenerations (παλιγγενεσίαι - 390A)[4]. The references to dismemberment here suggest that any basis of immortality in the myth of Dionysus may have lain in the story of his re-begetting or restoration by Zeus after being torn apart by the Titans[5], rather than in the story of his rescue of his mother. Neither aspect of the story is really comparable with resurrection in the Judaeo-Christian tradition, neither the indestructible life of the re-begotten divine child nor the ascent of the god to heaven[6], particularly if he somehow left his mortal remains at Delphi. That would not prevent a comparison with the Jewish or Christian doctrine, particularly once one wanted to compete with Jews or Christians.

Yet Dionysus has repeatedly been described as a dying and rising god; so, for instance, Bertram argues that he is a god of vegetation and foliage, depicting like Attis the vicissitudes of nature, dying in the winter, renewed in the spring[7]. In the second edition of his *Geschichte*, however, Nilsson

---

2 *Geschichte* 2, 365; Apollodorus, *Bibliotheca* 3.5.3 records that Dionysus brought his mother up from Hades, called her Thyone, and ascended (ἀνῆλθεν) with her to heaven (cf. Diod. S. 4.25.4; Paus. 2.31.2; 2.37.5; Plut., *Ser. num. vind.* 27.566A). This is rather hard to combine with accounts of his remains being buried at Delphi.

3 Le Corsu, *Isis* 74, interprets the ivy and pine-cones at the end of the *thyrsi* as symbols of immortality.

4 Cf. *Esu carn.* 1.7.996C (referred to in §2.2 n. 11 above).

5 Callimachus and Euphorion knew of Dionysus' dismemberment. Callimachus frg. 643 (Pfeiffer); Euphorion frgs 13, 36 (in Powell, *Collectanea* 32, 37); the latter at least knew of Rhea's putting the limbs together, as did Philodemus (*De pietate* 44=*Orph. Fr.* 36). Diod. S. 3.62.6 tells of Dionysus' third γένεσις when Demeter gathered his limbs. (Philodemus also seems to know of an Orphic tradition that Dionysus remained in Hades: *Orph. Fr.* ibid.; Clem. Alex., *Prot.* 2.18.2 and Eus., *Praep. ev.* 2.3.25 speak of Dionysus' remains being given to Apollo to bury — hence presumably the tradition of his burial at Delphi; cf. Jeanmaire, *Dionysos* 381).

6 See n. 1 above.

7 *RAC* 1, 925f; cf. Frazer, *Bough*[3] 7, 12–34; also Festugière, 'Mystères' 211; H. Metzger, 'Dionysos' 296–313 (and also n. 9 below on Nilsson's change of mind). It is true that rationalist explanations of his myths try to link his vicissitudes with, e.g., viticulture: Cornutus, *Theol. Graec.* 30 (Lang 58f) — that is at least evidence that in our period he seemed like a god who was born a second time (like the product of the trampled grapes); Diod. S. 3.62.5 gives a different version: the second birth is when the plant brings forth its fruit — §7 says that it is the third birth which produces the wine.

alters the similar opinion which he had held earlier: Plut., *Is. et Os.* 35.365A, at any rate, with its reference to the Thyiades raising Liknites cannot refer to a vegetation god, for this rite is performed every other year[8]; rather the god of the dead is aroused to participate in the rites, as in the *Orphic Hymns*[9]. God of the dead he may be, in some sense[10], but it should be noted that, despite the parallel which Herodotus draws between him and Osiris (2.42, 144)[11], he is not generally spoken of as king of the realm of the dead, although artists might merge him with Hades[12]. If he is a 'god of the dead' it is in the sense that he is a god in whom the dead put their trust (see later in § 5.1.3), who is present with his own in the world of the dead and offers them bliss there in his presence[13]. It is there that he is with them for the most part, although his worshippers still in this world look for his appearance amongst them; if they 'raise' him from the dead it is but for episodic spells of gracing their biennial rites[14]. Indeed the 'raising' here may be more like the 'rousing' of Iacchus in Aristophanes, *Ranae* 340, that is not so much a raising from the dead as a rousing from inactivity or lack of visible presence to lead the worshippers in their celebrations[15]. But the fact that he can still do so means that if he is a god who died then he himself has conquered death and still lives on.

---

8 *Orphic Hymn* 30 addresses Dionysus as τριετής; cf. the headings of *Hymns* 45 and 52, and 53.4f.

9 *Geschichte* 2, 364; *Mysteries* 39f; cf. *Geschichte* 1, 581. The earlier view can be found in the first ed. of his *Geschichte* 2, 347–9 (see also Athanassakis' ed. of the *Orphic Hymns* 128; H. Metzger, 'Dionysos' 313, distinguishes the Dionysus of Thracian origin from the god of vegetation who is of Phrygian origin; cf. Farnell, *Cults* 5, 127–32). Similarly the reference to the ἀνεγέρσεις of Dionysus in Plut., *Is. et Os.* 69.378E is an awaking from sleep primarily; cf. the preceding καθεύδειν ... ἐγρηγορέναι ... κατευνασμοί.
This seems a more significant point than Jeanmaire's observation that Dionysus is a tree-spirit rather than a grain-spirit (*Dionysos* 376); that could involve a similar annual cycle.
For the call for the presence of the god in the *Orphic Hymns* cf. *Hymns* 30, 42, 45–7, 50, 52f.

10 Nilsson, *Mysteries* 118: 'In Central Greece and South Italy Dionysus was clearly related to the dead in the classical age'; cf. 122ff; Bruhl, *Liber* 5; Fraser, *Alexandria* 1, 206. Burkert, *Religion* 438=ET 294, cites Harpocration s.v. λεύκη: 'initiates in the Bacchic rites are crowned with white poplar because both the plant and Dionysus son of Persephone are chthonic' (ed. Dindorf 1, 192; similarly Phot., *Lex.* s.v., ed. Porson 1, 216 – not in Naber).

11 Cf. Diod. S. 1.11.3; *Orphic Hymn* 42.9f.

12 Jeanmaire, *Dionysos* 384; Nilsson, *Mysteries* 118. This despite Heraclitus in Diels-Kranz, *Fragmente* §22 B 15; Zuntz, *Persephone* 408, holds that Heraclitus is stating a unity of opposites; he regards it as 'self-evident' that the two could not be identified (cf. also Aesch. frgs 5, 228, Nauck). For a different view based on non-literary evidence cf. H. Metzger, 'Dionysos' 314–23: in Greek art Dionysus is not associated with infernal deities but takes on their characteristics; also Otto, *Dionysus* 115–19.

13 *Pace* Festugière, 'Mystères' 196f.

14 Diod. S. 4.3.2 (ἐπιφανείαι of Dionysus), §3 (his παρουσία).

15 'Rise up, rouse yourself' is one possible translation of ἐγείρου (cf. the translations of Rogers,

3.2.3.3. Osiris is often regarded as a dying and rising god, but caution is necessary here. Wagner, we saw, denied that Osiris experienced a 'resurrection': Osiris merely 'continues to exist' as 'only a dead king' of the realm of the dead[1]. In this denial Wagner is to some extent justified, in that resurrection for Jews and Christians was normally part of God's new, final re-creation of the world that he had made. Bertram, too, makes a further point[2]: the mysteries of Osiris commemorated not his resurrection but the finding of his corpse, which was then followed by his fitting burial, leading to his entry into the world of the dead.

Moreover there is a tendency in the Egyptian texts to play down the reality of Osiris' or the king's preceding death[3]; Griffiths quotes from the *Pyramid Texts*:

> O King, thou hast not gone away; thou hast gone away alive[4].

He comments that here we have 'a doctrine of continued life rather than of resurrection or resuscitation after death'; 'resurrection' is not, strictly speaking, the right word to use here, although it is not entirely misleading in that Christian texts can also liken the death of believers to a sleep prior to their resurrection; here he compares Eph 5.14[5], to which we may add other Pauline texts like 1 Cor 15.51 and 1 Thess 4.13–15, as well as Acts 7.60[6]. A further Egyptian text underlines this tendency to play down the reality of death and at the same time introduces a further complicating element into the situation, namely the variety of Egyptian beliefs about the afterlife, at different periods and places as well as simultan-

---

'Come, arise, from sleep awaking', and v. Daele), cf. further §1.3.2.3 and n. 10; *Orphic Hymn* 53.3f – but there the sleep has been in the house of Persephone. His sleep has been in the realm of the dead. However Otto, *Dionysus* 80f, aptly comments of the 'raising' (ἐγείρωσιν) of Dionysus by the Thyiades in Plut., *Is. et Os.* 35.365A, that 'they awakened him as Liknites, as a child in the cradle. He had . . . just been born and had not yet gained consciousness.' This was, in other words, the waking of a sleeping infant and not the raising of one dead. But see Griffiths' ed. 435.

Notes on 3.2.3.3

1 Cf. Frankfort, *Kingship* 197f, 204ff, 289; Köster, *Einführung* 195; Nilsson, *Geschichte* 2, 686. West, *Poems* 141, even distinguishes him from Dionysus in this respect.

2 *RAC* 1, 921.

3 Cf. Greßmann, *Tod* 3: 'for a divine being death can only be a passage to new life'; also Eliade, *History* 1, 95; Frankfort, *Kingship* 281. But contrast Morenz, *Religion* 24f: the gods are created beings and so it is logical that, potentially at least, they should be subject to death (cf. *Book of the Dead* 154 – Budge 518); so 'mortality is by no means peculiar to Osiris' (cf. Plut., *Is. et Os.* 21.359C); so also Gardiner, *Attitude* 11f; Hornung, *Conceptions* 151ff.

4 *Origins* 66, quoting *Pyramid Texts* 134a (Sethe 1, 1). One could add many parallels here (cf., e.g., *Coffin Texts* §44=1.190, Faulkner 1, 36: 'Rise up to life, for you have not died', as well as the list in Breasted, *Development* 91f.

5 *Origins* 67; however not every ref. to death as sleep plays down the reality of death: cf. Morenz, *Religion* 188, 191f.

6 For Greek parallels cf. Leipoldt, *Tod* 89f, 93f (also Jewish parallels).

eously, as one local tradition fused with another and the beliefs of one period were piled upon their predecessors[7]:

> My father, Osiris-King has not indeed died the death, what has happened is that my father has become a glorious spirit[8].

That variety included different beliefs about the place of Osiris' existence, be it in the sky (perhaps identified with Orion)[9] or in the underworld[10], and different beliefs about the material nature or otherwise of the world to come[11]. What is perhaps safest is to speak, with Nock, of a 'triumphant reassertion of self'[12], a reassertion which could be expressed in more than one form, just as the god's reassertion could be variously expressed.

This uncertainty about the fate of Osiris is mirrored in, or is a reflection of, a variety of expectations as to the form in which the individual would survive death. The important thing from our point of view is that the main alternatives for each individual seem to have been becoming a glorious (astral) spirit or being identified with Re on the one hand[13], or

---

7 Gardiner, *Attitude* 28f, refers to 'a plethora of theories as to man's fate in the hereafter'; see also Brandon, 'Technique' 19; Breasted, *Development* chaps 1–5, 8; Eliade, *History* 1, 94ff; Erman, *Religion* 208ff; Griffiths, *Origins* 65f; Kees, *Totenglaube passim*, but esp. 14 and chap. 4; Morenz, *Religion* 204ff. Frankfort, *Kingship* 31, 184, seeks to find a rationale in what 'seems to involve (Osiris)' in two mutually exclusive destinies – the sun passes through both the heavens and the underworld.
  In particular there is evidence that some Egyptians held that for some (or all?) dead death was a dread and terrible reality: cf. Morenz, *Religion* 186ff, quoting from E. Otto, *Inschriften* 193 (period of Ptolemy XI). He also refers to Zandee, *Death*, for further documentation of this (see also Otto, *Inschriften* 46ff, for further examples). Moreover, however sanguine an Egyptian might be about the efficacy of a proper burial there were always those for whom the due performance of the rites was not possible: cf. Breasted, *Development* 63, 65f.
8 *Pyramid Texts* 1385*bc* (Sethe 5, 315), quoted by Griffiths, *Origins* 67ff (Morenz, *Religion* 205, however translates 'for my father possesses a spirit [in] the horizon'). Griffiths, *Origins* 66, puts this concept of death thus: 'Death is really only a sleep, a phase of tiredness'.
9 *Pyramid Texts* 819*c* (Sethe 4, 62) and other reff. quoted by Griffiths, *Origins* 13; cf. Breasted, *Development* 149; Kees, *Totenglaube* chaps 4f and pp. 207f (quoting also *Book of the Dead* 69.5, Budge 234).
10 Cf. Eliade, *History* 1, 94. In this respect 'living in death' would be an apter description of Osiris' fate. So H. Brunner summarizes Osiris' fate according to Egyptian myths thus: 'Yet Osiris cannot be awoken again to earthly life and so the lordship over the underworld with the dead is assigned to him' (*Grundzüge* 56).
11 Thausing, *Auferstehungsgedanke* 2ff.
12 'Cremation' 293; G. Bertram in *RAC* 1, 921, speaks of a 'return to life of the slain Osiris'.
13 Cf. Eliade, *History* 1, 94; Griffiths, *Origins* 65; Ringgren, *Religionen* 61; also Breasted, *Development* 10, 99ff, 274ff; Erman, *Literature* 2–4, quoting *Pyramid Texts* §§267, 335 (365*a*–369, Sethe 2, 81f; 546*a–c*, Sethe 3, 25), and pp. 4f; see also *Coffin Texts* §252 (3.352, Faulkner 1, 195).
  Perhaps this ascent to heaven was especially for the *ba* (soul); cf. *Coffin Texts* §§99–104 = 2.94–111, Faulkner 1, pp. 97–101; Morenz, *Religion* 205f. This raises the question of the relation of this to the carefully preserved and mummified corpse; cf. the contrasted texts quoted by Morenz, *Religion*, ibid.: in the one 'the *ba* belongs to heaven, the dead body to the nether world', in the other there is a prayer lest the *ba* be separated from the body.

remaining in the place of the dead, either as its king (Osiris) or as one of his protégés, on the other[14]; the idea of the dead being in an *interim state*, followed by a restoration of their former earthly state or by its replacement with a yet more glorious bodily condition, such as is involved in ideas of resurrection in the Judaeo-Christian tradition, is hard to reconcile with these beliefs. The burial rites were meant to ensure a person's entry *as quickly as possible* upon his or her future and ultimate state, of whatever kind[15]. The qualification 'as quickly as possible' is necessary because of Thausing's insistence upon an 'interim stage' between death and resurrection[16]; yet the difference remains between (1) a purposeful and necessary waiting for a process that is in motion in the individual to be fulfilled for him or her, and (2) a waiting for a future goal whose coming depends not upon the completion of a process in the individual but upon God's plans for the entire cosmos[17]. For a start the former is short and determinate, the period of mummification, the latter of indeterminate length as far as human knowledge is concerned[18]. The former is a transitional phase[19], in which the divine (and human) rescuing is taking place, the latter involves a state of being still requiring and looking for the divine rescue.

Again, however, we must ask the question how these different views of the fate of Osiris and the dead appeared to the Graeco-Roman world[20]. Evidently to some it again appeared like the (death and) burial of seed in the ground and its sprouting up to new life in the spring; Plutarch is critical of those interpreting Osiris in this way (*Is. et Os.* 65.377B), but the

---

14 The contrast can be seen most starkly in a text like *Pyramid Texts* 251*b–d* (Sethe 1, 234f). Breasted, *Development,* traces this to a conflict between popular religion locating Osiris' kingdom in the underworld and a royal, state theology built around the sun-god Re: 'Among the *people* Re is later, as it were, dragged into the Nether World to illumine there the subjects of Osiris . . . . In the *royal* and *state temple* theology, Osiris is lifted to the sky . . .' (160). See also Griffiths, *Origins* 232; Kees, *Totenglauben* 205f.

15 Cf. Brandon, *Man* 47: the Egyptian rites were designed 'to free the body from the immobility of death and restore to it the ability to receive food, to breathe, and to see and hear'; he adds in a note, 'There is, however, in Egypt no idea of a physical resurrection after the manner in which the Jews and Christians came to conceive of it.'

16 *Auferstehungsgedanke* 15ff; she likens the delay to that between conception and birth.

17 Cf. Nock, 'Cremation' 294: 'There was no corporate resurrection to await' in Egyptian beliefs.

18 An 'interim stage' (*Zwischenstadium*) may be appropriate enough for the first; in the latter we more often hear of an 'interim state' (*Zwischenzustand*) which suggests something longer-lasting.

19 Cf. Gardiner, *Attitude* 13: 'if all the precautions taken should prove successful, then physical death might be a mere transition from one state of life to another' (cf. 40 n. 19).

20 Note Breasted, *Development* 368: 'it was the religion of Egypt as viewed, interpreted, and apprehended by generations of Greeks, it was this Hellenized composite of old Egyptian religion and Greek preconceptions which passed out into the Mediterranean world . . .'; also Morenz, 'Problem' esp. 84.

interpretation was offered and it can probably claim considerable antiquity if this is the correct interpretation of the 'corn-mummies' representing Osiris[21]. For our purpose it is of no great consequence that texts can also be cited seemingly identifying Osiris with the Nile whose beneficent influence causes the grain to sprout[22], or with the soil or earth[23]; on the other hand, by the time which concerns us, all these, and other, identifications or associations had been made: the Osiris of the Graeco-Roman era was a many-layered deity who had assimilated to himself a great many attributes derived from his earlier association with a variety of Egyptian deities whom he had supplanted, as well as from Greek attempts to accommodate him to their world. But surveying the whole range of interpretations still leaves us with reason to doubt whether we have to do here with an exact parallel to the Judaeo-Christian doctrine of resurrection, or even a sufficiently close parallel that could give rise to Christian beliefs about Jesus and Christians' union with him; it is another matter when the question arises of parallels being drawn later when those Christian beliefs were already formed.

Yet there is a parallel in this, that the very fact that such care was taken with the preservation of the corpse suggests a very physical survival, presumably both for the god and for the devotees whose burial rites imitated his[24]. This could be described as a 'resurrection' in a sense, with the twofold qualification that (1) it followed hard upon death, the body being preserved from decomposition, and (2) that it was not 'resurrection' from the world of the dead but 'resurrection' into the world of the dead, the glorious kingdom of the god Osiris. Thus the world of the dead here plays a very different role compared with its very negative features in the Judaeo-Christian tradition[25]. But, interestingly, the one case of resurrection in this tradition which does come closest to Egyptian beliefs

---

21 Cf. Greßmann, *Tod* 8–11; also Brunner, *Grundzüge,* 127; de Vaux, 'Rapports' 38. One is illustrated, e.g., in E. Otto, *Art* pl. 15 (14th century B.C.E. – p. 69: 'the germinating seed symbolizes the resurrection of the god of fertility'). But see Griffiths, *Origins* 163ff – he argues that this was an earlier practice only later associated with the Osiris-cult. See also *Coffin Texts* §330 (4.168ff, Faulkner 1, 254f).

22 Cf. *Pyramid Texts* 589a (Sethe 3, 91) cited, along with other texts, by Breasted, *Development* 18ff (cf. Erman, *Religion* 40ff), an argument and interpretation which is criticized by Griffiths, *Origins* 151ff, in the light of his thesis that Osiris was originally god of the dead (cf. Kees, *Totenglaube* esp. 199, 218f), and that the references to (Nile) water must be seen in the light of the funerary cult. Certainly Plut., *Is. et Os.* 36.365B, calls moisture in general the ἀπορροή of Osiris, not Osiris himself.

23 Cited in Breasted, *Development* 21f; Griffiths, *Origins* 159, argues that his argument here is influenced by J. G. Frazer although his indebtedness is unacknowledged; see also Kees, *Totenglaube* 214f.

24 Cf. Le Corsu, *Isis* 3; also Breasted, *Development* 33.

25 Cf. Brandon, *Man* 47 n. 3, cited in n. 15 above.

in some respects is the resurrection of Jesus, in that he was raised to eternal life on the third day, before he could 'see corruption' (Ps 16.10 as quoted in Acts 2.27). Yet here the resemblance ends: Christians were 'buried with' Christ in their baptism (Rom 6.4), a rite that could not be described as imitating burial rites; they were baptized while still alive and, when they eventually died, there is no hint that their burial rites sought to imitate those of Jesus' burial (see further §5). Moreover the Egyptian cult did not influence the funerary practices of the Graeco-Roman world[26]; in turn this suggests that the idea of bodily survival inherent in it was probably lost sight of as well.

3.2.3.4. Origen clearly regarded *Tammuz*'s fate as a death and resurrection[1], although Jerome speaks rather of his coming to life again[2]. Against that Wolfgang Röllig baldly states 'There was no "resurrection" of Tammuz', although he grants that according to one tradition Tammuz was allowed to spend one half of the year in the upper world[3]. Yet the end of the *Descent of Ishtar to the Nether World*, an end that perhaps does not belong to the original[4], may read

> On that day that Tammuz ascends (?)
> With him ascend (?) the flute of lapis lazuli and the carnelian ring,
> With him the wailing men and wailing women ascend (?),
> May the dead too rise and smell the incense[5]!

This is essentially similar to the translation of E. Ebeling which Wagner rejects with the comment that this 'text . . . is usually rendered quite differently today'[6]. Most would agree that this is an unusually obscure text, yet Ringgren confidently affirms that it 'must yet refer to the god's return to life'[7]. (But not only Tammuz would be returning, but also other

---

26 Nock, 'Cremation' 293.

Notes on 3.2.3.4

1 *Comm. in Ezek.* 8.14 (Migne *PG* 13, 797D–800A)=Turchi, *Fontes* §298: ὡς ἀπὸ νεκρῶν ἀναστάντι.

2 *Comm. in Ezek.* 8.14 (Migne *PL* 25, 85f) =Turchi, *Fontes* §299: *revixisse . . . reviviscens.*

3 *KP* 5, 508; cf. *RGG*[3] 6, 609. This looks suspiciously like the result of assimilation, perhaps to Adonis. The relevant text is quoted in Jacobsen, *Treasures* 61; he alternates with his sister Geshtinanna (Jacobsen 62 suggests that they refer respectively to the alternating periods of storage of beer and wine).

4 Cf., e.g., Gurney, 'Tammuz' 153f, 160.

5 Translated following Ringgren, *Religionen* 127 (his question-marks; he acknowledges that it is hard to translate; ET 64 omits the question-marks; E. A. Speiser's translation in *ANET* 109 is essentially the same).

6 *Baptism* 143; Ebeling's translation in *AOT* 210 is not significantly different from Ringgren's.

7 Ibid. Yet cf. Yamauchi, 'Notes' 13: 'It would seem more plausible to explain the rising both of Tammuz and of the dead as the ascent of spirits to partake of the offerings made for the dead' (cf. 'Tammuz' 288).

dead as well, and that would conflict with what Brandon calls the 'pessimistic nature of Mesopot[amian] eschatology'[8].) If it does refer to this, then it looks like a later modification of the earlier story of Tammuz or Dumuzi who is consigned to the world of the dead as a substitute for Inanna, having formerly been her husband[9]. However, when Dumuzi/ Tammuz represented vital forces in nature and cycles of growth, then some restoration, some return to life, might be expected; the difficulty is to discover texts which actually speak of this[10].

For our purpose, however, it may be adequate to note that the dominant impression left by the cult of Tammuz was one of mourning[11]; he was the one for whom Ishtar 'ordained wailing year after year'[12]. And, more important still, it is likely that in the Graeco-Roman world Tammuz was hard to distinguish from the Phoenician Adonis[13], to whom we must now turn. Correspondingly, his role as a god who rose from the dead is linked to the question whether Adonis was regarded as resurrected[14].

3.2.3.5. Adonis, whom Origen and Jerome identified with Tammuz[1], was a parallel figure to that Mesopotamian figure. Again the Church Fathers speak of his 'resurrection', in the case of Cyril of Alexandria in language

---

8 *Dictionary* 600; cf. Frankfort, *Kingship* 281. In the *Descent of Ishtar* lines 19f raising the dead is spoken of as a threat of something to be avoided (*ANET* 107) – cf. Yamauchi, 'Tammuz' 286.

9 Gurney, 'Tammuz' 153; Kramer, *Sumerians* 153–60; Wagner, *Baptism* 143. Jacobsen, *Treasures* 63, suggests that the 'death' of Inanna represents the emptying of the storehouse in the later winter which is then replaced by a fulness achieved at the cost of the shepherd Dumuzi whose animals must die to provide fresh meat in late spring or early summer.

Gurney 154f mentions the account of Tammuz and Gizzida 'at the gate of Anu' (*Myth of Adapa* B.20, *ANET* 101) and argues that this must be a different version of the myth, perhaps an alternative where Tammuz goes straight to heaven (compare the similar ambivalence about the destination of the dead in Egyptian religion mentioned in the previous section).

10 G. Bertram in *RAC* 1, 923, confidently asserts that this is the case; but cf. the caution of Baudissin, *Adonis* 373.

It is perhaps implied in the Damu texts quoted by Jacobsen, *Treasures* esp. 70–2 (see too Langdon, *Psalms* 339f, and *Tammuz* 21–3; followed by E. O. James, *Religion* 115f), but these are different in character from the highly anthropomorphic texts concerning the fortunes of Dumuzi.

11 Ringgren, *Religionen* 128: 'his death and the lamentation for it were the completely dominant features of the Tammuz cult.' This rite took place in mid summer. Cf. Lambrechts, ' "Résurrection" ' 216.

12 *Gilgamesh Epic* 6.46 (*ANET* 84).

13 Cf. Preisendanz in *PRE* 2. Reihe 4, 2140.

14 Cf. Wagner, *Baptism* 145: 'It is only where Tammuz is identified with Adonis by the Christian writers . . . that he appears as a dying and resurrected god.' I doubt, however, whether this identification only emerged first in Christian writers.

Notes on 3.2.3.5

1 Cf. §3.2.3.4 nn. 1 and 2.

suspiciously reminiscent of the 'finding' of Osiris[2]. Again, however, the dominant impression left by the rites of this god or hero is one of mourning[3]. Despite that Lucian, *Syr. Dea* 6, says that on the day following the mourning of Adonis' death at Byblos ζώειν τέ μιν μυθολογέουσι καὶ ἐς τὸν ἠέρα πέμπουσι. The meaning of the last phrase is obscure[4], but Lambrechts suggests that the reference is to the erection of a cult statue like the Djed-pillar in the Osiris cult, and that the whole tradition of a celebration of Adonis' revivification is due to the influence of the Osiris rites, and that relatively late[5]. For such an influence of the Osiris cult on the Byblos cult of Adonis he can point to the beginning of *Syr. Dea* 7[6]:

> Some inhabitants of Byblos . . . say that the Egyptian Osiris is buried among them and that all the laments and the rites are performed not for Adonis but for Osiris[7].

Moreover, if Soyez is right in thinking that at Byblos as elsewhere in the Graeco-Roman world the festival of Adonis took place in mid July, at the rising of Sirius, then the point of time which in Egypt marked the fertilizing inundations of the Nile marked in Lebanon the death of vegetation under the burning summer sun. The prominence of mourning and death in the rites is then scarcely surprising; the idea of rebirth and new life is an alien importation[8]. However Atallah cautions against supposing

---

2 *Comm. in Isa* 18.1f (Migne *PG* 70, 441AB)=Turchi, *Fontes* §300: εὑρῆσθαι . . . τὸν ζητούμενον (cf. Procopius of Gaza in Migne *PG* 87.2, 2140AB). Hyginus, *Fabulae* 251.4 lists Adonis among those 'who have returned from the underworld by permission of the Fates', but this may refer to the tradition of the newborn child consigned to Persephone's keeping in a chest, i.e. before his tragic end. See also *Orph. Hymn* 56.11.

3 Attested from Sappho frg. 140 (Lobel-Page) onwards; see too Bion's *Lament for Adonis* (esp. lines 95f). Cf. Lambrechts, ' "Résurrection" ' *passim*; he maintains that even the 'gardens of Adonis' were symbols of premature withering, not of life; cf. Atallah, *Adonis* 211, 227f; Bianchi, 'Initiation' 166=161; Frankfort, *Kingship* 291; de Vaux, 'Rapports' 33f; Vernant in Detienne, *Gardens* xvi–xvii (but contrast xix?); also Detienne himself on 101–22. Contrast Schneider, *Mysterien* 48.
   Important here is Plato, *Phaedrus* 276B, which on the one hand stresses the rapid growth of the seeds thus planted (8 days instead of 8 months), but suggests on the other that such a mode of planting shows no concern for the seeds' bearing fruit.
   The fact that the withered gardens were thrown not only into springs but also into the sea tells against the view of Frazer and others that they were a magical means of ensuring supplies of water (cf. Eustathius on Hom., *Od.* 11.590).
   Whittaker, *Jews* 264, speaks of the gardens as symbols of Adonis' resurrection and death (in that order!); she regards the spectacle which Theocritus describes in *Idyll* 15 as a description of Adonis and Venus together on the former's 'one day of . . . resurrection'.

4 Soyez, *Byblos* 35, speaks of 'a sort of "resurrection" '. This particular phrase she translates 'et ils l'escortent en procession à l'air libre', i.e. out of an enclosed space (14, 39); cf. also Atallah, *Adonis* 261–3.

5 So too Soyez, ibid. 37f, 74.

6 Ibid. 233f; de Vaux, 'Rapports' 39ff, and also, for a later period in Rome, v. Graeve, 'Tempel'.

7 Tr. Attridge-Oden. The account goes on to describe the story of a head floating annually from Egypt to Byblos in 7 days. In chap. 6 too a comparison with Egyptian rites had been made.

8 *Byblos* esp. 73–5, appealing to Baudissin, *Adonis*.

that mourning was the only characteristic note of the *Adonia* all the time and everywhere[9]: perhaps, though, the rites at least ended on a note of mourning?

The influence of the Egyptian rites on the cult of Adonis at Alexandria is of course even more likely[10], and this would explain the references to a 'finding' of Adonis in the Church Fathers mentioned above. But it would be more damaging for Lambrechts' theory of a comparatively late influence of the Egyptian cult upon that of Adonis if the resurrection of Adonis were already to be found in the writings of Theocritus in the third century B.C.E. However, as Gow remarks in his commentary to *Idyll* 15[11], Theocritus 'has said as plainly as he can be expected to say that in Alexandria after the day of mourning nothing will be heard of Adonis for another year'; in other words Adonis' return is celebrated before his death is mourned and there is no immediate restoration of him to life:

> Look on us with favour next year too, dear Adonis.
> Happy has thy coming found us now, Adonis, and when thou comest again, dear will be thy return[12].

This would tend to confirm the suggestion made above that joy preceded mourning in the *Adonia*.

Noteworthy, too, is Lambrechts' scepticism about the suitability of the word 'resurrection' to describe the story of Adonis[13]: here we rather have the idea of the annual return of a god of vegetation for a brief stay upon earth, near to his beloved Aphrodite[14]. Implicit here in Lambrechts' verdict is perhaps a contrast with the finality, the once and for all achievement of victory that is inherent in the idea of 'resurrection' in the Judaeo-Christian tradition[15].

---

9 *Adonis* 270–3, criticizing Lambrechts.

10 See Damascius in Hopfner, *Fontes* 690: an image which the Alexandrians say is both Osiris and Adonis κατὰ μυστικὴν . . . θεοκρασίαν. Cf. also the tradition of the women of Alexandria sending a jar floating from Alexandria to say that Aphrodite had found Adonis (Cyril of Alexandria on Isa 18 – Migne *PG* 70, 441AB).

11 2, 264; although he finds the evidence presented by Glotz, 'Fetes', in the nearly contemporary *P. Petr.* 3, no. 142 (ed. Mahaffy-Smyly 332f) illuminating, he feels that the Fayum cult may have differed from the Alexandrian; it may have taken on an 'Egyptian tinge' (=assimilation to Osiris rites?); cf. also Atallah, *Adonis* 136–40; Bianchi, 'Initiation' 169=164.

12 Lines 143f, tr. Gow (1, 119, 121); cf. Bion, *Lament for Adonis* 94–8; also Atallah, *Adonis* 133; Bianchi, *History* 144; de Vaux, 'Rapports' 47ff.

13 ' "Résurrection" ' 237; cf. Atallah, *Adonis* 268f (citing Grandmaison and Lagrange); Bianchi, 'Initiation' 170=165; Colpe, 'Struktur' 27.

14 Thus the marriage or union *precedes* the death; cf. Bianchi, ibid. 166=161. In *Orph. Hymn* 56.11 we have perhaps an alternation between the underworld and Olympus, rather than just the earth.

15 G. Bertram, in *RAC* 1, 924, argues for belief in Adonis' resurrection from the depiction of him on sarcophagi, but Lambrechts, ' "Résurrection" ' 224, points out that, in contrast to Christian sarcophagi, a resurrection of Adonis is not portrayed; usually the scenes depicted are Adonis departing for the hunt, being wounded and then dying, with Aphrodite coming to his aid.

3.2.3.6. For *Attis* again our starting point is a Christian writer, Firmicus Maternus; Attis' followers claim that 'he whom they have buried a little earlier has come to life again' (*revixisse, Err. prof. rel.* 3.1). Nilsson points out that otherwise the myths have Attis remain dead[1], and he suggests that Firmicus is interpreting the myths of Attis in line with Eleusinian ideas; the Naassenes clearly blended the two[2]. Over against that one finds assertions to the effect that 'the theme of death and resurrection was. strongly expressed in the rites of Attis'[3], but again one needs then to raise the question, 'When, how early?' Certainly appeal to the rite of the *taurobolium*[4] does not help us, for we have no evidence of the rite earlier than the second century C.E., and then only as a sacrifice offered generally for the sake of the emperor and his realm, then later for the dedicator[5]. It is only later still, in the fourth century, that we find its reinterpretation as a rite of individual rebirth[6], and by then there is considerable evidence that Attis was thought of as a heavenly figure, triumphant over death[7].

There is too, it seems, good reason to be sceptical about whether the *Hilaria* on 25th March formed part of the March festival of the cult of Cybele at Rome earlier than the reign of Antoninus Pius (138–61) or even later[8]. Lambrechts again advocates the view that the rites of Attis in the first century C.E. were ones of mourning, terminating with the *Lavatio* on 27th March[9], and Vermaseren concedes that all the literary evidence for the institution of the *Hilaria* on the day following the *Sanguis*, the day of

---

Notes on 3.2.3.6

1 Cf. Hepding, *Attis* 100ff; also Zuntz, *Persephone* 18. For Lagrange, 'Attis' (1919) 449, Firm. here follows the account of Minucius Felix, *Octavius* 23.4; but Minucius does not mention Attis' death, but only his mutilation. Prümm, *Handbuch* 258, describes the revivification of Attis as only a late *Nebenform* of the legend.

2 *Geschichte* 2², 648f (cf. 686); cf. Wagner, *Baptism* 220; in one version Zeus grants Agdistis' request that his body might be preserved for ever (Arnobius, *Adversus nationes* 5.14 in Migne *PL* 5, 1110f). Vermaseren, *Cybele* 112, also recognizes that in earlier accounts of Attis he remains dead; cf. Gasparro, *Soteriology* 45, 47f, who sees Firm. the Christian reading elements into the Phrygian rites.

3 Griffiths, *Isis-Book* 297, quoting Hepding, *Attis* 195ff; Vermaseren, *Legend* 44ff. Contrast Lagrange, 'Attis' (1919) 438.

4 As in Hepding, ibid. 195ff.

5 Cf. Duthoy, *Taurobolium* 95, 117f, recognized by Hepding, ibid. 199.

6 *CIL* 6, 510=*ILS* 4152=*CIMRM* 520= Duthoy, ibid. no. 23 (376 C.E.). For Reitzenstein this was the original sense of the rite (*Mysterienreligionen* 45).

7 Jul., *Or.* 5.169C (cf. Sallust, *De diis et mundo* 4); see also Duthoy, ibid. no. 33, quoted by Vermaseren, *Cybele* 50; but see the different interpretation offered by Lagrange, 'Attis' (1927).

8 Duthoy also assigns the introduction of the *taurobolium* into the cult of Cybele to his reign (ibid. 116), following Lambrechts.

9 E.g. 'Fêtes'; cf. Fishwick, 'Cannophori' 194f, 200–2; Gasparro, *Soteriology* 56f; G. Sanders, 'Kybele' 281.

blood, is late. It has been suggested that the earliest is perhaps Valerius Flaccus' *Argonautica*, written perhaps towards the end of the first century C.E., where we read that (after the *Lavatio*?) 'Cybele is glad and festal torches gleam in the city streets'[10]; yet Vermaseren, following Lamb-rechts, notes that the order is unusual: if the *Lavatio* precedes the *Hilaria* this is strange, and so the reference is merely to the joyous returning from the Almo after bathing the goddess' statue[11]. Yet, he claims, the archaeol-ogical evidence is early[12]. By this he means the representations of a dancing Attis, although such figures are lacking from the terracottas in the Republican temple of Cybele in Rome. Moreover, he grants, such figures could be meant to represent either Attis triumphant after his sufferings *or* his carefree earlier life before his tragic fate[13]. It is only when we find representations of a winged Attis[14] that it becomes more plausible to plump for the first alternative. These figures date from the second century B.C.E. onwards. Yet one must again distinguish the representa-tions of him that are like a winged Eros; it is perhaps going too far when Vermaseren says that he then dances 'the hilaria after his resurrection as the new-born child Attis'[15]. Assimilation to Eros could explain his appear-ance. Far more impressive evidence can be found in the representations of an older and graver winged Attis[16], or of an Attis showing marked female characteristics[17].

Also significant here is the representation of a winged Attis escorting Ganymede to heaven found in one of the scenes depicted in an under-ground basilica near the Porta Maggiore in Rome, a construction that is generally regarded as dating from the first century C.E.[18] If Vermaseren is indeed correct in identifying this figure as Attis[19], which seems likely, then it seems that for at least some first century devotees of the Phrygian cult the mourning for Attis was not the last word; we should not expect this hope immediately to find its recognition in the official cult, nor even

---

10 8.240 (tr. Mozley).
11 *Cybele* 120–2; Gasparro, *Soteriology* 59, may read too much into this return from the Almo if she assumes that they can only be joyful if they are now certain of Attis' survival.
12 Ibid. 119.
13 Ibid. 123; he was less cautious in his assessment in *Legend* 47, where only the first possibility is mentioned.
14 Vermaseren, *Legend* pls 25.2–3, 26.2–4, 28.4, 31.1–2, and other examples listed on pp. 47–53; *CCCA* 2, nos 616–18, 637.
15 *Legend* 47 (on 46 he tells us that 'Attis received his wings under the influence of Eros').
16 E.g. ibid. pls 25.2–3.
17 E.g. ibid. pl. 26.4; *CCCA* 4, no. 133.
18 Already noted in §2.1 (*CCCA* 3, no. 344; see p. 97 on dating).
19 *Cybele* 56; so also G. Sanders, 'Kybele' 281f. But, curiously, Gasparro, *Soteriology*, makes little use of this evidence (cf. however 93 n. 42).

that it should find general acceptance among all the devotees of the cult[20]. Indeed as late as the time of Arnobius the myth of the cult seems to have stated that Attis' body remained incorruptible, with his hair still growing and his little finger in constant motion[21]. For Gasparro this survival cannot appropriately be called a return to life or resurrection[22]. Whether the promise of a like survival was enough to enthuse the followers of the Great Mother seems questionable[23], but anyway she concludes that 'even if the promise of a better lot in the hereafter was offered to the *mystai* of Cybele and Attis, it does not appear to have been the primary and specific objective of the esoteric cult'[24]. Part of the solution may be that many of them were not enthused with the thought of what awaited them in the world to come, for she points to a series of epitaphs where a future hope is strikingly lacking[25].

Plutarch too seems to know of a happier end to the story of Attis or at least of a Phrygian god: in *Is. et Os.* 69.378EF he tells us that the Phrygians believe that their god sleeps in the winter but awakes in the summer, and so they perform rites to lull him to sleep in the winter and in the summer ones to arouse him, in the manner of Bacchic rites. This sequence of two festivals may be confirmed by an inscription from the third century B.C.E. at Piraeus, seemingly referring to two festivals of Attis[26]. But Rome seems to have known of no festival of Cybele and Attis later in the year; that does not, however, rule out the possibility of the existence of one in the East, but it raises the question whether the god in question might be Dionysus[27] or possibly Sabazius.

Yet, even if we grant that some first century devotees believed in Attis' conquest of death, it does not necessarily mean that 'resurrection' is the right term to use of it. So G. Sanders points out that no bodily ascent of Attis is celebrated[28]; yet again I wonder whether this in itself precludes a comparison with some views of Jesus' triumph over death in which his ascension and exaltation were stressed, and little was said of his bodily

---

20 Cf. the evidence of v. Doren cited in §2.1 n. 62.

21 Arnobius, *Adversus nationes* 5.7 in Migne *PL* 5, 1097; cf. Paus. 7.17.12.

22 *Soteriology* 42; cf. too 125. Attis is 'surviving in death'.

23 *Pace* Gasparro, ibid. 63, 125. It might be preferable to follow Lagrange, 'Attis' (1919) 438ff, in seeing the story of Attis as primarily one of consecration to Cybele's service, not of his death, which would be a secondary addition.

24 Ibid. 104; cf. Lagrange, ibid. 470–80.

25 Ibid. 94f.

26 *CCCA* 2, no. 262.10 (*IG* 2.2, 1315); cf. Hepding, *Attis* 137 (he gives a slightly later date); Lagrange, 'Attis' (1919) 436f.

27 As suggested, e.g., by Rohde, *Psyche* 270f n. 28; v. Wilamowitz-Moellendorff, *Glaube* 2, 63; Lagrange, ibid. 437, suggests that Attis and Adonis have become confused here.

28 'Kybele' 286.

resurrection[29]. Again, however, this is a comparison which can only become credible once the traditions of Jesus' triumph have become established; the traditions about Attis are neither similar enough nor prevalent enough to have been likely to have had a formative effect on Christian beliefs about either Jesus' resurrection or that of his followers; the drawing of comparisons belongs to the stage of later rivalry and competition between the cult of the Great Mother and the increasingly prominent cult of the Christian Saviour.

3.2.3.7. Wagner left out of his reckoning the rites of *Mithraism* on the grounds that 'Mithras does not belong to the dying and rising gods, and no death and resurrection ritual has ever been associated with his cult'[1]. Yet Tertullian does say that Mithras *'imaginem resurrectionis inducit'*[2], and Vermaseren comments that the followers of Mithras 'firmly believed that by eating the bull's flesh and drinking its blood they would be born again just as life itself had once been created anew from the bull's blood'[3]. That in turn suggests that here again we have an instance of a Christian theologian, Tertullian, using a Christian term to describe something rather different in pagan thought, here probably the idea of spiritual rebirth[4].

3.2.3.8. One text needs perhaps to be considered separately, Firm. Mat., *Err. prof. rel.* 22.1. It should receive separate consideration because of the uncertainty as to which cult is here referred to. Firmicus tells of an image being laid flat on a litter at night and being mourned. Then a light is brought in and a priest anoints the throats of the mourners and murmurs quietly to them

> Have courage, initiates; for since the god has been saved
> we shall have salvation from our pains.

This has been taken to be a reference to the cult of Cybele and Attis[1], to

---

29 Whittaker, *Jews* 232, 235, talks happily enough of Attis' resurrection.

Notes on 3.2.3.7
1 *Baptism* 67.
2 *Praescr. haer.* 40.4 = Turchi, *Fontes* §341.
3 *Mithras* 103; yet he still speaks of their enacting a 'resurrection'.
4 Cf. *Nat.* 1.19.3f; *Apol.* 48 — the Christian hope of resurrection compared with the no less incredible doctrine of metempsychosis; cf. also 50.11, 'resurrection' through the 'eternity' conferred by pagan monuments; also Gordon, 'Cumont' 236.

Notes on 3.2.3.8
1 E.g., tentatively, Hepding, *Attis* 167; cf. Cumont, *Lux* 262f; Graillot, *Culte* 131; v. d. Leeuw, *Religion* 484; Whittaker, *Jews* 235 (one could compare Damascius in Photius, *Bibliotheca* 242. 131=6, 34, 345A).

that of Eleusis[2], or of Qsiris[3], or Adonis[4] or a composite deity[5]. The phrase in 22.3, *'iacentia lapidis membra componis.*, may perhaps suggest the gathering of the dismembered body of Osiris, and this cult is perhaps the one most iikely to be referred to here. However Cumont compared the *Carmen aureum* ascribed to Pythagoras with this passage[6], and Turcan points out that the idea of πόνος as a pledge of becoming a hero and immortal is of Pythagorean origin; he suggests here a fusion of the Hellenistic rites of Osiris with Neopythagorean theosophy[7].

At any rate the terms used are σώζω and σωτηρία, not 'resurrection'[8]; that language is used by the Christian writer (22.2): no oracle has spoken of that god's resurrection nor has he shown himself to any mortals after his death nor did he prepare the way by earlier signs or prophecies. If the cult referred to is that of Osiris then the comparison is not inappropriate; yet we should recall that the 'salvation' referred to is not quite identical with the Christian hope of resurrection; the deity was rescued from destruction and brought safely by means of the appropriate mortuary rituals to the world of the dead, as its king and as the prototype for the salvation of mortals. Moreover that salvation may still lie in the future (ἔσται), unless the future tense is a logical future, not a temporal.

3.2.3.9. This section is not easy to summarize, nor has it been easy to write. The question with which we started out, the possibility of influence of the ideas of the mysteries upon Christian ideas about resurrection led us to steer a hazardous course between the Scylla of so tight a definition of 'resurrection' that some Christian accounts of the phenomenon of Christ's resurrection would be excluded, and the Charybdis of overlooking fundamental differences of substance between various myths and the Christian story.

---

2 V. Magnien, *Mystères d'Eleusis* 130, in Atallah, *Adonis* 282f.

3 Cumont, *Religions* 226=*Religionen* 228 n. 46; Kuss, *Röm* 362; Lagrange, 'Attis' (1919) 448; Nilsson, *Geschichte* 2, 639; ed. Pastorino 225; Prümm, *Handbuch* 258; Vermaseren, *Cybele* 116; Wagner, *Baptism* 97.

4 Cf. Cumont, *Lux* 262f.; v. Graeve, 'Tempel' 346.

5 Atallah, *Adonis* 283, citing Ausonius, *Epigrams* 48.

6 *Lux* 404; he went as far as to say that Firm. was inspired by *Carmen aureum* 63ff (esp. 63, 66; v. d. Horst dates this work to the 2nd century C.E.).

7 Ed. 317; there is an extensive bibliography on the different origins ascribed to these rites on 313–15. The whole passage bears an extraordinary resemblance to a re-enactment of shamanic initiation experiences – cf. Eliade, *Chamanisme* esp. chap. 2: dismemberment and restoration, even the cry 'our shaman revives and comes (*va*) to help us' (ibid. 54=ET 44, 'Our shaman is returning to life and he will help us').

8 But cf. Widengren, *Religionsphänomenologie* 224.

Our investigation of those myths has been hampered by a number of factors: there is the existence of different layers of interpretation, sometimes even simultaneously, so that one and the same deity may mean a number of different things to different people, or sometimes even to the same people[1]. Again the syncretism which merges a number of different, but sufficiently similar, deities, either within the one country or between different countries, makes it difficult to give a coherent and unitary account of the fortunes of any particular deity. For related to that is the further difficulty that beliefs about one deity may influence those about another, or may even, as we have seen to be likely, be added on to those held about another deity. The problem becomes especially acute when the influence may be from the competing beliefs of Christianity itself.

But once a deity is seen as a symbol of, for instance, the natural cycle of vegetation, or perhaps even came into being as a symbol of that cycle, then it would seem appropriate to speak of that deity's death and resurrection. But is it? A number of scholars have insisted that it is far more appropriate to speak of the deity's return[2]. That point may be granted; the vegetation deity returns only to die again; it does not effect any final victory over death, at least not *qua* vegetation deity, although it may as a god of the dead or a solar deity. Nor, in the Graeco-Roman world, did its devotees see their own destinies in terms of resurrection. And so it is all the more significant when we see that non-Christians generally did not use the terms ἀνάστασις or ἐγείρω or their cognates of these deities[3], but only terms like ἀναβίωσις or παλιγγενεσία[4].

Nor is it clear that the devotees of these gods viewed them, *qua* vegetation deities, as connected with their own destinies beyond the grave. More often they were interested in the beneficent presence of the deity with them in this world with all its natural processes[5]. If they also believed

---

Notes on 3.2.3.9

1 Cf. §2.2. The difficulty is well illustrated by G. Bertram's art. on 'Auferstehung' in *RAC* 1, 920: originally these cults only lamented the death of the deity and did not celebrate its resurrection, but only when they became mysteries oriented towards the world to come; but they were often *Jenseitsmysterien* from a very early date (e.g. Eleusis).

2 Cf. also Bianchi, *History* 52.

3 Cf. Nock, 'Cremation' 302f: the idea of resurrection was 'to the faithful of the mystery religions . . . as foreign and repugnant an idea as to St Paul's hearers in *Acts*'.

4 Though it should be noted that these terms could be used of resurrection: e.g. Jos., *Ant.* 18.1.3 §14; *Ap.* 2.30 §218; 2 Macc 7.9; *Act. Jn* 53 (Lipsius-Bonnet 2.1, 177.32 – n.b. line 20); *Act. Thom.* 158 (ibid. 2.2, 269.1); also ἀνακαίνισις in *Act. Jn* 78 (ibid. 2.1, 190.6).

5 In other words their interests had more in common with Paul's assertion that Christ had become a 'life-giving spirit' (1 Cor 15.45) than with his insistence that he was the first-fruits of the resurrection of all (v 20); they were more interested in the deity's present power than in how it had attained to that power or in the implications of that manner of attainment for their future salvation.

that their gods would affect their future lives after they had died it was, as we shall see (§5), more by virtue of their beneficent presence and protection in the world to come (and when they are in a position to offer that to their devotees they have passed beyond the role of vegetation deities). Just as Wilckens comments on the failure of Jews to relate the resurrection of the Messiah to their own share in salvation[6], it seems to have been true that many devotees of the mystery-gods failed to draw from the fate of their deity any inferences concerning their own survival; not only .the Egyptian cult, but also the other Eastern cults seem to have had no impact on Graeco-Roman funerary practices[7].

It is when Christians came to express in their own terms the beliefs of non-Christians that we find the tendency to describe those beliefs as including the resurrection of the deity or of his devotees[8]. Now it is true that this means that they saw in those beliefs at least a superficial similarity to their own[9]. But that need not mean that the similarity was anything more than superficial. It is quite another thing to suggest that those beliefs somehow generated the Christian ones. Had the dominant Christian claim been, for instance, one to the effect that Jesus had ascended, had been snatched up to heaven, either pagan (or indeed Jewish) beliefs could have been adduced as possibly influential in the formation of the Christian belief, but 'resurrection' is another matter and it is this that is the dominant expression of Christian beliefs about Jesus and also of Christians' beliefs about their own destiny. Paul, it may be granted, used the natural cycle to illustrate the nature of resurrection[10], but illustrated by it not the inevitability of resurrection and new life, but rather the necessity of death and the discontinuity between the seed sown and the resultant plant.

---

6 *Resurrection* 102.

7 Nock, 'Cremation' 293: this is in contrast to the relationship between the Egyptian cult and Egyptian funerary rites.

8 Cf. G. Bertram in *RAC* 1, 928; 'it was the Christian apologists who seem to have been the first to apply the clear Christian and biblical concepts of death and resurrection to the Hellenistic mystery-deities'; he compares Just., *Dial.* 69.2, and goes on to comment that the conception of 'resurrection' was not really appropriate for what occurred in the Hellenistic myths, which expressed not so much the hope of resurrection as that of immortality and eternal life.

However Lucian, *Peregr. mort.* 40, tells of one legend in which Peregrinus appeared alive in white garments after his death, garlanded with wild olive; this seems to be in some tension with the story of the vulture flying up from Peregrinus' pyre saying 'I leave the earth and go to Olympus' (§§39f); but Peregrinus had earlier come under Christian influence (§§11ff) — were their ideas of resurrection responsible for the first version of Peregrinus' survival mentioned above?

9 Yet generally Christian apologists seem to have been more concerned about similarities between pagan *rites* and their own.

10 1 Cor 15.36ff; cf. §3.2.2.

Here again, then, a difference in terminology points to a difference in, and independence of, ideas[11]. If the gods of the mysteries were unlikely to have generated the idea of Jesus' resurrection[12], it is equally unlikely that they influenced the way in which Christians saw themselves as sharing in Jesus' resurrection. If it is hard to trace instances of the mystery-gods rising from the dead quite as Jesus was thought to have done, it is even harder to find evidence of the followers of the former believing that now in this world they shared their gods' escapes from death already (if they did escape)[13]. Perhaps the nearest that we come to this is in Firm. Mat., *Err. prof. rel.* 22.1 and there the rescue is spoken of as σωτηρία and the initiates' salvation may well still lie in the future.

3.3. A Present Resurrection?

It is now left to consider cases in which the language of resurrection is applied to present existence. We shall see that it is questionable whether the original impetus for this reinterpretation came from Hellenistic views of the body. This may be true of later, Gnostic traditions (§3.3.1) where the idea of resurrection was already firmly established in both Jewish and particularly Christian traditions, and Gnostic groups often found that they could not claim continuity with those traditions unless they made some attempt to integrate this idea within their own view of things. The evidence for a Hellenistic Jewish reinterpretation in *Joseph and Aseneth* is far from certain (§3.3.2). It is in the Palestinian Jewish Dead Sea Scrolls that we seem to find a 'realized eschatology', but even that description of their beliefs is doubtful; even more doubtful is whether one is correct to speak of an experience there of present 'resurrection' rather than 'exaltation'. With these last two areas of material we are dealing

---

11 Cf. §2.4.3. So Perkins, *Resurrection* 68 n. 55, remarks that 'resurrection has important structural differences from both the cyclic vegetation myths and the Orphic speculations, since it does not concern itself with patterns of return whether of nature or of the soul'.

12 Cf. Nock, 'Note' 50: 'The evidence at our disposal does not suggest any prototype so close as to lend probability to the supposition either that the Christians deliberately borrowed a story, or that they were consciously influenced by some model' in their account of Jesus' resurrection; after all this story was known to Paul within at most 10 years of Jesus' death. Yet despite this cf. Wells, *Jesus* e.g. 230–41.

13 It is expressly denied for Egyptian religion by Brunner, *Grundzüge* 136; Griffiths, *Isis-Book* 52, frankly admits that 'the concept . . . applied to spiritual regeneration in the present life is not clearly attested in the ancient tradition', but adds that 'perhaps it was a development in the Graeco-Roman phase'.

with the main evidence for Brandenburger's thesis that 'the idea of a resurrection that took place when one entered the community of the redeemed already existed . . . in certain circles in pre-Christian Judaism' and that thus, influenced by these circles, 'the idea of a present resurrection, if not even older, was found at least as early in Hellenistic-Jewish Christian churches as was the apocalyptic concept of a future resurrection'[1].

3.3.1. It seems to have been the prominence and centrality of the belief in resurrection in Christian tradition that impelled *Gnostic groups* to reinterpret this concept so as to reconcile it with their disparagement of the body. As evidence of this we can point to both (a) their clear dependence on Christian affirmations about the resurrection of Jesus and of Christians and (b) their consequent discomfort in living with such traditions. In other words the evidence points to a sequence in which the Christian assertion about a physical resurrection (in some sense) is followed by Gnostic attempts to reconcile those assertions with their own ways of thought. They adopted something foreign to those ways and then sought to accommodate it to them as best they could[1].

(a) The explicit appeal to Christian teaching on the resurrection, or at least an ostensible appeal, can be seen most clearly in the *Treatise on Resurrection* (*NHC* 1.4). For Rheginus, the recipient of the *Treatise*,

---

Notes on 3.3
1 'Auferstehung' 27.

Notes on 3.3.1
1 Cf. Sellin, '"Auferstehung"' 223: this accommodation belongs to later strata of Gnostic thought and where we find it it is one of the surest signs of Christian influence. Or, putting it more positively, Peel seems to think along similar lines when he tentatively suggests that 'the more Christianized the form of Gnosticism, the more tendency there is to conceive the postmortem state in terms of a "resurrection body" of some type' ('Eschatology' 163). Rudolph, *Gnosis* 205=ET 189, speaks of a possible modification of 'Jewish models', but I find it hard to give examples of such a direct influence of Jewish thought, unmediated by Christian tradition.
It is very clear from *Gos. Phil.* §11, 53.29–54.2, that the author understands by 'resurrection' something very different to normal usage, i.e. there is a revaluation of the term. Cf. also Rudolph, ibid. 168=ET 154: 'resurrection' is one of those events understood by Gnostics as 'symbolic incidents of cosmic significance and accordingly . . . subjected to entirely new interpretations' (cf. 184=171).
I am in this section assuming that Gnosticism is in some measure a phenomenon independent of Christianity, even if the latter religion played an important formative part in its development. The evidence of the use of the term 'resurrection' is most easily understood if we have here a case of a movement which seeks, in part, to grow up within the Christian church, but finds the traditions of the church, as usually understood, alien to its own convictions. That suggests that the origin of those convictions lies elsewhere than within Christianity, that Gnosticism is essentially something other than Christianity, however much the latter religion may have spawned Gnostic groups, nurturing them like some warbler with a cuckoo fledgeling in its nest.

'Catholic scripture and tradition appear to be authoritative, and therefore our gnostic author, who is probably a Valentinian, takes pains to phrase his explanation in these terms, at least in the opening paragraphs of the Treatise'[2]. The author sets himself alongside Rheginus in affirming a claim to Christian status: 'we' have received rest 'through our Saviour, our Lord Christ' (43.36f)[3]; 'we have known the Son of Man, and we have believed that he rose from the dead. This is he of whom we say, "He became the destruction of death . . ."' (46.14−19). The Christian presuppositions of the *Treatise* are clear, as is the Pauline content to the Christianity which the author assumes; Paul is 'the Apostle' to whom the author refers in 45.24, even if what follows is only 'a vague pastiche of Pauline formulae'[4]: 'we suffered with him, and we arose with him, and we went to heaven with him' (lines 25−8)[5]. Equally there is probably an unacknowledged allusion to Paul (1 Cor 15.54: cf. 2 Cor 5.4) in the use of the language of 'swallowing up' death immediately before and after (45.14, 20; 46.1; cf. 49.4)[6].

In the *Gospel of Philip*, too, Paul is quoted in logion 23: there 1 Cor 15.50 is appealed to (*NHC* 2.3, 56.32−34), a verse to which the Ophites also appealed[7]. There may also be an allusion to 2 Cor 5.3 in the opening allusion to 'Some who are afraid lest they rise naked'[8].

Another piece of evidence of the influence of Christian tradition is probably those passages in which Gnostics speak of a present resurrection

---

2 Layton, 'Vision' 209; however he stresses the utterly different views of the author: his theology is anything but orthodox, and his views and intentions are very different to Paul's (cf. 212f, 216, against W. C. v. Unnik; contrast Peel *Epistle* 180).

3 Cf. 44.13ff.

4 So Layton, 'Vision' 202 n. 55; for Lindemann, *Paulus* 400, *Treat. Res.* was almost unique among Gnostic texts in its use of Paul, but see Koschorke, 'Paulus'. On the Valentinian veneration of Paul cf. Pagels, *Paul* 1f and reff. there; for Paul as 'the apostle of the resurrection' cf. Clem. Alex., *Exc. Theod.* 23.2.

5 Cf. Lona, *Eschatologie* 397: it is impossible to miss the use of Paul's 'with Christ' language here; cf. Gaffron, 'Apologie' 222f; Ménard, *Traité*, 65f.

6 Layton, 'Vision' 210 ('It seems clear that the author intends to give the impression that his gnostic philosophy is that of the apostle himself'); cf. *Treatise* 123; Koschorke, 'Paulus' 198f; Perkins, *Resurrection* 357; R. McL. Wilson, *Gospel* 88. It is perhaps his debt to Paul that explains the reference to a '*spiritual* resurrection' in 45.40; Layton, *Treatise*, puzzles over the ref. to πνεῦμα rather than νοῦς here, but the answer probably lies in Paul's assertion of the resurrection of a 'spiritual body' in 1 Cor 15.44 (cf. 46) and his relegation of the ψυχικόν to the present world-order (and so the spiritual resurrection here swallows up the ψυχική as well as the σαρκική); cf. Koschorke, ibid. 199. Robinson, 'Kerygma' 35 n. 19, suggests that Eph 5.14 is reflected in 45.28−39 with its analogy of the sun and its rays.

7 See below. See also Pagels, '"Mystery"' 286 for Valentinian use of this verse; also Koschorke, ibid. 191f.

8 Cf. Pagels, *Paul* 98ff; Schenke in Leipoldt-Schenke, *Schriften* 42 n. 5. For the influence of Paul here see also Kretschmar, 'Auferstehung' 122−4: 'Despite the Johannine quotation our author remains above all an exegete of Paul's letters'.

as occurring in baptism, as in Colossians and Ephesians[9]. For elsewhere they prefer to attach it to another rite, particularly chrism[10], or to speak of it as conferred with knowledge[11], or as being equivalent to regeneration[12], or as being a disengagement from the flesh in this life[13], without any of these being specifically associated with any particular cultic act.

(b) Gnostic unease at Christian traditions of resurrection is signalled already towards the end of the first century C.E. by Cerinthus: Jesus, he maintained, suffered and rose, but the Christ had by then separated from Jesus and remained untouched by death[14]. He was spiritual; one could perhaps infer then that all other spiritual persons would be likewise immune. Here the point of Jesus being raised is not immediately apparent if it was the enduring life of the spiritual Christ that was important. The reason for this tradition of the resurrection's being retained is presumably that it was tradition, it was something given. Similarly Hippolytus tells us that according to Apelles, a follower of Marcion, Jesus died, rose, showed his flesh to his disciples and then returned it to the earth whence it had come and ascended to his Father[15]; here again the given tradition of Jesus' resurrection seems difficult to accommodate. Consequently it is not surprising to find the resurrection of others denied; it is perhaps more surprising how rare it is to find it said outright[16].

---

9 So *Gos. Phil.* §§76 (69.25f), 90 (73.1–8) – cf. Lona, *Eschatologie* 390f; Menander in Iren., *Haer.* 1.23.4=Harvey 1.17, and Tert., *De anima* 50.2; the Nicolaitans in Hipp.'s letter on resurrection to the Empress Mammaea (ed. Achelis 251); cf. Lona, ibid. 378 and n. 171 (further reff. to Just., *Apol.* 1.26.4; Tert., *De resurrectione mortuorum* 19.5); H.-F. Weiß, 'Paulus' 121f.

10 So *Gos. Phil.* §§92 (73.18f), 95 (74.18–20). This interpretation of §92 depends on a translation like W. W. Isenberg's in J. M. Robinson, *Library* 92: 'it is from the olive tree that we get the chrism, and from the chrism, the resurrection'; contrast R. McL. Wilson, *Gospel* 154 (meaning?).

11 See below on *Act. Pl and Thekl.* 14; also Simon and Carpocrates in Iren., *Haer.* 2.31.2=Harvey 2.48.2; Tert., *De resurrectione mortuorum* 19.2–6; cf. Gaffron, 'Apologie' 218f, 224f; Lona, *Eschatologie* 379 and n. 173.

12 Naassene interpretation of ?John 5.28 in Hipp., *Ref.* 5.8.23; *Exeg. Soul* (NHC 2.6) 134.6–12 (cf. Lona, ibid. 384; ed. Sevrin 108: 'the resurrection from the dead is a Christian formula, apparently the only one attested in *Exeg. Soul* apart from the *auctoritates* cited'); ?*Gos. Phil.* §67 (67.9–27; cf. §76, 69.25f). Much the same premises may lead to Simon's denial of resurrection in Pseudo-Clem., *Hom.* 2.22.5, if we are to see his reasons for this in §4: he himself is immortal and his body was incapable of decay. See also *Ep. apostolorum* 21.

13 Cf. on Layton's interpretation of *Treat. Res.* below. Ménard, *Traité* 18–20, interprets this above all as a recovery of oneself as one was originally; cf. Koschorke, 'Paulus' 199. Is something like this also what is meant by the 'spirits who have arisen from the dead' in *Thund.* (NHC 6.2) 21.17f (cf. 18.18–20)?

14 Iren., *Haer.* 1.26.1=Harvey 1.21.

15 Hipp., *Ref.* 7.38.4f; Cf. Pseudo-Tert., *Adversus omnes haereses* 6.6. Compare the views of Justin's *Baruch* in Hipp., *Ref.* 5.26.31f, where Jesus leaves his 'body of Eden' on the cross, i.e. the psychic and earthly nature, and goes up to the Good (ἀνέβη πρὸς τὸν ἀγαθόν); this underlines the awkwardness, even redundancy, of the resurrection in Apelles' account.

16 Resurrection of the flesh is denied in Epiph., *Haer.* 26.9.3; the same may be true of the *Testi-*

Others were prepared to find room for Jesus' resurrection by stressing the other-worldliness of the resurrection body. The Ophites held that it was formed of soul and spirit and appealed to 1 Cor 15.50[17]. The Valentinian Ptolemaeus seems to have held that a mortal body is raised after the passions have been put to flight[18], and Epiphanius mocks the Valentinians as denying the resurrection of the dead, 'saying something mysterious and ridiculous, that it is not this body which rises, but another rises from it, which they call spiritual'[19], ('Mysterious and ridiculous' perhaps, but still very Pauline.)

Since the *Treatise on the Resurrection* is often reckoned to be a product of the Valentinian school it is not surprising that it is often regarded as an example of how these Gnostics could incorporate the hope of resurrection, at least in its Pauline form, within their systems[20]. However it is equally plain that this cannot be done easily and scholars point to the tensions arising within the work[21].

Layton, however, sees the author of this work as boldly and consistently imposing his own meaning upon the term 'resurrection', in complete disregard for its orthodox sense[22]; his approach to Pauline exegesis is worlds apart from that of the deutero-Pauline exegetes who reinterpreted Paul's idea of dying and rising with Christ[23]. This consistency of approach which Layton can find in the *Treatise* where others have failed to detect it can only be maintained if we agree with his analysis of 47.4ff as a series of *aporiai* in which counter-arguments from an orthodox standpoint are summarily rejected; the author does not entertain the idea of a resurrected

---

mony of Truth (NHC 9.3), but the text of 34.26ff is so mutilated as to render interpretation a rather conjectural business; however cf. Wisse, ' "Opponents" ' 109f. 36.29—37.5 is clearer and is critical of 'carnal resurrection'; what is not clear is whether it was replaced by another sort of resurrection.

For further evidence of Gnostic difficulties in speaking of a final resurrection of the body cf. Lona, *Eschatologie* 376 and n. 167, citing Iren., *Haer.* 5.31.1; Pseudo-Tert., *Adversus omnes haereses* 1.5; 6.6; Just., *Dial.* 80.4.

17 Iren., *Haer.* 1.30.13=Harvey 1.28.7. The Archontics held that there was only a resurrection of the soul: Epiph., *Haer.* 40.2.5; cf. the views attributed to Basilides in Hipp., *Ref.* 7.27.10.

18 Clem. Alex., *Exc. Theod.* 61.7.

19 Epiph., *Haer.* 31.7.6, tr. Foerster-Wilson, *Gnosis,* 1, 237.

20 Cf. Peel, 'Eschatology' 160, and *Epistle* e.g. 26; Schenke, 'Auferstehungsglaube' 125; Wisse, ' "Opponents" ' 110—12. On Valentinian exegesis here cf. Pagels, ' "Mystery" '.

21 So Peel, *Epistle* 26: 'it is rather remarkable to see either how apparently inconsistent the author was in trying to hold his Gnostic views together with his use of the New Testament, or how little his Gnosticism has affected his exegesis.' Rudolph, *Gnosis* 209=ET 192, speaks of 'argumentation which really must have run contrary to the gnostic spirit'. Cf. Ménard, 'Épitre' esp. 191f; *Traité* esp. 15f; Schenke, ibid. 125f.

22 Contrast Wisse, ' "Opponents" ' 112 (cf. Lona, *Eschatologie* 403, 406; Schmöle, *Läuterung* 6); I do not find his 'Pauline' reading of the *Treatise* as convincing as Layton's. Cf. Rudolph, ibid.

23 'Vision' 212f.

or renewed flesh[24]. Rather ἀνάστασις is for him a metaphor for the disengagement of the superior element in human beings, the intellect, from the inferior, the flesh; as such it not only *can* be in the present for Christians; it is only relevant for them now, since once they are dead the bodily encumbrance will have been removed[25].

In this this *Treatise* is, Layton thinks, different from the *Gospel of Philip*[26]. There, in particular in the puzzling §23 (56.26—57.19) — and only in it? —, there seems to be talk of a 'resurrection flesh', although as R. McL. Wilson remarks, 'it is difficult to avoid the conclusion that the author is frankly inconsistent here'[27]: he seems to start by attacking the doctrine of the resurrection of the flesh (56.26—34) and end by defending a resurrection of some sort of flesh (57.9—19). The solution to this Wilson finds in §72 (68.26ff) which seems to distinguish between 'flesh' and 'true flesh' (although the text is fragmentary here); the former is probably spoken of as but an image of the true flesh[28]. (This discussion of resurrection reflects Paul's understanding of resurrection remarkably accurately)[29]. Here we may compare the observation of M. L. Peel that 'there are numerous passages in which the Gnostic is said to put on "another nature", or a "heavenly garment", or "bridal clothes", or some other type of clothing at the point of the departure of the pneuma-self from the body'[30]. In other words they 'thought in terms of the survival of *some*

---

24 'Vision' 198—208 (cf. his *Treatise* 77ff, 121f, 133); this passage accounts for two of the three reff. given by Peel, 'Eschatology' 159f, for the idea in this work of an ascent after death of one's invisible inward members covered by a new spiritual flesh. The third (45.39—46.2) speaks of our being drawn to heaven by Christ, like beams by the sun; 'this is the spiritual resurrection which swallows up the psychic in the same way as the fleshly' (Peel in Robinson, *Library* 51). Layton, *Treatise* 65, interprets the 'swallow up' here as 'makes irrelevant' (cf. 127 with n. 5) and this is more readily intelligible than Peel's interpretation of it as 'destroy' (*Epistle* 75; cf. Ménard, *Traité* 67), and Gaffron's of it as 'include, enclose'; this sense is intelligible as applied to 'death' in 1 Cor 15.54 (although there and even more in 2 Cor 5.4 there is also the nuance of 'superseding'), but neither 'death' nor 'our mortal nature' are quite the same as psychic and fleshly resurrection. See also Perkins, *Resurrection* 388 n. 74.

25 'Vision' 208; *Treatise* 126: he compares 49.15f, 'leave the state of dispersion and bondage, and then you already (ἤδη) have resurrection'. Cf. Altermath, *Corps* 79 n. 1. Brandenburger, 'Auferstehung' 18, on the other hand says that spiritual resurrection is the heavenly ascent that takes place at death. Kretschmar, 'Auferstehung' 125, thinks that *Treat. Res.* avoids speaking of the resurrection of the 'body' since this familiar Greek word meant for its Hellenistic author something mortal; 'flesh' on the other hand is a rarer term and lacks these unfavourable connotations.

26 'Vision' 208; contrast Rudolph, *Gnosis* 175, 209=ET 160, 192.

27 *Gospel* 87; cf. Lona, *Eschatologie* 392 and the critique of Schenke, 'Auferstehungsglaube' 124f there.

28 Cf. Ménard, *Évangile* 143; R. McL. Wilson, 'New Testament' 294. Lona, ibid. 394, argues that this 'true flesh' is the flesh of Christ (cf. Koschorke, 'Paulus' 192; Kretschmar, 'Auferstehung' 123f).

29 So Wilson, *Gospel* 12.

30 'Eschatology' 161; on this and the following page he gives a number of examples of this, not

type of "resurrection body" together with its identifiable personal characteristics'[31]. When we see that examples of this include a 'new man' that is put on in *Treat. Seth* 59.4 when Christ comes to his own and unites them with himself (59.9–11) then this may lend support to Wilson's suggestion[32] that in *Gos. Phil.* §23 the connection between the beginning and end of the section lies in the exposition of Jn 6.53 that lies between them, with its reference to eating Jesus' flesh which is the Word and to drinking his blood which is the Holy Spirit (57.6f)[33]. In both the *Second Treatise of the Great Seth* with its echo of Eph 4.24[34] and in the *Gospel of Philip* with its citation of the Fourth Gospel it would again seem that Christian traditions have been influential in the Gnostic authors' retention of a corporeal element in their expectations of eternal life.

Equally it needs to be said that this view in §23 is not typical of the whole work. In §21 it is denied that 'the Lord died first and (then) rose up'[35]; it is the other way round: he rose and then died. One dies, or is already dead[36], if one does not attain resurrection. Similarly in §90 much the same is said of Christians: it is denied that they die and then rise. Rather they have to receive the resurrection while still alive. The text then goes on possibly to imply that this gift comes at baptism, but more likely to imply a criticism of too high an evaluation of baptism by orthodox Christians [37]. Behind this reversal of the order of death and resurrection

---

all equally apposite; but note the 'splendid robe' of the *Hymn of the Pearl* (*Act. Thom.* 108.9, 14; 110.46f – Hennecke-Schneemelcher-Wilson 2, 498–500), Christ putting on imperishability in *Gos. Truth* (NHC 1.3, 20.32; cf. 1 Cor 15.53f, quoted also in Heracleon frg. 40, Foerster-Wilson, *Gnosis* 1, 177) and clothing himself in *Ap. James* (NHC 1.1, 14.36), the reff. to 'heavenly garments' in *Dial. Sav.* (NHC 3.5, 136.22; cf. 138.21; 139.2, 4), and to the 'new man' put on by souls in *Treat. Seth* (NHC 7.2, 59.4), and to Christ's 'incorporeal body' in *Apoc. Pet.* (NHC 7.3, 83.7f); cf. Rudolph, *Gnosis* 210f =ET 193f; on 204f =188 he also refers to the 'robes' of *Trim. Prot.* (NHC 13.1, 45.16f; 48.15–17), compare too the 'invisible spiritual body' of the soul in *Auth. Teach.* (NHC 6.3, 32.32).

31 Peel, ibid. 163.

32 *Gospel* 88; cf. Rudolph, *Gnosis* 210=ET 194.

33 This is rather different from the idea in Herm., *Sim.* 5 7.1f, appealed to as a parallel by Schenke, 'Auferstehungsglaube' 125, since there the spirit dwells in the flesh, but in *Gos. Phil.* there seems to be a possible word-play on the phrase 'in the flesh' once the flesh has been identified with Jesus' word.

34 Cf. *Gos. Phil.* §101, 75.21f; Wilson, 'New Testament' 292.

35 56.16f, tr. W. W. Isenberg in Robinson, *Library* 134; cf. §90, 73.1–4; Wilson, *Gospel* 85, asks whether the basis of this lies in texts like Acts 5.30 or 13.37 or statements about God's appointing of Jesus using ἀνίστημι.

36 Cf. the view of death in §4 (52.15–19); Güttgemanns, *Apostel* 69, points out that 'the Gnostic myth' prepared the way for the use of ἀνάστασις by speaking of the unredeemed state as drunkenness and sleep from which one must be aroused by the Redeemer. In n. 91 he gives Mandaean examples of a 'Weckruf' followed by an ascent of the soul.

37 So Wilson, *Gospel* 153; Ménard, *Évangile* 209. Lona, *Eschatologie* 388, sees here polemic against the early Christian kerygma.

presumably lies the conviction which was noted above, that in baptism, or the chrism, Christians are granted resurrection (§§76, 92, 95).

With this we may compare the repudiation of Paul's teaching on a future resurrection by Demas and Hermogenes in *Act. Pl and Thekl.* 14: it has already taken place in one's children and also in one's knowledge of God, if we follow the reading preferred by Hennecke-Schneemelcher[38].

From the above, I would suggest, it is implied that Gnostics who professed to be Christians found themselves confronted with a tradition of belief in resurrection, both the past resurrection of Jesus and the still future one of believers; this tradition, with its very different evaluation of bodily existence to their own[39], fitted ill with their own views. Some, however, could seize upon Paul's differentiation between different sorts of flesh as in 1 Cor 15.39 or different bodies in 1 Cor 15.44, and seek by this means some accommodation with Christian tradition and indeed might be in this respect more in tune with Paul's views than were many orthodox Fathers[40]. I find here, however, no hints of either a tradition that existed prior to Paul of a realized 'spiritual' resurrection or of a Gnostic concept of a spiritual body which Paul then adopts in 1 Cor 15; it is far easier to see here his own adaption of a theme found in Jewish traditions, of the bestowal of the Spirit upon God's people in the new age[41].

3.2.2. E. Brandenburger argues that in *Joseph and Aseneth*, a Hellenistic Jewish document, probably of pre-Christian date, entry into the Jewish community 'is described as renewal, a coming to life, even expressly as a raising of the dead'; intermingled with this are the motifs of inward communion with the angelic world and endowment with the spirit of wisdom and esoteric knowledge; this is all combined with clearly sacramental initiatory acts[1]. So he appeals to a text like 8.10–11[2]:

> O Lord, the God of my father Israel, the Most High, the Mighty One, who made all things alive (ζωοποιήσας) and called them from darkness into light and [from error into

---

38 Cf. Hennecke-Schneemelcher-Wilson 2, 357, and Schenke, 'Auferstehungsglaube' 123, against Lipsius-Bonnet 1, 245, and Wisse, '"Opponents"' 108f n. 33; cf. also Tert. cited above in n. 11.

39 Cf. Schenke, ibid.: 'two fundamentally different world-views and their anthropologies'.

40 Cf. Peel, 'Eschatology' 160; H. -F. Weiß, 'Paulus' 119.

41 Cf. Ménard, *Épître* 192–5, and *Traité* 16f, esp. the Jewish traditions contrasting Gen 2.7 with Ezek 37.14: *Gen. Rab.* 14.8, etc.

Notes on 3.3.2

1 'Auferstehung' 23; cf. Berger, 'Hintergrund' 402.

2 Ed. Philonenko=ed. Batiffol 49.17–50.3; tr. follows, with some modernization and alteration, that of D. Cook in Sparks, *Apocryphal OT* (square brackets denote words omitted by Philonenko).

truth] and from death into life; bless this virgin also, and give her life (ζωοποίησον)[3], and renew (ἀνακαίνισον) [her] with your [holy] spirit, . . . and may she eat the bread of your life, and may she drink the cup of your blessing, she whom you chose before she was begotten[4], and may she enter into your rest, which you have prepared for your elect.

It is true that a word like ζωοποιεῖν could appropriately be used of resurrection, but need it refer to it[5]? Its first use in this passage most likely refers to the creation of the world[6], and it is thus easier to see a reference here to the idea of the proselyte as a new creature[7]. It is interesting that if 'all things' is the object of 'called' (again aorist) then God's act of creation in the beginning may be described as a calling 'from death into life'. (It is more forced to describe it as a calling 'from error into truth'; this is omitted in two MSS; if genuine it would be a case of creation's being portrayed in terms more appropriate to conversion with which it is being compared.) This allusion to the creation is probably confirmed by the parallel, which Brandenburger notes (25), in Joseph's otherwise rather gratuitously complicated reference to the day of the week in 9.5 (=50.14—17), that 'this is the day on which God began to make all his created things'; this is intelligible as a symbolic allusion to the new creation which is about to take place.

In 15.4[8] an angel addresses Aseneth, telling her to have courage since 'from today you will be made new (ἀνακαινισθήσῃ), and refashioned (ἀναπλασθήσῃ) and given new life (ἀναζωοποιηθήσῃ), and you shall eat the bread of life and drink the cup of immortality, and be anointed with the unction of incorruption'. We have already seen (at the end of §2.4.2) that it is unlikely that this work regards salvation as mediated by these various actions of eating, drinking and being anointed, but rather as being accompanied by or, better, followed by them. Indeed a literal eating of bread, etc., is not seemingly indicated, for this promise is regarded as

---

3 Philonenko inverts the order of the ζωοποίησον and the εὐλόγησον and has the phrase τὴν παρθένον ταύτην after the latter.

4 Philonenko's text; Batiffol has a reference to Aseneth's being numbered with God's people whom he chose before all things were made; i.e. in Batiffol's text God's people are chosen before creation (so too C. Burchard in Charlesworth, *Pseudepigrapha* 2, 213), in Philonenko's Aseneth is chosen before her birth.

5 Sänger, *Judentum* 42, says that it 'kann' be used of a 'reale Totenauferstehung'; the point is, however, that it can be used of other things too.

6 Hence the aorist; cf. 8.2 (Battifol 48.19 follows MS D in reading the pres.). However Philonenko translates both this and καλέσας with a pres. ('donnes . . . appelles'). But in any case the choice would be between the original act of creation and *creatio continua*, since the neuter τὰ πάντα means that sub-human creatures are also in mind.

7 So the idea of a new creation is applied to all penitent Jews in *Midr. Ps* on 102.18; further reff. in Str. -B, 2, 421f and Sjöberg, 'Wiedergeburt' 53—69; cf. Charlesworth, *Pseudepigrapha and the NT* 133.

8 Batiffol 61.4—7; tr. following Cook.

fulfilled in the eating of a piece of honeycomb[9]. Nor is there any greater reason than with the previous passage for seeing this language as being specifically that of a spiritualized resurrection. Cavallin argues that the threefold ἀνα - 'indicates the idea of a *re*surrection rather than a continued spiritual life after death'[10]: ζωοποιεῖν is commonly used for resurrection. Here he compares *T. Abraham* A 18.11 and *Odes Sol.* 11.12, both also cited by Philonenko[11]. Yet these two texts are hardly enough to prove his point. For *T. Abraham* A 18 does not refer to the ultimate or eschatological fate of those restored to life[12]: Abraham's obduracy has led to a visitation of his house by the angel of death and this has brought about the untimely death of seven thousand of his household; in response to Abraham's intercession they are restored to their life in this world[13]. Elsewhere the longer recension of the work speaks only of the post-mortal fate of the soul, separated from the body[14]; in Abraham's case it is taken up to be with God[15], while his body is buried by the oak of Mamre (A 20.11). It is only the shorter recession which finds room for a resurrection: in B 7.15−16 Abraham is to be taken up to heaven at death, but his body is to remain on earth for seven thousand ages till the time when all flesh is raised. That this recension has passed through Christian hands is immediately plain from its Trinitarian closing benediction, even if its language suggests that it is generally older than the longer recension[16]. Arguably the reference to the resurrection is awkwardly inserted into the work, for elsewhere the shorter recension agrees with the longer in speaking only of the post-mortal fate of the soul[17]. Thus *T. Abraham* only supports the argument in this one maverick passage, and then only uses this term of restoration to continued this-worldly life; that it does so is hardly surprising.

Odes Sol. 11.12 comes from the one Ode surviving in Greek (in the *Bodmer Papyrus* 11)[18] and the Greek version does contain the word ἀνεζωοποίησεν; however the Syriac has 'And I became like the land that blossoms and rejoices in its fruits' instead of the Greek's 'And he enliv-

---

9 Ibid. 64.14f (not in Philonenko).

10 *Life* 1, 155f; cf. in *ANRW* 2.19.1, 297f.

11 Ed. 183; cf. Sänger, *Judentum* 42.

12 Cf. Cavallin, *Life* 1, 97.

13 Cf. B 14.5f.

14 Cf., e.g., A 1.7; 7.8, 10, 12; 15.7, 16.15; 20.9−12.

15 Cf., e.g., A 1.7; 3.3; 20.12.

16 James (ed. 34−49, esp. 49, also 51) argues that A is more original in its content but late in its language; B is an abridgment of the content but is generally in simpler, more original language (cf. Box's tr. xiii; E. P. Sanders in Charlesworth, *Pseudepigrapha* 1, 872 − but B on the whole shows less Christian influence).

17 Cf., e.g., B 4.9; 8.13−15; 9; 14.7, but contrast Delcor's ed. 62.

18 Cf. Charlesworth's ed. 9−12.

ened me through his incorruption'[19]. Although the *Ode* goes on to described the poet's entry into Paradise (16ff) 'the emphasis in this Ode
. . . is not upon an abode of the blessed after death'. This is rather a
'present and earthly' Paradise[20]. Thus it is doubtful whether this reviving
is meant to be an anticipation of, or substitute for, a post-mortal resurrection.

Sänger cites other texts as parallels to ἀναζωοποιεῖσθαι used of resurrection[21]:

(1) Deut 32.39; 4 Kgdms 5.7 LXX: both describe it as God's prerogative to kill and to make alive; the former used ζῆν ποιεῖν and the latter
ζωοποιεῖν. Few would argue that resurrection was in the minds of the
original writers of these passages and it is questionable how far it was in
those of the Greek translators[22].

(2) 2 Esdras 19.6 LXX speaks of God as the one who makes all things
alive (ζωοποιεῖς), but it is clearly speaking of his role in creation, both in
the past and in the present, but not in the eschatological future.

(3) *2 Apoc. Bar.* 85.15, 'Then he will make alive those whom he has
found'[23], clearly refers to a future consummation, and in the thought
of this work that could clearly involve a bodily resurrection (cf. §3.1.1).

(4) *Ep. Arist.* 16 and 234 again refer to God's work in creating and sus-
taining this world.
These examples, then, all serve to show the varied contexts in which the
idea of 'making alive (again)' could be used, and the difficulty of finding
support for this as the sole or even dominant reference of this language.

There is, however, one passage where some have seen an explicit allusion to the resurrection of the dead in *Joseph and Aseneth* and that is in
the strange incident in chap. 16 where bees emerge from the honeycomb
that has miraculously appeared in Aseneth's room or store. They surround
Aseneth (and in Batiffol's version form a comb upon her mouth and eat
it); the angel then tells them to depart, which they do. In Philonenko's
version they then fall dead; in Batiffol's it is only those which wished to
harm Aseneth who die. The dead bees are told to rise (ἀνάστητε) and they
rise (ἀνέστησαν) and depart to the court adjoining the house (and settle
on fruit-trees in Batiffol's version). The bees, Philonenko argues[24], are a

---

19 Tr. Charlesworth 52 and 55 n. 22.
20 Charlesworth, *Odes* 56 n. 29.
21 *Judentum* 42.
22 In Deut 32.39 it is parallel to ἰάσομαι.
23 So A. F. J. Klijn in Charlesworth, *Pseudepigrapha* 1, 652; Bogaert: 'sauvera'; Syr. *naḥê* (ed.
   Kmosko 1234.16).
24 Ed. 189, comparing the apocryphal *Apocalypse of John* 11 (dated to the 5th century by
   Hennecke-Schneemelcher-Wilson, *Apocrypha* 2, 753); cf. Cavallin, *Life* 1, 156, and in *ANRW*
   2.19.1, 298.

symbol of the resurrection. Yet, if so, they are hardly an unambiguous one, particularly in Batiffol's longer text: there all the bees rise (ἀνέστησαν) at the angel's command to go to their place (65.11) and go to heaven. Those wishing to harm Aseneth fall dead on the ground and it is only those· whom the angel touches and orders to rise and go to their place who do so; their place is seemingly the fruit-trees in the adjoining courtyard. If this is a symbol of the resurrection it is hard to see why only bees that do wrong are granted it, whereas the others depart straight to heaven. Yet arguably Batiffol's text, with its mention of two groups of bees, makes better sense of the twofold commands, to depart and to arise (65.10–11, 14–15), than Philonenko's, where the bees are told to go (ὑπάγετε) to their places (plural), leave Aseneth, fall dead, and are then told to rise and go to their place (singular)[25]. This repeated command in the shorter text is odd and it is surely better to say, as Burchard argues[26], that there is a lacuna in the shorter text after the first command and that the stinging bees are symbolic of people like Dan and Gad in chaps 24–8[27]; the symbolism is then not of 'dying and rising as man's future', but rather of dying and rising as a symbol of sin and forgiveness (he compares Lk 15.24, 32)[28]. Certainly it is worth noting that, despite his interpretation of chap. 16 Philonenko finds in 27.8, 'Your soul shall live for ever', a 'particularly clear statement of the doctrine of the immortality of the soul'[29]. At any rate, since the bees that sought to harm Aseneth rise, it is hardly likely that this is being offered as a symbol of present salvation for the redeemed.

Thus we find in *Joseph and Aseneth* no clear reference to the idea of resurrection, either in its traditional form or transposed to the present[30]; the language of 'making alive (again)' is applied more widely than just to raising from the dead, and so one cannot argue from the presence of the former that an allusion to the latter is intended; the background might equally well be the language of rescue or protection from woe, be it danger or darkness[31].

---

25 For Burchard Philonenko's version may be nearer the original language of the work, but it is likely that Batiffol's is nearer the scope and content of the original (*Zeuge* 60f; cf. Sänger, *Judentum* 10).

26 Cf. 'Text' 20.

27 Burchard in Charlesworth, *Pseudepigrapha* 2, 230; there does remain the problem why they land in Aseneth's garden, but in his *JSRHZ* ed. he suggests a possible solution in 28.7f.

28 Suggested by Professor Burchard in a personal communication.

29 Ed. 215; not that this necessarily excludes a resurrection of the body – cf. Cavallin's table in his *Life* 1, 197, under the signs 'RB' and 'IS' and §7.1.2 on 199 there.

30 Cf. E. P. Sanders, 'Covenant' 23 – he notes the absence of other traditional soteriological expressions like the redemption of Israel or its share in the world to come as well.

31 Cf., e.g., LXX of Ps 70.20; Qoh 7.12.

3.3.3. The evidence of the *Dead Sea Scrolls* is hard to evaluate. If they were the product of the literary output of a group of Essenes, as they are generally thought to be, then we are faced with Josephus' assertion that for the Essenes human bodies were corruptible and human souls immortal[1]; for the Pharisees, on the other hand, these immortal souls pass into another body (*Bell.* 2.8.14 §163; 3.8.5. §374)[2]. The distinction between the two implies that he thought that the Essenes believed in an incorporeal survival of the soul. One cannot simply dismiss this as a concession to Josephus' Hellenistic readers[3], for it then needs to be .explained why the same concession was not made with regard to the Pharisees. One could imagine that Josephus might well have been keener to commend *them* to his non-Jewish readers in view of his own sympathies with their traditions (*Vita* 2 §12). On the other hand, if Qumran's hope was for an eventual establishment of God's kingdom on earth, an earthly prolongation of their present communion with God and his angels[4], then it is unlikely that, if pressed to be specific, they would have expressed a hope for, or a belief in, a disembodied life for those who would participate in that kingdom; moreover, if they concentrated on the future of the group rather than of the individual, then the question of the individual members' survival and means of participation in that future may well have remained peripheral[5].

Certainly it is true that, as far as the evidence of the Scrolls goes, 'belief in the resurrection of the dead was not a central tenet of the Qumran faith'[6]. It would also probably be as well not to assume that all the community thought alike at all stages in its history[7]. However many scholars still maintain that they not only knew of this belief but shared

---

Notes on 3.3.3

1 Maier, 'Lehrer' 265, draws attention to *Bell.* 2.8.11 §154f with its adoption of the idea of the body as a prison of the soul and its express comparison with Greek views. Pryke, 'Eschatology' 56, holds that the Qumran sect's views were 'near to immortality of the soul', 'mystical' and at times 'dangerously near to gnosticism'.

2 Hipp., *Ref.* 9.27.1 holds that the Essenes said that the flesh would arise and be immortal as the soul is now (cf. Buitkamp, *Auferstehungsvorstellungen* 51f; Black, *Scrolls* 190f).

3 *Pace* Schubert, 'Entwicklung' 204.

4 Cf. Larcher, *Études* 122; Laurin, 'Question' 350–4; Schubert, ibid.; tentatively Vermes, *Scrolls* 186. Klinzing, *Umdeutung* 35, sees in 1QM 2 a future eschatological worship in the Jerusalem temple.

5 Cf. Laurin, 'Question' 355 (he compares 1QH 10.3f; 12.24–6; 1QH frg. 4); for another possible reason see Vermes in the following note.

6 Schürer-Black-Millar-Vermes, *History* 2, 582f; cf. Cavallin in *ANRW* 2.19.1, 277; Mansoor, *Hymns* 89; Vermes, *Scrolls* 197 suggests the reason that they were so little interested in this was because of their 'hope for the arrival of God's kingdom during the lifetime of the current generation'; the implication is presumably that their lives in blissful communion with God would just continue.

7 Cf. P.R. Davies, 'Eschatology'.

it[8]. That they should have known of it is hard to deny in the light of their use of the Book of Daniel[9], quite apart from other pseudepigraphal documents like *1 Enoch* which they possessed and which speak of resurrection. I doubt whether one can go further and say that the texts which we shall consider below, which use a language that suggests that of resurrection although they are in a different context to discussions of resurrection and future life, are unintelligible if the Qumran community had not believed in resurrection[10]. That they are but echoes (to us only?) of resurrection language and are in a different context may well be very significant.

There are these few passages which seem to use the language of resurrection. In a passage which refers to a future time of judgment (1QH 6.29–36) and thus in a context where we would expect to find mention of resurrection we read

> Hoist a banner,
> O you who lie in the dust!
> O bodies gnawed by worms,
> raise up an ensign for [the destruction of wickedness][11]!

Although the reference to lying in the dust may contain faint echoes of Dan 12.2, 'many of those who sleep in the dust of the earth', it is far from clear that this passage is being alluded to. It is even further from being clear that the writer of the *Hodayoth* is speaking of a resurrection[12]. On the one hand it is a *banner* that is to be raised, not those lying in the dust and 'gnawed by worms', and Cavallin is probably right to argue that the verbs 'wake' and 'rise' (6.29) are here used to refer to readiness for war[13]. More important, it is uncertain that the phrase 'bodies gnawed by worms' is a correction translation of תולעת מתים; Lohse translates this 'der Wurm der Toten' (lit. 'the worm of the dead') and explains it as a 'description of the lowliness and frailty of men'[14]. This may be

---

8 For a full list of earlier scholarly opinions on the subject cf. the introduction to Buitkamp, *Auferstehungsvorstellungen*, as well as pp. 66ff; also Bietenhard in *ANRW* 2.19.1, 748; Larcher, *Études* 116–22; G. Stemberger in *TRE* 4, 445. For the opposite view cf. Beresford, *Concept* 89.

9 See Bruce, 'Book'; cf. Cavallin, *Life* 1.63ff; Larcher, *Études* 122; Beale, *Use* esp. 56–8.

10 Schubert, 'Entwicklung' 203; however the use of the language of resurrection does not necessarily entail belief in resurrection in the normal sense (as we saw in dealing with Gnostic views in §3.3.1). But the more important question is 'How far was this really the language of resurrection?'

11 1QH 6.34 (tr. Vermes).

12 But cf. Bietenhard in *ANRW* 2.19.1, 748 n. 199; Cavallin in *ANRW* 2.19.1, 274f; Delcor, *Hymnes* 59; Hoffmann, *Toten* 132; Mansoor, *Hymns* 147, comments that 'this seems to be a reference to resurrection'; Rabin, *Studies* 73.

13 *Life* 1, 63.

14 *Texte* 157, 289 n. 30; for man as a 'worm' cf. Job 25.6; Ps 22.6(7).

equally true of 'you who lie in the dust'[15]. It is admittedly surprising to find Vermes translating this phrase in such a way as to suggest a literal resurrection of the body when the revision of Schürer's *History*, in which he plays a major role, suggests that such references as this 'may be simply metaphorical'[16]; that suggests a shift of opinion. Another possibility, perhaps even more suggestive of a metaphorical use of the phrase, is to take מתים as meaning 'of men'[17], and to see here a reference to Isa 41.14, 'Fear not, you worm (תולעת) Jacob, you men (מתי) of Israel'[18]! The phrase would then mean 'worm-like men', 'men who are as lowly as a worm'.

The other text which may speak of resurrection contains the same phrase and the same ambiguity[19]:

> For the sake of Thy glory
> Thou hast purified man of sin
> that he may be made holy for Thee
> with no abominable uncleanness
> and no guilty wickedness;
> that he may be one [with] the children of Thy truth
> and partake of the lot of Thy Holy Ones;
> that bodies gnawed by worms (תולעת מתים) may be raised from the dust
> to the counsel [of Thy truth],
> to the understanding [which comes from Thee];
> that he may stand before Thee
> with the everlasting host
> and with [Thy] spirits [of holiness],
> to be renewed together with all the living
> and to rejoice together with them that know[20].

---

15 Buitkamp, *Auferstehungsvorstellungen* 85, considers this a reference to the living, not the dead; cf. 3.13 where the rather similar phrase יושבי עפר is used (Lohse translates 'those who dwell on dry land' as opposed to the following 'those who who sail the seas'), and 1QM 11.13 where כורעי עפר, 'those bent to the dust' (Vermes) are parallel to 'the poor'; cf. Beresford, *Concept* 87; contrast Holm-Neilsen, *Hodayot* 121 n. 172; Kuhn, *Enderwartung* 49.

16 Schürer-Black-Millar-Vermes, *History* 2, 583; cf. Vermes, *Scrolls* 187; Pryke, 'Eschatology' 55. C. C. Black, 'Perspectives' 415, labels the reference to death here as 'mythological' rather than 'metaphorical'; in 11.3, 10–13 it is 'metaphorical'.

17 So Mansoor, *Hymns* 147 (yet he describes Wallenstein's paraphrase 'the worm-eaten bodies' as apt! This takes us back to Vermes' translation which surely intends something altogether different); further reff. in Kuhn, *Enderwartung* 79 n. 1.

18 However Holm-Nielsen, *Hodayot* 121 n. 172, argues that since 1QIsa[a] reads מיתי in 41.14 but מתי in 5.13 'the community's understanding of Isa 41:14 was of the dead Israel which God would resurrect' (which makes some assumptions about the degree of unity of thought of the community – cf. again P. R. Davies, 'Eschatology'; for a start 1QIsa[b] has מתי at 41. 14).

19 Evans, *Resurrection* 28, refers to the problem that words like 'rise' or 'eternal life' 'are notoriously ambiguous' in such a context.

20 1QH 11.10–14 (tr. Vermes).

This passage is of particular interest because it speaks of something already done by God for his elect[21]. In Vermes' translation it does indeed suggest a present resurrection[22]. Yet if we accept again the metaphorical rendering of תולעת מתים this reference is less clear[23]. The raising too might be metaphorical, as in Ps 113.7, '(God) raises the poor from the dust'[24]; after all, taken out of context this text too might seem to be a reference to resurrection, but in its context it is clearly not.

In fact much of the language of the Scrolls which might be interpreted as a form of 'realized eschatology' is perhaps best described as an exaltation of the lowly. So 1QH 3.19—36, which seemingly ends with a depiction of the final and still future consummation, begins with an affirmation of what God has done for the writer[25] :

> Thou hast redeemed my soul from the Pit . . .
> from the Hell of Abaddon (20) Thou hast raised me up (העליתנ י) to everlasting height (לרים עולם).

While there are no exact parallels to the language here in the Old Testament the language is similar to that used there of present salvation, be it from oppression, illness or the like[26]. Buitkamp concludes here too that the reference is simply to deliverance from a situation endangering life and agrees with Laurin that there is no eschatological reference here[27]. The

---

21 I wonder therefore whether Buitkamp, *Auferstehungsvorstellungen* 53, should really deal with this text under 'Zukunftshoffnung'. Delcor, *Hymnes* 236, likens it to the ideas of *Joseph and Aseneth*.

22 Cf. Nickelsburg, *Resurrection* 155f; also Brandenburger, 'Auferstehung' 23, Delcor, *Hymnes* 237; Kuhn, *Enderwartung* 84—8.

23 But cf. Hoffmann, *Toten* 132; Kuhn, *Enderwartung* 79.

24 Cf. 1 Sam 2.8. Holm-Nielsen, *Hodayot* 187 n. 23, who had seen a ref. to resurrection in 6.34 (see above), yet argues that 'there should not be any thought here of the resurrection of the dead; the expression should be understood figuratively to denote the opposed and despised. Kuhn, *Enderwartung* 88, observes that his interpretation involves taking עפר in 1QH 11.3 and 11.12 in different senses, in the former the human earthly mode of existence, in the latter the dwelling-place of the worm. The interpretation here still means a shift from what humans are made of to where they are. See also *Odes Sol.* 8.5.

25 Holm-Nielsen, *Hodayot* 66: 'the context does not seem to concern the future life, but rather a condition into which the psalmist has already been brought.'

26 Cf. Pss 9.13 (14); 27.5; 113.7 cited by Holm-Nielsen, ibid.; closer still is perhaps 30.3(4) which also uses the hiph. of עלה and refers to an already accomplished deliverance from Sheol (cf. also 40.2(3); 71.20; Jonah 2.7); contrast the futuristic Ezek 37.12f. Also comparable is the תרוממני of Ps 18.48(49).

27 *Auferstehungsvorstellungen* 74, quoting Laurin, 'Question' 346; the same holds good of 1QH 2.20f; 4.21f; 5.6; 7.29—31; 15.16, 23f; 17.15; 18.28—30 — these all speak '*only* of a rescue and redemption from a situation endangering life through God's help and forgiveness, but not of resurrection or immortality' (79). Contrast Gundry, *Sōma* 102 on 11.12—14, which, he holds, 'refers ultimately and mainly to blessed immortality of the soul far above the plane of flesh, not just to that proleptic association with angels while the covenanters are still earthbound'.

vivid language of being raised to everlasting height[28], of the 'everlasting Council' (סוד, line 21), of being 'with the host of the Holy Ones', the congregation of the Sons of Heaven' (line 22), 'the Spirits of knowledge' (lines 22f), may be reckoned as an elaboration of the Old Testament psalmist's experience of being in God's presence and with him now[29]. On the other hand Nickelsburg argues, following H.-W. Kuhn, that the imagery is 'strongly eschatological in tone' here and that therefore 'the blessings of the *eschaton* are already a reality for the author of the Qumran hymn'[30]. He concludes that this hymn would therefore not contain a reference to a future resurrection and life in the world to come, since, for its writer, 'the decisive eschatological event has already happened; he is already sharing in the new life'[31]. But before agreeing with this I would need to be more persuaded that references to '(eternal) inheritance' and 'lot' would be applied *primarily* to the eschatological salvation in contemporary thought and literature, and that it is *only* 'in descriptions of this salvation that the righteous are depicted in the presence of the angels'[32]. And here there is the fundamental problem that it was language used to describe this-worldly salvation or protological bliss which most often provided material and imagery for descriptions of eschatological salvation and bliss[33]. Surely, after all, neither the beginning nor the end are normally accessible for description; protological and eschatological descrip-

---

28 On the parallels to this phrase cf. Kuhn, *Enderwartung* 56f; it is a description of heaven.

29 Cf. Buitkamp, ibid. 75, citing Pss 41.13; 56.14; 116.9; 140.13(14); also 27.13; see too 1QH 6.13; 1QM 10.11.

30 *Resurrection* 153; Kuhn, *Enderwartung* §3.

31 *Resurrection* 154.

32 Nickelsburg, *Resurrection* 153; cf. Kuhn, *Enderwartung* 47, 73–5; Brandenburger, 'Auferstehung' 23, sees here rather a 'development of the esoteric thought of priestly (Levitical) circles' (which for Kuhn is one element in the imagery of this and other passages; he argues that the priestly community were also apocalyptists – 181–7; thus salvation was for them also eschatological); the connection between a priestly role and fellowship with angels is suggested in 4QD^b cited by Milik, *Years* 114, where a number of categories of persons, in part parallel to the list of disqualifications from priesthood in Lev 21.16–23, are barred from the community 'for the holy angels (are in the midst of it)'; cf. Klinzing, *Umdeutung* 107; it is true that much the same disqualifications re-appear in the eschatologically. oriented 1QSa 2.3–9, showing that the present priestly holiness of the community also made them ready for the last days, but CD 15.15–17, where most include 4QD^b, shows that this holiness was a feature of the community in the present. For Klinzing, however, priestly fellowship with angels is an eschatological idea (against J. Maier) – *Umdeutung* 128f; cf. Kehl, 'Erniedrigung' 390.

33 Aune, *Setting* 40, remarks that the use of paradisal imagery at Qumran would be called 'realized protology' in other religions. Are we so sure that it was 'realized eschatology' at Qumran? Scroggs, *Adam* 26f, comments on the problem of the phrase כול כבוד אדם in 1QS 4.23; CD 3.20; 1QH 17.15, a glory promised for the end but, he believes, a 'glory which was intended for man from the beginning but which has yet to be consummated', although he endorses P. Wernberg-Møller's verdict that this glory is identical to, or as great as, that possessed by Adam, even if he is unsure whether אדם is generic or individual (cf. *1 Enoch* 69.11); one could also compare the phrase 'all the inheritance of man/Adam' in 4QpPs 37 3.1f.

tions have a common starting point, a present perception of the ideal, and an awareness that the present does not square with that ideal, whether that awareness comes from rational analysis or ecstatic vision or religious imagination; the awareness of what the present is not is projected onto an ideal past or future. It will be difficult to establish that those using this language of present experience derived it only *via its eschatological application* rather than more directly. How sure can we be that those wishing to describe their present experience and those wishing to describe the future bliss did not both draw on the same reservoir, without the former feeling that they were doing so via the latter? After all the Qumran community knew both the Old Testament and some non-canonical apocalyptic texts. These contained depictions of both present and future bliss and spiritual privileges, and the former, the depictions of blessing in the present, could have inspired them as just that, depictions of something in the present. There is moreover the further problem of seeing quite how they would come to apply eschatological motifs, which they knew only *as eschatological motifs*, to their present existence. In the case of early Christianity we can see that the belief that Jesus had been finally rescued from death in resurrection meant that an unambiguously eschatological event had already taken place, and this could trigger off claims to the anticipation of various eschatological blessings in the experience of his followers, doubtless reinforced by the presence of ecstatic spiritual phenomena. However it is far harder to find such a catalyst in the experience of the Qumran community. Rowland suggests rather as an explanation of these claims contacts with the experiences of participation in heavenly worship which are recorded in the accounts by apocalyptic seers of their visionary ascents to heaven[34]. Although the enjoyment of such might be viewed as part of the eschatological bliss of the redeemed, yet this analogy suggests that the content of this expectation, as well as of this interpretation of the community's present experience, derived from the experiences recorded of certain individuals in the past, experiences which they had enjoyed in ecstasy[35]; the experiences of those individuals were now attrib-

---

34 *Heaven* 113–20; cf. Holm-Neilsen, *Hodayot* 68 n. 11.

35 Rowland, *Heaven* 78, traces this tradition back to the heavenly vision of Micaiah b. Imlah in 1 Kgs 22.19f; cf. further 199–202; at a later date one could also refer to the stories which Rowland sets out in synoptic form (284–8, 310–12), where visionary experiences involving encounter with 'ministering angels' are described (*y. Ḥag.* 77a; *b. Ḥag.* 14b); cf. Gruenwald, *Apocalyptic* 83, 92. On 470 (n. 106) Rowland refers to Philo, *Vit. cont.* 11f, with its Dionysiac language used of the Therapeutae; Kehl, 'Erniedrigung' 390, maintains that Qumran's fellowship with the angels was not ecstatic but resulted from a presence of heaven on earth, yet grants (n. 104) that since 4QŠir Šabb refers to a 'heavenly temple', heavenly event and presence of heaven on earth could merge into one another. Strugnell, however, refers to a 'preoccupation with the heavenly temple and cult' in 4QŠir Šabb ('Liturgy' 335); cf. Schürer-Black-

uted to the community as a whole[36], just as attributes of priests were predicated of the whole community, whether or not they were actually of priestly descent[37]. Indeed the enjoyment of proximity to heaven and participation in heavenly worship may be a facet of the priestly tradition which the community appropriated[38]. In short, this suggests that the community's experience of being lifted up to the heights[39] echoes the language of ecstatic rapture or exaltation of spirit rather than that of the eschatological raising of the body from death.

The Dead Sea Scrolls are thus surprisingly vague about their hopes for the future and at the same time make considerable claims for their present existence[40]. This may be no accident; the higher the claims that one makes for the present, the more difficult it becomes to express what more could be offered in a post-mortal existence, the less need there was to dwell upon what was to come[41]. For there are two sorts of a 'spiritual' resurrection which are very different in their nature and in their motivation: ideas of a spiritual resurrection in the future arise from the questions, 'How are the dead raised? With what kind of body do they come?' (1 Cor 15.35), questions which were by no means ones which exercised only Paul[42]. It is likely that Greek anthropological ideas acted as a stimulus to this sort of reflection. There is, however, no hint in the Dead Sea

---

Millar-Vermes, *History* 3.1, 462f — the 'main source of inspiration' for this text, so concerned with heavenly worship, is Ezek chaps 1, 10 and 40−8.

One could compare the ecstasy in which Job's daughters speak the language of angels in *T. Job* 48−50. It is true that R. P. Spittler (in Charlesworth, *Pseudepigrapha* 1, 834) assigns chaps 45−53 to a Montanist hand, but (a) one might then have expected a clearer reference to, and defence of, ecstatic 'prophecy', and (b) the characteristics of Hellenistic Judaism which he cites are found just as much in this section (835), and (c) he asks whether this is the 'source' of 1 Cor 13 (866); B. Schaller, however, suggests, on lexicographical grounds, a date in the 2nd century C.E. for the whole work (in *JSHRZ* 3.3, 312), and R. Thornhill (in Sparks, *Apocryphal OT* 619) suggests that the author knew the NT. See further §4.1.1 on 1 Cor 13.1.

36 Rowland, *Heaven* 120: 'the temporary privilege of the apocalyptic seer has now become a permanent feature of the corporate life of the group'.

37 Cf. Klinzing, *Umdeutung.*

38 Cf. Rowland, *Heaven* 118; on p. 63 he asks why *Levi* was chosen as the recipient of an apocalypse in *T. Levi* 2.6−5.3, speculating that it was because of the 'priestly privilege of close contact with God'. At this point Gruenwald's observation (*Apocalyptic* 96f) about the tradition of special experiences of priests taking incense into the Holy of Holies is relevant. Cf. also Maier, *Kultus* 21f, 133.

39 In *T. Job* 33.3 Job speaks of his throne being in 'the upper world' and Spittler (in Charlesworth, *Pseudepigrapha* 1, 855 n.) compares this with the Qumran community's fellowship with angels.

40 Cf. Kuhn, *Enderwartung* 176f.

41 Cf. Larcher, *Études* 121: the importance of joining the company of the angels and being always in God's presence quite overshadows the expectation of a bodily resurrection; also Kehl, 'Erniedrigung' 385.

42 Cf. above on rabbinic discussions and on *2 Apoc. Bar.* in §3.1.1.

Scrolls that this sort of anthropological question exercised the Dead Sea community. Indeed their views of the after-life as a whole remain notoriously vague[43]. It might be thought that their vagueness as to a future resurrection in whatever form would leave them more free to speak of a resurrection in the present; the term 'resurrection' would not be earmarked for the future, so to speak. The idea of a spiritual resurrection or exaltation in the present, on the other hand, arises from a different motivation to the other; it stems from the intensity of 'spiritual' experience in the present; it might be easier to express it in images suggestive of resurrection in a Jewish context because (a) 'resurrection' is more at home in that context, and (b) in a Jewish context there would not always be the same inclination to confine this exalting experience to the incorporeal self, the non-bodily part of the person; because body and soul are held together more closely than in Hellenistic thought it is easier to see the whole person, both body and soul, as involved in this present experience. (Hence Paul in 2 Cor 12.3 can contemplate the possibility that his ascent to heaven may have been in the body.) But, even so, the passages in the Scrolls at which we have just looked might equally well suggest a background of raising those humiliated and abased, not of raising the dead[44]. Thus this imagery would more aptly be described as that of exaltation rather than resurrection. Thus, although one could see how the Qumran community might have been readier than, say, Hellenistic converts of Paul's in Corinth to use the language of resurrection of their present condition, it does not seem to be established that they actually made this transference of the eschatological act to the present.

3.4. Conclusions

In the first section of this chapter (§3) I prefaced this study of the 'spiritualizing of "resurrection"' by pointing out some of the ambiguities which this title presented, and in particular some of the different things that the word 'resurrection' could mean.

However I have argued for a certain rather obstinate corporeality and physicality about the language of resurrection, both for Jews and for

---

43 Cf. Buitkamp, *Auferstehungsvorstellungen* 55. They were perhaps more informative on the lot of the damned: e.g. 1QS 2.8, 'the shadowy place of everlasting fire' (cf. 2.15; 1QpHab 10.5, 12f; cf. Larcher, *Études* 117f; but n.b. 1QS 5.13, 'eternal destruction'; 1QM 1.5, 10,16 – cf. Kuhn, *Enderwartung* 38).
44 Cf. the caution of Lona, *Eschatologie* 58 on this point.

Greeks, which only gradually and under considerable pressure yielded to attempts to introduce a figurative, non-corporeal and non-physical sense; in particular Gnostics who wished to remain, or to seem to remain, within the Christian fold found themselves caught between the Scylla of the inescapable presence of resurrection in Christian tradition and the Charybdis of their aversion to the physical body. By this period Christian orthodoxy tended to define resurrection as resurrection of the 'flesh', despite the relative sophistication of Paul's thought in 1 Cor 15 and his rejection of the idea that 'flesh and blood' would inherit God's kingdom (15.50); Paul's more immediate successors, the authors of Colossians and Ephesians, had, I argued (§1.4), extended his idea of Christians' death with Christ in baptism to include their resurrection with him then as well, and thus both the apostle and his followers provided canonical hand-holds for the Gnostics in their attempts to salvage an idea of 'resurrection' that was consonant with their anthropological ideas.

The suggestion that Jewish circles had anticipated the Gnostic in speaking of a present resurrection I viewed with some caution; it does not seem to me that a clear case can be made out for an unambiguous use of resurrection language either in *Joseph and Aseneth* or in the Qumran hymns. The former speaks of new life and creation for the redeemed and uses the symbol of restoration to life, perhaps to show the possibility of forgiveness even for the enemies of the elect; that is not the same as claiming that the eschatological act of resurrection would take place already, and indeed eschatology is not an interest of this work. In Qumran we found evidence of a heightened sense of the elect's present bliss coupled with the vaguest of indications of their expectations for the future; the concentration on the present privileges of the redeemed community perhaps discouraged precision about the future destinies of individuals. The language of exaltation used to describe their present state need not be derived from Jewish expectations for the future, but could as well be explained partly from the language of raising the abased in the Old Testament and partly from the ecstatic experiences of various prophetic and priestly figures of the past.

Further, the Graeco-Roman background of the New Testament and of contemporary Judaism would have offered little, if any, incentive or encouragement to speak of a present resurrection. As we have noted, the Graeco-Roman world shared the Jewish view that resurrection was something that involved the body. Even where pagan gods were thought to have risen from the dead in a way that was in any sense comparable with Jewish hopes and with Christian beliefs, it is hard to find any trace of a belief that their initiates and devotees already shared that resurrection. In chap. 5 we will see that this not surprising, since the idea of their sharing the fate of a dying and rising deity or hero (where it is appropriate to speak of a dying and rising figure at all) may be the product of modern scholars who have read Pauline ideas into the theology of the mystery-cults.

Thus it is more convincing to look for the origins of the idea of a resurrection that is already present within the Pauline tradition, as his followers reinterpreted the ideas of Romans 6 and imposed a symmetry upon the asymmetrical statements there concerning participation in Christ's death on the one hand and in his resurrection life on the other. One can then go on to see how not only logical consistency but perhaps also the demands of the particular polemical context in which Colossians was written may have led the author of that letter to assert that Christians were already secure with Christ, united with him in his risen and exalted state; this idea was then taken up and reinforced by Ephesians in its own characteristic way (see §1.4.3 above).

4. Life in the Spirit

We have seen (§1.3.3.3) how baptism was in early Christian tradition associated with the bestowal of God's spirit[1]. We have already seen (§1.2.3.2) and shall see again (§4.1) that this gift of the divine spirit, bestowed in the rite of baptism, seems to have played a prominent part in the life of the church at Corinth, and at the same time to have been responsible for a number of the problems which that church posed for Paul.

If this spirit was prominent in the experiences of this largely Gentile congregation, how then did they understand this experience? Here we must consider, however briefly, how such ecstatic phenomena as were manifested in Corinth were regarded in the Graeco-Roman world (§4.2); did their Graeco-Roman background supply a means of interpreting what they were experiencing? In this, of course, it will be necessary to avoid a one-sided handling of the idea of πνεῦμα such as characterized the work of the *religionsgeschichtliche Schule* and above all Leisegang's *Der heilige Geist*; yet in resisting such a derivation of the idea of πνεῦμα exclusively or even predominantly from the Greek-speaking world, and in making allowance for the influence of distinctively Jewish contributions to the concept we should not blind ourselves to the fact that Christian missionaries, speaking of, and demonstrating the power of, a divine spirit, brought their message and their experiences to converts who already had their own concept of the nature and manifestations of πνεῦμα. We must reckon with a fusion of traditions, in a mixture that Paul did not find wholly to his taste.

For we shall have to note an element here that was largely foreign to the Graeco-Roman world, namely the Judaeo-Christian concept that the divine spirit thus bestowed was the eschatological gift of God, a sign of the end-time (§4.3). Whereas we shall see that ecstasy and divine posses-

---

Notes on 4

1 In this chapter I shall try to avoid giving 'spirit' a capital letter on account of the well-known difficulties which this often presents (cf., e.g., Moule, *Spirit* 7–10); in particular it creates a distinction in English where there is none in Greek, and so may distort the presentation of material.

sion was for the Graeco-Roman world something episodic and temporary, there were Christians who claimed to be 'spiritual', not just at moments of high arousement, but seemingly always and permanently. But that raises the question how the non-Jewish hearers of the Christian gospel would understand this message of the eschatological outpouring of God's spirit as an interpretation of the ecstatic phenomena present among them; for we have seen in the previous chapter that 'resurrection' was unlikely to have suggested or commended itself to them as a description of what they were experiencing.

The claim to be possessed by, or of, the divine spirit has its parallel in the aspirations of philosophers of the time to be 'wise', not just sometimes but always, and that ideal was taken up by Hellenistic Jews and associated with the idea that it was God's spirit which gave wisdom (§4.4). 'Wisdom' was something else to which some Corinthian Christians at least seemingly laid claim.

Thus I shall try to argue that the roots of the exaggerated enthusiasm and realized eschatology of some early Christians lay, not in a sacramental theology of the mysteries which spoke of sharing already in the dying and rising of the mystery-deity, but in a far wider understanding of ritual in the Graeco-Roman world, as a quasi-magical bestowal of certain powers on its participants (§4.5). In this case the power bestowed was, for the Corinthian Christians especially, but perhaps also for others too, the gift of that spirit that was poured out in the end-time, bringing with it gifts of wisdom and insight as well as gifts of ecstatic utterance and the ability to work wonders. In Schweizer's words, 'the Corinthians understood the presence of the Spirit . . . as the new, eschatological life itself, as the apocalyptic "living with Christ" '[2], but they misunderstood it as inalienably and unconditionally theirs.

4.1. Spirit and Sacraments in 1 Corinthians

4.1.1. In investigating the part played by experiences of God's spirit and by spiritual phenomena in the life of the Corinthian congregation it may well be best to start towards the end of 1 Corinthians, in *chapters 12–14,* with Paul's extensive discussion of a question raised with him by the Corinthians in their letter to him, their question περὶ τῶν πνευματικῶν (12.1). Unless one is prepared to see fairly extensive later editorial work in

---

2 'Dying' 8.

the letter and to regard a verse like 14.1 with its reference to τὰ πνευματικά as a gloss[1], then it may be best to regard the πνευματικῶν of 12.1 as
a neuter also; it has, however, been suggested that it is a masculine, and
this usage is found in 2.(?13), 15; 3.1; 14.37 (cf. Gal 6.1). It is perhaps
more likely, in my opinion, that Paul raises the question in the neuter
form[2], but, as we shall see, it does not make a great difference to the
likely substance of the question if it was originally posed in the masculine[3]: the problem was one of how certain people were using the gifts
which they enjoyed, how certain πνευματικοί were exercising their
πνευματικά.

For it is clear from what follows that a problem was posed by those
who spoke in 'tongues'[4]. This is clearly implied by the practical instruction which follows in chap. 14. There we find Paul underlining first that
speaking in tongues is a communication with God, not one's fellows
(vv 2–5); for this reason 'prophecy' is to be preferred to 'tongues', unless
an 'interpretation' is supplied for the latter, so that the church may be
'built up'; clearly this only makes sense applied to speaking in tongues in
a public place, in the gatherings of the church.

For 'tongues' by themselves are unintelligible; they do not communicate a clear message (vv 6–11), and edifying communication should be the
Corinthians' goal (v 12; cf. 19); the tongues-speaker should therefore
pray for an interpreter (v 13). Even the tongues-speaker's mind does not

---

Notes on 4.1.1

1 Cf. Schmithals, *Gnosis* 89 n. 1, 163. Hurd agrees in reading 12.1 as a masculine, but without
questioning 14.1 (*Origin* 194 n.1); see also Bachmann, *1 Kor* 375; Bruce, *1–2 Cor* 116; Holtz,
'Kennzeichen' 365, 368f; House, 'Tongues' 144; Lake, *Epistles* 202; Painter, 'Paul' 242; Ruef,
1 Cor 126; J. Weiß, *1 Kor* 294.

2 So, e.g., Barrett, *1 Cor* 277f; Conzelmann, *1 Kor* 240; Grudem, *Gift* 156–60; Héring, *1 Cor*
122f; Isaacs, *Concept* 87; Klauck, *1 Kor* 85; Lietzmann-Kümmel, *1–2 Kor* 60 (the translation opts for the neuter, the comment is less certain); Martin, *Spirit* 8; Orr-Walther, *1 Cor* 276
(tentative); Robertson-Plummer, *1 Cor* 259; Senft, *1 Cor* 155.

3 So Barrett, ibid. 278; Morris, *1 Cor* 166. Ruef, *1 Cor* 126, in a sense has it both ways (!): 'One
suspects the Corinthians asked about "men" and Paul instructed them about "gifts" ' – despite
the efforts of Hurd, *Origin*, it is hard to be sure in what form the Corinthians posed the question; Ruef may well be correct in that the Corinthians were concerned as to who could call
themselves spirit-endowed, although it is not necessary that they actually used the adjective
'spiritual' to formulate their question.

4 Cf. Bachmann, *1 Kor* 375; K. Berger in *TRE* 12, 191; Conzelmann, *1 Kor* 247; G. Dautzenberg in *RAC* 11, 238; Halter, *Taufe* 135; Hartman, '1 Co 14,1–25' 149; Héring, *1 Cor* 122;
Hurd, *Origin* 188–90, 193; Orr-Walther, *1 Cor* 282; Painter, 'Paul' 243; Pearson, *Terminology*
46; Ruef, *1 Cor* 124; Schlatter, *Paulus* 331; Senft, *1 Cor* 158; Wendland, *1–2 Kor* 92; Wischmeyer, *Weg* 47; Wolff, *1 Kor* 105.
It may be unnecessary to follow House, 'Tongues' 144, and to argue that for the Corinthians
πνευματικός was 'a technical term . . . for "one who speaks in tongues" or "speaking in
tongues" '; it would be enough if in practice they ignored the claim to be 'spiritual' of anyone
not exercising this faculty.

Life in the Spirit

comprehend his utterance; it is all taking place on the level of 'spirit' (v 14). The unversed person (the ἰδιώτης) will be left out, unable to add his 'Amen' to the prayer that he does not understand (v 16).

Paul then appeals to Isa 28.11f, but in a manner which has left exegetes puzzled. He uses this text to show that 'tongues', presumably identified with Isaiah's 'strange tongues', are a sign (σημεῖον) for unbelievers, and prophecy is one for believers (vv 20–2). J. B. Phillips, for instance, went so far as to reverse the meaning of the text here[5]. The best solution of this problem seems to me to lie in the meaning given to 'sign' here. In its original context the 'strange tongues' were those of Assyrian invaders; not even this drastic judgment of, and punishment upon, God's people would bring them to their senses and cause them to listen to him. The sense of 'sign' here is thus that of a warning sign[6]: if God issues such a sign it means that those to whom he issues it are 'unbelieving', that they have need of such a mode of communication from God. To the believing and obedient he communicates intelligibly.

Paul then returns to the effect made upon those inexperienced in such matters (ἰδιῶται again) or even unbelievers (ἄπιστοι) who enter the assemblies of the church and are confronted by nothing but tongues-speakers. Paul does not remark that they will not listen, which might have been a reasonable inference from his quotation from Isaiah, but instead states that they will form the opinion that these Christians are mad (v 23). How much better, how much more impressive, how much more effective in communication if all speak in prophecy, that is in intelligible speech inspired by God's spirit (vv 24f).

It is perhaps reasonable to infer that there had been a danger of this happening in the meetings of the Corinthian church. Not only would this be damaging to the impression given by the church to outsiders, but it was damaging to ἰδιῶται too. This last term is one that occasionally occurs in the context of Greek cults, meaning those who do not belong

---

5 *New Testament* 346 n.: 'this is the sole instance of the translator's departing from the accepted text. He felt bound to conclude, from the sense of the next three verses, that we have here either a slip of the pen on the part of Paul, or, more likely, a copyist's error.'

6 So BAG 755a: as the 'sign of Jonah' in Lk 11.29f; Wolff, *1 Kor* 136 n. 353, points out that prophecy is also a sign, and has a positive role of upbuilding; however it is clear that the two signs do not have the same *effect* upon their hearers, and that stems in part from the different attitudes of those hearers, but the matter is complicated by the different nature of the two sorts of utterances, suggesting a different *purpose* as well in the one who inspires both. Whether Paul meant to imply this is open to question. Cf. also Barrett, *1 Cor* 323; Klauck, *1 Kor* 102; Orr-Walther, *1 Cor* 309; Robertson-Plummer, *1 Cor* 317; Weiß, *1 Kor* 332 (*Verstockungsmittel*); but see too Senft, *1 Cor* 179. (Further lit. in Hartman, '1 Cor 14,1–15' 168 n. 52.) But note the suggestion of Johanson that v 22 is a rhetorical question ('Tongues').

to the membership of a cult but yet share in its sacrifices[7]. It is also found in the context of the mysteries as one of the categories contrasted with the initiated[8]; it should not, however, be regarded as a technical term of the mysteries, but rather as the application to them of a term in general use for the unskilled in contrast to the expert[9]. Applied to a Christian context that suggests those who are not church members but attend their gatherings[10]. More significantly still, as Weiß notes, if not members they would not have been baptized[11]; if baptism was regularly associated with ecstasy and the bestowal of spiritual gifts, especially tongues-speaking, they would have no personal experience of this phenomenon except as hearers of it[12]. The two possible senses of ἰδιώτης which Conzelmann mentions, the non-ecstatic listener (as Lietzmann suggested here) or the non-Christian participant or catechumen (so Weiß, Bauer), may thus here coincide[13]. If 14.23 uses the term in the same sense as 14.16 then Paul's charge would be that the behaviour of the Corinthians reduces their sympathetic adherents to the same position as sceptical outsiders. Perhaps also significant here is Pausanias' use of the term of one who does not possess the skills of a seer (2.13.7): Amphiaraus was but an ἰδιώτης until

---

7 Poland, *Geschichte* 422; cf. 361f n. †*; *IG* 2, 610.4; *SIG*³ 987.28; 1013.6.

8 *SIG*³ 736.17 (ἰδιώτιες); H. Schlier in *TDNT* 3, 215, and BAG 371*a* evidently take the main contrast to be with the following reference to priestesses, but the word is one amongst a number of categories listed, initiates, children, etc.; cf. Schol. in Hom., *Od.* 3.332; also Philo, *Omn. prob. lib.* 3 (also *Spec. leg.* 3.134 – opposed to priests; cf. *OGIS* 90.52).

9 Despite the impression given by H. Schlier in *TDNT* 3, 215: 'It means the "layman" as compared with the expert . . . the layman as distinct from the priest . . . On this basis ἰδιώτης comes to have the general sense of "unskilled".' The 'basis' must be the first statement, not the particular religious application of it mentioned immediately before.

10 So Klauck, *1 Kor* 101, who holds them to be, not full Christians (*pace*, e.g., Lietzmann-Kümmel *1–2 Kor* 72), but non-Christian sympathizers frequenting Christian gatherings as guests; also Héring, *1 Cor* 151; Morris, *1 Cor* 195f; Weiß, *1 Kor* 329–31. Schlier, ibid. 217, is probably wrong to identify them with unbelievers; the ἰδιῶται may include those who are on the way to faith and church membership, but have not yet been baptized. (Their status would be rather like that of the 'God-fearers' in the Jewish synagogue – if one accepts the existence of that category, as I do, but cf. Kraabel, 'Disappearance'.) But cf. also Barrett, *1 Cor* 324f, who renders ἰδιώτης and ἄπιστος as 'unbelieving outsider'.

11 So Weiß, ibid. 330.

12 Wolff's observation (*1 Kor* 136 n. 355) that ἰδιώτης cannot refer to a group of adherents to the church, since these would be familiar with tongues-speaking, is better suited to v 23 than v 16; the incomprehension (and alienation?) of the latter would fit equally, would indeed fit better, such a group of adherents; this feeling of exclusion could easily lead to the harsher reaction of v 23, especially with the encouragement of the verdict of more sceptical complete outsiders. Senft, *1 Cor* 179, is bolder: ἰδιώτης changes meaning between 16 and 23 (so too Barrett, *1 Cor* 324; Bruce, *1–2 Cor* 133; Lietzmann-Kümmel, *1–2 Kor* 73).

13 Conzelmann, *1 Kor* 282; cf. Lietzmann-Kümmel, ibid. 72 (also Weiß, *1 Kor* 331; Wolff, ibid. 134); BAG 371*a*; Ruef's point is significant here, if somewhat poorly expressed (*1 Cor* 150): 'from the congregation's point of view everyone was an *outsider* as opposed to the ecstatic' – I take this to mean that they regarded all non-ecstatics as outsiders.

he entered the 'mantic house' of Phlius, but hereafter he began to divine (μαντεύεσθαι). Here the use of this word to mean one unskilled as opposed to an expert passes over into a religious context.

Paul condemns such behaviour because it is loveless; it is another offence against those for whom Christ died (8.11) and does not contribute to their upbuilding nor to that of the church as a whole. So, tellingly, chap. 13 had spelled out the fruitlessness of gifts like tongues-speaking if unaccompanied by love (13.1); the lists of gifts of the divine spirit in chap. 12 had relegated 'tongues' to the last position (12.10, 30*b*), even at the risk of seeming to go against the principles of mutual interdependence and equal importance which Paul expounds with the help of the analogy of the body and its many limbs (vv 14–26); a likely reason for this is that that risk had to be taken because the Corinthians had exalted this gift to a position of pre-eminence.

Then in chap. 14 Paul turns to practical orders for the conduct of church meetings (vv 26–33*a* or *b* (36))[14]; his concern is that all should contribute to upbuilding of the church (26), but there should not be disorder (33*a*), but rather a seemly order (40); this is not to stifle anyone, but to give all a chance to contribute in the different ways in which they can (26); no one person, no one gift should monopolize the service of worship, and if there are unintelligible 'tongues' they must be interpreted; if no one can interpret then there must be no 'tongues' (28). Even intelligible prophecy is subject to some sort of evaluation by those present (29).

As I have already indicated, these instructions make best sense if directed to a situation in which the dangers which Paul here seeks to avert were all too real: the gatherings of the Corinthian church were dominated above all by the competing incomprehensible utterances of the tongues-speakers; these held the limelight and insisted upon the exercise of their gifts to the detriment of the others[15]. The latter in turn must

---

14 Despite arguments to the contrary I am of the opinion that the command to women to keep silent is a later (deutero-Pauline) interpolation in the spirit of 1 Tim 2.11f; it conflicts with the evidence of 1 Cor 11.2–16 that women spoke in inspired utterances in the church gatherings at Corinth, it is forced to take it of utterances (λαλεῖν, 34; cf. 27f) of a different sort to the inspired utterances of 26–32 (*pace* Dunn, 'Congregation' 227 and n. 93; Ellis, 'Wives'; Grudem, *Gift* 239–55, following J. B. Hurley; Hill, *Prophecy* 135; Martin, *Spirit* 83–7), and would be evidence of a glaring limitation on the meaning of ἀδελφοί in 26 if it and the following ἕκαστος applied only to male members of the gatherings. Cf. Dautzenberg, *Prophetie* 257–73, and J. Kremer's response on behalf of the German-speaking group of participants to Dunn, 'Congregation' 236f; also Conzelmann, *1 Kor* 289f; Klauck, *1 Kor* 105f; Lietzmann-Kümmel, *1–2 Kor* 75 (but contrast 190); MacDonald, *Legend* 86–9; Ruef, *1 Cor* 154f; Senft, *1 Cor* 182f.

15 Cf. Dunn, 'Congregation' 217.

have felt repelled and alienated. 'Unbelievers' might write off those thus possessed as 'mad', but it is likely that those disposed to believe the Christian message or those who should have been fully part of the community would not have been able to dismiss those speaking in tongues so easily, at least without questioning the value to themselves of a community where such practices prevailed. Paul seems to imply that not all baptized Christians could or did in fact speak in tongues (12.29f), and it may be that we should see the main thrust of the enigmatic 12.2f as a reassurance of those who could not and did not: if they have been able to utter the baptismal confession of Jesus as Lord they *have* received God's spirit. That confession is the crucial test of its presence. That presence may then be manifested in a variety of ways (12.4–10), but these are all manifestations of that one spirit (12.11)[16].

The opening words of chap. 13 may also indicate another aspect of this phenomenon, that it was believed that those who spoke in tongues themselves spoke in the language of angels[17]; it may even be that this was what tongues-speaking was generally believed to be. We have already noted (§3.3.3 n. 34) the idea of speaking angelic languages in ecstasy in *T. Job* 48–50[18]; this would be a natural corollary of the idea that in earthly worship one participated in the worship of the heavenly court, that one spoke the language(s) of that court[19]. That surely suggests that a (or the?) prime impetus to the 'realized eschatology' reflected and criticized in 1 Cor 4.8 (see §1.2.3.1) lay in the experience of ecstatic utterances in the spirit, linked with the conviction that one was thus participating in the worship of heaven.

---

16 A line of exegesis first suggested to me in a seminar held by Dr G. Jeremias in Heidelberg in 1969.

17 Cf. Conzelmann, *1 Kor* 247; G. Dautzenberg in *RAC* 11, 237f; Delling, *Worship* 35 (cautious); Hartman, '1 Co 14, 1–25' 164, 167; Klauck, *1Kor* 95; Lincoln, *Paradise* 34; Martin, *Spirit* 43, Pearson, *Terminology* 46; Schlatter, *Paulus* 354; Schlier, 'Hauptanliegen' 148, 155; Weiß, *1 Kor* 337f; Wolff, *1 Kor* 105, 120; but contrast Bruce, *1–2 Cor* 125.

It is also tempting to see in the belief that in (ecstatic) worship one was participating in the heavenly worship of the angels an explanation for the enigmatic 'because of the angels' in 1 Cor 11.10; an appropriate dress was all the more important in worship because of the proximity of angels there; cf. Ellis, *Prophecy* 36.

18 Cf. *Apoc. Zephaniah* 8.4 (O. S. Wintermute in Charlesworth, *Pseudepigrapha* 1, 514)=3.4 of an anonymous apoc., tr. K. H. Kuhn in Sparks, *Apocryphal OT* 922=ed. Steindorff 13.6–11; *2 Enoch* 19.3 A (cf. 17). The ascending soul in *Corp. Herm.* 1.26 joins in the hymns of the beings in the ogdoad and hears those above the ogdoad singing.

19 Cf. K. Berger in *TRE* 12, 184. One may also compare the secret languages of shamans as they converse with spirits or gods; see Eliade, *Chamanisme*, e.g. 99f, 199, 229, 263, 313 (ET 96f, 183, 252f, 290, 347); cf. R. R. Wilson, 'Prophecy' 326. Note too the explanation of a case of 'possession' among the Dinka observed by G. Lienhardt and quoted by Gould, 'Making' 10.

4.1.2. *1 Corinthians 3.1* should also probably be regarded as strong evidence for the belief of some Corinthians that they were 'spiritual'. Paul could[1] not speak to them as spiritual, but rather as fleshly, though nevertheless infants in Christ. That makes better sense if they wished to regard themselves as 'spiritual' now[2]. It is not necessary, however, to assume that they did[3]; the term had, after all, been introduced by Paul in 2.13 and 15; if πνευματικοῖς in 2.13 might be a neuter[4] 2.15 is unambiguous: Paul recognizes the existence of 'spiritual' people who review everything, but are themselves exempt from scrutiny[5]. It is quite plausible that some Corinthians at least did already regard themselves as 'spiritual' people of this sort, and indeed perhaps regarded themselves as already such during Paul's time in Corinth; why, they may have wondered, had he not given them more fitting teaching (such as subsequent visitors to the church perhaps gave them)? To some such criticism Paul may well now be replying.

If we ask how these Corinthians could have come to speak of themselves as 'spiritual', then an answer lies close to hand in Gal 6.1: Paul himself had taught them to do so, for, as Pearson remarks[6],

> the occurrence of the term πνευματικός in Galatians does show that the term was not uncongenial to Paul, and that he could make use of the term by applying to its use his own criterion as to what it means to be 'spiritual'. . . . οἱ πνευματικοί in Galatians 6.1 are those who 'walk by the Spirit' and do not 'fulfill the desire of the flesh' (5.16). They are 'led by the Spirit' (5.18), and produce the 'fruit of the Spirit' (5.22) in their lives. . . . In short, it is clear that for Paul οἱ πνευματικοί are those who are ἐν Χριστῷ . . ., and who have received the eschatological gift of his Spirit.

Notes on 4.1.2

1 Most pass the aor. ἠδυνήθην by without comment, but cf. Bachmann, *1 Kor* 141; Wilckens, '1 Kor 2,1–16' 512; Barrett, *1 Cor* 79, prefaces his discussion of the verse with the words 'He now returns to the present situation', but the present is not introduced until the end of v 2. The implication is that they are no better than when he first preached to them. Ruef, *1 Cor* 21, is probably correct to imply that Paul is still continuing his defence of his seemingly wisdom-less preaching in Corinth; they were not ready for it, Paul argues. (To make too strong a break between chaps 2 and 3 obscures this.)

2 Cf. Jewett, *Terms* 121f; Painter, 'Paul' 237; Ruef, *1 Cor* 21; Winter, *Pneumatiker* 212, 222f; Wolff, *1 Kor* 97.

3 Cf. Grudem, *Gift* 158f.

4 Bachmann, *1 Kor* 134; Bruce, *1–2 Cor* 40; Conzelmann, *1 Kor* 86 (uncertain, but argues that the context favours a neuter); Fascher, *1 Kor* 128; Lietzmann-Kümmel, *1–2 Kor* 13f; Ruef, *1 Cor* 20; Senft, *1 Cor* 47. Contrast Héring, *1 Cor* 19f; Klauck, *1 Kor* 30; Robertson-Plummer, *1 Cor* 47; Weiß, *1 Kor* 65; Wilckens, '1 Kor 2,1–16' 511, etc. Barrett, *1 Cor* 76, understands λόγοις here (and by implication Moffatt, *1 Cor* 33?).

5 Cf. Winter, *Pneumatiker* 216, on this striking statement: Paul, he plausibly argues, takes up a principle of his opponents to turn it back on them, to rebut their criticisms of himself. (He calls it a 'Gnostic' principle, but in my opinion it is wider spread than this term would suggest; cf. Knox, *Paul* (1939) 116).

6 *Terminology* 5; moreover it is possible – but no more – that Paul himself had led the way in speaking in tongues in Corinth or at least had spoken of his own experience of the phenomenon (cf. 1 Cor 14.18).

And yet in 1 Cor 3.1 the Corinthians, although they are '(babes) in Christ', are not 'spiritual' but 'fleshly'. To be truly 'spiritual' may entail that one is 'in Christ', but it seems that the converse is not true: it is possible to be 'in Christ', but unspiritual. However, Pearson's point about Paul's positive view of being 'spiritual' holds good, and is confirmed by his positive use of the term in (2.13 and) 2.15, for the flow of the argument surely suggests that the 'spiritual' person is the same as the one who has Christ's mind, or spirit (רוח) in the Massoretic text of Isa 40.13, quoted in 2.16. Nor would it be surprising if the Corinthians gladly adopted this term to describe themselves; the appropriateness of such a designation to those who habitually exercised spiritual gifts that were incontrovertible (or so it seemed to them) evidence of God's power working in and through them is plain to see. Moreover it is likely that this term expressed for them the centre of their religious experience; with justification Halter observes that 'the possession of the spirit . . . was the alpha and omega of the Corinthians' enthusiasm, and that in connection with the sacrament'[7].

4.1.3. There are, however, also signs, strong ones, in 1 Corinthians that the Corinthians' claim to be 'spiritual' was in their eyes supported by their understanding of the rites of baptism and the Lord's supper. For in *1 Corinthians 10.3f* Paul speaks of the Israelites in the wilderness eating 'the same spiritual food' and drinking 'the same spiritual drink' from 'the spiritual rock which followed them', a rock which Paul identifies with Christ.

This passage is fraught with several enormous difficulties. The ones that chiefly concern us here are Paul's reason for calling the Israelites' food and drink 'spiritual' and what he means by calling them this. He could mean, it seems, at least four things:

(a) the manna and the water were of spiritual substance, i.e. made of $\pi\nu\epsilon\tilde{\upsilon}\mu\alpha$[1];

(b) they were given by the spirit[2]:

---

7 *Taufe* 158.

Notes on 4.1.3
 1 Cf. Senft, *1 Cor* 129 (appealing to E. Schweizer in *TDNT* 6, 418 on 1 Cor 12.13); Weiß, *1 Kor* 251 with 372f; also perhaps Conzelmann, *1 Kor* 196; Lincoln, *Paradise* 34 (of the Corinthians' interpretation of it as = angelic, heavenly); Lewy, *Ebrietas* 30, seems to say that the spiritual drink is the 'spirit streaming into the human spirit and making it capable of knowledge'.
 2 Bachmann, *1 Kor* 332; BAG s.v.; Carlson, *Baptism* 327; Morris, *1 Cor* 141; v. Soden, 'Sakrament' 365 (262f); Wolff, *1 Kor* 41. Hanson, *Jesus Christ* 16, has a variant, 'given by Christ'. E. Schweizer in *TDNT* 6, 437, seems to combine (b) and (c) ('comes directly from God's

(c) they mediated the spirit to their recipients[3]; or

(d) they pointed to higher, spiritual things[4].

But Paul does not just describe the manna and the water as 'spiritual', but the rock that followed them as well[5]. Unfortunately it is necessary to try to clarify first what Paul may have meant by applying this epithet to the rock. One obvious reason for calling the rock 'spiritual' would be that it was in fact Christ, and Christ is a life-giving spirit (1 Cor 15.45). But there are problems in the way of such a straightforward identification of the rock and Christ – apart from the oddness of the idea (to us at least)[6]. Although some have happily espoused that interpretation and have talked of a 'real presence' of Christ in the wilderness experience of the Israelites[7], we have to note that it is perhaps then surprising that Paul does not speak more directly of the Israelites being baptized into Christ, instead of adapting the Christian baptismal usage in order to speak of their being baptized into Moses (10.2)[8].

---

sphere and gives divine power') – endorsed by Neuenzeit, *Herrenmahl* 49. Klauck, *1 Kor* 70, on the other hand, translates 'given by God' in v 3 and 'giving life' in v 4 (moving to (c)?). Orr-Walther, *1 Cor* 245, seem to combine (b) and (d) – 'supplied by God's special action' and having 'a spiritual or typological significance' – , and Barrett, *1 Cor* 222, combines (tentatively) (c) and (d), but then apropos of the 'spiritual rock' quotes with approval Schlatter's 'that which comes from God and reveals him' – (b) and (d)? Halter, *Taufe* 159, 161f,. has 'spirit-filled and bestowing spirit' – (a) or (b) and (c)?

3 Dinkler, 'Taufaussagen' 89; Käsemann, 'Doctrine' 113 (16); Ruef, *1 Cor* 90.

4 Cf. K. Berger in *TRE* 12, 181 (typological sense of scripture); Bourke, 'Eucharist' 373 ('figures of the Eucharist'); Bruce, *1–2 Cor* 91; Ellis, *Use* 131 n. 3 ('in its typical or prophetic significance'); Martelet, 'Sacrements' 354–9 (among other senses is that of 'figuratif').

It is not clear to me where L. Goppelt's suggestion of 'according to the manner (so for *Art*) of the Spirit of God' (*TDNT* 6, 146) belongs; this he describes as a 'christological sense' in that the food and drink are 'the vehicle of the saving work of God mediated through Christ'.

5 The mobility of the rock is found in Jewish haggadah: *t. Sukk.* 3.11–13; *Tg. Onq.* on Num 21; *Bib. Ant.* 10.7; 11.5; cf. Str.-B. 3, 406–8; O. Cullmann in *TDNT* 6, 97; Ellis, *Prophecy* 209–11; but note Héring, *1 Cor* 86f, who prefers the view of Theodore of Mopsuestia that it was not the rock that did the following, but the power of Christ. Cf. also the critique of Ellis (and Goppelt) in Neuenzeit, *Herrenmahl* 50f.

6 So Wolff, *1 Kor* 42f, although he is persuaded of the pre-existence of Christ here, denies that the rock is being identified with him. All that Paul wants to say is that Christ gave the Israelites water from the rock. But then Paul has put it rather poorly! That is far from impossible.

7 Hanson, *Jesus Christ* 10–23; Robertson-Plummer, *1 Cor* 201; cf. also Barrett, *1 Cor* 223; Hamerton-Kelly, *Pre-existence* 131f; Klauck, *1 Kor* 71; Knox, *Paul* (1939) 123; Luz, *Geschichtsverständnis* 119, etc; Neuenzeit, *Herrenmahl* 52, rejects an identification of the rock and Christ, but argues for the latter's pre-existence and presence in the OT events.

8 It is unnecessary to suppose that any Jews had been accustomed hitherto to speak of their being baptized into Moses or even that the Corinthians had already spoken in such terms (Jeske, 'Rock' 247). Rather Paul describes the Israelites' experiences in Christian terms in order to highlight how they are 'types' (10.6; cf. 10.11) as a warning to the Corinthians (G. Barth, *Taufe* 83, vs Conzelmann; Meeks, '"Rose"' 65f). I am here arguing in precisely the opposite direction to Hanson, *Jesus Christ* 12f, who, assuming that Christ is pre-existent in 10.4, argues that Moses cannot be a type of him in 10.2 – he is a 'minister' to Christ, not his counterpart.

Nor is it likely that this phrase in 10.4 is an allegory in the strictest sense of the term[9]. That would presumably have to involve a two-stage identification: the rock represents wisdom[10], and Christ is wisdom (1 Cor 1.24, 30)[11]. This is not impossible, but it is important to recognize the complexity of the idea. And moreover we should note that Paul does not use the present tense as he does in Gal 4.24—6, although this is by no means a conclusive argument[12]. But anyway much allegorizing in the ancient world was not exclusively allegorical in the sense that it denied any sense to the allegorized text over and above the allegorical meaning. Philo at least was generally prepared to recognize more than one level of meaning in the Old Testament text and, although stressing the allegorical or symbolic meaning of it, yet granted the validity of the literal sense except where this was morally or theologically repugnant to him[13]. So P. Borgen comments that, for Philo, 'the symbolical, though higher and more important, practically never invalidates the literal'[14]. This would be preferable here since it would not involve denying that the rock was a rock; it could be really a rock just as the food and drink were really and literally food and drink[15]. So Dunn classifies Paul's exegesis here as 'typological' rather than 'allegorical' (appealing to the reference to τύποι and τυπικῶς in vv 6 and 11): Paul meant the Corinthians to 'see the rock then as an equivalent to Christ now'[16]. What Christ is to them now the rock was to Israel then[17]. As Christ was one sent by God's spirit and one

---

9 Cf. Jeske, 'Rock' 247: 'more than allegory' (echoing the more cautious words of Luz, *Geschichtsverständnis* 119, although he goes on to describe it as an allegory in 122); cf. Neuenzeit, *Herrenmahl* 51.

10 So Philo, *Leg. all.* 2.86f (cf. 87; *Det. pot ins.* 115—18 on Deut 32.13; *Som.* 2.221f — God as the rock and source of wisdom). Bourke, 'Eucharist' 376f, sees the background to the ideas here in wisdom traditions like those of Sir 15.3; 24.19—21, which also serve as the basis for the ideas of Philo. For the well of Num 21.18 as the Torah cf. CD 6.4.

11 Cf. Dunn, *Christology* 184.

12 Cf. the discussion in Dunn, ibid. 330 n. 78.

13 So Philo, *Quaest. in Gen.* 4.123, sees a value in the words 'And he gave him whatever was his' (Gen 24.36) both 'for those who receive external material things' and for 'the self-taught' who see in it a symbol (or one can also see in it a symbol of the self-taught — Marcus n.). Again Rebecca's scarf is 'a visible symbol of clear-shining virtue' (ibid. 4.143) and in 4.173 Philo speaks of the literal meaning as a 'parable'. Tobin, *Creation* chap. 6, makes the interesting suggestion that for Philo allegorical interpretation is largely in terms of his allegory of the soul, and most other interpretations are literal; moreover he is the earliest example of an allegorist who recognized the validity of different levels of interpretation simultaneously (155).

14 'Philo' 261.

15 *Pace* E. Schweizer in *TDNT* 6, 437 n. 707.

16 *Christology* 183f; cf. O. Cullmann in *TDNT* 6, 97 (not very lucid!) as well as Bourke, 'Eucharist' 375, and perhaps also J. Behm in *TDNT* 3, 738f. Luz, *Geschichtsverständnis* 122, sees this reference to Christ shattering the typology of the passage.

17 So Dinkler, 'Taufaussagen' 89, against Luz: this is a 'Vergleich', not an identification of Christ and the rock. This way of looking at the passage seems to me preferable to the proposal of

who brought life through the spirit, Paul would then be attributing the same epithet, 'spiritual', to his Old Testament counterpart, the rock.

However, this might seem to be special pleading in order to avoid the oddity of Paul's ideas here. It does, in my judgment, become just a little bit more plausible if Paul is reacting to others' formulations here. But rather than supposing that Paul has taken over the ideas of 10.1–4 whole-sale and has simply added the words 'and the rock was Christ'[18], I think it likelier that he works here with material from at least two different traditions:

(a) an already existing Christian midrash or midrashim on the Exodus events[19], and

(b) the application by the Corinthians and quite likely by other Greek-speaking Christians of the epithet 'spiritual' to the bread and wine of the Lord's supper[20]. I think it likelier, in other words, that Paul has put these two together rather than that he found the Corinthians or others already discussing the Exodus events in terms of 'spiritual' food and drink.

This rather obscure usage of the term 'spiritual' is certainly more readily explicable if the Corinthians were already accustomed to speaking of 'spiritual' persons and/or gifts, and if Paul in 10.3f picks up their usage of the term; it becomes even more intelligible if they were also accustom-

---

Lietzmann-Kümmel, *1–2 Kor* 181 (following Schlatter, *Paulus* 290; cf. Bachmann, *1 Kor* 332), that the rock was 'spiritual' 'because Christ by his almighty grace caused the water to come forth from the rock'. If Paul meant that he has expressed himself very poorly. Are these scholars reasoning as Wendland (*1–2 Kor* 71) does when he argues that Paul identifies Christ and the rock in the same sense as he believed the former to be at work in the Lord's supper?

18 I find it hard to believe that the Corinthians had already interpreted the Old Testament story of the Exodus allegorically in the Philonic manner, perhaps as pupils of Apollos who was himself schooled in Alexandrian exegesis (Jeske, 'Rock' 246f). For evidence of Old Testament exegesis of this sort being practised by the Corinthians is otherwise hard to find.
  Meeks, '"Rose"' 65, 72, thinks it 'very likely' that 'and the rock was Christ' is a Pauline gloss on an already existing homily.

19 Weiß, *1 Kor* 250, referred to 10.1–5 as a midrash (cf. Neuenzeit, *Herrenmahl* 45), and v. Soden, 'Sakrament' 345 (245), called it 'midraschartig'. More recently Meeks ('"Rose"' 65) has suggested that almost all of 10.1–13 is an already formed Christian homily. Paul may have been its author (71). V. Soden, ibid. 359 (257) n. 27, calls 1–12 a 'Schrifthomilie'. Certainly some pre-formed tradition is made the more plausible by the existence of features that seem hard to account for if these verses are formulated in the light of the Corinthian situation alone: 'grumbling', for instance, is not particularly relevant there as far as we know (but cf. Wischmeyer, *Weg* 99 – yet they seem to have been in more danger of an (unwitting?) provocation of God – 10.22 – rather than a deliberate grumbling at him); see too Luz, *Geschichtsverständnis* 118f. But see Halter, *Taufe* 155f, against the hypothesis of any quotation of pre-formed material here.

20 Luz, ibid., suggests that 'Hellenistic churches' applied the term 'spiritual' to the eucharistic bread and wine; cf. too L. Goppelt in *TDNT* 6, 146, comparing *Did.* 10.3: ' "spiritual food" and "spiritual drink" were probably current expressions for the distributed eucharist elements'; also Halter, ibid. 159; Käsemann, 'Doctrine' 114 (16); Wendland, *1–2 Kor* 71; but contrast Neuenzeit, *Herrenmahl* 49.

ed to apply it themselves to the Christian food and drink, the eucharistic bread and wine, although they may well not have been the first to do so. For Paul would then be taking up their usage and applying it himself to the Israelites' equivalent of this food and drink, the manna and the water that was miraculously provided for them, as well as, for good measure, to the following rock that was the source of the water; and, in his eyes, this had a role analogous to that of Christ who nourished and sustained them in the Lord's supper. The sense of 'spiritual' applied to the water and to the rock may thus have been somewhat different, but yet related: it applied to the giver and to his gift, but that gift is fundamentally the presence of the giver himself (cf. Rom 8.9*b* with 8.10*a*)[21]. But in that case the question of the meaning of the word 'spiritual' becomes a twofold one: what did the Corinthians mean by the term, and what did Paul? The answer in each case is not necessarily the same. For whatever the source of the usage, we must reckon with the possibility that it meant one thing for Paul, another for the Corinthians, and yet another for any precursors that the Corinthians may have had in this usage; yet we know so little (indeed nothing certain!) of this last group and their usage that it would be fruitless to speculate as to their understanding of it; rather we must content ourselves with asking, in the light of what we otherwise know of Paul and his Corinthian converts, what they might have meant respectively by the term.

It seems likely that the fourth sense (d) given above can be discounted as anachronistic: 'in its typical or prophetic significance'[22] may be a possible paraphrase of the modern usage of the term 'spiritual', but it is doubtful whether such a sense for the Greek adjective is likely at that time; it is another matter when the adverb πνευματικῶς is used with verbs describing the activity of interpreting a text (e.g. Rev 11.8, καλεῖται πνευματικῶς), although even there there is room for argument[23]; the use of the adjective outside a context speaking explicitly of the interpretation of texts or the like (and that would also include Origen's 'spiritual' exegesis of the Old Testament) is harder to interpret in this way. We should note that 'spiritual' was used by Church Fathers of the Christian antitypes of Old Testament types, but it is harder to find examples of the adjective applied to the Old Testament types themselves[24].

---

21 Cf. Käsemann, ibid. 114, 118 (16f, 19f).

22 Ellis in n. 4 above.

23 E. Schweizer in *TDNT* 6, 449, argues here against the sense 'allegorically': 'Jerusalem is seen with prophetic eyes and identified with the biblical Sodom and Egypt'; he also quotes with approval M. Rissi's 'corresponding to the measure of God'.

24 Cf. *LPGL* 1105; one possible exception which is cited here is Greg. Naz., *Or. theol.* 15.12 (Migne *PG* 35; 932C) – Eleazar as 'spiritual father' of Christian priests.

Of the other three possibilities the first (a) might come into the reckoning, particularly as the Corinthians', or Hellenistic Christians', interpretation of the Christian rites[25]; they might well have held that the spirit permeated the bread and wine, so that in eating and drinking them they also ate and drank the spirit. So demons could also be thought to permeate food offered to idols[26]. Such a material view of the spirit and its operations is unlikely to have found favour with Paul[27], but was possibly held by the Corinthians or other non-Jewish Christians. To read it into Paul's statements here and in 1 Cor 12.13 is perhaps to take too literally what may be but a figure of speech[28]. A more literal view of this held by the Corinthians would explain how they came to view the spirit as imparted to them necessarily and automatically by their eating and drinking, which seems to be the misapprehension that Paul seeks to correct in this entire passage.

The second sense of πνευματικός (b) has in its favour the fact that this is the same sense as in the reference to 'spiritual gifts': πνευματικά are gifts given by God's spirit. In the present passage Paul emphasizes rather *Christ* as the giver of gifts: Christ is likened to the rock in the wilderness from which the Israelites obtained their drink. Yet if we recall again that Christ is a 'life-giving spirit' (15.45) it is easy to see that the two, Christ and the spirit, are far from a mutually exclusive pair of alternatives. Christ who is himself spirit bestows a nourishment that is the spirit in Christians and bestows it upon them as they partake of the eucharistic bread and wine[29]. Yet for Paul there is nothing automatic about the receiving and possessing of this gift.

---

25 In *Joseph and Aseneth* 16.7f (14) Batiffol inserts an identification of the honeycomb to be eaten by all who follow God with 'the spirit of life' (64.5f), but this reading finds no place in the text followed by Philonenko or D. Cook (in Sparks, *Apocryphal OT*); see however C. Burchard in Charlesworth, *Pseudepigrapha* 2, 229 (his 16.14); the same is true on 2, 233 (19.11= Batiffol 70.1f) with its interesting 'spirit of life . . . spirit of wisdom . . . spirit of truth' breathed into Aseneth by Joseph's kiss; cf. Sänger, *Judentum* esp. 175–208.

26 Cf. v. Soden, 'Sakrament' 366 (263f) n. 32; also Lietzmann-Kümmel, *1–2 Kor* 50f (but see §5.1.3 below).
   If one could believe the account given by Lewy, *Ebrietas* 43f, of the Pythian priestess at Delphi inhaling the divine in the vapours issuing from the rock, and consuming it in the laurel berries and spring water, then this would be an obvious parallel, but see the critique of Fontenrose, *Oracle* chap. 7: the exhalations referred to by Plutarch were obviously imperceptible; see also Price 'Delphi' 138–41. According to Fascher, ΠΡΟΦΗΤΗΣ 58, there is evidence for spring water inducing inspiration in Apolline oracle-shrines, cf. 75 on Plutarch and Iamblichus.

27 But cf. E. Schweizer in *TDNT* 6, 418.

28 Cf. L. Goppelt in *TDNT* 6, 138f.

29 Wolff argues that Paul uses the term 'spiritual' here 'to emphasize God's activity through his spirit in this event' (*1 Kor* 41); compare too Kennedy's argument (*St Paul* 267f) that in using this adjective Paul had in mind Deut 8.3 and the words 'everything that proceeds from God's mouth'.

The third sense of πνευματικός (c) has this in its favour, that in the context of sacraments it would provide a close parallel to the idea that the spirit was meditated by the rite of baptism, as we saw was likely in §1.2.3.2 : if πνευματικός is translated in this sense then it would mean that this rite of the Lord's supper also mediated the spirit; this food and drink also were a means of mediating God's spirit to those who ate and drank. Such a view is intelligible, particularly on the Corinthians' lips: they believed that their possession of the spirit was mediated to them and maintained through the sacraments of baptism and the Lord's supper. Paul would not have quarrelled with this belief, but nevertheless he felt that he must remind them that this gift of the spirit is not inalienably, irrevocably theirs; it is something which can be quenched and stifled (cf. 1 Thess 5.19). Israel enjoyed their corresponding privileges (cf. Rom 9.4—5); they all shared the same food and drink which their God provided, but not all of them escaped his wrath subsequently. Far from it (v 5). This line of argument surely suggests that both sacraments were encouraging a false sense of complacency and self-confidence in the Corinthians, and it is plausible to suggest too that they gave them these false hopes because both were thought to mediate to their recipients the gift of God's spirit. As long as they had been baptized and went .on partaking of the Lord's supper they were receiving the spirit; continued spiritual experiences of ecstasy could only have reinforced this conviction. There would thus be a sacramental basis, as well as that of enthusiastic experience, underlying their conviction that they possessed the spirit of God. Paul and the Corinthians shared a common conviction that the sacraments mediated this spirit; where they differed was in their understanding of the implications of this for their subsequent lives, whether this gift was irrevocably theirs to be enjoyed unconditionally, or whether it was one that would be withdrawn from the unfaithful.

The exact sense of 'spiritual' here, for Paul and for the Corinthians, must perhaps remain uncertain. However n. 2 above will already have suggested that the various possibilities are not necessarily mutually exclusive: the spirit may be mediated by the bread and the wine by being in them; the spirit, or Christ as spirit, who gives them may with this gift and in this gift give itself or himself. Certainty may also be unattainable on the matter of the situation which Paul is seeking to correct in 1 Cor 10.1—13. There is at best a strong possibility, perhaps even probability, that this usage of Paul's points, polemically, to a conviction on the part of the Corinthians that their possession of the spirit depended upon, was reinforced by, their partaking of the bread and the wine of the Lord's supper. That possibility would become yet more likely if we see other reasons for supposing that the Corinthians' confidence in their own spiritual status and endowment rested upon their beliefs about the effect upon

them of this rite and that of baptism[30]. The importance to them of the
latter is surely indicated by one last piece of evidence, Paul's discussion
of the divisions in the Corinthian congregation in 1 Corinthians 1.

4.1.4. The stress that Paul lays in *1.12–17* upon the rite of baptism
strongly suggests that the divisions mentioned in v 12 had something to
do with the question of who had administered baptism to each Christian[1].
Otherwise it is hard to see why Paul emphasizes how few he baptized at
Corinth, or why he should then play down his role as a baptizer. However,
rather than see this bond between baptizer and baptized being formed
solely on the analogy of the relationship between the mystagogues of the
mystery-cults and their initiates[2], it seems plausible to see the bond as
also reinforced by the manner in which the divine spirit was bestowed by
the baptizer's laying of his hands upon the baptized[3]. Correspondingly it
would be as a result of this experience that the 'spiritual' at Corinth first
came to regard themselves as such, especially if the laying on of hands and
bestowal of the spirit at baptism manifested itself in their first experience
of ecstatic utterances[4].

Such a link between baptism and the gift of God's spirit should come
as no surprise if we recall that such a gift may well have been associated
with the rite from the earliest days of the church (see §1.3.3.3) ; certainly
in Gal 3.2–5 Paul seems to assume that that was how the Christian lives
of his Galatian converts began[5]. However Halter rightly warns us to be

---

30 Cf. Halter, *Taufe* 154: 'it seems that it was the sacraments, seen in Corinth as signs of eschatological salvation and that above all *qua* mediating knowledge (wisdom, authority, freedom) and
   the life-giving spirit, which were a strong support of the enthusiasm of the Corinthians, leading
   to moral carelessness or overconfidence and heedlessness'. Contrast Carlson, *Baptism* 333f.

Notes on 4.1.4

  1 Cf. Conzelmann, *1 Kor* 50; Halter, *Taufe* 573 n. 6; Thrall, *1–2 Cor* 19 (tentatively); Wilckens,
    Röm 2, 53. But contrast Bachmann, *1 Kor* 74 n. 2; Fascher, *1 Kor* 94.
  2 See Héring, *1 Cor* 7; Klauck, *1 Kor* 22; Lietzmann-Kümmel, *1–2 Kor* 8; Lohse, *Umwelt* 179
    (ET 242); Moffatt, *1 Cor* 11; Paterson, *'Man'* 106; Ruef, *1 Cor* 10 (tentatively); Senft,
    1 Cor 35; Weiß, *1 Kor* 19; Wilckens, *Weisheit* 12 (cf. 16), etc. (further reff. in Halter, *Taufe*
    577 n. 24); contrast Carlson, *Baptism* 315; Machalet, 'Paulus' 191f.
    For the reality of this bond between initiate and mystagogue cf. Apul., *Met.* 11.25 (the priest
    Mithras as Lucius *parens* now; in 11.22 they were already linked together astrologically); cf.
    Berner, *Initiationsriten* 87; Dieterich, *Mithrasliturgie* 52, 146–9.
  3 Cf. Haufe, 'Taufe' 564.
  4 Painter, 'Paul' 245, considers that on the whole it is probable that 'the πνευματικοί understood
    their position . . . as a result of initiation'.
  5 However Schnackenburg, *Baptism* 16, goes too far in asserting that 'the gift of the Spirit to
    the Christian is exclusively bound to baptism'; the evidence of Acts suggests otherwise, namely
    that baptism ought normally to be accompanied by the gift of God's spirit, but sometimes
    was not (esp. 8.12–16); also the gift of the spirit might sometimes precede baptism (10.45–8).
    It seems unlikely that the author of Acts invented such an irregularity.

cautious here ; such a reconstruction would involve certain assumptions
– for instance, that Peter had baptized some in Corinth, and that 'I am of
Christ' in 1.12 did not refer to a Christ-party that actually existed in
Corinth, but was either a gloss or Paul's own retort to the first three
slogans (a more likely suggestion in my opinion)[6]. Yet Halter's own alternative suggestion that the remarks about baptism in 1.14–17 are an
appendix of little importance seems equally problematic. One has to ask
why they were appended and why Paul considered them relevant here.

4.2. Ecstasy in the Graeco-Roman World

In the previous section we saw the importance probably placed by some
Corinthian Christians upon their possession of ecstatic, supernatural manifestations of the spirit; we saw the likelihood that the possession of these
was linked to their understanding of the Christian rites of baptism and the
Lord's supper. Here we have to ask how citizens of their world would have
understood these phenomena, in particular the ecstatic manifestations of
spiritual gifts; we shall return to the question of the link with the rites
of baptism and the Lord's supper later, in §4.5.

We shall see that the ancient world was familiar enough with ecstatic
possession by the divine in various forms (§4.2.1). This will lead us on to
consider the most helpful parallel to the Corinthians' experience, the·
concept of oracular inspiration as seen by philosophers and also appropriated by them as a metaphor for their own acquisition of truth (§4.2.2). In
this it will be remarked how often the divine spirit is an impersonal object
impinging upon the soul of the one inspired. For Paul such a view of the
spirit of God was not possible, but what of his Corinthian converts? How
would they have regarded the spiritual power let loose in their midst
(§4.2.3)?

4.2.1. Many of the religious cults in the Graeco-Roman world seem to
have, at one point or another, displayed *ecstatic features*. It may be going
too far to claim, as Schnackenburg does, that 'the chief means of the
Mysteries was ecstasy, and to induce this many natural means were ap-

---

6 *Taufe* 140f; Halter himself is not disposed to regard these as insuperable difficulties. On 'I am
of Christ' see §1.2.2.3 n. 3 above.

plied'[1], but it is not far from the truth. Certainly it was prominent in a number of oriental cults. One thinks immediately of the frenzied and bloodied devotion of the followers of Cybele[2], and the temple of the Syrian goddess at Hierapolis contained 'women who are frenzied and deranged'[3], and at the performance of their rites by the *Galli* frenzy ($\mu\alpha\nu\iota\eta$) comes on many, leading them to castrate themselves[4]. In the Egyptian cult, Plutarch tells us that the priests at the burial of Apis behave as do those possessed in Bacchic rites[5], and a second-century relief in the National Museum in Rome shows men and women dancing in ecstatic fashion in honour of Isis[6].

But of all the cults in the Graeco-Roman world that displayed ecstatic features, it is perhaps the Dionysiac which is the most obvious example. Some scholars have suggested that these rites influenced the Corinthian Christians in their understanding of their religious experience. So Hengel postulates that they 'misunderstood Paul's message along the lines of the ecstatic Dionysiac mysteries with which they were so familiar'; Livy's account of the suppression of the *Bacchanalia* (see §2.1 above) affords the closest parallel to the ecstatic phenomena in the Corinthian church; their vital spiritual experience lent itself to interpretation on the analogy of the mysteries[7]. Leipoldt too speaks of Christian worship in Corinth taking the same form as that of the Dionysiac cult[8]. F. C. Grant goes further, and speaks of an 'outbreak of corybantic paganism in the church at Corinth'[9]. Certainly this is an analogy that would readily have suggested

Notes on 4.2.1

1 *Baptism* 168; cf. Cumont, *Religions* 25, 215 n. 17=*Religionen* 27, 216 n. 17; Prümm, *Handbuch* 298; P. Wendland, *Kultur* 155.

2 As does Lucian when describing the antics of Alexander of Abonuteichos in *Alex.* 13. As early as Eur., *Hipp.* 141–4 the Greeks had known Cybele as one who could produce $\mu\alpha\nu\iota\alpha$ and make one $\ell\nu\theta\epsilon\sigma\varsigma$: cf. Gasparro, *Soteriology* 15 and further reff. there.

The heirs of the cult of Cybele were the Montanists: Nilsson, *Geschichte* 2, 656; it may be questioned, however, whether Montanus had been a devotee of Cybele (J. Wirsching in *KP* 3, 417), but that the charge was made underlines the similarity. House, 'Tongues' 137, observes that he could find no evidence for a temple of Cybele-Attis in Corinth in the first century; yet there was a temple of the former there when Pausanias visited the city (2.4.6); the other remains listed in *CCCA* 2.456–67 are mostly of fairly indeterminate date.

3 Lucian, *Syr. Dea* 43, tr. Attridge-Oden.

4 Ibid. 50f. We meet ecstatic priests of Atargatis also in Apul., *Met.* 8.27.

5 *Is. et Os.* 35.364EF.

6 H. von Hesberg in *ANRW* 2.17.2, 1056f (pl. 6); the presence of 'local visitors to the festival' depicted there underlines that we are not dealing with anything mysterious or secret here.

7 *Sohn* 46–9 and n. 56 (ET 28). Contrast Delling, *Worship* 38f (cf. 183–5). One should note, however, Henrichs' observation that 'the gradual demise of maenadism began in the Hellenistic period and was apparently complete by the third century A.D.' ('Maenadism' 155).

8 'Christentum' 53.

9 *Hellenism* 138; Dunn, 'Congregation' 209, describes the type of tongue-speaking practised by

itself at Corinth, with Delphi and the slopes of Parnassus, the location of the biennial winter rites of the maenads, lying on the far side of the Gulf of Corinth. Moreover, in so far as the Dionysiac experience of ecstasy, and that of many other ecstatic religions, was one of communion with the divine[10], it is likely that this is a real analogy, for Paul recognizes the tongues-speaking of the Corinthians – and himself – as a speaking to God (1 Cor 14.2).

And yet the most prominent mark of the Corinthian ecstasy seems to have been speaking in 'tongues', and this is not a feature of Dionysiac frenzy[11], nor for that matter is prophecy; that was more the province of Dionysus' neighbour at Delphi, Apollo[12]. We should not, however, claim that tongues-speaking was a widespread and recognized phenomenon in pagan religion of the day; for that there is hardly any evidence, despite the statement of F. C. Conybeare that the term

> was a repetition . . . of a phrase common in ancient religions. The very phrase γλώσσαις λαλεῖν . . . was not invented by the New Testament writers, but borrowed from ordinary speech[13].

---

the Corinthians as 'a near-Dionysiac frenzy', though quite what evidence he has for supposing that the kind which Paul himself practised was different is not clear to me; cf. also Painter, 'Paul' 242f.

10 Diod. S. 4.3.3 (τὴν παρουσίαν . . . τοῦ Διονύσου); cf. Cumont, *Lux* 254f; Henrichs, Maenadism' 135f; Portefaix, 'Concepts' 204f.

11 The allusion by J. Behm in *TDNT* 1, 722 to Aristoph., *Ran.* 357, γλώττης βακχεῖ is misleading; it is a partial quotation of the line

μηδὲ Κρατίνου τοῦ ταυροφάγου γλώττης βακχεῖ' ἐτελέσθη,

which Rogers translates 'or shared in the Bacchic rites (Stanford: 'tongue-rites') which old bull-eating Cratinus' words supply'; nearer to the sense required by Behm is v. Daele's translation 'accents bachiques', but this is still a far cry from the required sense. The allusion is to Cratinus' comedy which defeated Aristophanes' *Nubes* in 423 in Dionysiac festivals in which these plays were performed; it was in perfectly good Greek and not in the least ecstatic! Of course there were wild cries uttered by the maenads, but this is hardly the same as a speaking in tongues.

12 Cf. Guthrie, *Greeks* 200. However Fontenrose, *Oracle* 204–12, is sceptical of the widely held conception of a frenzied Pythia (n.b. esp. 207); the only reliable evidence of this is when something went wrong (Plut., *Def. orac.* 51.438B)! Lucan's account in 5.165–74, 190–3 owes more to Vergil's account of the Cumaean Sibyl than to any knowledge of the operations of the Delphic Oracle.

13 In *EBrit* 27 (1911), 10. Contrast G. Dautzenberg in *RAC* 11, 236; H. Kleinknecht in *TDNT* 6, 359; Wischmeyer, *Weg* 166. Harrisville, 'Speaking', argues that the term had its origins in pre-Christian Jewish circles. Some have claimed that the *Homeric Hymn to Apollo* 162f refers to a similar phenomenon, but cf. v.d. Horst, 'Parallels' 52f.

More restrained is the claim of Weiß, *1 Kor* 335, that γλῶσσαι or γένη γλωσσῶν was a technical term intelligible to Paul's readers; that is not the same as saying that they were accustomed to use the term; they merely understood it when it was used. And on 336f he lists a great many instances of it used of 'unintelligible statements' (or 'unintelligble words' in Greek usage); cf. Héring, *1 Cor* 128 and n. 14; Lietzmann-Kümmel, *1–2 Kor* 69; Thrall, *1–2 Cor* 98; Wendland, *1–2 Kor* 119, etc.

H. W. House quotes this with approval, but, despite the fact that showing this might have been thought to be the main point of his article on 'Tongues and the Mystery Religions of Corinth', he cites not a scrap of evidence for parallels to this aspect of the Corinthian Christians' beliefs and behaviour, whatever else can be paralleled in the mysteries. And the fact that before long early Christian writers found themselves at a loss to know quite what the phenomenon was surely means, not only that it had died out in their own Christian circles, but also that it was not something readily recognizable in their pagan environment[14].

Ecstasy was not, of course, the monopoly of mystery-cults[15], and often it was part of the public rites of oriental cults; that is true, for instance, of the cult of Cybele. It was also practised by individuals and in particular seers, prophets and diviners, and, either imitating them or perhaps also through genuine religious experience, by philosophers. Since prophecy was also a gift practised in the Corinthian church (implied, surely, by references such as 1 Cor 12.10, 28; 13.2; 14 *passim*, esp. 26, 29–32, 37), this parallel perhaps lies closer to hand[16]; moreover many of the other spiritual gifts which Paul lists were also the speciality of ecstatics of this sort: wisdom and knowledge (1 Cor 12.8), healing (ibid. 9, 28, 30), miracles (ibid. 10, 28f)[17]. One of the closest parallels to the phenomenon of speaking in tongues in the ancient world may be the utterances of the 'false prophet' Alexander of Abonuteichos, whom Lucian described as follows:

> Uttering a few meaningless sounds (φωνάς τινας ἀσήμους) such as might have been those of Hebrews or Phoenicians, he astounded the people for they did not know what he was saying except that he everywhere mentioned Apollo and Asclepius. (*Alex.* 13, *LCL* tr.)

Finally, not only were the maenads' hunting grounds close to Corinth, but so too was Delphi, the seat of Greece's most famous prophetic oracle, whose sanctity could at times be attributed to the presence of a πνεῦμα

---

14 See Currie, '"Speaking"'; Harrisville, 'Speaking' 48; Robertson-Plummer, *1 Cor* 257; also G. Dautzenberg, ibid. 244f; in 231 he compares the series of magical names and letters found in magical papyri and also supposed to derive from otherworldly languages; cf. Lietzmann-Kümmel, *1–2 Kor* 69; Weiß, *1 Kor* 338f.

Orig., *Cels.* 7.9, seems, however, to presuppose the continued existence of a comparable phenomenon: some prophets of whom Celsus knew who, after giving intelligible prophecies, 'then go on to add incomprehensible, incoherent, and utterly obscure utterances, the meaning of which no intelligent person could discover: for they are meaningless and nonsensical, and give a chance for any fool or sorcerer to take the words in whatever sense he likes' (tr. Chadwick).

15 Painter, 'Paul' 245, seems to make the mistake of equating 'pagan ecstatic religion' and the mysteries.

16 Cf. G. Dautzenberg in *RAC* 11, 230; H. Kleinknecht in *TDNT* 6, 346.

17 Cf. F. Pfister in *RAC* 4, 976–8.

or πνεύματα[18]. Moreover what was claimed to be the same god and the same spirit of prophecy evidently worked elsewhere than at Delphi; for evidence of that we need look no further than Acts, where in 16.16 Paul and his companions encounter a girl with a πνεῦμα πύθων; however one translates the phrase ('a spirit of divination' seems the most widely agreed), the allusion to the snake slain by Apollo at Delphi is clear, even if the manner of the possession was apparently different (Plut., *Def orac.* 9.414E): Fontenrose has underlined very clearly the evidence that normally the Pythia herself spoke clearly and coherently[19]. That such ecstatic manifestations would be familiar to the Corinthians is more than probable[20].

Despite Paul's careful distinction between tongues-speaking and prophecy in 1 Corinthians 14, these are arguments for considering prophetic and quasi-prophetic inspiration as our best key to understanding how the Corinthians were likely to have understood their possession of and by the divine spirit, at least as far as their pagan environment was concerned. This is particularly true if the Corinthians did not make the same distinction as Paul did between rational and conscious prophecy and ecstatic, unconscious tongues-speaking[21]. Yet Dautzenberg is surely right to argue that Paul and the Corinthians both understood it to be something other than pagan ecstasy, however similar it may have seemed to the outsider (1 Cor 14.23, μαίνεσθε); for a start Jewish parallels to the idea of participating ecstatically in angelic worship and language lay nearer to hand (see §4.1.1 on 1 Cor 13.1); furthermore they created their own terminology for the phenomenon which they experienced[22]. In short this experience takes on new dimensions from its being located within the expectations and world-view of Jews and Christians.

That Paul had this pagan background in mind, however, and that this had influenced the Corinthians' attitude to their possession of the spirit as well may be suggested by the enigmatic words of 1 Cor 12.2, even if the text and the translation of the verse are very much in doubt[23]. Conzel-

---

18 E.g. Pseudo-Arist., *Mund.* 4.395b; Iambl., *Myst.* 3.11; Plut., *Def. orac.* 50.437C (but cf. Fontenrose, *Oracle* 198); Strabo 9.3.5; cf. Lucan 5.132, 165; Valerius Maximus 1.8.10 (*spiritus*).

19 *Oracle* esp. 212.

20 Dunn, 'Congregation' 208, rightly notes the parallels between tongues and interpretation thereof on the one hand, and the ecstasy of the Pythia and the interpretation of her utterances by a priest on the other. Whether Pearson, *Terminology* 46, is right to give priority to the Hellenistic *Jewish* phenomenon of ecstatic prophecy as the background to the Corinthians' usage may be questionable; it could be argued that they would be more familiar with the non-Jewish phenomenon (and the Jewish phenomenon as described by Philo may be as much a literary convention as a reference to actual ecstasy – see §4.2.2 below).

21 See also §4.2.2 and nn. 13f there.

22 In *RAC* 11, 236f.

23 Cf. Chrys. *Hom. in 1 Cor* 29.1 (Migne *PG* 61, 241f); Barrett, *1 Cor* 278; Bruce, *1–2 Cor*

mann finds the argument of Weiß decisive here: Paul is drawing an analogy between the Corinthians and their previous experience as pagans (and not a contrast); he points to the passivity of those who are in the grip of a spirit; thus he must be appealing to their previous experience of ecstasy[24]. Although ἄγω and its compounds are not the commonest Greek terms for divine possession they are found occasionally, the uncompounded ἄγω particularly in Lucian; in a much-cited passage of his, *Dialogi mortuorum* 27 (19).1 (411), love represented as a δαίμων carries us away (ἄγει) as it wills, and we are powerless to resist[25]. Here as elsewhere in Lucian it is noteworthy that the uncompounded form of the verb is used, as is found in most modern texts of this passage of 1 Corinthians[26]. Nevertheless other interpretations of the verse are to be found[27].

4.2.2. In §2.4.1 we saw Plato paving the way for *philosophy*'s appropriation of the language of the mysteries to present its claims to reveal the truth. At the same time, in *Phaedrus* 249CD, he made use of the language of both ecstasy and enthusiasm: the philosopher separates himself (ἐξιστάμενος) from human pursuits and attends to the divine; the masses deem him mad, not knowing that he is inspired (ἐνθουσιάζων). Philo follows Plato in defining the fourth and best possible sense of ἔκστασις[1]

117; Hermann, *Kyrios* 70; Holtz, 'Kennzeichen' 372f; Klauck, *1 Cor* 85; Lietzmann-Kümmel, *1–2 Kor* 60; Moffatt, *1 Cor* 178; Senft, *1 Cor* 156; Thrall, *1–2 Cor* 87; Weiß, *1 Kor* 294; Wendland, *1–2 Kor* 92; Wolff, *1 Kor* 98. Painter, 'Paul' 242f, expressly links this verse to the Dionysus-cult; this is too specific, as is Martin's connection of it with Apollo (*Spirit* 9).

24 *1 Kor* 243.

25 Betz, however, lists several other instances of a similar usage (*Lukian* 40f n. 10): *Vera historia* 1.33; *Philopseudes* 14 (?25); *Syr. Dea* 36; *Dialogi meretricii* 4.5. Significantly he finds a similar sense in Rom 8.14; Gal 5.18; Lk 4.1, 9 (leading by the spirit of God or by the devil).

26 Wolff, however, seems to think that the compound ἀνήγεσθε would make such a reference more likely here (*1 Kor* 98 n. 176; cf. Maly, '1 Kor 12,1–3' 83); G. Strecker in *RAC* 5, 462, lists this as one of the terms used of translation, but of that there should be no question here (cf. Weiß, *1 Kor* 294): but cf. Héring, *1 Cor* 124.

27 One sees a reference to the unsatisfied search amongst the various cults (Bachmann, *1 Kor* 377), others simply a bondage to cults (Maly, ibid. 84–6; cf. Morris, *1 Cor* 167; Robertson-Plummer, *1 Cor* 259f), and Schlatter to their traditionalism (*Paulus* 331f); Orr-Walther, *1 Cor* 276, suggest that the figure is that of animals driven to sacrifice (which Héring, *1 Cor* 124, recognizes for ἀπαγόμενοι, but he distinguishes this from ἀνάγεσθαι). Conzelmann, *1 Kor* 242, rightly observes that (ἀν)άγειν could refer either to ecstasy or simply to domination by demons.

Notes on 4.2.2

1 In *Rer. div. her.* 249–66 the forms of ecstasy are described; apart from this form described above the other three are 'a mad fury producing mental delusion', extreme amazement at the unexpected, and passivity of mind. On the wider use of the term cf. A. Oepke in *TDNT* 2, 449f. Fascher, ΠΡΟΦΗΤΗΣ esp. 151f, observes that the Old Testament avoids the idea of Yahweh being in a human, and that Philo followed it in this. It would be wrong, however, to give the impression that he avoided the idea utterly, even if he understood it in a weakened sense,

as 'divine possession or frenzy' (ἔνθεος κατοκωχή τε καὶ μανία, *Rer. div. her.* 249). Abraham was an example of this, an 'inspired and God-possessed' man (ἐνθουσιῶν καὶ θεοφόρητος, 258); the experience showed him to be a prophet, as does the testimony of Gen 20.7, 'he is a prophet'. For Plato poets, too, were similarly inspired: the poet cannot produce his work 'until he has been inspired (ἔνθεος) and put out of his senses (ἔκ-φρων) and his mind is no longer in him'. He is possessed by a divine power, and the deity speaks through him; the same is true of soothsayers (χρησμῳδοί) and seers (μάντεις)[2].

In this the language of the entry of the divine into the human agent is clear enough (ἔνθεος, ἐνθουσιάζω, κτλ.); it enters the personality to possess it and use it (κάτοχος, κατέχω, κτλ.). The god is in the human person, even in his human body[3]. That body is thus often driven to action, wild or strange, beyond its normal powers, for there is within it that which is divine. As Burkert says,

> An ancient name and interpretation for an abnormal psychic state is *entheos*: 'within is a god', who obviously speaks from the person in a strange voice or in an unintelligible way and induces him to perform odd and apparently senseless movements. At the same time . . . it is said that a god seizes or carries a person, that he holds him in his power, *katechei* . . . .[4]

If we can trust Clement of Alexandria the early atomist Democritus attributed the enthusiasm of poets to the presence of divine spirit[5], and Pseudo-Longinus also attributes the inspiration of writers to 'a spirit not their own' such as moved the Pythia[6]. Thus we find evidence both of the wide range of phenomena which were regarded as the result of divine possession and of the attribution of this possession to 'spirit'.

I have already indicated above that Philo too uses ἔνθεος and similar terms of prophetic ecstasy. The prophets' words are not theirs, but another's, the echoes of another's voice; they become the 'vocal instru-

---

perhaps with the divine spirit as a mediator, as Fascher suggests was the view that later prevailed in Judaism (cf. 160).

2 *Ion* 534B–D, tr. Lamb.

3 Cf. Eur., *Ba.* 300. So too Apul., *Met.* 8.27 speaks of the *deum praesentia* in those inspired, and Poll., *Onom.* 1.15 seems to treat ἔνθεος and πλήρης θεοῦ as parallel terms. This is borne out by reff. like that of Longinus, *De sublimitate* 13.2 to ἀτμὸς ἔνθεος; hence Rohde, *Psyche* 259, is surely wrong to say that ἔνθεος refers to being in the god; 275 n. 50 is better: 'the ἔνθεος is completely in the power of the god; the god speaks and acts through him.' Jeanmaire, *Dionysos* 134, argues that it means literally 'in the hand of a god', but that again fails to do justice to Longinus' phrase. This view of prophecy seems, however, to be rejected by Lamprias in Plut., *Def. orac.* 9.414E.

4 Cf. Burkert, *Religion* 178 and n. 1 (ET 109f and 391 n. 1); also James, *Religion* 135; Nilsson, *Geschichte* 1, 577; F. Pfister in *RAC* 4, 955f; 5, 455f, 'Ekstasis' 183; Willoughby, *Regeneration* 75.

5 Diels-Kranz, *Fragmente* §68 B 18; cf. Leisegang, *Geist* 134.

6 *De sublimitate* 13.2 (tr. Russell 113); cf. 8.4; 9.13; 33.5 (δαιμόνιον πνεῦμα).

ments, the ὄργανα ἠχεῖα, of God and in this sense each of them is inspired by God (ἐνθουσιᾷ) and is possessed (κατεχόμενος)[7]. So too a thinker like Philo knows a voice in his soul as it is possessed by God and prophesies concerning things about which it has no knowledge (*Cher.* 27)[8].

But Burkert, who had prefaced the passage quoted above with the remark that Greek usage to describe ecstatic phenomena was 'varied and inconsistent', continues

> stepping out, *ekstasis*, is spoken of just as much not in the sense that the soul leaves the body, but that the person has abandoned his normal ways and his good sense and yet one can also say that his understanding (*nous*) is no longer in him. These various expressions can neither be reconciled systematically nor distinguished in terms of an evolution in the history of ideas; they mirror the confusion in the face of the unknown. The most common term is therefore *mania*, frenzy, madness[9].

This confusion is also mirrored in Paul's thought when he describes, untypically, the experience of being lifted up to the third heaven in 2 Cor 12.2f: he does not know whether it was in the body or without it, only God knows that. Still more relevant is the observation that Paul's distinction in 1 Cor 14 between mindless tongues-speaking and prophecy and other spiritual activities in which the mind participates may not have coincided with the Corinthians' understanding of their experiences: they may not have felt that they were leaving their minds behind when they engaged in speaking in tongues. This uncertainty as to the rationality or otherwise of such phenomena was, we shall see, also shared by Philo.

For, by the first and second centuries C.E., things were, if anything, even more confused than in the period about which Burkert speaks. For a start, that which he denies, that ecstasy was thought of as the soul's leaving the body, is found, as we shall see; yet if the influence of shamanism was felt in Greek religious experience and thought at an earlier period[10] it is perhaps unreasonable to deny that this manifestation of it

---

7 *Rer. div. her.* 259f; cf. 266; *Spec. leg.* 4.49; *Quaest. in Gen.* 1.42; compare also Epiph., *Haer.* 48.4.1 (Montanus); Iambl., *Myst.* 3.7 — the deity uses the possessed ὡς ὀργάνοις; Plato, *Ion* 534D; Plut., *Def. orac.* 9.414E (critizing the concept). On Plato's legacy here cf. Fascher, ΠΡΟΦΗΤΗΣ 69: Plato 'increased the seer's dependence on the deity in that he made the human being a mere organ and mouthpiece'.

8 Cf. *Som.* 2.252 — this voice is the invisible spirit (πνεῦμα).

9 As n. 4; cf. Nilsson, *Geschichte* 1, 577; F. Pfister in *RAC* 4, 944, and 'Ekstasis' *passim*.
   I find it difficult to endorse House's statement that 'ecstatic religion by its very nature is self-oriented' ('Tongues' 141), for it seems in a very real sense to involve a loss of self.

10 Eliade, *Chamanisme* esp. 19 (ET 5), defines a shaman as specializing in trances in which his soul leaves the body to undertake heavenly ascents or descents to the infernal regions.
   On the question of the relevance of shamanism for understanding various phenomena in Greek religion see Burkert, *Lore* 162–5 and 'ΓΟΗΣ'; Dodds, *Greeks* 140–7; Eliade, ibid. chap. 11; Rohde, *Psyche* chaps 8§3; 9§7; West, *Poems* 4f, 146–50, etc., but also the doubts and criticism of Bremmer, *Concept* esp. 47f.

was also experienced earlier, even if the term ἔκστασις does not happen to have been used for it[11], and even if there was a tendency for a time at least to play down the radicality of the idea; after all those who experienced something so drastic and spectacular were rather exceptional[12]. By the New Testament era, at any rate, it seems clear that this is one way in which ecstatic experience is interpreted.

As we have seen, Paul evidently regarded tongues-speaking as being done without the collaboration of the mind: the mind is literally 'fruitless' (1 Cor 14.14; cf. 14.15, 19)[13]. At times Philo has a similar view of prophecy, which, it seems, Paul implicitly distinguishes from tongues-speaking at precisely this point. It is therefore plausible to suggest, as Wischmeyer does, that 'the Corinthians . . . retained various features of the understanding of prophecy held by the Jews and the ancient world in general, which Paul confronts with his own understanding of prophecy'[14]. I have already mentioned the possibility of this difference of definition in §4.2.1; more precisely I would suggest that (a) for the Corinthians and for their environment, but not for Paul prophecy was ecstatic; they would not then distinguish comprehensible prophecy and incomprehensible tongues in terms of the presence or absence of the mind and consciousness of what one is saying; rather (b), with their love of wisdom which we shall consider below in §4.4, it is surely unlikely that they would regard the coming of God's spirit as replacing their minds; rather it is likelier that they would regard it as enhancing their rational powers.

And yet that most philosophical of Jews, Philo, does at times seem to share with Paul the view that the human mind is supplanted in ecstasy: the mind is evicted (ἐξοικίζεται) at the arrival of the divine spirit and the

---

Burkert, *Lore* 163, points to the interest of Heraclides and Clearchus (frgs 7 and 8) in shamanic experiences of the soul's independence of the body. Cf. too Suidas' account of Epimenides (E.2471, ed. Adler 2, 370=Diels-Kranz, *Fragmente* §3 A 2) and the life of Pythagoras contained in Phot., *Bibliotheca* 249.438B (Henry 7, 127); also Guthrie, *Greeks* 193–9.

For ecstasy defined as a 'spiritual contemplation' in which the soul leaves the body cf. Chrys., *Hom. in Acta* 22.1 (Migne *PG* 60, 172).

11 Cf. Rohde, *Psyche* 259f, 264; also James, *Religion* 135; against this F. Pfister in *RAC* 4, 952; 'Ekstasis' 183.

12 Cf. Burkert, 'ΓΟΗΣ' 48: in the documented historical period γοητεία (the Greek equivalent of shamanism) is something peripheral.

13 Cf. Iambl., *Myst.* 3.8, οὐ μετὰ διανοίας . . . τῶν λεγόντων.

M. Bouttier, in a response to Dunn, 'Congregation' 247, sees a polemic on Paul's part against the Platonic and Philonic view of inspiration. Pearson, *Terminology* 44, 47, plausibly argues that the Corinthians did not share Paul's distinction between irrational tongues-speaking and rational prophecy; both were for them ecstatic and that is all that mattered to them; cf. Bornkamm, 'Glaube' 133 (ET 38), and the dissertation of N. Engelsen cited by Callan, 'Prophecy' 136f.

14 *Weg* 52f; cf. Fascher, ΠΡΟΦΗΤΗΣ 184, who contrasts the ecstatic prophecy of the Corinthians with types of prophecy found elsewhere in the early church.

divine frenzy (*Rer. div. her.* 265); 'when the light of God shines, the human light sets; when the divine light sets, the human dawns and rises'[15]. In inspiration the prophet's 'reason (λογισμός) withdraws and surrenders the citadel of the soul to a new visitor and tenant, the Divine Spirit (τὸ θεῖον πνεῦμα)'[16]. 'Ecstasy . . . is nothing else than the departing and going out of the understanding'[17]. In this he draws upon a tradition going back to one strand of Plato's view of inspiration[18]: poets are not possessed of their wits (ἔμφρονες) when composing (*Ion* 534A)[19]; when they are inspired (ἔνθεος) they are out of their wits (ἔκφρων) and their mind (νοῦς) is no longer in them (534B)[20]. The god takes away their νοῦς and uses them and soothsayers and divine seers as his servants. Bousset and Greßmann see Philo here as not so much in opposition to Plato as developing his thought: the divine μανία of the philosopher was not in opposition to νοῦς, but for Philo it is[21]. But we shall see that Philo's view of this μανία is not clearly defined. Plato's description of prophecy is also echoed in Lucan's account of the Pythia's trance (5.165–74), and Leisegang points too to the Dionysiac possession which leads Pentheus' wife unwittingly to her gruesome slaughter of her husband in Euripides' *Bacchae*[22].

Plutarch, too, at times speaks of souls having the power to 'range amid the irrational and imaginative realms of the future', This power, however, is only released when one dreams or dies and the rational faculties (τὸ λογιστικὸν καὶ φροντιστικόν) are relaxed and released. The best seers are intelligent and follow the intelligence (νοῦς) that the soul has, and judge

---

15 *Rer. div. her.* 264, tr. Colson-Whitaker.

16 *Spec. leg.* 4.49, tr. Colson-Whitaker; cf. Balaam in *Vit. Mos.* 1.283.

17 *Quaest. in Gen.* 3.9, tr. Marcus; this is a striking change of usage. When Eur., *Ba.* 359, 850, says ἐξέστης φρενῶν/ἔκστησον φρενῶν (cf. 944) it clearly means that the subject departs from her or his wits (F. Pfister in *RAC* 4, 945; for further reff. cf. the following col.), a genit. of separation, but Philo often seems to make the mind the thing that does the departing (contrast *Rer. div. her.* 250); but he seems to have a good Platonic precedent for this alternative image, for in *Ion* 534B to be ἔκφρων means that one's νοῦς is no longer in one.

18 Cf. W. Bieder in *TDNT* 6, 374; on the evaluation of this tradition and what Plato himself believed about such phenomena cf. Dodds, *Greeks* 217f; for the tension in Plato's account see also Fascher cited in n. 26 below.

19 Cf. *Tim.* 71E; *Phaedrus* 244B, where the *mania* of prophetesses is contrasted with the state of σωφρονοῦσαι; also *Leg.*. 4.719C and Cic., *Div.* 1.37.80.

20 So too in *Apol.* 22C 'prophets and givers of oracles' say fine things, but know nothing of what they say, cf. also *Meno* 99D; Leisegang, *Geist* 167, argues that Plato's account of μανία provides the basis for Philo's description of ἔκστασις. Note, however, Fascher's observation that Plato mostly does not suggest that their utterances were unintelligible (ΠΡΟΦΗΤΗΣ 68); it is only in *Tim.* 72AB that μάντεις and prophets are distinguished, with Delphi particularly in mind; there the latter are needed to communicate the sense of the former's utterances.

21 *Religion* 449; cf. R. Meyer in *TDNT* 6, 822 n. 286; Holladay, *Aner* 157f.

22 *Geist* 126 and 128 n.; cf. Eur., *Ba.* 359.

what is probable. Yet the capacity to foretell the future is 'irrational and indeterminate in itself'; it receives impressions and perceptions in advance[23]. The imagery here is not as stark as Philo's; rational thought is not expelled here, but rather only relaxed or suspended, allowing the reception of impressions from a prophetic current ($\dot{\rho}\epsilon\tilde{v}\mu a$) and a most divine spirit ($\pi\nu\epsilon\tilde{v}\mu a$)[24].

Plutarch's insistence on the rationality of the best seers is perhaps in part explained by another passage, *Pyth. or.* 7.397 BC: the oracles at Delphi are not the god's composition, but he merely sets things in motion by imparting visions ($\phi a\nu\tau a\sigma i a\iota$), and then leaves the rest to the natural abilities of the prophetess[25]. (Does some such view of prophecy lie behind Paul's insistence on the evaluation of prophecy in 1 Cor 14.29?)[26] Admittedly some of the mental effort had been made unnecessary by the god's resorting to more prosaic language instead of the extravagant speech of poetry (24.406EF), yet Plutarch is concerned to insist that the prophetic skill is not godless or irrational. The soul is like material worked upon by the spirit that inspires it ($\dot{\epsilon}\nu\theta ov\sigma\iota a\sigma\tau\iota\kappa\dot{o}\nu \pi\nu\epsilon\tilde{v}\mu a$) and the exhalation ($\dot{a}\nu a\theta v\mu i a\sigma\iota\varsigma$?) as an instrument (wielded by the god?) or, changing the metaphor, a plectrum (48.436EF). Even when the divine afflatus has played its tune upon this inert soul, there is still scope for the activity of rational discernment to interpret and apprehend the heavenly message[27].

At other times ecstasy for Philo seems to involve the mind[28] : in *Rer. div. her.* 70 he speaks of the mind ($\delta\iota a\nu o i a$) being under the divine affla-

---

23 *Def. orac.* 40.432CD, tr. Babbitt; cf. the description of the impact of the divine inspiration upon the soul (and body) of the Pythian priestess in *Pyth. or.* 21.404E (cf. Philo, *Ebr.* 147); the bodily impact led to the experience being described in sexual terms: see Burkert, *Homo* 143 (ET 126); H. Kleinknecht in *TDNT* 6, 345; Verbeke, *Évolution* 269–71.

24 Verbeke, ibid. 281, notes the difference between Philo and Plutarch here in that for the former the mind makes way for something higher, for the latter it is, as it were, drugged to allow lower faculties to come into play. Here he thinks Philo is closer to Plato (285f).

25 For Antiphon (in Diels-Kranz, *Fragmente* §87 A 9) prophecy was entirely the opinion of a wise man (cf. Eur. frg. 973 (Nauck); F. Pfister in *RAC* 4, 962; also Gunkel's account of the biblical prophets – cf. R. R. Wilson, 'Prophecy' 322f!).

26 Plato's distinction of the $\dot{a}\phi\rho ov\epsilon\varsigma$ $\mu\dot{a}\nu\tau\epsilon\iota\varsigma$ and the $\ddot{\epsilon}\mu\phi\rho ov\epsilon\varsigma$ $\pi\rho o\phi\tilde{\eta}\tau a\iota$ who judge ($\kappa\rho i\nu\epsilon\iota\nu/\kappa\rho\iota\tau a i$) the inspired utterances of the former springs to mind here (*Tim.* 71E–72B); for further evidence of the need for reason and $\sigma\omega\phi\rho o\sigma\dot{v}\nu\eta$ to evaluate the utterances of prophets and seers cf. Fascher ΠΡΟΦΗΤΗΣ 68f.

27 Cf. the discussion of Socrates' $\delta a\iota\mu\dot{o}\nu\iota ov$ in *Gen. Socr.* 20.588E; also Callan, 'Prophecy' 129; for a discussion of Plutarch's views cf. Fascher, ibid. 70–5: the clear picture of the prophetess as the god's tool in *Pyth. or.* is complicated in *Def. orac.* by the introduction of daemons and of a material element as contributory to enthusiasm; Plutarch's view is not a unity (74).

28 At other times ecstasy is spoken of as a state of the soul (e.g. *Ebr.* 145–50, but n.b. the switch in 152 to speaking of $\nu o\tilde{v}\varsigma$ although 1 Sam 1.15 speaks of $\psi v\chi\dot{\eta}$).
Leisegang, *Geist* 181, rightly notes the tension between the description of ecstasy as replacing the mind in *Rer. div. her.* 264–6 and the earlier stress on the wise as the one worthy to be God's mouthpiece (259); Fascher, ibid. 69, emphasizes the tension in Plato's thought too

tus (ἐνθουσιῶσα) and no longer ἐν ἑαυτῇ²⁹; it is stirred and maddened by
a heavenly desire (ἔρως) and is drawn upwards by the truly existent One
with truth clearing its path for it. The same imagery is evoked by Gen
15.5 in *Leg. all.* 3.40f: God leads out the mind as far as is possible, away
from 'the needs of the body, the organs of sense, specious arguments,
the plausibilities of rhetoric, last of all itself'³⁰. It is led higher and higher
to explore the divine, seeking a change to a better place in which to dwell
(ibid. 84)³¹. In some ways Philo's language here is more like the ἔκτασις
which Pfister distinguishes from ἔκστασις, that is a stretching out (of the
mind here, not the soul) towards the divine³². One point of difference
is the rather perplexing idea of the mind leaving itself (see further n. 38
below). A different idea again is that the dying Moses is transformed from
a compound of soul and body into a single being of mind most like the
sun; as this purest νοῦς he is possessed and prophesies (*Vit. Mos.* 2.288).
The implication of that is that the purest state of the living is when the
mind is most free from the body and the lower soul; then they are readiest
for prophetic ecstasy. Or, in another change of imagery, Philo describes
the soul extending the goblet of its own reason (λογισμός) for the *logos*
to pour into it its own draught (*Som.* 2.249), although the idea of ecstasy
(or 'sober drunkenness' in his striking phrase) is not explicitly mentioned.

In view of the place that *logos*, reason, and rationality have in Philo's
thought, it is only natural that he should thus stress the mind's role in
ecstatic inspiration. It is, for instance, Melchizedek, who is λόγος, reason,
who gives to souls a drink that they may be possessed (κατασχέτοι) by an
intoxication more sober than sobriety itself (*Leg. all.* 3.82)³³. So great is

---

between the rationalist and the mystical. Callan, 'Prophecy' 133f, comments on the different
types of prophecy outlined by *Vit. Mos.* 2.188, ecstatic and non-ecstatic (the latter being
more important in Philo's eyes?). In the visions of Jewish apocalyptic seers too we are told at
times that 'understanding' is granted to the seer before his vision (Hultgård, 'Ecstasy' 219f,
citing *T. Levi* 2.3 and 4 Ezra 5.22).

29 Colson-Whitaker translate 'in its own keeping'; cf. Balaam in Jos., *Ant.* 4.6.5 §118, tr. Thackeray: 'no longer his own master'.

30 So too in Cic., *Divin.* 1.31.66 the *animus* is drawn out from the body in prophetic frenzy (cf.
1.50.113).

31 Cf. *Op. mund.* 69–71; *Conf. ling.* 95, and of the soul or mind in *Ebr.* 152 (it is just the self
in *Spec. leg.* 3.5); Pohlenz, 'Philon' 474, points to the parallel in Sen., *Naturales quaestiones*
1.7–13.
   F. Pfister in *RAC* 4, 951, appeals to the idea of ecstasy as a τροπὴ τοῦ νοῦ in Philo, *Leg all.*
2.31 as evidence of the mind staying in place but being changed; but τροπή can be used of
'putting to flight' as well as 'change'; the following τρέπεται παρά with the accus. which Colson-Whitaker translate 'turning . . . not of his own motion but of God's' surely more naturally
refers to a 'turning towards'.

32 Ibid. 954.

33 *Ebr.* 146 speaks of such a state resulting from grace (χάρις) filling the soul, cf. 147f.
   Also relevant here is Isaac's observation (*Concept* 38) that Philo associated spirit and reason

Philo's stress upon reason and philosophy that some scholars have been unwilling to take seriously or literally his claims to inspiration and ecstasy. Yet in *Migr. Abr.* 34f he describes how sometimes his mind has been barren and bereft of ideas, but at others he has

> suddenly become full, the ideas falling in a shower from above and being sown invisibly, so that under the influence of the Divine possession (ὑπὸ κατοχῆς ἐνθέου) I have been filled with corybantic frenzy and been unconscious of anything, place, persons present, myself, words spoken, lines written. For I obtained language, ideas, an enjoyment of light, keenest vision, pellucid distinctness of objects . . . .[34]

The ideas of Philo are, however, Pohlenz argues, not those of an ecstatic mystic, but simply those of one who follows the conventions of Greek philosophers and uses the language of the ecstatics[35]. For instance Philostratus describes Apollonius as 'divinely inspired (ὑποθειάζων) in his philosophy'[36]. Or more plausibly, as Brandenburger argues[37], Philo was heir to a tradition of wisdom theology which stressed the incapacity of the human mind as it was actually constituted (Wis 9.14f) to grasp the truths of God; some, Philo says (*Som.* 1.118f), presumably endorsing their view or at least not refuting it, hold that the divine *logos* only comes to aid those ready to acknowledge that the νοῦς cannot truly apprehend νοητά (or αἴσθησις αἰσθητά) in its own strength, and ready to let mind and sense-perception 'set' or retire from view, as it were. Be that as it may – for Brandenburger perhaps emphasizes one strand in Philo's all too complex thought to the neglect of others –, Verbeke has noted how Philo's own experience of ecstatic illumination seems to conflict with the otherwise more prominent view in his writings of the divine afflatus as displacing the reason[38]. Here we should note that, if Philo was, as a

---

in a way unparalleled except in 4 Macc 7.13f; cf. also Sandelin, *Auseinandersetzung* 27, pointing to *Plant.* 18 as evidence for the identification of spirit and *logos*.

34 Tr. Colson-Whitaker; cf. *Cher.* 27; *Som.* 2.252 (he hears the voice of the invisible spirit); *Spec. leg.* 3.1–5 (he looks fondly back on the time when he had leisure for philosophy, a time when he could contemplate the universe and all in it, and he seemed to be carried upwards in a sort of inspiration of soul).
  Isaacs, *Concept* 49, 51, argues that for Philo and Jos. this inspiration was not attributed to God's spirit, but that was limited to the canonical prophets and above all to Moses. Yet, if asked, whence would they have derived this experience in the present? And is this not contradicted by Philo, *Som.* 2.252, where Philo hears the invisible πνεῦμα?

35 'Philon' 474; cf. §2.4.2 above; also Jonas, *Gnosis* 2.1, 109, 214; a good example might be Plato, *Crat.* 396D (cf. 428C); but see also the critique in Hegermann, *Vorstellung* 8, 23. Jos. certainly seems to use ἔνθους of himself with all seriousness and meant quite literally (*Bell.* 3.8.3 §353; contrast too Bousset-Greßmann, *Religion* 450).

36 *Vit. Ap.* 1.3.

37 *Fleisch* 131f; cf. 151. One should also compare the attitude of the Qumran *Hodayot* to the ability of human powers to receive the divine; cf. Foerster, 'Geist' 127f; see also Schweizer, *Spirit* 32.

38 *Évolution* 254; cf. Fascher, ΠΡΟΦΗΤΗΣ 160. Philo's difficulties may perhaps be illustrated

rational expositor of the Law of Moses, reluctant to give the divine human mind, 'a portion (ἀπόσπασμα) of that divine and blessed soul' (*Det. pot. ins*. 90), a subordinate or even contrary role to the incursions of the spirit of God[39], then we might expect that the Corinthians, who also set so much store by wisdom, might also be reluctant to remove the mind from any share in any of their spectacular spiritual endowments, even ecstatic speech. Here they may well have parted company with Paul, who held an altogether less uncritical attitude towards both human wisdom and human powers and the gift of esctatic speech.

---

by comparing his seemingly totally paradoxical language about the soul's leaving itself in ecstasy. For not only is it to leave the body, the sense, and speech, but it is told to 'be a fugitive (ἀπόδραθι) from thyself also and issue forth (ἔκστηθι) from thyself' (an exegesis of Gen 12.1), for this is the state of 'persons possessed and corybants' (*Rer. div. her.* 69, tr. Colson-Whitaker – βακχευθεῖσα καὶ θεοφορηθεῖσα κατά τωα προφητικὸν ἐπιθειασμόν); one might compare here *PGM* 4.725f, where the visionary is released from his soul and is no longer in himself. Thus the ἐν ἐαυτῇ which we noted in *Rer. div. her.* 70 could be translated quite literally 'in itself' (compare our idea of 'being beside oneself'?). The soul, too, that is referred to in §69 is presumably the highest part of the soul, the soul of the soul, the mind (*Op. mund.* 66; *Rer. div. her.* 55; *Quaest. in Gen.* 2.59). In keeping with this we read in *Leg. all.* 3.41 of the mind ultimately leaving itself, of Isaac leaving 'himself and his own mind' (νοῦς; in 43 Moses leaves his soul and in 44 the mind leaves the soul, but 'soul' here is probably meant in its wider sense). But in 47 (cf. 48) Philo returns to the mind (διανοία), urging it to leave itself and seek diligently. In 47 that 'itself' is possibly the 'heavy encumbrances of the body or the self-conceits with which the νοῦς is familiar', but even there that is not quite what Philo says (ἀπο σαυτῆς) and in 41 bodily needs and 'itself' are distinguished. The more paradoxical Philo's statements become, the more tempting it is to take the idea of the mind or the soul's not being in itself not quite literally. When Philo tells us (in *Quaest. in Gen.* 3.9) that the mind possessed 'is no longer within itself, for it receives the divine spirit to dwell within it', it is possible that the 'within' here means 'in the power of, under the control of' (as in Colson and Whitaker's translation in *Rer. div. her.* 70 – cf. my 'Observations' 86, §7; F. Pfister in *RAC* 4, 948, suggests that the opposite to ἔξω εἶναι/γίνεσθαι, ἐν ἐαυτῷ γίνεσθαι, means simply 'to come to oneself (to one's senses)' and notes the alternative use of ἐπί with the dat. in Aristotle, *Eth. Eud.* 2.8.21.1225a27. Bevan, *Sibyls* 171, argues that Philo does not think of the suspension of the human mind *qua* percipient but only *qua* active.

More restrained is the language used in *Som.* 1.60 of a self-despair, a recognition of the nothingness of all created things, as a precondition for a perception of the One who exists (Jonas, *Gnosis* 2.1, 100, seems to go further than Philo actually does when he speaks of a 'Todesmoment' in Philonic ecstasy; this may be true elsewhere, however: Lewis, *Religion* 58).

But we are left with the impression of two contradictory images struggling with one another in Philo's thought, that of the mind leaving the body so that the divine spirit may replace it, presumably in the body, and that of the mind leaving the body in order that there, independent of the body, it may receive the divine afflatus; these two images also seem to correspond, at least partially, to the two basic forms of the union of humanity and deity in antiquity as Reitzenstein, *Mysterienreligionen* 381, describes them, the raising of humanity to God or the descent of God into humanity; cf. L. de Heusch in Lewis, ibid. 50; R. R. Wilson, 'Prophecy' 325. To attempt to combine the two, as well as to combine rational and irrational views of prophecy, is surely over-ambitious.

39 Bevan, ibid. 151, points out that the idea that the divine had displaced and superseded the soul of the one possessed 'would tend to a low view of the human soul' and also, we may add, of the human mind.

The presence in Philo, too, of the motif of the 'heavenly journey' of the mind towards God is all the more significant as a clue to the beliefs of the Corinthians in view of the signs of their belief that their spiritual endowment enabled them to converse in angelic languages (1 Cor 13.1). What they experienced in religious ecstasy Philo expresses in more intellectual terms: in his philosophical work he seemed borne upwards to accompany the heavenly bodies, to gaze down upon earthly things and the cares of mortal life (*Spec. leg.* 3.1f). As God is to the world so too the divine mind in human beings contemplates all things, ascending to the ether and the heavens, and reaching out even beyond them to the intelligible world, seeing sights there which fill that mind with an ecstatic frenzy. It could even see God himself were it not dazzled by the pure light streaming from him (*Op. mund.* 69–71)[40].

The temptation to compare with the ecstatic experiences of both the Corinthians and Philo the shaman's experience of the soul's leaving the body is all the stronger here since this journey of the soul is often viewed as a source of supernatural wisdom and knowledge[41]. This too is true of some of the figures from the Greek world who are often compared with shamans[42]: Suidas records the reputation of Epimenides, that his soul left his body and returned just as it pleased, 'wise in matters divine with a wisdom concerning inspiration and initiation'[43]. Hermotimus of Clazomenae's soul would leave his body, journeying to great distances and bringing back mantic lore and knowledge of the future[44]. There is,

---

40 Cf *Spec. leg.* 2.45 on the winged souls of those practising wisdom who tread the ether and contemplate the powers there; Plato *Phaedrus* 249C, also speaks of the winged mind of the philosopher. Cf. also *Corp. Herm.* 11.20; 13.11; *Anth. Pal.* 9.577; Cic., *Divin.* 1.50–1.114f; *PGM* 4.537ff (a passage which has certain suggestive parallels with Lucius' brief summary of his initiation ceremony in Apul., *Met.* 11.23); *Orphica* 26–31 (M. Lafargue in Charlesworth, *Pseudepigrapha* 2, 799); Pseudo-Aristotle, *Mund.* 1.391a11–16; Jones, 'Posidonius' 98, describes this idea of an imaginative flight of the mind through the universe as a philosophical commonplace.

41 Cf. Eliade, *Birth* 95, and *Chamanisme* esp. chaps 4, 6, 8f – he warns that this aspect in itself is not limited to shamans – see esp. 428f (ET 493), but significantly he adds that what distinguishes them is that they achieve their ascent by ecstasy. Cf. also Bevan, *Sibyls* 134; Halifax, *Voices* 19. Nearer to Paul's world still is that of the seers of the apocalypses: Dean-Otting, *Journeys* 4, remarks that different accounts of their heavenly ascents in Hellenistic Judaism are bound together by the idea that in those ascents one learns the secrets of the cosmos and gains a knowledge that is normally beyond human reach. She distinguishes these ascents from the shamanic by the fact that they are not theurgically induced (ibid. 27).

42 Cf. n. 10 above and Guthrie, *Greeks* 193–9; Jones, 'Posidonius', lists instances where 'by a supernatural ascent the soul of a living man gains visions which belong to souls not yet incarnate and to souls freed from the stains of the body' (99).

43 Ed. Adler 2, 370=E.2471 s.v. Ἐπιμενίδης=Diels-Kranz, *Fragmente* §3 A 2; Plut., *Solon* 12 7.84D (tr. Perrin 12.4: 'with a mystical and heaven-sent wisdom'); cf. Rohde, *Psyche* 331 n. 116 (see nn. 117f for further reff. to his resultant wisdom).

44 Pliny, *Hist. nat.* 7.52.174 (n.b. also ref. to Aristeas of Proconnesus – cf. Max. Tyr. 10.2.53a;

too, Plato's myth of Er (*Resp.* 10.614B–621B), and the other-worldly insights that Er gained by his 'death'. Timarchus, too, is described as undergoing an experience in the cave of Trophonius very similar to some accounts of shamanic soul-wanderings[45].

This comparison of the Corinthians' claims with those of shamans becomes all the more significant when we note Eliade's observation that 'shamans are "elect ones" and as such they have access to a sacred zone inaccessible to other members of the community'[46]. That seems an apt parallel to the impression left by the tongues-speaking Corinthians upon the ἰδιῶται of 1 Cor 14.16 and quite possibly to the estimate which the former held of their own status, particularly if they believed their tongues to be the language of heaven and their ecstatic worship to be a communicating with the heavenly realm. Without wishing to call the Corinthians shamans, I would suggest that their in many ways rather similar experiences produced similar attitudes in themselves and in those around them.

One can also here compare the again rather similar experiences which the ancients believed that one had in dreams, a similarity that is underlined by the fact that Leisegang can choose to illustrate the process of divine ecstasy as Philo sees it by looking at the latter's account of Jacob's dream at Haran (*Som.* 1.2–188)[47]. Likewise Cicero links prophecy and dreams by the fact that in both the *animus* has nothing to do with the body[48]. He also includes the famous example of a dream as a source of heavenly knowledge in his account of Scipio's dream in his *Republic*[49]. Xenophon too holds that in sleep the human soul is revealed at its most divine as it looks forward into the future in freedom (*Cyrop.* 8.7.21)[50]. Symptomatic of this close similarity between dreams and ecstasy is Hultgård's perplexity in deciding in a given case in Jewish apocalyptic texts whether references to sleep mean that the seer in question had a vision in a dream or whether 'sleep' is used as a metaphor for ecstasy[51].

In summary: the evidence of Philo which we have looked at in this section seems to be confused and conflicting[52]; this is in part due to the strangeness of the phenomena involved, but is also the product of an

---

38.3.132*a*; Suidas s.v.=A.3900; cf. Jones, 'Posidonius' 106); cf. Bevan, *Sibyls* 50; Rohde, ibid. 331 n 112.

45 Plut., *Gen. Socr.* 21–2.590A–592D; cf. Lucian, *Icaromenippus.*

46 *Chamanisme* 21 (ET 7).

47 *Geist* 207; cf. Bevan, *Sibyls* chap. 6.

48 *Divin* 1.50–1. 113–17 (cf. 1.30.63).

49 *Rep.* 6.9.9–end.

50 Cf. Pindar frg. 131 (96)=115f (Bowra).

51 'Ecstasy' 220f.

52 Cf. W. Bieder in *TDNT* 6, 374f.

allegorical exegesis : the text suggests different images, often conflicting ones, at different times. Yet the confusion would not have arisen had there not also been an underlying uncertainty as to the nature of the phenomena, a lack of a clear perception of its nature, such as we also noted in Paul (2 Cor 12.2f). The text of *Quis rerum divinarum heres sit* seems to reveal a fundamental inconsistency concerning the experience and the evaluation of the role of the mind in the highest, most divine form of ecstasy: is it ousted and displaced (as seemingly in Paul's view of ecstatic speaking in tongues), or is it that which sallies forth, leaving behind the impediments of earthly existence to commune with God and penetrate the mysteries of the heavenly world? Is it irrelevant to the imparting of divine truth, or is it, on the contrary, precisely that in human nature which is capable of receiving what God has to bestow? It is perhaps because he was aware of this tension that Philo insists paradoxically that ultimately the mind must leave itself behind. Leisegang plausibly traces Philo's difficulties here to his attempt to unite two very different concepts, the popular belief in the entry of demons or gods into the human soul, and Plato's view of the ascent of the mind to the world of the ideas[53]. Rather than following this distinction of popular and Platonic one may, however, be better to heed Bevan when he states that these two beliefs are two versions of 'the philosophic theory of inspiration', one in which 'the utterance was held to come from the soul of the ecstatic raised to abnormal powers of clairvoyance', the other in which it came 'from a wholly different personality which had superseded, for the time being, the soul of the ecstatic, and spoke through his lips'[54].

Plutarch's account too is not without tension when he insists on the rationality of the best seers, for, if the condition for the reception of the impressions of the future involves a relaxation of the mind's rational control, one might well think that the less rational one was the better[55]. This tension is, however, resolved more or less satisfactorily by his theory of co-operation between the divine and the human: the human reason is left to make sense of the impressions and revelations received.

We seem here, then, to have a range of interpretations of the phenomenon of ecstasy which extends from, at the one end, a replacement of the

---

53 *Geist* 182; cf. 206.
54 *Sibyls* 134 — on 171f he finds different Greek antecedents for these views which tie in more closely with Leisegang's distinction: one linking on to 'Greek ideas of μαντική, the Delphic oracle, and so on; the other links on to the Platonic doctrine that the soul, when free from the body, rapturously contemplates the eternal ideas . . .'. The point to be noted here is that the former is not only 'popular' as opposed to 'philosophic' or even 'Platonic', for it has left its mark on Plato too.
55 Cf. Plato, *Phaedrus* 244AB.

human mind by a divine spirit which uses the body and in particular the tongue of the one possessed as an instrument upon which it can play to, at the other, a view of it as an experience of purest rationality. So Philo sees Moses, as we saw above, as transformed at his departure from this life into mind most like the sun (*Vit. Mos.* 2.288), an experience which Leisegang is probably right to regard as the acme of ecstatic experience[56]. In between lie views which see ecstasy as involving a varying degree of participation by the mind, and which also estimate its value differently; this is further complicated by the differing views held of rationality and differing estimates of its value and importance.

For Paul, we saw, there is an absence of mind in tongues-speaking and consequently, if not a disparagement, at least a playing down of its value within the Christian community. That tongues-speaking was a problem at Corinth seems to indicate, however, that the Corinthians placed a rather different value upon it. We do not know whether they held that the mind was inactive during it or not, or even whether they had considered the question; after all Philo gives the impression of being in two minds on the matter. Perhaps, too, they had not considered its value to the community, but they were confident of its value to themselves, and we can be reasonably confident that they held that it enhanced the wisdom by which they set such great store (see § 4.4) rather than detracted from it, and indeed that it may have been the very source of that wisdom. One can perhaps therefore go further than Wilckens does when he observes[57] that the spiritual manifestations in early Christianity were not completely irrational, but included knowledge of the 'deep things of God', imparted in the rational λόγος σοφίας or λόγος γνώσεως, as well as in irrational tongues-speaking. For that is to accept Paul's estimate and distinction. I repeat: one cannot know what the Corinthians thought of this matter, but they would have had at least one strand of Philo's thinking about ecstasy on their side had they felt ecstatic speaking in tongues was also thoroughly rational, an enhancement of their powers of comprehension of the otherwise unseen mysteries of God.

4.2.3. Particularly in the passages of Plutarch which were considered in the previous section, with their language of 'streams' and 'exhalations' as well as 'breath' (πνεῦμα), it was noticeable how *impersonally* the spirit was conceived which was responsible for prophetic inspiration: it is impersonal in its nature and impersonal in its manner of impinging upon

---

56 *Geist* 168.
57 '1 Kor 2,1–16' 523.

humans[1]. It was, for instance, an instrument or plectrum (*Pyth. or.* 48.436F) manipulated presumably by Apollo to work upon the receptive soul of the prophetess. If this idea is less prominent in Philo[2], it is even less to be found in Paul, for whom the presence of the spirit is the presence of God or the presence of Christ (cf. Rom 8.9–11; 1 Cor 3.16; 6.19; 2 Cor 3.17)[3]. Ecstasy, however, as the presence of a god in the person of the one possessed was an idea readily intelligible to the Graeco-Roman world[4]; here the experiences and convictions of popular religion in that world and those of the Judaeo-Christian tradition converge: the differences concern rather the nature and character of the god who is thus present, whether he can be conceived of materially or not, and whether he possess ethical qualities or not, and, if so, to what degree, and how he reacts with human beings, whether forcing himself upon them or inviting them to respond[5].

However, from an impersonal view of the spirit, be it conceived of materially or immaterially, there could easily arise the idea that its benefits and effects were automatically conferred, automatically received; its presence could be detached from the grace of the God who gave it and whose presence it was. Jewett therefore rightly refers to a (he says 'the' which perhaps goes too far) 'typical Hellenistic misunderstanding about the Spirit' in that it 'was understood in an enthusiastic . . . manner as divine power which takes man over and grants him immediate immortal-

---

Notes on 4.2.3

1 For Verbeke, *Évolution* 255, Plutarch's 'mantic spirit' is very differently conceived from Philo's 'prophetic spirit'; the former is but an exhalation found at certain places; cf. 279f. Cf. also Pseudo-Aristotle, *Mund.* 4.395b26–9.

  Leisegang, however, comments (*Geist* 30) on the difficulty Philo found in liberating himself entirely from the 'hylozoistisch' ideas of Greek philosophy, and Käsemann, 'Doctrine' 115, 117 (17, 19) seems to suggest that Paul too had similar problems.

2 Leisegang, ibid. esp. 141, argues that Philo tended to avoid πνεῦμα precisely because of its material connotations. Cf. also Brandenburger, *Fleisch* 128; Hoffmann, *Toten* 82. Tobin, *Creation* 82, finds in *Rer. div. her.* 283 a criticism of Stoic views of the soul and the ether composing it precisely because they seemed to make it too material.

3 As also to some extent in Philo and Jos. – cf. Isaacs, *Concept* 25 (contrast Reitzenstein, *Mysterienreligionen* 337f); arguably this is true, too, of the Old Testament: cf. Schniewind, 'Antwort' 115f (cf. ET 94): 'The sphere of that which is traced to the spirit . . . ranges in the Old Testament from warfare and artistic skill to renewal of the heart. One speaks of the spirit everywhere that one experiences the *immediate presence* of the God who is *known from his revelation*. Thus it is not a matter of the "supernatural" as such, but of God's direct activity.' But one should also note Fascher's point, that the Jewish tradition avoided speaking of God's being in a person, preferring instead to speak of his spirit entering a person (see §4.2.2 n. 1).

4 Cf. Eur., *Ba.* 300 again and the reff. in §4.2.2 n. 3.

5 Cf. H. Kleinknecht in *TDNT* 6, 359: 'The secular Greek concept of πνεῦμα, whether understood physiologico-cosmologically, mantico-enthusiastically or in the last resort spiritually, is distinguished from the NT concept by the fact that the God who stands behind it is quite different'. Cf. Hermann, *Kyrios* 124f.

ity'[6]. This will be all the more significant when we come to consider the Corinthians' views of Christian rites in §4.5.

4.3. The Eschatological Gift of the Spirit

4.3.1. The pagan parallels considered in the previous section, and perhaps the Jewish ones too, were all of temporary phenomena, episodic possession by a deity or a spiritual force. However we saw that it was likely that the Corinthians dubbed themselves 'spiritual', implying *a more permanent possession of God's spirit*. Indeed Paul may have been accustomed to refer to some Christians, and perhaps, at least initially, to all, by this term. Not that this difference of usage need be absolute; after all the term 'prophet' was applied, not to those who prophesied all the time, strictly speaking, but presumably rather to those who did so regularly or habitually. The term 'spiritual' could then have been applied to those who regularly, but still only temporarily, manifested the powers of the spirit at work in them.

But Paul's expectation of the presence of the spirit differs markedly from this, especially when he insists that the spirit must be present in those who confess that 'Jesus is Lord' (1 Cor 12.3); since a Christian's whole life is lived out before the Lord and in acknowledgment of him (e.g. Rom 14.8f; Phil 1.20f), it is inevitable that that whole life should be seen as fashioned and moulded by the spirit. That is implicit in a passage like Rom 8.9−11: in 9*b* Paul says that one cannot belong to Christ without having his spirit; the converse would be equally true in his eyes, for if we have Christ, if he is in us, then 'the spirit is life, although our bodies may have been slain by sin (v 10)[1]; that 'spirit is 'the spirit of the One who raised Jesus from the dead' (v 11*a*). For if we are made alive by that spirit then we should also live our lives by it (Gal 5.25), though that by no means follows inevitably.

---

6 'Agitators' 210f apropos of Gal 5.25; cf. Käsemann, 'Doctrine' 115−17 (17−19).

Notes on 4.3.1

1 That is to take πνεῦμα in 10*c* as the indwelling divine spirit of 9*ab* and 11*a*, and not as spirit in the anthropological sense. For in the latter case I would expect 'our spirit is alive/lives', not 'the spirit is life' (='gives life'?); cf. Barrett, *Rom* 159. At most Paul is sliding over into an anthropological usage in which the spirit that gives us life is Christ's spirit in us; whether he goes so far as to make it mean the Christian's self determined by − but still distinct from? − Christ's spirit seems more doubtful (but cf. Wilckens, *Röm* 2, 132f and n. 543).

At the same time there was very likely a further element in early Christian beliefs about the spirit, shared by Paul and many others, which could not but have encouraged the use of 'spiritual' to refer to a permanent feature of Christian experience: that element was the belief that the spirit was the power of God poured out in the end-time and characterizing that end-time. As they believed that they were living in that end-time, it was all too understandable that the presence of that spirit should be seen as permanently marking their lives and experience.

For it seems to have been a conviction common to most, if not all, early Christians that the presence among them of the working of the spirit was a sign of their living 'in the last days' (Acts 2.17). Its presence in the individual's life is for Paul a 'pledge' of ultimate redemption (2 Cor 5.5; cf. 1.22) and for the author of Ephesians a 'pledge' of the inheritance of God's people, rightly described as 'a spirit of promise' (1.13f; cf. 4.30)[2]. Paul also uses the image of the 'first-fruits' to describe the spirit's presence as a token of the future redemption of the body (Rom 8.23), an image which he had used in 1 Cor 15 to describe the relation of Christ, the final Adam (v 45) to the rest of humanity who waited to share his resurrection (v 20). For the writer of Hebrews too the arrival of our salvation is attested by 'signs and wonders and miracles of all sorts and by the distribution of gifts of the holy spirit' (2.3f). Isaacs also sees in the Fourth Gospel as well as Paul the belief that 'πνεῦμα is associated with the dawning of the Messianic Age'[3]. That is correct, for entry into God's kingdom is only possible through birth of water and spirit (Jn 3.5), and the coming and now present 'hour' is one of worship of the Father 'in spirit and truth' (4.23).

Jewish expectations of the end do at least hint at a role to be played in it by the outpouring of God's spirit, but it can hardly be said that they do much more than hint at this, and Jesus himself perhaps did even less to encourage such hopes[4]. God's spirit, perhaps seen as a scorching, des-

---

2 Isaacs, *Concept* 87 n. 32, compares Gal 3.14, but 'the promise of the spirit' is more likely to refer to the spirit which has been promised, whereas in the context Ephesians' phrase may refer to a spirit whose presence is in itself a promise of things to come – so Bruce, *Eph* 265; Masson, *Eph* 147f (and n. 8 against those who simply translate the phrase as 'promised spirit'). Rowland, *Origins* 209, compares *t. Soṭa* 13.2 (?better 13.3f), where the idea is rather of the withholding of God's spirit even from deserving individuals, since the age was unworthy of it.

3 *Concept* 100; cf. 86.

4 So Isaacs, ibid. 84: 'πνεῦμα plays very little part in the eschatological thinking of the period', citing E. Sjöberg in *TDNT* 6, 384f, on the paucity of reff. in the apocryphal and pseudepigraphal literature; he does point, however, to the prominence of Ezekiel's prophecies in rabbinic expectations of the end-time. Cf. Foerster, 'Geist' 119.

The spirit was singularly and surprisingly inconspicuous in Jesus' teaching; cf. Barrett, *Spirit passim*, esp. 160; Schweizer, *Spirit* 47; but cf. K. Berger in *TRE* 12, 178f; Dunn, *Jesus* chaps 3f; Isaacs, *Concept* 139–42.

troying wind, is seen both as an instrument of judgment (Isa 4.4; 11.4; 30.28) and a means of salvation (Isa 26.18, LXX; 34.16). According to Isa 44.3 God had promised to pour out his spirit on Israel's descendants and his blessing on their offspring[5]. Ezekiel has God promising a new or different heart and a new spirit[6], but it remains unclear whether this 'spirit' is anthropological in sense or refers to an outpouring of the divine spirit or whether one should pose these as alternatives at all; should one rather speak of God's 'apportioned spirit'[7]? Above all there is the prophecy of Joel 2.28–32 (LXX 3.1–5) quoted in Peter's speech in Acts 2.17–21, where the fact that this is a mark of the end-time is underlined by changing Joel's 'after these things' to 'in the last days'. This text in Joel Isaacs describes as a 'universalizing' of earlier prophetic experience[8].

This theme continues in intertestamental Judaism: in *T. Levi* 18.11, in the days of the 'new priest' (18.2), 'the spirit of holiness shall be upon them', i.e. the saints, and in *T. Judah* 24.3 Judah tells his children that not only will God pour out the spirit on 'the star from Jacob', a sinless man from his race (24.1)[9], but that God will pour out 'the spirit of grace'

---

5 Cf. 32.15.

6 11.19; 36.26f; 37.14; cf. *4 Ezra* 6.26; *Jub.* 1.23.

7 11.19 and 36.26 seem to be anthropological with a 'different/new heart' and a 'new spirit' as parallels; 36.27 and 37.14, on the other hand, clearly speak of God's spirit; the echo of Gen 2.7 that has been seen here (e.g. by Zimmerli, *Ezek* 2, 257; cf. 261) suggests, however, that this is a revivification of humanity to be what God wanted it to be; it is not a 'supernatural' endowment except in the sense that all are 'supernaturally' endowed, i.e. owe their lives to One over and above them. The juxtaposition of 36.26 and 36.27 suggests that the alternatives 'anthropological' and 'theological' are misleading here.

Very suggestive here is Schade's allusion to *Gen. Rab.* 14.8 with its contrast of the inbreathing of soul into Adam in Gen 2.7 and the eschatological inbreathing of spirit in Ezek 37.14. He suggests that the Corinthians knew Paul's exegesis of Gen 2.7 in these terms, but misunderstood him to mean that the new being was not just already secured, but also realized (*Christologie* 79). This collocation of the two texts, Gen 2.7 with its reference to ψυχή and Ezek 37.14 with its reference to God's πνεῦμα bestowed in the end-time, is surely a more likely explanation of the contrast of ψυχικός and πνευματικός than one which concentrates on the exegesis of Gen 2.7 alone (cf. Pearson, *Terminology*; Wilckens, '1 Kor 2,1–16' 531–3); for Gen 2.7 alone cannot explain why ψυχή and πνεῦμα should be contrasted, for there it is apparently the presence of the latter (or πνοή) that results in Adam's becoming a living ψυχή. Cf. further W. H. Schmidt in *TRE* 12, 172, who also compares Ezekiel's vision with Gen 2.7. Yet with Pearson, ibid., and Horsley, 'Pneumatikos', as well as Brandenburger, *Fleisch* 135, 141, it is right to see Hellenistic Jewish wisdom circles that despaired of the unaided powers of human wisdom and intellect to comprehend the divine as the source of the framework of ideas, if not of the vocabulary, of this distinction. It is perhaps significant that this terminology emerges in early Christianity with its heightened eschatological expectation and awareness; this may have made it the readier to appropriate what was promised for the human race at the end in Ezekiel's prophecies.

8 *Concept* 83.

9 The endowment of God's servant and agent with the spirit is found in Isa 11.2; 42.1; 61.1, and is given an eschatological reference in *Pss. Sol.* 17.37(42); 18.7(8); *1 Enoch* 49.3 (and of

on them as well. *Jubilees* 1.23 foretells a time when Israel will return to their God and he will create for them a holy spirit to prevent them forsaking him again. The writer of the Qumran *Hodayoth* too is conscious of God's holy spirit upon him (1QH 7.6f; 12.12; 13.18f; 14.13; 16.9, 11f), and the *Community Rule* foretells a time when God will intervene to end all evil and will purge 'some of the sons of men' or 'the human frame' of all wickedness by a spirit of holiness, and will shed upon them or it the spirit of truth (1QS 4.21)[10].

It may be largely due to its lack of interest in eschatology that Hellenistic Judaism says little about the spirit in such a context[11]. However Book 4 of the *Sibylline Oracles* speaks of a day of judgment, after which the righteous will remain on earth 'and God will give them spirit and life and favor at once'[12]. It is also true that Hellenistic Judaism had within its possession the Septuagint with its scattered prophecies of an eschatological outpouring of God's spirit[13], ready to be used by an offshoot of Greek-speaking Judaism like the Greek-speaking early Christians, for whom the experience of spiritual phenomena had become characteristic and of central importance.

The relative prominence of the spirit of God in the lives of the earliest Christians and the interpretation of it as a sign of the end-time is thus not easily explicable on the grounds of Old Testament and Jewish inter-testamental beliefs that the outpouring of this spirit would be characteristic of the final age. For these references are, I feel, too isolated and sporadic to explain the centrality of the Christian conviction that this was how God's new age was now manifest, unless the spiritual phenomena that they experienced had first impelled them to seek some explanation

---

Enoch in 91.1); *T. Levi* 18.7; cf. further W. H. Schmidt in *TRE* 12, 172, and Foerster, 'Geist' 119.

Some see a reference to the Messiah mediating the spirit to God's elect in CD 2.12: so Charles translates 'through His Messiah He shall make them know His holy spirit' (2.10 in *Apocrypha* 2, 804), but Lohse emends the text to read מֹשִׁיחֵי and translates 'he taught them through those anointed by his holy spirit', i.e. the prophets; cf. 6.1; Rabin sees also a reference to the prophets here, but takes 'the holy spirit' to be the object of 'make known' (he sees in מֹשִׁיחוֹ an example of the plural suffix written without *yodh* — ed. 8).

10 The problems of this passage are enormous, concentrating upon the words in line 20,

אִישׁ מִכְּנֵי לוֹ וְזֵקֵק גֶּבֶר מַעֲשֵׂי כֹּל ... אֵל יְבָרֵר

with the succession of apparently singular pronominal suffixes. Contrast Vermes ('God will ... purify every deed of Man ...; he will refine for Himself the human frame ... his flesh ...') and Lohse (God will 'alle Werke des Menschen läutern und wird sich einige aus den Menschenkindern reinigen ... ihres Fleisches ...', cf. Wernberg-Møller, *Manual* 27, who then continues 'His flesh', cf. 85f). Principally the argument is over whether there is a reference to several people (*geber* taken collectively) or to an individual, a messianic figure. Cf. here in general Foerster, 'Geist' 126—32.

12 4.46, tr. J. J. Collins in Charlesworth, *Pseudepigrapha* 1, 385; cf. 4.189 (389).

13 Cf. Isaacs, *Concept* 83.

from the scriptures of what was happening in their midst. In other words, their conviction can only be plausibly explained if it was what they inter- preted as the outpouring of God's spirit 'in the last days' that had driven them to the Old Testament to seek an explanation; just as the disciples, in all probability taken by surprise and mystified by Jesus' death, sought an explanation in the Old Testament after his resurrection, so, perhaps equally mystified by the outbursts of ecstasy in their midst, they then sought the explanation for that too in the same scriptures.

This assertion that God's spirit had come finally and irrevocably, and had taken up residence in the lives of God's people might well have sounded strange to the ears of non-Jewish audiences. When speaking of ecstatic phenomena they were more accustomed to think of temporary, episodic irruptions of the divine into the human consciousness; the presence of the divine in all people from birth to death, which could be spoken of as 'spirit' (as an alternative to 'soul'), particularly under Stoic influence, was something quite different from the exceptional bestowal of the spirit of prophecy and ecstasy which remained 'an exceptional phenomenon imparted only in special circumstances to the elect'[14]. One has the impression of two quite different spheres of usage of the term 'spirit' in Greek literature with little or no attempt made to define the relationship of the one to the other. Early Christian assertions about their possession of the divine spirit would seem to combine the permanency of the first with the ecstasy of the latter.

What was true of the non-Jewish and non-Christian world would be true for Philo too, to a certain extent; for him human beings' possession of God's spirit, in the sense of an external, inspirational force, was episodic and could not be permanent (and hence it comes as no surprise that he does not know of a class of people who are 'spiritual')[15]. Yet this creates

---

14 H. Kleinknecht in *TDNT* 6, 358.

15 *Gig.* 19f (it does not remain for ever παρὰ τοῖς πολλοῖς ἡμῖν); cf. 28, 53 (only one sort of people enjoys the presence of the spirit, those who have divested themselves of created things and come with naked mind to God, like Moses), 55; *Deus imm.* 2; *Quaest. in Gen.* 1.90; yet in *Gig.* 47 he apparently still hopes to share Moses' experience. We will see, moreover, in §4.4 that Moses' experience was not one of continuous ecstasy (*Vit. Mos.* 1.175). Cf. Isaacs, *Concept* 19, 38, 46.

It is a weakness of Horsley, 'Pneumatikos', that although he heaps up parallels in Philo to other characteristics of the Corinthians, the designation of someone as 'spiritual' and the contrast with ψυχικός are unparalleled there. That needs further explanation – cf. n. 7 above and §4.4 below. It seems to me a dangerous assumption by Leisegang, *Geist* 224, that Philo knew of a class of 'spiritual' or 'gnostic' people, but chose ὁρατικοί instead to avoid the pagan connota- tions of the former terms; yet he grants that our first evidence of a group called πνευματικοί is late (indeed this term starts for us its history in this sense with Paul); cf. too Bieler, ANHP 2, 36; Jonas, *Gnosis* 2.1, 114. Sandelin also criticizes the view of Pascher, 'Οδός 129ff, that *Leg. all.* 1.31f, 37f, describes, not the creation of the natural man (as Philo says it does), but

a tension with those passages where he speaks seemingly of that same spirit as the stuff of the human mind or even of the soul, as we shall see in §§4.3.2 and 4.4, for that surely presupposes that all members of the human species have this spirit, however little they may use it (and thus the human race is divided into two sorts, those who do and those who do not — *Rer. div. her.* 57)[16]. This problem presumably arises because Philo is heir to a complex πνεῦμα-tradition, and in particular to one which embraces both the strands of Greek thought just mentioned, the spirit which inspires the few, the poets, seers and prophets, and also the spirit which plays a role in natural science and anthropology and is present everywhere and in everyone. Verbeke is, however, right to recognize that the Old Testament too, with its accounts both of the universal endowment of the human race in Gen 2.7 with the spirit of God and its accounts of the special endowment of prophets with seemingly this same spirit, had a decisive influence on Philo's pneumatology and shares no little responsibility for his incoherence[17]. Philo himself seems to acknowledge a twofold sense of πνεῦμα in *Gig.* 22, a physical sense of 'air' (which he here finds in Gen 1.2)[18] and the knowledge which every wise person has. That distinction is, however, inadequate to encompass the whole variety of senses in which he uses the term. But, at any rate, Wolfson is, in my view, correct to distinguish 'divine spirit' in the context of prophecy from the same term 'where the subject of discussion is the rational soul of man'[19]: the relationship between the two is not altogether clear in Philo's thought, nor are his statements about the two easily reconciled.

Yet even if the prophetic spirit remains for Philo something episodic and transitory, at least for most people, and especially for contemporaries whom he was not so inclined to idealize, two things can be said here; the

---

that of the heavenly man or the *pneumatikos*; rather Adam is seen as a (perfect) wise man (*Auseinandersetzung* 35f) as well as (elsewhere in the tractate) as one not yet perfected.

16 That is true here even when limiting πνεῦμα to the rational element in the soul; when one seeks to unify Philo's usage and to include the whole gamut of πνεῦμα-induced manifestations, as Laurentin does ('Pneuma' 397f), the problem is greater still: 'This pneuma causes all who possess it to be what they are — to the sick it gives his sickness, to the unfortunate his gaspings and anguish, to the Indian snakes a cruel greed, to athletes strength, to Moses' serpent the voraciousness to devour all the ones which the magicians had arraigned against him; and finally it is this breathing (πνεῦμα), this *aspiration,* or inspiration which allows Moses to pronounce divine words'. But then what are we to make of the affirmation that this spirit always bears the divine image (433)? Leisegang, ibid. 114, is on firmer ground in pointing to a striking contradiction here.

17 *Évolution* esp. 254, 257–9; cf. Leisegang, ibid. 76, but contrast 114f.

18 Cf. the definitions of 'spirit of God' in *Quaest. in Gen.* 1.90 (cf. *Det. pot. ins.* 83); presumably what Philo means here is that the sense of 'spirit' in question is not air in motion but the other (cf. Leisegang, ibid. 42).

19 *Philo* 2, 26f; but cf. 30f: the two are 'of the same nature and of the same order of existence'.

first, in anticipation of §4.4, is that the effects of those episodic and transitory experiences of inspiration live on and remain with their recipients, making them more specially gifted than their fellows, and in particular making them wise. The second is that, as we have seen, the early Christians set things on a different level to Philo – even in a different age! – by their contention that the final, eschatological outpouring of God's spirit had taken place and was continuing to take place in their experience. That was not, could not be, something merely transitory and episodic; it was final and enduring – by definition –, even if many of its more striking manifestations were not. If the confession of Jesus' lordship is the crucial criterion for the presence and activity of the eschatologically bestowed spirit of God, as Paul argues in 1 Cor 12.3, then, as we saw at the beginning of this section, that spirit is present in every aspect and at all points in a Christian's life, and not just at certain high points of ecstatic experience. That belief marked him and other early Christians off both from pagan experiences of ecstasy and from Philo, with his almost total reticence about the eschatological dimension to Jewish beliefs, let alone about any present realization of final hopes[20]. The elitism of some Corinthian Christians, on the other hand, may have been a reversion to views of spirit-possession current in the Graeco-Roman world, which saw it as present only in episodic and often spectacular bursts of ecstasy. Such a view withdrew the right to be considered 'spiritual' from those whose only claim to the possession of the divine spirit was the seemingly more prosaic one of acknowledging Christ's lordship, and was only manifested in more mundane gifts which were yet of great (for Paul, greater) service to the congregation. It is against such a position that Paul must argue in 1 Corinthians 12: God's spirit is in all who confess Jesus as their Lord, and it manifests itself in all sorts of ways, by no means all of them spectacular or overtly supernatural.

4.3.2. If, then, the spirit that was at work amongst the new Christian congregations was the eschatological outpouring of God's spirit that had been expected, what did they believe that it did to them? What did they believe that it gave them? One obvious answer would be spiritual gifts, speaking in tongues, prophecy, working miracles and the like. But these are episodic in character. What did they have when they were not speaking in tongues, prophesying or working miracles? It is unlikely that they

---

20 Cf. Wilckens, '1 Kor 2,1–16' 515 (although he only mentions Paul as differing from Philo in this respect, the same would be true of other Christians too, and especially those whom Paul had taught; he also mentions only the sudden appearance of ecstasy for Philo, but a corollary of this is the absence of spirit-possession at other times).

believed that they had 'resurrection', for, as we saw in the previous chapter, that term would at least initially have been seen in very literal and physical terms; one did not have it or need it unless one had very literally and physically died first, and anyway many non-Jewish Christians may have felt unsure whether they wanted it even then either, if it meant the renewal of their bondage to the body.

Another answer to which we will turn in the following section is 'wisdom', but a broader and more inclusive answer might be *'life'*[1]. After all Paul himself was accustomed to speak of the spirit as 'life-giving' (1 Cor 15.45; 2 Cor 3.6), and that was not a peculiarity of his[2]. It was a belief shared by other New Testament writers (Jn 6.63; 1 Pet 3.18), by Philo (*Op. mund.* 30; *Quaest. in Gen.* 1.4; 2.8; 4.5)[3], and by the writer of the Wisdom of Solomon (15.11)[4]. They inherited from the Septuagint the idea of a πνεῦμα ζωῆς (Gen 6.17; 7.15; Ezek 1.21; 10.17; 37.5 (as v.1. in 10); Jdt 10.13 – = 'living person')[5].

This association of 'spirit' and 'life' is all too intelligible: as πνεῦμα in the sense of 'breath' marked the presence of life, it is a very natural image[6]. While the LXX of Gen 2.7 used there neither ἐμπνέω nor πνεῦμα, but ἐμφυσάω and πνοή, Philo once quotes the verse with ἐνέπνευσε (*Plant.* 19); generally, however, with the exception that in *Leg. all.* 3.161 and *Det. pot. ins.* 80 he quotes this verse with πνεῦμα[7], he does observe that the text says πνοή and not πνεῦμα, and indeed can point to the difference to make the point that the mind of the man of Gen 1 had the superior and strong πνεῦμα, but the material mind of the one formed in Gen 2.7 only had the inferior, lighter πνοή (*Leg. all.* 1.42)[8]. Yet that does

---

Notes on 4.3.2

1 Sandelin, *Auseinandersetzung* 43f, comments on the close connection of 'wisdom' and 'life' in Israelite wisdom traditions (Prov 3.16, 18; 8.35; 16.22; Sir 4.12; Bar 4.1).

2 Sandelin, ibid. 44–7, derives it from wisdom traditions also used by Philo (*Leg. all.* 1.31f, 37f), cf. Bourke, 'Eucharist' 379.

3 Cf. Sandelin, 'Spiritus' 71: 'The spirit for Philo is a life-giving Spirit, although we do not find Paul's expression πνεῦμα ζωοποιοῦν in his writings'.

4 Cf. 15.16; Verbeke, *Évolution* 177f, 225, 237, traces this feature in Philo and in Wisdom in part to the influence of the Alexandrian doctor Erasistratus (3rd century B.C.E.), who had distinguished a πνεῦμα ζωτικόν and a πνεῦμα ψυχικόν.
On the roots of the idea of πνεῦμα as a source of life in Greek popular thought cf. Leisegang, *Geist* esp. 51f.

5 Cf. Job 7.7; 2 Macc 7.23: τὸ πνεῦμα καὶ ἡ ζωή to be restored in the resurrection; also 14.46; see further W. H. Schmidt in *TRE* 12, 172.

6 Colson-Whitaker translate it 'life-breath' in *Op. mund.* 29f; cf. the 'life-creating spirit-force' in the soil in *Spec. leg.* 4.217.

7 Cf. Wis 15.11 (and Sandelin, 'Spiritus' 72) and the Mandaean *Ginza R* 241 cited by Sandelin, ibid. 59f (*ruha*): 'Ptahil cast in Adam a sort of spirit from his own spirit'; also *Ap. John* 51.18 (Till)=*NHC* 3, 24.10=2, 19.26 (πνεῦμα); further reff. in Sandelin, ibid. 60–70.

8 Tobin, *Creation* 128, argues that the contrast of πνεῦμα and πνοή is a tradition which Philo inherited. It would then be one which he elsewhere ignores; he also compares *Plant.* 44 where

not deter him from repeatedly interpreting πνοή there as if it were πνεῦμα (*Op. mund.* 135, 144; *Leg. all.* 1.33, 37; *Rer. div. her.* 56f; *Spec. leg.* 4.123; ?*Quaest. in Gen.* 1.4; 2.59)[9]. This is all too natural, for it is πνευμα- τικὴ οὐσία that gives the soul its faculties (*Op. mund.* 67) and is the οὐσία of the soul (*Det. pot. ins.* 80)[10]. Its presence is life and all have it, even the wicked, who thus cannot plead ignorance as an excuse (*Leg. all.* 1.35).

All the same, life could also be gained in a deeper or metaphorical sense by the possession of wisdom, and thus gained more indirectly by the ministrations of God's spirit. For Bultmann has shown how Greek usage recognizes two senses, or levels of usage, of ζωή corresponding to two senses of ψυχή[11]: just as ψυχή could be either the vital principle in all animate creatures or 'the specifically human principle of self-awareness', so too 'life' could be either a natural phenomenon or specifically human life, including θεωρία, intellectual reflection, empowered by the mind that has come to us from *extra nos*. If one substitutes for the mind the divine spirit which the Corinthian Christians were so conscious of possess- ing, one can see how easily they, and other early Christians, could feel themselves to be the true possessors of life. So too in Hellenistic Judaism Philo (*Fug.* 97) speaks of the one who draws from the divine *logos*, the fount of wisdom, and gains the prize of eternal life (ζωή ἀίδιος) in place of death[12]. It remains true, however, that this true, eternal life is generally connected expressly with wisdom and the *logos* rather than with the in- breathing of the divine spirit. That connection would be an inference, a reading between the lines. On the borderline between this usage and that of natural life is Philo's exegesis of Gen 2.7 in *Leg. all.* 1.32, when he stresses that God's inbreathing there is of 'a power of true life'; the one thus inspired becomes a soul, not just any soul, but one that is 'rational and truly living'[13]. The truly living soul, in other words, is one that is rational. Relevant here is Cumont's observation apropos of texts like Cic., *Nat. deorum* 2.66.167, which speaks of great men receiving a divine afflatus, and says that

the man of Gen 1.26f is stamped with πνεῦμα, yet the contrast with the πνοή of Gen 2.7 is not explicit there.
It is also interesting to note that the plural of πνοή is used in Eur., *Ba.* 1094 of the frenzying inspiration of the maenads. Contrast *Anth. Pal.* 6.220.4.

9 Cf. Wis 15.11 and Verbeke, *Évolution* 225.
10 Cf. *Op. mund.* 135.
11 In *TDNT* 2, 834; cf. 836 and the ref. in n. 33 to Plato, *Resp.* 6.495C: 'According to idealistic philosophy, life is truly fulfilled as life in the νοῦς, in θεωρία, as the life of the philosopher'; also 837f.
12 Cf. *Rer. div. her.* 53: those 'truly living' have wisdom for their mother.
13 Cf. Leisegang, *Geist* 86f; Sandelin, *Auseinandersetzung* 31.

men were not all born equal: if each of them possessed the *psyche* which nourished and animated the body, yet all men did not equally receive the divine effluence (πνεῦμα) which gave reason. This reason, which distinguished man from the beasts, was akin to the fires of the stars; it established between man and heaven a community of nature (συγγένεια) which alone made it possible for him to acquire a knowledge of divinity ... .[14]

Plainly this statement refers to all in general; all humans are by definition rational and not beasts. And yet not all are equally rational. One could respond to that observation in two ways: one could apply something rather similar to the Pauline tension between indicative and imperative: all are rational, but still need to be urged to live rationally (Gal 5.25, substituting 'reason' for 'spirit'!). Or one could say that this rational power was unevenly distributed; one could perhaps even speak in terms rather like those of prophetic inspiration, although there would be the risk of denying reason to any not so inspired. If one was unwilling to go as far as that then the afflatus would have to be regarded as a sort of boosting, as it were, a 'topping up' of something in all of us by nature. By implication one then comes near to achieving some sort of relationship between the spirit in all of us and the spirit of inspiration (transferred from the realm of irrational prophecy to that of reason), but it is only an implication. The nearest that Cicero comes to such an explanation is perhaps in *Divin.* 1.49.110, where 'natural' divination is mentioned: this is possible because of the gods' own nature from which our rational souls (*animi*) have been formed; since the universe is filled with eternal understanding (*sensus*) and divine mind, human souls are moved by their contact with divine souls, but only some are actually so moved because the majority are distracted by this world's cares. Here there is an avoidance of the language of a (violent) divine irruption or afflatus: the divine is near, ready to be contacted by those ready to make contact[15].

However, although the Corinthians too prided themselves on their intellectual gifts of wisdom and knowledge (see the following section), we have seen evidence that they believed, not so much that they were living life on earth as it was meant to be lived, at its highest level of attainment, but that they believed that they were already living the life of heaven and the world to come; in other words, they believed that they already enjoyed 'eternal life'. The wisdom and knowledge that they had may have been regarded as heavenly, and it seems that Paul would not have quarrelled with that had theirs been a truly Christian wisdom and knowledge in

---

14 *After Life* 111; cf. 114.

15 Here Cic. seems to combine two of the three ways in which Posidonius said dreams came about (*Divin.* 1.30.64): (1) the *animus* foresees things because by nature it is akin to the gods; (2) the air is full of immortal *animi* stamped with the marks of truth; (3) the gods speak with those asleep. §110 has no equivalent for divination to the the third of these.

his eyes (1 Cor 2.6–16); the tongues which they spoke may well have been thought to be heavenly too, as we have seen above (§4.1.1 on 1 Cor 13.1); they had visions (14.26), and those were likely to be of the heavenly world and realities. Life in its fullest sense was already in their grasp, and particularly as they worshipped together ecstatically. But there is no need to suppose that they believed that they needed 'resurrection' for this; for such an entry into heaven and communion with the divine it might indeed be preferable to dispense with the body; Philo evidently thought so as we have seen in §4.2.2, and Paul himself might not have wanted to argue about that with regard to temporary experiences of ecstasy (2 Cor 12.3 – 'without the body'), however much he rejected it for the final, permanent state of the redeemed (1 Cor 15).

4.4. The Spirit of Wisdom

The prominence of the terms 'wisdom' and 'wise' in 1 Corinthians has frequently been noted[1], and the most obvious explanation for this is that the Corinthians emphasized, and set great store by, the possession of wisdom[2]. Some have seen this emphasis as having oriental roots, in mythology involving a personified wisdom as a redeemer[3], but, unless 1 Cor 1.22, 'Jews ask for signs, and Greeks seek wisdom', is 'rhetorical'[4], this verse suggests that we look somewhere nearer to Corinth for the roots of this preoccupation of the Corinthians with 'wisdom'[5].

In §1.2.3.1 I sought to understand 1 Cor 4.8, at least partly, against the background of the Cynic-Stoic traditions about the good and wise. This same stream of popular philosophy would also provide at least a

---

Notes on 4.4

1 σοφία 17x in 1 Cor (16x in chaps 1–3), 2x in the rest of the Pauline homologoumena (9x in Eph and Col); σοφός 11x in 1 Cor (10x in chaps 1–3), 4x in Rom (once in Eph).

2 Horsley, 'Wisdom' 231: 'These Corinthians had come into an intimate relationship with *sophia* as the means and probably also the content or object of their salvation. Possession of Sophia meant immortality and perfection' (cf. 235).

3 So, above all, Wilckens, *Weisheit* and in *TDNT* 7, 519–22, but, in response particularly to the criticisms of Scroggs, 'Paul', he abandoned this view: '1 Kor 2,1–16'. See also Funk, *Language* 292: 'It is thus possible, and exegetically more illuminating, to understand the correlation of sophia and Christ as specifically Pauline, in opposition to the Corinthian subordination of all the apostles as well as Christ to sophia' (cf. Conzelmann, 'Paulus' 237).

4 Davis, *Wisdom* 189 n. 26.

5 Cf. Barrett, *1 Cor* 55, who sees this 'wisdom' as 'gnosticism, . . . a pretended revelation of God which was in truth a human speculative construction' (I would avoid the term 'gnosticism' here!); cf. also Bachmann, *1 Kor* 94ff; Morris, *1 Cor* 45f.

partial basis for understanding the Corinthians' interest in wisdom and claims to be (truly) wise. It would then be Paul who counters this by appealing to Semitic wisdom traditions and identifying God's (true) wisdom with the crucified Christ, despite the paradoxicality of such assertion (1 Cor 1.24, 30)[6].

Yet however much the Corinthians' wisdom may have owed to their Graeco-Roman environment, and in particular to their education as members of that society (and probably those troubling Paul were of sufficient social standing to have enjoyed a good measure of that education), in one respect their belief in their wisdom was indebted to the Jewish world from which the Christian gospel had come to them: they linked their possession of it with their possession of the divine spirit. That is a claim which, to my knowledge, is never found in quite those terms in Graeco-Roman popular philosophy of the time[7]. The nearest that one comes to it is in Socrates' claim to divine or 'daemonic' inspiration: 'something divine and "daemonic" ($\theta\epsilon\hat{i}\acute{o}\nu\ \tau\iota\ \kappa\alpha\hat{i}\ \delta\alpha\iota\mu\acute{o}\nu\iota\iota\nu$)' came to him (Plato, *Ap.* 31D), which is his 'customary mantic skill given by the "daemon"', a divine sign (40AB)[8]. For, when Greek philosophers and others wish to affirm the divine origin of their wisdom, they generally preferred to use terms which more clearly indicated that a deity had endowed them. 'Spirit' by itself is too naturalistic to imply this, whereas terms like 'enthusiasm' and its cognates do, as we have seen, imply the presence of the divine, the god within them[9]. The claim that the wise possess God's spirit is, however, found in Jewish traditions and in particular in the writings of Philo: for the latter, for instance, the wise is such neither by natural constitution, nor by instruction, nor by practice, but

---

6 Cf. Barrett, 'Christianity' 283 (12): 'we lack clear exegetical evidence that any adversaries of Paul's at Corinth taught a $\sigma o\phi\acute{\iota}\alpha$-myth, in the sense of a story about a figure called $\sigma o\phi\acute{\iota}\alpha$ who descended through the powers for the redemption of mankind: this sort of myth arose rather in Paul's response to a $\sigma o\phi\acute{\iota}\alpha$ which was that of the powers themselves'; cf. Funk quoted in n. 3 above, and also Conzelmann, 'Paulus' 236: 'Paul latches on to *one* of the three main variants of Jewish wisdom speculation: that of the *vanished* wisdom, which once appeared in the world, offered itself, and then retired to heaven once more – and appears again, but this time not for the whole world, but for the circle of the elect. Paul now presses this material into the service of his *theologia crucis*, his understanding of the believer's existence and its dialectic'.

7 So Holladay, *Aner* 126, comments that in speaking of Moses' mystic vision in *Vit. Mos.* 1.158 Philo has seemingly 'departed from the Cynic-Stoic model of the ideal king in which the mystic vision of the king played no significant role'. His explanation is that Philo's source here is rather the Platonic ideal king of the *Republic*. Even that could take a more rational form – cf., e.g. Tiede, *Figure* 36–42 (n.b. too the telling quotation from Sen., *De vita beata* 26.8–27.1 on 59f).

8 Cf. *Euthyd.* 272E; Pseudo-Plato, *Theages* 129E, 130C.

9 Cf., e.g., Epimenides in Plut., *Solon* 12.7.84D, who is wise with an $\dot{\epsilon}\nu\theta o\upsilon\sigma\iota\alpha\sigma\tau\iota\kappa\dot{\eta}\ \kappa\alpha\hat{i}\ \tau\epsilon\lambda\epsilon\sigma\tau\iota\kappa\dot{\eta}\ \sigma o\phi\acute{\iota}\alpha$; Philostratus, *Vit. Ap.* 1.3, describes Apollonius as $\dot{\upsilon}\pi o\theta\epsilon\iota\acute{\alpha}\zeta\omega\nu\ \tau\dot{\eta}\nu\ \phi\iota\lambda o\sigma o\phi\acute{\iota}\alpha\nu$; for Neoplatonist and other reff. to divine wisdom, etc, cf. Bieler, ANHP 1, 75. On the meaning of $\dot{\epsilon}\nu\theta\epsilon o\varsigma$ cf. §5.2.2 n. 3.

by the gracious endowment of God[10], and being an heir to the biblical tradition of a divine spirit he is, like other Jews before him, less reluctant to attribute this endowment to God's spirit, seeing in it the source of the divine wisdom possessed by patriarchs and prophets of Israel's history.

For it was an association frequently found in Jewish circles, both amongst the Palestinian Jews of the Qumran community and others, and among Greek-speaking Jews in Alexandria, and stretches back into the Old Testament[11]. For the Qumran community endowment with God's spirit brings knowledge of God and his mysteries: the author of 1QH 12.11f declares that as 'one with understanding' (משכיל) he has come to know God by his spirit which God has set upon him[12], and this same spirit of holiness has enabled him to hearken to God's counsel (סוד). In 14.12f he exclaims 'Thou hast [shed] Thy Holy Spirit [upon me] and then drawn me near to understanding of Thee (לבינתך)'[13]. In 1QS 4.22, in an otherwise rather obscure and disputed passage, 'some of the sons of men' or the 'man' of 4.20 are purged by God's spirit of truth 'that (they or) he may instruct the upright in the knowledge of the Most High and teach the wisdom (חכמה) of the sons of heaven to the perfect of way'[14]; the presence of this spirit seems here to give knowledge possessed by angels, inviting a comparison again with the 'tongues of . . . angels' in 1 Cor 13.1. More prosaically, the diligent student of the Law is promised, if God so wills it, a filling with the spirit of understanding in Sir 39.6, and he will pour out words of wisdom.

The association of wisdom and the possession of God's spirit is clear in the Wisdom of Solomon[15]. This is above all most explicit in the parallelism of 9.17:

---

10 Cf. Leisegang, *Geist* 147–9, and also Bousset-Greßmann, *Religion* 448; see, e.g., Philo, *Poster. C.* 15f; *Gig.* 22–7, 47; *Plant.* 24; *Migr. Abr.* 34–42; *Rer. div. her.* 64; *Jos.* 116; *Praem. poen.* 45; *Quaest. in Gen.* 1.90.

11 Cf. Exod. 31.3; Deut 34.9; Job 32.7f.

12 Cf. 13.18f; in *T. Levi* 18.7 the eschatological priest has 'the spirit of understanding'; cf. *4 Ezra* 5.22. Compare here Foerster, 'Geist' 127: the giving of insight by God's spirit is often presupposed even where it is not expressly mentioned.

13 Tr. Vermes.

14 Tr. Vermes; on the complexities of this passage see §4.3.1 n. 10. With the 'spirit of truth' here compare the 'spirit of knowledge and the fear of God' in 1QSb 5.25. The prophets too had in the past given their revelation 'through God's spirit of holiness' (1QS 8.16; also Sir 48.24; *Jub.* 31.12). In *1 Enoch* 49.3 God's Elect One has in him 'the spirit of wisdom, the spirit which gives thoughtfulness, the spirit of knowledge . . .' (tr. E. Isaac in Charlesworth, *Pseudepigrapha* 1, 36); cf. too 91.1 and Enoch's endowment there for instructing his sons; Ezra prays for a similar endowment for his writing (*4 Ezra* 14.22).

15 Cf. Larcher, *Études* chap. 5. Pearson, *Terminology* 36, perhaps goes too far in suggesting that we have here 'a semi-hypostatic wisdom-figure . . . identified with the Holy Spirit'; would it not be enough to explain Wisdom's language if the presence of this spirit entailed wisdom and *vice versa*?

Who has learned thy counsel, unless thou hast given wisdom and sent thy holy Spirit from on high? (*RSV*)

This association may be hinted at too in 1.6, 'wisdom is a kindly ($\phi\iota\lambda\acute{\alpha}\nu$-$\theta\rho\omega\pi\sigma\varsigma$) spirit', or, more clearly, in 7.7:

. . . I prayed, and understanding ($\phi\rho\acute{\sigma}\nu\eta\sigma\iota\varsigma$) was given me; I called upon God, and the (or 'a'?) spirit of wisdom came to me. (*RSV*)[16]

The idea of wisdom as (the moist vapour of) God's breath ($\dot{\alpha}\tau\mu\acute{\iota}\varsigma$) in 7.25 also brings it near to the root meaning of $\pi\nu\epsilon\hat{\upsilon}\mu\alpha$ (from $\pi\nu\acute{\epsilon}F\omega$, I blow)[17]. Here and in earlier material Brandenburger argues that to some extent the wise man has replaced the prophet[18]; wisdom is regarded as pouring out her teaching like prophecy (Sir 24.33).

For Aristobulus Moses was noted for his wisdom and the divine spirit in him which attested his claim to be a prophet, and it is hard to resist the inference that he was wise because he had this prophetic spirit and *vice versa*[19].

Josephus too ascribes Daniel's wisdom to the same source in *Ant.* 10.11.3 §239, when Belshazzar says that he has learnt of him and his wisdom, namely that the divine spirit was with him[20]. This association is, Isaacs notes[21], unusual for Josephus, but not so much so for Philo. For him Joseph, like Daniel, was skilled in interpreting dreams, and Pharaoh wonders where one could find another such person who has a divine spirit in him (*Jos.* 116)[22]. *Gig.* 22f contains a discussion of some of the different senses of $\pi\nu\epsilon\hat{\upsilon}\mu\alpha$: it is air, the third element (as in Gen 1.2 – §22), but it is also pure knowledge ($\dot{\epsilon}\pi\iota\sigma\tau\acute{\eta}\mu\eta$) 'in which every wise man naturally shares'; this is clear from Exod 31.2f where Bezalel is 'filled . . . with divine spirit, with wisdom, with understanding, with knowledge . . .'; here we can find a definition of 'divine spirit'. Then, he continues, Moses had such a spirit, and it came upon the seventy elders, to enable them to surpass others; to do this they had to receive a share of that all-

---

16 See also Wis 1.5 (spirit of instruction); 7.22 ($\pi\nu\epsilon\hat{\upsilon}\mu\alpha$ $\nuo\epsilon\rho\acute{o}\nu$; various MSS here omit an $\dot{\epsilon}\nu$ to produce the statement that wisdom is a rational spirit, rather than that a rational spirit is in wisdom). Cf. Sir 39.6 and Davis, *Wisdom* 16–24; Verbeke, *Évolution* 227–31.

17 Isaacs, *Concept* 20.

18 *Fleisch* 124.

19 Frg. 2.4 according to the enumeration of A. Y. Collins in Charlesworth, *Pseudepigrapha* 2, 838 (=Eus., *Praep. ev.* 8.10.4).

20 This is a more literal rendering than that of Marcus for $\dot{\omega}\varsigma$ $\pi\acute{\upsilon}\theta\sigma\iota\tau\sigma$ $\pi\epsilon\rho\grave{\iota}$ $\alpha\dot{\upsilon}\tau\sigma\hat{\upsilon}$ $\kappa\alpha\grave{\iota}$ $\tau\hat{\eta}\varsigma$ $\sigma\sigma\phi\acute{\iota}\alpha\varsigma$ $\ddot{\sigma}\tau\iota$ $\tau\grave{\sigma}$ $\theta\epsilon\hat{\iota}o\nu$ $\alpha\dot{\upsilon}\tau\hat{\omega}$ $\pi\nu\epsilon\hat{\upsilon}\mu\alpha$ $\sigma\upsilon\mu\pi\acute{\alpha}\rho\epsilon\sigma\tau\iota$ . . .; four MSS have the definite article $\tau\acute{o}$, but Niese omits it.

21 *Concept* 46 n. 20.

22 Colson translates the anarthrous $\pi\nu\epsilon\hat{\upsilon}\mu\alpha$ $\theta\epsilon\hat{\iota}o\nu$ 'the spirit of God'. In *Rer. div. her.* 64 it is the purest mind which is inspired from above ($\kappa\alpha\tau\alpha\pi\nu\epsilon\upsilon\sigma\theta\epsilon\grave{\iota}\varsigma$ $\ddot{\alpha}\nu\omega\theta\epsilon\nu$) that can inherit incorporeal and divine things.

wise spirit (Num 11.17 – §24). What Moses has is 'the wise, the divine, the excellent spirit', which can be shared with others with 'no diminution in understanding and knowledge and wisdom'[23]. Later we read that 'the divine spirit of wisdom' remained long 'with Moses the wise'[24]. In other words, Philo too knows and uses the equation of spirit and wisdom[25]. The divine spirit is in the wise and in having it the wise has wisdom.

For Philo divine spirit is above all rational, and the mind is 'spiritual' (*Fug.* 133). So, while at times he speaks of spirit as empowering the soul in general (*Op. mund.* 67; *Det. pot. ins.* 80; cf. §4.3.2 above), it is above all that of which the mind is formed (*Rer. div. her.* 55)[26], and divine spirit is equated with reason or wisdom (ibid. 57; *Quaest. in Gen.* 1.90)[27]. We have therefore 'rational spirit' (λογικὸν πνεῦμα) within us (*Spec. leg.* 1.171, 277); this is the true human being and not the composite being formed by body and soul; it is the 'God-like creation with which we reason' (*Det. pot. ins.* 84). Yet, of course, not all use this 'God-like creation' as they should.

It is rather the wise and rational person who lives by this divine spirit (*Rer. div. her.* 57; cf. 64); potentially all are thus akin to God and the things of God (*Leg. all.* 1.38)[28]. But this is true above all of the one who is a real philosopher (*Plant.* 24). But not only philosophers have this generous measure of spirit; the angels too are of spiritual nature (*Quaest. in Gen.* 1.92)[29]. It should therefore come as no surprise if those at Corinth who considered themselves wise and filled with spirit believed themselves also akin to angels, as well as speaking in their languages (§4.1.1 above). When Philo tells of the spirit coming on Abraham (*Virt.* 217), we read of his being granted beauty of body (not a claim of the Corinthians as far as we know) and persuasiveness in his speech (which they probably did claim – hence 1 Cor 2.1, 4f); his hearers are granted understanding. Above all, though, it was Moses who was the possessor of God's spirit

---

23 §27, tr. Colson.

24 §47, tr. Colson. P. Schäfer in *TRE* 12, 174, describes the divine spirit and wisdom as 'gleichbedeutend' in Philo.

25 Cf. W. Bieder in *TDNT* 6, 373; Brandenburger, *Fleisch* 143, comparing *Gig.* 22–7 ('πνεῦμα θεῖον is expressly defined as nothing other than σοφία').

26 Cf. *Fug.* 133 (Dillon, *Platonists* 159 n. 1, points out how Stoic is the definition of νοῦς as ἔνθερμον καὶ πεπυρωμένον πνεῦμα); *Quaest. in Gen.* 2.59; Verbeke, *Évolution* 244, sees here an unresolved tension in Philo's thought.

27 Cf. *Gig.* 23–7, 47.

28 Cf *Quaest. in Gen.* 4.1.

29 Cf. *Abr.* 113 (though there πνευματικός is parallel to ψυχοειδής); cf. Wis 15.11; 16.14. Alternatively, in keeping with common Hellenistic Jewish usage, they are called 'spirits': *Quaest. in Gen.* 1.92; 2.8.

and wisdom *par excellence*[30]. Philo goes further than that, too: in *Quaest. in Exod*. 2.29, commenting on Moses' coming near to God in Exod 24.2, he speaks of the prophetic mind coming near to God; when divinely inspired and filled with God (ἐνθουσιᾷ καὶ θεοφορεῖται) it becomes like the monad, and thus comes near God in a sort of family relationship (κατὰ συγγενῆ τινα οἰκειότητα) and is changed into the divine; 'such men become kin to God and truly divine'[31]. (This offers a reasonably clear glimpse of what being a 'divine man' meant in Philo's eyes: not being God or even a god so much as being God-like, in a family relationship to him. In §5.2 we will see how 'deification' or 'identification' with the gods is probably to be understood similarly in the mysteries.) Elsewhere, however, Philo also says that even Moses was only spasmodically possessed by the spirit of God, and at other times spoke quite normally and calmly (*Vit. Mos*. 1.175). Does this not suggest that the difference between him and Philo was only a quantitative one, not a qualitative? Leisegang even suggests that Philo's depiction of Moses is based on his own spiritual experience, although in my judgment one would have to allow for a degree of idealization[32]. Yet that still permits the inference that at similar moments of possession Philo would feel himself to be 'divine', i.e. God-like. And so it is perhaps not correct to limit this experience to the past, to the prophets of the biblical period, as Isaacs wishes[33]. For a start there is then the problem of the source that Philo would then assume, not only for his own inspiration (see §4.2.2 above), but also for that of contemporary ascetics (*Mut. nom*. 39) and of the translators of the Septuagint (*Vit. Mos*. 2.37–40); in addition there is the fact that he seems in *Gig*. 47 at least to hope to share Moses' untrammelled enjoyment of God's spirit[34]. In *Fug*. 166–8 too there is no hint that the class of the self-taught wise is purely a feature of the past; it is new and higher than reason and truly divine, produced by a divinely-inspired frenzy (μανία). In *Fug*. 63 leaving this place and fleeing to the realm of the divine and becoming as far as possible like God ourselves is laid upon us as an obligation. Again in *Rer. div. her*. 182–4 there are two kinds of wisdom, the pure or divine and the mixed or human; but the former seems not to be limited to God as one might think, but rather the human mind (νοῦς) is

---

30 Cf., e.g., *Gig*. 24, 47, 54f; *Vit. Mos*. 1.175 (?2.40); Leisegang in Cohn-Wendland 7,16; see too Abraham in *Poster. C*. 27.
31 Tr. Marcus; cf. Holladay, *Aner* 155–60, who, however, perhaps underestimates the full force of this passage; he compares also *Vit. Mos*. 2.188 (160f).
32 *Geist* 159; he calls Philo a 'Doppelgänger' of Moses even if not on the same level.
33 *Concept* 49.
34 Note too the ἀεί of *Spec. leg*. 3.1, and also *Conf. ling*. 95; cf. too Davis, *Wisdom* 58. He has also been initiated by Moses into the 'great mysteries': *Cher*. 49.

the purest part of the soul and, inspired from above, may be preserved unharmed. Finally in *Gig* 22 one sense of God's spirit is the pure knowledge which every wise person properly shares[35]. The reason why Philo may be reluctant to ascribe this experience to people of the present, himself included, may be simply that they are still in the midst of their warfare with the flesh, in which defeat by the flesh may at any moment cause God to withdraw his spirit; he would then display a caution similar to that of Paul in 1 Cor 9.27 and Phil 3.12, as well as something of the depreciation of human worthiness to know the divine so characteristic of the Qumran *Hodayot*. With the dead who have run their race it is easier confidently to affirm their possession of God's spirit and their permanent enjoyment of it. But presumably he would at least be prepared to say that at those moments when possessed by the divine spirit and at others besides, when still controlled by the experience and knowledge granted in those heady moments, he was 'divine' and possessed divine wisdom, even if he had not advanced to so complete a possession of and by this spirit as to be able to call himself 'spiritual'[36]. At the same time we can well imagine how others, less inhibited and more frequently impelled by ecstatic experiences, might be far less modest and restrained in their claims for themselves.

For, although in Philo's works and in early Christianity the spirit was manifested in temporary ecstatic phenomena, the fact that it brought wisdom and made its recipients 'wise' indicates that it was not solely a passing phenomenon, any more than the outward beauty which Philo saw the spirit conferring on Abraham (*Virt.* 217, noted above); its ecstatic manifestations were but symptoms of a more permanent 'spirituality'[37]. On that Paul and his converts in Corinth were agreed; where they differed was in their appreciation, or lack of it, of the range and breadth of the symptoms of that one state of spirit-possession, and in the confidence which they placed in their own hold upon its more spectacular gifts, especially the wisdom and knowledge which it brought through mysterious utterances and perhaps also visionary experiences; it is likely that they felt that they were wise with an unearthly wisdom, and looked down upon those who did not share their insights (cf. 1 Cor 8.7–12). Moreover

---

35 Cf. too Sandmel, *Philo* 87f.

36 Cf. his consolation in *Spec. leg.* 3.4–6 that despite being immersed in civic cares he has planted in his soul a παιδεία ἵμερος, enabling him occasionally to rise above these worldly problems for a time, and to receive the light of wisdom.

37 So Socrates, having introduced the imagery of possession, rather with his tongue in his cheek, speaks of a resultant δαιμονία σοφία which he has and can go on to make use of it (and will even have it, so to speak, purified away! – Plato, *Crat.* 396DE, 428D).

they seemingly left the latter feeling that they had little to offer to the communal worship of the church (cf. §4.1.1 above).

Such a claim to wisdom on the part of the Corinthians is not entirely like the claims of either popular philosophy or other Jewish wisdom traditions. It placed far greater emphasis on the ecstatic manifestations of God's spirit than either of those did. It is true that, as we saw in §4.4.2[38], Philo was at times prepared to describe his mental processes in terms of ecstasy. Here he could build upon the precedent of Plato:

> Already for Plato the activity of the philosopher at its highest level was no longer a matter of calm, rational thought, but was rather an intuitive vision, profound inspiration (ἐνθουσιασμός), divine inebriation and divine frenzy (θεία μανία), heavenly love. Something of the wild, mystic and ecstatic religion of the Orphic mysteries echoed in his philosophy, although all here was raised to a purified, purged, and transfigured form, raised to a higher level[39].

There is some evidence also that wisdom was for popular Graeco-Roman philosophy something that one was deemed to have and to keep, and therefore to be as a result 'wise'. That might seem to follow almost inevitably once one divides humanity into the 'wise' and the 'foolish' with no intermediate category, as the Stoa did[40], and yet at the same time the Stoics granted that there had hardly been any wise at all in history, perhaps indeed not a single one[41]. Yet Pohlenz notes that Philo was less niggardly in his ascription of perfection than they: the Essenes, for instance, qualified (*Omn. prob.* 75–91), as well as the Seven Sages of Greece, the Magi and the Gymnosophists (ibid. 73f)[42]. Here Philo goes beyond the readiness of many Greek philosophers only to recognize as truly wise idealized figures of the past, and he makes the claim for a group in the present (admittedly probably only known to him by hearsay, although his account of the Therapeutae, with whom he must have had some contact, in *De vita contemplativa* is hardly any less fulsome in its praise). Apollo too, through his oracle at Colophon, apparently did not shrink from calling Apollonius of Tyana 'utterly wise' (Philostr., *Vit. Ap.*

---

38 See also the reff. in §4.2.2 nn. 8, 34.

39 Bousset-Greßmann, *Religion* 449; this philosophical precedent is more plausible than any direct dependence on the mysteries such as they also suggest (449f). (One should, however, question whether Orphic traditions ought to be singled out in this way as influential.)

40 Cf. Long, *Philosophy* 90, 178; Pohlenz, *Stoa* 1, 153f (cf. esp. *SVF* 1.227; also 3.544–684); also Tiede, *Figure* 113f on Philo's use of this dichotomy.

41 Pohlenz, ibid. 157f; cf. Sextus Emp., *Math.* 7=*Adversus logicos* 1.432; *Math.* 9=*Adversus physicos* 1.133; *SVF* 3.668; also 658, 662, and Diogenes of Babylon in 3.32 (p. 216); Sandbach, *Stoics* 47.
   At first sight Sen., *De consolatione ad Helviam* 5.2 might seem to be another example of this, but he does go on to speak of giving himself to wise men, implying that he knew of some (past or present?) – cf. *De tranquillitate animi* 7.4; *De constantia* 2.1; 7.1; *De ira* 2.10.6; *Ep.* 90.6.

42 Ibid. 378; cf. Cic., *Fin.* 2.12.37; Lucretius 5.8–10; Orig., *Cels.* 7.41; also Sen. in previous note.

4.1). The god and the Jewish philosopher seem to have been more generous with this epithet than were orthodox Stoics. Lewy, however, sees an
echo of Stoic thought in Philo when he holds that too much drinking
could not render the wise other than wise, for he would be 'soberly
drunken' – his was a *'character indelebilis'*[43]. Thus, even when the intoxication of divine inspiration and the divine gift of wisdom threatens to give
way to a baser kind of intoxication, it would seem, if Lewy's interpretation is correct, that the 'wisdom' of the wise endures. However, if the wise
were such rare birds (they are likened in this respect to the phoenix!)[44],
this remains somewhat hypothetical. To talk of the inalienable character
of an unrealizable, or almost unrealizable, ideal does not greatly help us in
determining the beliefs of less ideal, although perhaps more realistic and/or
less self-critical, sages or would-be sages. Philo, we saw above, was more
generous in his granting of the designation 'wise'; there are signs that others
too were not altogether satisfied with the rigours of the Stoic ideal, and
that they were prepared, while recognizing the lofty excellence of this ideal,
still to allow for a rank of the wise and good of the second class, who
'bore a certain resemblance and likeness to wise men'[45]. Perhaps their
wisdom may have been reckoned less permanent and inviolable. Yet we
must again question whether the Corinthian Christians were so modest or
so self-critical as to place any such limitations upon their possession of
this divine gift!

Those Hellenistic Jews who associated wisdom with the presence of
God's spirit also seem generally to have regarded this as something stable
and permanent, even if the spirit that conferred it was not necessarily
felt to be always present to the same degree or in the same manner.
Isaacs is therefore, to my mind, incorrect in saying that for them 'this
wisdom was thought of as a transient inspiration'[46], for in the Wisdom of
Solomon, where this association of wisdom and spirit is above all to be
found, there are those who are styled 'wise' (although the writer prefers

---

43 *Ebrietas* 27 and n. 2 citing Philo, *Fug.* 32; Sen., *Ep.* 83.27; Lewy 38f also deals with Philo,
Plant. 144, where Philo is more clearly citing the views of others, to the effect that the φρόνησις of the wise is proof against injury; cf. also 146–8.

44 Sen., *Ep.* 42.1 (yet at the same time he recognizes that there may be 'good' men who are
'good' in a less rigorous sense than perfection – those *secundae notae*); *SVF* 3.658. Holladay,
Aner 194, remarks that 'it was generally conceded that the Stoic Wise Man was an unattainable
goal'. Yet, though Stoics and others might shrink from calling themselves perfectly wise, the
same restraint did not keep them from calling others, perhaps idealized, 'wise' much as Philo
sees Moses. Again, in the case of the Corinthians, we have also probably to make allowance for
a rather un-Christian lack of modesty.

45 Cic., *Off.* 3.4.16, tr. Miller; cf. Long, *Philosophy* 213f, on Panaetius (cf. also Sen. in previous
note), 220 on Posidonius (Sen., *Ep.* 90.5).

46 *Concept* 38.

to speak of the 'righteous') and who die 'wise' (4.17)[47]; in every generation wisdom 'passes into holy souls', making them God's friends and
prophets, a title which again suggests how closely wisdom and spirit
were associated for the author (7.27). Although Isaacs may be right to
say that their numbers were few, yet Wisdom wishes it were otherwise,
for a multitude of them would save the world (6.24)[48]. They are, however, limited to those who 'aspire to a higher and moral life and who
humbly beg God for his help'[49]. Such humility, however, as we have
already suggested, does not seem to have been a characteristic of the
'strong' and 'wise' in the Corinthian church, at least in Paul's eyes; again
we can perhaps see only too easily how their confidence, fuelled by
repeated ecstatic and seemingly supernatural experiences, could have led
them into making extravagant claims about their spiritual status. It is an
easy step from Philo's premises that only the good and wise are true
prophets, or that goodness and righteousness go hand in hand, are co-
extensive with, possession and prophecy[50], to the assertion that those who
are possessed and prophesy are therefore both good and wise. The evidence seems to suggest that the Corinthians claimed the latter epithet on
the strength of their spirit-possession.

4.5. A Misunderstanding of Ritual?

H. von Soden saw in the Corinthians' sacramentally based (over-)con-
fidence a reflection of an assumption of Graeco-Roman religion: he
regarded their error (in Paul's eyes) as being the belief that 'those consecrated with Christ's sacraments are proofed against all powers and thus
have a boundless ἐξουσία'[1]. He then goes on to cite the well-known
Cynic critique of initiation into the mysteries, that 'Pataecion, the robber,
will have a better portion after death than Epaminondas, just because he
is initiate'[2]. And certainly this would be the most natural explanation of

---

47 Cf. 7.15.
48 Solomon himself was of course among their number (7.15–21).
49 Verbeke, *Évolution* 230.
50 E.g. *Rer. div. her.* 259f.

Notes on 4.5
  1 'Sakrament' 361 (259); Barrett, *1 Cor* 220; Halter, *Taufe* 154 (and bibliog. in 584 n. 6); Lake,
    Epistles 201.
  2 So Plut., *Aud. poet.* 4.21F (tr. Babbitt), quoting Diogenes' response to the sentiments of the

what Halter calls an 'incontestable fact, that the Corinthians overvalued baptism in their enthusiasm and considered it a magical rite (10.1ff; 15.29)'[3]. It would, however, be a mistake to limit this view of ritual acts to the initiations of the mysteries; magical practices of all sorts were rife everywhere, and any rite designed to affect someone or something's nature or status was liable to be interpreted on the analogy of magical rites.

We have just seen the reference by Halter to 1 Cor 15.29, and it is indeed hard to understand the Corinthians' (or some Christians')[4] practice of baptism for the dead except as implying a quasi-magical interpretation of the Christian rite[5]. The most natural sense of this verse[6] is surely that some Christians allowed themselves to be baptized vicariously on behalf of some persons who had died unbaptized, be they catechumens[7], or other Christians who had died without baptism[8], or even non-Christians[9]. One can compare here Jewish expiatory sin offerings on behalf of dead persons who are part of the community of faith, but yet have sinned, and one could compare the Jewish belief that this implied a hope of resurrection[10]. Yet it is hard to avoid the impression that such actions on the part of the Corinthians were in some measure different: the symbolism of washing is not that of a sin offering, and the way in which it is supposed to represent cleansing is different. For a start Jesus was widely believed to have died as a sufficient sin offering for his people; the motiva-

---

likes of Soph., frg. 753 (Nauck); cf. Diog. L. 6.39: 'It would be ludicrous . . . if Agesilaus and Epaminondas are to dwell in the mire, while certain folk of no account will live in the Isles of the Blest because they have been initiated' (Diogenes again; tr. Hicks). Prümm, *Handbuch* 217, likens the effect of the mysteries to magical rites.

3 Halter, *Taufe* 140.

4 Paul's argument does not demand that the Corinthians, or a group among them,.practised this rite,' but his argument has a great deal more force if they did (Wolff, *1 Kor* 190; cf. Wendland, *1–2 Kor* 130f: probably those denying the resurrection practised this; contrast Spörlein, *Leugnung* 82f).

5 Cf. Barrett, *1 Cor* 364; Conzelmann, *1 Kor* 327; Weiß, *1 Kor* 363; Wilckens, *Röm* 2, 53; contrast Preisker, 'Vikariatstaufe'.

6 For surveys of the many different interpretations of this rite cf. Rissi, *Taufe*; Spörlein, *Leugnung* 78–88; Wolff, *1 Kor* 185–91.

7 Cf. Barrett, *1 Cor* 364; Senft, *1 Cor* 202.

8 Cf. Moffatt, *1 Cor* 253; Preisker, 'Vikariatstaufe'. Presumably this is also what is meant by 'Ambrosiaster' – (Migne *PL* 17, 266) cf. n. 11 below.

9 Klauck, *1 Kor* 116; presumably included by Schniewind, 'Leugner' 126f; Schweitzer, *Mysticism* 285.

10 Cf. here 2 Macc 12.39–45, esp. 43f. As Rissi argues (*Taufe* 89), the action of those referred to in 1 Cor 15.29 is indeed a testimony to faith in resurrection – implicitly, although evidently they did not see it so; presumably it was for them a guarantee of disembodied survival (cf. §1.2.3.3 above; Wolff, *1 Kor* 191). But it was more than such a testimony (cf. Conzelmann, *1 Kor* 328f n. 123; Wolff, ibid. 188).

tion for a ritual to make a further sin offering *should* not have existed. That such a ritual existed is better explained if it was felt that it was necessary for the participation in salvation of the baptized or of another represented by him. Whereas Jews performed the ritual of sin offerings for sinful members of the community of faith, it is likely in view of the usual associations of Christian baptism as marking entry into the Christian community that it was felt that without it the dead were not even members of that saved community. That suggests a conviction of the indispensability of the ritual even if not its inevitable efficacy; it would have been believed that without baptism there was no salvation, even if it did not necessarily follow that salvation was inevitably or automatically produced by baptism. Thus this view, which Paul uses in his argument, but, to the embarrassment of many, does not disown, may not be incompatible with his argument in 10.1–13; there he seems (see §4.1.3 above) to reject the view that the rites of baptism and the Lord's supper guarantee salvation, not the view that they are necessary for salvation. If such a view is in tension with Paul's thought, it is perhaps to be felt more in Paul's playing down of the role of baptism in his ministry in 1.16f. Were baptism in his eyes as indispensable for the Corinthians' salvation as it seems to have been in the eyes of those baptizing for the dead, it is hard to see how he could have held his preaching of the gospel to be in any way adequate without its results being sealed in the baptizing of the saved. Yet presumably the views and the practice of those baptizing for the dead were used by him in an argument that is at least to a considerable extent *ad hominem*[11]: he could not share their concern for baptism, but their concern did at least give him a handhold in his argument with them.

Such a view could well have been encouraged in some Corinthians by the analogy of rites performed for the dead in Greek religion, especially in Orphic circles[12]. In particular Plato (*Resp.* 2.364E–365A) tells of books of Musaeus and Orpheus containing cures and purifications from wrong, not only for the living, but also for the dead. *Orph. Fr.* 232 quotes an Orphic passage from Olympiodorus which tells of rites (ὄργια) performed to secure the release of, or perhaps more likely from, lawless

---

11 So Klauck, *1 Kor* 115f; cf. 'Ambrosiaster' (Migne, *PL* 17, 266): *non factum illorum probat, sed fixam fidem in resurrectionem ostendit.*

12 Cf. Lietzmann-Kümmel, *1–2 Kor* 82, 194; Wolff, *1 Kor* 190; the inscr. cited by A. Oepke in *TDNT* 1, 542 (cf. Reitzenstein, *Vorgeschichte* 43f) is obscure: it is not clear whether the rite is performed for a dead person, and whether that person's καταλούεσθαι refers to a form of baptism, and if so whether it was sinful or not (see Oepke's n. 66 and Rissi, *Taufe* 62). The passage in the *Pistis Sophia* (128=210.25–212.35, Schmidt-Till) is relevant, but late; for other Gnostic parallels see Rissi, ibid. 7f; cf. also Wagner, *Baptism* 29 n. 101, 272 nn. 58f.

ancestors[13]. That these rites were not, as far as we know, baptisms or washings does not entirely rule out the validity of the precedent; they were rituals and that is perhaps enough to make this point[14].

Yet, however frequent the parallels may be to the understanding of ritual acts as quasi-magical in function, it would be far harder to find precise parallels to the idea of the ritual bestowal of spirit; at least this seems not to have been a way in which Graeco-Roman religion for the most part thought or spoke of the impingement of the divine upon the human world[15], with one possible exception in those rituals accompanying the consultation of oracles. Another possible exception to this may lie in some of the magical papyri, where amidst the ritual practices one finds the desire to receive a spirit so as to become immortal[16] or to become a spirit[17]. It is not clear that this reflects the ideas of the mysteries, let alone those at the time of the New Testament. Leisegang, however, argues that avoidance of talk of spirit may have largely been a matter of style[18]: Pollux's *Onomasticon* (1.15f) suggests a string of synonymous expressions, and it is these that we chiefly find, both in relation to cults and applied metaphorically to philosophers and others (see §2.4.2), except in literature which makes no stylistic pretensions. Whether this is, however, quite fair to a writer like the author of Luke-Acts, who seems to have quite considerable literary pretensions and yet speaks unusually frequently of spiritual endowment, is another matter. The greater prominence of this endowment in early Christianity, coupled with the usage of the Septuagint, have surely played a greater role here; another factor is the desire to avoid language which was too characteristic of pagan cultic experience.

However, once one makes allowance for the fact that this was the way in which Christians (and at least some Jews) in the Graeco-Roman world conceived of God acting upon them and their world, then, *mutatis mutandis*, one can see that there may be parallels in the belief that through initiation one received divine powers and thus a divine status of a sort; that there are such parallels we shall see in §5.2 below. If due allowance is made for the frequent association of the reception of bap-

---

13 West, *Poems* 99, translates 'release from their forefathers' unrighteousness'; this is more likely since λύσις is often followed by a genitive denoting that from which one is released (cf. LSJ s.v.); contrast Oepke, ibid.

14 *Pace* Rissi, *Taufe* 63.

15 Yet Reitzenstein, *Mysterienreligionen* 379f, suggests that the idea of receiving spirit in baptism is of Hellenistic origin.

16 Cf. *PGM* 4.500–10, 628f, 645–8; 7.559–62.

17 Cf. *PGM* 4.520f; cf. Zosimus, *De virtute* 2 (Berthelot-Ruelle 108.9, 17) – becoming a spirit through a sort of voluntary death.

18 *Geist* 122–5.

tism and manifestations of tongues and ecstatic phenomena (see §4.1.4 above), then it is not surprising that this result of baptism should be interpreted as the automatic result of the rite, bestowing this new nature upon the baptized unalterably and irrevocably[19].

The reference to the acquisition of divine powers or status in initiation might suggest a comparison with the concept found in Philo and in other religious and philosophical traditions of antiquity of certain sages and philosophers of the past as 'divine' ($\theta\epsilon\tilde{\iota}o\iota$). The studies of this concept by Holladay and Tiede[20] were shaped by the application of this concept to Christology and the study of the Christian Gospels, and this concern guided their accounts. Their analyses do, however, show that one has to ask of 'divine men' 'divine in what sense and by what criteria?', and that different groups may give different answers to both parts of this question. Once one recognizes that to call a sage 'divine' is not necessarily to imply that he is a god incarnate, let alone that he is a previously known god come to earth, but more often means simply that he possesses divine powers, godlike qualities, then one can better understand how Philo can happily use this adjective of human beings[21], particularly those in whom the divine spirit is at work, and in whom the divine element, the mind, rules; so too we can see that for some traditions being godlike shows itself particularly in the exercise of the divine rational element in human nature, but for others this divine power flowing through humans is displayed in more abnormal activities, ecstasy, powers of healing and the like. Different writers may place a different emphasis on these rational and non-rational manifestations of divine qualities and powers, but in the hagiography of the sages it is rare not to find some elements of both; one tradition may lay more weight on the heightening of the latent divinity in human nature, another on the irruption of unusual powers to supplement those possessed by the rest of humanity, but seldom are either totally absent. We have seen the 'daemon' that addresses the otherwise alarmingly rational Socrates; on the other hand even the most extravagantly charismatic figures of antiquity claimed the possession of a wisdom which they sought to impart rationally with their heightened

---

19 If this was the mistake of the Corinthians concerning baptism then it is altogether misleading to compare Acts 18.25, and to argue that Apollos might have been the cause of the Corinthians' views; Apollos' knowledge only of the baptism of John was hardly a misapprehension of the same sort, *pace* Horsley, 'Wisdom' 232.

20 Holladay, *Aner;* Tiede, *Figure;* cf. Paterson, 'Man'.

21 E.g. *Fug.* 168; *Vit Mos.* 2.188; *Virt.* 177. Tobin observes how in *Fug.* 63 Philo adopts the Middle Platonic ideal of $\delta\mu o\iota\omega\sigma\iota\varsigma$ $\theta\epsilon\tilde{\omega}$ – the one who is like God is holy, just and wise (*Creation* 18f), and one must flee from the earthly to the realm of the divine, and become as far as possible like God.

and supernaturally charged powers of reason. More important for our purpose is the recognition that they were regarded, at least by posterity, as 'divine' and as being 'divine' permanently and not just episodically. In the absence of many firsthand sources like Empedocles' claim to be an immortal god and no longer mortal[22] we are largely left with the eulogies or sneers of succeeding generations, but one does get the impression that sages like Philostratus' Apollonius of Tyana or Lucian's Alexander of Abonuteichos behaved as if they thought themselves, or wanted themselves to be thought, more godlike, more possessed of godlike qualities, than the common run of their fellow mortals. Their teachings, their extraordinary acts, were but symptoms and expressions of this exalted status. It may have been the particular contribution of the Judaeo-Christian tradition to see both the godlike in human nature and the divine power which impinged upon human nature from outside as being describable in terms of 'spirit'; both these manifestations of 'spirit' had their pagan precedents, but in separate traditions in pagan thought which had not come together before[23]; yet the features of the godlike man described in terms of the presence of such a spirit did not greatly differ from those of the godlike men recognized as such in the surrounding culture of the Graeco-Roman world. Nevertheless it may be true that the monotheism of the Judaeo-Christian tradition acted as a restraint which prevented being like God passing over into actually being a god. We shall see in §5.2 that there is reason to be cautious in evaluating how often this latter was really thought to happen even in pagan circles in the world into which the church was born.

Yet we must note that, although the likes of Philo was ready to employ the attribute 'divine' of mortals, to the discomfort of some modern scholars, yet to our knowledge this was not an epithet which the Corinthians appropriated for themselves, however prepared they may have been to make extravagant (in Paul's eyes at least) claims for themselves[24]. The point which I would want to make is simply that their attitudes and behaviour were comparable to those of what may, for want of a better term, be characterized as the 'divine men' of the Graeco-Roman world. For them the 'daemon' with which they were in contact, and the divine power that was channelled through them was identified as the eschatol-

---

22 Diels-Kranz, *Fragmente* §31 B 112.4.

23 It is striking how H. Kleinknecht's article in *TDNT* 6 draws mainly upon the Stoic tradition for most of the material on 'πνεῦμα in Natural Science and Philosophy' (352–7) and the Platonic for its use in 'manticism' (345–52).

24 Paterson, *'Man'* esp. 134, draws attention to the fact that in the ancient world whether one called someone 'wise', 'divine' or a 'magician' may depend more on whether one praises that person or criticizes him or her; the characteristics of these three categories are indistinguishable.

ogical outpouring of the divine spirit, enabling them to commune with the heavenly realm in angelic languages, and to impart to their fellow humans the secrets of that unseen realm which they had thus learnt.

Earlier we saw evidence that the Corinthians associated their receiving of this spirit with the ritual acts of baptism and the Lord's supper (§4.1.1–4). Does that mean that they believed that they received it inevitably, automatically and unconditionally? Probably it does, for this would then explain why Paul must stress that the comparable experiences of the Israelites in the wilderness brought no such security to them (1 Cor 10.1–13), and it is he who introduces the idea that one can partake in the Lord's supper 'unworthily', and stresses how dangerous this is to those who do so (11.27–31). Such an assumption on the part of at least some Corinthians could then only be confirmed for them when they continued to manifest what they regarded as incontrovertible proof of the presence of God's spirit in them, particularly in the form of wonderful utterances, the more wonderful the better.

4.6. Conclusions

The conclusions to be drawn from this chapter can be summarized as follows:

(1) we saw the value which the Corinthians seem to have placed upon their possession of the divine spirit, and in particular of spiritual gifts, notably the ability to speak in (?heavenly) tongues and their wisdom. It is likely that this confidence was based, at least in part, upon the mediation of this spirit to them by means of the Christian rites of baptism and the Lord's supper, and that these rites fostered in them an excessive self-confidence which Paul criticizes in 1 Cor 10.1–13.

(2) Paul plays down the importance of tongues-speaking, above all on the grounds of the harm which its unfettered use can have on the life of the Christian community, and of the impression that it makes on outsiders. He also contrasts it with prophecy, holding that tongues-speaking is done without the participation of the mind. He thus draws on one strand of Greek thought about ecstasy, but it is perhaps unlikely that the Corinthians, who prided themselves on their wisdom, would have agreed with that assessment of the experience. They could easily have found other assessments of the phenomenon of ecstasy in the Greek world which viewed it, and the role of the rational mind within it, more positively. Paul and the Corinthians would, however, have agreed on seeing tongues-speaking as something God-given.

(3) Moreover for both of them it was a sign of the eschatological out-pouring of God's spirit, ushering in the new, final age. It was a sign that they lived now in that new age, possessed of the powers of that age and of 'newness of life' (Rom 6.4). Thus there was a permanency and finality about the presence of the spirit that was lacking in the ecstatic phenomena of the Graeco-Roman world, including Hellenistic Judaism. The new age is here, at least proleptically, and its powers are enjoyed now.

(4) This new age is one in which God's people prophesy and the young men see visions and the elders dream dreams (Joel 2.28 in Acts 2.17); it is an age of spiritual gifts and heaven-sent knowledge, and the Corinthians seem to have prided themselves exceedingly on these. Too often, perhaps, the actual content of their wisdom may have been painfully human, the product of their environment, but they prided themselves that it was supernaturally given to them by God. God's spirit had taught them things which those not so endowed could never grasp. They were the truly wise, possessing a divine wisdom that was inseparably linked to the presence of the divine spirit within them.

(5) And that spirit was irrevocably theirs because, they believed, the Christian rites of baptism and the Lord's supper had both bestowed it upon them (in the case of baptism) and continued to impart it to them (in the bread and wine of the Lord's supper); this impression was only confirmed by the continued manifestation of ecstatic and supernatural gifts among them. (This, or something very like it, seems to me the most plausible reconstruction of the situation in the Corinthian church.)

(6) Yet the negative point can, and should, be made, that this surging confident life does not amount to 'resurrection'. That, I argued in the previous chapter, was something physical, bodily, and the traditions which I have used to illustrate the understanding of ecstasy in large measure viewed the body as wholly inimical to the reception of divine truth in ecstasy; that is true at least of those traditions which stress the participation of the mind in ecstasy, if not of those which see ecstasy as involving the mind's displacement and replacement. If I am correct in thinking that the Corinthians did not share Paul's view that the mind had no part in tongues-speaking, then it is likely that they approximated more to the position of those traditions that spoke of the mind's collaboration, and indeed enhancement, in ecstasy; and this it could do only by liberation from the body, transcendence of the body and its limitations, by leaving the world of the senses and soaring to a higher vision. To call this blissful life of vision 'resurrection' would be grotesque as long as the word retained its usual connotations.

(7) Rather this experience was true 'life', a life that stood in stark contrast to the 'death' that passed for life in the eyes of most mortals

(see further in chapter 6 below), and its source was the outpoured spirit of God, bestowed now in an act of new creation.

In trying to evaluate how early Christians in the Graeco-Roman world might have viewed this endowment with the eschatological spirit of God, particularly in its more striking manifestations, I have concentrated on the evidence of 1 Corinthians. There are good reasons for that: most of the evidence is there, and within the framework of the present enquiry such a restriction is all the more natural. For we saw how 1 Corinthians 15 played a prominent part in the hypothesis of an early Christian baptismal theology based on the soteriology of the mysteries. Moreover Romans was quite possibly written from Corinth. The church in that latter city may have been in some ways exceptional, but surely not altogether dissimilar to the rest of Paul's churches — and other congregations too — in the Graeco-Roman world. We know that the Thessalonians too needed advice about spiritual manifestations and especially prophecy, even if their problems may have been almost the opposite of those of the Corinthians; 1 Thess 5.19f suggests the danger that they placed too tight a rein upon these gifts. The Galatians' conversion had evidently been accompanied by impressive workings of the spirit of God (δυνάμεις, Gal 3.5; cf. v 3) and, as we have seen, Paul not only urged a spirit-led life upon them, but addressed them as 'spiritual' (5.25; 6.1). It is not unreasonable to suppose that in these churches too the presence of God's spirit was thought to bring 'life', even if they did not share the Corinthians' exaggerated claims that this life was already fully that of the age to come, even of heaven itself.

5. Union with Christ

In our preliminary look at the question of a unified theology of the mystery-cults (§2.3) we saw how for some scholars some form of union with, and conformity to, the deity was an essential ingredient of the mystery-cults. For C. Colpe, indeed, this is *the* decisive and distinctive characteristic of mystery-cults, that in them the initiate's fate is conformed to that of the deity in question[1]; other postulated characteristics are subordinated to this essential one: they had a secret doctrine which was their myth, telling of the fate of the deity to which humans must be conformed (but these stories seem to have been common knowledge!)[2]; their initiations drew human life into the mythical event(s); the rebirth which they effect is shaped by the god's destiny and leads to a deification which is given a specific sense by the story of the vicissitudes of their god.

Implicit in this is that the god with whom devotees are united is one who has died and come to life again, if rebirth comes through a conformity to that god's destiny[3]; so for G. van der Leeuw 'the essence of the Hellenistic mysteries consisted in the members "taking part" in the life and death of the saviour-god[4]. This is implicit in a good deal that is written on the background of Romans 6: so in a recent study Lona refers to the basic analogy between the mysteries and Paul's baptismal theology, in

---

Notes on 5

1 'Mithra-Verehrung' 381; cf. also (e.g.) M. Barth, *Taufe* 190f; G. Bertram in *RAC* 1, 920; Cumont, *After Life* 34, 122; Lohse, *Umwelt* 173=ET 234; Prümm, *Handbuch* 217f; Roetzel, *World* 46; Widengren in *HO* 1.8.2, 75; criticized in Burkert, *Religion* 415=ET 277 and 455 n. 13.

2 But cf. Isoc., 4.28=Turchi, *Fontes* §86: the εὐεργεσίαι shown to Demeter which are not to be heard by anyone except the initiates. Some of the benefits rendered by the royal house of Eleusis are clearly disclosed in the *Homeric Hymn*. However Richardson, *Hymn* 82, 259, sees a connection with the Orphic version of Demeter's story (*Orph. Fr.* 49) and a reference to information disclosed by the Eleusinians about Persephone's abduction.

3 So W. Fauth in *KP* 3, 1534, lists among characteristics of the mysteries the 'death and rebirth of the saviour deities as a promise for the initiates' destiny'; cf. Cumont, *After Life* 122.

4 *Religion* §73.1, 483.

the *Schicksalsgemeinschaft* between the human devotee and the deity[5]. But was the deity with whom one was united in the mysteries one who suffered death? Did salvation indeed come through sharing that deity's fate? We shall see that in the vast majority of cases it is hard to give an affirmative answer to either question. In this context it may be significant that when an international colloquium met to discuss the soteriology of oriental cults in the Roman Empire in Rome in 1979 they had before them a *'Hypothèse de travail'* which offered as a characterization of 'mystical' the definition of it as 'the experience of a profound reciprocal participation and interaction between the divine, cosmic and human spheres – either in the sense of certain deities' participation in a type of "vicissitude" characteristic of humans (disappearance and return, life and death), or in the sense of a ritual participation of humans in a destiny and a vicissitude in part bound up with those of the gods or the divine beings just mentioned . . .'[6]. Yet cautious and judicious in its choice of words though this definition was, the final conclusions of the colloquium, as summarized by R. Turcan, emphasized, as we have seen[7], the diversity of the oriental cults and expressly excluded Mithraism from this definition of the 'mystical'; the salvation offered by the cults was not only concerned with life after death but often linked this with salvation in this world 'in a biocosmic continuity and solidarity'[8]; the quest for salvation was different in different cults and also varied according to the spiritual and intellectual level attained by individual worshippers[9]. Considerable as these reservations are, we shall see that even more caution is warranted.

---

5 *Eschatologie* 167; he compares Bornkamm, 'Taufe' 35=ET 85 n. 5; Bultmann, *Theology* 1, 140; Frankemölle, *Taufverständnis* 106f (with considerable reservations); Gäumann, *Taufe* 45f; Hegermann, *Vorstellung* 143f (but note his reservation on 144); Schnelle, *Gerechtigkeit* 208f n. 418; Tannehill, *Dying* 10 (without mentioning this connection with the mysteries as far as I can see); but the list could be greatly lengthened. (E.g. v.d. Leeuw, ibid. 484, expressly associates Paul's language with the ideas of the mysteries quoted above.) However not all these expressly mention sharing the deity's fate as the common factor in Paul and the mysteries.

6 Bianchi-Vermaseren, *Soteriologia* xiv–xv.

7 §2.3 n. 10. On the non-death of Mithras cf. Bianchi, *Mysteria* xiv–xviii.

8 Cf. Bianchi, *Mysteries* 2, 4f. Contrast, e.g., van der Leeuw, *Religion* §34.6: 'the real purpose of the mysteries . . . was the attainment of eternal life'; or Gräßer, 'Kol 3,1–4' 163: 'that which was the essence of the mysteries: ascent into a "higher" existence, or as A. Dieterich has expressed it in the words of Hippolytus (*Ref.* 5.8.41): ἡ γένεσις ἡ πνευματική, ἡ ἐπουράνιος, ἡ ἄνω' (quoting *Mithrasliturgie* 164). Haufe, 'Mysterien' 102, simply states that the purpose of initiation was 'deification'. Against that F. C. Grant, *Hellenism* 11f makes the telling comment that immortality at this period would be taken for granted (except that epitaphs do not bear that out) and that what the mysteries were more concerned with was the quality or nature of the life that one enjoyed hereafter; the second point may stand even if the first is a questionable generalization.

9 Ibid. xvii.

5.1. How Did the Mysteries Promise Salvation?

It seems to me clear that there are a number of different ways in which we can conceive of the initiate of a mystery-cult looking for 'salvation' either in this world or the next[1]. In the first place (A) his initiation might assure him of a relationship to the deity of his choice in which he was confident of the favour of an all-powerful deity[2]. That deity had power to protect him both during his earthly life and beyond the grave.

A variation of this (A[1]) would be that in which the initiate anticipated *his own* demise and subsequent victory over death through the favour of the deity. Not only was he shown that the deity would protect him in the future and had the power to do so, but proleptically he experienced his future destiny in the cult's rites of initiation[3]. Here we meet the term 'iteration' in some works in the context of the initiations of the mysteries (although I shall myself avoid it): so Hoffmann explains this term thus: 'the initiates' happy lot in the world to come is regarded as the continuation of their celebration of the mysteries on earth'[4].

A second way (B) in which an initiate might look for salvation from death's powers was that he saw in the cult's proclamation that the deity of his choosing had shown in his own experiences that he was master over death or that she was its mistress[5]. This is a more specific form of the first

---

Notes on 5.1

1 Reitzenstein recognized that initiates in the mysteries expected different things of their initiations – help in this life, a promise of life after death, knowledge, enhancement of the divine in themselves (*Mysterienreligionen* 30).

2 So Theon of Smyrna 22f (Dupuis) describes the fifth and final act of initiation as εὐδαιμονία consisting in being beloved of the god and living in fellowship with the gods. Cf. Prümm, *Handbuch* 298.

3 Nock, *Conversion* 12, gives the impression that the rites of the mysteries were all of this type; some were (see below), but I would hesitate to generalize here. So too Bianchi, 'Initiation' 159 (154) suggests that this was typical of the mysteries; cf. Eliade, *Birth* 62.
  As an example: Burkert, *Religion* 425=ET 284 argues that the Samothracian mysteries worked on the principle that 'the encounter with fatal danger and the gods of death is intended . . . to protect from real death'.
  A similar principle would be at work here to that found by Dodds, *Pagan* 42f, in some of the dreams of Aelius Aristides, the desire 'to evade some imagined threatening evil by its pre-enactment in a harmless symbolic form'. Feuillet, 'Mort' 490f, quotes with approval H. Riesenfeld's rather similar view of Christian baptism ('Descente' 213f). As we shall see, however, Paul's view differs in that the anticipation of the Christian's death takes place not only in the rite of baptism, but also took place on Calvary, and takes place too in the Christian's daily life (Feuillet 492).

4 *Toten* 31; cf. too Berner, *Initiationsriten* e.g. 31; Sänger, *Judentum* 112. I am uncertain how generally recognized this term is, at least in the English-speaking world.

5 Cf. G. Widengren in *HO* 1.8.2, 75: 'the initiate found the grounds for his confidence that God can actually bestow lifegiving redemption in the saving fact that God had suffered the same

way of salvation, in which a specific demonstration was given of the ability of the deity to do this particular thing for his or her devotees. Now it shows that he or she has the power to conquer his or her own death and subsequently to enjoy life in some form, even if only reigning in the world of the dead. The one who trusts in this deity need not fear that world either, for he has there one who can and will receive him kindly and give him a blessed afterlife.

A third type of salvation (C) to which an initiate conceivably might look might rest in his own likeness to the death-conquering deity in some way or other. It is not simply, as with type B, that the deity shows its life-giving power by surviving death itself; there the fact that it has conquered death gives the grounds for confidence that this power cannot prevail against the deity or those whom it protects. Rather the initiate somehow expects to share the deity's fate, thus gaining the assurance that he will share the deity's victory. This pattern, *if* it can be found, will give us a partial approximation at least to the view of Christian initiation that Paul expresses in Romans 6 and a closer one still to Paul's view of the subsequent Christian life as a 'carrying around the putting to death (νέκρωσις) of Jesus' (2 Cor 4.10).

But the closest parallel would be type D, in which the initiate is assured of salvation by already participating in the deity's past death and victory over death in the cult. This ritual re-enactment would give him the confidence that he would indeed share that victory ultimately[6].

There may well be other possibilities or variations on these possibilities, but these may suffice for a broad schematic characterization of the possibilities, some of which may be found to remain theoretical possibilities not actually attested in any cult. The differences between these types may perhaps be shown more clearly with the aid of the following diagram:

---

fate. He had died but risen again. [He quotes Firm. Mat., *Err. prof. rel.* 22.1] . . . The redemption of the god gave the guarantee for the individual's redemption'. But then he goes a stage further: 'Initiation meant a dying with the deity' − very Pauline language, indeed distinctively so, as we shall see below, and taking us over into type D below.

6 Eliade, *Birth* 131, argues for something very much like this in the mythology giving the origins of initiation rites in archaic cultures: a supernatural being attempted to renew humans by killing them and bringing them to life again 'changed' (cf. the Demophoön story at Eleusis − §5.1.2), but they killed that being. Later rites celebrated the death of this deity, 'reactualized on the occasion of each new initiation'. Initiatory death is thus the repetition of the death of the deity who founded the mystery (but at Eleusis this was Demeter, and she did not die). Initiands imitate the deity's fate, its death by violence, and so share 'in the supernatural condition of the founder of the mystery'. However true this may be for the wider world of ancient myths (and I have my doubts − is this again generalizing too much?) I find it hard to recognize this in the Graeco-Roman mysteries and their myths and rites.

Type	Initiate's experiences	Basis of initiate's hopes	Nature of initiate's hopes	Basic role of deity
A	Belonging to deity	Favour of deity	Protection now and hereafter	Protector
A¹	Belonging to deity and anticipation of future protection	Ditto	Ditto	Ditto
B	Seeing deity's victory/ rescue	Power of deity	Protection hereafter	Protector and forerunner
C	Sharing deity's suffering at some future time	Ditto	Sharing deity's victory in hereafter	Prototype and pattern
D	Present cultic sharing in deity's suffering and victory	Power of deity anticipated in cultic death and resurrection	Death already conquered in rite	Representative?

These are not, of course, mutually exclusive; we will see that elements of one or more of them may be present at the same time in a given cult. But for the present this framework may provide a useful viewpoint from which to chart our way through the complex and entangled terrain that is the world of the mysteries.

5.1.1.1. Which of these types of expectation do the mysteries in fact reflect? What is perhaps our prime source, Apuleius' account of the initiation of Lucius, seems for the most part to suggest that the hopes of the initiate were of type A or A¹. *Isis* introduces herself to him as 'queen of the spirits of the departed, first of the inhabitants of heaven', having at her beck all the regions of the skies and earth and even the underworld; correspondingly she is identified as 'Stygian Proserpina' by the Sicilians (Apul., *Met.* 11.5). Therefore she promises Lucius that after he has been restored to human form he will live in her service a life 'full of glory (*gloriosus*)'; when he has finished his allotted time and passes down to the underworld there too he will worship her as she shines in the darkness and reigns in the world of the Styx[1]. Moreover, if faithful, he may expect to have his time of earthly life extended beyond the bounds

---

Notes on 5.1.1.1

1 Cf. Tibullus 1.3.58: Venus is expected to guide him into the Elysian fields (cf. Bücheler, *Carmina* 1109.27f), Reitzenstein, *Mysterienreligionen* 158f, sees here the influence of oriental mysteries upon beliefs about Venus.

assigned by fate (11.6)[2]. Prior to his initiation he is also reminded how the goddess holds in her hand 'the gates of hell and the guarantee of life' (11.21, tr. Griffiths)[3]. This all seems to fit in with Nock's general observation about the mysteries that the initiate not only found in them confirmation of views that he already held 'of the nature of the soul and its hope of bliss and of the symbolic expression of natural processes', but gained 'a sense of intimate and special personal relationship to the universe and the spiritual forces underlying its operations'[4]. It seems too to confirm Vidman's view that the devotees of Isis expected from her protection from the dangers of this life as well as the gift of salvation in the next[5].

Lucius' Isis corresponds closely to the Isis of the Isis-aretalogies (11.5—6 indeed echo these proclamations of Isis' power). In particular we find there too that she is mistress of fate[6]. In the *Hymns of Isidorus* from Medinet Madi those 'in the power of death' are saved when they call upon Isis to be present[7]. Missing, however, from these is the thought of Isis ruling in the underworld; the aretalogies proclaim her as mistress of all aspects of life on earth, but are on the whole strikingly silent about the extension of her power to the underworld[8]. In one Egyptian hymn of praise to Isis, however, her control is extended to the underworld[9].

---

2 Cf. Junker, *Pylon* 76.3—6: 'Isis who bestows life, . . . who lengthens the years of him who is devoted to her and causes his rule to last for ever'. (Cf. 'Isis, giver of life' — 1.13; 4.2; 13.3, etc.; Otto, *Gott* e.g. 145f nos 21—3; cf. 137 nos 18—21; 160 no. 28; Junker, 'Preis' 271.6, 14).

3 Cf. Witt, *Isis* 22, 30f. One could perhaps compare here the practice of putting an image of Nut on coffins or corpses in the hope that 'the goddess might give birth anew to the dead together with the stars which she continually brings to the world in such great numbers every evening' (H. Brunner, *Grundzüge* 128; similarly the sungod Re — 129).

J. G. Griffiths, *Isis-Book* 307 wonders how Wagner, *Baptism* 112 (Griffiths less aptly cites 120f), following Nilsson, *Geschichte* 2, 636, could deny that Isis promises immortality. This is to overlook the *campos Elysios incolens* of 11.6; see too Berner, *Initiationsriten* 105; Klauck, *Herrenmahl* 131.

4 *Conversion* 115.

5 'Isis' 142; this is confirmed by Plutarch's remark (*Is. et Os.* 27.361D—G) that the stories of Isis' sufferings are included in her rites 'as a lesson in godliness and an encouragement for men and women who find themselves in the clutch of like calamities' (tr. Babbitt).

6 Cyme (*IG* 12 Suppl., 99.55f); Andros (*IG* 12.5, 739.171—3); cf. Vanderlip, *Hymns* 95.

7 1.29, 34 (Vanderlip 17—19); cf. 2.7f (Vanderlip 35f). It is, however, possible that this concerns deadly peril in this life: cf. J. G. Griffiths, *Isis-Book* 166, who yet grants that this may concern life after death.

Compare here the power of the Cabiri as outlined by Diod. S. 5.49.5f; Schol. on Aristoph., *Pax* 277f = Turchi, *Fontes* §179.

8 The *Hymns of Isidorus* in fact seem to think of heaven as the place of the blessed departed (4.31f, Vanderlip 63—5). Possible exceptions are the references to Isis as 'fire of Hades' in the *Hymn of Mesomedes* (Peek, *Isis-hymnus* 145.9) and in *P. Oxy.* 1380.127: Isis is 'the glad face in Lethe'.

9 Junker, 'Preis' 271.8.

Yet perhaps Lucius' account of his actual initiation suggests that this was rather of type A[1] (not just A): his reference to approaching the boundary of death and 'treading on Prosperpine's threshold' and his vision of gods celestial and subterranean could be interpreted as anticipating his own death[10]; thus his experience could be described as a voluntary death (11.21): he has passed through the gates of hell and been guaranteed life through this proclamation of, and vision of, Isis' power[11]. 'Lucius had made the journey *mysterio*; it could hold no terrors for him when it had to be made *re vera*'[12]. There would then be an analogy here to the visionary experience recounted by Aelius Aristides, which he describes as an 'initiation' (τελετή)

> in which there were ladders, which delimited the region above and below the earth, and the power of the god [here Sarapis] on each side, and there were other things, which caused a wonderful feeling of terror, and cannot perhaps be told to all, with the result that I gladly beheld the tokens. The summary point was about the power of the god, that both without conveyance and without bodies Sarapis is able to carry men wherever he wishes[13].

This suggests that a conviction of the god's sovereign power was the chief message imparted by the visionary experience of initiation. There seems little reason to go further and suggest that in the case of Lucius' initiation the initiate participates in Isis' cosmic rule[14], although it is true that if the initiate has the favour of the one who thus rules he can draw upon her power; yet this power, like salvation itself, remains for him *precaria* (11.21), a matter of a gracious response of the all-powerful goddess to her devotee.

We also read that he passed through all the elements[15]. At the dead of night he saw the sun shining brightly. He approached the gods below and

---

10 §23; cf. Bleeker, 'Isis' 13f; Dibelius, 'Isis Initiation' 77; Reitzenstein, *Vorgeschichte* 17 (except that he attaches too much importance to Lucius' 'baptism' and says that it is Apuleius' baptism and initiation; it may also have been, but it is Lucius' that is described); also Kuss, *Röm.* 361 (although he speaks of Lucius' becoming Osiris – see next section).
It may be significant to note here how often initiatory rites do include descent to the underworld and ascent to heaven; cf. Eliade, *Birth* esp. 78: obviously these denote different experiences, but both 'spectacularly prove that he who has undergone them has transcended the secular condition of humanity and that his behaviour is purely that of a spirit'.

11 Cf. §21; Dibelius, ibid. 81, tentatively speaks of a union with Isis (cf. n. 54 in *Botschaft* 2, 54). Segal in ANRW 2.23.2, 1350, asks whether Lucius' initiation involved an experience of ascent and an ecstatic encounter with Isis which admitted one eternally to the company of the gods; however the permanence of this experience is questionable, for Lucius is still subsequently dependent upon further visions and dreams for guidance about yet more initiations.

12 Nock, 'Cremation' 300.

13 *Or. 49=Or. sacr.* 3.48, tr. Behr; cf. §5.1.1.4 below.

14 *Pace* Dibelius, 'Isis Initiation' 81, followed by Berner, *Initiationsriten* 101.

15 Egyptian parallels are noted in Griffiths' nn. on the passage (296–308); see also now Bergman, '*Per omnia*'. Vermaseren-v. Essen, *Excavations* 144f, suggest strong parallels existed in Mithraic initiations.

above[16] and worshipped them close at hand[17]. This may be the more significant in that Spiegel argues for a stage in the burial rites of the *Pyramid Texts* where the *ba* of the dead symbolically passed through the underworld[18]. He does so in the company of Re-Atum, whose son he is (§217)[19]; repeatedly it is proclaimed that the dead king (Unas) has the right to decide who will live and who will die (153c, etc.). He is not identified with Osiris but rather replaces him (§218)[20]. It is only in §219 that the argument from analogy appears: if Osiris lives, the king lives (167b, etc.)[21]. This is followed by symbolically passing through a narrow entry into a middle chamber representing the world above, in this case the earth on which we live; the narrowness symbolizes the difficulty of the soul's passage back into the upper world[22]. The dead king is then presented as Horus (§§220f)[23], in a text reflecting the coronation ritual of lower Egypt[24]. Into the following similar section (§222)[25] a typical mortuary text describing an ascent to heaven has been inserted according to Sethe[26]. This succession of a journey to the underworld followed by a coronation that is mingled with a heavenly ascent is certainly suggestive in the context of Apuleius' account of Lucius' experiences. Was the rite which he experienced an adaptation of Egyptian funeral rites? That it was may be suggested by the earlier reference to the rites as 'like a voluntary death . . . and a life obtained by grace'[27]. Yet in so far as this was a ritual anticipation for the living of what were essentially burial rites this

---

16 That is the order; curiously Griffiths reverses it (ed. 99), despite the fact that the preceding passage suggests that the visit to the underworld was first on his itinerary. Cf. Bergman, ibid. 680f.

17 I find it hard to share Bergman's confidence that here we have the authentic formulae of the Isiac cult, even slightly stylized (ibid. 674); contrast Griffiths' ed. 296.

18 'Auferstehungsritual' 361–7; *Auferstehungsritual* 44f, 181–205, quoting *Pyramid Texts* §§217–219, 152a–193c, Sethe 1, 52–78.

19 It is noteworthy how Seth is spoken of positively in 153a, as joint lord of Upper Egypt with Nephthys (Sethe 1, 58); the story of Seth's destruction of Osiris is absent here.

20 Spiegel, *Auferstehungsritual* 188 n. 7. Now Seth (and Thoth) are viewed as hostile (163d; cf. Sethe 1, 70).

21 Spiegel, 'Auferstehungsritual' 363, speaks of the king's *ba* as the 'new Osiris'; but it is only in 193a–c that a bodily identity seems to be spoken of; even this may be misleading – Sethe speaks of their bodies being 'doubles' of one another (*Dubletten* – 1, 98).

22 Spiegel, *Auferstehungsritual* 44.

23 194a–198d, Sethe 1, 99–108 – or 'a Horus' (Sethe 1, 106).

24 Sethe 1, 100.

25 199a–213b, Sethe 1, 115–117.

26 Sethe 1, 118: 207a–210c, 212a–213b.

27 §21: J. G. Griffiths (95) translates *precaria salus* thus; one might suggest 'obtained in answer to prayer'; that salvation is so obtained shifts the emphasis away from the due performance of the rite, which would reduce it to the level of magic, towards a greater stress on the sovereign will of the goddess. Cf. Braun, ' "Stirb" ' 146: 'ein bittweise geschenktes Heil'.

conforms to the pattern of type A^1, as I suggested above. Association with the gracious goddess now bestows upon Lucius the sort of powers that the magical formulae in Setne's book of Thoth confer in Egyptian legend: the first gives the power to enchant all of creation and to discover its secrets, the second bestows the power, even in Hades, to see Re shining in heaven and the moon rising[28]. However, tempting as the comparison with some facets of Egyptian funerary rites may be, we have to note that there is no trace in Apuleius' account of elements like the distinctive funerary rite of 'the opening of the mouth'; this basis in Egyptian ritual must therefore remain very much unproven. Some of the parallels could equally well derive from some common source of Egyptian religious ideas. Moreover, as we shall see, there is really no trace of Lucius' identification with Osiris, about whom the description of this stage of Lucius' experiences is conspicuously silent. If funerary rites have been used to furnish the contents of this mystery initiation then the borrowing has been highly eclectic.

There is another problem here: in the passages of the *Pyramid Texts* just cited Isis is mentioned but is hardly very prominent, let alone described as the primary source of salvation. That is a development for which evidence is somewhat scanty in the intervening years, although there is nothing intrinsically improbable in it. Bergman, indeed, points to what may constitute evidence for this development, in texts like *Coffin Texts* §1095[29], the *Book of Amduat*, 7th hour[30], and the *Book of the Day*, 6th hour[31]. These and evidence like the position of Isis and Nephthys in the *Book of Gates*[32] mean that 'one can easily understand that Isis was predestined to become mistress of cosmic navigation and also the one who decides the world's destiny and consequently the destinies of men . . . '[33].

---

28 Cf. F. L. Griffith, *Stories* 20f, 93, 103. One might compare the powers appropriated by the authors of the Greek magical papyri: cf. Vermaseren, 'Sotériologie' 17.

29 Bergman, *'Per omnia'* 690: 'This is Isis who is before him as Maᶜet, she shows him the paths when crossing the sky, that he may imitate what Reᶜ does' — 7.379, tr. Faulkner 3, 152. Bergman has 'en Mâat'.

30 Ed. Hornung 2, 131: 'this magic of Isis and of the Oldest Magician is performed to keep Apophis away from Re in the West, in the hidden place of Duat. Thus does one perform it on earth. He who performs it is one who is in the ship of the Sun in heaven and in the earth.' (Cf. his *Unterweltsbücher* 134). Bergman, *'Per omnia'* 690, has 'pour faire retirer Apophis de Rê'. Also relevant here is a text that Bergman cites (693), from Bresciani-Pernigotti, *Assuan*, B. 15, 66f: 'You are worshipped in the nocturnal ship of the sun, they rejoice before you in the day-time ship of the sun . . . Re desires that you should be in his ship to chase away the serpent Apophis with your magic' (Ptolemy IV).

31 Ed. Piankoff 16: ' "Rise up, rise up, let the gods who are in the ship rise up to repulse Apophis, let Seth stretch out ('pose'?) his hand to cause Apophis to fall", says Isis in her incantations.'

32 Cf. Hornung, *Unterweltsbücher* 197ff, esp. 306—8 (so Bergman, ibid. 690f).

33 Ibid. 691; cf. Bleeker, 'Isis'.

5.1.1.2. Others, however, have compared with Paul's language of dying and rising with Christ Egyptian beliefs about the identification of the dead with *Osiris*. This would certainly be the most plausible place to start looking for parallels, for he, alone perhaps of all the mystery-gods, provided in his fate the pattern for the experiences of succeeding generations of human beings[1]. Brandon, for instance, claims to find in Romans 6 'a most striking parallel to the Osirian rite'[2]. This rite he illustrates from the ancient *Pyramid Texts*[3]: these reflect a 'ritual, which was performed on behalf of the deceased person', and which 're-presented or re-enacted the sequence of actions, which, it was believed, had originally led to the revivification of the dead Osiris'[4]. This process was ritually re-enacted in embalming. Part of the liturgy consisted in the assertion that the dead, originally the king, shared the fate of Osiris. As Osiris did not die, neither did the king[5]. This led to talk of an actual identification in which Osiris' body was asserted to be that of the dead[6]. It may be, however, that this was subsequently qualified as an identification of the *ba* of the deceased and the *ba* of Osiris[7]. Or again perhaps we should never speak of 'identification' except as redefined by Hornung, that is as meaning 'that through his own efforts the human being takes on a previously determined role that bears the name Osiris'[8]. This he likens to an actor's taking on the role

---

Notes on 5.1.1.2

1 A point made by H. Wißmann in *TRE* 4, 443: 'In general the belief in the victory over death ascribed to particular deities had no consequences for their devotees' views on the fate of mortals beyond the grave', but Osiris was an exception. Reitzenstein, on the other hand, treats Osiris as a pattern for all those 'religions, in which a magic process unites one with the gods who have experienced a death and a resurrection'; in them their respective gods rise again (*Mysterienreligionen* 73).

2 *History* 26; cf. 'Technique' 32; Enslin, *Paul* 81f; Griffiths, *Isis-Book* 52; but Bonnet, *Reallexikon* 359, which Brandon cites in *Man* 66, comments that this is no union with the god in the fellowship of an Osiris-mysticism; rather it is a magical fiction in which Osiris' name has magical properties.

3 Cf. H. Kees in *HO* 1.2, 58–60.

4 *History* 21; cf. J. G. Griffiths, *Origins* 3; also Greßmann, *Tod* 15.

5 Cf., e.g., *ANET*[3] 32f (*Pyramid Texts* §219, 167a–193c, Sethe 1, 72–8).

6 Cf. the text in the previous note and those cited in Griffiths, *Origins* 64, 218, 229; Griffiths notes that the process by which these beliefs evolved was a gradual one. 'As a ruling god of the dead, Osiris is at first an object of fear and terror; then he becomes a god with whom the deceased king associates in a friendly way . . .; and this advantage is finally pressed home by a direct identification with Osiris' (216).

7 Defined by L. Žabkar as 'the manifestation of the power of a deceased king or god or the king or god himself in a state in which his power is manifest' (*A Study of the Ba Concept in Ancient Egyptian Texts*, Studies in Ancient Oriental Civilization 34, Chicago, 1968, 160, quoted by Griffiths, *Origins* 221). Appeal is made here to *Coffin Texts* §492 (6.72, Faulkner 2, 134).

8 *Conceptions* 96 (in keeping with his reassessment of the 'syncretism' involved in forms like 'Amon-Re'); cf. Griffiths, *Origins* 222; Junge, 'Isis' 107. On the question of a possible development of this idea of 'identification' in the Hellenistic age cf. Morenz, 'Problem' esp. 82–5: The Greeks were not so concerned to keep human and divine distinct. For further discussion of the term 'identification' see below, §5.2.

of Mephistopheles in a play: if he plays it well 'then he *is* Mephistopheles, at any rate within the limited spatial and temporal sphere of the world of the stage'. As the king played the part of Horus in his life, so he played that of Osiris in his death. It is true that the Egyptians were far more inclined than we to identify the bearer of a role with the role itself and to let the king act not only in a manner like (*wie*) that of a god, but as (*als*) a god[9]. He sees signs that kings were not completely identified with Osiris in references to the kings of Upper and Lower Egypt reigning in the world to come 'in the presence of Osiris'. Similarly a series of apparent inconsistencies are resolved when we regard the Pharaoh not as a god or a 'god-king', but a man acting in a divine role[10].

Berner too questions the appropriateness of 'identification' as a term to describe what is happening in the mysteries (he is speaking in general terms but apropos of the Eleusinian rites, not of the Egyptian cult): rather there is operative here a 'symmetrical way of thinking by analogy using symbols': the divine and the human activity and spheres are related symmetrically and this is grasped by analogy. Only such a symmetrical relationship enables us to understand in the case of Eleusis how the various stages in the ritual could produce a change in the existence of the individual initiate[11]. Yet when he comes to the rites of Isis he seems to recognize the appropriateness of language of identification, although all the same keeping that of analogy[12]. This distinction might, I suggest, only be really plausible if we could assume that the Egyptian mysteries of the Graeco-Roman world owed more to the funerary rites of Egypt performed on the dead than to the Greek mysteries performed for the living.

Simon is also critical of the comparison of union with Christ with the relationship of Osiris' devotees to their god: there is no sign that they could say that they had put on Osiris or that he lived in them. Rather their salvation lay in following the pattern of Osiris rather than in mystic assimilation to him; he was just the model for, the first beneficiary of, the saving power of Isis[13]. With the language of a 'pattern' or a 'model' we

---

9 So Griffiths, *Isis-Book* 317, compares *Coffin Texts* §485 (6.62*i*–*k*, Faulkner 2, 130): 'I am in the retinue of Hathōr . . . I have put on the cloak of the Great Lady, and I am the Great Lady'; cf. §5.2 and n. 24.

10 *Geschichte* 24f and 61 n. 55.

11 *Initiationsriten* 28f ('mit Symbolen arbeitendes symmetrisches Analogiedenken'); he goes on expressly to contrast this with language of 'identification of the initiate with the deity or the deity's fate'.

12 Ibid. 115f; so too Griffiths is happy enough to talk still of identification with Osiris ('Concept' 203). It was, moreover, not only Osiris with whom the dead might be identified: Brandon, 'Significance' 42, points out that 'union' with Re can become identification with him: in *The Story of Si-nuhe* the flesh of the divine king merges with him who made him (*ANET*[3] 18).

13 'École' 267; cf. Eliade, *History* 1, 99 – Osiris as a paradigmatic model.

come near to Hornung's talk of a 'role' to be played, although the idea is
not quite the same. But, as we shall see in §5.2, playing a role (or following a pattern) may nevertheless be life-transforming and indeed life-
constituting.

However some have seen in Lucius' appearance in Apul., *Met.* 11.24 a
clear statement of his actual identification with Osiris, while others have
also suggested that he re-enacted the fate of Osiris in his initiation: in
particular his baptism (§23) recalled the drowning of Osiris in the Nile[14].
But this is perhaps surprising, since no mention has been made hitherto
of Osiris; it is not Osiris but Isis who rules in the underworld, we have
been told[15]; Anubis, but not Osiris, features in the procession in §11; and
when Lucius is initiated into the rites of Osiris at Rome, he tells us that
'although the principle of the deity himself and of his faith was associated,
and indeed was at one, with that of Isis, yet a very great distinction was
made in the rites of initiation' (§27, tr. Griffiths)[16]. In the light of this it
is doubtful whether it is enough to say that these rites were 'identical as
far as their profound meaning was concerned' but were 'clothed in different outward trappings'[17]. It might be that the answer lies in seeing Osiris
in these rites as very much a passive figure, victim of a violent death but
restored to life by the power of his sister-wife[18]. Or perhaps he was passed
over completely. The emphasis in the Osiris-rites, on the other hand,
might well have been laid far more on the power of Osiris, 'the great god

---

14 Griffiths, *Isis-Book* 298, argues against Dibelius that although it is never mentioned that the
initiate shares Osiris' fate, 'the concept is so basic, however, in the Egyptian tradition that it
can scarcely be avoided' (cf. 307); cf. Malaise, *Conditions* 232; Salditt-Trappmann, *Tempel*
64; also Kuss, *Röm.* 361. Contrast Carlson, *Baptism* 194; Dey, Παλιγγενεσία 91; Dibelius,
'Isis Initiation' 77 (also 108 n. 40); Köster, *Einführung* 195=ET 1, 190; Krämer, 'Isisformel'
94; Wagner, *Baptism* 105f.
15 Köster, *ibid.*
16 V. d. Leeuw, *Religion* §66.3, 458, refers to 'Osiris mysteries' in ancient Egypt which took
the form of a mock battle between the forces of Osiris and his enemies. These would be very
different indeed from what is described at Cenchreae! Another form, likewise dissimilar to anything there, might be the 'mystery' of Osiris referred to by Bleeker, 'Initiation' 56, in which
Osiris' death and resurrection 'were actualized by shaping his broken and reconstructed body
in certain moulds'; this may be supported by Firm. Mat., *Err. prof. rel.* 22.3 – see below.
17 Malaise, *Conditions* 235.
18 Cf., e.g., Eliade, *History* 1, 98; n.b. Griffiths, *Origins* 232: it is Horus who saves, not Osiris –
see also Köster, *Einführung* 195=ET 1, 190; Witt, *Isis* 249. This is in tension with the dominant
role ascribed to Osiris by Frankfort, *Kingship* e.g. 183, 289 (Isis is in 'total dependence' upon
Osiris; 'Osiris dominates Isis'). But we need not go further into this discussion, for it is clear
that by the Hellenistic age Isis has become a very dominant figure.
The only clear instance of Osiris' playing an active role in the salvation of his devotees is in the
prayer to him to give cold water to the dead, a function which he fulfils as beneficent king of
the underworld: cf. Vidman, *Sylloge* 459–62 (the last he dates to 1st century C.E. – contrast
Zuntz, *Persephone* 370), 778.

and supreme parent of the gods', the 'unconquered' one (§27)[19]. Thus we may well have to remain very tentative about Osiris' playing an explicit part in the cult of Isis at Cenchreae, bearing in mind also that in the Greek East Sarapis had largely displaced Osiris and that even in the Latin West the latter only appears infrequently[20]. That Osiris is worshipped in Rome by no means implies that he figures at all prominently in Cenchreae; after all Sarapis too was worshipped in Corinth[21], although he does not figure at all in Apuleius' account. But even if Osiris did play a subordinate part in the Isis rites, it would be far more plausible to see the moment of his subjection to death, and the initiate's re-enactment of that, in the point in the rites where Lucius 'trod on Proserpina's threshold' (§23), rather than in the ritual bath just before[22]. But more likely still is that Òsiris' death was not re-enacted but that he was foremost among the 'infernal gods' whom Lucius mentions that he had met and worshipped.

It is, nevertheless, true that devotees of Isis in the festivals of that goddess did re-enact her search for the dead Osiris and rejoiced with her at his rediscovery; that is attested by the cry 'We have found; let us join in rejoicing'[23]! That is, however, re-enacted *in public* and it is a re-enactment of *Isis'* experience, not Osiris'; the devotees mourn with Isis[24] and share her subsequent joy. If a hope for the devotees' survival is implicit in this joy (and it may be reading too much into it to see this here)[25],

---

19 Cf. Brandon, *Man* 36; it seems to me highly speculative when Hölbl, 'Gottheiten' 166, suggests the contents of the Roman rites of Osiris-initiation. What we do have is the hope of living for ever with Osiris in Vidman, *Sylloge* 463; Griffiths may therefore be right to see his saving role confined to the world of the dead (*Origins* 233); cf. also Kees, *Totenglauben* 352.

20 Cf. Vidman, *Isis* 10–15; a comparison of the maps for the distribution of finds relative to the cults of Isis and Osiris at the end of Malaise, *Inventaire* (maps 10 and 11) will make the point immediately. Cf. Nock, 'Cremation' 300: 'a god who is a little in the background in the hellenistic cult'. See also Griffiths, *Isis-Book* 188; Sänger, *Judentum* 127; Tran Tam Tinh, *Essai* 100 (in the festival celebrating discovery of Osiris' body Isis plays the leading role – cf. *P. Oxy.* 1380.187–9, 242f – 'thou madest great Osiris immortal').

21 For Corinth the presence of Sarapis is attested from 3rd–2nd century B.C.E. onwards – Vidman, *Sylloge* 34*a*.

22 The bath in §23 is, according to Griffiths, *Isis-Book* 286f, probably the usual washing preliminary to any act of worship; there is a tension between this statement and his endorsement of Reitzenstein's association of the baptism with rebirth (289 following Reitzenstein, *Mysterienreligionen* 220f), although he criticizes him (298) for too great use of the *Rhind Funerary Papyrus* 1 and the idea of apotheosis by drowning found there.

23 Sen., *Apocolocyntosis* 13; Firm. Mat., *Err. prof. rel.* 2.9: εὑρήκαμεν συγχαίρομεν.

24 So Minucius Felix, *Octavius* 22.1; Paulinus of Nola, *Carmina* 19.111–116 in Hopfner, *Fontes* 648; cf. Greßmann, *Tod* 7, 36. I wonder whether Nock ('Note' 48) has conceded too much in saying that devotees of the mystery-gods sympathized with the deity who suffered, if by that is meant the one mourned for rather than the one who suffers loss and bereavement (cf. on Eleusis below).

25 But cf. Dunand, *Culte* 3, 281: 'one can grant that all the faithful participating in these ceremonies may have hoped to be identified with Osiris and to benefit themselves in the after-life, from the protection of Isis' (applying particularly to the Egyptian rites).

then it is likely that that hope rested on the power of the faithful Isis to restore the dead to life[26]. Certainly many looked to her for healing[27], and her restoration of Osiris to life can be regarded as yet another manifestation of this power and that of her magic[28]. It is possible that the same search and finding played its part in the mysteries of Isis[29], yet it might also be possible that the assertion that this was part of the mysteries too[30] was made solely on the basis of what was known about the cult from its public aspects, had not Plutarch clearly indicated that the mysteries of Isis contained images (εἰκόνες) and allusions (ὑπονοίαι) and representations (μιμήματα) of the contests (ἆθλοι) and struggles (ἀγῶνες) that she had endured and her wanderings (πλάναι)[31]. That remark is all the more authoritative in a work addressed to an initiate of Osiris (*Is. et Os.* 35.364E). Yet there is no hint of it in Apuleius' account either of the public rites of Isis which he describes or, particularly, of the secret initiation ceremony[32]. Was it then part of the rites of Osiris or of Isis which he experienced at Rome? Did Plutarch too know similar rites?

This absence of references to the story of Osiris in Apuleius' account of Lucius' initiation coupled with the strong indications of solar imagery, especially in §24 where Lucius appears adorned like the sun, suggests that he was primarily identified with the sun, or at least enacted the role of the sun, visiting the domains of Osiris (the underworld) but then passing through the heavens and the upper world as well[33]. But even so Dibelius remarks that Apuleius' description reminds us 'less of the mythical experiences of the deity than of her cosmic domain'; there is no suggestion that the initiate shares the same fate as Osiris[34]. Again here we see an enact-

---

26 Cf. Simon and Eliade quoted above (§3.1.1.2 n. 13).

27 See Dunand, *Culte* 3, 258–61.

28 Bleeker, 'Isis' 8; Dunand, ibid. 262, 278f; Le Corsu, *Isis* 20–5.

29 Cf. Tran Tam Tinh, 'Sarapis' 113; Dunand, ibid. 249: 'perhaps the themes developed in the November festival were in fact taken up again in the mysteries, but accompanied by instruction given to the initiates concerning the double meaning, mythical and symbolic, of the actions represented'; cf., however, Le Corsu, *Isis* 50.

30 Athenag., *Suppl.* 22.9 (ed. Schoedel; =Hopfner, *Fontes* 344).

31 *Is. et Os.* 27.361D.

32 But cf. Griffiths' ed., e.g. 298, 307, 313. The absence of this story in Apul.' account of the public rites is less significant; after all his account is confined to the festival of the *navigium Isidis* and the daily cult of her sanctuary. (It is true that Re and Osiris tended to merge in many strands of Egyptian thought or at least to 'interpenetrate' each other, but can we assume that this remained the case, if the tendency to merge them arose from a particular tension between two competing theologies at a certain period of Egyptian history?)

33 So Bergman, *'Per omnia'* esp. 692, appealing to Reitzenstein, *Mysterienreligionen* 228, and Dibelius; cf. Liebeschuetz, *Continuity* 221.

34 'Isis Initiation' 77; v. Gennep, *Rites* 157, holds that the identification of the dead Osiris and the dead with the sun were originally separate rituals, although he sees them as later merged. Morenz, *Religion* 211, speaks of the dead being 'absorbed into the substance' of Osiris; the theology of Heliopolis had them ascending to heaven and accompanying the sun-god on his

ment of a deity's fortunes (the sun's) under the guidance of the goddess
Isis; Lucius, symbolically trusting her power to convey him through the
underworld and out again to the life beyond, henceforth will trust her
power to protect him in this world and beyond the grave[35]. It may be that
symbolically he is portrayed as Horus, or a Horus (as the Egyptian kings
were regarded), and assimilated to Horus as a sun-god[36]; the message of
the rite to those witnessing Lucius' attire is that as the great goddess
protects the sun(-god) on his daily journey, so she will protect this mortal
and grant him as glorious a destiny; she it is who orders the 'bright heights
of heaven'[37] and the silent underworld (§5). He has become a son of Isis[38].

5.1.1.3. Continually, too, it must be borne in mind that, as we have
already seen, identification with Osiris is in Egyptian rites part of a
funerary ritual; it is performed on the *dead* to speed their passage to a
happy after-life, it is not performed on the living to give assurance that
after death they will pass to this after-life. For Klauck only this would
qualify these rites as those of mysteries[1]; certainly it would be odd if there
were mysteries that were *only* relevant for the dead. Evidence that this
ritual for the dead was performed for the living in the Graeco-Roman
period is elusive[2].

We saw that the possible Egyptian precursors to Lucius' initiation which
we considered earlier were usually funerary rites, not initiations; the
experiences of the deity were also a pattern for those of the dead. But
any closer analogy to Romans 6 at the stage of the *Pyramid Texts* at least

---

journey (not the same as identification with him); cf. 107, where it is clearer that he views
these as alternatives.

35 Compare here the Egyptian texts cited above in §5.1.1.1 nn. 30f which tell of Isis' protection
of the sun in his travels.

36 Cf. Bergman, *'Per omnia'* 692, quoting the *Hymn to Isis* from Aswan: 'You (Isis) rejoice in
your son Horus, when he opens his eye in the heavens; his face illumines the earth at dawn,
when he has placed his eye as the sun. He is Re.' (Text in Bresciani-Pernigotti, *Assuan* B.13,
62f.) See also Pascher, 'Οδός 78f. Sänger, *Judentum* 139, comments that reff. to Osiris as sun-
god are infrequent, but cf. Plut., *Is. et Os.* 52.372D, and *P. Salt* 825, 18.1−2, as quoted by
Junge, 'Isis' 106 (Derchain's 'C'est Râ et c'est Osiris' is enigmatic − 144; Junge has 'Re ist es
und dieser ist Osiris'); contrast P. Wendland, *Kultur* 117.

37 Here I depart from Griffiths' 'starry', for 'luminosa' surely refers to more sources of light than
just the stars.

38 Cf. Vidman, *Sylloge* 585: after his death a 16-year-old boy will bear the name of Isis' son. Yet
Nilsson, *Geschichte* 2, 688, holds that in the mysteries, in distinction to Christianity, initiates
were never referred to as children of the mystery-deity.

Notes on 5.1.1.3

1 *Herrenmahl* 126 − contrast J. G. Griffiths, *Isis-Book* 316, who moves directly from initiation
to funerary rites.

2 Yet Cumont, *After Life* 203, argues that the rites of dying and rising gods in general were a
development of funerary ritual; cf. (tentatively) Griffiths, *Isis-Book* 31.

is impossible because (a) those for whom the rites were performed were very literally dead[3] and (b) the rites re-enacted the actions either of the gods Re or Horus or of the goddesses Isis and Nephthys or other Egyptian deities[4], so that the hope of immortality is as much based on their power to save (and so is of type A) as on any power inherent in Osiris himself[5]. Indeed Wagner goes so far as to maintain that even as king of the underworld Osiris needs the protection of benevolent gods[6]. It could, of course, be pointed out that Jesus too was dependent upon the power of God to rescue him from death (Rom 8.11, etc.); yet there still remains the difference that the Egyptian rites focus on the actions of the saving deities, not on the sufferings of the saved one.

But what of more recent periods in the history of Egyptian religion? The burial rites performed for the Pharaohs came to be more widely used; the queens of the Sixth Dynasty and later nobles and others were exalted as the Pharaohs had previously been, by association with Osiris[7]. But the fundamental point still remains that these were rites for the dead and they imitated the experiences and actions of the saviour gods and goddesses, not the saved god Osiris; they are performed by the living on behalf of the dead. It is the latter whose experiences and hopes were made to cor-

---

3 Cf. Bianchi, 'Iside' 29.

4 Isis is particularly prominent in the *Hymn to Osiris* quoted by Erman, *Literature* 143: 'His sister protected him, she that held the foes aloof and warded off the deeds of the miscreant by the beneficent things of her mouth . . . . Beneficent Isis, that protecteth her brother, that sought for him without wearying, that traversed the land mourning, and took no rest until she found him . . . '. Horus too is praised (144): ' "The son of Isis hath protected his father . . ." '; cf. Brandon, 'Significance' 42f: the whole funerary process 'was conceived as ritually accomplishing on behalf of the deceased what had once been done, so it was believed, by the deities Isis, Nephthys and Anubis to save the dead body of Osiris from physical disintegration.' Cf. Moret, *Mystères* 37f. On the enhanced role of Anubis at a later period cf. Vermaseren, *Mithras* 199, 202.

5 Griffiths, *Origins* 232 n. 60, holds it to be a fundamental difference between Christian beliefs and Egyptian ones that the former were concerned with a historical person, the latter with a god of the dead. It is Horus and other deities who have saved Osiris (233); cf. E. Otto in *HO* 1.8.1, 43: 'the character of the god (Osiris) is passive'.

6 *Baptism* 119; presumably he is thinking of a text like Junker, *Stundenwachen,* with its repeated mention of protecting deities who defeat Osiris' enemies for him (2, 35, etc.) or Junker-Winter, *Geburtshaus* 199, where Isis is 'she who protects her brother from enemies; cf. also Moret, *Mystères* 36; Zandee, *Death* 221–3; or else (less naturally?) when the re-ascent of Re after his rest in Osiris' realm is described as Horus' triumph over his father's enemies (cf. Assmann, *Lieder* 104f with n. 81 and 110f). See also again E. Otto as in the previous n.: 'even his existence in the kingdom of the dead is a shadowy and suffering one'.

7 Griffiths, *Origins* 230: he argues that even when the earlier texts spoke only thus of the king, he was regarded as a 'corporate personality which embodied his subjects' (cf. *Pyramid Texts* 371a, Sethe 2, 90, quoted on 231); his elevation may have brought a similar status to his people. Cf. also Bonnet, *Reallexikon* 347; Frankfort, *Kingship* 208f; Morenz, *Religion* 55; Ringgren, *Religionen* 61f.

respond to those of slain Osiris[8]. Moreover, as Frankfort notes[9], the rites
never apparently represent the dying of Osiris; they present him as one
already dead, to whom the living may assimilate their dead.

Though both funerary rites and initiatory ones are 'rites of passage',
these Egyptian ones remained the former as far as we have any firm evidence. Morenz argues strongly that they were never anything else as far as
the Egyptians were concerned. That Hellenistic influence changed this
by transferring funerary rites to the living as an initiation in a mystery is
unproven, but possible, as I granted above. Junge suggests that the Graeco-
Roman mysteries of Isis and particularly of Osiris were rather an extension of the secret rites and dramas performed by priests and a few others
in the inner rooms of temples as documented by Junker in his edition of
the *Stundenwachen*[10]. In that case the rites would be more concerned
with the perpetuation of the existence of the god and the continuation of
his beneficent presence, offering a hope of immortality hereafter in the
kingdom where he continued to exercise his kingly power despite the continual efforts of opposing evil forces to suppress him[11]. This would be an
extension of the pattern of type B in which the rites would assure the
worshippers that the victory of the god still prevailed. Whether the Hellenistic rites were transferred funerary rites or were the successors of these
latter rites they still do not provide any *close* parallel to Paul's idea of
union with Christ.

However, some have seen in a passage of Firmicus Maternus the evidence that hitherto has eluded us: in 22.3 he describes rites which are
probably those of the Egyptian cult –

> It is an idol that you bury, it is an idol which you mourn, it is an idol which you bring
> forth from the grave; wretched one, do you rejoice at having done so? You set your god
> free, you arrange his inert stone limbs in place, you restore senseless rock. May your
> god thank you, and bestow like gifts upon you, and desire you to participate in him-
> self. May you die as he dies; may your life be like his.

R. Turcan's comment on this passage is perhaps over-hasty: 'the ritual of
the mysteries causes the devotees to share in the death and resurrection

---

8 Cf. Moret, *Mystères* 37ff; also Junge, 'Isis' 100.

9 *Kingship* 185, 204.

10 'Isis' 107; on 109 he seems to suggest, however, that the initiatory rites were part of the Egyptian cult of the dead, which is then qualified on the following page by the suggestion that they
   were based on the similar initiation rites for Egyptian priests; this confusing set of identifications is perhaps explicable by noting that all three rites, funerary, initiatory and those for consecrating priests, (a) prepared the recipients for fellowship with the gods and (b) marked a
   transition from one life to another.

11 Cf. Kees, *Totenglauben* 352, quoting the *British Museum Stele* 574: 'that the god may be fav-
   orable to me in judgment, when I am "there"' (tr. Breasted, *Records* 1, 277 §613); he also
   quotes from *Louvre Stele* C15 (but see the strengthened criticism of Moret's interpretation of
   this stele in the 2nd ed. of 1956, 252).

or rebirth of the god'[12]. For we should recall that this is the ironic comment of a Christian critic, viewing these rites and their meaning from a Christian perspective, perhaps even a Pauline perspective. The resemblance to Paul may, however, be more apparent than real; Firmicus may simply be wishing that in the future the god's devotees may come to share his fate, his death – a very real one – which they re-enact, and also his life – an illusory one. We have to note that the rites are performed upon an image of the god, not upon the worshippers. There is no ritual anticipation by the worshipper of his own burial and rescue from the grave[13]. Now it is true that the rescue of the god may have offered the worshipper the hope that he too would one day be rescued in a similar manner, but the confidence that he had is more likely to have been either in the efficacy of the ritual to do the same for him after his own death and burial or in the power of Isis to do the same for him as she did for Osiris or in both of these together[14]. The likely pattern of hopes here is thus again of type B, as with the suggestion above of the derivation of the Graeco-Roman Osiris mysteries from ritual re-enactments of Osiris' burial and rescue.

5.1.1.4. We have already seen that in the second century C.E. the orator (and hypochondriac?) Aelius Aristides gives some insight into his relations with *Sarapis*. Although the latter was not commonly a mystery-god[1], Aelius views his relations with him almost as those of an initiate (*Or.* 49.48=*Or. sacr.* 3.48)[2]: after a vision convincing him of Sarapis' power, enabling him to carry mortals whithersoever he wishes, Aelius concludes 'such was the initiation ($\tau\epsilon\lambda\epsilon\tau\acute{\eta}$)'. Sarapis can also, we find, bless his devotees in this life, purifying the soul with wisdom and giving health

---

12 Ed. 319; Pastorino, ed. 227 notes the view of G. Heuten that one could not have a better statement of the 'essential doctrine' of the mysteries, that association with the god guarantees the initiate's resurrection (in the latter's comm. on Firm., Bruxelles, 1938); surprisingly Simon too sees in 'sic moriaris ut moritur; sic vivas ut vivit' the 'very essence of the mysteries' ('*Schule*' 140f).

13 Contrast Hölbl, 'Gottheiten' 166: . . .'The Osiris initiation, in which the initiand symbolically suffered Osiris' death'.

14 But note the caution – again perhaps excessive – of MacMullen, *Paganism* 55: 'It should really not be taken for granted . . . that people who believe a god might rise from the dead also believed in such a blessing for themselves as well. The conjecture needs support – and finds none.'

Notes on 5.1.1.4

1 For evidence of Sarapis as a mystery-god cf. Klauck, *Herrenmahl* 133 nn. 284–6 (generally late – 3rd century; by this period mysteries were thoroughly fashionable); *contra* see the authorities named in n. 283.

2 Cf. §5.1.1.1 above. His relations with Asclepius are similarly described in *Or.* 48.28, 32; 50.7. Tr. Behr.

to the body and even granting the possession of money (45.18), enriching life both spiritually and materially (45.19, cf. 20). The hopes and expectations here seem to be of type A, though some of the experiences, like that of 49.48, may have been a foretaste of future protection and so of type A^1.

Cumont also points to a series of funerary bas-reliefs where the dead are portrayed as wearing the *kalathos* of Sarapis. Here he finds a continuation of Egyptian beliefs, in which the dead person is assimilated to the god of the dead[3]. Instead, that is, of becoming Osiris he becomes Sarapis. However this is still a funerary practice for the dead and not an initiation for the living. Nor was Sarapis a mystery-god in the usual sense, although he may have been viewed in a similar way by Aelius; there is at least no myth of *his* sufferings.

5.1.1.5. In *summary*, then, the complex evidence of the Egyptian cults shows us clearly the initiate and the goddess Isis entering into a relationship in which the initiate throws himself upon the sovereign power of Isis to protect him in this world and the next. The rites which are alluded to in Apuleius' account may well have been as it were a preview of the exercise of that power, but there is no hint in Lucius' initiation into the rites of Isis that he was identified with Osiris or re-enacted Osiris' sufferings. Conceivably he was identified with Horus, her son.

Identification with Osiris or Sarapis, in some sense (see further §5.2), did take place, in funerary rites. The influence of these upon the mysteries of Osiris in the Graeco-Roman world, let alone upon the mysteries of Isis, is hard to demonstrate. Devotees of Isis did, however, unite with her in her searching for Osiris and her subsequent joy at his discovery; this was a matter of public knowledge. The ministrations of Isis and her helpers which resulted in Osiris' being found and restored to life were evidently re-enacted in some mysteries too, and it is possible that these formed the content of the rites of Osiris to which Apuleius refers and which were so different from those of Isis at Cenchreae. Yet did they not too show the power of the goddess Isis to save (perhaps this is what Apuleius means by the *inunita ratio numinis religionisque* in 11.27)? The great god Osiris would remain a passive figure in these rites. At least that would be the inference that we would be justified in drawing if Firm. Mat., *Err. prof. rel.* 22.3 refers to this rite (see also §5.1.5 below). Instead of being, as it were, safely escorted through his own death as in Lucius' initiation at Cenchreae the initiate would contemplate the power of the

---

3 *Religions* 75=*Religionen* 74.

goddess to save Osiris, as ritually depicted before his eyes, receiving thence the confidence that she would do the same for him and thus bring him into fellowship with the great god Osiris. Whereas the former pattern was that of type A[1], the latter would have been of type B.

5.1.2. The *Eleusinian* rites are a difficult problem: unquestionably the form of the rites reflects the myth of Demeter's search for her daughter[1]. The σύνθημα which Clement of Alexandria and Arnobius quote (see above §2) refers to two prominent elements in that search, Demeter's fasting and drinking of cyceon offered to her which ends that fast:

> . . . for nine days queenly Deo wandered over the earth with flaming torches in her hands, so grieved that she never tasted ambrosia and the sweet draught of nectar, nor sprinkled her body with water. . . . A long time she sat (in the house of Celeus) . . ., never smiling, and tasting neither food nor drink, until careful Iambe . . . moved the holy lady with many a quip and jest to smile and laugh and cheer her heart. Then Metaneira filled a cup with sweet wine and offered it to her, but she refused it, for she said it was not lawful for her to drink red wine, but made them to mix meal and water with soft mint and give her to drink. And Metaneira mixed the draught (κυκεών) and gave it to the goddess as she bade. So the great queen Deo received it to observe the sacrament (ὁσίης ἕνεκεν)[2].

Various artistic representations of the initiation of Heracles and others suggest that other parts of the rites, whether they were part of the actual initiation or preparatory rites for those especially defiled[3] (and Berner's insistence upon the *Stufenstruktur* of the initiatory rites of the mysteries may mean that this is an unnecessary distinction, except in so far as some stages may not have been obligatory for all), also echoed the experiences of the goddess when Iambe 'placed a jointed seat for her and threw over

---

Notes on 5.1.2

1 Lact., *Inst. epitome* 18 (23).7; also Clem. Alex., *Prot.* 2.12.2 (the rape of Kore is also celebrated). Cf. Burkert, *Homo* 304=ET 275. In Samothrace too there is a ritual searching for Harmonia, daughter of Electra or Electryone, and Burkert infers 'a myth about Harmonia's abduction parallel to the fate of Persephone' (*Religion* 424=ET 284, citing Ephorus in *FGH* 70 frg. 120).
And yet Clem. Alex., *Prot.* 2.20.1, puzzlingly tells us that initiates are forbidden so to act that they might seem to imitate the sorrowing goddess, but this (τοῦτο, sing.) may only refer to sitting at the well.

2 *Homeric Hymn to Demeter* 47–50, 198–211 (tr. Evelyn-White); Richardson, *Hymn* 211, translates the last phrase 'for the sake of the rite'; so too Kane, 'Meal' 340: 'Clearly, the phrase should be regarded as a reference to the *ritual* associated with this incident in the myth'; Evelyn-White's translation he rightly regards as 'certainly too bold or too ambiguous'. Cf. Speiser, 'Mysterien' 367: in the fasting of the initiates 'we have the ritual repetition of the mythology of Demeter, and thus a move towards identifying the initiate with the diety'; cf. Kuss, *Röm.* 347.

3 So Mylonas, *Eleusis* 207.

it a silvery fleece'[4]. The Lovatelli urn depicts Heracles holding a pig and a hooded Heracles sitting on a stool, his bare feet resting on a ram's skin, a priestess holding a winnowing fan over his head[5]. A sarcophagus from Torre Nova shows a comparable scene: again a hooded figure on a stool with bare feet placed on a ram's fleece, with a female figure standing behind with burning torches[6]. Akin to this is a relief in the National Museum of Naples[7]. Bianchi includes in this series a plate of a terracotta relief from the Museo Nazionale delle Terme in Rome which he compares with the left and middle scenes on the Lovatelli urn[8]. When we turn to the *Homeric Hymn to Demeter* we can see how closely the posture of the seated figure corresponds to Demeter's in the house of Celeus: Iambe fetches a 'jointed stool' ($\pi\eta\kappa\tau\grave{o}\nu$ $\check{\epsilon}\delta o\varsigma$) for her to sit on and throws over it a 'silvery fleece'; she sits with veiled face on the stool ($\delta\acute{\iota}\phi\rho o\varsigma$)[9]. Now it is true that we would infer from this that the fleece was on the stool and not under her feet and that her face was covered by something lighter than the heavy cloak covering the initiates' heads. All the same, it is hard to resist the conclusion that the initiates' posture reflects that of the mourning Demeter[10]. Moreoever Hesychius tells us that enthronement ($\theta\rho\acute{o}\nu\omega\sigma\iota\varsigma$) was part of the preparatory rites for initiates[11].

Demeter's drink of cyceon too had its place in the initiatory rites as we saw when looking at the formula quoted by Clement of Alexandria and Arnobius in §2; one of the actions mentioned there is the drinking of cyceon[12].

Yet the difficulty mentioned at the start of this section remains: in all this it is clearly Demeter's actions that are copied, not those of her

---

4 *Hom. Hymn to Demeter* 195f (tr. Evelyn-White); cf. Richardson, *Hymn* 211.

5 See Bianchi, *Mysteries* pl. 50; Kerenyi, *Eleusis* pl. 12 (pp. 56f); Leipoldt-Grundmann, *Umwelt* 3, pl. 31; Mylonas, *Eleusis* pl. 83.

6 See Bianchi, ibid. pl. 84; Kerenyi, ibid. pl. 11 (54); Leipoldt-Grundmann, ibid. pl. 34; Mylonas, ibid. pl. 84.

7 See Bianchi, ibid. pl. 49.

8 Ibid. pls 51f.

9 Lines 195–8.

10 Cf. Burkert, *Homo* 294–6 =ET 266–9; *Religion* 427 = ET 286, who describes this as a propitiatory rite.

11 S. v. $\theta\rho\acute{o}\nu\omega\sigma\iota\varsigma$ (Latte 2, 331); cf. Plato, *Euthyd.* 277D. Dio Chrys., *Or.* 12.33 might suggest that $\theta\rho o\nu\iota\sigma\mu\acute{o}\varsigma$ was part of initiation itself, but perhaps it is inexact to distinguish a necessary preamble from the subsequent rites. If this rite was part of the preliminary rites, then it is unlikely that Farnell is correct in suggesting that it was 'aimed at producing the impression of deification in the mortal' (*Cults* 3, 301; cf. Graillot, *Culte* 184).

12 Richardson, *Hymn* 347: the drink may have been basically an 'agricultural' ritual, but the initiate would also 'have felt that he was following the example of the goddess, sharing her food as well as her fast, and performing an act that had been "consecrated" by her'; cf. Kane, 'Meal' 340f. Burkert, *Homo* 303 (ET 274f) finds in our uncertainty as to the stage at which cyceon

ill-fated daughter who dies and is brought back, albeit temporarily[13]. As with the case of the public (and the secret?) rites of Isis it is the mourning of the one left on earth that is copied, just as presumably joy follows when death gives up its prisoner, at least for a season[14]. The fact that the initiates and worshippers align themselves with Demeter and Isis, not Kore and Osiris, underlines the difference between their expectations and those of types C and D outlined above. In other words, in these two cults the 'mystic sympathy' of the devotees of which Kennedy speaks is a sympathy with the grief of the mother and the sister/wife, not with the vanished daughter or husband/brother[15]. Moreover, as has been noted by several scholars, the *telestērion* where the rites took place contained 'no true entrance to the nether world, no chasm, no possibility of acting out a journey into the underworld'[16].

One possible exception to this is the sacrifice of pigs at the festival of the *Thesmophoria* and before initiation. Clement of Alexandria explains the former by referring to the pigs of Eubouleus which were swallowed up by the earth along with Persephone (*Prot.* 2.17.1)[17]; this fits the symbolism of the *Thesmophoria* in which the pigs' bodies were cast afterwards into underground caverns, but it is not clear how they were disposed of after the preliminary sacrifice in initiation. It seems that the initiands also each sacrificed a pig on their own behalf[18]; however this last observation may be based on the rationale of sacrifice in general, and conflicts with the suggestion that 'the pig-sacrifice had the character of an anticipatory sacrifice of a maiden'[19], and the tradition that pigs had thus to die because a herd of them had obscured the tracks left by Hades

---

was drunk 'an indication that it probably belonged to the secret central portion of the festival' (but cf. Richardson, ibid. 213).

13 Cf. Colpe in *Gn.* 48f; Kerenyi, *Eleusis* 144f.

14 Apollodorus in *FGH* 244 frg. 110(b): Kore is summoned by the hierophant with a gong; cf. Lact., *Inst.* 1.21.24 and *epitome* 18 (23).7; Burkert, 'ΓΟΗΣ' 40.

15 *St Paul* 206. However, quite whether one should call this 'mystic' is questionable if by that one means part of the secret mysteries, for this sympathy found expression in public rites.

16 Burkert, *Religion* 429=ET 288; cf. Mylonas, *Eleusis* 17. Contrast the similar sanctuary at the oracle of the dead near Ephyre in Thesprotia, of which Garland, *Way* 3, comments that 'it differs from Eleusis in that it was constructed over a vaulted subterranean chamber where, presumably, the encounter with the dead would take place'.
Others make more of the adjacent grotto dedicated to Pluto: cf., e.g., Schneider, *Mysterien* 16.

17 Cf. schol. on Luc. 275.24–276.3 (Rabe); Burkert, *Religion* 367, 427=ET 243, 286; *Homo* 283–92=ET 256–64.

18 Burkert, ibid. 285=ET 258, translates the ὑπὲρ ἑαυτοῦ of schol. on Aristoph., *Ach.* 747 'in his stead' (cf. 292=ET 264) and argues that a life was exchanged for a life. That is true if the ὑπέρ is identical with the ἀντί of Porphyry, *Abst.* 2.28, which he also cites; that may, but need not, be the case.

19 Burkert, ibid. 286=ET 259. This would hardly square with a sacrifice of a pig in the place of a male initiand.

in his abduction of Persephone[20]. All in all, it is hard to see at all clearly in this a vicarious death of the initiands with Persephone.

It is perhaps also tempting to see some connection between the bright blazing light that was so characteristic of the rites and accompanied their climax[21] and the puzzling incident in the *Homeric Hymn* in which Demeter hides the infant Demophoön in the fire at night[22]:

> And the child grew like some immortal being, not fed with food nor nourished [at the breast: for by day rich-crowned] Demeter would anoint him with ambrosia as if he were the offspring of a god and breathe sweetly upon him as she held him in her bosom. But at night she would hide him like a brand in the heart of the fire, unknown to his dear parents. (235–40)

The parents wondered at his growth, 'for he was like the gods face to face'; but Demeter's hopes of making him immortal[23] were frustrated by Metaneira's interrupting her one night and crying out in distress

> Demophoön, my son, the strange woman buries you deep in fire and works grief and bitter sorrow for me. (248f)

In fury the goddess tells her that she has spoiled her plans for Demophoön and that he will now not escape death and the fates. But

> I am that Demeter who has share of honour and is the greatest help and cause of joy to the undying gods and mortal men. (268f)[24]

She commands a temple to be built at Eleusis and says that she will teach her rites (ὄργια) so that they may win her favour by performing them[25].

---

20 Ovid, *Fasti* 4. 465f.

21 Ael. Arist., *Or.* 22.11; Clem. Alex., *Prot.* 2.22.1; Dio Chrys., *Or.* 12.33; Himerius, *Or.* 8.8; 29.1; 60.4; Hipp., *Ref.* 5.8.40; Plut., *Prof. virt.* 10.81E; *Them.* 15.1. Kerenyi also refers to *Milan Papyrus* 20 where an initiate states '[I have beheld] the fire whence [and] I have seen the Kore' (*Eleusis* 83f).

   Is there perhaps also here a connection with the practice which v. d. Leeuw mentions (*Religion* 193) of ἀμφιδρομία, in which a naked man runs round a fire with a newborn infant, 'the fire's potency being thereby extracted'?

   Yet, equally, some of the reff. cited above may refer to the light accompanying the discovery of Kore (Apul., *Met.* 6.2; cf. also Lact. in n. 1 above). V. d. Leeuw, too, expressly connects it with the idea of 'baptism of fire' (195); Eliade, *Birth* 7, 138 n. 13, gives a number of examples of an ordeal by roasting near a fire in initiation ceremonies, which may be comparable here. Cf. Burkert, *Religion* 384=ET 255, Nilsson, *Geschichte* 1, 95 (a more prosaic interpretation).

22 An incident borrowed by the cult of Isis seemingly: Plut., *Is. et Os.* 15–16.357A–D; cf. ed. Griffiths 320f, 324f; Klauck, *Herrenmahl* 125 n. 232; Le Corsu, *Isis* 61; Richardson, *Hymn* 238.

23 Burkert's reading between the lines that Metaneira's reaction was all too correct and that Demeter *was* trying to kill Demophoön, a child sacrifice to correspond to the loss of her daughter (*Homo* 309=ET 280), conceivably may reflect the hidden origins of the cult but certainly runs counter to the message of the *Hymn*; it cannot surely tell us much about the expectations of participants in an even later period. Richardson, *Hymn* 240, sees here the idea of a 'burning away or purging the mortal parts', or releasing the divine in mortals by fire.

24 Tr. Evelyn-White.

25 Cf. Burkert, *Homo* 326=ET 296: 'one can only hope that the gods will be merciful'.

Later she keeps this promise (476). Then a blessing is pronounced on those who have seen (ὄπωπεν) these rites; in contrast the one who has not experienced them enjoys no share of the blessings they confer but must simply remain in the gloomy underworld (480–2). Again the evidence is at best suggestive, implying that the rites assure initiates that, though they will die as Demophoön did[26], yet they have in Demetèr a very great help and joy that will not desert them in the world to come. The place in the rites of the boy specially chosen for initiation 'from the hearth' may point to a role in which a boy plays the part for all initiates of the child whom Demeter wished to bring to immortal life through seeming death[27]. The association of her daughter in the rites may have been a further comfort, assuring them of the powerful protection of the queen of the underworld[28], but attention centres rather on the power of the mother, to bless both in this life and in the next[29]. The rites may also have shown her power in recalling her daughter to life when the latter was summoned in the rites by a gong[30]. The hope offered for the world to come is very clearly attested for the Eleusinian rites[31], but it is signif-

---

26 It might be tempting to suggest that the attempted deification of Demophoön prefigured the rites, and the intentions, of the mysteries, but Eliade, *History* 1, 292, states, rather categorically, that 'initiation of the "mystery" type differs radically from the initiation interrupted by Metaneira. The initiate into the Eleusinian mysteries did not obtain immortality.' To introduce talk of 'cremation' at this point is perhaps misleading (but cf. Kerenyi, *Eleusis* 94); the recollection of this incident could legitimately have assured the initiate of the will and the ability of the goddess to immortalize human beings. The blazing light so characteristic of the Eleusinian rites might then have symbolized this power of the goddess.

27 Cf. Burkert, *Homo* 309=ET 280f. It may be more plausible to see initiates' hopes resting on this incident – for Demophoön was like them a mortal – rather than on the rescue of Kore (*pace* Kuss, *Röm.* 351); see too Kerenyi, *Eleusis* 94. Yet Burkert argues that the hearth referred to is probably 'the state hearth of the Prytanes at the marketplace'; but in the instances of the phrase cited ἀφ' ἑστίας seems to qualify μυεῖσθαι and that is surely more easily understood if the hearth is actually where the initiation takes place (*IG* 1² 6.108f; Harpocration, ed. Dindorf 1, 69.13f; Bekker, *Anecdota* 1, 204.19f; Clinton, *Officials* 98–114, esp. 98–100 and no. 7, 110 no. 38; 112f, no. 51 and ?54f).

28 Burkert, *Religion* 251=ET 161, suggests that fundamentally Demeter too is a chthonic deity (cf. the evidence quoted in n. 27 – ET 411: Plut., *Fac. lun.* 28.943B; Cic., *De legibus* 2.25.63).

29 Cf. Alderink, 'Structure' 8, 12f; Bianchi, *Mysteries* 2, 4; Kroll, 'Elysium' 32; Speiser, 'Mysterien' 370, 372, suggests that Demeter had this power as the one who gives life to corn, by analogy she ensures eternal life to her human devotees.
There is the suggestion that the mysterious announcement that 'the Mistress has given birth to a holy boy, Brimo to Brimos' (Hipp., *Ref.* 5.8.39) is a reference to Demeter's son Plutos, wealth given in the ear of corn manifested to the initiates (ibid. 40); cf. Burkert, *Religion* 430=ET 288; *Homo* 318–21=ET 288–91 – Dumuzi was also represented by a blade of wheat.
One of the gold leaves from Thurii seems to express a similar confidence based upon the protection of the daughter, Persephone: 'I sank into the bosom of the Mistress, the chthonic queen' (*Orph. Fr.* 32c=Diels-Kranz, *Fragmente* §1 B 18); the verb is reminiscent of the language of the formula quoted by Clem. Alex., *Prot.* 2.15.3 (ἔδυν/ὑπέδυν).

30 Cf. n. 14 above (Apollodorus).

31 Not only is there the promise of the *Homeric Hymn* quoted above but cf. Pindar frg. 137

icant that Burkert, commenting on the hope of bliss in the next world promised to initiates, concludes 'whence it [the Eleusinian rite] could draw its force of conviction remains a mystery to us'[32]. However texts like Aristophanes, *Ranae* 312–459 give a vivid picture of the Eleusinian procession (coupled with references to Dionysiac rites and with Orphic elements)[33] being celebrated still in Hades.

Here we should note again the importance of the Eleusinian cult for our investigation: we saw in §2.3 the position of these rites as a pattern inspiring the formation and transformation of other rites. If they do not include the idea of sharing in the deity's fate as postulated by advocates of a common theology of the mysteries, then one major source for such a unified theology is removed, and it is far less likely that a unified theology built around this idea existed in the various cults. In fact we have found only a sharing in the experiences of the deity who mourned, not the one who was mourned for, as we saw in the case of the Egyptian cult also.

5.1.3. It is hard to find in all the variegated cult of *Dionysus* instances of the initiate identifying himself with the sufferings of the god. Already we have seen[1] that one possible example ought to be eliminated: the rending and eating of raw flesh was not an imitation of Dionysus' fate at the Titans' hands for there he was cooked and, moreover, he was not captured as the result of pursuit and chase[2]. Yet at the same time the possibility of assimilation to the *ōmophagia* exists, for Plut., *Esu carn.* 7.996C refers to his dismemberment by the Titans (διαμελισμός) and their tasting of his blood. However, even if the parallel were closer, the eating would be a re-enactment of the violence of the Titans, not a con-

---

(Snell); Soph. frg. 753 (Nauck)=837 (Pearson); Isoc., 4.28 (cf. Turchi, *Fontes* §§86, 151f); *IG* 2/3², 3361=Peek, *Vers-Inschriften* 879; Ael. Arist., *Or.* 22.10; Krinagoras of Lesbos in *Anth. Pal.* 11.42.3–6; Cic., *De legibus* 2.14.36. See too Dey, Παλιγγενεσία 63f.

32 *Religion* 431=ET 289.

33 Cf. Graf, *Eleusis* 40: if we can trust the schol. on *Ran.* 314 then here we have 'evidence of the amalgamation of Dionysiac, Eleusinian and Orphic elements within the context of Eleusinian ritual of the late fifth century'. Rightly he sees clear evidence of the Eleusinian colouring of the passage (45–50).

Notes on 5.1.3

1 §2.2 esp. n. 15.

2 Cf. Klauck, *Herrenmahl* 116f – but it seems to go beyond all the evidence to argue that 'at the time of Euripides the story of the sufferings of Dionysus-Zagreus was used to interpret the rite of *ōmophagia*'. Plut. is evidence (perhaps) of the opposite influence, the *ōmophagia* colouring the story of the rending by the Titans, where originally the eating of blood would not have been so prominent. Moreover *ōmophagia* is possibly earlier than the story of the rending by the Titans (see §2.2 n. 10).

forming to the suffering victim[3]. Yet precisely that sort of re-enactment seems to be assumed by Firm. Mat., *Err. prof. rel.* 6.5, which tells of Cretans who re-enacted all that the child did or had done to him in his death; 'they tear a live bull with their teeth, summoning up the cruel feast by their annual commemorations'. Despite Pastorino's comments[4] there does not seem to be a close correlation between the rites and the myth as we know it. Nearer the truth is his reference to a merger between Cretan rites and the ordinary Dionysiac cult[5]; in such a union lies perhaps the explanation why rites and myth seem out of step, with the practices of one cult wedded to the mythology of another. Nor is it impossible that Firmicus, by mentioning the two rites one after the other, the re-enactment and the *ōmophagia*, has made them seem more closely connected than was apparent to their participants. Certainly it seems easier to see the rite of *ōmophagia* as an imitation of a god who was himself a wild and savage hunter and eater of raw flesh (ὠμάδιος, ὠμηστής)[6].

It is also true that, as Burkert notes apropos of the Dionysiac mask, 'the merging of god and votary which occurs in this metamorphosis is without parallel in the rest of Greek religion: both votary and god are called Bacchus'[7]. Others speak of this phenomenon in more guarded terms. Nock speaks of a 'spiritual union'[8], Bruhl of their being like him, not united with him[9]. Guthrie speaks of the youth leading the Bacchic rites being filled with the spirit of Dionysus and being called by his

---

3 Contrast W. F. Otto, *Dionysus* esp. 191f; Henrichs, 'Maenadism' 144f, quoting Harpocration (=Suidas N.123) and Phot., *Lex.* s.v. νεβρίζειν; only the latter seems to support this point; Diod. S. 4.3.3 only speaks of their imitating the maenads of old.

4 Ed. 84; to want to find a ref. to a bull in the *Gurob Papyrus*' mention of a goat and a ram seems forced.

5 Ibid. 84f; he implies that this merger had not always been as complete as it was by Firmicus' time.

6 Cf. n. 43 below. West, *Poems* 153, derives ζαγρεύς from ζάγρη, a pit for catching animals – which suggests a more guileful way of catching one's prey than that practised by the maenads. Cf. W. Fauth is *PRE* 9A, 2222–6 for other possible etymologies. For Dionysus as an eater of raw flesh cf. the reff. in *PRE* 18/1, 342f, 378. He is described as ταυρόφαγος in Soph., *Tyro* frg. 607 (Nauck). Or did the god merely get these epithets from the behaviour of his followers? But then would they have behaved thus without believing that their god somehow sanctioned it?

7 Burkert, *Religion* 252=ET 162; yet this is not without parallel if we look further afield than Greece – see §5.2. Cf. also Henrichs, 'Identities' 158: the shared title points to 'a more substantial and deeper identification' than is indicated, e.g., by the claim of a ruler to be a 'new Dionysus'. Cf., e.g., Eur. frg. 472.15 (Nauck); Kaibel, *Epigrammata* 821. Whether it is right to see the mask as expressing this merging is doubtful: it is depicted set on posts, not worn by humans, and indeed is often too large to be worn with any comfort. Cf. Otto, *Dionysus* chap. 6, esp. p. 88.

8 Nock, *Conversion* 24.

9 *Liber* 9.

name[10], for in the ecstasy the Dionysiac worshipper was one with the god
who had entered into him[11]. This introduces a further element in this
union: the filling with the god in ecstasy as we observed earlier in chapter
4. Burkert elsewhere argues that the god was also believed to enter his
followers in the form of the wine which they consumed[12], and Klauck
that they were filled with the god through eating him in the form of a
rent sacrificial victim[13]; presumably this might be true however tame and
domesticated the rite became. Yet only in the last case would there be
a question of union with a god who suffers, and this we have just seen
again to be a most dubious interpretation of the rite: the rite does not
match the myth. The presence of the god in the other two ways, in
ecstasy and in wine, is the presence of the god in overwhelming power,
not as a suffering victim.

Burkert backs up the assertion that the consumption of wine filled one
with Dionysus by appealing to the myth of Dionysus' dismemberment — he
was 'dismembered to serve as wine for sacramental drinking'[14], although
he grants that this only emerges in the works of 'late Hellenistic allegor-
ists', in Diodorus and Cornutus[15]. Moreover he concedes that the story of
Dionysus' dismemberment 'describes not the preparation of the wine . . .
but, rather, a bloody initiation sacrifice with boiling and roasting'. To
postulate a different, but analogous, myth of dismemberment lying
behind the *Anthesteria*, one which perhaps 'always . . . existed only in
allusions and disguises', seems to carry imaginative reconstruction too
far[16]; when Philostratus appeals to the influence of Orphic theology at
the *Anthesteria*[17] it is more natural to think of the Orphic mythology
which we know, rather than to invent a further parallel account. And even
if such a myth existed, the drinkers of wine would again be imitating the
actions of the Titans, not those of their victim.

It may therefore be safer to stick with Klauck's formulation: 'grapes
and wine are signs of the god's epiphany'[18]. Further he hesitates to go. On

---

10 *Greeks* 148; cf. Eur., *Ba.* 115, 141 (the name of the god here is Βρόμιος); but cf. below and
   Kirk, *Bacchae* 39: Dionysus leads them in person.
11 Ibid. 174; but Gasparro, *Soteriology* 14f, insists that this is not a re-evocation of the god's
   vicissitudes; rather it is a rite placing the devotee in an immediate relationship to the deity.
12 *Homo* 249=ET 224f; cf. Eur., *Ba.* 284; *Cycl.* 520–8; Phanodemus in *FGH* 325 frg. 12, and
   Philochorus in *FGH* 328 frg. 5 (I think it hard to appeal to Plato, *Leg.* 6.773D here). Cf.
   Cumont, *After Life* 120.
13 *Herrenmahl* 111 (see below); contrast Otto, *Dionysus* 132; von Wilamowitz-Moellendorff,
   Glaube 2, 67.
14 *Religion* 361=ET 238.
15 Diod. S. 3.62.7; Cornutus, *Theol. Graeca* 30.
16 *Homo* 249f=ET 225f.
17 *Vit. Ap.* 4.21.
18 *Herrenmahl* 107.

the one hand there is the denial of any closer identification by Cicero (*Nat. deorum* 3.16.41); on the other hand seeming identification may be the result of poetic licence[19] or the result of allegorizing (which asserts not so much that grapes or wine are Dionysus but rather that Dionysus is the grape and the wine). He concludes that 'the sources do not give a completely clear picture. But we can affirm a close connection of Dionysus with wine, which goes beyond a mere metonymy and poetic metaphor'[20].

However, when he turns to the *ōmophagia*, Klauck is prepared to see it as a theophagy, the actual eating of the god[21]. He puts together the three data, (1) that the god, who can assume animal form, delights in eating raw flesh, (2) that his followers tear apart living animals, and (3) that his representative (he refers to his cousin Pentheus) was torn apart and offered for a meal, and concludes that Dionysiac worshippers subsequently distributed pieces of raw flesh 'in the belief that by eating the bloody flesh they were consuming the substance of the god'. Yet he grants that this conclusion is controversial[22]. The rigour of logic may indeed not be the best guide here; express evidence of this belief is hard to find; nearest are the passage from Firmicus Maternus noted above[23] and the remark of a scholiast on Clem. Alex., *Prot.* 2.119.1[24] that 'Dionysiac initiates were wont to eat raw flesh, performing this rite as a sign of the dismemberment which Dionysus suffered at the hands of the maenads'. This is poor evidence for the significance attached to the rite in the first century C.E., if indeed the rite was prominent at all: for Klauck, for instance, it had more or less passed into oblivion and did not suit the Roman mysteries of Dionysus of the imperial period[25]. Is it therefore

---

19 He cites (108f) Eur., *Cycl.* 519f (see above n. 12); Prop. 3.17.19 (does this quite make his point?), etc.

20 Ibid. 109 (the first sentence is quite an understatement!).

21 Ibid. 109–12; cf. Lietzmann-Kümmel, *1–2 Kor.* 50f (and 183). On cannibalism as identification with a deity cf. Eliade, *Birth* 69, 71; for initiands behaving like wild animals cf. 81.

22 Protagonists of both views are listed in nn. 131f on p. 111; note too McGinty, *Interpretation* 115, 225 n. 27, on Nilsson's change of mind; add to 131 Eliade, *History* 1, 365; Jensen in *HRG* 3, 184. For a stern rebuttal cf. esp. Festugière, 'Mystères' 196; Kane, 'Meal' 334–6: the *ōmophagia* is a sign of a union with the god already effected, not a means to it; in Eur., *Ba.* 138f Dionysus delights in it (but cf. Kirk, *Bacchae* 41), but is not himself the one eaten; his role is to madden the Bacchants. Despite Kirk's reservations, if the the purpose of the rite was, as he goes on to say, 'to bring the worshipper as close as possible to the life, power, and liberation of wild Nature, which Dionysus represented' then it is surely natural to think of Dionysus himself also behaving thus.
Cumont, *Religions* 64=*Religionen* 62f, points to the primitive idea that in drinking the blood of the slain one imbibed the qualities of the one slain (cf. 108f =107).

23 *Err. prof. rel.* 6.5.

24 Ed. Stählin 318.5–7.

25 Ibid. 115; Kane, 'Meal' 335, with justice questions the centrality or importance accorded to this act in some modern accounts; cf. Henrichs, 'Maenadism' 148–52.

perhaps significant that when Plutarch asks why the women of Elis call on Dionysus to come 'with bull's foot' this is not one of the possible explanations which he offers[26]? And anyway is it not hard to speak of identification with the eater(s) and the one eaten at the same time? Klauck's first two premises suggest identification with or imitation of the eater and not the one eaten, and his third premise seems to be a dubious interpretation of Pentheus' role.

Identification with Dionysus is for him also presupposed by the enigmatic line from two of the gold plates from Thurii:

A kid, I/you fell into milk[27].

For Dionysus himself is represented at times as a kid[28]. Moreover one plate has just told the one addressed that he has changed from a mortal to an immortal[29]. Yet it would be rash to build too much upon an interpretation of this line, an interpretation upon which, moreover, Zuntz for one has poured such learned scorn and ridicule[30].

Central to Dionysiac initiation in the Graeco-Roman period seems to have been the revelation of a phallus[31], which cannot be described as in any way symbolic of the god's suffering. Perhaps, rather, as a symbol of fertility and life-giving power, it may point to the god's power, a power which will enable him to restore life to his followers after death. After all he is a god whose life could not be destroyed by death or a hero who was, like Heracles, accorded Olympian immortality[32]: when his mother Semele was incinerated by the heat of Zeus' lightning his father Zeus sewed him in his own thigh and brought him to the time of birth there[33]. Not only that, but Dionysus brought his mother back from death[34], and brought immor-

26 *Quaest. Graec.* 36.299AB.

27 *Orph. Fr.* 32c.11 and 32f.4=Diels-Kranz, *Fragmente* §1 B 18.11 and 20.4; cf. Angus, *Mystery-Religions* 40.

28 Apollodorus, *Bibliotheca* 3.4.3; Hesych. s.v. Εἰραφιώτης (but should Ἔριφος be Ἐρίφιος? – Zuntz, *Persephone* 323f); Otto, *Dionysus* 168.

29 *Orph. Fr.* 32c.10=Diels-Kranz, *Fragmente* §1 B 18.10.

30 Ibid. 323–7; he prefers to follow Nilsson in seeing here a proverb, referring to 'the attainment of a supreme good' and comparing the phrase Ἔφυγον κακόν· εὗρον ἄμεινον (Demosth., *Or.* 18.259=Turchi, *Fontes* §14).

31 Cf. the reff. in §2.1 nn. 45f; also Klauck, *Herrenmahl* 113 (but contrast 163 where ōmophagia is described as the most important cultic act – see Kane in n. 25 above!)

32 Cf. the reff. in Vermaseren-Simoni, *Liber* 55–8; this would make him a prototype for his followers. (It is important here to distinguish eternal existence such as the Olympians had by nature, and immortality; cf. Talbert, 'Concept' 420f).

33 Eur., *Ba.* 3, 6–9, 88–100, 243–5, 286f; Pind. frg. 85 (Snell)=75(Bowra); Hdt. 2.146.2; cf. Nilsson, *Geschichte* 2, 365. However Linforth, *Arts* 358, argues that Dionysus' rebirth is given a cosmic interpretation in allegorical accounts, not an individualistic one, and thus that there is no reason to suppose that it ever encouraged his followers to believe that '"we are risen with him"'.

34 Cf. §3.2.3.2 above. Also *Anth. Pal.* 3.1 (the title suggests that the bringing up from Acheron

tality through the gift of Zeus to his beloved Ariadne[35]. He seems to have enjoyed an unparalleled popularity as a god of the dead, offering restored life in the world to come to his devotees, as the frequent Dionysiac scenes on sarcophagi attest[36]. This life to come would, however, be in the underworld; for, as Nilsson comments, 'the adherents of the Bacchic mysteries did not believe that they would rise up from the dead; they believed that they would lead a life in eternal bliss and joy in the other world'[37]. Similarly Burkert argues for a form of 'iteration': the holy way of ecstatic bliss in this world as the Bacchants raged through the mountains corresponds to the holy way that the initiates would follow in the world to come; 'afterlife is repetition of the mysteries'[38]. The sentiment is most clearly illustrated from the kindred cult of Sabazius by the depiction in' the catacomb of Praetextatus of the priest of Sabazius, Vincentius, and his wife, Vibia, banqueting in the world to come[39]. Or, looked at the other way, as J. G. Griffiths says, in particular apropos of the cult of Isis but also with reference to the mysteries in general: 'The new life . . . is viewed as *beginning at once*, and here is a significant idea shared by the other Mystery Religions and also by Christianity'[40].

At the same time there is also an imitation of the followers of Dionysus as recounted in the myths about him and thus an imitation of the god whom they copy[41]. It is the actions of these earlier followers which the rending of living animals and the eating of their raw flesh by later devotees

---

was also a bringing to heaven); Paus. 2.31.2; 37.5; Plut., *Quaest. Graec.* 12.293D; *Ser. num. vind.* 27.566A. Culianu, ' "Ascension" ' 286, argues that this last ref. indicates that at this period 'the posthumous fate of the soul was analogous to that of Semele'; cf. too Vermaseren-Simoni, *Liber* 48–50, on a disc from Taranto.

35 *ALGM* 1, 541f; cf. H. von Hesberg in *ANRW* 2.17.2, 1179.

36 Ferguson, *Religions* 137: 'the Mystery-religions, with the sole exception of Dionysus, play next to no part in the sarcophagi' (cf. 149). Even the sceptical MacMullen (*Paganism* 53) is prepared to grant that the Dionysiac cult may have promised life after death.

37 'Mysteries' 184; cf. *Geschichte* 2, 367; Zuntz, *Persephone* 408, 411 – 'but not in Hades', a surprising qualification; where else might the 'other, mystic realm' be for most Greeks of the classical period? This bliss was not confined to the world to come – cf. Weil, 'Péan' 403 (πόνων . . . ὄρ]μον [ἄλυπον]); also Matz, Τελετή 28.

38 *Religion* 437=ET 293; cf. Bücheler, *Carmina* 1233; Plut., *Ser. num. vind.* 27.565F; cf. Culianu ' "Ascension" ' 286; Cumont, *After Life* 201 sees a similar significance in Dionysiac meals. It is surprising that Gasparro, *Soteriology* 17, does not seem to recognize this 'eschatological' element in earlier Dionysiac traditions; one should not dismiss the evidence from a Dionysiac inscription in Cumae as relevant only in the Orphic atmosphere of Magna Graecia, for there is the evidence from Athens of Aristophanes' *Ranae* with its cocktail of Eleusinian, Dionysiac and Orphic elements – see above in §5.1.2.

39 One of these is reproduced as fig. 3 in Cumont, *Religions* 61=*Religionen* fig. 4, two others also in Leipoldt-Grundmann, *Umwelt* 3, pls 68–70.

40 'Concept' 202 – cf. 215 on the Dionysiac cult.

41 Otto, *Dionysus* 16.

copy[42]. In this they imitate the god himself[43]. Yet the stories told of these earlier followers also often make them the victims of persecution, a persecution directed at the god himself and which he shares, as is most graphically and vividly portrayed in Euripides' *Bacchae*, where the god leads the maenads incognito. How far then does Otto's observation take us, when he comments that Dionysus was 'the persecuted god, the suffering and dying god, and all whom he loved, all who attended him, had to share his tragic fate'[44]? At precisely this point Euripides' story does not fit his account, for there the persecuted god does not die, but instead lures his would-be persecutor to his own death. Again, if we go further back, to the account of the persecution of the maenads by Lycurgus in Hom., *Il.* 6.130ff, we find that Dionysus flees into the sea and is there received by Thetis (135−7); this is no death but escape, as befits an immortal. Whatever fate his unfortunate attendants suffer does not overtake their leader, with the one exception of a single tradition from amongst others concerning his conflict with Perseus[45]. Again, legend tells that Icarius, an Attic peasant to whom the god first revealed the art of viticulture and of making wine, was slain by his fellows on suspicion of poisoning them, and his daughter committed suicide[46]. Dionysus is one who brings death to his followers, but almost all the stories just mentioned show him escaping[47]. His followers in all ages copy his fury and share the hostility directed against him, but lack the immortality to save them from the consequences. The one exception which we have noted is hardly a very firm foundation upon which to base any theory of a prevailing soteriology involving a suffering god.

---

42 Ibid. 109; cf. Diod. S. 4.3.3.

43 Dionysus is himself a hunter − Eur., *Ba.* 1192 (Dodds' ed. doubts whether there is any allusion here to Zagreus) −, even an eater of raw flesh (cf. 127): Eur. *Ba.* 135−9; further reff. in Klauck, *Herrenmahl* 110 n. 124.

44 Ibid. 49; cf. 76−8, 103.

45 The only possible exception to this that Otto can cite (ibid. 216 n. 10) is the schol. on Hom., *Il.* 14.319: Perseus killed Dionysus by hurling him into the Lernaean lake (ed. Erbse 3, 641). Further reff. to this tradition can be found in *ALGM* 3/2, 2016, which argues that this is a local tradition of considerable antiquity connected with the Lernaean mysteries (similarly K. Meuli in *PRE* 12, 2090). Other accounts of the end of this story exist and of the connection of Dionysus with Lerna (Nonnus, *Dionys.* 47.496−741; Paus. 2.23.7; *PRE* 12, 2088).

46 Eratosthenes, ed. Robert 77.

47 Otto, *Dionysus* 103f, points to the tradition of the tomb at Delphi (Plut., *Is. et Os.* 35.365A − cf. §3.2.3.2 above) as evidence that Dionysus was regarded as having died; cf. Ps.-Clem., *Recg.* 10.24.2 − buried in Thebes.
But according to tradition Dionysus' remains came to be at Delphi as a result of his death at the hands of the Titans − reff. in Burkert, *Homo* 140=ET 123 n. 41; see too Otto, *Dionysus* 194!

5.1.4. What then of the mourning for dead *Attis* and *Adonis*? With both Tammuz (§3.2.3.4) and Adonis (§3.2.3.5) we noted the dominant character of the rites as ones of mourning. Again therefore the rites enable their practitioners to identify with the experience of loss suffered by the bereaved partner and not with the experience of the one slain[1].

The devotees of Cybele also joined with the goddess in mourning her dead lover[2], and we saw that some scholars held that this was the dominant impression left by these rites in the first century (§3.2.3.6)[3]. Yet possibly even then the gloom of the mourning may have been relieved by hope for life triumphant over the grave. What we do not find is any suggestion in the evidence that this hope was based upon assimilation to Attis in his death and restoration to life. Rather the hopes seemed to rest either upon the powers of Attis to escort the soul to immortality, if Vermaseren's interpretation of the Porta Maggiore decorations is correct[4], or upon the powers of the Great Mother to rescue her own; perhaps this latter confidence might be enhanced by the belief that she had also thus rescued Attis from death[5]. Graillot points to the presence of terracotta figurines of the goddess found in graves as evidence of this hope[6]. There is too the evidence of the Neoplatonist Damascius, but it is late, to the effect that initiates could descend into a subterranean passage at Hierapolis, filled with toxic vapours, and return unharmed, and that he fell asleep at Hierapolis and dreamt that he became Attis and that the *Hilaria* were celebrated in his honour at Cybele's behest, signifying 'our salvation from Hades'[7]. It seems clear that a quasi-death took place here, in the form of an ordeal, but there is no express statement that this was thought to be a death like that of Attis, even if the life that was promised as a result was his. And if we remember the manner of Attis' death we can easily understand why Damascius might shrink from making that compari-

---

Notes on 5.1.4.

1 Cumont, *Religions* 101=*Religionen* 100. Soyez, *Byblos* 39f, interprets the shaving of the head by worshippers in Luc., *Syr. Dea* 6, as sealing their union with death or the deity or both, but grants that such a shaving was above all a practice of mourning. What justification is there for seeing more in it than this? (Luc. compares the shaving of heads in mourning for Apis.)

2 Graillot, *Culte* 119.

3 Cumont, *Lux* 264, compares the 'Precatio Terrae Matris' in Riese, *Anthologia* 1.5.13 ('cum recesserit anima, in te refugiemus').

4 §3.2.3.6 and n. 18, but esp. §2.1 and nn. 60f.

5 From the 2nd century cf. the silver dish from Parabiago in *CCCA* 4, 268 (pl. 107); also H. von Hesberg in *ANRW* 2.17.2, 1188f.

6 *Culte* 176; Vermaseren, *Cybele* 76, also argues that the representation of Cybele on 'sepulchral monuments implies that the deceased was, in some way, compared and identified with the main character of the story in question'.

7 In Photius, *Bibliotheca* 242.345a. It seems likely that the Egyptian cult of Osiris may have influenced this account.

son. It is safer to follow Gasparro here, who sees in the Damascius passage evidence which, though late, perhaps points to an earlier assurance derived from the rites of the March festival of Cybele, in which the devotee was granted an immediate and intimate relationship with the gods, and a promise of the Great Mother's benevolent protection, as well as a guarantee of future blessing, just as she had blessed Attis[8]. This would seem to combine elements of expectations of types A and B above.

A closer identification with the fate of Attis is not entailed in the worshippers of Cybele's dressing themselves as animals or mythical companions of the goddess[9]. This might be compared with the public procession of the *Navigium Isidis* depicted by Apuleius (*Met.* 11.8–11). If Clement of Alexandria's version of the formula of the cult of Cybele[10] is correct, then initiation into it may have involved entry into the 'bridal chamber' with her, and this would have been a treading where Attis had trod (or a lying where he had lain), but not a sharing in his suffering. However Nilsson suggests that the παστός here is the innermost sanctuary of the temple, and points to the institution of the Isiac *pastophori*, carrying representations of the shrine in procession; thus, he argues, a sexual union with the goddess had no place in the Phrygian cult[11].

We have seen (§3.2.3.6) that the *taurobolium* was only relatively late interpreted as bestowing salvation upon the one who underwent the rite. Moreover there is no suggestion anywhere in the ancient sources that the one who thus submitted to this gory showerbath was imitating the experiences of Attis[12]. Simon rightly concludes that the link between this rite and Attis is not quite clear[13]. In general Gasparro is right to conclude that

---

8 *Soteriology* 63; in §3.2.3.6 above we saw, however, that the form of survival sometimes affirmed for Attis was not exactly an enthralling prospect.

9 Yet Graillot, *Culte* 133, sees here an analogy to the initiation rites, entailing an intimate communion like the sacred marriage that there took place.
  Klauck, *Herrenmahl* 124, argues also for an imitation of, and communion with, the goddess in the form of the initiates' sacred meal (milk and herbs?).

10 §2 and n. 24 (*Prot.* 2.15.3).

11 *Geschichte* 2, 648; Vermaseren, *Cybele* 117; Klauck, *Herrenmahl* 121 rightly draws attention to Firmicus' ref. to *interiores partes* of the temple in *Err. prof. rel.* 18.1; so also Gasparro, *Soteriology* 81f; contrast Hepding, *Attis* 193ff who takes παστός here in its more usual nuptial sense.

12 Duthoy, *Taurobolium* 108f (this observation does not seem vulnerable to the criticisms summarized by Vermaseren, *Cybele* 107). But cf. Schneider, *Mysterien* 47: the blood of this bloodbaptism was that of Attis. The baptized, he continues, now offers his own blood to Attis, perhaps even to the point of castration. Yet the rites of self-mutilation are attested early, the *Taurobolium* relatively late, and what evidence is there that they were thus connected in thought? But see also Lohse, *Umwelt* 177=ET 240: in the *taurobolium* the one undergoing the rite experienced the death of the god and was filled with divine powers; cf. P. Wendland, *Kultur* 155.

13 'École' 362; cf. Lagrange, 'Attis' (1919) 456–9.

There is little basis in the documents in our possession for the idea, so frequently advanced, that the *mystes* of Attis was submitted to a ritual containing a symbology of death and resurrection to a new life[14].

The nearest that she comes to tracing a link between the *taurobolium* or *criobolium* and Attis is the special treatment given to the genitals of the victim which, she argues,

confirms the specificity of the taurobolium 'sacrifice' as a rite pertaining to a religious context in which the practice of eunuchism and its mythical roots in the traditions concerning Attis confer a particular importance on this aspect of the cultic practice[15].

The link, however, is still between the (dedicatory?) self-castration of Attis and one aspect of the sacrifice, and not between the death of Attis and that of the sacrificial victim.

Only in one case do we really find an imitation of Attis' sufferings and that is in the self-castration of some of the followers of Cybele, the *Galli*. It is true that less serious self-inflicted wounds might be regarded as tokens of this more drastic sacrifice, yet less serious wounds might also be regarded simply as expressions of sympathetic grief. Whether one limits the imitation of Attis' suffering to self-castration or whether one extends it also to these lesser wounds, however, this is clearly the nearest that we have yet come to the idea of conforming to the sufferings of a god or hero[16]. So the account of the Attis myth in Luc., *Syr. Dea* 15 tells us that some hold that the *Galli* 'imitate Attis' ("Αττεα μιμέονται), although he himself knows another, more plausible explanation (presumably the story of Combabus in 20–7?). Wagner, however, takes issue with those quoted by Lucian for another reason: 'the self-emasculation of the Galli is not a genuine, deliberate *imitatio* of Attis, its object is rather assimilation to the goddess', i.e. becoming female like her[17]; 'when the Gallus strove to be assimilated to the deity, his objective was not Attis but Cybele'[18]. Nevertheless one could reply that Attis was the pattern and the prototype for this assimilation[19]; even if devotion to the goddess had not been his motive — rather in one version of the myth his self-castration was the result of a madness inspired by the goddess as a punishment[20] — yet

---

14 *Soteriology* 82.
15 Ibid. 110; yet she is careful to note that, particularly in the earlier phases of the rite's development, there should be no question of its being a substitute for the castration of a *Gallus* (e.g. when performed at the expense of, and supervised by, a woman or performed *pro salute imperatoris*) – 116.
16 Klauck, *Herrenmahl* 119, speaks of the myth standing in a *Homologieverhältnis* to the rite. Cf. Angus, *Mystery-Religions* 60, 140; Turcan, 'Salut' 175.
17 *Baptism* 266; cf. 238f; Lagrange, 'Attis' (1919) 423.
18 Ibid. 239.
19 So Lagrange, 'Attis' (1919) 430; Prümm, *Handbuch* 258.
20 This is the version found in Ovid, *Fasti* 4.222–44 (but cf. Hepding, *Attis* 100ff on the other

the practice of naming priests of Cybele Attis[21] suggest that his was an example that was not regarded as abhorrent or as something to be avoided, but rather as endowed with honour and prestige. Moreover Lucian shows that to some observers it could seem otherwise than Wagner supposes, and for our purpose that may be as significant as the views of adherents of the cult, and indeed some adherents too may have seen things similarly.

5.1.5. It is against this pattern of mourning for the dead god or hero that the quotation of Firm. Mat., *Err. prof. rel.* 22.1 should be set. As we saw (§3.2.8) the cult from which this couplet derives is much disputed and we would do well to reach our decisions about its implications for our present enquiry without making any assumptions about the identity of the saved god. My own preference is for Egyptian rites particularly if the origin of the quotation is the same as the following references in 22.3 (see §5.1.1.2 above).

The chief point is to note that the worshippers are said to mourn, not to identify themselves with the one mourned. If they are also referred to in 22.3 then they perform various actions to symbolize the liberation and restoration of the deity in question. If the Egyptian cult is in view then it is the actions of Isis and her helpers which they imitate, and not those of the slain Osiris.

Yet out of the successful outcome to their ministrations comes a hope for 'salvation' from troubles; it is not specified that the troubles include death, but this is likely if the one mourned and restored was also dead. Yet it should not necessarily be limited to death, particularly if we recall the breadth of the promises uttered by Isis to her followers (§5.1.1.1). Moreover we should note again that the salvation lies in the future. Had the initiates really believed that they were dying as the god died and living as the god lived, expressing this in the present as at the end of 22.3, then we should have expected a perfect or at least a present tense to correspond to the perfect 'the god has been saved'; instead we have a future. It is not, however, suggested that salvation comes by passing through the same tribulations as the god. In short the pattern here seems to be of type B; the symbolic restoration to life of the god gives the hope that the same power will in the future bless them too[1].

---

versions: in Paus. 7.17.12 it is the daemon Agdistis that causes the frenzy; in Luc., *Syr. Dea* 15 Rhea deliberately castrates Attis for her service).
21 See § 5.2 below.

Notes on 5.1.5
1 Cf. Nock, 'Christianity' 95: 'The joy spoken of is a joy in sympathy with divine joy, the deliver-

5.1.6. In *summary* we can say that we have seen plenty of evidence of the truth of the Christian apologist Athenagoras' statement that the mysteries disclosed the 'sufferings' (πάθη) of the gods (*Suppl.* 32.1); however, if anything they concentrated on the sufferings of the bereaved deities, not on those of the partners who died, and we found little evidence that initiates were conformed to the latter as opposed to the former or sympathized with them.

The one instance where there seems, on balance, to be evidence to suggest an imitation of, or identification with, one who suffered something more than an emotional trauma was in the case of the Attis cult, in the self-castration of Cybele's beloved according to one version of the myth of the cult. Yet the cult's devotees did not carry their imitation as far as the death which was the result of Attis' self-inflicted wound, nor is there any indication that they regarded their act as being a quasi-death. The *taurobolium* and *criobolium*, again, developed an individual initiatory role only later and there is no evidence that it was ever regarded as making up for this deficit in conformity to Attis. Furthermore it would surely be grotesque to suggest that Christian baptism developed its theology from either of these practices: the *taurobolium* and *criobolium* are anyway too late attested for this to be plausible and without them, and them interpreted in this relationship to Attis' death, it is implausible in the extreme to suggest that Christians would have seen any resemblance between their initiation and that of the *Galli*, much less would have wanted to see an analogy.

Rather the mysteries seem to have concentrated on assuring their initiates of the power of the god or goddesses into whose rites they were entering. They were shown his or her power both in this life and in the next. They may in some cases have enacted proleptically and symbolically their salvation through their deity in the world to come. In the case of the Egyptian rites at least they will have been made aware of the power that Isis had once exercised in rescuing Osiris from death and will have thus been given confidence that she had the power to do that for them too both in this life and the next (Firm. Mat., *Err. prof. rel.* 22.1). Lastly, it is possible that the Eleusinian initiates too were reminded of Demeter's power shown in bringing her daughter up again from the realm of the dead.

---

ance is a deliverance in harmony with the god's deliverance, not a deliverance brought by his sufferings: it is the spiritualisation of a rite concerned with death and revival of the life of the fruits of the earth'; hence, he argues, there is a considerable difference to the Christian doctrine of redemption. And Wagner, *Baptism* 98: the god's salvation is not the ground but the 'type' of the worshippers' salvation. Contrast, e.g., Reitzenstein, *Mysterienreligionen* 400, who sees sharing in the god's fate symbolized by their being anointed (Turcan, ed. 316, is sceptical of this interpretation and thinks the throat might need lubrication after so much lamentation!).

5.2. Identification and Deification

When dealing with the Egyptian cults (§5.1.1.2) we came across the problem of the term 'identification', which, when the one with whom one is identified is a god, might seem to imply also deification. We saw statements which seemed to imply that certain dead human individuals were Osiris; these could be taken in much the same way as statements like 'James I of England was James VI of Scotland' and 'this James was the first king of both England and Scotland'. However we also saw that it was suggested (by Hornung) that becoming Osiris was regarded more like playing a role in a play. Yet these two can be hard to distinguish at times. In Dürrenmatt's *'Die Physiker'* we meet three scientists confined to a psychiatric institution for imagining that they were respectively Newton, Einstein and Solomon; only as the play progresses does it emerge that their delusions are feigned to escape the implications of their knowledge and their profession – a play within a play: in the end they find that there is no escape and that they must resign themselves to live the rest of their lives in the institution and the play ends with their recalling their roles, the assumed identities that they must now live out for the rest of their lives. *'Ich bin Newton. . . .' 'Ich bin Einstein. . . .' 'Ich bin Salomo. . . .'*[1] Do they simply play a role, or are they recognizing that this is now the only identity that they have?

Another instance of the problems of the language of apparent identification is the anthropologist E. E. Evans-Pritchard's handling of statements by the Nuer people to the effect that something is *Kwoth*, Spirit. Applied to phenomena like rain or lightning or diseases this predication means that these things are signs or manifestations of divine activity. When it is said that a snake or crocodile is Spirit, the reverse is not true: Spirit is not a snake or crocodile; rather these reptiles represent Spirit to some people. Lévy-Bruhl was wrong to regard this as the pre-logical language of a primitive people which permitted contradictions. Such statements are not taken literally (Evans-Pritchard looks too at the assertion that twins are birds); they recognize the difference between the two things seemingly identified. Such statements do not mean

> that something is other than it is but that in a certain sense and in particular contexts
> something has some extra quality which does not belong to it in its own nature[2].

Again, we speak of 'identifying' ourselves with someone or something in the sense that their interests, their feelings, their experiences or the

---

Notes on 5.2
  1 Ed. 361.
  2 'Problem' 146.

like become ours, are shared by us. This is the language of 'solidarity'. 'Identification' in this sense would very aptly describe the experiences of the devotees of Eleusis or of the cult of Isis who re-enacted or saw re-enacted the mourning and searching of the grief-stricken goddesses, who stood therefore in solidarity with those goddesses just as mourners express their solidarity with the bereaved by their presence at a funeral. It is an expression of 'sympathy' in the truest sense of that word, a suffering with another, a bearing of some portion of their grief, an acknowledgement that their loss is a shared one. Or we 'identify' ourselves with a cause, by making it ours, giving ourselves to its service.

So we should distinguish for a start at least three senses of 'identification' that are relevant to our discussion:

(a) identification in a strict sense such as is involved in 'James I of England was James VI of Scotland',

(b) identification of oneself with a role to be played, and

(c) identification of oneself with someone or something in solidarity and sympathy.

Two further things need to be said here: (1) playing a role need not be a superficial matter, but can be a life-transforming one. Just as the roles that they had adopted were for the three *Physiker* to be their lives from now on, so even the playing of a part in a play may leave the actress or actor a different person if they have so entered into the characterization that they see things, experience things differently in the future. (2) Playing a role is not, of course, the best phrase to use when speaking of funerary rites; the one identified with Osiris is really past playing anything. Yet one can transfer this sense to this situation if one looks at the whole setting in which the restoration of Osiris is re-enacted; the dead is cast in the role, albeit inertly and passively, by those performing the active roles of Osiris' restorers and rescuers. It is, of course, another matter when incidents from the life (before or after death) of Osiris, as opposed to his death, are re-enacted and it is another matter too when we meet devotees of the other mystery-gods re-enacting scenes from the lives of those gods.

When looking at the Egyptian rites above (§5.1.1.2) we saw that it was disputed whether or not Lucius is depicted as a solar Osiris in Apul., *Met.* 11.24; I suggested that it might rather be as a solar Horus or one like a solar Horus that he appears (§5.1.1.3). The issue that concerns us here is not so much with which god he is identified as whether he is identified with a god at all and, if so, in what sense. Widengren poses the problem thus[3]: arguing that Lucius is *quodam modo renatus* and that redemption means new life and rebirth, he continues:

---

3 In *HO* 1.8.2, 71.

It is indeed perfectly clear that in Apuleius' description of initiation the initiate, who voluntarily died and returned from the underworld through all the elements, appeared as a divine being before the public; he was placed on the stage as a statue (*Standbild*) of the sun-god, *ad instar Solis*. Thus it cannot be doubted that the purpose of the initiation was this, to become a god through rebirth. The initiate was *renatus* and *instar Solis*. But the real problem remains as to how one conceives of this new being. Probably one thought of it as a lengthening of normal life and at the same time as an existence of a higher, divine kind. Lucius . . . is in the future to live *gloriosus*, 'glorified', and at the same time *beatus*, 'blessed'. One can hardly speak of a true immortality, or at least our sources are insufficient to justify such an assertion.

This passage shows with a remarkable candour the scholar's perplexity when confronted with this passage: is Lucius' attire simply a role to be played or is it to be taken in full seriousness as meaning that he is now a god? Widengren steers a *via media* — eventually. After seeming to choose the latter interpretation he opts for a far more mundane explanation, one not involving 'true immortality', although in a sense many in that day and age expected that they, or at least their souls, were by nature immortal[4].

Now it is certainly true that rebirth can mean renewed this-worldly life: when Lucius is restored to human form and can speak again once more instead of braying, his tongue is *renata* (*Met.* 11.14) and he is described by by-standers as *renatus quodam modo* because Isis has formed him anew in human form (11.16). All this is *before* his initiation. Isis, however, in granting initiation into her secrets to human beings made them *quodam modo renatos* and set them again on paths of a new salvation (*salus*, 11.21). Lucius' transformation, from ass to human, was undoubtedly very substantial; was his second, his initiation, which is described in identical terms, any less substantial[5]? Moreover his presentation in this fashion does seem to be saying something about his nature or status now that he has been initiated; this may seem to mean more than those cases where priests and devotees may have assumed the attire of a god for the purpose of portraying them in a drama or even representing them in a procession such as is described earlier in *Met.* 11.8—11. Lucius is consecrated (*sacratus*) in or by his robes and proceeds to celebrate 'the most happy birthday of my initiation'[6]. One might well compare this scene to that scornfully described in Prudentius, *Peristephanon* 10.1048: when the bloodstained priest — decidedly less glorious in his appearance than Lucius — emerges from the *taurobolium* 'they all stand apart and do

---

4 Cf. the rather incautious comment of F. C. Grant quoted in §5 n. 8; but it might receive support from Zuntz, *Persephone* 85, except that that only expressly refers to a period before (but only just before) the Atomists and Epicurus came upon the scene.

5 Widengren, 'Reflections' (1965) 301, argues that Greek mystery texts always speak of the μεταμορφοῦσθαι of initiates (a rather vague reference!).

6 11.24, tr. Griffiths.

him reverence'[7]. Apuleius does not mention Lucius receiving such homage but it is perhaps presupposed[8], although one may ask whether in either case it was directed towards the humans so much as the deities in whose name they stood there. (One must allow for Prudentius' scorn causing him to make things seem more ridiculous than they were. Moreover Lagrange notes appositely that the honour may have been due to the *tauroboliatus* as an *archigallus*, and not just to anyone who had undergone the rite[9].) Again, Xenophon of Ephesus describes his heroine Anthia as being worshipped as Artemis, although others, rather than taking her to be the goddess herself, took her to be someone else fashioned by the goddess in her likeness (*Ephesiaca* 1.2.7). That surely suggests that there may have been different perceptions simultaneously of what Lucius' experience implied. Yet the repeated *quodam modo* warns us that Apuleius at least was conscious that 'rebirth' here was a figure of speech, as indeed it always is[10]. The question is, to what sort of reality this metaphor is applied, a change of nature or of status, something that Lucius now has or merely has in prospect. The change, at any rate, was not so outwardly manifest as the previous one from asinine form to human, but may none the less have been just as real and important in the eyes of Lucius and Apuleius and the onlookers[11].

When comparisons are drawn between Lucius' solar crown and those of Roman emperors, following the precedent of Hellenistic monarchs[12], we can see that we are dealing with a sort of role-play that some, but perhaps only a few, took with the utmost seriousness, indeed with a seemingly megalomaniac literalness, but others treated with levity or ridicule: the latter can be evidenced by the coolness shown by some Roman emperors towards their eastern subjects' desire to deify them[13] as

---

7 Tr. Thomson.
8 So Reitzenstein, *Mysterienreligionen* 42f; he rises as a god (46).
9 'Attis' (1919) 456.
10 Cf. Nicodemus' question in Jn 3.4! I must confess to being somewhat puzzled by Wagner's contrast between a 'spiritual rebirth' which Lucius' initiation is not and an embarking on a new course of life, dead to the world, dedicated to the service of Isis (*Baptism* 113). Nash's observations on this (*Christianity* 175) I also find rather beside the point.
11 For Reitzenstein, *Mysterienreligionen* 39f, 193, this is a change of nature, an entering of a new life.
   For the veneration of what are plainly still humans, though endowed with divine qualities, cf., e.g,. Hes., *Theog.* 91; *Joseph and Aseneth* 18.11.
12 Cf. Dieterich, *Nekyia* 41f; Ferguson, *Religions* 45f; see, e.g., Smallwood, *Documents* (1967) 124, 126, 129, 143f.
13 Compare Claudius' letter to the Alexandrians (e.g. in Smallwood, ibid. 370); cf. Habicht, 'Zeit' 76–85 for further examples. Earlier, Gardner suggests (*Leadership* xxiii), the educated subjects of Hellenistic kings are unlikely to have taken seriously the honours accorded to a human as being those accorded to an Olympian god.

well as by the more anecdotal evidence such as Suet., *Vespasian* 23, in which
the dying Vespasian is supposed to have quipped 'Woe's me. I think that
I'm becoming a god'; the former is harder to gauge for we are dependent
upon second-hand sources and do not have immediate access to the
thoughts of the likes of Gaius Galigula so that we might tell whether they
really believed themselves to be divine or not and, if so, in what sense[14].
And yet at the same time this very instance raises the question whether,
if the mysteries *were* proclaiming their initiates to be divine in any comparable sense, this would not be construable as in some way subversive,
trespassing upon imperial prerogatives, and thus treasonable[15]. After all
the more restrained earlier emperors waited until their deaths for deification, at least in Rome, and reckoned it sufficient during their lives to be
the sons of their now divine parents. While deification of the dead as
practised in the Egyptian cult might be tolerable, deification of the
living was another matter[16]. Does that not suggest that a display such as
Apuleius describes had to be generally understood in a different sense, as
making less drastic claims for the nature and identity of the one thus
displayed?

That suggests that we would be wiser to see this ritual act as making
more modest claims for the initiate. Comparable problems arise with the
Roman triumph where the *triumphator* was dressed as Jupiter and originally 'was looked upon as the god manifesting himself', but this was an
idea which 'was no longer alive during the time of the Roman republic'[17]
for it was not acceptable to the Romans[18]. So, with regard to Lucius,
Nilsson argues that this was no deification, but merely a human playing

---

14 Versnel, *Triumphus* 86f, points to the example of the 'famous hypomanic physician' of the 4th
century B.C.E., Menecrates, who 'called and felt himself Zeus' (cf. Athen., *Deipnosophistae*
7.289A).

However Pliny, *Panegyricus* 11.2 (Mynors) asserts that Trajan deified the dead Nerva because
he believed he was a god, in contrast to the unworthy motives behind earlier deifications. Yet
Bowersock, 'Intellectuals' 199, argues that Domitian's claim to be *deus* and not just *divus*
caused genuine shock and outrage. Habicht, 'Zeit' 85, remarks that Caligula abandoned the
restraint of preceding and succeeding emperors and claimed full divinity for himself.

15 Cf. the garb of C. Silius in Tac., *Ann.* 11.31: was there in his ivy crown an echo of the claim
to be a 'new Dionysus' as Hellenistic rulers had claimed and as M. Antonius, the great-grand-
father of Messalina, had also claimed (e.g. Plut., *Ant.* 24.4f; Huzar, *Mark Antony* 193–9,
2004f)? Cf. Fraser, *Alexandria* 1, 204f; Henrichs, 'Maenadism' 159. One of the charges seemingly brought against Apollonius of Tyana according to Philostr., *Vit.Ap.* 7.20f; 8.5; 8.7.7, is
that he allowed himself to be worshipped as a god by the Greeks.

16 Within Hellenistic Judaism, on the other hand, we find a readiness to 'deify' in some sense a
man like Moses, but not to ascribe to such persons immortality in the sense of attaining to
divine prerogatives after death: cf. Talbert, 'Concept' 430, citing Jos., *Ant.* 3.7.7 §180 with
4.8.48 §326; Philo, *Vita Mos.* 1.158 with 2.291 – but contrast 288 (Talbert 424); see also
the discussion of this whole concept of 'divinity' in Holladay, *Aner.*

17 Versnel, *Triumphus* 92 (the rites go back to the Etruscans and their royal ritual).

18 Ibid. 90.

the role of a god; he compares Paus. 7.18.12 where Artemis in a procession is represented by a priestess, and Chariclea's appearance from the temple of Artemis in Heliodorus, *Aeth.* 3.4.1–6[19]. Yet we have already argued that such appearances in dramatic reconstructions and in processions are not, at first sight, quite comparable to Lucius' experience. Dey, however, goes slightly further: Lucius' crown need only mean his exaltation and being marked out for a special destiny[20], yet that is already taking us beyond the mere playing of a part in a drama; it says something about Lucius' own existence and status.

Priests, priestesses and worshippers seem often in the ancient world to have been seen and depicted wearing the clothes and insignia of their deities. Godwin comments of the statue of a priestess of Isis in the Capitoline Museum that it 'could equally well be a statue of Isis herself, for the priestess in her ritual clothing and gestures imitates and in a certain sense incarnates the goddess for the worshippers'[21]. Similarly a bust in the Vatican Museum models the portrait of a priest of Asclepius or of a doctor on the god of healing himself[22]. Such wearing of divine dress, we may suggest, symbolizes not so much deification or admittance to the ranks of gods as fellowship with the gods, dedication and belonging to the one whose garb is worn, and at the same time the possession in one's life of the divine qualities and powers characteristic of that deity[23]. If that is what such dressing up means and if that is how it was generally regarded then, after all, there is not such a great difference between Lucius' enrobing and the wearing of divine garments by priests, in processions and elsewhere. The term *sacratus* applied to Lucius points to the extension of priestly functions and status to initiates of the goddess.

It is thus perhaps significant when J. G. Griffiths quotes apropos of Plut., *Is. et Os.* 3.352B from Spell 485 of the Egyptian *Coffin Texts*: 'I have put on the cloak of the Great Lady, and I am the Great Lady' (Hathor)[24]; for when one turns from this seemingly straightforward

---

19 *Geschichte* 2, 690 and n. 6; Zuntz, *Persephone* 92, comments that humans engaged in cultic activities in Greek religion might wear divine crowns; for an example cf. the frieze of dancing maidens from the *propylon* of the *temenos* at Samothrace and the comments of Lehmann-Spittle, *Samothrace* 5, 221f.

20 Παλιγγενεσία 97; Sänger, *Judentum* 80, gives a similar evaluation to *Joseph and Aseneth* 5.6.

21 *Mystery Religions* 122 (Malaise, *Inventaire* -Latium, Villa Adriana 29, 110f, describes this as a statue of Isis); cf. 147: an Eleusinian initiate dressed like Heracles (assimilation here, then, not to the mystery deity but to the prototype heroic initiand; cf. §5.1.2).

22 Lippold, *Skulpturen* 3/2, 449=Pl. 190.7 which is presumably that meant by Ferguson, *Religions* 110; for royal identification with Isis cf. Fraser, *Alexandria* 1, 240–6; Le Corsu, *Isis* 86.

23 Cf. Zuntz, *Persephone* 325; also Meeks. 'Image' 184: 'the assimilation of the power of the deity represented by the new garb'.

24 Griffiths' ed. 317; the quotation of the *Coffin Text* is from Faulkner's ed. 2, 130; cf. also §5.1.1.2 n. 9.

identification (though it may not be quite as straightforward as it seems) to the text of Plutarch we see that he makes no mention of any such straightforward identification as a consequence of wearing Isis' garments: the garments are, rather, symbolic of the Isiac religion and when the dead wear them it indicates that they go to the other world bearing those truths and only them. The true devotee of Isis is marked not by his clothing but by the fact that he is one who examined rationally the received truths of that religion (352C). This makes sense as a philosophical restatement of the belief that in wearing these robes one was protected by Isis' power and also received divine powers from her; that is a more modest claim than saying one was the deity. We may note that Zuntz holds it 'axiomatic that no Greek cult of any kind ever aimed to achieve identity of god and worshipper, alive or dead. That kind of aspiration existed in Egypt'[25]. That distinction seems still to be true at this relatively late period.

Some such reserve is all the more appropriate if Versnel is correct in arguing that the 'humanity' of the mystery-gods, i.e. their having suffered as humans do, at the same time provided the possibility of 'identification' and communion and also, paradoxically, made them greater and more majestic than the old gods, so that the relationship between humans and their gods was displayed in the first instance in self-abasement and surrender[26]. In that case identification in the strict sense becomes all the less appropriate, however much identification in the sense of solidarity or sympathy is made easier. This is perhaps confirmed by the fact that Lucius in his initiation worships the gods below and above (Apul., *Met.* 11.23); he may be close to them (*de proxumo*) but is not on the same level or of the same rank as them and so his appropriate response is still that of a worshipping human. It is unlikely that his public manifestation after his initiation changed that.

Such an interpretation may help us to understand better the background to the Pauline and deutero-Pauline language of 'putting on' Christ, language which in its turn may have had its place already in early Christian baptismal traditions, perhaps aided by the reclothing necessary after the act of baptism. The Christian who puts on Christ does not thereby become Christ, but does share the character and consecration to God of

---

25 *Persephone* 325. More cautious is Vidman, *Isis* 172, who holds that the evidence does not exist to show us whether or not the Greeks of the Hellenistic period believed in the identification of the dead with Osiris; but the Romans took over the belief from the Egyptians (at least as regards the dead; cf. his *Sylloge* 585f). Dunand, *Culte* 2, 144–8, points to a number of funerary *stelai* from 1st–2nd century Athens that represent dead women as Isis. However they do not wear Isis' crown and so are still mortals (148).

26 'Religion' 62.

Christ (Rom 13.14; cf. Eph 4.24; Col 3.10, 12) and does belong to Christ (Gal 3.27f) and is part of that new humanity created by God in Christ. Moreover it seems to me undoubtedly true that the widespread convention of attiring priests and worshippers in the manner of their deities would have made this particular New Testament usage a great deal more intelligible in the Graeco-Roman world, and may indeed have suggested to early Christians this step beyond the language of the Septuagint which speaks of a metaphorical wearing or putting on of moral or religious qualities like righteousness. For all around them they saw the adherents of the various pagan cults 'putting on' their deities, dressing up as them and imitating their actions.

Besides wearing the dress of a particular deity union of some sort with a deity might be signalled in another way, bearing that deity's name. And yet just as wearing the dress of a deity had its parallels outside the sphere of the mystery-cults, e.g. in the Roman triumph or even more in the imperial propaganda, so too with names we need to recall that under the Roman Empire freedmen bore the *nomen gentile* and *praenomen* of their patrons[27].

In the case of the Dionysiac rites we noted (§5.1.3) the merging of god and devotee which took place in the latter's frenzied possession by the deity and which was marked by the devotee's being called Bacchus. At first sight it might seem as if this was a merely temporary state, an episodic, though recurrent, experience of bliss, yet Henrichs argues that the hopes of Dionysiac initiates for life after death indicate 'that the follower of Dionysus has finally acquired a lasting Dionysiac identity, either as a permanent member of the god's eternal entourage, or more ambitiously, as another Dionysus who has accomplished his own apotheosis through identification with one of Dionysus' mythical roles'[28]. Matz suggests that these two alternatives in fact mark different stages in the development of the Dionysiac mysteries; the evidence of sarcophagi suggests that the old belief in which the deceased simply joined the θίασος of Dionysus in the world to come prevailed into the time of Hadrian and the early Antonine period; from the late second century on a change is evident, with more stress on the individuality of the deceased, and with his becoming a new Dionysus[29]. In other words, for the period in which we are interested this merging with the deity or being placed on the same level as it is not so pronounced and may not have existed at all in this form.

---

27 Cf. H. Rix in *KP* 4, 660; Steinwenter in *PRE* 13, 106.
28 'Identities' 160.
29 Cf. Τελετή 41f (also in *Gn.* 32, 550f). Zuntz, *Persephone* 325, is more cautious: 'new Dionysus' applied to kings was the empty rhetoric of court-ceremonial; the dead might be thought of as divine, as gods, but not identified with one of the known gods.

We also referred above (§5.1.4) to Damascius' dream that he became Attis and so was delivered from death. Becoming Attis was a feature well attested in the cult of Cybele in that the high priests at Pessinus bore this name[30], although the fact that Damascius recounts his experience in this form might at this late date conceivably owe something to the Egyptian cult of Osiris and the idea of becoming Osiris. Hepding argues that Catullus' Attis too was another such priest, or a *gallus* of some sort, who had imitated his master and was called by his name[31].

In the various instances that we have looked at, in which followers of a god wore the attire or bore the name of that god, we have seen reason to be cautious, in a Graeco-Roman context and particularly where a living being was concerned as opposed to a corpse, about taking the identification with the god in too rigorous a sense. Rather these badges marked the initiate's or priest's belonging to the god, being under the god's protection, having access to, or possession of, the god's powers. It is thus comparable with a phenomenon which we can note in the Greek magical papyri where the authors identify or unite themselves with various gods in order to obtain those gods' powers[32]. These were divine powers and thus the initiate might be said to be deified to this extent, yet the powers remained the gods' and the initiate's possession of them remained derivative, dependent upon his contact with the deity and upon his or her gracious favour[33]. Isis, we recall, offered Lucius salvation in answer to prayer (*precaria salus*, Apul., *Met.* 11.21). In each instance of the deity's favour the initiate and his life becomes an epiphany, an incarnation of that divine power and presence; such a mark of Isis' favour was Lucius' initiation, in which her beneficent power was made available to him. Thus when Reitzenstein affirms that it was a 'basic view of the mysteries that they unite one with god and make one divine' we can readily assent to the first part but must ask of the second 'Divine in what sense'[34]? Not,

---

30 Hepding, *Attis* 126 (cf. 78f nos 2, 6, 8; Sherk, *Rome* §29); Vermaseren, *Cybele* 98.

31 *Attis* 140; cf. Dioscorides in *Anth. Pal.* 6.220 (see Hepding, ibid. 139)

32 Cf. Vermaseren, 'Sotériologie' 18; a particularly good example is cited by Reitzenstein, *Poimandres* 20f: 'I am you (Hermes) and you I' (=*PGM* 2.850). This is a pretence in Nock's eyes ('Papyri' 188) who sees this as a feature common to the papyri and to Egyptian magical literature.

33 Too often 'deification' has been treated as if it were immediately evident what the word means or would mean for the ancient world, where generally the divine world and the human world were seen not as wholly disparate, for some gods suffered human weaknesses and failings and some were even subject, albeit temporarily, to death and mortality, and some humans could command or invoke divine powers. The disparity of the two worlds was therefore not usually felt so keenly as in the Judaeo-Christian tradition. Cf. Talbert, 'Concept', and Holladay, *Aner* esp. 57–9, 189–94.

34 *Mysterienreligionen* 26; cf. Bowersock, 'Intellectuals' esp. 189, 198f, on the range of meaning of θεῖος; also Holladay as in the previous note, and n.b. Bieler, ANHP 2, 114.

we have seen, in the sense that the initiate becomes one of the gods that already exist or even that his role and status are completely equivalent to theirs, but only in the sense that he shares the powers which that god makes available to his devotees[35]. And that involves not so much a change of nature or substance as a change of status and potential[36]. In some sense that makes him 'divine', but then he may often have been viewed as 'divine' in some sense before his initiation, by virtue of being rational, possessing an immortal soul, or the like[37]. It makes him 'divine' too, in much the same way as a magician's special knowledge makes him 'divine'[38] and possessed of 'divine' powers, or as some philosophers claimed that their wisdom made them 'divine'[39]. For the initiate also had special knowledge and insight granted to him[40]. In that respect too he or she might be godlike[41], but that is not to say that he or she was identified with a previously existent god. We would do well to note here Bicker- man's comment apropos of representation of Roman rulers (and their spouses) as deities that these only need indicate that at certain moments

---

35 Cf. Bowersock, ibid 180: it was not until the time of Julian that prayers were offered to em- perors dead or alive (cf. 182). Junge, 'Isis' 110, argues that the Isis initiation was like the con- secration of an Egyptian priest which in turn was analogous to funeral rites, since priests and the dead were in a similar position: the latter enjoyed eternal life in fellowship with the deity, the former anticipated this bliss in fellowship with the deity in the innermost temple. But we noted the absence of distinctive funerary elements in Lucius' initiation.

36 Cf Talbert, 'Concept' 420 and n. 9. Thus some qualification is perhaps necessary of Eliade's remark that 'to show something ceremonially . . . is to declare a sacred presence, to acclaim the miracle of a hierophany' (*Birth* 43).

37 And so Reitzenstein, *Mysterienreligionen* 30, speaks of 'an enhancement of the divinity of one's own self', i.e. enhancement is different from replacement of the wholly non-divine by the divine. So he speaks (ibid. 40) of being raised to a better nature (which need not be a totally different nature?).

38 And yet still dependent on the aid and co-operation of a yet higher power as the example of the witch Erichtho in Lucan 6.744f shows – she threatens to resort to an appeal to a god yet more infernal than the infernal (748f.). Nock ('Papyri' 192) comments how prominent depend- ence on divine grace is in the *Mithras-Liturgy* – cf. *PGM* 1, 4.499, 642. Cf. on this and on philo- sophers' 'divinity' Paterson, 'Man'.

39 Cic., *Tusc.* 1.21.48; Dio Chrys., *Or.* 69.1; Epict., *Diss.* 1.9.22–6; Epicurus, *Ep. ad Menoecum* 135 (Bailey 92); *Ep. Heraclitus* 4 (ed. Malherbe); Lucretius 5.8–10, 51; cf. 1.731–3; Plut., *Alex. fort. virt.* 9.331A; Sen., *Ep.* 53.11.

40 E.g. Eur., *Ba.* 73. Eliade, *Birth* 78, says of the experiences of descent to the underworld and as- cent to the heavens in initiatory rites that the one who has undergone them 'has transcended the secular condition of humanity and . . . his behavior is purely that of a spirit'. Reitzenstein, *Mysterienreligionen* 169, observes that, although the soul is only fully deified at death, it is also deified in receiving revelation (which can therefore be represented as either a death or a prelim- inary for death).

41 So too the Pythagorean apologists (of whatever date) for the divine powers of the Hellenistic kings, preserved by Stobaeus, justified this because (ideal) kings were most godlike (e.g. Dioto- genes §61 ed. Delatte 39.10–12; Ecphantus §64, ibid. 27.5–7; 28.1f); so too for Pliny, *Panegyricus* 7.5 (Mynors), a ruler should be chosen who is most godlike; cf. also Bowersock, 'Intellectuals' 189.

they were represented as exercising some functions of those gods or as enjoying their protection[42]. Instructive too here is the anthropologist V. W. Turner's comment on initiation rites in general that

> The arcane knowledge or *'gnosis'*, obtained in the liminal period [see §6.2 below] is felt to change the inmost nature of the neophyte, as a seal impresses wax, with the characteristics of his new state. It is not a mere acquisition of knowledge, but a change in being[43].

That new being for the initiates in the mysteries of the Graeco-Roman world was a more godlike being; they enjoyed a more godlike status and exercised more godlike functions; well might they receive the veneration of their less fortunate fellow mortals. They were 'deified' in the sense of becoming (more) godlike and possessed of divine powers, but not in themselves, but through their access to the favour and power of their tutelary deity; they were 'identified' with that deity, but not in the fullest or most strict sense; rather they were at one with the deity, communing with it and at the same time representing it to their fellow mortals.

5.3. The Background of the Pauline 'with Christ' Language

In turning to consider Paul's view of baptism and that of early Christians we have to note that two considerations weigh heavily against any derivation of the idea of dying and rising with Christ from the soteriology of the mysteries:

(1) hard as we may search we will find no true parallel there to Paul's characteristic 'with Christ' language[1]. It is true that there is the συγχαίρ-ωμεν of the Isis initiates[2], but that is a present rejoicing with a goddess who rejoices that her bereavement is over, not a past dying or rising with the slain god; only the latter, as we have seen (§1.3.3.5), would provide us with a true parallel to Paul's soteriology[3]. Lohmeyer rightly rejects,

---

42 *'Consecratio'* 3.
43 *Forest* 102; cf. Eliade, *Birth* x.

Notes on 5.3

  1 *Pace* Bonnard, 'Mourir' 110; cf. also §§1.3.2.3 n. 8, 1.3.3.5. Tannehill rightly cautions against regarding 'with Christ' as a formula (*Dying* 6; so too Luz, *Geschichtsverständnis* 305f; contrast, e.g., Dupont, ΣΥΝ ΧΡΙΣΤΩι 10; Gäumann, *Taufe* 55; W. Grundmann in *TDNT* 7, 782; Hoffmann, *Toten* 301; Lohmeyer, 'Σὺν Χριστῷ' *passim*), but it is perhaps more than a motif; it is a novel use of language, more novel perhaps than the idea that it expresses (see below).
  2 Cf. §5.1.1.2 n. 23; cf. Paul's use of this compound in 1 Cor 12.26.
  3 Cf. Bonnard 'Mourir' 111.

too, as a parallel the use of σὺν θεῷ/θεοῖς in Greek literature, for this refers simply to the 'helpful assistance which the gods have provided for people in their deeds and journeyings' and this sense is 'in sharp contrast to the meaning of Paul's formula'[4].

(2) Although one does find assertions to the effect that in baptism 'the neophyte was . . . ritually assimilated to Christ in his death'[5], this is not true: Christ did not die by drowning but by crucifixion, and the Christian rite is not outwardly a re-enactment of Christ's death[6]. Schnackenburg finds an attempt to make it this in the *Apostolic Constitutions* 3.17: 'the water stands for (ἀντί) burial . . . the going down (into the water) is dying with him, the coming up rising with him'[7]. But so late a witness to this idea hardly suggests that it was responsible for the original use of this rite.

But if this idea and this language were not borrowed from the mysteries how did they arise? We can perhaps more easily parallel the idea than the language. An obvious parallel and an often cited one is the Mishnaic text relating to the Passover, *Pesaḥ*. 10.5:

> In any generation a man must so regard himself as if he came forth himself out of Egypt, for it is written, 'And thou shalt tell thy son in that day saying, "It is because of that which the Lord did for me when I came out of Egypt"' (Exod 13.8). . . . He brought us out from bondage to freedom, from sorrow to gladness, and from mourning to a festival-day, and from darkness to great light, and from servitude to redemption . . .[8].

---

4 'Σὺν Χριστῷ 228f; cf. Dupont, ΣΤΝ ΧΡΙΣΤΩΙ 9, 21 (but n.b. 191); W. Grundmann in *TDNT* 7, 773f; the antecedents to Paul's language cited by Cranfield, *Rom* 1, 311f, are largely of this type too (and of these only Ps 139 (140).14 (13) even has σύν as opposed to μετά; cf. Grundmann, ibid. 780 − not noticed by Gäumann, *Taufe* 55? See too the Greek of *1 Enoch* 1.9.) These might provide a parallel to living 'with Christ' (Rom 6.8*b*), but not if that involves also a being made like his risen state (6.5) and certainly no parallel to dying with him (6.8*a*).

5 Brandon, Significance' 47; contrast, e.g., Carlson, *Baptism* 219.

6 Cf. Dibelius, 'Isis Initiation' 95; 'baptism ought really to be a dying, but the form of the action contradicted that, unless one interpreted it − as Luther later did − as a veritable "being drowned". So . . . it is understood as an imitation of Christ's burial − a forced interpretation, for the burial is not a salvific act of Christ. That fact proves . . . that this evaluation of baptism was not original and that the baptismal ritual . . . arose from another world of symbols. The Christian congregation probably borrowed baptism, as an eschatological sacrament, from the circle of John the Baptist.' He continues, 'the Christians of the hellenistic world felt the need to understand it as a hellenistic mystery. Here the analogy of the mysteries explains everything'. Here the problems arise in my opinion. Cf. also M. Smith, 'Transformation' 112.

7 *Baptism* 55; Schweizer, *Lordship* 91=*Erniedrigung* 142, also finds a contrast with the mysteries in the view of the Christian life as a following of Jesus in his sufferings.

8 Tr. Danby; he notes that the first sentence is lacking in older versions (cf. ed. Beer 195f). Davies, *Paul* 103 n.2, comments 'Nevertheless, the theme is constant throughout the Haggadah and underlies the whole rite'.
 In thus turning to Jewish ideas here I find myself in conflict with Brandon, 'Technique' 30: 'In interpreting the death by crucifixion of Jesus of Nazareth soteriologically, the Apostle Paul had to draw on concepts which were alien to Jewish religion'. (I also find hard to accept his claim immediately following this that Paul was the first to see that death as saving all as opposed to just a martyrdom for Israel; I take 1 Cor 15.3 to be traditional.)

W. D. Davies finds the same idea embodied in the liturgy of the *Passover Haggadah* which he thinks was probably arranged by Gamaliel II (80–120 CE) and thus goes back to an earlier ritual. He quotes the response

> We were slaves to the Pharaoh in Egypt, and the Lord our God brought us forth from thence . . . .

Moreover there is added to the Mishnah passage just quoted the statement,

> Not our ancestors alone did God redeem then, but he did us redeem with them as it is said (Deut 6.23): 'And he brought us out from thence that he might bring us in to give us the land which he sware unto our fathers'[9].

Equally it is possible to trace this idea back into the Old Testament, even if the expressions of it are not so striking; so Schweizer cites Amos 3.1,

> Hear this word that the Lord has spoken against you, O people of Israel, against the whole family which I brought up out of the land of Egypt[10].

In this the solidarity and unity of the nation from generation to generation is clearly expressed. In the passages relating to the Passover quoted above we also find the idea of a ritual in which the participants find themselves, as it were, in some sense participants also in a past act of redemption, an event experienced by a past generation of God's people. Paul on the other hand says that the ritual of baptism is a participation in a saving event experienced not by a whole generation, but by one person, and does so in a succinct form of language not paralleled in the Mishnah, although the *Passover Liturgy*'s 'he did us redeem with them' comes as near to Paul's language as anything that we have seen[11]. Despite that this is in general a closer analogy than the 'eschatological sacrament' of John's baptism to which Dibelius refers (though as an explanation of the earliest Christian baptismal theology, not Paul's)[12]; the latter looks forward,

---

9 *Paul* 102f; the 'with them' of the second quotation translates עמהם (Marks-Löwy 24) which Fleg curiously translates 'en eux' as if switching to a parallel to Paul's 'in Christ'. E. P. Sanders, *Paul* (1977) 512f criticizes Davies' attempt to explain the idea of a dying and rising with Christ from Exodus typology; cf. too Schnackenburg, *Baptism* 186 and 'Todes- und Lebensgemeinschaft' 49: but Davies *has* rightly perceived the *Grundstruktur* of Paul's thought; his fault is to have 'overlooked the fact that Paul is not using specific Jewish theologoumena, but trying to encompass his new and special teaching about Christ with the categories that lay to hand, or, better, he is attempting to express and describe theologically, in his own way, the unique reality of Christ as he grasps it in faith.' Put another way, Davies was wrong to specify these ideas as peculiarly connected with the Exodus; rather they are basic ideas, ways of looking at things, to which the Jews had given classic expression in their Passover liturgy.

10 *Lordship* 47=*Erniedrigung* 68f.

11 Anderson, *Jesus* 275 asks 'Does not [Rom 6.11f] also echo the liturgy of the Jewish Passover, in which the member of the Jewish community is summoned to recapitulate in his own history the historical events of Israel?' He then cites Knox, *Paul* (1939) 97f. But see n. 9 above.

12 See n. 6 above.

anticipates participation in a future event, whereas the former and Paul both look back and treat the rite as a re-enacting of a past participation in a past event. Schweizer, more appropriately, refers to the idea of Adam including all generations 'in' himself; though he toys with that idea of influence from the mysteries which I have argued against, he concludes that this is far more important and relevant to the understanding of Paul's thought[13].

To my mind this is the likeliest background to Paul's thought, and it is clear from a passage like Romans 6 that he expected it to be intelligible to his readers in Rome[14]. Perhaps it was, but then it need not be the case that Paul was always actually intelligible to his readers; 1 Cor 5.9f shows that he was not. Perhaps in this case he expected Jewish and Christian tradition to have made them sufficiently familiar with such ideas, or he may have expected the preceding development of the contrast between Adam and Christ to have prepared their minds for this usage. However such an explanation is not available for the daring statement of Gal 2.19, but then in the passionate argument of that letter he probably did not stop to consider too long the best way of making his thought clear (and 2.19 is not the only example in the letter of less than transparently clear statements).

Anyway, although in the Graeco-Roman world the sense of oneness and unity between a representative figure like a ruler and his people was perhaps not as vivid as in the ancient Near East[15], yet traces of it do remain. At the accession of Gaius Caligula the people of Assos affirmed that the world's joy knew no measure, and that 'every city and every race' desired to see the god since 'the most pleasant age for the human race had now begun'[16]. Nero too was hailed as 'saviour and benefactor of the world'[17], and previous Roman emperors and leaders had been addressed in much the same way[18]. Yet the blessing brought by these rulers to their subjects seems to have been thought of more as the beneficent work of a god or godlike figure incarnate amongst them rather than of a man acting representatively on their behalf[19]. However the end result

---

13 *Erniedrigung* 143.
14 That is, they would be familiar with the idea rather than with this precise terminology (*pace* Gäumann, *Taufe* 55).
15 The ruler-cult of the Hellenistic kings, too, perhaps concentrated more on the divine status of the ruler rather than this representative role, with its concomitant sense of the involvement of the subjects in their ruler's fortunes. There was, too, a sense of alienation between many subjects and their rulers: cf., e.g., Polyb. 15.24.4.
16 *SIG*³ 797=Smallwood, *Documents* (1967) 33.
17 E.g. *OGIS* 668=Smallwood, ibid. 419.
18 For reff. cf. W. Foerster in *TDNT* 7, 1008, 1010–12.
19 Cf. for a slightly later period Sauter, *Kaiserkult* 163–5.

seems to have been much the same: the well-being of the many was dependent on that of the one; so Messala insisted that the prosperity (*felicitas*) of Rome depended upon Augustus' good fortune[20], and there is also the story that when Augustus was sailing past the Gulf of Puteoli the crew and passengers of an Egyptian ship that had just arrived heaped praises on him and burnt incense, saying that 'through him they lived, through him they sailed the seas, through him they enjoyed freedom and good fortunes'[21]. The *Acta fratrum Arvalium* for 22nd January, 86 CE speaks of Domitian as the one 'on whose safety the well-being of all depends'[22]. On such ideas as these Paul could build as he proclaimed his 'Lord' to his converts in the Graeco-Roman world.

Wilckens, however, makes a further suggestion to explain the origin of these ideas and this language in Paul's letters[23]. Paul's 'with Christ' language originates in Christian traditions concerning following Jesus even in his crucifixion. It is true that one can point to the fact that two others were 'crucified with' (συνεσταυρωμένοι, Mk 15.32; cf. Matt 27.44, σvσταυρωθέντες σὺν αὐτῷ; Lk 23.2, σὺν αὐτῷ ἀναιρεθῆναι) Jesus and that Peter confidently spoke of his readiness to 'die with' (συναποθανεῖν, Mk 14.31; cf. Matt 26.35, σὺν σοὶ ἀποθανεῖν) him. The latter example underlines the problems of this line of explanation acutely: Peter did not die with Jesus in the sense that he intended, but rather took flight with the others; in Paul's sense he did nevertheless die with Jesus as one of those for whom Jesus died. 'With Christ' used in Mark's sense is a natural Greek usage[24]; in Paul's sense it is anything but usual and it is better to explain it as his striking adaptation of that usage for a new purpose, to express an idea that nevertheless has old roots, in the solidarity of the many with a founding father or fathers of the race or group.

Schweizer, on the other hand, considers the 'with Christ' statements about an eschatological fellowship with Christ after the parousia to be original and thinks of a progressive extension of this being 'with Christ' back into even the earthly life of the believer (1 Thess 5.10). Now it is true that this eschatological 'with Christ' usage is far more readily explicable than its application to the present or the past[25]. But then Schweizer asserts, 'That the eschatological meaning of the expression "with Christ"

---

20 Suet., *Aug.* 58.
21 Ibid. 98.2; C. Habicht in discussion of Bickerman, *'Consecratio'* 32, comments that Augustus was praised for bringing peace and undisturbed trade, not for protection from storms – that was the role of other deities.
22 McCrum-Woodhead, *Documents* 13.39f; cf. further reff. in Sauter, *Kaiserkult*, esp. 11–13.
23 *Röm* 2, 60f; Braumann, *Taufverkündigung* 54f, makes a similar suggestion. Kayes's appeal to 2 Cor 7.2f (*Structure* 88) seems to me no more apposite than this gospel material.
24 Cf. LSJ s.v. συναποθνῄσκω.
25 Cf. Dupont, ΣΥΝ ΧΡΙΣΤΩΙ 24 (n.b. 36f).

is the original one is also proved by II Cor. xiii.4: "We are weak *in* Christ, but shall live with him"[26]. The change in preposition is certainly striking, but 'proof' is far too strong a term; after all the very ease with which one might understand a future living with Christ might well explain why Paul has changed the preposition. And chronologically it is quite significant that as early as 1 Thess 5.10 Paul may be using the phrase of present communion with Christ. Likewise, Schweizer claims, the eschatological phrase was extended to the rite of baptism, which 'brings the eschatological being with Christ', 'is the anticipation of the change of the aeons'[27]. But we have argued that Paul's 'with Christ' language in this context does not just mean that the baptized were 'with Christ' in their baptism, whatever that might mean[28], but that their baptism signified, pointed to the fact, that they were already 'with' him in his past death and resurrection. True, these were 'eschatological events'[29], but I doubt whether that makes the idea of our being involved in them any more easily intelligible. After all the eschatological being 'with Christ' understood in the sense of Jewish apocalyptic and the fellowship of the redeemed with the Messiah is no nearer the 'with Christ' of Paul's baptismal theology than is the sense in which Jesus' two fellow-victims were 'with him' at his crucifixion and his disciples wanted to be but failed to be[30]. Might the clue not better be found in the sense of solidarity with a representative to which I have alluded? Since one has been 'with' (σύν) one's representative in his representative act (whether or not it is protological or eschatological or neither is not of primary importance) it is only natural that one expects the full consequences of that participation to unfold in a life

---

26 'Dying' 2; contrast Kramer, *Christos* §38, 145: 'the sacramental σύν is the presupposition of the eschatological' (ET 147 gets it the other way round!); cf. Gäumann, *Taufe* 58.

27 Ibid. 5f; cf. Carlson, *Baptism* 251; Hahn, 'Verständnis' 141, also 'Taufe' 23.

28 Was he 'with' them in their baptism as Lohmeyer ('Σὺν Χριστῷ' 251) suggests: 'he dies in each baptism and the baptized dies *with him*, and he is raised in each baptism, as the baptized is raised with him'? I doubt it. Paul at least never says that, and that may well be significant.

29 Bornkamm, 'Taufe' 39=ET 75: 'Christ's death and resurrection are . . . eschatological occurrences'; the Christ-event is therefore 'not an event that becomes past in the sense of other events, transcended by other events, but an event that means "once and for all" and includes a "no longer" (Rom. 6.9)' (40=76). Rather the many are included in this event because it involves God's appointed representative for the many and it is eschatological because God speaks his last word there which will not be superseded or made redundant or invalidated by any subsequent word; what he speaks to succeeding generations of individuals, e.g. in baptism, is but a repetition, a reinforcing, an echo of that last word.

30 Rightly seen by Tannehill, *Dying* 88 n. 14: Schweizer's postulated 'development would involve a considerable change in the original meaning' of the apocalyptic 'with Christ' language. Carlson, *Baptism*, makes much of Beker's used of the term 'apocalyptic theology' to explain Paul's language here. To be convinced of the value of this as an explanation I would need to see more sign in other apocalyptic texts of similar ideas of sharing in a representative's past experiences or even of Paul's striking personifications of sin, death and the law as hostile powers.

with him now and hereafter, and that life with him hereafter should also be, according to Jewish apocalyptic imagery, one in his fellowship ($\mu\epsilon\tau\acute{a}$)[31]. That is to suggest that the idea of solidarity with a representative may be logically, and perhaps also chronologically, prior to the idea of eschatological communion[32]. And Paul could as well have coined his $\sigma\acute{u}\nu$ language to express the former before he used it of the latter.

Some scholars have sought the presuppositions of the 'with Christ' language in the contrast of Adam and Christ that is found in Rom 5.12–21[33]; however, since Paul has earlier used the idea of our having died with Christ in a context where there is no mention of Adam or of Christ as the eschatological Adam, in Gal 2.19, we should not make the former idea too dependent on the latter. It is true, nevertheless, that the explanation which I am offering for the former means that there is a real affinity between it and the latter idea, and that both draw upon the same background of ideas.

5.3.1. Elsewhere I have, albeit briefly, pointed to a passage which may be held to confirm this backgound for Paul's ideas, in the argument of *Galatians 3*[1]. There Paul speaks of the Gentiles being blessed not only in Abraham (v 8) but also with him (v 9)[2]. Here he appeals expressly to the Old Testament, echoing Gen 12.3 and 18.18[3]. There the Septuagint uses

---

31 In n. 4 above it was noted that few of the comparable OT texts use $\sigma\acute{u}\nu$; $\mu\epsilon\tau\acute{a}$ is commoner.

32 W. Grundmann in *TDNT* 7, 783, argues that Paul speaks as he does in 2 Cor 4.14 'out of the conviction that fellowship has been set up between Christ and His community, this being grounded in the death of Christ for us' (1 Thess 5.10); cf. ibid. 785: 'The offering "for us all" is the basis of the "with him" '; also Hoffmann, *Toten* 307.

33 Cf. Wagner, *Baptism* 290: 'The train of thought in Rom. VI has to be seen against the background of the Adam-Christ parallel which is elaborated in Rom. V.12ff.' – also lit. in n. 131 (he goes on to refer to Judaistic Gnostic speculations about Adam, which I consider less plausible – cf. my 'Body' and 'Structure'); also Schmidt, *Röm* 107.

Notes on 5.3.1

1 Most recently in 'Observations'.

2 Bruce, *Gal* 157, comments that 'In using the preposition $\sigma\acute{u}\nu$, Paul conveys the precise force of Heb b^e, translated $\dot{\epsilon}\nu$ in the LXX in Gen 12:3 and 18:18'. However, as his subsequent appeal to C. G. Montefiore suggests, b^e might be translated 'with' in the sense of 'by means of' but this is not the commonest sense of $\sigma\acute{u}\nu$ (but see LSJ s.v. A7); moreover Dos Santos' *Index* 21 shows that, despite all the Greek equivalents for b^e used in the LXX, $\sigma\acute{u}\nu$ is not found there; $\dot{\epsilon}\nu$ is by far the commonest translation. That suggests that Paul intended more than just an equivalent of b^e in v 9.

3 Bruce *Gal* 156, sees in 3.8 a conflation of Gen 12.3 and 18.18 (cf. Bonnard, *Gal* 66); Sanders, *Paul* (1983) 21, 53 n. 24, argues that the latter is Paul's primary text as it contains the word $\check{\epsilon}\theta\nu\eta$; Lindars *Apologetic* 225, argues that 12.3 is primary 'because the argument turns on the fact that the promise has already been made before 15.6'. (But is there a conflation with Rom 4 – n.b. v 10 – here?)

ἐν which I have argued has primarily an instrumental, causal sense here[4]. The σύν phrase could then serve to make more precise the way in which Abraham is the means or channel of blessing to the nations: it is by being associated with him as recipients of his blessing. In other words God associated them with him, and in blessing him he intended also to bless them, viewing Abraham as their representative[5].

God thus spoke, Paul suggests, his word of blessing to all nations through Abraham, but Abraham could only be that channel of blessing by hearing, believing and obeying[6]; the nations could only appropriate that blessing by imitating his faith, by being those ἐκ πίστεως (v 9).

If this usage is analogous to that of Romans 6 it suggests that in the latter passage God has also associated us with Christ, not this time as co-recipients of the pronouncement of a blessing, but as co-recipients of his verdict upon human sin. They receive that verdict together with their representative and in his person; it remains for them, however, to work out for themselves the implications and the consequences of that verdict, to treat themselves, in other words, as 'dead to sin'[7]. Schweizer also rightly remarks that

> with Paul the unity of the members with the body consists above all in the fact that they 'carry the death of Jesus in their body', because they, as he himself, are persecuted, exposed to humiliation and suffering until they also share with Jesus in his exaltation to the glory of the Father[8].

---

4 But distinguished from διά perhaps by the additional nuance which it conveys of association as the basis on which Christ is this instrument or means; cf. my 'Observations'.

5 So Bouttier, *En Christ* 43, says of σύν in σύν Χριστῷ when used of the salient events of Christ's life: 'God's plan has joined (*associé*) us together with the destiny of Jesus Christ'; cf. Bonnard, *Gal* 67: 'the solidarity between (σύν) Abraham and the Galatians is based . . . on a single decision of God, announced in Abraham and now applied to Christians of pagan background (*pagano-chrétiens*).'

6 Burton, *Gal* 161: for Paul the ἐν σοί meant 'in thee, because by this exercise of faith in God thou hast given occasion to the establishment and announcement of the principle that God's approval and blessing are upon those that believe'.

7 G. Barth, *Taufe* 102, sees in the parallelism of Rom 6.5–7 and 8–10 evidence that the baptismal event and the Christ-event are not just analogous; the former is not just a repetition of the latter as a comparison with the mysteries might suggest (and this holds good even on our account of them above – they do repeat and imitate the actions of the deities, only not usually their death and restoration, but more often the grieving and the restoring of the dead, i.e. they imitate the actions of deities, not their passions); rather the two are identical. One might be better to say that for Paul the imitation came later, was a consequence of, both the Christ-event and the baptismal event which echoes it (and *is*, to that extent, a repetition of it, i.e. a restatement of the divine pronouncement in it).

8 *Lordship* 48=*Erniedrigung* 71. It seems to me dangerous, however, to appeal here to a different 'Hebrew conception of time' (47=68). The character of events like Christ's death and resurrection when viewed as divine statements which we must hear and to which we must respond seems a better explanation.

Dunn too stresses the perfect tense used in Gal 2.19, 6.14, and Rom 6.5 and argues that for Paul the Christian crucified with Christ still hangs on his cross; this vivid language shows that it is incumbent upon the Christian to be conformed to Christ in his death until that time when they can take the form of his risen state[9]. These expositions underline the fact that, despite the impression given by Paul's aorists that death with Christ was something past[10], that death continues on into the present[11].

Christ, then, is like Abraham, a representative figure through whom God speaks and acts towards the human race; they were 'with' him when God spoke and acted just as they were 'with' Abraham. The 'with' language thus arises out of this idea of the solidarity of the race with its representative and not out of any idea gleaned from the mysteries. After all Abraham was no dying and rising saviour figure and yet similar language was used of him. That surely suggests that Paul's thinking here is influenced more by his Jewish background than by the mysteries[12]. Regardless of how the original writers saw the nations being blessed with Abraham Paul, I suggest, saw this as analogous to the blessing that would come through Christ and was pronounced on them 'with Christ'. Here, significantly, he draws on ideas of solidarity with, and representation by, a single figure, our 'forefather Abraham' (Rom 4.1) in the singular rather than the whole generation of 'our fathers' who came out of Egypt (1 Cor 10.1) as in the *Passover Haggadah*. And those who are in solidarity with, and represented by, this single figure are not limited to ethnic Israel but are drawn from 'all nations'[13].

---

9 *Jesus* 331f; it might also be suggested that this idea of bearing the likeness of the suffering earthly Jesus (cf. 1 Cor 15.49) is the main reason why Paul in Rom 6.5 inserts τῷ ὁμοιώματι and does not simply say σύμφυτοι γεγόναμεν τῷ θανάτῳ αὐτοῦ. Hoffmann, *Toten* 307f, stresses the importance of *Gleichgestaltung* in the statements about our present and our future life with Christ, in addition to the idea of fellowship.

10 In Gal 2.19 we find the aor. ἀπέθανον and the pf. συνεσταύρωμαι (Paul is inclined to use the pf. of the pass. of σταυρόω – contrast the aor. act. of 5.24 and the aor. pass. of Rom 6.6; with ἀποθνῄσκω he habitually uses the aor.); the pf. of Rom 6.5 is surrounded by the aor. in 6.2–4, 6–10 (except for δεδικαίωται in 7); cf. further Schnackenburg, 'Todes- und Lebensgemeinschaft' 37 (although he sees the effect of the action of *baptism* enduring rather than the effect of union with Christ's death on the cross; contrast Frankemölle, *Taufverständnis* 103f; Hoffmann *Toten* 305f n. 87.

11 Contrast Lohmeyer, 'Σὺν Χριστῷ' 220f!

12 Cf. Schnackenburg, 'Todes- und Lebensgemeinschaft' 53. *Pace* Schweizer, *Lordship* 46=*Erniedrigung* 69 I see no particular reason either to emphasize the Hellenistic influence on reflection about the *Stammvater* as a background to Paul's thought; it was there, but Paul makes little use of the figure of Jacob=Israel and I doubt whether Hellenistic spatial ideas have played any great part in the formulation of 'in Adam' or 'in Christ' (the former I see as formed on the analogy of the latter); see my 'Observations' 88, 94 n. 24.

13 Sanders, *Paul* (1977) 514, speaks of 'covenantal' categories being transcended by the determination of the world's fate by Adam; by implication what Christ did in contrast to Adam also transcends covenantal categories. Rather Paul uses 'participationist transfer terms'.

At first sight, however, the receiving of a blessing with Abraham is very different from dying and rising with Christ. Yet it need not be, particularly, if the emphasis is placed upon the death and resurrection of Jesus as divine pronouncements, so to speak, as a verdict of condemnation and a promise of life[14]. Thus Klaiber comments on 2 Cor 5.14–21 that 'the judgment of Jesus' death is passed upon the whole human race'[15]. In other words, although the 'with Christ' language is not used there, in that one died for all, all died and died with him (2 Cor 5.14) in passing under that same divine judgment as was passed upon Jesus when he was 'made sin' on our behalf, in order that we might likewise share his restoration and vindication and fellowship with, and status before, God – all of which Paul sums up in the word 'righteousness' (2 Cor 5.21). Rightly G. Otto applies the same ideas to Romans 6: 'What happened to Christ happened too to all with him who ever are or will be Christians. He is the inauguration of $\kappa \alpha \iota \nu \acute{o} \tau \eta \varsigma$ $\zeta \omega \tilde{\eta} \varsigma$ and thus it is inaugurated for all Christians'[16]. Schlatter too, also commenting on Romans 6, interprets Paul's ideas along rather similar lines[17].

> [Christ] includes [believers] in God's judgment laid on him, and by that they are made dead too. . . . the sinner is judged in that God's Son has suffered death for him and has produced from his death that act of grace that promises righteousness to those who believe in him.

5.3.2. Does this mean then that the explanation of Paul's 'with Christ' language lies in the much-used concept of *'corporate personality'*? That certainly is the conclusion of Mußner as well as many others apropos of

---

14 In my use of the term 'solidarity' and my stress on the participation of all in Christ's representative death and resurrection in the past I may seem near to the position of 'Protestant antisacramentalism' alluded to by Bonnard, 'Mourir' 109f (he cites K. Barth, M. Barth, R. Bultmann and O. Cullmann as examples of it). Yet the stress upon the word-character of the rite of baptism here does perhaps allow me to do greater justice to the rite of baptism than he suggests that these scholars do; it would be a sort of 'echo' or re-proclamation of that which was declared in Christ's death and resurrection, declared now in its validity for the individual in question.

15 *Rechtfertigung* 82; cf. Beker, *Paul* 194 ('to be "crucified with Christ" . . . means to be subjected to God's judgment'); Bouttier, *En Christ* 45; G. Otto, *Formulierungen* 35. Bonnard, 'Mourir' 111f, also comes near this in his talk of a 'dialogue with God' – the rite of baptism 'maintains and renews . . . an encounter (*face-à-face*), a union (*alliance*) created by the initial redemption. The judgment signified by Christ's crucifixion and resurrection has but the character of an accomplished and definitive fact.' The reverse is also true: the events of Christ's death and resurrection have the character of judgments, decisions of God.

16 *Formulierungen* 40.

17 *Gerechtigkeit* 196f; cf. 200f.

Galatians 3[1]: he expounds Gal 3.9 in a similar way to that of the previous section of this study and appeals expressly to the idea of 'corporate personality'. Betz demurs: Paul only regards Adam and Christ in this way, not Abraham[2]. Yet the similarity of the language used of all three figures suggests that they were regarded in much the same way: either all three are examples of 'corporate personality' or none are.

Hitherto I have spoken of 'solidarity' with Christ and 'representation'[3] by him and that choice of words has been deliberate. I am strongly aware of the difficulties of the term 'corporate personality' as a term[4], although thoroughly appreciative of the idea expressed by it as long as exaggerated claims are not made for it.

For any appeal to this concept will have to come to terms first with the articles of two British Old Testament scholars. The first, by J. R. Porter, deals with 'the legal aspects of the concept of "corporate personality" in the Old Testament'; it questions 'how far Israelite law envisages the "psychic community" or the "psychical unity" ': rather it 'operated on the basis of the individual rather than the group, and was concerned to fix individual guilt and inflict individual punishment'; yet at times it was recognized that 'a man can possess persons in much the same way that he possesses property' (hence, e.g., Achan's household were forfeit in Josh 7?) and they held 'beliefs about the contagious nature

---

Notes on 5 3.2

1 Mußner, *Gal* 222; cf. Best, *Body* 56; Hoffmann, *Toten* 310; Schnackenburg, 'Todes- und Lebensgemeinschaft' 44 and 'Adam-Christus-Typologie' 48, 50; Wagner, *Baptism* 292f.

2 *Gal* 143 n. 41.

3 Cf. G. Otto, *Formulierungen* 37: what Paul is saying in Rom 6 is only intelligible against the background of the idea of representation. Tannehill, *Dying* 2, speaks rather of the dominant influence of the motif of Christ as 'inclusive *anthropos*', Frankemölle, *Taufverständnis* 102, of the 'corporate "new Adam" '. Schnackenburg, 'Adam-Christus-Typologie' 50, finds within 'corporate personality' the categories of 'solidarity, representation, and *Vikariation*'. Schweizer, *Lordship* 54=*Erneidrigung* 76, distinguishes four conceptions of representation: (1) the representative is the end of history and its meaning is fulfilled in him; (2) he is 'father' of the race and is determinative of the destiny of succeeding generations; (3) he is an 'inclusive personality' including many in himself as a vessel contains water; (4) he acts vicariously, delivering many by doing or suffering what all ought to have done or suffered. All seem to me thoroughly applicable to Pauline Christology with the possible exception of (3); that may be in Heb 7.5, but I am not persuaded that Paul had this imagery in mind. The other three must, however, be understood in the context of the 'word' character of Christ's experiences outlined above, as well as qualified 'by the fact that Jesus had called men to follow him' (ibid. 55=76).

4 Cf. my 'Body' 83—5: is it the individual Christ or all those represented by him that are the 'corporate personality' (Dodd, *Rom* 86 prefers the latter – they are the 'corporate personality', Christ is their 'inclusive representative'; contrast Best *Body* 59, 'the idea of Christ as an inclusive or corporate personality')? Is it that one or a group *is* a 'corporate personality' or is it something that one *has*? (One speaks usually of being a person of a certain character and having a certain personality, but not so in this instance apparently. Would one be better to speak of a group as a corporate person which has a corporate personality?)

of blood, holiness, sin and uncleanness' (so Achan's household might be infected by the stolen holy objects?), aspects of Israelite thought which had in large measure given rise to the belief in the notion of 'corporate personality' and which we do not share[5].

Five years later, in 1970, there appeared the second article, by J. W. Rogerson, re-examining the idea of 'corporate personality'. For Rogerson found that H. W. Robinson, that great proponent of this idea and this phrase, 'nowhere defined what he meant' by it[6]. He traces Robinson's use of the idea to the work of Sir Henry Maine on *Ancient Law*; yet Maine was suggesting, not that an individual in ancient society had no consciousness of individuality, but that he had no individual rights. Robinson, in other words, was making a further claim, about the psychology of primitive people, and here he was dependent upon 'Spencer and Gillen's *The Northern Tribes of Central Australia* which describes societies dominated by the ideas of identity of substance between the clan and the eponymous totem, and the magico-biological unity of members of the same clan'[7]. Robinson, curiously, can speak of this phenomenon as 'a primitive survival in Hebrew thought that was gradually superseded by individual moral responsibility' and yet hold that it was still operative in Jewish thought in the first century C.E.[8] This he does by seeing the two ideas of corporate personality and individual responsibility being merged (perhaps held together in creative tension?) so that 'the individualism of the Old Testament is usually, if not always, conceived as realized in and through the society which is based upon it'[9]. Here we see another meaning of the phrase, that 'a man cannot be treated as an isolated individual, but must be viewed as a member of society', and this sense stems from 'a modern understanding of man and his community', a sense that was supposed to be self-evident to modern readers[10].

Later the anthropological and psychological sense of the phrase became dominant in Robinson's writings, under the influence of L. Lévy-Bruhl and his views on primitive, pre-logical thought. Under the same influence, and therefore the same strictures, come the writings of such as D. S. Russell, A. R. Johnson and R. P. Shedd; they also at times show an odd tendency to illustrate a supposedly primitive mentality from experience of the present day. Rightly, for we are not so individualistic as to be

---

5 'Aspects' 379f.

6 'Conception' 2.

7 Ibid. 5.

8 Ibid. 6.

9 H. W. Robinson, *The Christian Doctrine of Man* (Edinburgh, 1911) 34, quoted by Rogerson, ibid.

10 Rogerson, ibid. 7.

unable to be 'deeply concerned for the well-being of (our) President or
. . . monarch' or to identify ourselves with 'the needs and hopes of (our)
family, . . . town or . . . country'[11]. We need but look at fans' identification with the fortunes of their football team[12].

Significantly, however, Rogerson, although he advocates that we should
'drop the term corporate personality completely', yet notes that Old
Testament phenomena like 'the "I" of the Psalms and the idea of the
hopes of the people being centred in the king' remain, even if 'corporate
personality' is not invoked to explain them; it need not be, since, as
Rowley noted, 'the corporate use of "I" (is) something known to modern
worshippers' and so need not be seen as evidence of primitive thought[13].
It is a fact that 'the hopes of the Israelites were centred on their king',
but 'these hopes depended on something other than the inability to distinguish clearly between the king and the community of which he was
head'. At the same time in the case of the Servant Songs of Deutero-
Isaiah there is 'a tension between an individual prophet, his immediate
circle, and the whole nation for which they stand'[14].

Thus the gravamen of Rogerson's criticism is directed not so much
against the reality of the Old Testament data as against Robinson's evaluation and explanation of them. The Old Testament writers do often speak
in the terms which suggested to him his theory or theories of 'corporate
personality'. Rogerson seems, however, to suggest that it is not enough
to appeal instead to 'modern experience'[15]; that would be correct, to my
mind, in so far as that 'modern experience' is in turn in need of evaluation
and explanation, and there may be as much to distinguish it from biblical
phenomena as unites them.

For a start it would be grotesque to compare Paul's Christology with
the relationship between a football team and its fans, at least at anything
deeper than the most superficial level. But the problem is more complex

---

11 Ibid. 13.

12 Cf. Turner, *Process* 3: 'in matters of religion, as of art, there are no "simpler" peoples, only
some peoples with simpler technologies than our own. Man's "imaginative" and "emotional"
life is always and everywhere rich and complex.. . . Nor is it entirely accurate to speak of the
"structure of a mind different from our own". It is not a matter of different cognitive structures, but of an identical cognitive structure articulating wide diversities of cultural experience.'
Cf. too M. I. Finley's introduction to Easterling-Muir, *Religion* xiv: the current approach to
Greek religion, drawing on Evans-Pritchard and others, 'rejects the very notion of "primitive"
or of a "rational" as against a "non-rational" (or even "irrational") approach to the questions
to which religion addresses itself'.

13 Yet Hasenfratz, *Lebenden* 5, includes among characteristics of 'archaic' or 'primitive' thought a
'collective mentality'; it may be true that such a thought is different from ours, but the difference may be of degree rather than kind.

14 Ibid. 14f.

15 Ibid. 16.

still. In comparing Christ with Adam Paul would not have questioned the tradition of Adam as literally the ancestor of the whole human race. He was only too aware of the symbolic nature of Adam's name, as he discloses by his introduction of him as an otherwise unnamed ἄνθρωπος in Rom 5.12 and his reference to Christ as 'the eschatological Adam' in 1 Cor 15.45; Adam and ἄνθρωπος are for him interchangeable and the former is not just the proper name of an individual (the same holds good perhaps of Israel as the proper name of a patriarch and of the race sprung from him), but is a generic name. But the legitimacy of that ambivalence is underpinned by a physical solidarity that it does not have for us once we abandon the idea of a single common ancestor; we cannot think of ourselves as already in Adam's loins (cf. Heb 7.5). We have to do without the myth of the fall of this ancestor. Yet does the force of Paul's theology suffer too greatly as a consequence? After all he does elsewhere use the symbolic nature of Adam's name to the full, in his allusion to the fall story in Rom 1.23 and behind the description of the encounter of the human personality (not further specified) with God's command in 7.7–13[16]. And the account of 5.12–21 may be reinforced in a different way to that of the myth of the fall by our contemporary awareness of our interrelationship in responsibility and guilt; in the affluent developed world we are, for instance, inextricably part of an economic order that unfairly exploits the developing and underdeveloped parts of our world. As we face intractable problems of our times like the conflicts in Ireland and the Middle East we become conscious that we bear the legacy of the past, that indeed the parents' sins weigh upon future generations, and yet we are not thereby exonerated; we cannot wash our hands of it.

As regards the Christ side of the comparison, Paul could not claim a physical underpinning for our relationship with Christ anyway and would not want to do so. Our solidarity with him is created by the same spirit of God that breathed in Jesus and guided him through his life to the grave and beyond it. If he is our representative it is not because like football fans we have tied our hopes to the fortunes of others but because, we claim, God has tied our destinies to that of this one individual. He represents us because, we believe, God chose him to do so. In him we see the pattern of what God willed humanity to be. In what happened to him, both in its fearfulness and in its expressible hopes, we see ourselves before God and in God's eyes, as our Creator sees us and chooses to regard us. We are thereby called and challenged to align ourselves with that pattern of God's working and choosing. If the death to sin and to the world which that involves seems fearful, yet it is the gateway to life as it was for Christ.

---

16 Cf. my 'Adam'.

Paul's language of our dying with Christ then is probably his own; at least I have found no convincing enough parallel to it which might explain whence he derived it. But the ideas which he expresses by this language are not so novel; they are one with the tradition which he inherited from Israel of a series of representative figures upon whose actions the destinies of successive generations in some measure depend and with whom these generations either did align themselves as they did with the actions of Adam[17] or should align themselves as they were called to do with the actions of the righteous patriarchs. As we noted above (§5.3), if his Graeco-Roman audience was not so accustomed to talk and think in those terms that might have made Paul's ideas rather less immediately intelligible to them, and yet not, I argued, wholly unintelligible. But if they hunted around in their own stock of ideas to find parallels to help them appreciate Paul's thought, it is not necessarily the gods of the mysteries to whom they would turn for illumination; they were accustomed to apply the title of 'saviour' far more widely and we saw that they would have seen their rulers and leaders as playing a representative role upon which their destinies and well-being depended. They could far more easily have conceived of these as fellow human beings upon whose fortunes their own in large measure depended, rather than the exalted deities whose vicissitudes were described in the myths of the mysteries. The former, however, were there on earth as agents of the gods and instruments of blessing put there by them to promote the well-being of the human race.

5.4. Conclusions

Yet, lest we come to the conclusion that Paul's soteriology has nothing in common with that of the mysteries, we must note that in §5.1 we looked at various ways in which the initiates into the mysteries might have expected salvation as a result of their initiation. We have certainly seen the questionable basis upon which so many theories of Paul's or Hellenistic Christianity's dependence upon the mysteries have been built, namely the idea of the initiate's dying and rising with the mystery-deity in the rite of initiation; we have also argued for a very different basis for Paul's distinctive language of dying 'with Christ'. A large part of the case

---

17 This I take to be the force of Rom 5.12*d*; see my 'Structure' and the Jewish intertestamental parallels cited there (349–51).

which I have presented rests upon the argument that the initiates in the mysteries did not in fact see their relationship to the mystery-deity in that way at all nor did they expect their salvation to come in any analogous way.

They did, however, perhaps always rest their hopes upon the power, now and hereafter, of the deity or deities with whom they were entering into a relationship in their initiation. Moreover, at least in the case of some of the Egyptian rites, they could see in the fate of Osiris a prototype of the way in which Isis could rescue them too (cf. § §5.1.1.1—5 and 5.1.5 on Firm. Mat., *Err. prof. rel.* 22.3). We also saw (in §5.1.2) the possibility that the Eleusinian mysteries offered hope to the initiates by pointing to two possible examples of Demeter's salvific power, in rescuing her daughter and in her thwarted plan to deify Demophoön.

Paul too knew of Christ as a prototype and example of the saved, rescued by the power and the divine spirit of his Father. This is clear in a number of passages: in Rom 8.11 he tells his readers that, if the spirit of the God who raised Jesus from the dead dwells in them, that same God will also make their mortal bodies alive through that same spirit and in 8.29 he speaks of God's purpose that his children should be fashioned ($\sigma\acute{\nu}\mu\mu\rho\rho\phi\rho\varsigma$) in the image of his Son, that the latter might be the firstborn ($\pi\rho\omega\tau\acute{\rho}\tau\rho\kappa\rho\varsigma$) among many brothers and sisters[1]. The same idea is implicit in the description of Christ as the firstfruits ($\dot{\alpha}\pi\alpha\rho\chi\acute{\eta}$) of the still future resurrection of all in 1 Cor 15.20—23, on a still future day when at last we will bear the image of the heavenly man, the eschatological Adam (v 49)[2]. The association of this hope with Christ's role as eschatological Adam suggests that its background lies in Jewish traditions of some sort, rather than in any soteriology of the mysteries, although in some ways the end result is rather similar; Paul has, in other words, reached a position comparable to that of the mysteries, but by a different route.

However in the case of Paul's thought it must be stressed that these ideas do not arise in the context of any ritual. There is no enactment of Christ's death and resurrection presupposed by the passages which we have just considered, and we do not know of any such rituals at this stage in the church's history; passion-plays lie still in the future. The Christian rite of initiation, baptism, is, as we have seen (§5.3), no re-enactment of

---

Notes on 5.4

1 Phil 3.21 differs from this in that it suggests that it is Christ, not God (cf. also 2 Cor 5.5) or God's spirit, who will transform us.

2 Accepting, along with the majority of commentators, the v.l. $\phi\rho\rho\acute{\epsilon}\sigma\rho\mu\epsilon\nu$ rather than the aor. subjunctive, although the latter is well-attested. To read an imperative here might well undermine Paul's polemic at this point, for he wants to stress that the realization of a heavenly nature is a matter for the future (see my ' "Man" ' 301f).

Christ's death and resurrection or ritual representation of the initiate's death and resurrection on the analogy of Christ's. Rather than from ritual the hope of a future sharing in Christ's salvation seems to stem both from the idea of his representation of all humanity, and from the experience of the power of the divine spirit, which, as we saw in §4.3.1, was regarded as the proleptic presence of the power of the coming age. The presence now of that spirit effected a transformation in the present (2 Cor 3.18), but a transformation that evidently will not be complete this side of death (cf. 5.1−5).

What some of the mystery rituals do have in common with the rite of Christian baptism is the aspect of a ritual anticipation of the future, ultimate destiny of the individual who undergoes the rite. The pronouncement of the forgiveness of sins which the baptized hears in this rite (cf. §1.3.3.2), the verdict of acquittal (cf. 1 Cor 6.11, ἀπελούσασθε . . . ἐδικαιώθητε), anticipates the final verdict of the Judge of all (cf. Rom 8.33). It marks the start of the life of the new age for the one baptized (cf. Rom 6.4, ἐν καινότητι ζωῆς περιπατήσωμεν). But this assurance is not granted by copying Christ's death and resurrection or witnessing a representation of it, in the way that the ritual re-enactment of Isis' restoration of Osiris could evoke faith in the devotee that she would one day restore him or her in the after-life. It lay rather in the conviction brought by the Christian message that Christ's death had been for the sins of all (1 Cor 15.3) and that his resurrection lifted all to that restored relationship with God which Paul could describe as δικαιοσύνη (Rom 4.25), peace and grace (5.1f) as well as newness of life. Thus, although again Paul arrives at a similar goal to the mysteries, a confidence for the world to come in the light of what has already been experienced, once more the route by which he has reached that goal is different. Just as he reached the conviction that Christ was a prototype for our salvation by a different, non-ritual route, so too here he reaches this goal of confidence for the future in the light of present experience in a different way; the ritual of baptism plays its part in this experience, it is true, but not by portraying before Christians' eyes Christ crucified and risen, but by reminding them that they had already been caught up in, involved in, Christ's past death and resurrection, in that God had addressed his word of condemnation and of restoration and restitution to them too, as represented by the eschatological Adam, Christ. Nor was the forgiveness and the new life merely anticipated in the rite, to remain a matter of promise alone, but that life began from that moment on, and was there to be walked in (Rom 6.4). This striking, paradoxical combination of realized and not yet fully realized eschatology is hard to parallel in the mysteries. It is most easily accounted for by the experience of what were regarded as the tokens already of the new age, the manifestations of the outpoured spirit of God in the church, combined with an awareness of the old age; what was generally regarded as a part of the end, resurrection, had also already taken place in the case of Jesus, but yet he was still to be manifested in the fullness of his power. The error of the Corinthians had been, in part at least, their stressing of the realized power of the new age present in their congregation, to the neglect of the powers of death and the old age still at large there. Paul, for his part, was content to live with the tension and the paradox of this combination, of power in the midst of weakness.

6. Life through Death

Much of what we have said, particularly in the previous chapter, seems to have been negative at least as regards Paul's relationship with the thought of the mysteries: his 'with Christ' language and ideas cannot be derived from those cults. Thus far we might seem just to have confirmed Wagner's conclusions, although by a somewhat different route (cf. §1.3 above). But if we deny too much the similarity between Paul's thought and that of his Graeco-Roman environment we make it difficult to see how much of what he said and wrote could have been understood and appreciated by his hearers and readers in his Gentile churches. It is true that some of his ideas may indeed have been hard for them to grasp and appreciate, but too great a gap would make it hard to account for his success; *all* of his hearers *should* then have reacted like the majority of his audience in Athens are portrayed as doing in Acts 17.32, either mocking or at least postponing any response. Was there not a common framework of ideas within which his readers could, for instance, understand his teaching about the Christian rite of initiation and its implications? And yet are there at the same time distinctive features of his teaching which differentiate it from comparable rites in his environment? We have in the last chapter seen the distinctiveness of his language and ideas of dying 'with Christ'; we must now turn more to the matter of dying as such.

6.1. 'Stirb und werde'

Such a point of contact seems to be suggested by the influential article of Herbert Braun on ' "Dying and Becoming" in Antiquity and in the New Testament'. There he points to what he regards as a common dialectic of death and life ('Stirb und werde') running through ancient literature, including especially the mystery-religions. He finds it attested in rabbinic sources[1] and in Stoic thought[2]; above all it is clearly present in Jesus' call

---

Notes on 6.1

1 E. g. *b. Ber.* 63*b*; *b. Giṭ.* 57*b*; *b. Šabb.* 83*b*; *b. Tamid* 32*a*.

to lose one's life in order to save it (Mk 8.35 pars; cf. Lk 17.33; Jn 12.25). The motif of the seed buried in the ground in order to give new life is a commonplace[3], although the stress on the necessity of death before the new life is a distinctive Christian emphasis. The true 'Stirb und werde', however, he finds in the view that dying in itself contains life hidden in it, dying *per se*, that is, and not dying undergone with some ulterior purpose like gaining life thereby (136), the idea of 'life *in* death' as opposed to 'life *through* death'.

Braun then turns to that sense of 'Stirb und werde' which thinks of dying as the passage to life[4]. Here he introduces a number of passages of considerable importance for our topic:

(1) Plutarch's *Quaestiones Romanae* 5 (264D–265B) describes two explanations for the custom of requiring those who have supposedly died abroad to enter their houses by the roof. The second is to compare the Greeks' treatment of those for whom a funeral and burial had been conducted in the mistaken belief that they were dead. One Aristinus, treated as an outcast for this reason, sought help from the Delphic oracle and was advised to deliver himself into the hands of women to treat as a newborn child, being washed and wrapped in swaddling clothes and suckled.

And yet does this really describe the principle of 'Stirb und werde'? Is it not rather that the one who has been formally buried is counted as dead; an individual once buried, who desires to exist, has to submit to a new beginning of life[5]. The 'becoming' is necessary because of a prior supposed 'dying'; it is not that the becoming takes place in dying, but rather the becoming is necessary as a result of such a ritual dying. (The assumption seems to be that the rites are effective, so effective as to render dead those for whom they are performed, regardless of whether or not they actually are dead. This is relevant for our purpose here in that is shows the importance and significance of ritual for the ancient world; see further at the end of §6.2 and also above in §4.5). Yet this incident does at the same time illustrate the ties existing between different 'rites of passage' (see below): various actions normally following a birth are performed to reverse the effects of the rites of death; admittedly some rites accompanying birth, like that of the *Amphidromia*, are not mentioned but could have been equally appropriate.

---

2 Epict., *Diss.* 3.20.4–8; 4.1.163–5 (ἀποθνῄσκων σῴζεται).

3 Ibid. 4.8 36; Plut. frg. 104 (Sandbach); *b. Ketub.* 111*b*; *b. Sanh.* 90*b*; *Pirqe R. El.* 33.

4 There seems to be here a certain tension between pp. 136 and 145, the former suggesting that what I call 'life in death' is the true sense of 'Stirb und werde', the latter that it is 'life through death'; so too in the examples of Beardslee, 'Saving' 61–3.

(2) Apuleius' account of Lucius' initiation into the mysteries of Isis includes a description of Lucius' 'voluntary death' (*Met.* 11.21) and his being described as 'in a certain manner reborn' (11.16), although that refers to Lucius' having resumed human shape after his earlier transformation into an ass, and not to the consequences of his initiation into the rites of Isis[6]. But for Lucius 'salvation means', in Braun's words, 'apart from the betterment of life in this world, also something else, . . . namely a most intimate union with the deity, even if there is no talk here of sharing the deity's fate, which, as in the case of Osiris [he here cites Firm. Mat., *Err. prof. rel.* 22.1], includes the initiates' being saved with the deity; that is still true even if one does not wish to understand as a deification Lucius' being presented to the people as the sungod after his initiation' (147; cf. §5.2 above). Here we do indeed see a case of life, or salvation (*salus*) through death (cf. §5.1.1.1 above).

(3) In the so-called *Mithras-Liturgy* of *PGM* 4.475−723 there seems to be a reference to a cultic process of death leading to the salvific vision; the one who experiences this passes through pressing need (503f) and 'pressing and bitter and inexorable necessity' (605f, tr. Meyer), which Braun argues is a cultic process analogous to death[7]. At this point he appeals to the Stobaeus fragment quoted above in §2.4.1: at death the soul 'has an experience like that of men who are undergoing initiation into great mysteries, and so the verbs τελευτᾶν (die) and τελεῖσθαι (be initiated), and the actions they denote, have a similarity'. Then it goes on to compare the soul's progress with that of the initiate who passes through darkness and terrors of all kinds before emerging into a spacious land of light and the company of 'pure and holy men'. Yet it must be noted that the fragment uses the mysteries to illustrate the experience of death and not *vice versa*; it does *not* say that initiation is like death, but that death is like initiation[8]. The former point, as we shall see below (§6.2), can be far more adequately made on the basis of other evidence.

On the basis of these texts Braun turns to the Pauline corpus where he finds a similar process, though dying and coming to life are there mediated, not by visionary experiences, but by a cultic, sacramental process.

---

5 Cf. Garland *Way* 100f, who agrees with Harrison that a 'rebirth' is necessary because there is something seriously wrong with one who is thus neither really dead nor really alive. For a further example of this, resolved only by eventual death, cf. Bloch-Parry, *Death* 13.

6 Hence the reference to his 'reborn tongue' (*Met.* 11.14); he could now speak instead of just braying. The ref. to Lucius' being reborn is *before* his initiation which only begins in §22 with the goddess's permission to proceed. It is also true, however, that the same phrase, *renatus quodam modo*, is used of initiates in §21 (cf. Griffiths, *Isis-Book* 258f, 308); but there is no word of their being reborn *in aeternum* (MacMullen, *Paganism* 53); see further above in §5.2.

7 On *PGM* 4.718−22 cf. below in §6.4.1.

8 So Harrison, *Epilegomena* 16, rightly speaks (in general and not apropos of this passage) of 'death as an initiation' and views the latter as '*the* rite of paramount importance'.

In deriving true life and salvation from such a sacramental process our New Testament texts are clearly at one with the texts relating to the mysteries, whether this true life is seen as being more something already present (Rom 6.11; Col 3.1) or more something in the future (Col 3.4; 2 Tim 2.11); it is true that the expectation of the resurrection (Rom 6.5) and the presence of the resurrection (Rom 6.4; Col 3.1) are the special Judaeo-Christian form in which life as salvation was expected or enjoyed (153).

This sacramental 'Stirb und werde' has its origins in 'oriental Hellenism' (ibid.) and the origin of this *topos* in the mystery concepts that he has already outlined should be plain (152). But perhaps it is only plain to those whose perspective is somewhat circumscribed and limited to only a small range of the relevant and available material. After all Braun does preface his article with the comment that the 'dialectic of death and life' is part of the 'spiritual stock' of the human race (136), and to this we must now turn.

6.2. Rites of Passage

So is Braun's narrow derivation of 'Stirb und werde' in the New Testament from 'oriental Hellenism' correct? I would suggest that it is not and that the phenomenon is far wider than his analysis suggests and is something basic to initiatory rites of all sorts and to all other 'rites of passage', to use the term introduced by the anthropologist Arnold van Gennep.

By this phrase van Gennep denoted the special acts by which individuals progress from one stage of life to another, from one occupation to another, or from one group to another. These special acts or rites can be subdivided into three sets of rites, those of separation (pre-liminal), transition (liminal — Turner uses here the word 'margin'), and incorporation (post-liminal — here Turner's word is '(re)aggregation')[1]. The purpose of these rites, be they at birth, puberty, marriage, parenthood, promotion to a higher class, specialization in one's occupation, or death, is always

> to enable the individual to pass from one defined position to another which is equally well defined. Since the goal is the same, it follows of necessity that the ways of attaining it should be at least analogous, if not identical in detail . . . [2].

Notes on 6.2

1 Cf. Turner, *Process* 94; *Forest* 94. Harrison, *Epilegomena* 14, speaks of 'expulsion' and 'impulsion'.

  This structure may help to explain the *Stufenstruktur* of the initiation rites of the mysteries to which Berner repeatedly points in his *Initiationsriten*.

2 *Rites* 3 (cf. Huntington-Metcalf, *Celebrations* 8f); *Rites* 88–93 deals with the mystery-cults but the account given of them is now rather dated and inaccurate (the translator also seems to have thought that Attis was female! – 92).

I quote this passage because it prepares us for the similarity of structure
between various rites of passage, as well as a certain mutuality, reciprocity
or interchangeability between the various rites. As Harrison puts it, 'what
is effective and salutary for one crisis may be effective and salutary for
another'[3]. So van Gennep points to 'some resemblances in the details of
certain birth and funeral rites' (52), stemming from the belief that the
earth is the home both of children before they are born and of the
dead[4]. In Cairo the rites for entry into Moslem brotherhoods are largely
'identical with those of the marriage contract' (98). In Christian orders
'entry into the order of the Carmelites includes funeral rites followed
by rites of resurrection' (ibid.). Van der Leeuw also points to the ordination rite in which Benedictine novices prostrate themselves between four
candles, are covered by a shroud and have the *Miserere* sung over them[5].
Van Gennep also mentions the presence in Kol funeral rites in India of
the singing of marriage songs and a marriage procession (152)[6]; he points
too to the rites consecrating 'sacred virgins' in the Roman Pontifical,
modelled on marriage-rites, making them the spouses of Christ (98–100),
and he compares the ritual for consecrating Hindu sacred prostitutes
(100). The ordination of a priest and the celebration of his first mass
can take the form of a marriage, even combined with nuptial rites as in
parts of the Tirol (106f). (Widengren also mentions that the covenant

---

This analogy or identity is underlined by the use of the same term for those involved in a variety
of rites of passage: cf. Turner, *Forest* 95f.

3 *Themis* 507 (she speaks of the various transition points in life as crises); the imagery of both
marriage (Lewis, *Religion* 190) and biological birth (Halifax, *Voices* 5) are held to be appropriate for describing shamanic initiation.

4 Cf. Samter, *Geburt* 4; v.d. Leeuw, *Religion* 194. For burial as 'a kind of birth' in more recent
Greek belief cf. Danforth, *Rituals* 99; for this imagery elsewhere cf., e.g., Huntington-Metcalf,
Celebrations 115f, and Bloch-Parry, *Death passim* – but note 20f in contrast to the previous
reference; a further good example from Zulu culture is found on pp. 24f, from Hindu on 80f;
85. At the same time Huntington notes that for v. Gennep the 'liminal phase of funerals is . . .
not entirely interchangeable with the liminal phases of other rituals. He carefully left room for
a special relevance' of symbols of regeneration and growth to the ritual of death (*Celebrations*
12).

5 *Religion* 198; Dr Cavallin, himself of this order, first drew my attention to this illustration.
Hasenfratz, *Lebenden* 34, goes further: the subsequent monastic garb marks the wearer as
belonging to the realm of the dead (cf. 23). For funerals as part of initiation cf. Bloch-Parry,
Death 13, 82, 146f (J. Middleton), 219–22 (Lugbara rainmakers and Hindu ascetics and
Merina circumcision rites and royal baths); see also §6.3 below. Turner, *Process* 35f, mentions
that Ndembu rites for infertility include the singing of songs from circumcision-rites, funerary
initiation, initiation into divining, a traditional women's cult, and initiation into hunters' cults.

6 Cf. v. d. Leeuw, *Religion* 200; also Bloch-Parry, *Death* 81; Barley, *Structures* 74, 87f, 106f,
mentions the Dowayos' treatment of a dead body as a candidate for circumcision and *vice
versa* (cf. 84: 'care is taken to establish correspondences at all stages' between burial and circumcision).

meal of the Parsi Bābakīyah contained marriage ceremonial[7].) 'Marriage ceremonies' too 'may be analogous, and are sometimes identical in every detail, to adoption ceremonies'; 'although cases where marriage is regarded as a rebirth are rare, those where it is an initiation or an ordination are not' (141). Van der Leeuw also points to the Kikuyu practice whereby a child before circumcision would lie beside its mother on a bed and cry like one newborn[8].

Such examples could be multiplied at great length, but we need to bring our enquiry closer to the world of the New Testament. When we look at the Greek world we do indeed find that some Greeks at least were aware of the similarity between their various rites of passage. Artemidorus of Ephesus (second century C.E.) tells us in his work on the interpretation of dreams that

> To dream that one is dead . . . signifies marriage for a bachelor. For both marriage and death are considered to be critical points (τέλη) in a man's life, and one is always represented by the other (ἀεὶ . . . δείκνυται ὑπ᾽ ἀλλήλων)[9]. . . . marriage is also similar to death and is represented (σημαίνεται) by death . . . . If a sick man dreams that he is marrying a maiden, it portends (σημαίνει) his death. For the same things that happen to a bridegroom happen to a dead man[10].

For evidence of this last remark Lawson points us to the following resemblances between Greek marriage rites and funeral rites[11]:

(1) the washing of the bride and groom and the washing of the dead[12]; the boy that brought the water for the former is depicted over the tombs of those that died unmarried[13].

(2) 'Anointing and arraying' for marriage or burial, usually in white robes[14]. Sometimes the bridal dress was used for the burial of the be-

---

7 'Reflections' (1980) 661.
8 *Religion* 197f.
9 2.49, tr. White. Whether this is the right way to translate τέλη is doubtful; cf. Fustel de Coulanges, *City* 44: 'Pollux [roughly contemporary with Artemidorus] . . . says, that in ancient times . . they designated [marriage] simply by the word τέλος, which signifies sacred ceremony, as if marriage had been . . . the ceremony sacred above all others'. The reference is to Poll., *Onom.* 3.3.38.
10 2.65, tr. White.
11 *Folklore* 555–60; cf. for modern Greece Danforth, *Rituals* 74–91; also v. Gennep, *Rites* 152, mentioned above.
12 So one of the things that Socrates does in his last moments is to bathe (Plato, *Phaedo* 116A); so too Oedipus and Alcestis in n. 14 below; cf. Garland, *Way* 24 (also 15f).
13 Cf. Harpocration s.v. λουτροφόρος καὶ λουτροφορεῖν; 'a clear case of the importation of a ceremony closely connected with marriage into the funeral rites of the unmarried' (Lawson, *Folklore* 556; cf. also the discussion on 594).
14 See Alcestis' preparations for death in Eur., *Alc.* 158–61: washing and magnificent clothes. Oedipus in Soph., *Oed. Col.* 1602f, washes himself and dresses 'in the manner ordained by custom'; cf. Artemid., *Oneirocr.* 2.3; also Garland, *Way* 24, and Danforth, *Rituals* 79.

trothed or newly wed[15]; crowns, chaplets or garlands were used in both ceremonies[16].

(3) Associated with both marriage and funerals are the apple, the quince or the pomegranate[17].

These parallels point, he believes, to the view that death was 'a marriage with the house of Hades' rather than a transference of funeral rites to weddings, a 'cynical and . . . distempered' view[18]. But to pose these as alternatives may be inappropriate; is it not better to see both rites as drawing on a common stock of ideas and images to express a common ritual structure? As Danforth remarks, 'marriage and the journey to distant lands are important metaphors for the experience of death, since they involve painful separation'[19].

A 'sacred marriage' may have been part of some mystery initiations, but, as Burkert comments, the evidence for the institution of a 'sacred marriage' in Greece is 'scanty and unclear'; while almost certainly 'sexual elements play a role in mystery initiations . . . there is hardly any clear evidence'[20]. There was a union between the wife of the Athenian king and Dionysus at the *Anthesteria*, but this was not a mystery initiation. One perhaps finds clearer evidence later in the imperial period, particularly in the form of the abuse of this idea, both by Alexander of Abonuteichos (Luc., *Alex.* 39) and by Decius Mundus (Jos., *Ant.* 18.3.4. §§ 66–80)[21]. Clearer, perhaps, is the idea that marriage was an initiation; not only could it be conducted by a priestess of Demeter (Plut., *Praec. coniug.* 138B), perhaps not so significant a point in itself, but in an inscription from Cos brides are referred to as αἱ τελεύμεναι[22]. Chariton, too, refers

---

15 Cf. Chariton *De Chaerea et Callirhoe* 1.6.2; Eur., *Tro.* 1219–21; Peek, *Vers-Inschriften* 1238.3f; Garland, *Way* 25 (Danforth, *Rituals* 13: the custom continues; cf. 79f).

16 Cf. Garland, ibid. 26 and 139.

17 From contemporary Greek customs Danforth, *Rituals* 79, adds the procession from home to church.

18 Ibid. 559f; cf. 597–602. Conversely he finds in Soph., *Antigone* a reflection of the view in Greek folklore that death is a marriage (550; cf. esp. *Ant.* 804f, 810–16, 891f, 1203–7, 1241f); however this imagery may spring naturally from the story in which Antigone will die instead of being wed to Creon's son Haemon. For other possible parallels in Greek tragedy cf. Garland, *Way* 72f.

19 *Rituals* 33

20 *Religion* 176 (ET 108); Nilsson, *Geschichte* 1; 122; *Religion* 44. The Church Fathers, of course, tended to make the most of what hints they could find. Lawson, *Folklore* 576f, and others are less guarded than Burkert (e.g. E. O. James, *Religion* 133, and Deubner, *Feste* 84, although he admits how dependent we are on Christian sources, notably Asterius; also Prümm, *Handbuch* 233; M. Smith, 'Transformation' 105; cf. Mylonas, *Eleusis* 311).

21 Yet this raises the interesting question whether a devotee of these cults really believed that intercourse with a god, as opposed to a human playing the part of a god, took place in these cults; was Paulina unusually gullible?

22 Paton-Hicks, *Inscriptions* 386.4f; cf. Lawson, *Folklore* 590. Leipoldt, *Tod* 87, finds a relation-

to the first night of wedlock as the νὺξ μυστική[23]. Harrison even speaks of marriage as *'the* mystery *par excellence'*[24].

'Rebirth' too has its place in the imagery of the mysteries. Dey in his study of this idea was perhaps properly sceptical about some of the exaggerated claims for its prominence in these rites[25]. Yet even he was forced to grant that it is found there; even if its use in a *taurobolium* inscription is late[26] we cannot escape the imagery on a number of different levels in Apul., *Met.* 11 (see §5.2 above), coupled with the reference to the *festissimus natalis sacrorum* in 11.24[27]. Anyway the references to a *(dies) natalis* or a *natalicium* in connection with a *taurobolium* or a *criobolium* are found from as early as the end of the second century onwards, and Gasparro is probably correct to infer that, when a father and son are together *crioboliati natali suo*, the reference is more likely to be to a shared spiritual birthday than to the coincidence of a joint physical birthday[28]. In view of the evidence of the idea in rites of passage elsewhere it is perhaps surprising that we do not find it attested earlier or more widely in the mysteries. It was, as Nock puts it, a 'natural metaphor for a new phase of life on a new plane'[29], and Widengren likens initiation-rites to those surrounding birth in particular[30].

All this is perhaps explicable when we note Turner's comment on the 'rich variety of symbols' which many societies employ to describe the

---

ship between initiation and marriage stemming from the fact that initiation was originally an introduction to the worship of a family (forced?).

23 *De Chaerea et Callirhoe* 4.4.9.

24 *Epilegomena* 17.

25 E.g. Παλιγγενεσία 36f. It may be dangerous, for instance, to infer too much from the reference to Brimo's giving birth to the 'holy child Brimos', however the Naassenes may have interpreted this (Hipp., *Ref.* 5.8.40f, tr. Foerster-Wilson). To speak of the *Homeric Hymn to Demeter* promising Eleusinian initiates 'a new birth to a blessed immortality' (James, *Religion* 126) attributes to it an idea and image not found there. Still, Nilsson (*Geschichte* 2, 688) concludes that words corresponding to 'rebirth' were current in the mysteries; cf. Lohse, *Umwelt* 173=ET 234; M. Smith 'Transformation' 106.

26 *CIL* 6, 510 dated to 376 C.E. (Dey, ibid. 73; Duthoy, *Taurobolium* 18 – no. 23). Duthoy 104 considers this to express 'the expectations of an enthusiastic *tauroboliatus* rather than a dogma accepted by all'. The same phrase is used in a dedication to Mithras by a *tauroboliatus* and *criobolatus* in *CIL* 6, 736, but this is now regarded as a forgery (Cumont, *Textes* 1, 179 – no. 584).
Vermaseren and v. Essen, *Excavations* 118–26 (cf. Vermaseren, *Mithras* 44) also point to a graffito in the Sta Prisca *Mithraeum* at Rome bearing the words *natus prima luce* (dated 202 C.E.); but cf. M. Guarducci, 'Graffito' – the reference is to the founding of the *Mithraeum* when Mithras was born there, so to speak.

27 Grudgingly Dey, ibid. 100, grants that here we may at least have rebirth in a figurative sense (Nilsson, *Geschichte* 2, 688 also grants that this was a metaphorical interpretation of the rites rather than their basis).

28 *Soteriology* 113f, citing *AE* 1956, no. 255 (Duthoy, *Taurobolium* no. 78).

29 'Question' 462.

30 *Religionsphänomenologie* 219; cf. James, 'Rituals' 151.

'ambiguous and indeterminate attributes' of those in transition, in the 'liminal' state:

> liminality is frequently likened to death, to being in the womb, to invisibility, to dark-
> ness, to bisexuality, to the wilderness, and to an eclipse of the sun or moon[31].

Not only do we see here a common stock of symbols, but some of them, those of death and birth, are properly bound to particular rites of passage. But because these symbols are of wider application, they, and the language and imagery of their associated rites, are found in the structure of rites connected with other transitions, as metaphors to express the meaning of those rites. The ancient world, Harrison argued, felt this similarity of structure, yet did not formulate it (at least before we come to later writers like Artemidorus), but 'expressed it by the similarity of rites'[32].

In the light of all this it is perhaps the more intelligible that in Romans 6 Paul refers not just to our dying with Christ but also to our being buried with him (6.4; cf. Col 2.12). It may be no accident that in expounding the significance of one rite, the Christian initiation-rite of baptism, he appeals to another rite undergone by Christ, and undergone with Christ by those whom he represented[33]. And just as that ritual

---

31 *Process* 95; cf., e.g., Barley's description of the Dowayo 'clowns' (*Structures* 73); Eliade, too, in *Birth* xiv, speaks of the recurrent use of symbols of darkness, cosmic night, the 'telluric womb', a hut, the belly of a monster, to describe the initiatory death which marks the reversion to a latent mode of being rather than annihilation. Many similarities may stem from other factors – e.g. that at a number of different pivotal points in human existence evil spirits need to be warded off (Samter, *Geburt* 27; the following pp. give many examples of this; also his 'Hochzeitsbräuche' 131, and Huntington-Metcalf, *Celebrations* 76; 106f; Widengren, *Religionsphänomenologie* 219). But even so the need to ward off these spirits particularly at these times surely stems from the fact that they are seen as critical periods of time when the participants are especially exposed and vulnerable. Or, in funeral rites, the souls of the departed may be viewed as dangerous, during 'a period when the soul is homeless, miserable, and malicious' (Huntington-Metcalf, *Celebrations* 73; cf. 84, and Bloch-Parry, *Death* 23). O. Harris' contribution to the last-named work suggests an example of these two factors working together (ibid. 45–73). Or some of the practices at birth, marriage, and death may stem from the sacredness of the one involved, a sacredness stemming from their being in transition according to Garland, *Way* 46f; Leach, *Culture* 78, refers to being 'contaminated with holiness'. In short it seems unwise to generalize here!

32 *Epilegomena* 16.

33 M. Barth *Taufe* 202–4, considers this a point of difference between Paul and the mysteries. He even goes so far as to say that it is 'probable that [Paul] distances himself from the thought of the mysteries by the choice of the idea of "being buried with Christ" ' (204). It is true that it is hard to find 1st century parallels in the mysteries in which the 'death' taking place there is symbolized by a burial. Possible parallels are both later and disputed: was the descent into a pit in the *taurobolium* a burial? Was there a ritual burial in Mithraic initiations? – cf. §6.3 and the opinion of R. Turcan quoted there (n. 17). The clearest parallel may be Procl., *Theologica Platonica* 4.9 (Saffrey-Westerink 4, 30), who mentions that 'in the most secret of initiations the *theourgoi* order the body to be buried except for the head'; in which rites this takes place is not stated, but it is the clearest evidence of a feigned burial as opposed to a feigned death in a mystery context; Lewy-Tardieu, *Oracles* 205, 444(*g*), link this with the rites envisaged in the

marked for the ancient world (and marks it still for ours) the safe passage of the person buried from one state to another, so Paul may by this reference underline the certainty and the finality of the transition which Christians have passed through[34], from being 'in sin' (Rom 6.2) to being 'in Christ' (6.11), from 'death' to 'life' (6.13)[35]. It is not that he is simply carried along by the series of saving acts listed in the credal formula of 1 Cor 15.3f, but that he deliberately chooses this item because by its nature it formally seals and marks ritually the due accomplishment of a passage from one state to the other. The one rite is used to interpret the other: the rite that marked Christ's passage from death to his life 'to God' that lay beyond the grave is used as a metaphor of the passage in baptism from 'death' through death with Christ and burial with Christ to life with him 'to God'[36].

At the same time Markus Barth underlines that Paul does not say that Christians are put to death with Christ in baptism, but 'buried'[37]. Their death is presupposed, is already behind them[38]. He rejects, however, the

---

Chaldean Oracles. But certainly if one looks further afield to other initiation-rites parallels can be found – cf. §6.3 nn. 1, 3, 39; M. Smith, 'Transformation' 108f. Barth is, however, correct to deny any parallel to the idea of being buried *with the saving deity*; that is equally true of *dying* with Christ as I have argued in the previous chapter. Moreover, unlike any other ritual parallels, it is doubtful how far one can speak of the Christian's burial being represented in baptism, if by that one means a dramatic representation of the act of burial; it is in water, not the ground, that he or she is immersed (and immersed they probably were usually, *pace* Barth 208; cf. Meeks, *Christians* 150). It may be better to speak of an *interpretation* of the Christian rite in terms of another rite.

34 Cf. M. Barth, ibid. 281f; Fazekaš, 'Taufe' 308f; Halter, *Taufe* 49f.

35 It is therefore a 'confirmation' (*Bestätigung*) of the Christian's death to sin and destiny of new life (M. Barth, *Taufe* 235), but it is more than that: as any rite of passage it effects the transition from the old state to the new. As 'performative utterances' 'make' something true ('I name this ship . . .', 'I hereby declare you man and wife', etc.) so declaratory, proclaiming acts declare something to be the case and are a *sine qua non* for that thing's being the case (e.g. regardless of physical age a person is not regarded as adult until he or she has passed through the appropriate puberty rites and actually is not a member of the adult group; so too a person is not a church member until he or she has undergone the appropriate rites). I approve of Barth's description of baptism as a *Tatzeugnis*, but am less happy with his assertion that it is less an 'An- und Zuspruch' than an act of obedience and faith (282). It also seems to me forced to say that Paul speaks of Christians' burial because it 'documents a hope beyond the grave' (283) unless one thinks of burial as a rite marking a passage from one existence to another; still it marks ('documents' if one will) the *passage* rather than the nature of the new existence. The fact that it is a sharing in *Christ's* burial of course gives rise to hope, for his burial was a passage to a glorious new existence (so Barth, ibid. and 301), and not just, for instance, an act consigning us to a drab and cheerless world of souls.

36 Col 2.11f mentions a further 'rite of passage', circumcision. If Barth, *Taufe* 249, is correct in interpreting 2.11 by means of 2.15 – and this may well be correct – then Christ's 'circumcision' is perhaps his death (just as the rite of baptism is used apparently as a metaphor for death in Mk 10.38f and Lk 12.50); cf. Lohmeyer, *Kol* 109; R. P. Martin, *Col* 82f; Moule, *Col* 96.

37 *Taufe* 230.

38 Cf. also ibid. 232, 244.

idea that they were already buried with Christ when he was buried. It must be granted that Paul does not say that, or even imply it, but the reason may well be that he only comes to use this idea, this experience of Christ, in the context of a description of a rite which expresses the individual Christian's involvement in Christ's death; I do not share Barth's conviction that the idea of our having been buried with Christ after his crucifixion is either inappropriate or impossible[39]; Paul rather chooses or happens to use the idea of burial with Christ otherwise. He uses it in a context where he is concerned to stress the Christian's irrevocable break with sin. At the same time I agree with Barth when he insists that a reference to burial with Christ is appropriate here since burial marks a death that has already taken place; I would go further, however, and argue that, as a rite of passage and when used as a metaphor for the Christian initiation rite, it makes effective for the individual that prior death; there is a very real sense in which that person is not effectively 'dead' without that rite[40]. Meeks may be right here to see the element of 'death' symbolized in the ritual of baptism by the baptizand's stripping off of his or her clothes[41]; in that case the Christian's 'death' is not just a matter of the past at Golgotha but that past death with Christ is represented in this ritual symbolism and becomes present for the individual there. However. it may be going too far to say that the ritual of the present is 'necessary', at least in God's eyes[42]; its effect is rather upon the meaning of a person's life both to that person and to those around him or her; its meaning is pastoral and social (or ecclesiological) rather than theological, controlling how that individual sees himself or herself and how his or her fellow-Christians and non-Christians regard that person[43]. It is *a*, though not, surely, the (only), means by which Christ's death and resurrection affect an individual's life and that of the community of the baptized. And yet this is an issue and a set of distinctions which probably

---

39 There should be no question of a re-burial (Barth, ibid.) — that would be to mistake the function of the Christian initiation rite as, as it were, an echo of the divine verdict passed in Christ's death and resurrection, or, to use more biblical language, a 'proclamation' of those events (1 Cor 11.26). Paul is not afraid to speak of 're-dying', so to speak – even daily (1 Cor 15.31)!

40 Cf. the critiques of Barth in Carlson, *Baptism* 222–6; Fazekaš, 'Taufe' 314–16.

41 *Christians* 154–6; 'Image' 184.

42 Contrast, e.g., Schlier, 'Lehre' 326f.

43 I would not like to contrast 'cognitive' and 'causative' as does, e.g., Schlier, 'Lehre' 324, for an act may have a 'causative' effect by means of a 'cognitive' — if another person recognizes my raised hand as a signal my raising of it causes them to stop; cf. also Meeks, 'Image' 182; M. Smith, 'Transformation' 104.

So a person may reach a certain age but may not be counted as adult without certain rites and may also be helped to behave in an adult way by those rites, to see herself or himself as an adult as well as to be seen as such by others (cf. n. 35 above).

Paul never contemplated; baptism is simply presupposed by him and he assumes that all Christians have been baptized.

6.3. Death and Resurrection/Return in Rites of Passage

Time and again van Gennep also refers to the participants in rites of initiation (or sometimes puberty-rites) as being regarded or treated as if they had died and been resurrected[1]. So it is with some Australian tribes (75) and among some American Indians (76f); the inhabitants of the region of the lower Congo are considered dead during their trial period and in their rites of reintegration 'act as if they were newly born (resurrected) and must relearn all the gestures of ordinary life' (81; cf. 138). Brahman ceremonies include a ritual death and rebirth (105f), as do some initiation ceremonies for Australian magicians; the experiences of some Ural-Altaic shamans include an experience of death and departure 'to the land of the spirits, the gods, or the dead', followed by a return to life and rebirth (108);

> in all the shaman's ceremonial actions one finds the recurring series of trances, death, voyages of the soul to the other world, return, and application of the knowledge acquired in the sacred world to a particular case (illness, etc.). (109)

Similar experiences occur in Carib *peai*-initiation (ibid.) and one becomes a *kiranga* among the Barundi of Tanzania by, *inter alia*, falling down in a faint as if dead and sleeping there for three or four days (109f). In Egyptian religion he points to parallels between funerary rites, daily worship, the inauguration of temples, and the ritual of enthronement:

> the death and rebirth, simultaneously, of Ra, Osiris, the king, the priest, and every deceased man who was 'pure' certainly constitutes the most extreme case known to me of a dramatic representation of the death and rebirth theme. (159f)

Notes on 6.3

1 Cf. Dieterich, *Mithrasliturgie* 159; Eliade, *Birth* xii and *passim*; Harrison, *Epilegomena* 15; *Themis* 20; James, 'Ritual', esp. 147; Turner, *Forest* 96 – 'rebirth' would be a far apter term than 'resurrection' here, for Turner goes on to describe as the second major aspect of the liminal *persona* their being symbolized by being likened to, or treated as embryos or newborn or sucklings. See also Widengren, *Religionsphänomenologie* 219; Eliade, *Birth* also tends to use 'resurrection' and 'rebirth' interchangeably although, when he does cite cases of the imagery of 'resurrection', it is sometimes subsidiary to the main rite of initiation; thus (12f) when a medicine man is buried and rises from the grave this shows the initiands the divine power exercised by and through the medicine man. At other times, however, 'resurrection' or restoration to life would be an appropriate description of the imagery (e.g. Frazer, *Bough*[3] 7.2, 235–7, 252f, etc. – a classic statement of this pattern in initiatory contexts is found in 225–78).

Thus he was critical of Mannhardt and Frazer and their followers[2] who had studied the Hellenistic mysteries because

> they failed to see them as groupings of rites of passage which are at once cosmic, religious, and economic, and which constitute only a small part of a far vaster category . . ..
> Death, the transition, and resurrection also constitute an element in ceremonies of pregnancy, childbirth, initiation into associations with no agricultural purpose, betrothal, marriage and funerals. (92; cf. 182–4)[3]

(A similar criticism might be levelled against Braun's study mentioned above.) It is thoroughly in keeping with this when Leach observes that 'birth/death is a self-evident "natural" representation of beginning/end' and that therefore 'death and rebirth symbolism is appropriate to all rites of transition and is probably manifest in a wide variety of cases'[4].

J. P. King's study of Romans 6 observes, correctly, that the rite of baptism falls under the category of 'rites of passage'; following van Gennep he argues that such rites fall into three stages, separation, transition, and (re)-incorporation (110f)[5]. The first stage, he argues, is almost always depicted as a kind of death: 'the rituals of the sub-category of the separation phase in almost all rites of passage are of the form of death-related ceremonials' (126); frequently these rites involve a simulation of death (131). In these assertions King is largely dependent on secondary literature and it is to be regretted that when he does turn to primary sources it is to illustrate the 'rite of passage' patterns in death and burial in Graeco-Roman society[6]. At this point he fails to raise clearly enough the far more interesting question (for our present purpose, and arguably also for his) whether other rites of passage bore the character of death and burial in that society; in other words instead of showing that all rites of passage there, birth, initiation, baptism, etc., tended to be deaths and

---

2 The same criticism might be levelled against the more recent book of Hasenfratz, *Lebenden* 4, in that he implies that only the mysteries provided a contemporary example of dying and new birth as a background for Rom 6.

3 So for instance Turner, *Process* 27–41, describes the rite of *Isoma* among the Ndembu of Zambia, which is for the cure of infertility: two holes in the ground represent respectively the grave and the womb; they are connected by a tunnel and the couple being treated move from the hole of life to that of death and back again a number of times. Again, on 'the installation rites of the Kanongesha of the Ndembu' he tells us that 'the chief-elect dies from his commoner state. Imagery of death abounds in Ndembu liminality.' (100) Eliade, *Chamanisme* chap. 2, also documents the prevalence of this pattern in shamanic initiations (esp. 45=ET 33), and observes how hard it is at times to distinguish tribal initiations, entry into secret societies, and shamanic initiations (73f =ET 65f); cf. Halifax, *Voices* 4–15, 66f; Lewis, *Religion* 70, 190. See further Bloch-Parry, *Death* 219f; Eliade, *Birth passim*, esp. 30–5; v.d. Leeuw, *Religion* 197; Widengren, *Religionsphänomenologie* 221f. Nock, 'Christianity' 117=*Essays* 101, limits this too much to puberty-rites of initiation.

4 *Culture* 79.

5 Cf. Bianchi, *Mysteries* 3f.

6 Cf. also now Garland, *Way*.

burials in some sense or other he shows that deaths and burials conformed to the patterns of rites of passage. In fact, in the case of the one other rite of passage in the ancient world which he considers, the manumission of slaves, he cites no trace of the idea of slaves 'dying to' their previous servile existence[7].

Now Gäumann does stress that the 'voluntary death' undertaken by Lucius in his initiation in Apul., *Met.* 11 shows that 'the idea of a death that takes place in the cult and a subsequent renewal is thoroughly at home in Hellenistic religious experience'[8] — but not, Ridderbos reminds us[9], in their washings or baptisms. Burkert confirms Gäumann's point for Greek initiation rites of an earlier period: the 'marginal existence' of initiands is marked, *inter alia*, by 'torments and threats, as if the young people were to be killed or devoured by a monster. In this way a dimension of death and new life is introduced'[10]. Significantly it is not the initiations of the mystery-cults of which he is primarily speaking, but initiations of boys and girls to adult status. But it has its place in mystery initiations too, for he mentions the whipping apparently to be endured in Dionysiac initiation according to the frescoes in the Villa of the Mysteries in Pompeii[11]. This would be confirmed by the Stobaeus fragment to which Braun appeals: ordeals and the threat of death were characteristic of the mysteries[12]. The reference to treading on Proserpina's threshold in Apul., *Met.* 11.23, does however introduce a further dimension: the threat of death may well have taken the form of a ritual enactment or, as I argued above (§5.1.1.1), a ritual anticipation of death[13]. It is, however, of the nature of the evidence for this that the earlier evidence is on the whole fairly controversial, since it either on the one hand consists

---

7 *Death* 274–92.
8 *Taufe* 43; cf. 44f; also Nilsson, *Geschichte* 2, 692; Reitzenstein, *Vorgeschichte* 17; Rostovtzeff, *Italy* 76–8; M. Smith, 'Transformation' 107–12. D. Levi, *'Mors'*, esp. 23, claimed to find this 'death' of the Isis-initiate depicted in a mosaic from Antioch-on-the-Orontes (House 20–0); so too Witt, *Isis* 161 and pl. 34; but Norris, 'Isis', esp. 204, thinks that Demeter, not Isis, may be depicted (cf. Griffiths, *Isis-Book* 300).
9 *Paul* 24.
10 *Religion* 391=ET 260; cf. 395=264; also *Homo* 325f (ET 295f) apropos of Eleusis. V.d. Leeuw, *Religion* 195, argues that circumcision and mutilation, which were often part of such rites in other cultures, were an 'intimation of death' (cf. 196: various tests and purifications as approximations to death); cf. Eliade, *Birth* 23f, 35; *Chamanisme* 91=ET 84f; Leach, *Culture* 79. At the same time these trials might be understood as tests of those about to enter the ranks of warriors (cf. Widengren, *Religionsphänomenologie* 220f; but contrast the encounter with quasi-dead recounted on 222).
11 Ibid 436=ET 292.
12 Procl., *In Alcibiadem* 1.142, speaks of 'shewings of secret apparitions and secret signs that startle (καταπλήττονται) the would-be initiates' (tr. O'Neill).
13 Cf. Reitzenstein, *Vorgeschichte* 17; however Griffiths, *Isis-Book* 297, rejects the idea that a threat of death is implicit here.

in reading between the lines of what few texts we have or in interpreting as best we can practices or archaeological finds or, on the other hand, it is relatively late. Yet the nature of the late evidence accords so well with general patterns discernible in rites of initiation and passage in other cultures that we can with greater confidence expect that in this matter at least they reflect earlier beliefs and practices.

We have for instance seen (§5.1.2) the possibility that in the account of Demeter's immersing Demophoön in the fire we have the reflection of a ritual involving a life-giving death. Certainly it bears, as we noted then, a strong resemblance to certain initiatory rituals which include the ordeal of 'roasting' near a fire[14]. In dealing with the Eleusinian cult we saw too that the initiands each sacrificed a pig 'on their own behalf' and this may therefore have involved a vicarious death, as Burkert argues; what remains doubtful is whether that death was in any way identified with that of Persephone[15].

In the rites of Mithras, especially as depicted in the paintings of the *Mithraeum* in Sta Maria Capua Vetere, Vermaseren sees a clear expression of the ordeals and death-like experiences of the Mithraic initiates at various stages of their progress through the cult's rites[16]: the initiate is pushed naked and blindfolded by the mystagogue; he kneels while a priest approaches with a sword or stick, or lies on the ground as if dead. Turcan comments on these paintings:

> Ritual nakedness, bandaging of the eyes, the feigning of death, physical and psychological tests of endurance belong to the typology of secret societies in general.

Yet he doubts whether a case has been made out for the identification of graves for a ritual burial in certain *Mithraea*; in that at Carrawburgh, for instance, are goat and sheep bones — it is a refuse pit. But at Capua he sees signs of a more characteristic ritual: a helmeted figure seems to

---

14 This seems a firmer line of connection with this theme than that which Kerenyi (*Eleusis* 142) detects in the symbolism of an Apulian vase on which two worshippers approach a shrine containing a poppy to perform rites for the dead: 'This cult at a grave, which was the scene of a divine epiphany in the form of a plant, was based on the myth' in which 'a mythical being dies, but though attended by pain and bloodshed, his death is only an apparent one.' To obtain immortality one must take death upon oneself as he did, and this the dead had done and lived on likewise. This seems to me to read more into the vase (reproduced on 143) than I can.

15 §5.1.2 and nn. 18–20.

16 *Mithras* 131–5; cf. 'Mithras' 107; Beck, 'Soteriology' 535f; certain details of the Capua *Mithraeum* paintings are found in figs 51–3 in the work first mentioned; cf. *CIMRM* 1, 187f, 193=figs 57f, 60 (also *CAH* pls to vol. 5, 164a; Merkelbach, *Mithras* 287–90); for fuller reproductions cf. Vermaseren, *Mithriaca* 1. Vermaseren-v. Essen, *Excavations* 144f, argue that in this respect too the Mithraic initiations resemble those described by Apuleius. There is, however, nothing to connect these rites with the life effected through the bull's death in Mithraic mythology.

test an initiate with a torch levelled at his face[17]. Vermaseren infers that this scene was also depicted on a marble base from Velletri; unfortunately this is no longer discoverable[18], and so this interpretation must remain tentative. Gregory of Nazianzus also refers to the 'ordeals' and 'brandings' (καύσεις) of the Mithraic initiates[19], and a suspect text of Lampridius says that in the Mithraic rites it was customary to say or imitate something to 'produce an impression of terror' (*ad speciem terroris*)[20].

Tudor and Oppermann also find a similar symbolic death in the cults of the Thracian rider-gods[21]. The rite of the *occultatio*, alluded to in some monuments simply by a dagger, is sometimes depicted more fully: two persons spread a ram's skin over a kneeling figure (a feigned burial?)[22]; in three cases[23] the animal itself is slaughtered above the initiate and 'in this way the symbolic death of the neophyte is represented by the actual death of the sacrificial victim'.

I have also mentioned already the graphic account of the ordeals involved in mysteries described by the Neoplatonist Damascius[24]: under a shrine of Apollo in Hierapolis is an underground corridor filled with toxic gases which no living creature can pass through and live. But those initiated (he uses the perfect tense, so that this suggests that this was not part of the initiation itself but a subsequent experience) may pass through and remain there unharmed. Damascius and the philosopher Dorus did so. It is not clear from the account what relation this experience bears to the dream which is subsequently recounted in which he becomes Attis and is thus saved from Hades. Here we certainly have the theme of death and rescue from death in a mystery context, but it is not quite clear what relation this death has to initiation.

Ordeals in the rites of Dionysus were mentioned previously, but it is hard to glean anything further from the rites of this god that bears on

---

17 *Mithra* 84–6; he is presumably referring to *CIMRM* 1, 188=fig. 58; Vermaseren earlier identified the torch as 'a sword or staff'; *CAH* pls to vol. 5, 164*a* as 'a wreath on a sword'; Merkelbach, *Mithras* 288: 'he holds in his right hand a staff or a spear, in the left perhaps a crown'; however in *Mithriaca* 1, 28 (where a coloured reproduction is given as pl. 22) Vermaseren says 'His right hand is not visible, it is possible that it is concealed by his cape, but in his outstretched left hand he holds a flaming torch near the head of the *mystes*. This person who is subjecting the *mystes* to a fire test, is certainly a *miles.*'
18 *Mithriaca* 1, 28f=*CIMRM* 1, 609.
19 *Or.* 4.70 in Migne *PG* 35, 592; but see the doubts of Ries, *Culte* 169; also Beskow, 'Branding' 489f (Gregory had Iranian practices in mind).
20 Script. Hist. Aug., *Commodus* 9 (tr. Magie).
21 Tudor in *CMRED* 2, 243–9; Oppermann, 'Reitergötter' 526.
22 Cf. *CMRED* 1, Index s.v. *Occultatio*. See on Procl., *Theologia Platonica* 4.9 in §6.2 n. 33 above.
23 *CMRED* 1.13, 27, 47.
24 In Phot., *Bibliotheca* 242.131 (344*b*–345*a*); cf. §5.1.4 above.

this theme. Interesting for their own sake, but probably not relevant to our immediate purpose are some bone plates from Olbia, which Burkert dates to the fifth century B.C.E.[25], and which contain on them the words ΒΙΟΣ-ΘΑΝΑΤΟΣ-ΒΙΟΣ as well as ΔΙΟΝ[   ] and ΔΙΟ[   ] and ΟΡΦΙΚ[   ]; Burkert sees here a contrast to Heraclitus' antithesis of life and death[26]; 'perhaps', he conjectures, 'this suggests that death is not the end but a transition'[27]. Yet perhaps this does not apply to death in general, but only death for those possessing the Orphic teachers' lore and who had been purged by their rites; perhaps it applies to the death of those who were devotees of the god Dionysus and who expected to enjoy his enlivening presence in the world to come. West, too, finds traces of two types of initiatory death in the myths (not the rites) of Dionysus, both that of tribal and fraternity initiation in which an ancestral spirit or spirits ritually capture and kill the initiate, and that of shamanic initiations where in hallucinations evil spirits kill the initiate, often by cutting him to pieces and boiling his flesh[28]. Yet there is no reason to suppose that the Olbia plates refer to an initiatory death, rather than to physical death; the 'transition' is not so much a rite as the soul's fate. Nor do they state, on Burkert's interpretation, that life is death or *vice versa* as Heraclitus might (see §6.4.1 below), but that death follows life and is itself followed by life. All that we have here that is relevant to our purpose is the idea of physical death as a transition from one life to another.

More to the point, if Eliade's interpretation is correct[29], is Demosthenes' reference to wiping Sabazius initiates with clay and bran (*Or.* 18.259); for, Eliade argues,

> what we have here is a form of archaic initiation ritual, well known in primitive societies: the novices rub their faces with powder or ashes in order to resemble ghosts; in other words, they undergo a ritual death.

In addition he notes that 'when they took part in the Dionysiac festivals, the Argives covered their faces with chalk or plaster' (the source for this is Nonnus, *Dionys.* 47.732f). This ritual, he thinks, has found its way into the myth of the Titans' destruction of Dionysus[30].

For an example of a quasi-death in consulting an oracle we have Pausanias' account of the underground oracle of Trophonius (9.39.5−14): there

---

25 'Funde' 36f; cf. West, *Poems* 17f.

26 Cf. §6.4.1. nn. 11f.

27 Ibid., he compares Pindar frg. 137 (=121 Bowra): the initiate knows life's end, but knows too its divinely given beginning.

28 Ibid. 143−5; the manner of Dionysus' death at the hands of the Titans suggests the latter, but details like their coating their faces with gypsum and the objects with which they deceive the divine child suggest ritual imitation of their deadly actions.

29 *History* 1, 370f.

30 Cf. n. 28 above.

the one who will descend sacrifices to find out whether Trophonius will receive him well. After anointing and washing he drinks the waters of *Lēthē* and *Mnēmosunē*, worships the image of Trophonius, and then proceeds to the *manteion* in a linen tunic with ribbons and country boots; he descends on a ladder to lie on his back with honeyed barley cakes[31] in his hands and is drawn into the oracle chamber. After seeing or hearing what is to come he returns upwards, feet first, by a small hole. After disclosing his experiences to priests he is received by his relatives in a state of a paralysis of terror, unconscious of himself and his surroundings, a state from which he subsequently recovers, as did Pausanias and others whom he had met. The similarities both to the experience of death and that of initiation are immediately apparent. Plutarch gives a somewhat different impression, however (*Gen. Socr.* 21–2. 590A–592E): Timarchus descended into the oracle for two nights and a day, so that most despaired of him 'and his family were lamenting him', but he ascended again 'with a radiant countenance'[32]. His experience had been of seeming to hear a crash and to feel a blow on his head so that it split and released his soul to witness the heavens and the underworld[33]. Yet, despite the impression given on his return, if anything the likeness to death in this experience is even clearer than in Pausanias' description.

A further trace of the pattern of 'life through death' is detectable in some ancient novels. This holds good whether or not one regards them as allegories of the mysteries[34]. Beck, for instance, is sceptical of this claim with regard to Iamblichus' *Babyloniaca*, but recognizes in it an 'extraordinary emphasis on *Scheintod*'[35]; this might come, directly or indirectly, from Mithraism (Merkelbach's suggestion) or it might be the result of a general yearning for spiritual change; in that case 'Iamblichus is putting into art (somewhat ineptly perhaps) what those of his age longed for and experienced in its most intense form in the rites of the cults'[36]. Merkelbach could find no correspondence to any particular

---

31 Philostr., *Vit. Ap.* 8.19, tells us that these are to appease the snakes that attack him as he descends; cf. schol. on Aristoph., *Nub.* 506–8; Suidas, s.v. Τροφωνίου κατὰ γῆς παίγνια.

32 Tr. de Lacy-Einarson; as they comment this belies the proverbial gloom of those who had experienced this oracle (461).

33 Cf. Culianu, '*Lunam*' 154–62; he sees here a close connection between this rite and initiation (156).

34 Cf. the classic statement in Merkelbach, *Roman*; also Kerenyi, *Romanliteratur* esp. 42f. Contrast Perry, *Romances* 336 n. 17 and lit. cited there: 'this is all nonsense to me'! Also the more careful critique of Turcan, 'Roman', who concludes that the mysteries and these stories may have a common ancestor in ancient tribal stories and rites, but, though parallel, these two traditions do not quite coincide (199).

35 'Soteriology' 534; so too in Xenophon of Ephesus, *Ephesiaca*, e.g. 3.7.1, ἡ δοκοῦσα τεθνηκέναι; cf. Kerenyi, ibid. 32–4; Merkelbach, ibid. 101.

36 Ibid. 536.

cult in Chariton's *Chaereas and Callirhoe* and yet there too one finds the theme of 'life through death', despite Merkelbach's accusation that the author had completely missed the mystic point[37]: Callirhoe describes her vicissitudes with the words 'I have died, I have come alive again' (τέθνηκα, ἀνέζησα, 3.8.9)[38]. With some justification, therefore, Kerenyi remarked that 'in general we can affirm that it is a rule of the Greek novel that its hero and heroine must die and rise again, a rule which none of the pieces of literature extant in a complete form abandons entirely'[39].

Again, Morton Smith, following H. Lewy, finds the same theme embodied in the ritual enjoined by the *Chaldean Oracles*: the ascent of the theurgist's soul was the climax of their principal sacrament. There, after preliminary lustrations, the neophyte lies on the ground with his body covered, or he is buried, all except for his head. Sacrifices for the dead are offered up as he lies there, and his soul is called forth to ascend to heaven[40]. Morton Smith then goes on to argue that the same beliefs lay behind passages in the *Paris Magical Papyrus* (see §6.4.1 below) and certain Hermetic texts.

At the same time there are pieces of evidence that have been adduced for the theme of 'life through death' in the mysteries which I would not want to produce in its support. In §2, for instance, I noted the statement of Firmicus Maternus (*Err. prof. rel.* 18.1) that the *symbolum* of the cult of Cybele and Attis was uttered so that 'the one who is about to die (*moriturus*)' might be admitted to the inner parts of the temple; Dibelius compared this, we saw, with Lucius' voluntary death, but I argued that this reference to the forthcoming death of the devotee of Cybele and Attis was Firmicus' own ironic and polemical comment: these pagan rites were lethal for the spiritual wellbeing of the participants. Nilsson, in addition to upholding this as a possible interpretation of Firmicus' words, also discounts the idea that the one who underwent the *taurobolium* was dying ritually; that is particularly true of its earlier period when the rite was performed for the emperor's wellbeing[41]. It seems unwise, too, to suppose that entry into the παστός of Cybele (Clem. Alex., *Prot.*

---

37 *Roman* 159.
38 Griffiths, *Isis-Book* 21, criticizes Nock for denying the echo of the mysteries in this passage. Achilles Tatius, too, makes Leucippe write to Clitophon: 'On your account I became a sacrificial victim and a purificatory offering and already I have died twice' (5.18.4).
39 *Romanliteratur* 25; the only apparent exception he sees is Longus' *Daphnis and Chloe,* and even he could not really avoid it (26); chap. 2 of Kerenyi's book is devoted to the theme of 'death and resurrection'.
40 'Transformation' 108f, citing Lewy-Tardieu, *Oracles* 204–11, who actually also quote here Procl., *Theologia Platonica* 4.9 (cf. §5.2 n. 33) which speaks of the body's being buried (θάπτειν), not just lying on the ground.
41 *Geschichte* 2, 653f, 686; contrast, e.g., Angus, *Mystery-Religions* 97.

2.15.3) refers to a descent to Hades[42]; much depends on how that was represented in ritual: did it for instance involve a descent into a subterranean chamber[43]?

Kennedy, following Reitzenstein, also made much of *Paris Papyrus* 47[44]; in this 'remarkable passage' Apollonius, whom Milligan describes as 'a κάτοχος in the Serapeum'[45] writes to his 'father' Ptolemaeus:

> I swear by Serapis . . . that all things are false and your gods with the rest, because they have cast us into a great forest, where we may possibly die: and even if you know (ἴδῃς) that we are about to be saved, just then we are immersed (βαπτιζώμεθα) in trouble[46].

With no little understatement Milligan comments of this passage that 'its general meaning is far from clear'[47], but Kennedy asserts that Apollonius is blaming Ptolemaeus and the gods for delaying his full initiation[48]. Where Kennedy follows Reitzenstein in reading 'we cannot die (οὐ δυνάμεθα)' Milligan reads οὖ, 'where'[49]. This seems preferable: the 'great forest', 'death' and 'baptism' are vivid metaphors for the difficulties in which Apollonius finds himself[50], which in fact seem to entail no more serious fate than that shame will prevent him showing his face in Tricomia again, having been deceived by the gods and having wrongly put his trust in dreams (lines 23–30). It would then be wrong to make too much of the parallelism between death and baptism. Kennedy was following the earlier editions of Reitzenstein's *Mysterienreligionen*; by the third edition of 1927 the latter was more doubtful whether conclusions could be drawn from Apollonius' letter written 'in wild passion and incoherent language'; 'it is better to leave such passages aside'. All that is certain is that Ptolemaeus was led by dreams to prophesy and to imagine that certain gods spoke through him (207).

Thus it is true that 'life through death' is attested in the mystery-rites and that this would provide an analogy to Paul's teaching on baptism and one which would lie close to hand. The Stobaeus fragment quoted by Braun would be an apt enough description of the experience common to many, if not all, of the mysteries. But its presence in the mysteries would be only one analogy among several and, moreover, it could be

---

42 Vermaseren, *Cybele* 117f, comparing *Orph. Fr.* 32c=Diels-Kranz, *Fragmente* §1 B 18.8.
43 Cf., e.g., Eliade, *Birth* 61–4.
44 *St Paul* 230f; this is no. 7 in Milligan, *Selections,* no. 100 in Hunt-Edgar, *Papyri* 1.
45 *Selections* 21.
46 Tr. Milligan, lines 2–13; Hunt-Edgar, *Papyri* 1, 289, have 'sink outright' for βαπτιζώμεθα.
47 Ibid. 21.
48 Fuller evidence for this is found in further papyri written by Ptolemaeus and cited by Reitzenstein, *Mysterienreligionen* 202f (72–80 in earlier edd.).
49 Hunt-Edgar, *Papyri* 1, 288, also has οὖ.
50 Milligan, *Selections* 22 n., compares the metaphorical use of βαπτίζω and βάπτισμα in Mk 10.38

argued that the idea lay near to hand in any rite of passage, and was therefore a natural image to use in the context of an explication of the Christian initiatory rite. Again, however, the point needs to be made that, had Paul regarded the idea as one peculiar to pagan cults, all the evidence suggests that he would have avoided it; if, on the other hand, it was an idea and imagery more widely spread than simply belonging to the beliefs and practices of pagan religion, then it is more easily comprehensible that he should use it without any hint of contrast or rivalry with other rites. Simon may be correct in stating that the similarities between the Isiac initiation of Lucius and Paul's teaching on baptism boil down to a general analogy: there is a symbolic death and salvation graciously bestowed in the form of a new birth or a new creation; this analogy, he suggests, could be the result of the influence of certain 'structures of the human spirit' rather than of any more direct influence[51]. Perhaps we can be rather more precise: for the rather vague phrase about 'structures of the human spirit' we can substitute a reference to a standard pattern or structure amongst initiatory rites in general, as well as amongst other rites of passage[52]. In this respect we then find here a further illustration of the basic correctness of Widengren's judgment upon the general relationship between Christianity and the oriental mysteries as regards their outward form:

> Probably Christianity was not influenced directly by the oriental mystery-religions in any significant way, but it formed a parallel phenomenon, and thus from the phenomenological point of view it is to be regarded as a mystery-religion. The similarities are above all to be attributed to similar presuppositions[53].

This perhaps also relieves us of the need to decide whether Jewish proselyte baptism existed early enough as a rite to influence Paul's theology of baptism[54]. The same pattern has been detected there, but may simply reflect this common initiatory structure. If the rite and practice did exist that early, then it is of course more likely that it influenced primitive Christianity than that early Christians deliberately aped the

---

51 'École' 268 ('basic structures of the human mind' in 'Schule' 140).

52 Compare Huntington's ref. apropos of v. Gennep to 'a universal logic of human social life' (*Celebrations* 11). Bloch and Parry remark that 'almost everywhere religious thought consistently denies the irreversible and terminal nature of death by proclaiming it a new beginning'; they add that 'conception and birth are the most striking and obvious symbols available for asserting such a dogma' (*Death* 9); cf. too Leach quoted above at n. 4.

53 *HO* 1.8.2, 80; his following remarks about the use by Paul and others of the language of the mysteries need to be qualified in the light of §2.4.3 above.

54 On the question cf. Beasley-Murray, *Baptism* 18–31; Flemington, *Doctrine* 3–11; (his appeal to Epict., *Diss.* 2.9.20 is persuasive; Epict. would hardly be familiar with a very recent Jewish innovation); Rowley, *Moses* 211–19; most recently Schürer-Black-Millar-Vermes, *History* 3, 174.

rituals of the pagan mysteries. The point is, however, that no direct dependence on either *need* be postulated; we do not have to choose between one and the other. Not that the oft cited saying of *m. Pesah.* 8.8=*m. ᶜEd.* 5.2, 'He that separates himself from his uncircumcision is as one that separates himself from a grave', is relevant here[55]; the point in that saying is surely that the state of uncircumcision is as unclean as that of contact with the grave; it is therefore an argument for a gap of seven days between circumcision and ritual cleansing as enacted in Num 19.16−19 for those who had been in contact with a grave[56]. It is not saying that the passage from uncircumcision to circumcision is like the passage involved in burial; if anything the opposite would be the likely view of Jews, and so it is more natural that the passage should be regarded as a new birth or a new creation[57]. Otherwise one would be ignoring the difference between death as a state from which one is redeemed and death as the means of redemption, a distinction similar to the one noted above in §1.3.1.2. It is therefore hard to see how the symbolism of this particular rite or its interpretation by Jews could have contributed much to the development of the metaphor of baptism as a death.

6.4. 'Life through Death' and 'Life in Death'

6.4.1. 'Life through death' is thus, I would suggest, a theme that lies near to hand by virtue of the very nature of baptism as an initiation and rite of passage, part of the structure of such ritual. Although I concluded above that King's study perversely allowed itself to be deflected into an area of investigation that was really of no direct relevance to his main area of enquiry (§6.3), yet his dissertation does have the considerable merit of raising the questions about this topic of 'life through death' in probably their most fruitful form, namely 'whether or not baptism, as admittedly an initiation rite, has the same *structure and existential effects* for the Christian as other forms of initiation had for the adherents of the mysteries' (58; cf. 75). Both baptism and initiation into the mysteries fall under the common category of rites of passage, in which 'the dominant symbolism is the passage from a death event of some sort to an

---

55 *Pace* Simon, 'École' 263f − and yet he goes on to recognize that the Christian is baptized into death (rather than baptized out of it, or as well as this).

56 Beasley-Murray, *Baptism* 28f; cf. Daube, *New Testament* 108 (but contrast 110!); Wagner, *Baptism* 288 n. 123.

57 *Gen. Rab.* 39.14; *b. Yebam.* 22*a*, 48*b*, 62*a*, 97*b*; *b. Bek.* 47*a*; cf. Daube, ibid. 112f.

immortalization of some kind as an event of total transformation of the passage person' (108 — 'immortalization' is perhaps too sweeping). And yet, most significantly, he notes that

> what distinguishes baptism[1] from other initiatory rites . . . is not the particular details of its ritual procedures or the understanding of what happens essentially up (*sic*) the initiate in the ritual process. Rather, it is the connection drawn in the traditions of the early church between baptismal-death and Jesus' death and resurrection, as well as the specific inferences drawn from that sort of redemptive participation for the life of the *Christian* initiate (162).

The examples given in the previous section offer some quite striking parallels to Paul's view of 'life through death' in Romans 6; the theology of Christian initiation in King's eyes is thus comparable to that of other initiatory rites. And yet two cautions must be uttered here: the first is that, whereas Romans 6 speaks of death (with Christ) leading to life — compare the ἵνα, 'in order that', of 6.4 —, Paul elsewhere speaks, not of 'life through death', but also of 'life *in* death'. The second, to which we shall turn in §6.4.2, stems from the distinctiveness of this 'with Christ' language to which King draws attention.

The theme of *'life in death'* is particularly prominent in 2 Corinthians: there Paul speaks of 'constantly carrying about in our body the putting to death (νέκρωσις) of Jesus, in order that Jesus' life too might be revealed in our body. For we who are alive are constantly being delivered up to death for Jesus' sake, in order that Jesus' life might be revealed in our mortal flesh' 4.10f)[2]. Of his ministry he says that 'we are dying and, look, we are alive' (6.9), a statement which is one of the most vivid of a series of paradoxical antitheses (6.8–10) rather reminiscent of 1 Cor 7.29–31[3].

Windisch calls the whole description of 6.8–10 'nearer to the Old Testament and Stoic thought in character than specifically Christian'[4], although Bultmann demurs, since rightly he sees that in particular the sentence just quoted must be understood in the light of 4.10f.[5] Yet Windisch is correct inasmuch as the antithetical paradoxes, i.e. the stylistic form of Paul's utterances here, are thoroughly at home in contempor-

---

Notes on 6.4.1

1 Presumably he means baptism as Paul sees it.

2 Cf. Gal 2.19f.

3 Curiously N. Schneider, *Eigenart* 56, 62, lists 2 Cor 6.8 among examples of oxymoron in Paul's writings, but not 6.9 although the construction flows on from v 8 into v 9; later he quotes with approval Bultmann's comment apropos of 2 Cor 7.10 (in *TDNT* 4, 321) that λυπή is a necessary part of Christian existence (ibid. 93); could the same not be said of death in 6.9? Cf. Beardslee, 'Saving' 67.

4 *2 Kor* 208 (the citation of Epict. below is on 207f).

5 *2 Kor* 175.

ary popular philosophical writings[6]. He cites for instance Epict., *Diss.*
2.19.24, but the nearest that that text gets to Paul's words is the contrast
of 'though dying . . . happy (εὐτυχοῦντα)'; Paul's form of the antithesis
is sharper and it may be correct to see the Old Testament's influence
behind the juxtaposition of life and death (Windisch also compares Ps 117
(118).17: 'I shall not die but I shall live'). Another factor which may have
made it possible for Paul to go further than the Graeco-Roman parallels
did is his awareness of the dynamic power in his own life, the power
of the life-giving Spirit that was Christ (1 Cor 15.45; cf. §4 above), and
the traditions of Jesus' teaching (see below).

Braun may therefore be right to distinguish a true 'dying and becoming'
as lying in the view that death itself contains life within it rather than in
the view that life is something lying on the far side of the dying; dying,
in other words, is the life and not just a pathway to that life, a necessary
(and perhaps even evil) preliminary to a still future bliss (136)[7]. Unfortunately that distinction and that insight tend to get lost from sight, as
we noted (§6 n. 4), amongst the examples which he subsequently cites,
but such a paradoxical view of life and death *is* found in some of his
examples. So, for instance, in the Jewish material quoted the nearest
to this is *b. Tamid 32a.*

> He (Alexander of Macedon) said to them. What shall a man do to live? They replied:
> Let him mortify himself. What should a man do to kill himself? They replied: Let him
> keep himself alive[8].

This comes in the context of a series of questions posed by Alexander to
'the elders of the south country', in a section headed by the question so
reminiscent of Stoic and Cynic traditions, 'Who is called wise?' It therefore comes as no surprise here that Fischel concludes that 'this is a Hebrew-
Aramaic version of Alexander's encounter with the Indian Gymnosophists,
a theme of Graeco-Roman sources'[9].

It is perhaps only to be expected that this idea should also be found in
the Stoic and Cynic traditions of the Graeco-Roman world with their
love of the paradoxical. Already we find this in Plato where Socrates
quotes a fragment of Euripides with approval,

> Who knows whether life is death
> and death is life?

---

6 Cf. Bultmann, *Stil* 24–30: rightly he draws attention (27) to the Cynic motto of 'adulterating
the coinage' (Diog. L. 6.20f); also Zmijewski, *Stil* 423.

7 Contrast 145 – see §6.1 n. 4.

8 Soncino tr.

9 *Literature* 151 n. 124; cf. Wallach, 'Alexander'. For the Greek version cf., e.g., v. Thiel, *Leben*
128–31 (3.6) and 242–7, and Plut., *Alex.* 64.

and goes on to suggest that we are really dead. (There follows the reference to 'the wise' who say that we are now dead and that the body is a tomb[10].) According to Sextus Empiricus Heraclitus said much the same:

> Heraclitus states that both life and death exist both in our state of life and in our state of death; for when we live our souls are dead and buried within us, and when we die our souls revive and live[11].

This is put more succinctly and vividly in Heraclitus' own words.

> Immortal mortal, mortal immortal, living their death, dying their life[12].

In large measure it was the theme of supposed life as in fact death which dominated philosophers' imagination[13]. If death were in fact life then martyrdom or suicide would be a natural corollary, and there was an understandable reluctance to dwell too much on this possibility[14]. Socrates, however, had taken the former route to life, and it is thus perhaps no accident that a pseudonymous Cynic letter attributes to him the view that the philosopher's life is a metaphorical dying:

> The philosopher does nothing other than to die, since he disdains the demands of the body and is not enslaved by the pleasures of the body; and this is nothing other than the separation of the soul from the body, and death is nothing other again than the separation of the soul from the body[15].

The corollary of that, though it is not expressly stated, is that the philosopher's life is the true life, for the philosopher has separated himself from the body or at least from its demands. It is Socrates, too, of whom Epictetus speaks in one passage quoted by Braun: 'dying he is saved' (*Diss.* 4.1.165). Here we approach most closely to Paul's theme of 'life in death'.

---

10 *Gorg.* 492E–493A; the quotation may be from another edition of the *Phrixus* which contains the version
τίς δ' οἶδεν εἰ ζῆν τοῦθ' ὅ κέκληται θανεῖν,
τὸ ζῆν δὲ θνῄσκειν ἐστί;
Others suggest the *Polyeidus* (Dodds' comm. 300).

11 *Pyrrh. hyp* 3.230, tr. Bury.

12 Diels-Kranz, *Fragmente* §22 B 62; cf. 77, 88.

13 Cf., e g., Epict., *Diss.* 1.19.9; Sen., *De tranquillitate animi* 5.5; Philo too (*Leg. all.* 1.107f) makes use of this, quoting something that bears resemblances to both Heraclitus frg. 62 and frg. 77, but differs from both (curiously Diels-Kranz, *Fragmente* seems to omit this citation): Ζῶμεν τὸν ἐκείνων θάνατον, τεθνήκαμεν δὲ τὸν ἐκείνων βίον. See also *Det. pot. ins.* 49; *Poster. C.* 45; *Gig.* 14; *Rer. div. her.* 53, 292; *Vit. Mos.* 1.279; cf. *Quaest in Gen.* 1.70; *Quaest. in Exod.* frg. 1 (Marcus 258). The constant translation of 'die to' in the LCL Philo underlines the similarity of Philo's thought to Paul's use of ἀποθνῄσκειν with the dat., although Philo (? following Heraclitus) generally uses the accus. (which I would prefer to infer behind *Quaest. in Gen.* 4.240 rather than Marcus' dat.); but cf. *Vit. Mos.* 1.29.

14 Cf. Diog. L. 6.4!

15 Tr. S. Stowers in Malherbe, *Epistles* 257, 259 (=*Epistles of Socrates and the Socratics* 14.8). Apollonius of Tyana denies the reality of Socrates' death in Philostr., *Vit. Ap.* 8.2 (and of Vespasian's in 8.7.2).

Yet here we are dealing with very different traditions to those of the initiations of the mystery-cults. Nock observes that to Paul

> Baptism meant dying with Christ sacramentally; and the notion of sacramental death is not foreign to paganism; but (to Paul) Christian life meant dying with Him every day[16].

Rather, as we have seen, dying as life at least had its points of contact in some pagan traditions, though not those of sacramental rites; perhaps life as a dying had its place in those traditions too, though it was never so vividly expressed in those terms, as we shall see; yet it is never a dying *with a deity*. It occurs rather in philosophical traditions where suffering deities were far removed, and where there was more interest in playing with recoined words[17].

The nearest that one comes to the theme of 'life in death' in the context of the mysteries is perhaps in a passage near the end of the *Mithras-Liturgy*, also cited by Braun:

> While being born again, I am passing away;
> while growing and having grown, I am dying;
> while being born from a life-generating birth,
> I am passing on, released to death[18].

Strictly this is a theme of 'death in life' rather than 'life in death', but the one might be regarded as the obverse of the other, with the emphasis laid on the liberation of the soul from bodily and normal ties[19]. It should be emphasized that, though the thought of this text owes much to the mysteries, it is an interpretation that could be placed upon them in certain circles, and is in no way built into their initiatory structures in the same way as 'life through death'.

For it has to be noted that whereas 'life through death' is very much a dominant theme in rites of passage, 'life in death' is not, at least in its

---

16 'Christianity' 106=*Essays* 93; contrast Godwin, *Mystery Religions* 13, on the followers of Mithras!

17 Cf. n. 6 above. Distinguish this from the re-evaluation of values mentioned by Hasenfratz, *Lebenden* 4, although the two can be related to one another. The instances he mentions are of, e.g., treating the living as if dead; where the two come near is when one regards these living as being in effect, at least for a certain stage in their lives, dead.

18 *PGM* 4.718–22, tr. Meyer:
παλιν γενόμενος ἀπογίγνομαι,
αὐξόμενος καὶ αὐξηθεὶς (720) τελευτῶ,
ἀπὸ γενέσεως ζωογόνου γενόμενος, εἰς ἀπογενεσίαν ἀναλυθεὶς πορεύομαι.
The text cited by M. Smith, 'Transformation' 110f, from earlier in *PGM* 4 (lines 154–285) is more easily construed as an example of 'life through death', a ritual burial preceding the acquisition of 'a nature equal to a god's' (lines 174–8, 219f).

19 Reitzenstein, *Mysterienreligionen* 181, denies that this refers to the mortal body; rather it refers to the initiate's 'self': 'the human in him must perish if the god is born or he is born as god'. But the former might be simpler, especially since the goal is immortality (477), to be given over to immortal birth and to his 'underlying nature' (502f), though mortal to be improved (517f); the liberation from the human power of the soul is only temporary however (523–5).

sharpest and most paradoxical form, and indeed could not be if van Gennep's analysis has anything in it, for it would collapse the stated, episodic structure of the rites into one: the separation would become the incorporation and the incorporation the separation, and there would be no transition. It is perhaps then not surprising that 'life in death' does not appear in Romans 6; life is there the goal of our death (v 4) and it replaces the deadness of our former state (v 13; cf. §1.3.12).

Yet it would perhaps have been at least theoretically possible for Paul to have accommodated the imagery of 'life in death' within his references to Christian initiation, for Turner notes how

> logically antithetical processes of death and growth may be represented by the same tokens, for example, by huts and tunnels that are at once tombs and wombs, . . . by nakedness (which is at once the mark of a newborn infant and a corpse prepared for burial), and by innumerable other symbolic formations and actions[20].

In other words the paradoxical language of Paul lay near to hand within the stock of symbols used to express the meaning of such ritual transitions.

The reversal of values with which Paul describes apostolic existence, and the transcending of distinctions, or opposites, which he sees as marking the new creation and the new age (Gal 3.28; 6.15)[21], bears a surprising resemblance to some of the characteristics of 'liminal' or 'marginal' existence as described in anthropologists' descriptions of rites of passage. Turner noted that it might be likened to bisexuality (cf. Gal 3.28?)[22] and continues

> Liminal entities . . . may be represented as possessing nothing. They may . . . even go naked, to demonstrate that as liminal beings they have no status, property, insignia, secular clothing indicating rank or role, position in a kinship system. . . . Their behaviour is normally passive or humble . . . . It is as though they are being reduced or ground down to a uniform condition to be fashioned anew and endowed with additional powers to enable them to cope with their new station in life[23].

---

20 *Forest* 99.

21 Cf Martyn, 'Antinomies'.

22 *Process* 102 speaks rather of sexlessness and this would be an even apter comparison (*Forest* 98 is rather more precise: bisexuality and asexuality are alternatives); cf. also Eliade, *Birth* 26, 44. If Gal 3.28 does have its origin in baptismal traditions, the abolition of differences between the sexes in baptismal and other initiatory rites (*Process* 103) is surely significant. But in most rites of passage this is a temporary state. For Paul it is the mark of eschatological existence. Relevant here, too, may be the practice of being baptized naked, and not being ashamed, as Adam and Eve were unashamed in Paradise – cf. J. Z. Smith, 'Garments' 222–8. There is thus in baptism an eschatological reversion to the primal state. If that is so then ritual nudity here surely has a different significance to the ritual nudity found in mystery initiations (cf. Smith, ibid. 218f n. 6).

23 *Process* 95; the following pages illustrate this well; cf. *Forest* 98f; Meeks, *Christians* 157; Samter, *Geburt* 114.

When we compare Paul's descriptions of the apostolic condition and the characteristics of the new creature, it is as if he had taken the imagery and the symbolism of the transitional state, and was saying that this limbo-like state between normal conditions was in fact the final state, or, in the case of the apostles, the state in which they must live out the rest of their earthly lives[24]. There is a certain logic to that, for after all rites of passage order life as we know it, are supportive of the *status quo* and the established order of society. Paul is speaking of a revolution that has overthrown that order (or should do so, if it is allowed to carry on its work of subversion and is not domesticated or tamed), and it is perhaps only natural that his mind turns to the images used elsewhere for the limbo-like existence of those in passage from one slot in society to another. So, if the social order is normally represented as an enclosed world (cf. the rectangle in the figure below), progression from one level or stage in that order is by means of stepping temporarily outside that world, into the realm of 'death', non-existence, in order to enter it again at another level or stage:

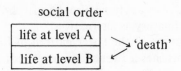

But for Paul the Christian steps outside of that ordinary world, whatever his or her place in it, be it as Jew or Greek, male or female, slave or free, into a new world, and becomes a new creature in a new creation, ordered anew by its Creator.

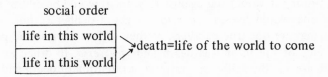

It is not surprising, either, that he then finds himself echoing the utterances of those in the Cynic tradition, with their critique of, and contempt for, so many of the established values and practices of contemporary society; they too were subversive in relation to the *status quo*. Yet,

---

24 In this he was not alone, as Turner notes (*Process* 107f, 111–13, and chap. 4 on 'communitas'); however, with the likes of St Francis he speaks of him viewing 'his friars as liminars in a life that was merely a passage to the unchanging state of heaven' (143f); that is different from saying that 'liminality' is ultimate reality. Cf. also Meeks, ibid., following Turner, as well as his 'Image' 182, 207f.

as I indicated earlier, the vivid imagery of (true) life as a death or a dying is not one that the Cynic tradition availed itself of, to my knowledge, at least in this positive sense of death; ordinary life as a death in a pejorative sense was, as we saw[25], an image taken up by philosophers of varying traditions. Paul has gone beyond them in the daring and the vividness of his imagery of the true life being found in death[26].

We noted earlier (§1.3.3.3) that Paul does not use the imagery of rebirth; the distinctions that I have drawn above may suggest a good reason why he does not: rebirth is a natural image to use when the idea to be conveyed is one of ending one life and then, subsequently, beginning another. It is not a helpful or natural image when that life is seen as manifested in the very dying. It is the former idea which is dominant in the mysteries (although perhaps not so all-pervasive as some would have us believe) and other forms of initiation-rites and rites of passage. The latter is prominent in Paul's thought, although the former is not absent, as we have seen. Indeed, where the former, life through death, is present, to the exclusion of life in death or life as death, there is no reason why Paul should not have used the image of rebirth; that he does not do so in Romans 6 may be more an accident than anything else: he just did not think of using it or chose to use other imagery as alternatives.

If rites of initiation are not the source of the latter pattern of life in death, and if philosophical traditions never went the length of this paradox, a more likely precursor would be Jesus' sayings about losing one's life (here $\psi\upsilon\chi\acute{\eta}$) and gaining it and vice versa[27], for they could easily be interpreted as meaning that in gaining one's life one loses it and *vice versa*, and not just as saying, as Braun suggests, that one must die in order to live (subsequently)[28]; indeed the form of the saying about gaining one's life and losing it would tell against this, for it would be odd to suggest that anyone would live *in order to* die (by a deliberate purpose); either the sayings are not true parallels, or they in fact express the paradoxical presence of life in and as death and *vice versa*. In other words, life and death are not the deliberate purpose or intention of death and life

---

25 See n. 13 above.
26 Cf. Beker, *Paul* 197: 'in Paul . . . a dialectical relation between the death and resurrection of Christ intersects the consecutive relation. And this may well be Paul's unique contribution to the theology of the cross. Life is not just life after death but also life in the midst of death . . . '.
27 Matt 10.39; 16.25f; Mk 8.35f; Lk 9.24f; 17.33; John 12.25. Even if these were originally 'eschatological reversal sayings' (Perrin, *Jesus* 52) it would have been quite possible subsequently to treat these futures as logical, and the gaining and losing as therefore simultaneous (as in John 12.25a; cf. also Mk 8.36).
28 Cf. §6.1; so too Beardslee, 'Saving' – is this really so paradoxical (58) if the life is not in the dying rather than just coming through it?

respectively, but rather their paradoxical concomitants each hidden in the other incognito.

Thus, if 'life in death' expresses the true 'Stirb und werde', as Braun claimed, or if it merely represents another version of the theme, more paradoxically put, it is a theme whose claim to be derived from 'oriental Hellenism' is slender; that claim can be made for 'life through death', with the qualification that it is far wider spread than 'oriental Hellenism', although 'oriental Hellenism' may have been the principle expression of this imagery present in the New Testament world. Stylistically the way that Paul speaks of 'life in death' may owe something to popular Greek philosophy, but his philosophical contemporaries or near-contemporaries never put this paradox in quite that pregnant form. For the explanation of that we are better to look to Jewish and above all Christian tradition stemming ultimately from the teaching of Jesus, even if Paul was unaware of the sayings just cited.

6.4.2. Even when speaking of the initiatory death in baptism Paul is, as we have seen, speaking not so much of the baptized person dying himself or repeating Christ's experience for himself, but rather of the Christian acknowledging an experience already previously undergone by Christ on his behalf; in fact he goes further, and says that the Christian in some sense shared in that experience in the past *with Christ*. King rightly, as we saw, here drew a distinction between Paul's view of baptism on the one hand and other initiation-rites on the other, in that the latter do not share this connection with the death and coming to life of the deity, that is in this case Jesus[1].

Bloch and Parry refer to funerary rites as 'representing death as part of a cyclical process of renewal'[2]. Such a cyclic view is inherent also not only in the analogies to the natural processes of the growth and decay of vegetation seen in the case of the mystery-deities (cf. §3.2.3.9), but also in the prominent role given to corn in the Eleusinian rites, culminating in the revelation of an ear of corn (so Hipp., *Ref.* 5.8.39). Yet Paul's view is anything but cyclic; at the basis of Christian baptism is our involvement in a death of Christ that occurred 'once and for all time' (Rom 6.10); Christ does not die afresh as his would-be followers are baptized into his death; rather they are related to that single past death and to an event that is eschatological in the sense of being God's final, decisive

---

Notes on 6.4.2

1 *Death* 162; cf. also §1.3.3.1 above.

2 *Death* 15.

act that can be neither repeated nor superseded, ushering in a new creation (2 Cor 5.17; Gal 6.15) that is not part of a recurrent cycle like some
Stoic παλιγγενεσία. What God has once thus renewed needs no further
renewal – in a sense.

Again, Eliade stresses the links in many initiation rites with primal
time, a mythical period when the world was made[3]. For Paul, however,
it is very different, as Eliade recognizes[4]: the link is not with protological
time but with eschatological time, with that moment when God brought
his new world into being and when the eschatological Adam/man was
fashioned (1 Cor 15.45). Even when the link with the very first time is
lacking, when the reference is, as often in the Graeco-Roman mysteries,
to some other event, occurring when the world is already formed as we
know it, yet its reference is to a pre-history, and involves deities and
figures of a past which can in no way be described as located firmly in
our history as was the victim of an execution by the Roman *praefectus*
of Judaea in the time of the emperor Tiberius. That the lives and destinies of Christian initiates should be caught up in, and determined by,
such a death of such a deity was a novelty in the ancient world.

Thus, despite similarities, Paul's talk of 'life through death' and 'life
in death' have a basis and a rationale and a point of reference that is very
different from that of contemporary Graeco-Roman religion and thought.
In so far as he and his fellow-Christians ordered themselves in a way that
was analogous to other groupings in Graeco-Roman society and in other
societies too, it is to be expected that there would be analogies in the
way that they spoke of belonging to, and coming to belong to, the Christian group. But the analogies come to an end at the point where they
differed from their contemporaries, in their understanding that their
God had finally decided the fate of the world and its inhabitants in the
events in the life of a Galilean religious teacher and that their destinies
and those of all peoples were ineluctably affected by this teacher's igno-
minious death and subsequent fate.

---

3 *Birth* xii–xiv, 5f and *passim* – e.g. 48: 'to perform the ritual is to reactualize primordial
time'.
4 *Birth* 117: 'For the earliest Christian communities, the resurrection of Jesus *could not be*
identified with the periodic death and resurrection of the God of the mysteries. Like Christ's
life, suffering and death, his resurrection had occurred in history.'

6.5. Conclusions

In considering Braun's important article we saw two weaknesses: the first was that he had unduly limited the provenance of the idea of 'dying and becoming' to 'oriental Hellenism'; it is rather something far more fundamental and widespread than that. Even more mistaken would be to limit it to the mysteries, although they were a prominent contemporary example of it. The second criticism concerned a certain laxity in definition, both in his failure to delimit sharply enough what were instances of this theme and in the failure to distinguish clearly enough what I chose to designate as the themes of 'life through death' and 'life in death', the distinction between death as a means to the final state and death as itself the final state.

Paul's mention of Christians' burial with Christ in Rom 6.4 is thoroughly appropriate in a context dealing with baptism; anthropology is familiar with the phenomenon of rites relating to one 'passage' borrowing from those relating to another, and of the one becoming a metaphor for the other. But for Paul it is not just any burial, but burial *with Christ*, a sharing of his burial, and that is a feature unparalleled in other non-Christian rites. (We saw in §5.1.1.2–3 that it was doubtful whether this idea could be found in Egyptian rites, either the ancient ones of burial or the newer ones of initiation as found in the Graeco-Roman world; certainly the language used bore no resemblance to Paul's.)

Death and restoration to life are metaphors frequently used in rites of initiation and other rites of passage the world over. It is no surprise, then, that this imagery was known in the ancient Greek world and in the Graeco-Roman world. It was by no means limited there to rites of initiation into the mysteries, but was found in other rites as well, and was used also as a metaphor for other initiation-like experiences, like consulting an oracle. Bearing in mind the repugnance with which early Christians viewed the pagan rites (see §2.4.3) it is surely wiser to say here that they would not have borrowed this idea from their pagan rivals, but drew it from the general stock of ideas of their time, and indeed of most other times as well. This was an imagery that was current then in their environment as it has been and is in a multitude of other cultures. We should bear in mind that, had they felt it to be peculiarly at home in, or the possession of, the mysteries, the evidence suggests that they would have avoided it as contaminated.

We also saw that Paul makes vivid use too of the theme of 'life in death', which owes much to the Stoic and Cynic traditions' love of paradoxical modes of expression; for them what is commonly thought of as life is in fact death, and, in particular when they reflected upon Socrates' martyrdom, death was seen as salvation or, as Paul would put it more starkly, life. The parallels to such language are thus in philosophical plays on words rather than in the thought of the mysteries, but at the same time, since the destiny of the Christian is to be set in a 'marginal' mode of existence, the theme of 'life in death' arises out of the symbolism of the Christian's transition from the old life to the new; whereas for most initiates 'death' is a necessary path to 'life', for the Christian 'death' is the destination, for what in other rites is a limbo-like interim state between two positions in the established order of things is for the Christian the paradoxical enjoyment of God's order of things, which is in revolutionary fashion subversive of the established order.

At the same time Paul parts company with his non-Christian contemporaries in that for him the Christian has died with Christ and the 'dying' that takes place in baptism is but an 'echo', a realization, of a past death with Christ, a death that took place once and for all, unrepeatable and final. It is again, in other words, the 'with Christ' which marks off Paul's theology from the ideas of his contemporaries; neither Paul's language nor his ideas find any adequate analogy in the mysteries or in rites of initiation elsewhere.

7. Conclusions and Postscript

We have looked at the widespread theory that the initiation-rites and the theology of the Graeco-Roman mysteries influenced Greek-speaking Christians and their baptismal theology, inducing them to suppose that their deity too had bestowed upon them a share in his resurrection in the Christian initiation-rite. We saw the weakness of the exegetical foundations upon which the theory of this influence had been built:

(1) the Corinthian Christians are unlikely to have been of the view that the resurrection had already happened when it is clear that Paul understands them to be saying that there is no resurrection. It is true that it is difficult to be sure quite what they did say or that Paul is altogether fair in his representation of their views and in his own counter-arguments. Yet still the theory with which we are dealing remains one of the less probable solutions of this *crux interpretum*.

(2) In Romans 6 Paul does presuppose some knowledge on the part of the Roman Christians of the interpretation which he is offering them, but it does not follow from this that they are already familiar with his 'with Christ' language from some other source. Moreover, if he is deliberately setting out to correct an 'enthusiastic' misunderstanding of baptism on the analogy of pagan initiation-rites in Rom 6.4, he is amazingly unguarded in his language in 6.13.

(3) Furthermore, how plausible is it that the authors of Colossians and Ephesians, probably followers of his, espoused a view of an already realized resurection, if Paul had earlier set his face against the idea? Is it not likelier that they had developed this idea as a logical extension of Paul's thought in Romans 6? In other words these later writings represent a later stage in the development of Pauline theology within the Pauline community rather than a reversion to an earlier, pre-Pauline baptismal theology.

Not that it is impossible for the mysteries to have influenced Paul and his Christian predecessors. The mysteries were indeed alive and well and flourishing in their day; they were part of the fabric of Graeco-Roman religion and society at the time in which the early church came into being. But they had become so much part of that world that one could pick up ideas and terms ultimately derived from them without really being aware of their source. Both Jews and Christians in that age did that. What is striking is that Christians in the first century, unlike their Jewish contemporary, Philo of Alexandria, did not present their faith as a counter-mystery; they did not deliberately and consciously imitate the language and the propaganda of the mysteries, but rather seem to have eschewed any language that would have seemed too like that of the mysteries. Yet if this rejection was conscious, or even if it was unconscious, this may well be described as influencing them, negatively, in their thought and their proclamation of their message. It is, however, quite another matter to suggest that early Christians set out to borrow the soteriology of the mysteries and to set it at the heart of the exposition of their own rites.

Still, we must not forget that the mysteries were only a part, albeit an important and influential one, of Graeco-Roman religion. Even the cults that had mysteries usually also had public rites too. Moreover some patterns which we can detect in the mysteries, like that of initiation viewed as a dying and coming to life again, were not peculiar to them, but were more widespread both in Graeco-Roman religion and in rites of passage in other settings and other ages. Arguably this is a thoroughly natural, even self-evident, metaphor to employ for all such rites.

Dying and coming to life again may be a widespread idea, then, but not dying and rising with the past death and resurrection of a deity. Even if many (but not all) of the mysteries did worship a hero or deity who was thought to have died and to have come to life again in some form or other, we have found no evidence that the initiates in any of their rites believed that in their initiations they were experiencing in themselves the death and resurrection of their deity, let alone that this idea was common to all or many of them. We must indeed abandon the idea of a common theology of the mysteries existing before such a unity was imposed upon them by the rise to dominance of Neoplatonist philosophy. Any unity that existed amongst them previously extended no further than the shared assumptions and world-view of the age, and even that probably varied with the levels of sophistication and education of individual initiates. There is little sign that the officials of any of the cults sought to interpret the experiences of these cults within the framework of an official theology, let alone that that theology included the belief that they shared the sufferings and restoration of the deity already in their initiation, still less that they had already died with the deity when he or she died in the primordial founding events of the cult. Only this last belief would, I believe, offer a true parallel to the thought of Paul.

Instead we must look elsewhere for the source of the beliefs of Paul and of his too-enthusiastic followers in Corinth. The latter, I have argued, most likely derived their beliefs from their interpretation of the Christian rites and their attendant spiritual phenomena, which they regarded as bestowing upon them unconditionally divine gifts of life and wisdom; the spirit of God heightened their mental powers so that they could perceive divine mysteries and participate in heavenly worship. Yet this heightened experience could not easily have been construed as 'resurrection', since the associations of that term were far too physical, implying a restoration of a body; I have argued that in all probability the Corinthian 'strong' sought and expected liberation from the body and imagined that they had already in essence gained it in their heady ecstatic experiences. The belief that this experience was a sign of the presence of God's new age would have encouraged the conviction that this gift of the divine spirit was permanent and enduring, and not merely fleeting and episodic like the ecstasies experienced in other cults of the Graeco-Roman world. From henceforth they were, they believed, citizens of a new age and a new world, and nothing could take that citizenship from them.

The belief in an already realized 'resurrection' that took place in baptism was not, I have argued, part of their convictions. Such a belief is later firmly attested in Christian Gnostic texts; there it could claim the support of the deutero-Pauline writers of the letters to the Colossians and the Ephesians. I have argued that this should be seen as a development of the idea of 'resurrection' that was only really possible and necessary within Christian traditions or traditions that sought to seem Christian. Otherwise the normal connotations of the term militated too strongly against its use in this sense, and the motivation for such a daring recoining of the term is elsewhere hard to find. The evidence for this reinterpretation in *Joseph and Aseneth* and in the *Dead Sea Scrolls* is hardly overwhelming.

Paul did, however, make important concessions to the sensibilities of his Graeco-Roman readers in 1 Corinthians 15, by stressing the otherness of the 'spiritual body' that would be resurrected. Yet he could not bring himself to speak of resurrection in the present, for life now was lived out in the all too mortal physical body that was still subject to the ravages of the last enemy, death. Christ's death and burial could, however, be shared now, and he wrote in these terms in writing to his readers in the Roman church as well as to his Galatian converts. The background to this lies perhaps in a world less familiar to them than to Paul, although I have argued that it would not have been altogether incomprehensible, altogether without its points of contact, to them: the roots of such language lie in the idea, so pervasive in the Old Testament and Judaism, of the involvement of subsequent generations in the earlier actions of a representative figure or figures, and in the solidarity of a race with one another down through its history. But now, in Paul's thought, the earlier generation has shrunk to but one figure, the eschatological human being, Christ, and the race has broadened to the whole of humanity. That one person died and with him all for whom he died; that past death is declared afresh in baptism, as the baptized says her or his 'Amen' to the past representative act, pledging herself or himself to live henceforth in solidarity both with the representative and all those represented by him; at the same time she or he receives the promise of new life uttered in the vindication of that same representative person by his resurrection from the dead. Those today that can share something of these ideas and thus can catch something of Paul's vision of the significance of Christ will find that this Christian apostle of the first century C.E. still speaks in the twentieth; for those who cannot he will remain an enigma; it is the task of the Christian interpreter to try to make him less enigmatic to her or his contemporaries, to try to bridge the gap of centuries, and to awaken an understanding of what he was trying to express.

It is the role of the study of the background of the New Testament to be ancillary to the interpretation of the New Testament – but an indispensable ancillary. I am conscious that in some ways this study has made the hermeneutical task of interpreting both the ancient mysteries and Paul more difficult. For we can no longer interpret either in the light of the other: the mysteries were not saying the same thing as Paul, nor was Paul borrowing his ideas from the mysteries. Each must now be considered in its own light. The interpretation of Paul is my task, and it is only just beginning. Yet it is, I hope, not an inconsiderable beginning, to have set a large warning sign at the entry to what I believe to be a 'dead-end' in Pauline studies, the interpretation of Paul's doctrine of union with Christ as derivative from the mystery-cults of his day.

Abbreviations

In general the conventions of the following have been used:
(1) for Biblical, Jewish and Gnostic works and for some reference works and periodicals the guidelines adopted by the *Journal of Biblical Literature* 95 (1976), 331–46;
(2) for most periodicals, serials, etc., S. Schwertner's *Abkürzungsverzeichnis* for *Theologische Realenzyklopädie* (Berlin/New York, 1978);
(3) for classical and patristic sources G. Kittel, tr. G. W. Bromiley, *Theological Dictionary of the New Testament* 1 (Grand Rapids, 1964), xvi–xxxix, supplemented by the revised list in the *Theologisches Wörterbuch zum Neuen Testament* 10.1 (Stuttgart, etc., 1978), 53–85, although sometimes a slightly longer form has been used for the sake of greater clarity. For some forms cf. (ed.) N.G.L. Hammond, H.H. Scullard, *The Oxford Classical Dictionary* (Oxford, 1970^2) ix–xxii.

In the footnotes the titles of modern works and articles have been abbreviated, usually to a single word or phrase (see bibliography). Biblical commentaries have usually been designated by the appropriate abbreviation for the Biblical book.

In addition the following have been used:

BCNH=Bibliothèque Copte de Nag Hammadi
BDR=F. Blaß, A. Debrunner, F. Rehkopf, *Grammatik des neutestamentlichen Griechisch*, Göttingen, 1979[15]
CCCA=Corpus cultus Cybelae Attidisque, ed. M. J. Vermaseren, EPRO 50, Leiden, 1977–
CIMRM=Corpus inscriptionum et monumentorum religionis Mithriacae, ed. M. J. Vermaseren, Hague, 1956–60
CMRED=Corpus monumentorum religionis equitum Danuvinorum, ed. D. Tudor, EPRO 13, Leiden, 1969, 1976–
DNTT=Dictionary of New Testament Theology, ed. C. Brown, Exeter, 1975–8
Grimm-Thayer=C. L. W. Grimm, J. H. Thayer, *A Greek-English Lexicon of the New Testament,* Edinburgh, 1896[4]
Hennecke-Schneemelcher-Wilson=E. Hennecke, W. Schneemelcher, R. McL. Wilson, *New Testament Apocrypha*, London, 1963–5, 1973–4[2]
JSNT=Journal for the Study of the New Testament (Sheffield)
Lipsius-Bonnet=R. A. Lipsius, M. Bonnet (ed.), *Acta apostolorum apocrypha,* Leipzig, 1903, repr. Darmstadt, 1959
NHC=Nag Hammadi Codices
OrRR=Die orientalischen Religionen in Römerreich, ed. M. J. Vermaseren, EPRO 93, Leiden, 1981
SEG=Supplementum epigraphicum Graecum (Leiden)
SVF=Stoicorum veterum fragmenta, ed. J. von Arnim, index by M. Adler, BSGRT, Leipzig, 1903–24

Bibliography

As far as possible the works cited have been separated into primary (1) and secondary (2) literature, although this distinction presents problems when editions of texts and commentaries on them are combined. In the interests of space reviews, and articles in standard works of reference, have been omitted from the bibliography and are merely referred to in the notes, as have texts identified adequately in the lists of abbreviations referred to above, and separate references to authors in a standard series like Migne's *Patrologia* where these can be conveniently cited in the notes. Works have generally been cited with a one-word abbreviated title; generally this should be easily recognizable as the first noun of the full title, but the form used is specified in the bibliography below. Where it has not been possible to consult a work first-hand then what bibliographical details are known, together with a reference to the source of the information, have been included in the notes.

1. Primary

(When titles are not specified the edition in question is of the extant works of the relevant author.)

Achilles Tatius, ed./tr. S. Gaselee, LCL, London/New York, 1917.
Aelius Aristides, ed. B. Keil, Berlin, 1898;
−−, ed./tr. C. A. Behr, Leiden, 1981.
Aeschylus, ed./tr. H. W. Smyth, LCL, London/New York, 1922−26 (revised H. Lloyd Jones, 1957).
Anthologia graeca, ed. H. Beckby, München, 1957−8[1];
−−, tr. W. R. Paton, LCL, London/New York, 1916−18.
Anthologie grecque 1: Anthologie Palatine, ed./tr. P. Waltz *et al.*, Paris, 1928−.
Antisthenes, *Fragmenta*, ed. F. D. Caizzi, Testi e documenti per lo studio dell' antichita, Milano, 1966.
Apocalypse of Baruch, ed./tr. P. Bogaert, SC 144−5, Paris, 1969;
−−, ed. M. Kmosko, in (ed.) R. Graffin, *Patrologia syriaca* 1.2, Paris, 1907, cols 1056−1306.
Apocalypse of Elijah, ed./tr. W. Schrage, JSHRZ 5.3, Gütersloh, 1980.
Apollodorus, *The Library*, ed./tr. J. G. Frazer, LCL, London/New York, 1921.
Apostolic Constitutions, ed. P. A. de Lagarde, Leipzig/London, 1862;
−−, ed. G. Ültzen, Rostock, 1853.
Apostolic Fathers, ed./tr. K. Lake, LCL, London/New York, 1912−13.
Apuleius, ed. R. Helm, BSGRT, Leipzig, 1955−9;
−−, *Apologia and Florida*, ed./tr. H. E. Butler, Oxford, 1909;
−−, *Metamorphoses*, ed./tr. W. Adlington, LCL, London/New York, 1915;

––, *The Isis-Book (Metamorphoses, Book XI)*, ed./tr. J. G. Griffiths, EPRO 39, Leiden, 1975.

Aristophanes, ed. F. W. M. Geldart, SCBO, Oxford, 1906–7;

––, ed./tr. V. Coulon, H. van Daele, CUFr, Paris, 1923–30;

––, ed./tr. B. B. Rogers, LCL, London/New York, 1924;

––, *The Frogs*, ed. W. B. Stanford, London, 1963³.

Aristotle, ed. U. C. Bussemaker, Scriptorum Graecorum bibliotheca, Paris, 1848–74;

––, *De anima*, ed. R. D. Hicks, Cambridge, 1907;

––, *De anima*, ed. W. D. Ross, SCBO, Oxford, 1956;

––, *Fragmenta*, ed. V. Rose, BSGRT, Leipzig, 1886;

––, *Fragmenta selecta*, ed. W. D. Ross, SCBO, Oxford, 1955;

––, *Select Fragments*, ed./tr. W. D. Ross, Oxford, 1952;

––, *Atheniensium respublica; Ethica Eudemia; De virtutibus et vitiis*, ed./tr. H. Rackham, LCL, London/New York, 1935;

––, *Ethica Nicomachea*, ed./tr. H. Rackham, LCL, London/New York, 1926;

––, *Sophistici elenchi; De generatione et corruptione; De mundo*, ed./tr. E. S. Forster, D. J. Furley, LCL, London/Cambridge MA, 1955.

Arnobius, *Adversus nationes*, ed./tr. A. H. Bryce, H. Campbell, ANCL 19, Edinburgh, 1871.

Artemidorus, *Onirocritica*, ed. R. A. Pack, BSGRT, Leipzig, 1963;

––, ed./tr. R. J. White, Noyes Classical Studies, Park Ridge NJ, 1975.

Asmussen, J. P. (ed.), *Literature=Manichean Literature: Representative Texts Chiefly from Middle Persian and Parthian Writings*, Persian Heritage Series 22, Delmar NY, 1975.

Assmann, J. (ed.), *König=Der König als Sonnenpriest: ein kosmographischer Begleittext zur kultischen Sonnenhymnik in thebaischen Tempeln und Gräbern*, ADAI. Ä 7, Glückstadt, 1970.

Athenaeus, ed./tr. C. B. Gulick, LCL, London/New York, 1927–41.

Athenagoras, *Legatio; De resurrectione*, ed./tr. W. R. Schoedel, Oxford, 1972.

Augustine, *De civitate Dei*, ed./tr. D. S. Wiesen, G. E. McCracken, W. M. Green *et al.*, LCL, London/Cambridge MA, 1957–72.

Ausonius, ed./tr. H. G. Evelyn White, LCL, London/New York, 1919–21.

Bekker, I. (ed.), *Anecdota=Anecdota Graeca*, Berlin, 1814–21.

Berthelot, M., Ruelle, C.-E. (ed.), *Collection des anciens alchemistes grecs*, Paris, 1888.

Betz, H. D. (ed.), *Papyri=The Greek Magical Papyri in Translation including the Demotic Spells*, Chicago/London, 1985.

Biblia hebraica, ed. R. Kittel *et al.*, Stuttgart, 1954¹¹.

Breasted, J. H. (ed./tr.), *Records=Ancient Records of Egypt*, Chicago, 1906–7.

Book of the Dead, ed./tr. E. A. W. Budge, London, 1951².

Bresciani, E., Pernigotti, S. (ed./tr.), *Assuan*, Biblioteca di studi antichi, sezione egittologica 16, Pisa, 1978.

Buecheler, F. (ed.), *Carmina=Carmina latina epigraphica*, Anthologia latina 2.1–2, Leipzig, 1897, 1930².

Callimachus, ed. R. Pfeiffer, Oxford, 1949–53;

––, ed./tr. A. W. Mair, LCL, London/New York, 1921.

Chairemon, ed. H.-R. Schwyzer, KPS 4, Leipzig, 1932.

Chaldean Oracles, ed./tr. E. des Places, CUFr, Paris, 1971.

Chariton, ed. W. E. Blake, Oxford, 1938;

––, ed./tr. G. Molinié, CUFr, Paris, 1979.

Charles, R. H. *et al.* (ed./tr.), *Apocrypha=The Apocrypha and Pseudepigrapha of the Old Testament*, Oxford, 1913.

Charlesworth, J. H. *et al.* (ed./tr.), *Pseudepigrapha=The Old Testament Pseudepigrapha*, London, 1983–5.

Cicero, *De finibus bonorum et malorum*, ed./tr. H. Rackham, LCL, London/New York, 1914;

––, *De natura deorum*, ed. A. S. Pease, Cambridge MA, 1955–8;

––, *De natura deorum; Academica*, ed./tr. H. Rackham, LCL, London/New York, 1933;

––, *De officiis*, ed./tr. W. Miller, London/New York, 1913;

––, *De re publica; De legibus*, ed./tr. C. W. Keyes, LCL, London/New York, 1928;

−−, *De senectute; De amicitia; De divinatione,* ed./tr. W. A. Falconer, LCL, London/New York, 1923;

−−, *Tusculanae quaestiones,* ed./tr. J. E. King, LCL, London/New York, 1927.

Clearchus: F. Wehrli, *Die Schule des Aristoteles: Klearchos,* Basel/Stuttgart, 1969[2].

Clement of Alexandria, *Excerpta ex Theodoto,* ed. O. Stählin, GCS 17, Leipzig, 1909;

−−, *Paedagogus,* ed. O. Stählin, GCS 12, Leipzig, 1905;

−−, ed./tr. H.-I. Marrou, M. Harl *et al.,* SC 70, 108, 158, Paris, 1960−70;

−−, *Protrepticus,* ed. O. Stählin, GCS 12, Leipzig, 1905;

−−, ed./tr. G. W. Butterworth, LCL, London/New York, 1919;

−−, ed./tr. C. Mondésert, SC 2, Paris, 1949;

−−, *Stromata,* ed. O. Stählin, GCS 15, 17, Leipzig, 1906−9;

−−, ed./tr. A. le Boulluec, P. Voulet, SC 278−9, Paris, 1981.

[Clement of Rome], ed. B. Rehm, GCS 42, 51, Berlin, 1953, 1965.

Coffin Texts, ed./tr. R. O. Faulkner, Warminster, 1973−8.

Cornutus, *Theologiae Graecae compendium,* ed. C. Lang, BSGRT, Leipzig, 1881.

Corpus Hermeticum, ed./tr. A. D. Nock, A. -J. Festugière, CUFr, Paris, 1945−54.

Cumont, F: V. M. (ed.), *Textes=Textes et monuments figurés relatifs aux mystères de Mithra publiés avec une introduction critique,* Bruxelles, 1896−9.

Delatte, L. (ed.), *Les traités de la royauté d' Ecphante, Diotogène et Sthénidas,* BFPUL 97,Liège/Paris, 1942.

Demetrius of Phalerum, ed. F. Wehrli, Basel, 1949.

[Demetrius], *De elocutione,* ed. W. R. Roberts, Cambridge, 1902.

Demosthenes, ed. S. H. Butcher, W. Rennie, SCBO, Oxford, 1903−31.

Des Places, *Oracles:* see *Chaldaean Oracles.*

Didascalia, ed. H. Achelis, J. Flemming, *Die älteste Quellen des orientalischen Kirchenrechts* 2, TU 25.2, Leipzig, 1904.

Diehl, E. (ed.), *Anthologia lyrica Graeca,* Leipzig, 1950[3].

Diels, H. (ed.), *Poetarum=Poetarum Graecorum fragmenta* 3.1: *Poetarum philosophorum fragmenta,* Berlin, 1901.

Diels, H., Kranz, W. (ed./tr.), *Fragmente=Die Fragmente der Vorsokratiker,* Berlin, 1959/60[9].

Diezinger W., 'Toten'='Unter Toten freigeworden. Eine Untersuchung zu Römer III−VIII', in *NT* 5 (1962), 268−98.

Dio Cassius, ed. J. Melber, BSGRT, Leipzig, 1890−1928;

−−, ed./tr. E. Cary, LCL, London/New York, 1914−27.

Dio Chrysostom, ed./tr. J. W. Cohoon, H. L. Crosby, LCL, London/New York, 1932−51.

Diodorus Siculus, ed./tr. C. H. Oldfather *et al.,* LCL, London/New York, 1933−67.

Diogenes Laertius, ed./tr. R. D. Hicks, LCL, London/New York, 1925.

Dionysius of Halicarnassus, *Antiquitates Romanae,* ed./tr. E. Cary, LCL, London/New York/Cambridge MA, 1937−50.

Dungan, D. L., Cartlidge, D. R. (ed.), *Sourcebook=Sourcebook of Texts for the Comparative Study of the Gospels: Literature of the Hellenistic and Roman Period Illuminating the Milieu and Character of the Gospels,* SBLSBS 1, Missoula, Montana, 1973[3].

Edmonds, J. M. (ed.), *The Greek Bucolic Poets,* LCL, London/New York, 1912.

Ehrenberg, V., Jones, A. H. M. (ed.), *Documents=Documents Illustrating the Reigns of Augustus and Tiberius,* Oxford, 1949.

1 Enoch: ed. R. H. Charles, Oxford, 1893;

−−, ed. M. Black, *Apocalypsis Henochi Graeca,* PVTG 3, Leiden, 1970;

−−, ed. J. T. Milik (with the collaboration of M. Black), *Books=The Books of Enoch: Aramaic Fragments of Qumrân Cave 4,* Oxford, 1976;

−−, ed. M. A. Knibb, Oxford, 1978;

−−, ed. S. Uhlig, JSHRZ 5.6, Gütersloh, 1984;

−−, ed. M. Black, SVTP 7, Leiden, 1985.

2 Enoch: ed./tr. A. Vaillant, Textes publiés par l' Institut d'Études Slaves 4, Paris, 1952.

Epictetus, ed./tr. W. A. Oldfather, LCL, London/New York, 1926−8.

Epicurus, ed./tr. C. Bailey, Oxford, 1926.

Epiphanius, *Panarion*, ed. K. Holl, GCS 25, 31, 37, Leipzig, 1915–33; GCS 31 ed. J. Dummer, Berlin, 1980[2].

Eratosthenes, *Catasterismi*, ed. C. Robert, Berlin, 1963[2].

Erman, A. (ed./tr.), *Literature=The Literature of the Ancient Egyptians*, London, 1927.

Eunapius, ed./tr. W. C. Wright, LCL, London/New York, 1922.

Euripides, ed. G. Murray, SCBO, Oxford, 1902–13;

——, ed./tr. A. S. Way, LCL, London/New York, 1912–16;

——, *Bacchae*, ed. E. R. Dodds, Oxford, 1960[2];

——, ed./tr. G. S. Kirk, Cambridge, 1979 (repr. of 1970).

Eusebius, *Hieronymi Chronicon*, ed./tr. R. Helm, GCS 47, Berlin, 1956;

——, *Historia ecclesiastica*, ed./tr. J. E. L. Oulton, H. J. Lawlor, LCL, London/New York, 1927–8;

——, *Praeparatio evangelica*, ed. R. Helm, GCS 43, Berlin, 1954.

Eustathius, *Commentarius ad Homeri Odysseam*, ed. G. Stallbaum, Leipzig, 1825–6.

Firmicus Maternus, *De errore profanarum religionum*, ed. K. Ziegler, BSGRT, Leipzig, 1907;

——, ed./tr. A. Müller, BKV 11, Kempten/München, 1913, 205–88;

——, ed. A Pastorino, Biblioteca di Studi Superiori 27, Firenze, 1969[2];

——, ed./tr. R. Turcan, CUFr, Paris, 1982;

——, *Mathesis*, ed. C. Sittl, BSGRT, Leipzig, 1894.

Foerster, W., Wilson, R. McL. (ed./tr.), *Gnosis=Gnosis: a Selection of Gnostic Texts*, Oxford, 1972–4.

Fränkel, M. (ed.), *Inschriften=Die Inschriften von Pergamon*, Sonderausgabe aus den Altertümer von Pergamon 8.1–2, Königliche Museen zu Berlin, Berlin, 1890–5.

Goodspeed, E. J. (ed.), *Die ältesten Apologeten*, Göttingen, 1914, repr. 1984.

Gow, A. S. F. (ed.), *Bucolici Graeci*, SCBO, Oxford, 1952.

Griffith, F. L. (ed./tr.), *Stories=Stories of the High Priests of Memphis: the Sethon of Herodotus and the Demotic Tales of Khamuas*, Oxford, 1900.

Harpocration, ed. W. Dindorf, Oxford, 1853, repr. Groningen, 1969.

Heliodorus, *Aethiopica*, ed./tr. R. M. Rattenbury, T. W. Lumb, J. Maillon, CUFr, Paris, 1935–43.

Heraclides Ponticus, ed. F. Wehrli, *Die Schule des Aristoteles*, Basel, 1953.

Heraclitus, *Quaestiones Homericae*, ed./tr. F. Buffière, CUFr, Paris, 1962.

Heraclitus of Ephesus, ed. R. Mondolfo, L. Taran, Biblioteca di Studi Superiori 59, Firenze, 1972.

Herodotus, ed. C. Hude, SCBO, Oxford, 1927[3].

Hesiod, ed./tr. H. G. Evelyn-White, LCL, London/New York, 1936[3];

——, *Opera et dies*, ed. T. A. Sinclair, London, 1932;

——, ed. M. L. West, Oxford, 1978.

Hesychius of Alexandria, ed. K. Latte, Copenhagen, 1953–.

Himerius, ed. A. Colonna, Scriptores Graeci et Latini consilio Academiae Lynceorum editi, Roma, 1951.

Hippolytus of Rome, *Exegetische und homiletische Schriften*, ed. G. N. Bonwetsch, H. Achelis, GCS 1, Leipzig, 1897;

——, *Refutatio omnium haeresium*, ed. P. Wendland, GCS 26, Leipzig, 1916;

——, ed./tr. F. Legge, Translations of Christian Literature, Series 1: Greek Texts, London, 1921.

Homer, ed. D. B. Monro, T. W. Allen, SCBO, Oxford, 1906–12.

Homeric Hymns, ed. H. G. Evelyn-White, LCL, London/New York, 1936[3].

Hopfner, T. (ed.), *Fontes=Fontes historiae religionis Aegypticae*, Bonn, 1922.

Horace, *Carmina; Epodi*, ed./tr. C. E. Bennett, LCL, London/New York, 1914.

Hornung, E. (ed./tr.), *Unterweltsbücher=Ägyptische Unterweltsbücher*, Zürich/München, 1972;

——, *Buch=Das Buch der Anbetung des Re im Westen*, Aegyptiaca Helvetica 2–3, 1975–6;

——, *Schrift=Die Schrift des verborgenen Raumes*, ÄA 7, Wiesbaden, 1963–7.

Horsley, G. H. R. (ed.), *Documents=New Documents Illustrating Early Christianity* 1: *A Review of the Greek Inscriptions and Papyri Published in 1976*, Macquarie University, 1981.

Horst, P. C. van der (ed.), *Les vers d'or pythagoriciens*, Leiden, 1932.

Hunt, A. S., Edgar, C.C. (ed./tr.), *Papyri=Select Papyri,* LCL, London/New York, 1932–4.
Hyginus, *Fabulae,* ed. H. I. Rose, Leiden, 1963².

Iamblichus, *De mysteriis,* ed./tr. E. des Places, CUFr, Paris, 1966;
––, *De vita Pythagorica,* ed. L. Deubner, U. Klein, BSGRT, Stuttgart, 1975.
Irenaeus, *Adversus haereses,* ed. W. W. Harvey, Cambridge, 1857.
Isocrates, ed./tr. G. Norlin, L. van Hook, LCL, London/New York/Cambridge MA, 1928–45.

Joseph and Aseneth, ed. M. Battifol, Studia patristica 1–2, Paris, 1889–90;
––, tr. E. W. Brooks, Translations of Early Documents, Series 2: Hellenistic-Jewish Texts, London, 1918;
––, ed./tr. M. Philonenko, StPB 13, Leiden, 1968;
––, tr. C. Burchard, JSHRZ 2.4, Gütersloh, 1983.
Josephus, ed. B. Niese, Berlin, 1955²;
––, ed./tr. H. St J. Thackeray, R. Marcus *et al.,* LCL, London/New York/Cambridge MA, 1926–65.
Jubilees, ed./tr. R. H. Charles, London, 1902;
––, ed./tr. K. Berger, JSHRZ 2.3, Gütersloh, 1981.
Julian, ed./tr. W. C. Wright, LCL, London/New York, 1913.
Junker, H. (ed.), 'Preis'='Ein Preis der Isis aus den Tempeln von Philae und Kalabsa', in *AAWW* 1957.18, Wien, 1958, 267–76;
––, *Pylon=Der große Pylon des Tempels der Isis in Philä,* DÖAW.PH Sonderband, Wien, 1958;
––, *Stundenwachen=Die Stundenwachen in den Osirismysterien nach den Inschriften von Dendera, Edfu und Philae,* DAWW.PH 54, Wien, 1910.
Junker, H., Winter, E. (ed.), *Geburtshaus=Das Geburtshaus des Tempels der Isis in Philä,* DÖAW. PH Sonderband, Wien, 1965.
Justin Martyr, ed. J. C. T. Otto, Jena, 1847–9.

Kaibel, G. (ed.), *Epigrammata=Epigrammata Graeca ex lapidibus conlecta,* Berlin, 1878.

Lactantius, ed. S. Brandt, G. Laubmann, CSEL 19, 27, Prag/Wien/Leipzig, 1890, 1897.
Langdon, S., *Psalms=Sumerian and Babylonian Psalms,* Paris, 1909.
Lehmann, K., Lewis, N. (ed.), *Samothrace* 1: *The Ancient Literary Sources,* London, 1959.
Lehmann, K., Fraser, P. M. (ed.), *Samothrace* 2: *The Inscriptions on Stone,* London, 1960.
Leipoldt, J., Schenke, H.-M. (ed.), *Schriften=Koptisch-gnostische Schriften aus den Papyrus-Codices von Nag-Hamadi,* ThF 20, Hamburg-Bergstedt, 1960.
Lenger, M.-T. (ed.), *Corpus=Corpus des ordonnances des Ptolemées,* MAB.L 2nd series 64, Bruxelles, 1980.
Leutsch, E. L. A., Schneidewin, F. G.(ed.), *Paroemiographi Graeci,* Göttingen, 1839–51.
Lidzbarski, M. (ed./tr.), *Ginza=Ginza: der Schatz oder das große Buch der Mandäer,* QRG 13.4, Göttingen, 1925, repr. 1978.
Livy, ed./tr. E. T. Sage, LCL, London/New York/Cambridge MA, 1922–59.
Lobel E., Page, D. L. (ed.), *Poetarum Lesbiorum fragmenta,* Oxford, 1955.
[Longinus], *De sublimitate,* ed. D. A. Russell, Oxford, 1964.
Lucan, ed./tr. J. D. Duff, LCL, London(New York, 1928.
Lucian, ed./tr. A. M. Harmon *et al.,* LCL, London/New York, 1913;
––, *De dea Syria,* ed./tr. H. W. Attridge, R. A. Oden, SBLTT 9: Graeco-Roman Religion Series 1, Missoula, 1976.
Lucretius, ed./tr. C. Bailey, Oxford, 1947.
Lycophron, ed. E. Scheer, Berlin, 1881, 1908;
––, ed./tr. A. W. Mair, LCL, London/New York, 1921.
Lydus, Johannes, *De mensibus,* ed. R. Wuensch, BSGRT, Leipzig, 1898.
Lysias, ed. C. Hude, SCBO, Oxford, 1913.

McCrum, M., Woodhead, A. G. (ed.), *Documents=Select Documents of the Principates of the Flavian Emperors Including the Year of Revolution, A. D. 68–96,* Cambridge, 1961.

Malherbe, A. J. *et al.*, (ed./tr.), *Epistles=The Cynic Epistles*, SBLSBS 12, Missoula, 1977.
Marinus, *Vita Procli*, ed. J. F. Boissonade, Scriptorum Graecorum bibliotheca, Paris, 1850.
Maximus of Tyre, ed. H. Hobein, BSGRT, Leipzig, 1910.
Merkelbach, R. (ed.), 'Der orphische Papyrus von Derveni', *ZPE* 1 (1967), 21–32.
Midrash on the Psalms, ed./tr. W. G. Braude, Yale Judaica Series 13, New Haven, 1959.
Midrash Rabbah, ed./tr. H. Freedman, M. Simon, London, 1939.
Milligan, G. (ed.), *Selections=Selections from the Greek Papyri*, Cambridge, 1912.
Minucius Felix, *Octavius*, ed./tr. G. H. Randall, LCL, London/New York, 1931;
– –, ed./tr. J. Beaujeu, CUFr, Paris, 1964.
Mishnah, ed./tr. H. Danby, Oxford, 1933;
– –, *Die Mischna-Pesachim*, ed./tr. G. Beer, Gießen, 1912;
– –, *Tractate Sanhedrin: Mishnah and Tosefta*, ed./tr. H. Danby, Translations of Early Documents, Series 3: Rabbinic Texts, London/New York, 1919.
'*Mithras Liturgy*', ed./tr. M. W. Meyer, SBLTT 10, Graeco-Roman Religion Series 2, Missoula, 1976.
Mynors, R. A. B. (ed.), *XII panegyrici Latini*, SCBO, Oxford, 1964.

Nauck: see *Tragicorum Graecorum fragmenta*.
NHC: *Library=The Nag Hammadi Library in English*, ed./tr. J. M. Robinson *et al.*, Leiden, 1977;
– –, (NHC 1.4) *Treatise on Resurrection: The Epistle to Rheginos: a Valentinian Letter on the Resurrection*, ed./tr. M. L. Peel (=*Epistle*), London, 1969;
– –, ed./tr. B. Layton (=*Treatise*), HDR, Missoula, 1979;
– –, ed./tr. J. E. Ménard (=*Traité*), BCNH Textes 12, Québec, 1983;
– –, (NHC 2.1, 3.1, 4.1) *Apocryphon of John: Die drei Versionen des Apocryphon des Johannes im koptischen Museum zu Alt-Kairo*, ed./tr. M. Krause, P. Labib, ADAI.K 1, Wiesbaden, 1962;
– –, (2.3) *Gospel of Philip*: ed./tr. R. McL. Wilson (=*Gospel*), London, 1962;
– –, ed./tr. J. E. Ménard, (=*Évangile*), Strasbourg/Paris, 1967;
– –, (NHC 2.6) *Exegesis on the Soul*: ed./tr. J. -M. Sevrin, BCNH Textes 9, Québec, 1983.
New Testament: *The New Testament in Modern English*, tr. J. B. Phillips (=*New Testament*), London, 1958;
– –, *The Greek New Testament*, ed. K. Aland *et al.*, United Bible Societies, 1975[3];
– –, ed. E. Nestle, K. Aland, Stuttgart, 1979[26].
Nonnus, *Dionysiaca*, ed. A. Ludwich, BSGRT, Leipzig, 1909–11.
Numenius: E. -A. Leemans, *Studie over den Wijsgeer Numenius van Apamea met Uitgave der Fragmenten*, MAB.L 37.2, Bruxelles, 1937;
– –, ed./tr. E. des Places, CUFr, Paris, 1973.

Odes of Solomon, ed./tr. J. H. Charlesworth, Oxford, 1973.
Olympiodorus, *In Platonis Phaedonem commentaria*, ed. W. Norvin, BSGRT, Leipzig, 1913.
Orators, Minor Attic, ed./tr. K. Maidment, J. O. Burrt, LCL, London/Cambridge MA, 1941, 1954.
Origen, *Contra Celsum*, ed. P. Koetschau, GCS 2–3, Leipzig, 1899.
Orosius, ed. C. Zangemeister, BSGRT, Leipzig, 1889.
Orphic Hymns, ed./tr. A. N. Athanassakis, SBLTT 12, Graeco-Roman Series 4, Missoula, 1977.
Ovid, *Fasti*, ed./tr. J. G. Frazer, LCL, London/New York, 1931;
– –, *Metamorphoses*, ed./tr. F. J. Miller, LCL, London/New York, 1916.

Page, D. L. (ed.), *Poetae=Poetae melici Graeci*, Oxford, 1962.
Papyrus Salt 825 (BM 10051); rituel pour la conservation de la vie en Égypte, Le, ed./tr. P. Derchain, MAB.L 58.1, Bruxelles, 1965.
Passover Haggadah, ed./tr. D. W. Marks, A. W. Löwy, London, 1887[3];
– –, ed./tr. Rabbi Back, E. Fleg, Paris, 1962.
Paton, W. R., Hick, E. L. (ed.), *Inscriptions=The Inscriptions of Cos*, Oxford, 1891.
Pausanias, ed./tr. W. S. Jones, H. A. Ormerod, LCL, London/New York, 1918–35.
Peek, W. (ed.), *Vers-Inschriften=Griechische Vers-Inschriften* 1: *Grab-Epigramme*, Berlin, 1955;

−−, *Isishymnus=Der Isishymnus von Andros und verwandte Texte*, Berlin, 1930.
Pesiqta de Rab Kahana, ed./tr. W. G. Braude, I. J. Kapstein, London, 1975.
Petronius, *Satyricon*, ed./tr. M. Heseltine, LCL, London/New York, 1913.
Philo of Alexandria, ed. L. Cohn, P. Wendland, Berlin, 1896–1915 (index by J. Leisegang, 1926);
−−, ed./tr. F. H. Colson, G. H. Whitaker, R. Marcus, LCL, London/New York/Cambridge MA, 1929–62;
−−, *Fragments=Fragments of Philo Judaeus*, ed. J. R. Harris, Cambridge, 1886.
[Philo], *Liber antiquitatum biblicarum*, ed./tr. M. R. James, Translations of Early Documents, Series 1: Palestinian Jewish Texts (Pre-Rabbinic), London, 1917;
−−, ed./tr. G. Kisch, Publications in Mediaeval Studies of the University of Notre Dame 10, Notre Dame, 1949;
−−, ed./tr. D. J. Harrington *et al.*, SC 229–30, Paris, 1976.
Philostratus, *Heroicus*, ed. L. de Lannoy, BSGRT, Leipzig, 1977;
−−, *Vita Apollonii*, ed./tr. F. C. Conybeare, LCL, London/New York, 1912.
[Phocylides], ed./tr. P. W. van der Horst, SVTP 4, Leiden, 1978;
−−, ed./tr. N. Walter, JSHRZ 4.3, Gütersloh, 1983.
Photius, *Bibliotheca*, ed./tr. R. Henry, CBy, Paris, 1959–77;
−−, *Lexicon*, ed. R. Porson, Cambridge, 1822;
−−, ed. S. A. Naber, Leiden, 1864–5.
Piankoff, A. (ed./tr.), *The Litany of Re*, BollS 40.4, New York, 1964;
−−, *Le livre du jour et de la nuit*, Bibliothèque d' Étude 13, Cairo, 1942.
Pindar, ed./tr. J. Sandys, LCL, London/New York, 1915;
−−, ed. C. M. Bowra, SCBO, Oxford, 1935;
−−, ed. B. Snell, BSGRT, Leipzig, 1964[3].
Pirqe Rabbi Eliezer, ed./tr. G. Friedlander, New York, 1916.
Plato, ed. C. F. Hermann, M. Wohlrab, Leipzig, 1873–94[2];
−−, ed. J. Burnet, SCBO, Oxford, 1903–10;
−−, ed./tr. H. N. Fowler *et al.*, LCL, London/New York, 1913–29;
−−, *Gorgias*, ed. E. R. Dodds, Oxford, 1959.
[Plato], *Axiochus*, ed./tr. J. P. Hershbell, SBLTT 21, Graeco-Roman Religion Series 6, Chico CA, 1981.
Plautus, ed./tr. P. Nixon, LCL, London/New York, 1916–38.
Pliny the Elder, *Historia naturalis*, ed./tr. H. Rackham *et al.*, LCL, London/New York/Cambridge MA, 1938–63.
Plotinus, ed./tr. A. H. Armstrong, LCL, London/Cambridge MA, 1966–;
−−, *Enneades*, ed./tr. E. Bréhier, CUFr, Paris, 1924–38.
Plutarch, *Vitae parallelae*, ed./tr. B. Perrin, LCL, London/New York, 1914–26;
−−, ed./tr. R. Flacelière *et al.*, CUFr, Paris, 1957–83;
−−, ed. K. Ziegler, H. Gärtner, BSGRT, Leipzig, 1959–80;
−−, *Moralia*, ed./tr. F. C. Babbitt *et al.*, LCL, London/New York/Cambridge MA, 1927–;
−−, *De Iside et Osiride*, ed./tr. J. G. Griffiths, Univ. of Wales, 1970.
Pollux, ed. E. Bethe, Lexicographi Graeci 9, Leipzig, 1900.
Polybius, ed./tr. W. R. Paton, LCL, London/New York, 1925.
Porphyry, ed. A. Nauck, Leipzig, 1886[2];
−−, *De abstinentia*, ed./tr. J. Bouffartigue, M. Patillon, CUFr, Paris, 1977–;
−−, *Vita Plotini*, ed./tr. A. H. Armstrong, LCL, London/Cambridge MA, 1966.
Powell, J. U. (ed.), *Collectanea=Collectanea Alexandrina: reliquiae minores poetarum Graecorum aetatis Ptolemaicae 323–146 A.C.: epicorum, elegiacorum, lyricorum, ethicorum*, Oxford, 1925.
Proclus, *In Platonis Alcibiadem I commentarius*, ed./tr. L. G. Westerink, Amsterdam, 1954;
−−, ed./tr. W. O'Neill, Hague, 1965;
−−, *In Platonis Rem Publicam commentarii*, ed. W. Kroll, BSGRT, Leipzig, 1899;
−−, *In Platonis Timaeum commentarii*, ed. E. Diehl, Leipzig, 1903–6;
−−, *Theologia Platonica*, ed./tr. H. D. Saffrey, L. G. Westerink, CUFr, Paris, 1968–.
Propertius, ed./tr. H. E. Butler, LCL, London/Cambridge MA, 1952.
Prudentius, ed./tr. H. J. Thomson, LCL, London/Cambridge MA, 1949–53.

Pyramid Texts, ed./tr. K. Sethe, Glückstadt/Hamburg, 1935–62.

Quandt, W. (ed.), *De Baccho ab Alexandri aetate in Asia Minore culto,* Diss. philol. Halenses 21.2, Halle, 1913.
Qumran Texts: *The Dead Sea Scrolls in English,* ed./tr. G. Vermes, Harmondsworth, 1962;
––, *Die Texte aus Qumran,* ed./tr. E. Lohse (*=Texte*), München, 1964;
––, (CD) *The Zadokite Documents,* ed./tr. C. Rabin, Oxford, 1958²;
––, (1QH) *Hodayot: Psalms from Qumran,* ed./tr. S. Holm-Nielsen (*=Hodayot*), AThD 2, Aarhus, 1960;
––, *The Thanksgiving Hymns,* ed./tr. M. Mansoor (*=Hymns*), STDJ 3, Leiden, 1961;
––, *Les Hymnes de Qumran (Hodayot),* ed./tr. M. Delcor (*=Hymnes*), Paris, 1962;
––, (1QS) *The Manual of Discipline,* ed./tr. P. Wernberg-Møller (*=Manual*), STDJ 1, Leiden, 1957;
––, (4Q Serek Širot ʿolat haššabbat) 'The Angelic Liturgy at Qumran . . .', ed./tr. J. Strugnell (='Liturgy'), in *Congress Volume, Oxford, 1959,* VT.S 7, Leiden, 1960, 318–45.

Rice, D. G., Stambaugh, J. E. (ed./tr.), *Sources=Sources for the Study of Greek Religion,* SBLSBS 14, Missoula, 1979.
Riese, A. (ed.), *Anthologia=Anthologia Latina* 1, BSGRT, Leipzig, 1894.
Rießler, P. (ed./tr.), *Schrifttum=Altjüdisches Schrifttum außerhalb der Bibel,* Heidelberg, 1966².

Sallust, *De diis et mundo,* ed./tr. A. D. Nock, Cambridge, 1926;
–'–, ed./tr. G. Rochefort, CUFr, Paris, 1960.
Schmidt, C., Till, W. (ed./tr.), *Koptisch-gnostiche Schriften* 1: *Die Pistis Sophia; die beiden Bücher des Jeû; unbekanntes altgnostisches Werk,* GCS 45 (13), Berlin, 1954².
Scholia: Scholia Aristophanica, ed. W. G. Rutherford, London, 1896;
––, *Scholia Graeca in Euripidis tragoedias . . .,* ed. W. Dindorf, Oxford, 1863;
––, *Scholia Graeca in Homeri Iliadem,* ed. W. Dindorf, E. Maass, Oxford, 1875–88;
––, *Scholia Graeca in Homeri Iliadem,* ed. H. Erbse, Berlin, 1969–83;
––, *Scholia Graeca in Homeri Odysseam,* ed. W. Dindorf, Oxford, 1855;
––, *Scholia in Iuvenalem vetustiora,* ed. P. Wessner, BSGRT, Leipzig, 1931;
––, *Scholia in Lucianum,* ed. H. Rabe, BSGRT, Leipzig, 1906;
––, *Scholia vetera in Pindari carmina,* ed. A. B. Drachmann, BSGRT, Leipzig, 1903–27;
––, *Scholia in Sophoclis tragoedias vetera,* ed. P. N. Papageorgius, BSGRT, Leipzig, 1888.
Scriptores Historiae Augustae, ed./tr. D. Magie, LCL, London/New York, 1932.
Seneca, *Moral Essays,* ed./tr. J. W. Basore, LCL, London/New York, 1928–35;
––, *Ad Lucilium epistulae morales,* ed./tr. R. M. Gummere, LCL, London/New York, 1917–25;
––, ed. L. D. Reynolds, SCBO, Oxford, 1965;
––, *Apocolocyntosis,* ed./tr. W. H. D. Rouse, LCL, London/New York, 1913;
––, *Naturales quaestiones,* ed./tr. T. H. Corcoran, LCL, London/Cambridge MA, 1971–2.
Septuaginta, ed. A. Rahlfs, Stuttgart, 1962⁷.
Servius, *In Vergilii Bucolica et Georgica commentarii,* ed. G. Thilo, Leipzig, 1887.
Sextus Empiricus, ed./tr. R. G. Bury, LCL, London/New York/Cambridge MA, 1933–49.
Sherk, R. K., *Rome=Rome and the Greek East,* Cambridge, 1984.
Smallwood, E. M. (ed.), *Documents* (1966)*=Documents Illustrating the Principates of Nerva, Trajan and Hadrian,* Cambridge, 1966;
––, *Documents* (1967)*=Documents Illustrating the Principates of Gaius, Claudius and Nero,* Cambridge, 1967.
Sophocles, ed./tr. F. Storr, LCL, London/New York, 1912–13.
Sparks, H. F. D. *et al.,* (ed./tr.), *Apocryphal OT=The Apocryphal Old Testament,* Oxford, 1984.
Spiegel, J., *Auferstehungsritual=Das Auferstehungsritual der Unas-Pyramids: Beschreibung und erläuterte Übersetzung,* ÄA 23, Wiesbaden, 1971.
Statius, ed./tr. J. H. Mozley, LCL, London/New York, 1928.
Steindorff, G. (ed./tr.), *Die Apokalypse des Elias, eine unbekannte Apokalypse und Bruchstücke der Sophonias-Apokalypse,* TU N. F. 2.3a, Berlin, 1899.

Stobaeus, ed. C. Wachsmuth, O. Hense, Berlin, 1884–1912.
Stone, M., Strugnell, J. (ed./tr.), *Books=The Books of Elijah*, SBLTT 18, Missoula, 1979.
Strabo, ed./tr. H. L. Jones, LCL, London/New York, 1917–32.
Suetonius, ed./tr. J. C. Rolfe, LCL, London/New York, 1914.
Suidas, ed. A. Adler, Leipzig, 1928–38.
Sukenik, E. L. (ed.), *The Dead Sea Scrolls of the Hebrew University*, Jerusalem, 1955.

Tacitus, *Annales*, ed. C. D. Fisher, SCBO, Oxford, 1906;
––, *Historiae*, ed. C. D. Fisher, SCBO, Oxford, 1911.
Talmud, Babylonian, ed./tr. I. Epstein, London, 1935–52.
Talmud, Jerusalem, ed./tr. M. Hengel *et al.*, Tübingen, 1975–.
Targums of Onkelos and Jonathan ben Uzziel on the Pentateuch with the Fragments of the Jerusalem Targum from the Chaldee, ed./tr. J. W. Etheridge, London, 1865.
Tertullian, ed. E. Dekkers *et al.*, CChr. SL 1–2, Turnholt, 1954;
––, *Apologia; De spectaculis*, ed./tr. T. R. Glover, LCL, London/Cambridge MA, 1960;
––, *De resurrectione mortuorum*, ed./tr. E. Evans, London, 1960.
Testament of Abraham, ed./tr. M. R. James, TaS 2, Cambridge, 1892;
––, ed./tr. G. H. Box, S. Gaselee, Translations of Early Documents Series 2, Hellenistic Jewish Texts, London, 1927;
––, ed./tr. M. Delcor, SVTP 2, Leiden, 1973.
Testament of Job, ed./tr. B. Schaller, JSHRZ 3.3, Gütersloh, 1979.
Theocritus, ed./tr. A. S. F. Gow, Cambridge, 1950.
Theon of Smyrna, ed./tr. J. Dupuis, Paris, 1892.
Thiel, H. van (ed./tr.), *Leben=Leben und Taten Alexanders von Makedonien*, TzF 13, Darmstadt, 1974.
Tibullus, ed./tr. M. Pochont, CUFr, Paris, 1924.
Till, W. (ed./tr.), *Die gnostischen Schriften des koptischen Papyrus Berolinensis 8502*, TU 60, Berlin, 1955.
Tosefta, ed./tr. J. Neusner, New York, 1977–81.
Tragicorum Graecorum fragmenta, ed. A. Nauck, BSGRT, Leipzig, 1926².
Turchi, N. (ed.), *Fontes=Fontes historiae mysteriorum aevi Hellenistici*, Collezione ΓΡΑΦΗ 3, Roma, 1923.

Valerius Flaccus, ed./tr. J. H. Mozley, LCL, London/New York, 1934.
Valerius Maximus, *Factorum et dictorum memorabilium libri novem cum Iulii Paridis et Ianuarii Nepotiani epitomis*, ed. K. Kempf, BSGRT, Leipzig, 1888².
Vanderlip, V. F. (ed./tr.), *Hymns=The Four Greek Hymns of Isidorus and the Cult of Isis*, ASP 12, Toronto, 1972.
Varro, *Saturarum Menippearum fragmenta*, ed. R. Astbury, BSGRT, Leipzig, 1985.
Vergil, *Eclogae*, ed. R. Coleman, Cambridge, 1977.
Vidman, L. (ed.), *Sylloge=Sylloge inscriptionum religionis Isiacae et Sarapiacae*, RVV 28, Berlin, 1969.

Walz, C., *Rhetores=Rhetores Graeci*, Stuttgart, 1832–6.

Xenocrates: ed. R. Heinze, *Xenokrates: Darstellung der Lehre und Sammlung der Fragmente*, Leipzig, 1892, repr. Hildesheim, 1965.
Xenophon, *Anabasis*, ed./tr. C. L. Brownson, LCL, London/Cambridge MA, 1947;
––, *Cynegeticus*, ed./tr. E. Delebecque, CUFr, Paris, 1970;
––, *Cyropaedia*, ed./tr. W. Miller, LCL, London/New York, 1914;
––, *Hellenica*, ed./tr. C. L. Brownson, LCL, London/New York, 1918–21;
––, *Scripta minora*, ed. E. C. Marchant, LCL, London/Cambridge MA, 1971;
––, *Symposium; Apologia Socratis*, ed./tr. O. J. Todd, LCL, London/Cambridge MA, 1947.
[Xenophon], *Atheniensium respublica*, ed./tr. G. W. Bowersock, LCL, London/Cambridge MA, 1971.
Xenophon of Ephesus, *Ephesiaca*, ed./tr. G. Dalmeyda, CUFr, Paris, 1926.

2. Secondary

Abbott, T. K., *Eph-Col=The Epistles to the Ephesians and to the Colossians*, ICC, Edinburgh, 1897.

Aland, K., 'Entstehung'='Entstehung des Corpus Paulinum', in id., *Neutestamentliche Entwürfe* (München, 1979) 302–50.

Albert K., *Religion=Griechische Religion und platonische Philosophie*, Hamburg 1980.

Alderink, L. J., *Creation=Creation and Salvation in Ancient Orphism*, American Classical Studies 8, Chico, 1981;

— —, 'Structure'='Mythical and Cosmological Structure in the Homeric Hymn to Demeter', in *Numen* 29 (1982), 1–16.

Alföldi, A., '*Regna*'='*Redeunt Saturnia regna* 7: Frugifer-Triptolemos im ptolemäischen Herrscherkult', in *Chiron* 9 (1979), 553–606.

Allo, E. -B., *1 Cor=Saint Paul: première épître aux Corinthiens*, EBib, Paris, 1956[2].

Altermath, F., *Corps=Du corps psychique au corps spirituel: interprétation de 1 Cor 15, 35–49 par les auteurs chrétiens des quatres premiers siècles*, BGBE 18, Tübingen, 1977.

Althaus, P., *Röm=Der Brief an die Römer*, NTD 6, Göttingen, 1954[8].

Anderson, H., *Jesus=Jesus and Christian Origins: a Commentary on Modern Viewpoints*, Oxford, 1964.

Angus, S., *Mystery-Religions=The Mystery-Religions and Christianity: a Study in the Religious Background of Early Christianity*, London, 1925.

Armstrong, A. H., 'Plotinus', in id. (ed.), *The Cambridge History of Later Greek and Early Medieval Philosophy* (Cambridge, 1967) 193–268.

Assmann, J., *Lieder=Liturgische Lieder an den Sonnengott: Untersuchungen zur altägyptischen Hymnik* 1, MÄS 19, Berlin, 1969.

Atallah, W., *Adonis=Adonis dans la littérature et l'art grec*, EeC 62, Paris, 1966.

Athanassiadi-Fowden, P., *Julian=Julian and Hellenism: an Intellectual Biography*, Oxford, 1981.

Aune, D. E., *Setting=The Cultic Setting of Realized Eschatology in Early Christianity*, NT.S 28, Leiden, 1972.

Bachmann, P., *1 Kor=Der erste Brief des Paulus an die Korinther*, KNT 7, Leipzig, 1905.

Balsdon, J. P. V. D., *Gaius=The Emperor Gaius (Caligula)*, Oxford, 1934.

Baltensweiler, H., *Ehe=Die Ehe im Neuen Testament: exegetische Untersuchungen über Ehe, Ehelosigkeit und Ehescheidung*, AThANT 52, Zürich, 1967.

Barley, N., *Structures=Symbolic Structures: an Exploration of the Culture of the Dowayos*, Cambridge/Paris, 1983.

Barrett, C. K., 'Christianity'='Christianity at Corinth', in *BJRL* 46 (1964), 269–97, repr. in *Studies in Paul* (London, 1982) 1–27;

— —, *1 Cor=A Commentary on the First Epistle to the Corinthians*, BNTC, London, 1968;

— —, 'Immortality'='Immortality and Resurrection', in *LQHR* 190 (1965), 91–102, repr. in (ed.) C. S. Duthie, *Resurrection and Immortality* (London, 1979) 68–88;

— —, *Rom=A Commentary on the Epistle to the Romans*, BNTC, London, 1962;

— —, *Spirit=The Holy Spirit and the Gospel Tradition*, London, 1947.

Barth, G., 'Erwägungen'='Erwägungen zu 1. Kor. 15,20–28', in *EvTh* 30 (1970), 515–27;

— —, *Taufe=Die Taufe in frühchristlicher Zeit*, Biblisch-theologische Studien 4, Neukirchen, 1981.

Barth, K., *Dogmatik 4.4=Kirchliche Dogmatik 4.4: Das christliche Leben: die Taufe als Begründung des christlichen Lebens*, Zürich, 1967;

— —, *Rom=The Epistle to the Romans*, Oxford, 1933 (ET of 1929[6]).

Barth, M., *Eph=Ephesians*, AncB 34/34a, Garden City, 1974;

— —, *Taufe=Die Taufe – ein Sakrament? Ein exegetischer Beitrag zum Gespräch über die kirchliche Taufe*, Zollikon-Zürich, 1951.

Bartsch, H. W., 'Argumentation'='Die Argumentation des Paulus in 1. Kor 15.3–11', in *ZNW* 55 (1964), 261–74;

— —, 'Eschatology'='Early Christian Eschatology in the Synoptic Gospels', in *NTS* 11 (1964–5), 387–97;

— —, 'Taufe'='Die Taufe im Neuen Testament', in *EvTh* 7 (1948–9), 75–100.

Baudissin, W. W., *Adonis=Adonis und Esmun: eine Untersuchung des Glaubens an Auferstehungs-götter und an Heilgötter*, Leipzig, 1911.

Bauer, K.-A., *Leiblichkeit=Leiblichkeit – das Ende aller Werke Gottes: die Bedeutung der Lei-blichkeit des Menschen bei Paulus*, StNT 4, Gütersloh, 1971.

Baumbach, G., 'Irrlehrer'='Die von Paulus im Philipperbrief bekämpften Irrlehrer', in (ed.) Tröger, *Gnosis* 293–310.

Baumgarten, J., *Paulus=Paulus und die Apokalyptik: die Auslegung apokalyptischer Überlieferun-gen in den echten Paulusbriefen*, WMANT 44, Neukirchen, 1975.

Beale, G. K., *Use=The Use of Daniel in Jewish Apocalyptic Literature and in the Revelation of St John*, Lanham, etc., 1984.

Beardslee, W. A., 'Saving'='Saving One's Life by Losing It', in *JAAR* 47 (1979), 57–72.

Beare, F. W., *Phil=A Commentary on the Epistle to the Philippians*, BNTC, London, 1959.

Beasley-Murray, G. R., *Baptism=Baptism in the New Testament*, London, 1963.

Beaujeu, J., 'Religion'='La religion de la classe sénatorial à l'époque des Antonins', in (ed.) M. Renard, R. Schilling, *Hommages à J. A. Bayet* (CollLat 70, Bruxelles, 1964) 54–75.

Beck, R., 'Soteriology' ='Soteriology, the Mysteries, and the Ancient Novel: Iamblichus *Babylonia-ca* as a Test-Case', in Bianchi-Vermaseren, *Soteriologia* 527–40.

Becker, J., *Auferstehung=Auferstehung der Toten im Urchristentum*, SBS 82, Stuttgart, 1976.

Beet, J. A., 'Sadducees'='The Corinthian Sadducees', in *Exp.* 2nd Ser. 1 (1881), 33–43, 147–57.

Beker, J. C., *Paul=Paul the Apostle: the Triumph of God in Life and Thought*, Philadelphia, 1980.

Bell, H. I., *Cults=Cults and Creeds in Graeco-Roman Egypt*, LMA, Liverpool, 1953.

Benoit, P., 'Rapports'='Rapports littéraires entre les épîtres aux Colossiens et aux Éphésiens', in *Exégèse et theologie* 3 (Paris, 1968), 318–34 (repr. from *Neutestamentliche Aufsätze*, FS J. Schmid, Regensburg, 1963, 11–22).

Beresford, A. J., *Concept=The New Testament Concept of Resurrection against Its Background*, Diss. Oxford, 1971.

Berger, K., *Auferstehung=Die Auferstehung des Propheten und die Erhöhung des Menschensohnes: traditionsgeschichtliche Untersuchungen zur Deutung des Geschickes Jesu in frühchristlichen Texten*, StUNT 13, Göttingen, 1976;

––, 'Hintergrund'= 'Zum traditionsgeschichtlichen Hintergrund christologischer Hoheitstitel', in *NTS* 17 (1970–1), 391–425.

Bergman, J., 'Beiträge'='Kleine Beiträge zum Naassenertraktat', in (ed.) G. Widengren, *Proceedings of the International Colloquium on Gnosticism, Stockholm, August 20–25, 1973* (Stock-holm, 1972), 74–100;

– , *'Per omnia'='Per omnia vectus elementa remeavi:* Réflexions sur l'arrière-plan égyptien du voyage de salut d'un myste isiaque', in Bianchi-Vermaseren, *Soteriologia* 671–708.

Berner, W. D., *Initiationsriten=Initiationsriten in Mysterienreligionen, im Gnostizismus und im antiken Judentum*, Diss. Göttingen, 1973.

Beskow, P., 'Branding'='Branding in the Mysteries of Mithras?', in Bianchi, *Mysteria* 487–501.

Best, E., *Body=One Body in Christ: a Study of the Relationship of the Church to Christ in the Epistles of the Apostle Paul*, London, 1955;

––, 'Dead'='Dead in Trespasses and Sins (Eph. 2.1)', in *JSNT* 13 (1981), 9–25;

––, *Rom=The Letter of Paul to the Romans*, CNEB, Cambridge, 1967;

––, *1–2 Thess=A Commentary on the First and Second Epistles to the Thessalonians*, BNTC, London, 1972.

Betz, H. D., 'Formation'='The Formation of Authoritative Tradition in the Greek Magical Papyri', in Meyer-Sanders, *Self-Definition* 3, 161–170;

––, *Gal=Galatians: a Commentary on Paul's Letter to the Churches in Galatia*, Hermeneia, Phila-delphia, 1979;

––, *Lukian=Lukian von Samosata und das Neue Testament: religionsgeschichtliche und paräne-tische Parallelen: ein Beitrag zum Corpus Hellenisticum Novi Testamenti*, TU 76, Berlin, 1961;

––, 'Problem'='The Problem of Rhetoric and Theology according to the Apostle Paul', in (ed.) A. Vanhoye, *L'apôtre Paul: personnalité, style et conception du ministère* (BEThL 73, Leuven, 1986) 16–48;

idem (ed.), *Writings=Plutarch's Theological Writings and Early Christian Literature*, SCHNT 3, Leiden, 1975.

Bevan, E. R., *Sibyls=Sibyls and Seers,* Cambridge MA, 1929.

Bianchi, U., *Essays=Selected Essays on Gnosticism, Dualism and Mysteriosophy,* SHR 38, Leiden, 1978;

−−, *History=The History of Religions,* Leiden, 1975;

−−, 'Initiation'='Initiation, mystères, gnose. (Pour l'histoire de la mystique dans le paganisme gréco-oriental', in id., *Essays* 159−76 (repr. from Bleeker, *Initiation* 154−71);

−−, 'Iside'='Iside dea misterica. Quando?', in (ed.) Cattedra di Religioni del mondo classico dell' Università degli Studi di Roma, *Perennitas: studi in onore di Angelo Brelich,* Roma, 1980, 9−36;

−−, 'L'orphisme'='L'orphisme ,a existé', in id., *Essays* 187−95 (repr. from *Mélanges d'histoire des religions offerts à H. C. Puech,* 1974, 129−37);

idem, (ed.), *Mysteria=Mysteria Mithrae: Proceedings of the International Seminar on the 'Religio-Historical Character of Roman Mithraism, with Particular Reference to Roman and Ostian Sources',* Rome and Ostia, 28−31 March, 1978, EPRO 80, Leiden, 1979;

−−, *Mysteries=The Greek Mysteries,* IoR 17.3, Leiden, 1976;

idem (ed.), *Origins=The Origins of Gnosticism: Colloquium of Messina, 13−18 April, 1966,* SHR 12, Leiden, 1967;

−−, 'Problème' (1965)='Le problème des origines du gnosticisme et l'histoire des religions', in *Numen* 12 (1965), 161−78, repr. in id., *Essays* 219−36;

−−, 'Problème (1967)='Le problème des origines du gnosticisme', in id., *Origins* 1−27, repr. in id., *Essays* 237−63.

Bianchi, U., Vermaseren, M. J. (ed.), *Soteriologia=La soteriologia dei culti orientali nell'Impero Romano, Atti del Colloquio Internazionale su la soteriologia dei culti orientali nell'Impero Romano, Roma, 24−28 Settembre, 1979,* EPRO 92, Leiden, 1982.

Bickermann, E., *'Consecratio',* in Boer, *Culte* 3−25 (discussion 26−37).

Bidez, J., *Vie=Vie de Porphyre le philosophe néo-Platonicien,* Recueil de travaux publiés par la Faculté de Philosophie et Lettres, Université de Gaud 43, Gaud/Leipzig, 1913.

Bieler, L., ANHP=ΘΕΙΟΣ ANHP: *das Bild des "göttlichen Menschen" in Spätantike und Frühchristentum.* Wien, 1935−6, repr. Darmstadt, 1976.

Black II, C. C., 'Perspectives'='Pauline Perspectives on Death in Romans 5−8', in *JBL* 103 (1984), 413−33.

Black, M., *Rom=Romans,* NCeB, London, 1973;

−−, *Scrolls=The Scrolls and Christian Origins: Studies in the Jewish Background of the New Testament.* Edinburgh, 1961.

Bleeker, C. J. (ed.), *Initiation=Initiation: Contributions to the Theme of the Study-Conference of the International Association for the History of Religions Held at Strasburg, September 17th to 22nd, 1964,* SHR 10, Leiden, 1965;

−−, 'Initiation'='Initiation in Ancient Egypt', in id., *Initiation* 49−58;

−−, 'Isis'='Isis as Saviour Goddess', in Brandon, *God* 1−16.

Blinkenburg, C., *Studien=Archäologische Studien,* Kopenhagen/Leipzig, 1904.

Bloch, M., Parry, J. (ed.), *Death=Death and the Regeneration of Life,* Cambridge, 1982.

Bömer, F., 'Untersuchungen'='Untersuchungen über die Religion der Sklaven in Griechenland und ·Rom. Dritte Teil: Die wichtigsten Kulte der griechischen Welt', in *AAWLM.G* 1961 no. 4, 243−509.

Boer, W. den (ed.), *Culte=Le culte des souverains dans l'empire romain,* Entretiens sur l'antiquité classique 19, Vandoeuvres-Genève, 1973.

Bonnard, P., *Gal=L'épître de saint Paul aux Galates,* CNT(N) 9, Neuchâtel, Paris, 1953, 1972[2];

−−, 'Mourir'='Mourir et vivre avec Jésus-Christ selon Saint Paul', in *RHPR* 36 (1956), 101−12;

−−, *Phil=L'épître de saint Paul aux Philippiens,* CNT(N) 10, Neuchâtel, Paris, 1950.

Bonnet, H., *Reallexikon=Reallexikon der ägyptischen Religionsgeschichte,* Berlin, 1952.

Borgen, P., 'Philo'='Philo of Alexandria', in (ed.) M. E. Stone, *Jewish Writings of the Second Temple Period* (CRI 2, Assen/Philadelphia, 1984) 233−82.

Bornkamm, G., 'Glaube'='Glaube und Vernunft bei Paulus', in id., *Studien zur Antike und Urchristentum* (BEvTh 28, München, 1959) 119−37, ET: id., *Early Christian Experience* (London, 1969) 29−46;

−−, 'Hoffnung'='Die Hoffnung im Kolosserbrief. Zugleich ein Beitrag zur Frage der Echtheit des

Briefes', in *Studien zum Neuen Testament und zur Patristik* (FS E. Klostermann, TU 77, Berlin, 1961) 56–64, repr. in id., *Geschichte und Glaube* 2 (BEvTh 53, München, 1971) 206–13;

– –, 'Lehre'='Die neutestamentliche Lehre von der Taufe', in *ThBl* 17 (1938), 42–52;

– –, 'Taufe'='Taufe und neues Leben bei Paulus', in id., *Das Ende des Gesetzes: Paulusstudien* (BEvTh 16, München, 1966), 34–50, ET: id., *Early Christian Experience* (London, 1969) 71–86.

Boulanger, A., 'Salut'='Le salut selon l'orphisme', in (ed.) L. H. Vincent, *Mémorial Lagrange* (Paris 1940) 69–70.

Bourke, M. M., 'Eucharist'='The Eucharist and Wisdom in First Corinthians', in *SPCIC 1961* (AnBib 17–18, Roma, 1963) 367–81.

Bousset, W., *Hauptprobleme=Hauptprobleme der Gnosis*, FRLANT 10, Göttingen, 1907;

– –, *Kyrios=Kyrios Christos: Geschichte des Christusglaubens von den Anfängen des Christentums bis Irenaeus*, Göttingen, 1913, 1965[5].

Bousset, W., Greßmann, H., *Religion=Die Religion des Judentums*, HNT 21, Tübingen,1966[4].

Bouttier, M., *En Christ=En Christ: étude d'exégèse et de théologie pauliniennes*, EHPhR 54, Paris, 1962.

Bowersock, G. W., 'Intellectuals'='Greek Intellectuals and the Imperial Cult in the Second Century A.D.', in Boer, *Culte* 179–206 (discussion 207–12);

– –, *Julian=Julian the Apostate*, London, 1978.

Boyancé, P., *Culte=Le culte des Muses chez les philosophes grecs: études d'histoire et de psychologie religieuses*, BEFAR 141, Paris, 1937;

– –, 'Mystères'='Sur les mystères d'Eleusis', in *REG* 75 (1962), 460–82;

– –, 'Remarques'='Remarques sur le salut selon l'orphisme', in *REA* 43 (1941), 166–71.

Brakemeier, G., *Auseinandersetzung=Die Auseinandersetzung des Paulus mit den Auferstehungsleugnern in Korinth: eine Untersuchung zu 1 Korinther 15*, Diss. Göttingen, 1968.

Brandenburger, E., *Adam=Adam und Christus: exegetisch-religionsgeschichtliche Untersuchung zu Römer 5,12–21 (1. Kor. 15)*, WMANT 7, Neukirchen, 1962;

– –, 'Auferstehung'='Die Auferstehung der Glaubenden als historisches und theologisches Problem', in *WuD* N. F. 9 (1967), 16–13;

– –, *Fleisch=Fleisch und Geist: Paulus und die dualistische Weisheit*, WMANT 29, Neukirchen, 1968.

Brandon, S. G. F. (ed.), *Dictionary=A Dictionary of Comparative Religion*, London, 1970;

– –, *God=The Saviour God*, Manchester, 1963;

– –, 'Kings'='Divine Kings and Dying Gods', in *HibJ* 53 (1955), 327–33;

– –, *History=History, Time and Deity*, Manchester, 1965;

– –, *Man=Man and His Destiny in the Great Religions*, Manchester, 1962;

– –, 'Significance'='The Significance of Time in Some Ancient Initiatory Rituals', in Bleeker, *Initiation* 40–8;

– –, 'Technique'='The Ritual Technique of Salvation in the Ancient Near East', in idem (ed.), *The Saviour God* (Manchester, 1963) 17–36.

Braumann, G. *Taufverkündigung=Vorpaulinische christliche Taufverkündigung bei Paulus*, BWANT 82, Stuttgart, 1962.

Braun, H., *Jesus=Jesus of Nazareth: the Man and His Time*, Philadelphia, 1979 (ET of Stuttgart, 1969);

– –, ' "Stirb" '='Das "Stirb und werde" in der Antike und im Neuen Testament', in id., *Gesammelte Studien zum Neuen Testament und seiner Umwelt* (Tübingen, 1967[2]) 136–58, repr. from (ed.) E. Wolf, W. Matthias, *Libertas Christiana* (FS Delekat, BEvTh 26, München, 1957) 9–29.

Breasted, J. H., *Development=Development of Religion and Thought in Ancient Egypt*, New York, 1912.

Bréhier, E., *Philon=Les idées philosophiques et religieuses de Philon d'Alexandrie*, Paris, 1908.

Bremmer, J., *Concept=The Early Greek Concept of the Soul*, Princeton, 1983.

Brown. R. E., *Conception=The Virginal Conception and Bodily Resurrection of Jesus*, London/Dublin, 1973.

Bruce, F. F., 'Book'='The Book of Daniel and the Qumran Community', in (ed.) E. E. Ellis, M. Wilcox, *Neotestamentica et semitica: Studies in Honour of Matthew Black* (Edinburgh, 1969) 221–35;

——, *Col; Eph=The Epistles to the Colossians, to Philemon, and to the Ephesians*, NIC, Grand Rapids, 1984;

——, *1–2 Cor=1 and 2 Corinthians*, NCeB, London, 1971;

——, *Gal=The Epistle of Paul to the Galatians: a Commentary on the Greek Text*, New International Greek Testament Commentary, Exeter, 1982;

——, *Rom=The Epistle of Paul to the Romans*, TNTC, London, 1963.

Bruhl, A., *Liber=Liber Pater: origine et expansion du culte dionysiaque à Rome et dans le monde romain*, BEFAR 165, Paris, 1953.

Brunner, H., *Grundzüge=Grundzüge der altägyptischen Religion*, Grundzüge 50, Darmstadt, 1983.

Budischovsky, M.-C., *Diffusion=La diffusion des cultes isiaques autour de la Mer Adriatique 1: Inscriptions et monuments*, EPRO 61, Leiden, 1977.

Buffière, F., *Mythes=Les mythes d'Homère et la pensée grecque*, CEA, Paris, 1956.

Buitkamp, J., *Auferstehungsvorstellungen=Die Auferstehungsvorstellungen in den Qumrantexten und ihr alttestamentlicher, apokryphischer, pseudepigraphischer und rabbinischer Hintergrund*, Diss. Groningen, 1963.

Bujard, W., *Untersuchungen=Stilanalytische Untersuchungen zum Kolosserbrief als Beitrag zur Methodik von Sprachvergleichen*, StUNT 11, Göttingen, 1973.

Bultmann, R., *Christianity=Primitive Christianity in Its Contemporary Setting*, London, 1960 (ET of Zürich, 1954[2]);

——, *2 Kor=Der zweite Brief an die Korinther*, ed. E. Dinkler, KEK 6, Göttingen, 1976;

——, *Stil=Der Stil der paulinischen Predigt und die kynisch-stoische Diatribe*, FRLANT 13, Göttingen, 1910;

——, *Theology=Theology of the New Testament*, London, 1952–5 (ET of Tübingen, 1948–53).

Burchard, C., 'Text'='Zum Text von "Joseph und Aseneth"', in *JSJ* 1 (1970), 3–34;

——, *Untersuchungen=Untersuchungen zu Joseph und Aseneth: Überlieferung – Ortsbestimmung*, WUNT 8, Tübingen, 1965;

——, *Zeuge=Der dreizehnte Zeuge: traditions- und kompositionsgeschichtliche Untersuchungen zu Lukas' Darstellung der Frühzeit des Paulus*, FRLANT 103, Göttingen, 1970.

Burger, C., *Schöpfung=Schöpfung und Versöhnung: Studien zum liturgischen Gut im Kolosser- und Epheserbrief*, WMANT 46, Neukirchen, 1975.

Burkert, W., 'Craft'='Craft versus Sect: the Problem of Orphics and Pythagoreans', in Meyer-Sanders, *Self-Definition* 3, 1–22, 183–9;

——, 'Funde'='Neue Funde zur Orphik', in *Informationen zum altsprachlichen Unterricht* 2 (1980), 27–42;

——, 'ΓΟΗΣ'='ΓΟΗΣ: zum griechischen "Schamanismus"', in *RMP* 105 (1962), 36–55;

——, *Homo=Homo necans: Interpretationen altgriechischen Opferriten und Mythen*, RVV 32, Berlin/New York, 1972 (ET: Berkeley/Los Angeles/London, 1983);

——, *Lore=Lore and Science in Ancient Pythagoreanism*, Cambridge MA, 1972 (ET of Nürnberg, 1962);

——, 'Orpheus'='Orpheus und die Vorsokratiker: Bemerkungen zum Derveni-Papyrus und zur pythagoreischen Zahlenlehre', in *AuA* 14 (1968), 93–114;

——, 'Orphism'='Orphism and Bacchic Mysteries: New Evidence and Old Problems', in *Center for Hermeneutical Studies in Hellenistic and Modern Culture: Colloquy* 28 (Berkeley, 1977), 1–8;

——, *Religion=Griechische Religion der archaischen und klassischen Epoche*, RM 15, Stuttgart, etc., 1977 (ET: Oxford, 1985).

Burton, E. de W., *Gal=A Critical and Exegetical Commentary on the Epistle to the Galatians*, ICC, Edinburgh, 1921.

Caird, G. B., *Letters=Paul's Letters from Prison*, NCB.NT, Oxford, 1976.

Callan, T., 'Prophecy'='Prophecy and Ecstasy in Graeco-Roman Religion and in 1 Corinthians', in *NT* 27 (1985), 125–40.

412 *Bibliography*

Carcopino, J., *Aspects=Aspects mystiques de la Rome païenne*, Paris, 1942;

−−, *Études =Études romaines* 1: *La basilique pythagoricienne de la Porte Majeure*, Paris, 1927.

Carlson, R. P., *Baptism=Baptism and Apocalyptic in Paul*, Diss. Union Theol. Seminary, Richmond VA/Ann Arbor MI, 1983.

Cavallin, H. C. C., *Life=Life after Death: Paul's Argument for the Resurrection of the Dead in 1 Cor 15* 1: *An Enquiry into the Jewish Background*, CB.NT 7.1, Lund, 1974.

Cerfaux, L., 'Influence'='Influence des mystères sur le Judaïsme alexandrin avant Philo', in *Muséon* 37 (1924), 28–88.

Charlesworth, J. H., *Pseudepigrapha and the NT=The Old Testament Pseudepigrapha and the New Testament: Prolegomena for the Study of Christian Origins*, MSSNTS 54, Cambridge, 1985.

Christ, F., 'Leben'='Das Leben nach dem Tode bei Pseudo-Phokylides', in *ThZ* 31 (1975), 140–9.

Clemen, C., *Einfluß=Der Einfluß der Mysterienreligionen auf das älteste Christentum*, RVV 13.1, Gießen, 1913.

Clinton, K., *Officials=The Sacred Officials of the Eleusinian Mysteries*, in TAPhS N.S. 64.3, Philadelphia, 1974.

Cole, S. G., *Theoi=Theoi Megaloi: the Cult of the Great Gods at Samothrace*, EPRO 96, Leiden, 1984.

Coleiro, E., *Introduction=An Introduction to Vergil's Bucolics with a Critical Edition of the Text*, Amsterdam, 1979.

Collange, J.-F., *Phil=The Epistle of Paul to the Philippians*, London, 1979 (ET of CNT(N), Neuchâtel/Paris, 1973).

Colpe, C., 'Einführung'='Einführung in die Geschichte und neue Perspektiven', in *OrRR* 1–40;

−−, 'Mithra-Verehrung'='Mithra-Verehrung, Mithras-Kult und die Existenz iranischer Mysterien', in (ed.) J. Hinnells, *Mithraic Studies: Proceedings of the First International Congress of Mithraic Studies* 2 (Manchester, 1975), 378–405;

−−, 'Struktur'='Zur mythologischen Struktur der Adonis-, Attis- und Osiris-Überlieferungen', in (ed.) W. Röllig, *Lisan mithurti* (FS W. v. Soden, Neukirchen, 1969) 23–44.

Conzelmann, H., *Eph; Kol=Der Brief an die Epheser; Der Brief an die Kolosser*, HNT 8, Göttingen, 1981[15];

−−, *1 Kor=Der erste Brief an die Korinther*, KEK 5, Göttingen, 1969;

−−, 'Paulus'='Paulus und die Weisheit', in *NTS* 12 (1965–6), 231–44;

−−, 'Schule'='Die Schule des Paulus', in (ed.) C. Andresen, G. Klein, *Theologia crucis – signum crucis* (FS E. Dinkler, Tübingen, 1979) 85–96.

Cosi, D. M., 'Salvatore'='Salvatore e salvezza nei misteri di Attis', in *Aevum* 50 (1976), 42–71.

Coutts, J., 'Ephesians i.3–14'='Ephesians i.3–14 and I Peter i.3–12', in *NTS* 3 (1956–7), 115–27;

−−, 'Relationship'= 'The Relationship of Ephesians and Colossians', in *NTS* 4 (1957–8), 201–7.

Crahay, R., 'Élements'='Éléments d'une mythopée gnostique dans la Grèce antique', in Bianchi, *Origins* 323–39.

Craik, E. M., *Aegean=The Dorian Aegean*, London, etc., 1980.

Cranfield, C. E. B., *Rom=A Critical and Exegetical Commentary on the Epistle to the Romans*, ICC, Edinburgh, 1957–9.

Croissant, J., *Aristote=Aristote et les mystères*, BFPUL 51, Liége/Paris, 1932.

Culianu, I. P., ' "Ascension" '='L' "ascension de l'âme" dans les mystères et hors les mystères', in Bianchi-Vermaseren, *Soteriologia* 276–302;

−−, '*Lunam*='*Inter lunam terrasque* . . .': incubazione, catalessi ed estasi in Plutarco', in (ed.) Cattedra di Religioni del mondo classico dell' Università degli Studi di Roma, *Perennitas: studi in onore di Angelo Brelich* (Roma, 1980) 149–72.

Cuming, E. J., ''Εποτίσθημεν'='Εποτίσθημεν (I Corinthians 12.13)', in *NTS* 27 (1980–1), 283–5.

Cumont, F. V. M., *After Life=After Life in Roman Paganism*, New Haven, 1922;

−−, *Lux=Lux perpetua*, Paris, 1949;

−−, *Religions/Religionen =Les religions orientales dans le paganisme romain*, AMG 24, Paris, 1924[4] (German translation: Stuttgart, 1981[8]).

Currie, S. D., ' "Speaking" '= ' "Speaking in Tongues": Early Evidence outside the New Testament Bearing on "Glōssais Lalein" ', in *Interp.* 19 (1965), 274–94.

Dahl, N. A., 'Adresse'='Adresse und Proömium des Epheserbriefs', in *ThZ* 7 (1951), 241–64;

––, 'Observations'='Form-critical Observations on Early Christian Preaching', in id., *Jesus in the Memory of the Early Church* (Minneapolis, 1976) 30–6, ET of (ed.) W. Eltester, *Neutestamentliche Studien für Rudolf Bultmann* (BZNW 21, Berlin, 1954) 3–9;

––, 'Paul'='Paul and the Church at Corinth according to I Cor. i.10–iv.21', in (ed.) W. R. Farmer, C. F. D. Moule, R. R. Niebuhr, *Christian History and Interpretation: Studies Presented to John Knox* (Cambridge, 1967) 313–335.

Danforth, L. M., *Rituals=Death Rituals of Rural-Greece*, Princeton, 1982.

Daube, D., *New Testament=The New Testament and Rabbinic Judaism*, London, 1956.

Dautzenberg, G., *Prophetie=Urchristliche Prophetie: ihre Erforschung, ihre Voraussetzungen im Judentum und ihre Struktur im ersten Korintherbrief*, BWANT 104, Stuttgart, 1975.

Daux, G., 'Inscriptions'='Trois inscriptions de la Grèce du Nord', in *CRAI* 1972, 478–93.

Davenport, G. L., *Eschatology=The Eschatology of the Book of Jubilees*, StPB 20, Leiden, 1971.

Davies P. R., 'Eschatology'='Eschatology at Qumran', in *JBL* 104 (1985), 39–55.

Davies, W. D., *Paul=Paul and Rabbinic Judaism: Some Rabbinic Elements in Pauline Theology*, London, 1955[2].

Davis, J. A., *Wisdom=Wisdom and Spirit: an Investigation of 1 Corinthians 1.18–3.20 against the Background of Jewish Sapiential Traditions in the Greco-Roman Period*, Lanham, etc., 1984.

Dean-Otting, M., *Journeys=Heavenly Journeys: a Study of the Motif in Hellenistic Jewish Literature*, Judentum und Umwelt 8, Frankfurt a. M., etc., 1984.

Deichgräber, R., *Gotteshymnus=Gotteshymnus und Christushymnus in der frühen Christenheit: Untersuchungen zu Form, Sprache und Stil der frühchristlichen Hymnen*, StUNT 5, Göttingen, 1967.

Delatte, A., *Études=Études sur la littérature pythagoricienne*, BEHE 217, Paris, 1915.

Delling, G., *Worship=Worship in the New Testament*, London, 1962 (ET of Göttingen, 1952 revised).

Denney, J., *Rom=St Paul's Epistle to the Romans*, in The Expositor's Greek Testament 2 (London, 1900), 555–725.

Des Places, E., 'Platon'='Platon et la langue des mystères', in *Annales de la Faculté des lettres et sciences humaines d'Aix* 38 (1964), 9–23, repr. in *Études Platoniciennes 1929–1979* (EPRO 90, Leiden, 1981) 83–98.

Detienne, M., *Dionysos=Dionysos Slain*, Baltimore/London, 1979;

––, *Gardens=Gardens of Adonis: Spices in Greek Mythology*, Hassocks, Sussex, 1977 (ET of Paris, 1972).

Deubner, L., *Feste=Attische Feste*, Berlin, 1932.

Dey, J., Παλιγγενεσία=Παλιγγενεσία: *ein Beitrag zur Klärung der religionsgeschichtlichen Bedeutung von Tit 3.5*, NTA 17.5, Münster, 1937.

Dibelius, M., 'Isis Initiation'='The Isis Initiation in Apuleius and Related Initiatory Rites', in (ed.) F. O. Francis, W. A. Meeks, *Conflict at Colossae: a Problem in the Interpretation of Early Christianity Illustrated by Selected Modern Studies*, SBLSBS 4, Missoula, 1975[2] (ET of SHAW.PH 8, 1917, also in (ed.) G. Bornkamm, H. Kraft, *Botschaft und Geschichte* 2, Tübingen, 1956);

––, *Pastoralbriefe=Die Pastoralbriefe*, HNT 13, Tübingen, 1931[2].

Dibelius, M., Conzelmann, H., *Pastoralbriefe=Die Pastoralbriefe*, HNT 13, Tübingen, 1955[3].

Dibelius, M., Greeven, H., *Kol; Eph=An die Kolosser, Epheser; an Philemon*, HNT 12, Tübingen, 1953[3].

Dieterich, A., *Mithrasliturgie=Eine Mithrasliturgie*, Leipzig/Berlin, 1910;

––, *Nekyia=Nekyia: Beiträge zur Erklärung der neutestamentlichen Petrusapokalypse*, Leipzig, 1893.

Diezinger, W., 'Toten'= Unter Toten freigeworden. Eine Untersuchung zu Römer III–VIII', in *NT* 5 (1962), 268–98.

Dillon, J. M., *Platonists=The Middle Platonists, 80 B.C. to A.D. 220*, London, 1977;

––, 'Self-Definition'='Self-Definition in Later Platonism', in Meyer-Sanders, *Self-Definition* 3, 60–75.

Dinkler, E., 'Römer 6.1–14.'='Römer 6.1–14 und das Verhältnis von Taufe und Rechtfertigung bei Paulus', in Lorenzi, *Battesimo* 83–103;

--, 'Taufaussagen'='Die Taufaussagen des Neuen Testaments: neu untersucht im Hinblick auf Karl Barths Tauflehre', in (ed.) K. Viering, *Zu Karl Barths Lehre von der Taufe* (Gütersloh, 1971) 60–153.

Dobschütz, E. von, *Life=Christian Life in the Primitive Church,* Theological Translation Library 13, London, 1904 (ET of *Die urchristlichen Gemeinden,* Leipzig, 1902).

Dodd, C. H., *Rom=The Epistle of Paul to the Romans,* MNTC, London, 1932.

Dodds, E. R., *Greeks=The Greeks and the Irrational,* Sather Classical Lectures 25, Berkeley/ Los Angeles, 1968 (repr. of 1951);

--, *Pagan=Pagan and Christian in an Age of Anxiety: Some Aspects of Religious Experience from Marcus Aurelius to Constantine,* Cambridge, 1965.

Dörrie, H., 'Kontroversen'='Kontroversen um die Seelenwanderung im kaiserzeitlichen Platonismus', in *Hermes* 85 (1957), 414–35;

--, 'Mysterien'='Mysterien (in Kult und Religion) und Philosophie', in *OrRR* 341–62.

Doren, E. van, 'Évolution'='L'évolution des mystères phrygiens à Rome', in *AnCl* 22 (1953), 79–88.

Dos Santos, E. C. (ed.), *Index=An Expanded Hebrew Index for the Hatch-Redpath Concordance to the Septuagint,* Jerusalem, n.d.

Doughty, D. J., 'Presence'='The Presence and Future of Salvation in Corinth', in *ZNW* 66 (1975), 61–90.

Drijvers, H. J. W., 'Quq'='Quq and the Quqites: an Unknown Sect in Edessa in the Second Century A.D.', in *Numen* 14 (1967), 104–29:

--, 'Ursprünge'='Die Ursprünge des Gnostizismus als religionsgeschichtliches Problem', in (ed.) K. Rudolph, *Gnosis und Gnostizismus* (WdF 262, Darmstadt, 1975), 798–841.

Dürrenmatt, F., *Komödien,* Zürich, 1957–66.

Dunand, F., *Culte=Le culte d'Isis dans le bassin oriental de la Méditerranée,* EPRO 26, Leiden, 1973.

Dunn, J. D. G., *Baptism=Baptism in the Holy Spirit: a Re-examination of the New Testament Teaching on the Gifts of the Spirit in Relation to Pentecostalism Today,* SBT 2nd Series 15, London, 1970;

--, *Christology=Christology in the Making: a New Testament Inquiry into the Origins of the Doctrine of the Incarnation,* London, 1980;

--, 'Congregation'='The Responsible Congregation (1 Co 14.26–40)', in Lorenzi, *Charisma* 201–36 (discussion on 237–69);

--, *Jesus=Jesus and the Spirit: a Study of the Religious and Charismatic Experience of Jesus and the First Christians as Reflected in the New Testament,* London, 1975;

--, *Unity=Unity and Diversity in the New Testament: an Inquiry into the Character of Earliest Christianity,* London, 1977.

Dupont, J., *Gnosis=Gnosis: la connaissance religieuse dans les épîtres de Saint Paul,* DGMFT Series 2.40, Louvain/Paris, 1949;

--, ΣΥΝ ΧΡΙΣΤΩΙ=ΣΥΝ ΧΡΙΣΤΩΙ: *l'union avec le Christ suivant Saint Paul* 1: '*Avec le Christ*' *dans la vie future,* Bruges/Louvain/Paris, 1952.

Duthoy, R., *Taurobolium=The Taurobolium: Its Evolution and Terminology,* EPRO 10, Leiden, 1969.

Easterling, P. E., Muir, J. V. (ed.), *Religion=Greek Religion and Society,* Cambridge, 1985.

Eliade, M., *Birth=Birth and Rebirth: the Religious Meanings of Initiation in Human Culture,* New York, 1958;

--, *Chamanisme=Le chamanisme et les techniques archaïques de l'extase,* Paris, 1951 (ET: BollS 76, New York, 1964);

--, *History=A History of Religious Ideas,* Chicago/London, 1978–82.

Ellis, E. E., 'Christ'='Christ Crucified', in (ed.) R. Banks, *Reconciliation and Hope: New Testament Essays on Atonement and Eschatology* (FS Leon Morris, Exeter, 1974) 69–75;

--, *Prophecy=Prophecy and Hermeneutic in Early Christianity: New Testament Essays,* WUNT 18, Tübingen, 1978;

--, *Use= Paul's Use of the Old Testament,* Edinburgh, 1957;

--, 'Wives'='The Silenced Wives of Corinth (1 Co 14.34–5)', in (ed.) E. J. Epp, G. D. Fee, *New*

Testament Textual Criticism: Its Significance for Exegesis (FS B. M. Metzger, Oxford, 1981) 213–20

Enslin, M. S., *Paul=Reapproaching Paul*, Philadelphia, 1972.

Erman, A., *Religion=Die Religion der Ägypter: ihr Werden und Vergehen in vier Jahrtausenden*, Berlin/Leipzig, 1934.

Ernst, J., *Eph; Kol=Die Briefe an die Philipper, an Philemon, an die Kolosser, an die Epheser*, RNT, Regensburg, 1974.

Evans, C. F., *Resurrection=Resurrection and the New Testament*, SBT 2nd Series 12, London, 1970.

Evans-Pritchard, E. E., 'Problem'='A Problem of Nuer Thought', in (ed.) J. Middleton, *Myth and Cosmos: Readings in Mythology and Symbolism* (Austin/London, 1967) 127–48.

Farnell, L. R., *Cults=The Cults of the Greek States*, Oxford, 1896–1909.

Fascher, E., 'Anastasis'='Anastasis – Resurrectio – Auferstehung', in *ZNW* 40 (1941–2), 166–229;

––, *1 Kor=Der erste Brief des Paulus an die Korinther* 1, ThHK 7.1, Berlin, 1980²;

––, 'Korintherbriefe'='Die Korintherbriefe und die Gnosis', in Tröger, *Gnosis* 281–91;

––, ΠΡΟΦΗΤΗΣ=ΠΡΟΦΗΤΗΣ: *eine sprach- und religionsgeschichtliche Untersuchung*, Geißen, 1927.

Fazekaš, L., 'Taufe'='Taufe als Tod in Röm 6.3ff', in *ThZ* 22 (1966), 305–18.

Fellmann, R., 'Belege'='Belege zum Sabazioskult im frühkaiserzeitlichen Legionslager von Vindonissa', in (ed.) S. Sahin, E. Schwertheim, J. Wagner, *Studien zur Religion und Kultur Kleinasiens* (FS F. K. Dörner, EPRO 66, Leiden, 1978) 1, 284–94;

––, 'Sabazios-Kult'='Der Sabazios-Kult', in *OrRR* 316–40.

Ferguson, J., *Religions=The Religions of the Roman Empire*, London, 1970.

Festugière, A. J., *Ideal=L'ideal religieux des Grecs et l'évangile*, Paris, 1932;

––, 'Mystères='Les mystères de Dionysos', in *RB* 44 (1935), 192–211, 366–96;

––, *Religion=Personal Religion among the Greeks*, Sather Classical Lectures 26, Berkeley, 1954 (repr. 1960);

––, *Révélation=La révélation d'Hermes Trismégiste: l'astrologie et les sciences occultes*, EtB, Paris, 1944–54.

Feuillet, A., 'Mort'='Mort du Christ et mort du Chrétien d'après les épîtres pauliniennes', in *RB* 66 (1959), 481–513.

Fischel, H. A., *Literature=Rabbinic Literature and Greco-Roman Philosophy: a Study of Epicurea and Rhetorica in Early Midrashic Writings*, StPB 21, Leiden, 1973.

Fischer, U., *Eschatologie=Eschatologie und Jenseitserwartung im hellenistischen Diasporajudentum*, BZNW 44, Berlin, 1978.

Fishwick, D., 'Cannophori'='The *Cannophori* and the March Festival of Magna Mater', in *TPAPA* 97 (1966), 193–202.

Flemington, W. F., *Doctrine=The New Testament Doctrine of Baptism*, London, 1948.

Foerster, W., 'Geist'='Der heilige Geist im Spätjudentum', in *NTS* 8 (1961–1), 117–34.

Fontenrose, J., *Oracle=The Delphic Oracle: Its Responses and Operations*, Berkeley, etc., 1978.

Frankemölle, H., *Taufverständnis=Das Taufverständnis des Paulus: Taufe, Tod und Auferstehung nach Röm 6*, SBS 47, Stuttgart, 1970.

Frankfort, H., *Kingship=Kingship and the Gods: a Study of Ancient Near Eastern Religion as the Integration of Society and Nature*, Chicago, 1948.

Fraser, P. M., *Alexandria=Ptolemaic Alexandria*, Oxford, 1972.

Frazer, J. G., *Bough³=The Golden Bough: a Study in Magic and Religion*, London, 1925–30³.

Frickel, J., *Erlösung=Hellenistische Erlösung in christlicher Deutung: die gnostische Naassenerschrift*, NHS 19, Leiden, 1984;

––, 'Naassener'='Naassener oder Valentinianer?', in (ed.) M. Krause, *Gnosis and Gnosticism* (NHS 17, Leiden, 1981) 95–119.

Friedrich, G., 'Lk 9.51'='Lk 9.51 und die Entrückungschristologie des Lukas', in (ed.) P. Hoffmann, N. Brox, W. Pesch, *Orientierung an Jesus: zur Theologie der Synoptiker* (FS J. Schmid, Freiburg, etc., 1973) 48–77.

Froitzheim, F., *Christologie=Christologie und Eschatologie bei Paulus*, FzB 35, Würzburg, 1979.

Früchtel, U., *Vorstellungen=Die kosmologischen Vorstellungen bei Philo von Alexandrien: ein Beitrag zur Geschichte der Genesisexegese*, ALGHL 2, Leiden, 1968.

Fuchs, E., 'Herrschaft'='Die Herrschaft Christi: zur Auslegung von 1. Korinther 6.12–20', in (ed.) H. D. Betz, L. Schottroff, *Neues Testament und christliche Existenz* (FS H. Braun, Tübingen, 1973) 183–93.

Fuller, R. H., *Formation=The Formation of the Resurrection Narratives*, London, 1980.

Funk, R. W., *Language=Language, Hermeneutic, and Word of God: the Problem of Language in the New Testament and Contemporary Theology*, New York, 1966.

·Fustel de Coulanges, N. D., *City=The Ancient City: a Study on the Religion, Laws, and Institutions of Greece and Rome*, Garden City NY, 1956 (ET of Paris, 1864).

Gäumann, N., *Taufe=Taufe und Ethik: Studien zu Römer 6*, BEvTh 47, München, 1967.

Gaffron, H. G., 'Apologie'='Eine gnostische Apologie des Auferstehungsglauben: Bemerkungen zur "Epistula ad Rheginum" ', in (ed.) G. Bornkamm, K. Rahner, *Die Zeit Jesu* (FS H. Schlier, Freiburg, 1970) 218–27.

Gager, J. G., 'Body-Symbols'='Body-Symbols and Social Reality: Resurrection, Incarnation and Asceticism in Early Christianity', in *Religion* 12 (1982), 345–63.

Gardiner, A. H., *Attitude=The Attitude of the Ancient Egyptians to Death and the Dead*, Cambridge, 1935.

Gardner, J. F. (ed.), *Leadership=Leadership and the Cult of the Personality*, London/Toronto, 1974.

Garland, R., *Way=The Greek Way of Death*, London, 1985.

Gasparro, G. S., 'Interpretazioni'='Interpretazioni gnostiche e misteriosofiche del mito di Attis', in (ed.) R. van den Broek, M. J. Vermaseren, *Studies in Gnosticism and Hellenistic Religions Presented to Gilles Quispel on the Occasion of His 65th Birthday* (EPRO 91, Leiden, 1981) 376–411;

——, *Soteriology=Soteriology and Mystic Aspects in the Cult of Cybele and Attis*, EPRO 103, Leiden, 1985.

Gennep, A. van, *Rites=The Rites of Passage*, London/Henley, 1960, 1977 (ET of Paris, 1901).

Georgi, D., 'Hymnus'='Der vorpaulinische Hymnus Phil 2.6–11', in (ed.) E. Dinkler, *Zeit und Geschichte* (FS R. Bultmann, Tübingen, 1964) 263–93.

Glotz, G., 'Fêtes'='Les fêtes d'Adonis sous Ptolemée II', in *REG* 33 (1920), 169–222.

Gnilka, J., *Eph=Der Epheserbrief*, HThK 10.2, Freiburg, etc., 1971;

——, *Kol=Der Kolosserbrief*, HThK 10.1, Freiburg, etc., 1980;

——, *Phil=Der Philipperbrief*, HThK 10.3, Freiburg, etc., 1968;

——, *Philemonbrief=Der Philemonbrief*, HThK 10.4, Freiburg, etc., 1982.

Godet, F., *1 Cor=Commentary on St Paul's First Epistle to the Corinthians*, Edinburgh, 1886–7.

Godwin, J., *Mystery Religions=Mystery Religions in the Ancient World*, London, 1981.

Goodenough, E.R., *Introduction=An Introduction to Philo Judaeus*, Oxford, 1962[2];

——, *Light=By Light, Light: the Mystic Gospel of Hellenistic Judaism*, New Haven, 1935;

——, 'Mystery'='Literal Mystery in Hellenistic Judaism', in (ed.) R. P. Casey, S. Lake, A. K. Lake, *Quantulacumque* (FS K. Lake, London, 1937) 227–41.

Goodspeed, E. J., *Meaning=The Meaning of Ephesians*, Chicago, 1933.

Goppelt, L., *Theologie=Theologie des Neuen Testaments*, UTB 850, Göttingen, 1978[3].

Gordon, R. L., 'Cumont'='Franz Cumont and the Doctrines of Mithraism', in (ed.) J. Hinnells, *Mithraic Studies* (Manchester, 1975) 1, 215–48;

——, 'Mithraism'='Mithraism and Roman Society: Social Factors in the Explanation of Religious Change in the Roman Empire', in *Religion* 2 (1972), 92–121.

Gould, J., 'Making'='On Making Sense of Greek Religion', in Easterling-Muir, *Religion* 1–33.

Gräßer, E., 'Kol 3,1–4'='Kol 3,1–4 als Beispiel einer Interpretation secundum homines recipientes', in *ZThK* 64 (1967), 139–68.

Graeve, V. von, 'Tempel'='Tempel und Kult der syrischen Götter am Janiculum', in *JdI* 87 (1972), 314–47.

Graf, F., *Eleusis=Eleusis und die orphische Dichtung Athens in vorhellenistischer Zeit*, RVV 33, Berlin/New York, 1974.

Graillot, H., *Culte=Le culte de Cybèle mère des dieux à Rome et dans l'empire romain*, BEFAR 107, Paris, 1912.

Grandjean, Y., *Aretalogie=Une nouvelle aretalogie d'Isis à Maronée*, EPRO 49, Leiden, 1975.

Grant, F. C., *Hellenism=Roman Hellenism and the New Testament*, Edinburgh/London, 1962.

Grant, R. M., 'Wisdom'='The Wisdom of the Corinthians', in (ed.) S. E. Johnson, *The Joy of Study: Papers on New Testament and Related Subjects Presented to Honor F. C. Grant* (New York, 1951) 51–5.

Greßmann, H., *Tod=Tod und Auferstehung des Osiris nach Restgebräuchen und Umzügen*, AO 23.3, Leipzig, 1923.

Griffiths, J. G., 'Concept'='The Concept of Divine Judgement in the Mystery Religions', in Bianchi-Vermaseren, *Soteriologia* 192–219;

— —, *Origins=The Origins of Osiris and His Cult*, SHR 40, Leiden, 1980;

— —, 'Search'='In Search of the Isles of the Blessed', in *GaR* 16 (1947), 122–6.

Grosheide, F. W., *1 Cor=Commentary on the First Epistle to the Corinthians*, NIC, Grand Rapids, 1953.

Grudem, W. A., *Gift=The Gift of Prophecy in 1 Corinthians*, Washington, 1982.

Gruenwald, I., *Apocalyptic=Apocalyptic and Merkavah Mysticism*, AGJU 14, Leiden/Köln, 1980.

Guarducci, M., 'Graffito'='Il graffito *natus prima luce* nel Mitreo di Santa Prisca', in Bianchi, *Mysteria* 153–63.

Güttgemanns, E., *Apostel=Der leidende Apostel und sein Herr: Studien zur paulinischen Christologie*, FRLANT 90, Göttingen, 1966.

Gundry, R. H., *Sōma=Sōma in Biblical Theology with Emphasis on Pauline Anthropology*, MSSNTS 29, Cambridge, 1976.

Gunkel, J. F. H., *Verständnis=Zum religionsgeschichtlichen Verständnis des Neuen Testaments*, Göttingen, 1903.

Gurney, O. R., 'Tammuz'='Tammuz Reconsidered: Some Recent Developments', in *JSSt* 7 (1962), 147–60.

Guthrie, W. K. C., *Greeks=The Greeks and Their Gods*, London, 1950;

— —, *History=A History of Greek Philosophy*, Cambridge, 1962– ;

— —, *Orpheus=Orpheus and Greek Religion: a Study of the Orphic Movement*, London, 1935, 1952[2].

Habicht, C., 'Zeit'='Die augusteische Zeit und das erste Jahrhundert nach Christi Geburt', in Boer, *Culte* 41–88 (discussion on 89–99).

Hahn, F., 'Taufe'='Die Taufe im Neuen Testament', in (ed.) H. Breit, M. Seitz, *Taufe* (CPH, Stuttgart, 1976) 9–28;

— —, 'Verständnis'='Das Verständnis der Taufe nach Römer 6', in (ed.) Protestantischer Landeskirchenrat der Pfalz, *Bewahren und Erneuern* (FS R. Y. Schaller, Speyer, 1980), 135–53.

Halifax, J., *Voices=Shamanic Voices: a Survey of Visionary Narratives*, Harmondsworth, 1980.

Halter, H., *Taufe=Taufe und Ethos: paulinische Kriterien für das Proprium christlicher Moral*, FThSt 106, Freiburg, etc., 1977.

Hamerton-Kelly, R. G., *Pre-existence=Pre-existence, Wisdom and the Son of Man: a Study of the Idea of Pre-existence in the New Testament*, MSSNTS 21, Cambridge, 1973.

Hanson, A. T., *Jesus Christ=Jesus Christ in the Old Testament*, London, 1965.

Hanson, R. P. C., *Allegory=Allegory and Event: a Study of the Sources and Significance of Origen's Interpretation of Scripture*, London, 1959.

Harnisch, W., *Existenz=Eschatologische Existenz*, FRLANT 110, Göttingen, 1973.

Harrison, J. E., *Epilegomena=Epilegomena to the Study of Greek Religion*, Cambridge, 1921;

— —, *Themis=Themis: a Study of the Social Origins of Greek Religion*, Cambridge, 1912.

Harrison, P. N., *Paulines=Paulines and Pastorals*, London, 1964.

Harrisville, R. A., 'Speaking'='Speaking in Tongues', in *CBQ* 38 (1976), 35–48.

Hartman, L., '1 Co 14.1–25'='1 Co 14.1–25: Argument and Some Problems', in Lorenzi, *Charisma* 149–69 (discussion on 170–99);

— —, 'Name'='Into the Name of Jesus', in *NTS* 20 (1973–4), 432–40.

Harvey, A. E., *Jesus=Jesus and the Constraints of History*, BaL 1980, London, 1982.

Hasenfratz, H. P., *Lebenden=Die toten Lebenden: eine religionsphänomenologische Studie zum sozialen Tod in archaischen Gesellschaften*, BZRGG 24, Leiden, 1982.

Haufe, G., 'Mysterien'='Die Mysterien', in Leipoldt-Grundmann, *Umwelt* 1, 101–26;

––, 'Taufe'='Taufe und Heiliger Geist im Urchristentum.', in *ThLZ* 101 (1976), 561–6.

Haulotte, E., *Symbolique=Symbolique du vêtement selon la Bible*, Theol(P) 65, Paris, 1966.

Hawthorne, G., *Phil=Philippians*, Word Biblical Commentary 43, Waco, 1983.

Hegermann, H., *Vorstellung=Die Vorstellung vom Schöpfungsmittler im hellenistischen Judentum und Urchristentum*, TU 82, Berlin, 1961.

Heitmüller, W., *'Im Namen Jesu'='Im Namen Jesu': eine sprach- und religionsgeschichtliche Untersuchung zum Neuen Testament, speziell zur altchristlichen Taufe*, FRLANT 1.2, Göttingen, 1903;

––, *Taufe* (1903)=*Taufe und Abendmahl bei Paulus: Darstellung und religonsgeschichtliche Beleuchtung*, Göttingen, 1903;

––, *Taufe* (1911)=*Taufe und Abendmahl im Urchristentum*, RV 1.22–3, Tübingen, 1911.

Hengel, M., 'Christologie'='Christologie und neutestamentliche Chronologie', in (ed.) H. Baltensweiler, B. Reicke, *Neues Testament und Geschichte: historisches Geschehen und Deutung im Neuen Testament* (FS O. Cullmann, Zürich/Tübingen, 1972) 43–67;

––, *Judaism=Judaism and Hellenism: Studies in Their Encounter in Palestine during the Early Hellenistic Period*, London, 1974 (ET of WUNT 10, Tübingen, 1973²);

––, 'Osterglaube'= 'Ist der Osterglaube noch zu retten?', in *ThQ* 153 (1973), 252–69;

––, *Sohn=Der Sohn Gottes: die Entstehung der Christologie und die jüdisch-hellenistische Religionsgeschichte*, Tübingen, 1975 (ET: London, 1976).

Henrichs, A., 'Identities'='Changing Dionysiac Identities', in Meyer-Sanders, *Self-Definition* 3, 13–60;

––, 'Glimpses'='Greek and Roman Glimpses of Dionysos', in (ed.) C. Houser, *Dionysos and His Circle: Ancient through Modern* (Cambridge MA, 1979) 1–11;

––, 'Maenadism'='Greek Maenadism from Olympias to Messalina', in *HSCP* 82 (1978), 121–60.

Hepding, H., *Attis=Attis, seine Mythen und sein Kult*, RVV 1, Gießen, 1903.

Héring, J., *1 Cor=The First Epistle of St Paul to the Corinthians*, London, 1962 (ET of CNT(N), Neuchâtel Paris, 1959²);

––, 'Saint Paul'= 'Saint Paul a–t–il enseigné deux résurrections?', in *RHPhR* 12 (1932), 300–20.

Hermann, I., *Kyrios=Kyrios und Pneuma: Studien zur Christologie der paulinischen Hauptbriefe*, StANT 2, München, 1961.

Hersman, A. B., *Studies=Studies in Greek Allegorical Interpretation*, Chicago, 1906.

Hickling, C. J. A., 'Centre'='Centre and Periphery in the Thought of Paul', in (ed.) E. A. Livingstone, *Studia Biblica* 3: *Papers on Paul and Other New Testament Authors* (JSNT Suppl. Series 3, Sheffield, 1980) 199–214.

Hill, D., *Prophecy=New Testament Prophecy*, London, 1979.

Hölbl, G., 'Gottheiten'='Andere ägyptische Gottheiten: Juppiter Ammon, Osiris, Osiris-Antinoos, Nil, Apis, Bubasis, Bes, Sphinx, Hermes-Thot, Neotera-Problem', in *OrRR* 157–92.

Hoffmann, P., *Toten=Die Toten in Christus: eine religionsgeschichtliche und exegetische Untersuchung zur paulinischen Eschatologie*, NTA N.F. 2, Münster, 1966, 1978³.

Holladay, C. R., *Aner=Theios Aner in Hellenistic Judaism: a Critique of the Use of This Category in New Testament Christology*, SBLDS 40, Missoula, 1977.

Holtz, T., 'Kennzeichen'='Das Kennzeichen des Geistes (1 Kor. xii.1–3)', in *NTS* 18 (1971–2), 365–76.

Holtzmann, H. J., *Lehrbuch=Lehrbuch der neutestamentlichen Theologie*, Freiburg/Leipzig, 1897.

Hornung, E., *Conceptions=Conceptions of God in Ancient Egypt: the One and the Many*, Ithaca NY, 1982 (ET of Darmstadt, 1971);

––, *Geschichte=Geschichte als Fest: zwei Vorträge zum Geschichtsbild der frühen Menschheit*, Libelli 246, Darmstadt, 1966.

Horsley, R. A., 'Elitism'=' "How can some of you say that there is no resurrection of the dead?" Spiritual Elitism in Corinth', in *NT* 20 (1978), 203–31;

––, 'Pneumatikos'='Pneumatikos vs Psychikos: Distinctions of Spiritual Status among the Corinthians', in *HThR* 69 (1976), 269–88;

––, 'Wisdom'='Wisdom of Word and Words of Wisdom', in *CBQ* 39 (1977), 224–39.

Horst, P. W. van der, 'Parallels'='Hellenistic Parallels to the Acts of the Apostles (2.1–47)', in *JSNT* 25 (1985), 49–60.

Houlden, J. L., *Letters=Paul's Letters from Prison*, PNTC, Harmondsworth, 1970.

House, H. W., 'Tongues'='Tongues and the Mystery Religions of Corinth', in *Bibliotheca sacra* 140 (1983), 134–50.

Hughes, P. E., *2 Cor=Paul's Second Epistle to the Corinthians*, NIC, Grand Rapids, 1962.

Hultgård, A., 'Ecstasy'='Ecstasy and Vision', in (ed.) N. G. Holm, *Religious Ecstasy: Based on Papers Read at the Symposium on Religious Ecstasy Held at Åbo, Finland, on the 26th–28th of August, 1981* (SIDA 11, Stockholm, 1982), 218–25.

Huntington, R., Metcalf, P., *Celebrations=Celebrations of Death: the Anthropology of Mortuary Ritual*, Cambridge, 1979.

Hurd, J. C., *Origin=The Origin of 1 Corinthians*, London, 1965.

Huzar, E. G., *Mark Antony=Mark Antony: a Biography*, Minneapolis, 1978.

Hyldahl, N., 'Auferstehung'='Auferstehung Christi – Auferstehung der Toten (1. Thess. 4.13–18)', in (ed.) S. Pedersen, *Die paulinische Literatur und Theologie* (Teologiske Studier 7, Århus/Göttingen, 1980) 119–36.

Isaacs, M. E., *Concept=The Concept of Spirit: a Study of Pneuma in Hellenistic Judaism and Its Bearing on the New Testament*, Heythrop Monographs 1, London, 1976.

Jacobsen, T., *Treasures=Treasures of Darkness: a History of Mesopotamian Religion*, New Haven, 1976.

Jaeger, W., 'Ideas'='The Greek Ideas of Immortality', in (ed.) K. Stendahl, *Immortality and Resurrection* (New York, 1965) 97–114.

James, E. O., *Religion=Comparative Religion: an Introductory and Historical Study*, London, 1938;

– –, 'Rituals'='Initiatory Rituals', in (ed.) S. H. Hooke, *Myth and Ritual: Essays on the Myth and Ritual of the Hebrews in Relation to the Culture Pattern of the Ancient East* (London, 1933) 147–71.

James, M. R., 'Clement'='Clement of Alexandria and Plutarch', in *ClR* 14 (1900), 23–4.

Jannoray, J., 'Inscriptions'='Inscriptions delphiques d'époque tardive', in *BCH* 70 (1946), 247–61.

Jeanmaire, H., *Dionysos=Dionysos: histoire du culte de Bacchus*, Paris, 1951.

Jeremias, J., *Baptism=Infant Baptism in the First Four Centuries*, London, 1960 (ET of Göttingen, 1958).

Jervell, J., *Imago=Imago Dei: Gen 1,26f im Spätjudentum, in der Gnosis und in den paulinischen Briefen*, FRLANT 58, Göttingen, 1960.

Jeske, R. L., 'Rock'='The Rock Was Christ: the Ecclesiology of 1 Corinthians 10' in (ed.) D. Lührmann, G. Strecker, *Kirche* (FS G. Bornkamm, Tübingen, 1980) 245–55.

Jewett, R., 'Agitators'='The Agitators and the Galatian Congregation', in *NTS* 17 (1970–1), 198–212;

– –, 'Redaction'='The Redaction of 1 Corinthians and the Trajectory of the Pauline School', in *JAAR* Supplement (Dec. 1978) B 389–444.

– –, *Terms=Paul's Anthropological Terms: a Study of Their Use in Conflict Settings*, AGJU 10, Leiden, 1971.

Johanson, B. C., 'Tongues'='Tongues, a Sign for Unbelievers? A Structural and Exegetical Study of I Corinthians xiv.20–25', in *NTS* 25 (1978–9), 180–203.

Johnston, G., *Eph=Ephesians, Philippians, Colossians and Philemon*, CeB, London, 1967.

Jonas H., *Gnosis=Gnosis und spätantiker Geist* 1: *Die mythologische Gnosis*, Göttingen, 1964[3]; 2.1: *Von der Mythologie zur mystischen Philosophie*, Göttingen, 1966[2];

– –, *Religion=The Gnostic Religion: the Message of the Alien God and the Beginnings of Christianity*, Boston, 1963[2].

Jones, R. M., 'Posidonius'='Posidonius and the Flight of the Mind through the Universe', in *CP* 21 (1962), 97–113.

Junge, J., 'Isis'='Isis und die ägyptischen Mysterien', in *Aspekte der spätägyptischen Religion* (GOF.Ä 4.9, Wiesbaden, 1979) 93–115.

Jungkuntz, R., 'Fathers'='Fathers, Heretics and Epicureans', in *JEH* 17 (1966), 3–10.

Käsemann, E., 'Apocalyptic'='On the Subject of Primitive Christian Apocalyptic', in *Questions* 108–37 (ET of *ZThK* 59, 1962, 257–84=*Versuche* 2, 105–31);

––, 'Doctrine'='The Pauline Doctrine of the Lord's Supper', in *Essays on New Testament Themes* (SBT 41, London, 1964) 108–35 (ET of *EvTh* 7, 1947–8, 263–83=*Versuche* 1, 11–34);

––, *Questions=New Testament Questions of Today*, London, 1969;

––, 'Questions'='New Testament Questions of Today', in *Questions* 1–22;

––, *Röm=An die Römer*, HNT 8a, Tübingen, 1974[2];

––, *Testament=The Testament of Jesus: a Study of the Gospel of John in the Light of Chapter 17*, London, 1968;

––, *Versuche=Exegetische Versuche und Besinnungen* 1, Göttingen, 1964[3]; 2, Göttingen, 1965.

Kaiser, H., *Bedeutung=Die Bedeutung des leiblichen Daseins in der paulinischen Eschatologie* 1: *Studien zum religions- und traditionsgeschichtlichen Hintergrund der Auseinandersetzung in 2 Kor 5.1–10 (und 1 Kor 15) im palästinensischen und hellenistischen Judentum*, Diss. Heidelberg, 1974.

Kane, J. P., 'Meal'='The Mithraic Cult Meal in Its Greek and Roman Environment', in (ed.) J. R. Hinnells, *Mithraic Studies* (Manchester, 1975) 2, 313–51.

Kaye, B. N., *Structure=The Thought Structure of Romans with Special Reference to Romans 6*, Austin, 1979.

Kearns, C., 'Interpretation'='The Interpretation of Romans 6.7', in *SPCIC* 1 (AnBib 17, Roma, 1963) 301–7.

Keck, L. E., Furnish, V. P., *Letters=The Pauline Letters*, Nashville, 1984.

Kee, H. C., 'Setting'='The Socio-Cultural Setting of *Joseph and Aseneth*', in *NTS* 29 (1983), 394–413.

Kees, H., *Totenglauben=Totenglauben und Jenseitsvorstellungen der alten Ägypter: Grundlagen und Entwicklung bis zum Ende des mittleren Reiches*, Leipzig, 1926, 1956[2].

Kehl, N., 'Erniedrigung'='Erniedrigung und Erhöhung in Qumran und Kolossä', in *ZThK* 91 (1969), 364–94.

Kennedy, H. A. A., *St Paul=St Paul and the Mystery-Religions*, New York/London, 1913.

Kerenyi, K., *Dionysos=Dionysos: Archetypal Image of Indestructible Life*, AIGR 2, London, 1976;

––, *Eleusis=Eleusis: Archetypal Image of Mother and Daughter*, AIGR 4, London, 1967 (revised ET of Zürich, 1962);

––, *Romanliteratur=Die griechisch-orientalische Romanliteratur in religionsgeschichtlicher Beleuchtung*, Tübingen, 1927, 1962[2].

King, J. P., *Death=Death, Burial and Baptism in Rom 6.1–14*, Diss. Emory Univ. GA, 1977.

Kirby, J. C., *Ephesians=Ephesians: an Inquiry into the Structure and Purpose of the Epistle to the Ephesians*, Montreal, 1968.

Kirk, G. S., Raven, J. E., *Philosophers=The Presocratic Philosophers: a Critical History with a Selection of Texts*, Cambridge, 1960.

Klaiber, W., *Rechtfertigung=Rechtfertigung und Gemeinde: eine Untersuchung zum paulinischen Kirchenverständnis*, FRLANT 127, Göttingen, 1982.

Klauck, H. J., *Herrenmahl=Herrenmahl und hellenistischer Kult: eine religionsgeschichtliche Untersuchung zum ersten Korintherbrief*, NTA N. F. 15, Münster, 1982;

––, *1 Kor=1 Korintherbrief*, Neue Echter Bibel 7, Würzburg, 1984.

Klinzing, G., *Umdeutung=Die Umdeutung des Kultus in der Qumrangemeinde und im Neuen Testament*, StUNT 7, Göttingen, 1971.

Knox, J., *Rom=Romans*, IntB, New York/Nashville, 1954.

Knox, W. L., *Paul (1925)=St Paul and the Church of Jerusalem*, Cambridge, 1925;

––, *Paul (1939)=St Paul and the Church of the Gentiles*, Cambridge, 1939.

Köberlein, E., *Caligula=Caligula und die ägyptischen Kulte*, BKP 3, Meisenheim am Glan, 1962.

Köster, H., *Einführung=Einführung in das Neue Testament im Rahmen der Religionsgeschichte und Kulturgeschichte der hellenistischen und römischen Zeit*, Berlin/New York, 1980 (ET: Philadelphia, 1982);

––, 'Purpose'='The Purpose of the Polemic of a Pauline Fragment (Philippians iii)', in *NTS* 8 (1961–2), 317–32.

Koschorke, K., 'Paulus'='Paulus in den Nag-Hammadi-Texten: ein Beitrag zur Geschichte der Paulusrezeption im frühen Christentum', in *ZThK* 78 (1981), 177–205.

Kraabel, A. T., 'Disappearance'='The Disappearance of the "God-Fearers"', in *Numen* 28 (1981), 113–26.

Krämer, H., 'Isisformel'='Die Isisformel des Apuleius (Met. XI 23,7) – eine Anmerkung zur Methode der Mysterienforschung', in *WuD* 12 (1973), 91–104.

Kraft, H., *Entstehung=Die Entstehung des Christentums*, Darmstadt, 1981.

Kramer, S. N., *Sumerians=The Sumerians*, Chicago, 1963.

Kramer, W., *Christ=Christ, Lord, Son of God*, SBT 50, London, 1966 (ET of AThANT 44, Zürich, 1963).

Kretschmar, G., 'Auferstehung'='Auferstehung des Fleisches: zur Frühgeschichte einer theologischen Lehrformel', in *Leben angesichts des Todes* (FS H. Thielicke, Tübingen, 1968) 101–37.

Kroll, J., 'Elysium', in *Arbeitsgemeinschaft für Forschung des Landes Nordrhein-Westfalen, Geisteswissenschaften* 2 (Köln-Opladen, 1953), 7–35.

Kruse, C., *Foundations=New Testament Foundations of Ministry*, London, 1983.

Kümmel, W. G., *Introduction²=Introduction to the New Testament*, London, 1975[2] (ET of Heidelberg, 1973[17]);

––, *New Testament=The New Testament: the History of the Investigation of Its Problems*, London, 1973 (ET of OA 3.3, München, 1970[2]).

Kuhn, H.-W., *Enderwartung=Enderwartung und gegenwärtiges Heil: Untersuchungen zu den Gemeindeliedern von Qumran*, StUNT 4, Göttingen, 1966.

Kuhn, K. G., 'Epheserbrief'='Der Epheserbrief im Lichte der Qumrantexte', in *NTS* 7 (1960–1), 334–46;

––, 'Rm 6.7', in *ZNW* 30 (1931), 305–10.

Kuss, O., 'Frage'='Zur Frage einer vorpaulinischen Todestaufe', in *MThZ* 4 (1953), 1–17; *Röm=Der Römerbrief*, Regensburg, 1957–.

Lähnemann, J., *Kolosserbrief=Der Kolosserbrief: Komposition, Situation und Argumentation*, StNT 3, Gütersloh, 1971.

Lagrange, M. J., 'Attis' (1919)='Attis et le christianisme', in *RB* 28 (1919), 419–80;

––, 'Attis' (1927)='Attis ressuscité?' in *RB* 36 (1927), 561–6;

––, *Rom=Saint Paul: épître aux Romains*, EtB, Paris, 1931.

Lake, K., *Epistles=The Earlier Epistles of St Paul: Their Motive and Origin*, London, 1911.

Lambrechts, P., 'Fêtes'='Les fêtes "phrygiennes" de Cybèle et d'Attis', in *BIHBR* 27 (1952), 141–70;

––, '"Résurrection"'='La "résurrection" d'Adonis', in *Mélanges Isidore Lévy* (AIPh 13, Bruxelles, 1955), 207–40.

Lang, F. G., *2. Korinther 5.1–10=2. Korinther 5.1–10 in der neueren Forschung*, BGBE 16, Tübingen, 1973.

Langdon, S., *Tammuz=Tammuz und Ishtar: a Monograph upon Babylonian Religion and Theology*, Oxford, 1914.

Lapide, P., *Resurrection=The Resurrection of Jesus: a Jewish Perspective*, Minneapolis, 1983 (ET of Stuttgart/München, 1977).

Larcher, C., *Études=Études sur le livre de la Sagesse*, Paris, 1969.

Larsson, E., *Christus=Christus als Vorbild: eine Untersuchung zu den paulinischen Tauf- und Eikontexten*, ASNU 23, Uppsala, 1962.

Latte, K., *Religionsgeschichte=Römische Religionsgeschichte*, HAW 5.4, München, 1960.

Laurentin, A., 'Pneuma'='Le Pneuma dans la doctrine de Philon', in ALBO 2.24=EThL 27 (Louvain, 1951), 390–437.

Laurin, R. B., 'Question'='The Question of Immortality in the Qumran Hodayot', in *JSSt* 3 (1958), 344–58.

Lawson, J. C., *Folklore=Modern Greek Folklore and Ancient Greek Religion: a Study of Survivals*, Cambridge, 1910.

Layton, B., 'Vision'='Vision and Revision: a Gnostic View of Resurrection', in (ed.) B. Barc,

Colloque international sur les textes de Nag Hammadi (Québec 22–25 août, 1978) (BCNH Etudes 1, Québec/London, 1981) 190–217.

Leach, E., *Culture=Culture and Communication: the Logic by Which Symbols Are Connected: an Introduction to the Use of Structuralist Analysis in Social Anthropology*, Cambridge, 1976.

Le Corsu, F., *Isis=Isis: mythe et mystères*, Collection d'études mythologiques, Paris, 1977;

— —, 'Oratoire'='Une oratoire pompéien consacré à Dionysos-Osiris', in *BSFE* 51 (1968), 17–31.

Leenhardt, F. J., *Rom=The Epistle to the Romans*, London, 1961 (ET of CNT(N), Neuchâtel/ Paris, 1957).

Leeuw, G. van der, *Religion=Religion in Essence and Manifestation: a Study in Phenomenology*, London, 1938 (ET of Tübingen, 1933).

Lehmann, P. W., Spittle, D., *Samothrace 5=Samothrace 5: The Temenos*, BollS 60.5, Princeton, 1982.

Leipoldt, J., 'Christentum'='Das Christentum als Weltreligion im Kreise der Weltreligionen', in (ed.) G. Mensching, *Handbuch der Religionswissenschaft* 1.4 (Berlin, 1948), 37–72;

— —, 'Taufe'='Die altchristliche Taufe religionsgeschichtlich betrachtet', in *WZ(L).GS* 3 (1953–4), 63–74;

— —, *Tod=Der Tod bei Griechen und Juden*, Leipzig, 1942.

Leipoldt, J., Grundmann, W., *Umwelt=Umwelt des Urchristentums*, Berlin, 1975–6[4].

Leisegang, H., *Geist=Der heilige Geist: das Wesen und Werden der mystisch-intuitiven Erkenntnis in der Philosophie und Religion der Griechen* 1.1, Leipzig/Berlin, 1919, repr. Darmstadt, 1967;

— —, *Gnosis=Die Gnosis*, KTA 32, Stuttgart, 1955[4].

Levi, D., '*Mors*'='*Mors voluntaria*: Mystery Cults on Mosaics from Antioch', in *Ber.* 7 (1942), 19–55.

Lewis, I. M., *Religion=Ecstatic Religion: an Anthropological Study of Spirit Possession and Shamanism*, Harmondsworth, 1971.

Lewy, H., *Ebrietas=Sobria ebrietas: Untersuchungen zur Geschichte der antiken Mystik*, BZNW 9, Gießen, 1929.

Lewy, H., Tardieu, M., *Oracles=Chaldaean Oracles and Theurgy: Mysticism, Magic and Platonism in the Later Roman Empire*, Paris, 1978.

Liebeschuetz, J. H. W. G., *Continuity=Continuity and Change in Roman Religion*, Oxford, 1979.

Lietzmann, H., *Röm=An die Römer, HNT 3.1*, Tübingen, 1906.

Lietzmann, H., Kümmel, W. G., *1–2 Kor=An die Korinther I–II*, HNT 9, Tübingen, 1949[4].

Lincoln, A. T., *Paradise=Paradise Now and Not Yet: Studies in the Role of the Heavenly Dimension in Paul's Thought with Special Reference to His Eschatology*, MSSNTS 43, Cambridge, 1981.

Lincoln, B., 'Mithra(s)'='Mithra(s) as Sun and Saviour', in Bianchi-Vermaseren, *Soteriologia* 505–23.

Lindars, B., *Apologetic=New Testament Apologetic*, London, 1961.

Lindemann, A., *Aufhebung=Die Aufhebung der Zeit: Geschichtsverständnis und Eschatologie im Epheserbrief*, StNT 12, Gütersloh, 1975;

— —, *Kol=Der Kolosserbrief*, ZBK, Zürich, 1983;

— —, *Paulus=Paulus im ältesten Christentum*, BUTh 58, Tübingen, 1979.

Linforth, I. M., *Arts=The Arts of Orpheus*, Berkeley/Los Angeles, 1941.

Lippold, G., *Skulpturen=Die Skulpturen des Vaticanischen Museums*, Deutsches Archäologisches Institut, Berlin, 1956.

Lipsius, R. A., *Phil=Der Brief an die Philipper*, HC 2, Freiburg/Leipzig, 1893.

Lloyd, A. C., 'Neoplatonists'='The Later Neoplatonists', in (ed.) A. H. Armstrong, *The Cambridge History of Later Greek and Early Medieval Philosophy* (Cambridge, 1967) 269–325.

Lobeck, C. A., *Aglaophamus=Aglaophamus sive de theologiae mysticae Graecorum causis*, Königsberg, 1829.

Lohmeyer, E., *Kol=Die Briefe an die Philipper, an die Kolosser und an Philemon*, KEK 9, Göttingen, 1964[13];

— —, 'Σὺν Χριστῷ', in (ed.) K. L. Schmidt, *Festgabe für A. Deißmann zum 60. Geburtstag* (Tübingen, 1927) 218–57.

Lohse, E., 'Bekenntnis'='Ein hymnisches Bekenntnis in Kolosser 2.13c–15', in (ed.) A. Descamps,

A. de Halleux, *Mélanges bibliques en hommage du R. P. Béda Rigaux* (Gembloux, 1970) 427–35;

– –, *Col=Colossians and Philemon*, Hermeneia, Philadelphia, 1971 (ET of KEK, Göttingen, 1968[14]);

– –, *Grundriß=Grundriß der neutestamentlichen Theologie*, ThW 5, Stuttgart, 1974;

– –, 'Taufe'='Taufe und Rechtfertigung bei Paulus', in *KuD* 11 (1965), 308–24=*Einheit des Neuen Testaments: exegetische Studien zur Theologie des Neuen Testaments* (Göttingen, 1973) 228–44;

– –, *Umwelt=Umwelt des Neuen Testaments*, GNT 1, Göttingen, 1971 (ET: London, 1976);

– –, 'Wort'='Wort und Sakrament in den paulinischen Theologie', in (ed.) F. Viering, *Zu Karl Barths Lehre von der Taufe* (Gütersloh, 1971) 44–59.

Lona, H. E., *Eschatologie=Die Eschatologie im Kolosser- und Epheserbrief*, FzB 48, Würzburg, 1984.

Long, A. A., *Philosophy=Hellentistic Philosophy: Stoics, Epicureans, Sceptics*, London, 1974.

Lorenzi, L. de (ed.), *Battesimo=Battesimo e giustizia in Rom 6 e 8*, Serie monografica di 'Benedictina', sezione biblico-ecumenica 2, Roma, 1974;

– –, *Charisma=Charisma und Agape (1 Ko 12–14)*, ibid. 7, Roma, 1983.

Luck, U., 'Weisheit'='Weisheit und Leiden', in *ThLZ* 92 (1967), 253–8.

Lüdemann, G., *Paulus 1=Paulus, der Heidenapostel 1: Studien zur Chronologie*, FRLANT 123, Göttingen, 1980;

– –, *Paulus und das Judentum*, TEH 215, München, 1983.

Lührmann, D., *Offenbarungsverständnis=Das Offenbarungsverständnis bei Paulus und in paulinischen Gemeinden*, WMANT 17, Neukirchen, 1965.

Luz, U., *Geschichtsverständnis=Das Geschichtsverständnis des Paulus*, BEvTh 49, München, 1968.

Macchioro, V., *Orpheus=From Orpheus to Paul: a History of Orphism*, London, 1930.

MacDonald, D. R., *Legend=The Legend and the Apostle: the Battle for Paul in Story and Canon*, Philadelphia, 1983.

McGinty, P., *Interpretation=Interpretation and Dionysos: Method in the Study of a God*, RaR 16, Hague, etc., 1978.

Machalet, C., 'Paulus'='Paulus und seine Gegner: eine Untersuchung zu den Korintherbriefen', in (ed.) W. Dietrich, P. Freimark, H. Schreckenberg, *Theokratia* (FS K. H. Rengstorf, Leiden, 1973) 2, 183–203.

McHugh, J., 'Present'='Present and Future in the Life of the Community (I Cor 4.6–13 in the Context of I Cor 4.6–21)', in (ed.) L. de Lorenzi, *Paolo a una chiesa divisa (1 Co 1–4)* (Serie monografica di 'Benedictina', sezione biblico-ecumenica 5, Roma, 1980) 177–88.

MacMullen, R., *Paganism=Paganism in the Roman Empire*, New Haven/London, 1981.

Magie, D., *Rule=Roman Rule in Asia Minor to the End of the Third Century after Christ*, Princeton, 1950.

Maier, G., 'Lehrer'='Die jüdischen Lehrer bei Josephus: einige Beobachtungen', in (ed.) O. Betz, K. Haacker, M. Hengel, *Josephus-Studien: Untersuchungen zu Josephus, dem antiken Judentum und dem Neuen Testament* (FS O. Michel, Göttingen, 1974) 260–72.

Maier, J., *Kultus=Vom Kultus zur Gnosis: Studien zur Vor- und Frühgeschichte der 'jüdischen Gnosis': Bundeslade, Gottesthron, und Märkabah*, Kairos(St) 1, Salzburg, 1964.

Maiuri, A., *Pompei=Pompei: i nuovi scavi e la Villa dei Misteri*, Itinerari dei musei e monumenti d'Italia, Roma, 1935[2].

Malaise, M., *Conditions=Les conditions de pénétration et de diffusion des cultes égyptiens en Italie*, EPRO 22, Leiden, 1972;

– –, *Inventaire=Inventaire préliminaire des documents égyptiens découverts en Italie*, EPRO 21, Leiden, 1972.

Malherbe, A. J., *Aspects=Social Aspects of Early Christianity*, Baton Rouge/London, 1977;

– –, 'Beast'='The Beasts of Ephesus', in *JBL* 87 (1968), 71–80.

Maly, K., '1 Kor 12, 1–3'='1 Kor 12,1–3, eine Regel zur Unterscheidung der Geister?', in *BZ* 10 (1966), 82–95.

Manson, T. W., *Studies=Studies in the Gospels and Epistles*, Manchester, 1962.

Martelet, G., 'Sacrements'='Sacrements, figures et exhortation en *1 Cor* x,1–11', in *RSR* 44 (1956), 323–59, 515–59.

Martin, R. P., *Col=Colossians and Philemon,* NCeB, London, 1974;

––, *Phil* (TNTC)=*The Epistle of Paul to the Philippians,* TNTC, London, 1959;

––, *Phil* (NCeB)=*Philippians,* NCeB, London, 1976;

––, *Spirit=The Spirit and the Congregation: Studies in 1 Corinthians 12–15,* Grand Rapids, 1984.

Martyn, J. L., 'Antinomies'='Apocalyptic Antinomies in Paul's Letter to the Galatians', in *NTS* 31 (185), 410–24.

Marxsen, W., 'Auslegung'='Auslegung von 1 Thess. 4,13–18', in *ZThK* 66 (1969), 22–37;

––, 'Erwägungen'='Erwägungen zur neutestamentlichen Begründung der Taufe', in *Apophoreta* (FS E. Haenchen, BZNW 30, Berlin, 1964) 169–77;

––, *Introduction=Introduction to the New Testament,* Oxford, 1968 (ET of Gütersloh, 1964);

- –, *Resurrection=The Resurrection of Jesus of Nazareth,* London, 1970 (ET of Gütersloh, 1968).

Masson, C., *Eph=L'épître de Saint-Paul aux Éphésiens,* CNT(N) 9.2, Neuchâtel/Paris, 1953.

Matz, F., Τελετή=Διονυσιακὴ τελετή: *archäologische Untersuchungen zum Dionysoskult in hellenistischer und römischer Zeit,* AAWLM.G 15, Wiesbaden, 1964.

Mearns, C. L., 'Development' (1980–1)='Early Eschatological Development in Paul: the Evidence of I and II Thessalonians', in *NTS* 27 (1980–1), 137–57;

––, 'Development' (1984)='Early Eschatological Development in Paul: the Evidence of 1 Corinthians', in *JSNT* 22 (1984), 19–35.

Meeks, W. A., *Christians=The First Urban Christians: the Social World of the Apostle Paul,* New Haven/London, 1983;

––, 'Image'='The Image of the Androgyne: Some Uses of a Symbol in Earliest Christianity', in *HR* 13 (1974), 165–208:

––, ' "Rose" '=' "And rose up to play": Midrash and Paraenesis in 1 Corinthians 10:1–22', in *JSNT* 16 (1982), 64–78.

Mellor, R., 'Archaeology' ='Archaeology and the Oriental Religions in the West', in *Ancient World* 7 (1981), 129–38.

Ménard, J.-É., *'Épître*'='L'*Épître à Rhéginos* et la résurrection', in *Proceedings of the XIIth International Congress of the International Association for the History of Religions* (SHR 31, Leiden, 1975) 189–99.

Merk, O., *Handeln=Handeln aus Glauben: die Motivierungen der paulinischen Ethik,* MThSt 5, Marburg, 1968.

Merkelbach, R., *Mithras,* Königstein, 1984;

––, *Roman=Roman und Mysterium in der Antike,* München/Berlin, 1962;

––, *Weihegrade=Weihegrade und Seelenlehre der Mithrasmysterien,* Rheinisch-Westfälische Akademie der Wissenschaften, Vorträge 257, Opladen, 1982.

Metzger, B. M., 'Considerations'='Considerations of Methodology in the Study of the Mystery Religions and Early Christianity', in *HThR* 48 (1955), 1–20.

Metzger, H., 'Dionysos'='Dionysos Chthonien d'après les monuments figurés de la période classique', in *BCH* 68–9 (1944–5), 296–339.

Meyer, B. F., Sanders, E. P. (ed.), *Self-Definition 3=Jewish and Christian Self-Definition 3: Self-Definition in the Graeco-Roman World,* London, 1982.

Meyer, H. A. W., *1 Kor=Kritisch-exegetisches Handbuch über den ersten Brief an die Korinther,* KEK 5, Göttingen, 1856[3] (ET: Edinburgh, 1879).

Meyer, H. A. W., Heinrici, G., *1 Kor=Handbuch über den ersten Brief an die Korinther,* KEK, Göttingen, 1888[7].

Meyer, H. A. W., Weiß, B., *Röm=Handbuch über den Brief des Paulus an die Römer,* KEK, Göttingen, 1886[7].

Michaelis, W., 'Teilungshypothesen'= 'Teilungshypothesen bei Paulusbriefen: Briefkompositionen und ihr Sitz im Leben', in *ThZ* 14 (1958), 321–6.

Michel, O., *Röm=Der Brief an die Römer,* KEK, Göttingen, 1966[13].

Milik, J. T., *Years=Ten Years of Discovery in the Wilderness of Judaea,* SBT 26, London, 1959 (ET of Paris, 1957).

Mitchell, H., *Economics=The Economics of Ancient Greece,* Cambridge, 1940.

Mitton, C. L., *Eph=Ephesians*, NCeB, London, 1976;

– –, *Epistle=The Epistle to the Ephesians: Its Authorship, Origin and Purpose*, Oxford, 1951.

Moffatt, J., *1 Cor=The First Epistle of Paul to the Corinthians*, MNTC, London, 1938.

Momigliano, A., *Claudius=Claudius, the Emperor and His Achievement*, Oxford, 1934.

Moore, G. F., *Judaism=Judaism in the First Centuries of the Christian Era (the Age of the Tan- naim)*, Cambridge, 1927–30.

Morenz, S., *Begegnung=Die Begegnung Europas mit Ägypten*, SSAW.PH 113.5, Berlin, 1968;

– –, 'Problem'='Das Problem des Werdens zu Osiris in der griechisch-römischen Zeit Ägyptens', in (ed.) P. Derchain, *Religions en Égypte hellénistique et romaine, Colloque de Strasbourg, 16–18 mai, 1967* (Paris, 1969), 75–91;

– –, *Religion=Egyptian Religion*, London, 1973 (ET of Stuttgart, 1960).

Moret, A., *Mystères=Mystères égyptiens*, Paris, 1913.

Morris, L., *1 Cor=The First Epistle of Paul to the Corinthians*, TNTC, London, 1958.

Moule, C. F. D., *Birth=The Birth of the New Testament*, BNTC, London, 1966[2];

– –, *Col=The Epistles to the Colossians and to Philemon*, Cambridge Greek New Testament, Cambridge, 1958;

– –, 'Death'='Death "to Sin", "to Law", and "to the World": a Note on Certain Datives', in (ed.) A. Descamps, A. de Halleux, *Mélanges bibliques en hommage au R. P. Béda Rigaux* (Gembloux, 1970) 367–75=id., *Essays in New Testament Interpretation* (Cambridge, 1982) 149–57;

– –, *Idiom Book=An Idiom Book of New Testament Greek*, Cambridge, 1963;

– –, *Spirit=The Holy Spirit*, London, 1978;

– –, *Worship=Worship in the New Testament*, ESW 9, London/Richmond VA, 1961.

Mrozek, S., 'Répartition'='À propos de la répartition chronologique des inscriptions latines dans le Haut-Empire', in *Epig.* 35 (1973), 113–18.

Müller, D., *Ägypten=Ägypten und die griechischen Isisaretalogien*, ASAW.PH 53.1, Berlin, 1961.

Murphy, D. J., *Dead=The Dead in Christ: Paul's Understanding of God's Fidelity: a Study of 1 Corinthians 15*, Diss. Union Theological Seminary, New York, 1977.

Murphy-O'Connor, J., 'Slogans'='Corinthian Slogans in 1 Cor 6:12–20', in *CBQ* 40 (1978), 391–6.

Murray, J., *Rom=The Epistle to the Romans* 1, NIC, Edinburgh/London, 1960.

Mußner, F., *Gal=Der Galaterbrief*, HThK 9, Freiburg, etc., 1974;

– –, 'Tauflehre'=Zur paulinischen Tauflehre in Röm 6.1–6: Versuch einer Auslegung', in id., *Praesentia salutis: gesammelte Studien zu Fragen und Themen des Neuen Testaments* (Düsseldorf, 1967) 189–96, revised from *TThZ* 63 (1954), 257–64.

Mylonas, G. E., *Eleusis=Eleusis and the Eleusinian Mysteries*, Princeton, 1961–2.

Nagel, G., ' "Mysteries" '='The "Mysteries" of Osiris in Ancient Egypt', in (ed.) J. Campbell, *The Mysteries* (PEY 2, BollS 30, Princeton, 1955) 119–34 (ET from *ErJb* 11, 1944).

Nash, R. H., *Christianity=Christianity and the Hellenistic World*, Dallas, 1984.

Neuenzeit, P., *Herrenmahl=Das Herrenmahl: Studien zur paulinischen Eucharistieauffassung*, StANT 1, München, 1960.

Nickelsburg, G. W. E., *Resurrection=Resurrection, Immortality and Eternal Life in Intertestamental Judaism*, HThS 26, Cambridge MA/London, 1972.

Niederwimmer, K., *Askese=Askese und Mysterium; über Ehe, Ehescheidung und Eheverzicht in den Anfängen des christlichen Glaubens*, FRLANT 113, Göttingen, 1975.

Nilsson, M. P., *Feste=Griechische Feste von religiöser Bedeutung mit Ausschluß der Attischen*, Leipzig, 1906;

– –, *Geschichte=Geschichte der griechischen Religion*, HAW 5.2.1–2, München, (1) 1967[3], (2) 1961[2];

– –, *Mysteries=The Dionysiac Mysteries of the Hellenistic and Roman Age*, Skrifter utgivna av Svenska Institutet i Athen 8°.5, Lund, 1957;

– –, 'Mysteries, ='The Bacchic Mysteries of the Roman Age', in *HThR* 46 (1953), 175–202;

– –, 'Orphism'='Early Orphism and Kindred Religious Movements', in id., *Opuscula selecta* 2 (Skrifter utgivna av Svenska Institutet i Athens 8.2.2, Lund, 1952), 628–83, repr. from *HThR* 28 (1935), 181–230;

– –, *Religion=Greek Popular Religion*, New York, 1940=*Greek Folk Religion*, New York, 1961.

Noack, B., *'Teste'='Teste Paulo:* Paul as the Principal Witness to Jesus and Primitive Christianity', in (ed.) S. Pedersen, *Die paulinische Literatur und Theologie* (Teologiske Studier 7, Ȧrthus/ Göttingen, 1980) 9–28;

––, 'Zitat'='Das Zitat in Ephes. 5.14', in *STL* 5 (1951), 52–64.

Nock, A. D., 'Christianity'='Early Gentile Christianity and Its Hellenistic Background', in (ed.) A. E. J. Rawlinson, *Essays on the Trinity and the Incarnation* (London, etc., 1928) 51–156= *Essays* 1, 49–133;

––, *Conversion=Conversion: the Old and the New in Religion from Alexander the Great to Augustine of Hippo,* Oxford, 1933;

––, 'Cremation'='Cremation and Burial in the Roman Empire', in *Essays* 1, 277–307, repr. of *HThR* 25 (1932), 321–58;

––, *Essays=Essays on Religion and the Ancient World,* ed. J. Z. Stewart, Oxford, 1972;

––, 'Mysteries'='Hellenistic Mysteries and Christian Sacraments', in *Mn.* Ser. 4.5 (1952), 177– 213=*Essays* 2, 791–820;

––, 'Note'='A Note on the Resurrection', in (ed.) A. E. J. Rawlinson, *Essays on the Trinity and the Incarnation* (London, etc., 1928) 47–50;

––, 'Papyri'='Greek Magical Papyri', in *Essays* 1, 176–94, repr. of *JEA* 15 (1929), 219–35;

––, 'Question'='The Question of Jewish Mysteries', in *Gn.* 13 (1937), 156–65, repr. in *Essays* 1, 459–68;

––, 'Vocabulary'='The Vocabulary of the New Testament', in *JBL* 52 (1933), 131–9=*Essays* 1, 341–7.

Norris, F. W., 'Isis'='Isis, Sarapis and Demeter in Antioch of Syria', in *HThR* 75 (1982), 189–207.

O'Brien, P. T., *Col=Colossians, Philemon,* Word Biblical Commentary 44, Waco, 1982.

Ollrog, W. H., *Paulus=Paulus und seine Mitarbeiter: Untersuchungen zu Theorie und Praxis der paulinischen Mission,* WMANT 50, Neukirchen, 1979.

O'Neill, J. C., *Rom=Paul's Letter to the Romans,* Harmondsworth, 1975.

Oppermann, M., 'Reitergötter'='Thrakische und danubische Reitergötter und ihre Beziehungen zu orientalischen Kulten', in *OrRR* 510–36.

Orr, W. F., Walther, J. A., *1 Cor=1 Corinthians,* AncB, New York, 1976.

Osten-Sacken, P. von der, ' "Christologie" '=' "Christologie, Taufe, Homologie" – ein Beitrag zu Apc Joh 1,5f', in *ZNW* 58 (1967), 255–66.

Otto, E., *Art=Egyptian Art and the Cults of Osiris and Amon,* London, 1968;

––, *Gott=Gott und Mensch nach den ägyptischen Tempelinschriften der griechisch-römischen Zeit: eine Untersuchung zur Phraseologie der Tempelinschriften,* AHAW.PH 1964.1, Heidelberg, 1964;

––, *Inschriften=Die biographischen Inschriften der ägyptischen Spätzeit: ihre geistesgeschichtliche und literarische Bedeutung,* PÄ 2, Leiden, 1954.

Otto, G., *Formulierungen=Die mit syn verbundenen Formulierungen im paulinischen Schrifttum,* Diss. Berlin, 1952.

Otto, W. F., *Dionysus=Dionysus, Myth and Cult,* Dallas, 1981 (ET of Frankfurt, 1933).

Pagels, E. H., ' "Mystery" '=' "The Mystery of the Resurrection": a Gnostic Reading of 1 Corinthians 15', in *JBL* 93 (1974), 276–88;

––, *Paul=The Gnostic Paul: Gnostic Exegesis of the Pauline Letters,* Philadelphia, 1975.

Painter, J., 'Paul'='Paul and the πνευματικοί at Corinth', in (ed.) M. D. Hooker, S. G. Wilson, *Paul and Paulinism: Essays in Honour of C. K. Barrett* (London, 1982) 237–50.

Pascher, J., Ὁδός='Η βασιλικὴ ὁδός: der Königsweg zu Wiedergeburt und Vergottung bei Philon von Alexandreia,* SGKA 17.3–4, Paderborn, 1931.

Paterson, G. A., 'Man'='The 'Divine Man' in Hellenistic Popular Religion,* Diss. Drew Univ., 1983/ Ann Arbor, 1984.

Pearson, B. A., *Terminology=The Pneumatikos-Psychikos Terminology in 1 Corinthians: a Study in the Theology of the Corinthian Opponents of Paul and Its Relation to Gnosticism,* SBLDS 12, Missoula, 1973.

Peel, M. L., 'Eschatology'='Gnostic Eschatology and the New Testament', in *NT* 12 (1970), 141– 65.

Percy, E., *Leib=Der Leib Christi* (σῶμα Χριστοῦ) *in den paulinischen Homologumena und Anti-legomena*, LUÅ N. F. 1.38.1, Lund/Leipzig, 1942;

––, *Probleme=Die Probleme der Kolosser- und Epheserbriefe*, SHVL 39, Lund, 1946.

Perdrizet, P., 'Mên', in *BCH* 20 (1896), 55–106.

Perkins, P., *Resurrection=Resurrection: New Testament Witness and Contemporary Reflection*, Garden City NY, 1984.

Perrin, N., *Jesus=Jesus and the Language of the Kingdom: Symbol and Metaphor in New Testament Interpretation*, Philadelphia, 1976;

––, *New Testament=The New Testament: an Introduction*, New York, etc., 1974.

Perry, B. E., *Romances=The Ancient Romances: a Literary-Historical Account of Their Origins*, Berkeley/Los Angeles, 1967.

Pesch, R., 'Entstehung'='Zur Entstehung des Glaubens an die Auferstehung Jesu', in *ThQ* 153, (1973), 201–28.

Pfister, F., 'Ekstasis', in (ed.) T. Klauser, A. Rücker, *Pisciculi: Studien zur Religion und Kultur des Altertums* (FS F. J. Dolger, AuC. E 1, Münster, 1939) 177–91.

Pfleiderer, O., *Christianity=Primitive Christianity: Its Writings and Teachings in Their Historical Connections*, London, 1906–11 (ET of Berlin, 1887);

––, *Origins=Christian Origins*, London, 1906 (ET of München, 1905).

Picard, C., 'Patère'='La patère d'Aquileia et l'eleusinisme à Rome débuts de l'époque impériale', in *AnCl* 20 (1951), 351–81.

Platner, S. B., Ashby, T., *Dictionary=A Topographical Dictionary of Ancient Rome*, Oxford, 1929.

Pleket, H. W., 'Aspect'='An Aspect of the Emperor Cult: Imperial Mysteries', in *HThR* 58 (1965), 331–47.

Pötscher, W., '"Auferstehung"'='Die "Auferstehung" in der klassischen Antike', in *Kairos* 7 (1965), 208–15.

Pohlenz, M., 'Philon'='Philon von Alexandrien', in *NAWG* 1942.2, 410–87;

––, *Stoa=Die Stoa: Geschichte einer geistigen Bewegung*, Göttingen, 1948.

Pokorný, P., 'Christologie'='Christologie et baptême à l'époque du christianisme primitif', in *NTS* 27 (1980–1), 368–80;

––, *Epheserbrief=Der Epheserbrief und die Gnosis: die Bedeutung des Haupt-Glieder-Gedankens in der entstehenden Kirche*, Berlin, 1965;

––, 'Epheserbrief'='Epheserbrief und gnostische Mysterien', in *ZNW* 53 (1962), 160–94.

Poland, F., *Geschichte=Geschichte des griechischen Vereinswesens*, Preisschriften von der Fürstlich Jablonowskischen Gesellschaft 38, Leipzig, 1909.

Polhill, J. B., 'Relationship'='The Relationship between Ephesians and Colossians', in *RExp* 70 (1973), 439–50.

Portefaix, L., 'Concepts'='Concepts of Ecstasy in Euripides' "Bacchanals" and Their Interpretation', in (ed.) N. G. Holm, *Religious Ecstasy: Based on Papers Read at the Symposium on Religious Ecstasy Held at Åbo, Finland, on the 26th–28th of August, 1981* (SIDA 11, Stockholm/Uppsala, 1982), 201–10.

Porter, J. R., 'Aspects'='The Legal Aspects of the Concept of "Corporate Personality" in the Old Testament', in *VT* 15 (1965), 361–80.

Preisker, H., 'Vikariatstaufe'='Die Vikariatstaufe I Cor 15,29 – ein eschatologischer, nicht sakramentaler Brauch', in *ZNW* 23 (1924), 298–304.

Price, S., 'Delphi'='Delphi and Divination', in Easterling-Muir, *Religion* 128–54.

Prümm, K., *Handbuch=Religionsgeschichtliches Handbuch für den Raum der altchristlichen Umwelt: hellenistisch-römische Geistesströmungen und Kulte mit Beachtung des Eigenlebens der Provinzen*, Roma, 1954.

Pryke, J., 'Eschatology'='Eschatology in the Dead Sea Scrolls', in (ed.) M. Black, *The Scrolls and Christianity: Historical and Theological Significance* (TCSPCK 11, London, 1969) 45–57.

Rabin C., *Studies=Qumran Studies*, ScJ 2, Oxford, 1957.

Räisänen, H., *Paul=Paul and the Law*, WUNT 29, Tübingen, 1983.

Rahner, H., *Myths=Greek Myths and Christian Mystery*, London, 1963.

Reicke, B., 'Setting'='The Historical Setting of Colossians', in *RExp* 70 (1973), 429–38.

Reinach, S., *Cultes=Cultes, mythes et religions*, Paris, 1923 (5, 61–71=*RAr* 1919, 162–72).

Reitzenstein, R., *Erlösungsmysterium=Das iranische Erlösungsmysterium: religonsgeschichtliche Untersuchungen*, Bonn, 1921;

— —, *Mysterienreligionen=Die hellenistischen Mysterienreligionen nach ihren Grundgedanken und Wirkungen*, Darmstadt 1966, repr. of 1927[3];

— —, *Poimandres=Poimandres: Studien zur griechisch-ägyptischen und frühchristlichen Literatur*, Leipzig, 1904, repr. Darmstadt, 1966;

— —, 'Religionsgeschichte'='Religionsgeschichte und Eschatologie', in *ZNW* 13 (1912), 1–28;

— —, *Vorgeschichte=Vorgeschichte der christlichen Taufe*, Stuttgart, 1929, repr. Darmstadt, 1967.

Reitzenstein, R., Schaeder, H. H., *Studien=Studien zum antiken Synkretismus aus Iran und Griechenland*, SBW 7, Leipzig/Berlin, 1926.

Resch, A., *Agrapha=Agrapha: außercanonische Schriftfragmente*, TU 5, Leipzig, 1889; TU 15.3–4, Leipzig, 1906[2].

Rese, M., 'Formeln'='Formeln und Lieder im Neuen Testament: einige notwendige Anmerkungen', in *VF* 15 (1970), 75–95.

Richardson, N. J., *Hymn=The Homeric Hymn to Demeter*, Oxford, 1974.

Ridderbos, H., *Paul=Paul: an Outline of His Theology*, London, 1975 (ET of Kampen, 1966).

Ries, J., *Culte=Le culte de Mithra en Orient et en Occident*, Centre d'Histoire des Religions Louvain-la-Neuve, Collection Information et Enseignement 10, Louvain-la-Neuve, 1979.

Riesenfeld, H., 'Descente'='La descente dans la mort', in *Aux sources de la tradition chrétienne: mélanges offerts à M. Goguel* (Neuchâtel/Paris, 1950) 207–17.

Ringgren, H., *Religionen=Die Religionen des alten Orients*, GAT, Göttingen, 1979 (ET: London, 1973).

Rissi, M., *Taufe=Die Taufe für die Toten: ein Beitrag zur paulinischen Tauflehre*, AThANT 42, Zürich, 1962.

Robertson, A., Plummer, A., *1 Cor=A Critical and Exegetical Commentary on the First Epistle of St Paul to the Corinthians*, ICC, Edinburgh, 1914.

Robinson, J. A. T., *Redating=Redating the New Testament*, London, 1976.

Robinson, J. M., 'Kerygma'='Kerygma and History in the New Testament', in id., H. Köster, *Trajectories through Early Christianity* (Philadelphia, 1971) 20–70, repr. from (ed.) J. P. Hyatt, *The Bible in Modern Scholarship* (Nashville/New York, 1965) 114–50.

Roetzel, C. J., *Letters=The Letters of Paul: Conversations in Context*, Atlanta, 1975, 1982[2]/London, 1983;

— —, *World=The World That Shaped the New Testament*, Atlanta, 1985.

Rogerson, J. W., 'Conception'='The Hebrew Conception of Corporate Personality: a Re-Examination', in *JThS* N. S. 21 (1970), 1–16.

Rohde E., *Psyche=Psyche: the Cult of Souls and Belief in Immortality among the Greeks*, New York, 1966, repr. of London/New York, 1925 (ET of Tübingen, 1921[8]).

Roloff, D., *Gottähnlichkeit=Gottähnlichkeit, Vergöttlichung und Erhöhung zu seligem Leben: Untersuchungen zur Herkunft der platonischen Angleichung an Gott*, UaLG 4, Berlin, 1970.

Roon, A. van, *Authenticity=The Authenticity of Ephesians*, NT.S 39, Leiden, 1974.

Rostovtzeff, M. I., *Italy=Mystic Italy*, New York, 1927.

Rowland, C., *Heaven=The Open Heaven: a Study of Apocalyptic in Judaism and Early Christianity*, London, 1982;

— —, *Origins=Christian Origins: an Account of the Setting and Character of the Most Important Messianic Sect of Judaism*, London, 1985.

Rowley, H. H., *Moses=From Moses to Qumran: Studies in the Old Testament*, London, 1963;

— —, *Relevance=The Relevance of Apocalyptic: a Study of Jewish and Christian Apocalypses from Daniel to the Revelation*, London, 1963[3].

Rudolph, K., *Gnosis=Die Gnosis: Wesen und Geschichte einer spätantiken Religion*, Leipzig, 1977/Göttingen, 1978 (ET: Edinburgh, 1983);

— —, ' "Gnosis" '=' "Gnosis" and "Gnosticism" –the Problems of Their Definition and Their Relation to the Writings of the New Testament', in (ed.) A. H. B. Logan, A. J. M. Wedderburn, *The New Testament and Gnosis: Essays in Honour of Robert McL. Wilson* (Edinburgh, 1983) 21–37.

Ruef, J., *1 Cor=Paul's First Letter to Corinth*, PNTC, Harmondsworth, 1971.

Russell, D. A., *Plutarch*, London, 1972.

Russell, D. S., *Method=The Method and Message of Jewish Apocalyptic 200 B.C.–A.D. 100*, London, 1964.

Sänger, D., *Judentum=Antikes Judentum und die Mysterien: religionsgeschichtliche Untersuchungen zu Joseph und Aseneth*, WUNT 2, Reihe 5, Tübingen, 1980.

Sahlin, H., 'Beschneidung'='Die Beschneidung Christi: eine Interpretation von Eph. 2:11–22', in *SyBU* 12 (1950), 5–22.

Salditt-Trappmann, R., *Tempel=Tempel der ägyptischen Götter in Griechenland und an der Westküste Kleinasiens*, EPRO 15, Leiden, 1970.

Samter, E., *Geburt=Geburt, Hochzeit und Tod: Beiträge zur vergleichenden Volkskunde*, Leipzig/Berlin, 1911;

— —, 'Hochzeitsbräuche', in *NJKA* 19 (1907), 131–42.

Sanday, W., Headlam, A. C., *Rom=A Critical and Exegetical Commentary on the Epistle to the Romans*, ICC, Edinburgh, 1902[5].

Sandbach, F. H., *Stoics=The Stoics*, London, 1975.

Sandelin, K.-G., *Auseinandersetzung=Die Auseinandersetzung mit der Weisheit in 1. Korinther 15*, Meddelanden från Stiftelsens för Åbo Akademi Forskningsinstitut 12, Åbo, 1976;

— —, 'Spiritus'='Spiritus vivificans: Traditions of Interpreting Gen 2.7', in (ed.) G. Lindeskog, *Opuscula exegetica Aboensia in honorem R. Gyllenberg octogenarii* (AAAbo Ser. A 45.1, Åbo, 1973) 59–75.

Sanders, E. P., 'Covenant'='The Covenant as a Soteriological Category and the Nature of Salvation in Palestinian and Hellenistic Judaism', in (ed.) R. Hamerton-Kelly, R. Scroggs, *Jews, Greeks and Christians: Religious Cultures in Late Antiquity: Essays in Honor of William David Davies* (SJLA 21, Leiden, 1976) 11–44;

— —, 'Dependence'='Literary Dependence in Colossians', in *JBL* 85 (1966), 28–45:

— —, *Paul* (1977)=*Paul and Palestinian Judaism: a Comparison of Patterns of Religion*, London, 1977;

— —, *Paul* (1983)=*Paul, the Law, and the Jewish People*, Philadelphia, 1983.

Sanders, G., 'Kybele' = 'Kybele und Attis', in *OrRR* 264–97.

Sandmel, S., *Philo=Philo of Alexandria; an Introduction*, New York, 1979.

Sauneron, S., *Priests=The Priests of Ancient Egypt*, Evergreen Profile Books 12, New York/London, 1960.

Sauter, F., *Kaiserkult=Der römische Kaiserkult bei Martial und Statius*, TBAW 21, Stuttgart/Berlin, 1934.

Schade, H. -H., *Christologie=Apokalyptische Christologie bei Paulus: Studien zum Zusammenhang von Christologie und Eschatologie in den Paulusbriefen*, GTA 18, Göttingen, 1981.

Schenk, W., '1. Korintherbrief'='Der 1. Korintherbrief als Briefsammlung', in *ZNW* 60 (1969), 219–43.

Schenke, H.-M., 'Auferstehungsglaube'='Auferstehungsglaube und Gnosis', in *ZNW* 59 (1968), 123–6;

— —, *Gott=Der Gott 'Mensch' in der Gnosis: ein religionsgeschichtlicher Beitrag zur Diskussion über die paulinische Anschauung von der Kirche als Leib Christi*, Göttingen, 1962;

— —, 'Hauptprobleme'='Hauptprobleme der Gnosis: Gesichtspunkte zu einer neuen Darstellung des Gesamtphänomens', in *Kairos* 7 (1965), 114–123, repr. in (ed.) K. Rudolph, *Gnosis und Gnostizismus* (WdF 262, Darmstadt, 1975) 585–600;

— —, 'Weiterwirken'='Das Weiterwirken des Paulus und die Pflege seines Erbes durch die Paulus-Schule', in *NTS* 21 (1974–5), 505–18.

Schenke, H.-M., Fischer, K. M., *Einleitung=Einleitung in die Schriften des Neuen Testaments 1: Die Briefe des Paulus und Schriften des Paulinismus*, Gütersloh, 1978.

Schille, G., *Hymnen=Frühchristliche Hymnen*, Berlin, 1965.

Schillebeeckx, E., *Jesus=Jesus: an Experiment in Christology*, London, 1979.

Schlatter, A., *Gerechtigkeit=Gottes Gerechtigkeit: ein Kommentar zum Römerbrief*, Stuttgart, 1959[3];

— —, *Paulus=Paulus der Bote Jesu: eine Deutung seiner Briefe an die Korinther*, Stuttgart, 1934;

— —, *Theologie=Die korinthische Theologie*, BFChTh 18.2, Gütersloh, 1914.

Schlier, H., *Eph=Der Brief an die Epheser: ein Kommentar*, Düsseldorf, 1957;

– –, 'Hauptanliegen'='Über das Hauptanliegen des 1. Briefes an die Korinther', in *EvTh* 8 (1948– 9), 462–73, repr. in id., *Die Zeit der Kirche: exegetische Aufsätze und Vorträge* (Freiburg, 1956) 147–59;

– –, 'Lehre'='Zur kirchlichen Lehre von der Taufe', in *ThLZ* 72 (1947), 321–36;

– –, *Röm=Der Römerbrief*, HThK 6, Freiburg, etc., 1977.

Schmidt, H. W., *Röm=Der Brief des Paulus an die Römer*, ThHK 6, Berlin, 1962.

Schmithals, W., 'Corpus'='The *Corpus Paulinum* and Gnosis', in (ed.) A. H. B. Logan, A. J. M. Wedderburn, *The New Testament and Gnosis: Essays in Honour of Robert McL. Wilson* (Edinburgh, 1983) 107–24;

– –, *Gnosis=Die Gnosis in Korinth: eine Untersuchung zu den Korintherbriefen*, Göttingen, 1965[2] (ET: Nashville/New York, 1971);

– –, *Paulus=Paulus und die Gnostiker: Untersuchungen zu den kleinen Paulusbriefen*, ThF 35, Hamburg-Bergstedt, 1965;

– –, *Römerbrief=Der Römerbrief als historisches Problem*, Gütersloh, 1975;

– –, 'Verhältnis'='Das Verhältnis von Gnosis und Neuem Testament als methodisches Problem', in *NTS* 16 (1969–70), 373–83.

Schmöle, K., *Läuterung=Läuterung nach dem Tode und pneumatische Auferstehung bei Klemens von Alexandrien*, MBTh 38, Münster, 1974.

Schnackenburg, R., 'Adam-Christus-Typologie' ='Die Adam-Christus-Typologie (Röm 5.12–21) als Voraussetzung für das Taufverständnis in Röm 6.1–14', in Lorenzi, *Battesimo* 37–55;

– –, *Baptism=Baptism in the Thought of St Paul*, Oxford, 1964 (ET of MThS 1, München, 1950);

– –, *Eph=Der Brief an die Epheser*, EKK 10, Zürich, etc., 1982;

– –, 'Tauflehre'=' "Er hat uns mitauferweckt"; zur Tauflehre des Epheserbriefes', in *LJ* 2 (1952), 159–83;

– –, 'Todes- und Lebensgemeinschaft'='Todes- und Lebensgemeinschaft mit Christus: neue Studien zu Röm 6.1–11', in *MThZ* 6 (1955), 32–53, repr. in id., *Schriften zum Neuen Testament: Exegese in Fortschritt und Wandel* (München, 1971) 361–91.

Schneider, C., *Mysterien=Die antiken Mysterien in ihrer Einheit und Vielfalt: Wesen und Wirkung der Einweihung*, Hamburg, 1979.

Schneider, N., *Eigenart=Die rhetorische Eigenart der paulinischen Antithese*, HUTh 11, Tübingen, 1970.

Schnelle, U., *Gerechtigkeit=Gerechtigkeit und Christusgegenwart: vorpaulinische und paulinische Tauftheologie*, GTA 24, Göttingen, 1983.

Schniewind, J., 'Antwort'='Antwort an Rudolf Bultmann: Thesen zum Problem der Entmythologisierung', in (ed.) H. W. Bartsch, *Kerygma und Mythos: ein theologisches Gespräch*, ThF 1 (Hamburg-Volksdorf, 1955), 77–121, ET: *Kerygma und Myth* 1 (London, 1953), 45–101;

– –, 'Leugner'='Die Leugner der Auferstehung in Korinth', in id., *Nachgelassene Reden und Aufsätze* (ed. E. Kähler, Berlin, 1952) 110–39.

Schottroff, L., *Glaubende=Der Glaubende und die feindliche Welt: Beobachtungen zum gnostischen Dualismus und seiner Bedeutung für Paulus und das Johannesevangelium*, WMANT 37, Neukirchen, 1970.

Schrage, W., 'Kirche'='Ist die Kirche das "Abbild seines Todes"? Zu Röm 6,5', in (ed.) D. Lührmann, G. Strecker, *Kirche* (FS G. Bornkamm, Tübingen, 1980) 205–19;

– –, 'Stellung'='Die Stellung zur Welt bei Paulus, Epiktet und in der Apokalyptik: ein Beitrag zu 1 Kor 7, 29–31', in *ZThK* 61 (1964), 125–54.

Schubert, K., 'Entwicklung'='Die Entwicklung der Auferstehungslehre von der nachexilischen bis zur frührabbinischen Zeit', in *BZ* 6 (1962), 177–214;

– –, 'Problem'='Das Problem der Auferstehungshoffnung in den Qumrantexten und in der frührabbinischen Literatur', in *WZKM* 56 (1960), 154–67.

Schürer, E., *Geschichte=Geschichte des jüdischen Volkes im Zeitalter Jesu Christi*, Hildesheim, 1964 (repr. of Leipzig, 1901–9; ET: Edinburgh, 1890–1, of Leipzig, 1886–90[2]).

Schürer, E., ed. M. Black, F. Millar, G. Vermes, *History=The History of the Jewish People in the Age of Jesus Christ (175 B.C.–A.D. 135)*, Edinburgh, 1973–.

Schütz, J. H., 'Authority'='Apostolic Authority and the Control of Tradition: I Cor. xv', in *NTS* 15 (1968–9), 439–57;

— —, *Paul=Paul and the Anatomy of Apostolic Authority,* MSSNTS 26, Cambridge, 1975.

Schulz, A., *Nachfolge=Nachfolge und Nachahmen: Studien über das Verhältnis der neutestamentlichen Jüngerschaft zur urchristlichen Vorbildethik,* StANT 6, München, 1962.

Schweitzer, A., *Mysticism=The Mysticism of Paul the Apostle,* London, 1953[2] (ET of Tübingen, 1930);

— —, *Paul=Paul and His Interpreters: a Critical History,* London, 1912 (ET of Tübingen, 1911).

Schweizer, E., 'Dying'='Dying and Rising with Christ', in *NTS* 14 (1967–8), 1–14;

— —, *Erniedrigung=Erniedrigung und Erhöhung bei Jesus und seinen Nachfolgern,* AThANT 28, Zürich, 1962[2];

— —, *Gemeinde=Gemeinde und Gemeindeordnung in Neuen Testament,* AThANT 35, Zurich, 1959 (ET: SBT 32, London, 1961);

— —, *Kol=Der Brief an die Kolosser,* EKK, Zürich, etc., 1976;

— —, 'Letter'='The Letter to the Colossians – Neither Pauline nor Post-Pauline?', in *Mélanges théologiques* (FS S. Dockx, BEThL 43, Gembloux, 1976) 3–16;

— —, *Lordship=Lordship and Discipleship,* SBT 28, London, 1960 (ET of revised ed. of *Erniedrigung,* 1955);

— —, *Spirit=The Holy Spirit,* London, 1981 (ET of Stuttgart, 1978).

Scott, E. F., *Col=The Epistles of Paul to the Colossians, to Philemon and to the Ephesians,* MNTC, London, 1930.

Scramuzza, V. M., *Claudius=The Emperor Claudius,* Cambridge, 1940.

Scroggs, R., *Adam=The Last Adam: a Study in Pauline Anthropology,* Oxford, 1966;

— —, 'Paul'='Paul: σοφός and πνευματικός', in *NTS* 14 (1967–8), 33–35;

— —, 'Romans vi.7'='Romans vi.7, ὁ γὰρ ἀποθανὼν δεδικαίωται ἀπὸ τῆς ἁμαρτίας', in *NTS* 10 (1963–4), 104–8.

Selby, P., *Look=Look for the Living: the Corporate Nature of Resurrection Faith,* London, 1977.

Sellin, G., ' "Auferstehung" '=' "Die Auferstehung ist schon geschehen": zur Spiritualisierung apokalyptischer Terminologie im Neuen Testament', in *NT* 25 (1985), 220–37.

Senft, C., *1 Cor=La première épître de Saint Paul aux Corinthiens,* CNT(N) 7, Neuchâtel/Paris, 1979.

Siber, P., *Mit Christus=Mit Christus leben: eine Studie zur paulinischen Auferstehungshoffnung,* AThANT 61, Zürich, 1971.

Simon, M., 'École'='À propos de l'école comparatiste', in (ed.) R. Hamerton-Kelly, R. Scroggs, *Jews, Greeks and Christians: Religious Cultures in Late Antiquity: Essays in Honor of William David Davies* (SJLA 21, Leiden, 1976) 261–70;

— —, 'Schule'='The Religionsgeschichtliche Schule Fifty Years Later', in *RelSt* 11 (1975), 135–44.

Simpson, E. K., Bruce, F. F., *Eph=The Epistles to the Ephesians and Colossians,* NIC, Grand Rapids, 1957.

Sjöberg, E., 'Wiedergeburt'='Wiedergeburt und Neuschöpfung im palästinischen Judentum', in *StTh* 4 (1950), 44–85.

Smith, J. Z., 'Garments'='The Garments of Shame', in *HR* 5 (1966), 217–38.

Smith M., 'Transformation'='Transformation by Burial (I Cor 15.35–49; Rom 6.3–5 and 8.9–11)', in *Eranos* 52 (1983), 87–112.

Soden, H. von, 'Sakrament'='Sakrament und Ethik bei Paulus: zur Frage der literarischen und theologischen Einheitlichkeit von 1 Kor 8–10', in *MThSt* 1 (1931), 1–40, repr. in id., *Urchristentum und Geschichte* (Tübingen, 1951) 239–75, and (ed.) K. H. Rengstorf, *Das Paulusbild in der neueren deutschen Forschung* (WdF 24, Darstadt, 1969) 338–79.

Solmen, F., *Isis=Isis among the Greeks and Romans,* Martin Classical Lectures 25, Cambridge MA/London, 1979.

Soury, G., *Démonologie=La démonologie de Plutarque: essai sur les idées religieuses et les mythes d'un Platonicien éclectique,* CEA, Paris, 1942.

Soyez, B., *Byblos=Byblos et la fête des Adonies,* EPRO 60, Leiden, 1977.

Speiser, F., 'Mysterien'='Die eleusinischen Mysterien als primitive Initiation', in *ZE* 60 (1928), 362–72.

Spiegel, J., 'Auferstehungsritual'='Das Auferstehungsritual des Unaspyramide', in *ASAE* 53 (1956), 339–439.

Spörlein, B., *Leugnung=Die Leugnung der Auferstehung: eine historisch-kritische Untersuchung zu 1 Kor 15*, BU 7, Regensburg, 1971.

Stambaugh, J. E., *Sarapis=Sarapis under the Early Ptolemies*, EPRO 25, Leiden, 1972.

Steinmetz, F. J., *Heils-Zuversicht=Protologische Heils-Zuversicht: die Strukturen des soteriologischen und christologischen Denkens im Kolosser- und Epheserbrief*, FTS 2, Frankfurt, 1969.

Stemberger, G., *Leib=Der Leib der Auferstehung: Studien zur Anthropologie und Eschatologie des palästinischen Judentums im neutestamentlichen Zeitalter (ca 170 v Chr – 100 n Chr)*, AnBib 56, Roma, 1972.

Stowers, S. K., *Diatribe=The Diatribe and Paul's Letter to the Romans*, SBLDS 57, Chico, 1981.

Strack, H. L., *Introduction=Introduction to the Talmud and Midrash*, Philadelphia, 1931, repr. New York, 1972.

Talbert, C. H., 'Concept'='The Concept of Immortals in Mediterranean Antiquity', in *JBL* 94 (1975), 419–39.

Tannehill, R. C., *Dying=Dying and Rising with Christ: a Study in Pauline Theology*, BZNW 32, Berlin, 1966.

Tate, J., 'Beginnings'= 'The Beginnings of Greek Allegory', in *ClR* 41 (1927), 214–5;

— —, 'Cornutus'='Cornutus and the Poets', in *CQ* 23 (1929), 41–5;

— —, 'History'='On the History of Allegorism', in *CQ* 28 (1934), 105–19;

— —, 'Plato'='Plato and Allegorical Interpretation', in *CQ* 23 (1929), 142–54; 24 (1930), 1–10.

Thausing, G., *Auferstehungsgedanke=Der Auferstehungsgedanke in ägyptischen religiösen Texten*, SOA 16, Leipzig, 1943.

Theißen, G., 'Schichtung'='Soziale Schichtung in der korinthischen Gemeinde: ein Beitrag zur Soziologie des hellenistischen Urchristentums', in *ZNW* 65 (1974), 232–72;

— —, 'Starken ='Die Starken und Schwachen in Korinth: soziologische Analyse eines theologischen Streites', in *EvTh* 35 (1975), 155–72.

Thiselton, A. C., 'Eschatology'='Realized Eschatology at Corinth', in *NTS* 24 (1977–8), 510–26.

Thrall, M. E., 'Christ'='Christ Crucified or Second Adam? A Christological Debate between Paul and the Corinthians', in (ed.) B. Lindars, S. S. Smalley, *Christ and Spirit in the New Testament* (FS C. F. D. Moule, Cambridge, 1973) 143–56;

— —, *1–2 Cor=I and II Corinthians*, CNEB, Cambridge, 1965.

Thüsing, W., *Per Christum=Per Christum in Deum: Studien zur Verhältnis von Christozentrik und Theozentrik in den paulinischen Hauptbriefen*, NTA N.F. 1, Münster, 1968[2].

Thyen, H., 'Βάπτισμα'='Βάπτισμα μετανοίας εἰς ἄφεσιν ἀμαρτιῶν', in (ed.) J. M. Robinson, *The Future of Our Religious Past: Essays in Honour of Rudolf Bultmann* (London, 1971=ET of *Zeit und Geschichte*, Tübingen, 1964), 131–68.

Tiede, D. L., *Figure=The Charismatic Figure as Miracle Worker*, SBLDS 1, Missoula, 1972.

Tobin, T. H., *Creation=The Creation of Man: Philo and the History of Interpretation*, CBQ.S 14, Washington DC, 1983.

Tondriau, J., 'Décret'='Le décret dionysiaque de Philopator', in *Aeg.* 26 (1946), 84–95.

Tran Tam Tinh, V., *Essai=Essai sur le culte d'Isis à Pompéi*, Paris, 1964;

— —, 'Sarapis'='Sarapis and Isis', in Meyer-Sanders, *Self-Definition* 3, 101–117.

Tröger, K.-W., *Gnosis=Gnosis und Neues Testament: Studien aus Religionswissenschaft und Theologie*, Gütersloh, 1973.

Tuckett, C. M., '1 Corinthians'='1 Corinthians and Q', in *JBL* 102 (1983), 607–19.

Turcan, R.-A., *Mithra=Mithra et le mithriacisme*, Paris, 1981;

— —, *Mithras=Mithras Platonicus: recherches sur l'hellénisation philosophique de Mithra*, EPRO 47, Leiden, 1975;

— —, 'Roman'='Le roman "initiatique": à propos d'un livre récent', in *RHR* 163 (1963), 149–99;

— —, 'Salut'='Salut mithriaque et sotériologie néoplatonicienne', in Bianchi-Vermaseren, *Soteriologia* 173–89;

— —, *Sénèque=Sénèque et les religions orientales*, CollLat 91, Bruxelles, 1967.

Turner, V., *Forest=The Forest of Symbols: Aspects of Ndembu Ritual*, Ithaca, 1977;

— —, *Process=The Ritual Process: Structure and Anti-Structure*, London, 1969.

Vaux, R. de, 'Rapports'='Sur quelques rapports entre Adonis et Osiris', in *RB* 42 (1933), 31–56.

Verbeke, G., *Évolution=L'évolution de la doctrine du pneuma du stoicisme à S. Augustin: étude philosophique*, Bibliothèque de l'institut supérieur de philosophie, Université de Louvain, Paris/Louvain, 1945.

Vermaseren, M. J., *Cybele=Cybele and Attis: the Myth and the Cult*, London, 1977;

– –, *Legend=The Legend of Attis in Greek and Roman Art*, EPRO 9, Leiden, 1966;

– –, *Mithras =Mithras, the Secret God*, London, 1963;

– –, 'Mithras'='Mithras in der Römerzeit', in *OrRR* 96–120;

– –, *Mithriaca* 1–4, EPRO 16, Leiden, 1971–82;

– –, 'Religions'='Hellenistic Religions', in (ed.) C. J. Bleeker, G. Widengren, *Historia religionum* 1 (Leiden, 1969), 495–532;

– –, 'Sotériologie'='La sotériologie dans les papyri graecae magicae', in Bianchi-Vermaseren, *Soteriologia* 17–30.

Vermaseren, M. J., Essen, C. C. van, *Excavations=The Excavations in the Mithraeum of the Church of Santa Prisca in Rome*, Leiden, 1965.

Vermaseren, M. J., Simoni, P., *Liber=Liber in deum: l'apoteosi di un iniziato Dionisiaco*, EPRO 53, Leiden, 1976.

Vermes, G., *Scrolls=The Dead Sea Scrolls: Qumran in Perspective*, London, 1982[2].

Versnel, H. S., 'Religion'='Römische Religion und religiöser Umbruch', in *OrRR* 41–72;

– –, *Triumphus =Triumphus: an Inquiry into the Origin, Development and Meaning of the Roman Triumph*, Leiden, 1970.

Vidman, L., *Isis=Isis und Sarapis bei den Griechen und Römern*, RVV 29, Berlin, 1970;

– –, 'Isis'='Isis und Sarapis', in *OrRR* 121–56.

Vielhauer, P., *Geschichte=Geschichte der urchristlichen Lituratur: Einleitung in das Neue Testament, die Apokryphen und die Apostolischen Väter*, Berlin, 1975.

Vogel, C. J. de, *'Sōma-Sēma* Formula'='The *Sōma-Sēma* Formula: Its Function in Plato and Plotinus Compared to Christian Writers', in (ed.) H. J. Blumenthal, R. A. Markus, *Neoplatonism and Early Christian Thought*, (FS A. H. Armstrong, London, 1981) 79–95.

Vogliano, A., Cumont, F., Alexander, C., 'Inscription'='The Bacchic Inscription in the Metropolitan Museum', in *AJA* 37 (1933), 215–70.

Volz, P., *Eschatologie=Die Eschatologie der jüdischen Gemeinde im neutestamentlichen Zeitalter nach den Quellen der rabbinischen, apokalyptischen und apokryphen Literatur*, Tübingen, 1934, repr. Hildesheim, 1966.

Wacker, M.-T., *Weltordnung=Weltordnung und Gericht: Studien zu 1 Henoch 22*, FzB 45, Würzburg, 1982.

Wagner, G., *Baptism=Pauline Baptism and the Pagan Mysteries: the Problem of the Pauline Doctrine of Baptism in Romans VI.1–11, in the Light of Its Religio-Historical 'Parallels'*, Edinburgh, 1967 (ET of AThANT 39, Zürich, 1962).

Walbank, F. W., *World=The Hellenistic World*, Glasgow, 1981.

Wallach, L., 'Alexander'='Alexander the Great and the Indian Gymnosophists in Hebrew Tradition', in *PAAJR* 11 (1941), 47–83.

Wallis, R. T., *Neoplatonism*, London, 1972.

Walter, N., ' "Eschatologie" '=' "Hellenistische Eschatologie" im Neuen Testament', in (ed.) E. Gräßer, O. Merk, *Glaube und Eschatologie* (FS W. G. Kümmel, Tübingen, 1985) 335–56;

– –, 'Paulus'='Paulus und die urchristliche Jesustradition', in *NTS* 31 (1985), 498–522.

Wedderburn, A. J. M., 'Adam'='Adam in Paul's Letter to the Romans', in (ed.) E. A. Livingstone, *Studia Biblica 1978* 3: *Papers on Paul and Other New Testament Authors* (JSNT Suppl. Series 3, Sheffield, 1980) 413–30;

– –, 'Body'='The Body of Christ and Related Concepts in I Corinthians', in *SJTh* 24 (1971), 74–96;

– –, 'Chronologies',='Some Recent Pauline Chronologies', in *ET* 92 (1981), 103–8;

– –, ' "Man" '='Philo's "Heavenly Man" ', in *NT* 15 (1973), 301–26;

– –, 'Observations'='Some Observations on Paul's Use of the Phrases "in Christ" and "with Christ" ', in *JSNT* 25 (1985), 83–97;

434   Bibliography

−−, 'Paul'='Paul and the Hellenistic Mystery-Cults: on Posing the Right Questions', in Bianchi-
    Vermaseren, *Soteriologia* 817−33;
−−, 'Structure'='The Theological Structure of Romans v.12', in *NTS* 19 (1972−3), 332−54.
Weil, H., 'Péan'='Un péan delphique à Dionysos', in *BCH* 19 (1895), 393−418.
Weiß, H.-F., 'Motive'='Gnostische Motive und antignostische Polemik im Kolosser- und im Ephe-
    serbrief', in Tröger, *Gnosis* 311−24;
−−, 'Paulus'='Paulus und die Häretiker: zum Paulusverständnis in der Gnosis', in (ed.) W. Eltester,
    Christentum und Gnosis (BZNW 37, Berlin, 1969) 116−28.
Weiß, J., *1 Kor=Der erste Korintherbrief*, KEK 5, Göttingen, 1925¹⁰.
Wells, G. A., *Jesus=The Jesus of the First Christians: a Study in Christian Origins*, London, 1971.
Wendland, H. D., *1−2 Kor=Die Briefe an die Korinther*, NTD 7, Göttingen, 1954⁶.
Wendland, P., *Kultur=Die hellenistisch-römische Kultur in ihren Beziehungen zum Judentum und
    Christentum* (revised by H. Dörrie), HNT 2, Tübingen, 1972⁴.
Wengst, K., *Formeln=Christologische Formeln und Lieder des Urchristentums*, StNT 7, Gütersloh,
    1972.
Wessetzsky V., 'Osirisglauben'='Über den Osirisglauben der Römerzeit', in *Studia Aegyptiaca* 2, Az
    Eötvös Loránd Tudományecyetem ókori történeti tanszékeinek Kiadvanyai 17 (1976), 139−
    44.
West, M. L., *Poems=The Orphic Poems*, Oxford, 1983;
−−, 'Tragica VI', in *BICS* 30 (1983), 63−82.
Wettstein, J., *Novum Testamenttum=Novum Testamentum Graecum*, Amsterdam, 1752, repr.
    Graz, 1962.
Whittaker, J., 'Plutarch'='Plutarch, Platonism and Christianity', in (ed.) H. J. Blumenthal, R. A.
    Markus, *Neoplatonism and Early Christian Thought* (FS A. H. Armstrong, London, 1981)
    50−63.
Whittaker, M., *Jews=Jews and Christians: Graeco-Roman Views*, Cambridge Commentaries on Writ-
    ings of the Jewish and Christian World 200 B.C.−A.D. 200 6, Cambridge, 1984.
Widengren, G., 'Reflections' (1965)='Some Reflections on the Rites of Initiation (in the Light of
    the Papers Presented at Strasburg)', in Bleeker, *Initiation* 187−309;
−−, 'Reflections' (1980)='Reflections on the Origin of the Mithraic Mysteries', in (ed.) Cattedra
    di religioni del mondo classico dell'Università degli Studi di Roma, *Perennitas: studi in onore
    di Angelo Brelich* (Roma, 1980) 645−68;
−−, *Religionsphänomenologie*, Berlin, 1969.
Wiegand, T., 'Bericht'='Vierter vorläufiger Bericht über die Ausgrabungen der Königlichen Museen
    zu Milet', in *SPAW* 1905, 533−48.
Wilamowitz-Moellendorff, U. von, *Glaube=Der Glaube der Hellenen*, Berlin, 1931−2, 1955², repr.
    Darmstadt, 1984.
Wilckens, U., '1 Kor2,1−16'='Zu 1 Kor 2,1−16', in (ed.) C. Andresen, G. Klein, *Theologia crucis
    signum crucis* (FS E. Dinkler, Tübingen, 1979) 501−37;
−−, *Resurrection=Resurrection: Biblical Testimony to the Resurrection: an Historical Examina-
    tion and Explanation*, Edinburgh, 1977 (ET of Gütersloh, 1974);
−−, *Röm=Der Brief an die Römer*, EKK 6, Zürich, etc., 1978−82;
−−, *Weisheit=Weisheit und Torheit: eine exegetisch-religionsgeschichtliche Untersuchung zu 1.
    Kor. 1 und 2*, BHTh 26, Tübingen, 1959.
Wili, W., 'Mysteries'='The Orphic Mysteries and the Greek Spirit', in (ed.) J. Campbell, *The Myster-
    ies* (PEY 2, BollS 30, Princeton, 1978) 64−92 (ET of *ErJb* 11, 1944, 61−105).
Williams, R.R., 'Catechesis'='The Pauline Catechesis', in (ed.) F. L. Cross, *Studies in Ephesians*
    (London, 1956) 89−96.
Willoughby, H. R., *Regeneration=Pagan Regeneration: a Study of Mystery Initiations in the
    Graeco-Roman World*, Chicago, 1929.
Wilson, J. H., 'Corinthians'='The Corinthians Who Say There Is No Resurrection of the Dead', in
    ZNW 59 (1968), 90−107.
Wilson, R. McL., *Gnosis=Gnosis and the New Testament*, Oxford, 1968;
−−, 'Gnosis'='Gnosis and the Mysteries', in (ed.) R. van den Broek, M. J. Vermaseren, *Studies in
    Gnosticism and Hellenistic Religions Presented to Gilles Quispel on the Occasion of His 65th
    Birthday* (EPRO 91, Leiden, 1981) 451−7;

– –, 'Nag Hammadi'='Nag Hammadi and the New Testament', in *NTS* 28 (1982), 289–302;

– –, 'New Testament'='The New Testament in the Nag Hammadi Gospel of Philip', in *NTS* 9 (1962–3), 291–4;

– –, 'Soteriology'='Soteriology in the Christian-Gnostic Syncretism', in Bianchi-Vermaseren, *Soteriologia* 848–65.

Wilson, R. R., 'Prophecy'='Prophecy and Ecstasy: a Reexamination', in *JBL* 98 (1979), 321–37.

Windisch, H., *2 Kor=Der zweite Korintherbrief*, KEK 6, Göttingen, 1924[9].

Winter, M., *Pneumatiker=Pneumatiker und Psychiker in Korinth; zum religionsgeschichtlichen Hintergrund von I. Kor. 2,6–3,4*, MThSt 12, Marburg, 1975.

Wischmeyer, O., *Weg=Der höchste Weg: das 13. Kapitel des 1. Korintherbriefes*, StNT 13, Gütersloh, 1981.

Wisse, F., ' "Opponents" '='The "Opponents" in the New Testament in Light of the Nag Hammadi Writings', in (ed.) B. Barc, *Colloque international sur les textes de Nag Hammadi (Québec, 22 –25 août, 1978)* (BCNH Études 1, Québec/Louvain, 1981) 99–120.

Wissowa, G., *Religion=Religion und Kultur der Römer*, HAW 5.4, München, 1912[2].

Witt, R. E., *Isis=Isis in the Graeco-Roman World*, London, 1971.

Wolff, C., *1 Kor=Der erste Brief des Paulus an die Korinther* 2: *Auslegung der Kapitel 8–16*, ThHK 7.2, Berlin, 1982.

Wolfson, H. A., 'Immortality'='Immortality and Resurrection in the Philosophy of the Church Fathers', in (ed.) K. Stendahl, *Immortality and Resurrection* (New York, 1965) 54–96;

– –, *Philo=Philo: Foundations of Religious Philosophy in Judaism, Christianity and Islam*, Cambridge MA, 1947.

Yamauchi, E. M., *Gnosticism=Pre-Christian Gnosticism: a Survey of the Proposed Evidence*, London, 1973;

– –, 'Notes'='Additional Notes on Tammuz', in *JSSt* 11 (1966), 10–15;

– –, 'Tammuz'='Tammuz and the Bible', in *JBL* 84 (1965), 283–90.

Zandee, J., *Death=Death as an Enemy According to Ancient Egyptian Conceptions*, SHR 5, Leiden, 1960.

Zeller, E., *History=A History of Greek Philosophy from the Earliest Period to the Time of Socrates*, London, 1881 (ET of Leipzig, 1876).

Zemmrich, J., 'Toteninseln'='Toteninseln und verwandte geographische Mythen', in *IAE* 4 (1891), 217–44.

Ziesler, J., *Christianity=Pauline Christianity*, Oxford/New York, 1983.

Zimmerli, W., *Ezek=Ezekiel*, Hermeneia, Philadelphia, 1979–83 (ET of BKAT 13.2, Neukirchen, 1969).

Zmijewski, J., *Stil=Der Stil der paulinischen "Narrenrede": Analyse der Sprachgestaltung in 2 Kor 11,1–12,10 als Beitrag zur Methodik von Stiluntersuchungen neutestamentlicher Texte*, BBB 52, Köln/Bonn, 1978.

Zuntz, G., 'Fresco'='On the Dionysiac Fresco in the Villa dei Misteri at Pompeii', in *PBA* 49 (1963), 17–201;

– –, *Persephone=Persephone: Three Essays on Religion and Thought in Magna Graecia*, Oxford, 1971.

INDICES

1. Index of Passages Cited from Ancient Literature

1.1. Old Testament

1.2. Old Testament Apocrypha

1.3. Old Testament Pseudepigrapha

1.4. Qumran Writings

1.5. New Testament

1.6. Rabbinic Writings

1.7. Jewish Hellenistic Writings

1.8. Graeco-Roman Secular Writings

1.9. Egyptian Writings

1.10. Other Ancient Near Eastern Texts

Descent of Ishtar to the Nether World (ANET)
   19–20   201

Myth of Adapa (ANET)
   B.20   201

Gilgamesh Epic (ANET)
   6.46   201

1.11. Collections of Manuscripts, Papyri, Inscriptions, etc.

Année épigraphique
   1956 no. 255   367

Bodmer Papyri
   11   220

Clinton, *Officials*
   7, 38, 51, 54–5   319

Corpus cultus Cybelae Attidisque
   2, 180, 182   124
       262.10   206
       309   124
       432   112, 124
       456–67   250
       469, 479   112
       616–18, 637   205
       650   112
   3, 14–199   101
       220, 310   107
       344   106, 205
       362, 365, 366,
       446   124
   4, 3   107
       20   101
       21, 29, 35, 40, 42
                         107
       45   124
       69, 85   107
       133   205
       147, 169, 194,
       203, 210, 229,
       248, 259   107
       268   124, 327
   7, 46   124
       59, 81, 85, 131,
       182   107

Corpus inscriptionum et momumentorum re-
ligionis Mithriacae
   1, 187–8   374
       188   375
       193   374
       520   204
       594   112
       609   375

Corpus inscriptionum Graecarum
   2, 3173   109

Corpus inscriptionum Latinarum
   3 Suppl. 12321   108
   6, 504   142
       510   142, 204, 367
       736   367
       1675, 1779   142
       10098   101, 105f
       33961   101
   10, 1406   101

Corpus momumentorum religionis equitum
Danuvinorum
   1, 13   375
       27   375
       47   375

Cumont, *Textes*
   584   367

Duthoy, *Taurobolium*
   23   204, 367
   33   204
   78   367

'Εφημερὶς ἀρχαιολογική
   3.3 (1885) 150.13–
       14   99

Fränkel, *Inschriften*
   1, 248.54   111

Gurob 'Mystery-Papyrus' (in Diels-Kranz,
   Fragmente §1)
   Frg. B 23   93, 116, 321

Hepding, *Attis*
   nos. 2, 6   340
       7–8   112
       8   340

Hunt-Edgar, *Papyri*
   100   379
   208 (=*BGU* 6,
       1211)   144

Inscriptiones Graecae
   1², 6.108–9   319
   2², 610.4   237
       1672   102

1.12. Early Christian Writings and New Testament Apocrypha

1.13. Nag Hammadi Codices and Other Gnostic Texts
(including Mandaean and Manichaean)

2. Index of Medieval and Modern Authors Cited
(excluding most editors and translators of texts and references cited in Index 1)

3. Index of Subjects

Wissenschaftliche Untersuchungen zum Neuen Testament

Begründet von Joachim Jeremias und Otto Michel
Herausgegeben von Martin Hengel und Otfried Hofius

1. Reihe

43
Helmut Merklein
Paulus und Jesus
1987. X, 479 Seiten.
Broschur und Leinen.

42
Otto Betz
Jesus
Der Messias Israels
1987. VII, 482 Seiten. Leinen.

41
Mathias Rissi
Die Theologie des
Hebräerbriefs
1987. X, 140 Seiten. fadengeh.
Broschur

40
Carl J. Bjerkelund
Tauta Egeneto
1987. XII, 162 Seiten. Leinen.

39
David G. Meade
Pseudonymity and
Canon
1986. VII, 257 Seiten. Leinen.

38
Chrys C. Caragounis
The Son of Man
1986. IX, 310 Seiten. Leinen.

37
Ernst Bammel
Judaica
1986. VI, 331 Seiten. Leinen.

36
Jarl E. Fossum
The Name of God
and the Angel of
the Lord
1985. XIII, 378 Seiten. Leinen.

35
Erich Gräßer
Der Alte Bund im
Neuen
1985. VIII, 345 Seiten.
Broschur und Leinen.

34
Folker Siegert
Argumentation bei
Paulus
1985. VIII, 320 Seiten. Leinen.

33
Markus-Philologie
Hrsg. von H. Cancik
1984. X, 415 Seiten. Leinen.

32
Hildebrecht Hommel
Sebasmata. Band 2
1984. VII, 415 Seiten. Leinen.

31
Hildebrecht Hommel
Sebasmata. Band 1
1983. X, 382 Seiten. Leinen.

30
Seyoon Kim
"The 'Son of Man'"
as the Son of God
1983. X, 118 Seiten. Broschur.

29
Heikki Räisänen
Paul and the Law
2. Auflage 1987. XXXI, 320
Seiten. Leinen.

28
Das Evangelium
und die Evangelien
Hrsg. von P. Stuhlmacher
1983. VIII, 455 Seiten. Leinen.

27
Klyne Snodgrass
The Parable of the
Wicked Tenants
1983. X, 140 Seiten. Broschur.

26
Folker Siegert
Nag-Hammadi-Register
1982. XXVI, 383 Seiten.
Leinen.

25
Gerhard Maier
Die Johannesoffen-
barung und die Kirche
1981. IX, 676 Seiten. Leinen.

24
Günter Schlichting
Ein jüdisches
Leben Jesu
1982. XVI, 292 Seiten. Leinen.

23
Marcel Simon
Le christianisme
antique et son contexte
religieux.
Scripta varia. 2 Bände.
1981. 1: XX, 370 Seiten;
2: VI, S. 371–852. Leinen.

22
Otto Bauernfeind

Kommentar und
Studien zur Apostel-
geschichte

1980. XVIII, 492 Seiten.
Leinen.

21
August Strobel

Die Stunde der
Wahrheit

1980. VII, 150 Seiten.
Broschur.

20

Drei hellenistisch-
jüdische Predigten

Erl. von F. Siegert
1980. 109 Seiten. Broschur.

19
Gerd Theißen

Studien zur Soziologie
des Urchristentums

2. Aufl. 1983. VI, 364 Seiten.
Broschur und Leinen.

18
E. Earle Ellis

Prophecy and
Hermeneutic in
Early Christianity

1978. XVII, 289 Seiten. Leinen.

16
Karlmann Beyschlag

Simon Magus und
die christliche Gnosis

1974. VII, 249 Seiten. Leinen.

15
Andreas Nissen

Gott und der
Nächste im antiken
Judentum

1974. IX, 587 Seiten.
Leinen.

14
Otfried Hofius

Der Vorhang vor dem
dem Thron Gottes

1972. VIII, 122 Seiten.
Broschur.

13
Helmut Merkel

Die Widersprüche
zwischen den
Evangelien

1971. VI, 295 Seiten,
Broschur und Leinen.

12
Gerhard Maier

Mensch und freier
Wille

1971. VII, 426 Seiten, Broschur
und Leinen.

11
Otfried Hofius

Katapausis

1970. IX, 281 Seiten, Broschur
und Leinen.

10
Martin Hengel

Judentum und
Hellenismus

2. Auflage 1973.
XI, 693 Seiten, Broschur und
Leinen.

8
Christoph Burchard

Untersuchungen
zu Joseph und
Aseneth

1965. VII, 180 Seiten, Broschur
und Leinen.

7
Ehrhard Kamlah

Die Form der
katalogischen
Paränese im Neuen
Testament

1964. VIII, 245 Seiten,
Broschur und Leinen.

5
Friedrich Rehkopf

Die lukanische
Sonderquelle

1959. VIII, 106 Seiten.
Broschur.

1
Karl G. Kuhn

Achtzehngebot
und Vaterunser
und der Reim

1950. III, 51 Seiten. Broschur.

J.C.B. Mohr (Paul Siebeck)
Tübingen

DATE DUE

MAR 1 0 '89		
NOV 1 9 1997		
JUL 2 9 1999		
AUG 2 5 1999		
SEP 1 5 1999		
SEP 2 6 2001		
FEB 1 0 2002		